THEATRICAL MOVEMENT:

a bibliographical anthology

edited by
BOB FLESHMAN

The Scarecrow Press, Inc.
Metuchen, N.J., & London
1986

PN
2071
.G4
T46

Library of Congress Cataloging in Publication Data
Main entry under title:

Theatrical movement.

    Includes bibliographies.
    1. Movement (Acting)--Addresses, essays, lectures.
2. Movement (Acting)--Bibliography. 3. Performing arts--
Addresses, essays, lectures. 4. Performing arts--Bibli-
ography. I. Fleshman, Bob, 1930-
PN2071.G4T46   1986   792'.028   85-1795
ISBN 0-8108-1789-6

ACKNOWLEDGMENTS

Many of the contributors of articles were most generous in recommendations that raised the quality of this work. They came to my rescue in many ways.

Ernest Ferlita, S.J., my department chairman, gave his patience and continued support during the long period of preparation. I am grateful to him.

The Department of Drama, College of Arts and Sciences, Loyola University in New Orleans, supported this work through reduced class loads, covering the many miscellaneous expenses incurred, and handling many other details of the book's preparation. A succession of departmental secretaries have worked on the volume, but I would especially like to thank the last, Maureen Lazaravish, who caught the brunt of the work.

Special appreciation, as explained in the Preface, is due Diane Lazier Carney and Dr. Drid Williams.

CONTENTS

The Americas

PREFACE

This volume is a result of my long association with two wonderful women, Diane Lazier Carney and Dr. Drid Williams. They are very much a part of the life of this work, its history and its spirit.

Diane Lazier Carney

Long before the present project was conceived--as early as 1970-- there was another publication plan, a bibliography of mime and related subjects by Diane Carney with me acting in an advisory capacity. Over the years lists and card files of bibliographical materials were built, until finally those "related subjects" took on a special importance for us. The concept changed and we began the present work as coeditors.

It soon became obvious that Ms. Carney's administrative and teaching responsibilities with Hysell Ballet Arts in New Orleans, plus her other directorial and artistic assignments, made it impossible for her to fulfill the role of coeditor and the full responsibility was shifted to me. Much credit for the early work on this volume must go to Diane Carney: the wealth of back-up material from the original effort, important contributions to the concept and design of this volume, shared responsibility for the first probings for contributors and, above all, her continued concern and personal support.

Diane is a person of great energy, excitement and delight; by sharing those special qualities with me on many occasions, not just on this work, she has added to my life when I was very low in such personal resources. This work certainly would not have been done without her help.

Dr. Drid Williams

The seed for such a project as this probably goes back to the late 1950's, when I first knew Drid Williams and studied at her New York City studio. As brief as that study period was, it was pivotal to my continued work in theatrical movement because of her breadth of knowledge about human movement and her intense, personal

ix

means of sharing that knowledge. In the mid-1970's, following her studies at Oxford University, Dr. Williams came to New Orleans, at which time I encountered her work in anthropology of human movement, which is so much a part of this volume.

Dr. Williams has contributed to this work in many ways beyond writing a key article. From her reservoir of knowledge and professional friendships, she guided me through many difficulties including the location of excellent scholars to handle many of the chapters, especially those for movement performance in other cultures. Her keen criticism given during numerous visits and telephone calls helped keep the work focused.

With her sense of integrity, backed by her forceful personality, Dr. Drid Williams does not make it easy for her students or for her friends to compromise. In a period of much relaxed standards, it is exactly that element that makes her of such great value as a teacher and as a friend. While I have no illusion that all the various articles presented in this volume meet her special sense of standards, nevertheless, much of whatever strength this volume has must be credited to Dr. Drid Williams. This work could not have been done without her help.

About This Work

The classical concept of an anthology is that of a collection of literary flowers, beautiful poems and epigrams. The term has come to include other forms of literature, such as an anthology of short stories or a science fiction anthology. In this case, the term is extended to mean a collection of bibliographical essays with the purpose of guiding the reader through the literature of special areas of study. The approach taken for this project was explained in the following description, sent to prospective contributors:

> This volume is a guide for those working in theatre, dance and related movement forms who are seeking a basic understanding of various areas of human movement beyond their own particular disciplines. It will supply such a worker with a compass and a map, so to speak, to use as he or she scouts out new areas of study. It will help the reader to move surefootedly, without stumbling across too many wrong paths or getting lost. It may save him or her the fate of many other such adventurers who started out on similar excursions but eventually threw up their hands out of confusion and gave up their search.
> This is an anthology of bibliographical information about theatrical movement, covering a wide range of subjects. It is composed of many sections, some short and some long, each representing a different area of human movement. Each section will be the work of a person known for his or

her accomplishment in the particular area. By placing
these sections together, we wish to create a strong, au-
thorative bibliographical overview of human movement as it
relates to theatrical presentation.

Each section has two parts: first, an essay which
orients the reader to the subject area, and second, a basic
bibliography which lists published material with which the
reader should be familiar....

Briefly and tersely, the essay introduces and defines
the particular area of human movement. It breaks the field
down into its component parts and explains the major points
of view. It may require a short historical survey. The
thrust of the essay, however, is in its discussion of the
literature of the field in such a way that the reader, who
probably knows very little about this new area, can find
his or her way safely through the unfamiliar material. This
requires from the contributor a solid evaluation of the literature of the field....

The structure will vary from one section to another.
Each will be shaped by the nature of its field.

There is often a desire and need to go beyond one's own
field, into related movement forms. It is awkward, indeed
often difficult, to find the information needed. Once found,
there is often a nagging feeling of insecurity about its validity and place within its own field. A bibliographical anthology, with contributions by recognized leaders, will be a
great service to all working in the many areas and forms of
human movement.

In the execution of such a bibliographical guide, there are
several main difficulties related to the nature of the literature being covered. The problems are especially acute when dealing with
other cultures, but they run through all areas of the study. First,
the state of scholarship is not equally developed in all areas. A
good example of this can be seen by comparing the sections on the
Middle East and Asia. The indigenous forms in the Middle East to
a great extent have been flattened by the impact of Western influence, and only very recently have there been attempts to redis-
cover and develop those original sources. Because of a cultural
bias against representational arts and especially ones using the human body as the medium of expression, little scholarly work has
been done in the area of movement performance, and of that even
less has found its way into Western publications. Asia, on the other
hand, is composed of many cultures that have practiced many forms
of theatrical arts for many centuries; the amount of scholarship has
been great both in Asia and the West. Second, the natures of the
literature of a particular area of study vary according to the purpose and audience, forming various groupings of literature, ranging
from popular magazine articles to detailed scholarly works for other
scholars. These groupings must be understood if they are to be of
value in a bibliographical anthology. Third, a literary work is the

product not only of an individual with special interests, but of a
person working within a particular discipline. Each discipline holds
special points of view and methods, and the various disciplines are
not necessarily obligated to be wholly compatible with one another.
These and similar problems are discussed in relationship to Indian
performance, in the chapter South Asian Performance, by Phillip
Zarrilli and Rhea Lehman.

It is important to note that this work is not intended to be a
comprehensive scholarly work of carefully aligned information; such
a publication is not possible for this work. The present work must
content itself to be a simple guide, nowhere near a comprehensive
one, to further study and work in the areas of human movement and
performance. Still, in some ways and in certain cases, this work
does go beyond what the playful metaphor in the description might
suggest, that of simple excursions and little outings.

The prospectus ended with the following statement:

All human movement forms and concepts are related to each
other insofar as they grow out of the universal nature of
the human body and human mind. Yet, the body and its
movement can be viewed in many ways: a self-regulating
system to meet the biological needs of the organism; an
expressive instrument of individual feelings, emotions and
thoughts; an extension of these into social action and interaction; as part of the structure of various cultures; and
even as a part of some grand scheme of the meaning of
things. The different layers of meaning are understood in
the different lights of various approaches and disciplines.
Somewhere within these various levels of meaning, or running throughout them, is a sense of artistic movement and
theatrical performance.

Part One: Preliminary Studies

The original shape of the project had a much larger vision and
was to include a more expansive coverage of the great variety of
Euro-American performance forms with some emphasis on the developing "theatre of movement," detailed coverage of movement training
techniques, a rounded study of dance as a theatrical form, and a
more complete investigation of studies in the human sciences as they
relate to theatrical movement. However, as the work progressed, it
became obvious that it would have to be limited to preliminary studies; thus, the scope was trimmed and the framework tightened.

The process of this condensation betrays both the origin of
the work--mime and related subjects--and a certain bias in my belief that mime, in its basic process although by no means in all of
its developed forms, is generic to theatrical movement. However,
I hope that this will not be misunderstood as the thesis of the book.

While Part One is, as its heading suggests, a preliminary study only, its main value is that it starts an important process. The inclusion of articles of human movement studies in the sciences provides a context for a meeting of the two worlds of the human sciences and the human arts, offering hope for a more meaningful relationship between them.

Part Two: Movement Performance in Other Cultures

The significance of this book may be in its attempt to cover movement performance in other major cultures. However, when dealing with theatrical movement of other cultures many problems arise.

It becomes immediately obvious that "theatrical movement" is an inadequate and misleading term because our concept of theatre is quite different from the concepts that produce movement forms in other cultures. For this part of the book the term has been shifted from "theatrical movement" to "movement performance."

The distinction made in our culture between acting and dancing is by no means universally held, and material on theatre runs throughout many of the articles side-by-side or interlocked with material we would generally consider to be dance.

There may also be confusion between theatre and ritual. In our own culture we probably would not think the traditional Roman Catholic Mass to be theatre, although we recognize the dramatic and theatrical elements in its structure and execution. However, in viewing a movement performance of another culture, because we are unlinked to the basic, penetrating dynamics of that culture as a whole, we tend to see a "theatrical reality" built upon a sense of theatre of our own culture.

In general, we tend to look at the products of another culture as they seem to us to relate to our own cultural forms and experiences. This is the primary difficulty in dealing with various other cultures in their various movement performance forms. It takes hard work to begin to understand the unique cultural systems, which differ from our own. Many of the authors of this part of the book have discussed this problem in passing, but it is the focus of Drid Williams' article, "(Non) Anthropologists, the Dance, and Human Movement."

A Variety of Approaches

The authors contributing to this volume come from many different disciplines, each working within the special approaches of his or her professional training. There are theatre scholars and historians, anthropologists, ethnomusicologists, librarians, and others in areas of study and practice of human movement in the humanities and human sciences.

On the one hand, this variety of approaches adds a richness to our learning experience, giving a breadth of meaning and a multidimensional view. On the other hand, a unified approach would help insure that we are all talking from the same base about the same subject. Many of the approaches are not always compatible, some are contradictory to others, and a few seem to be quite hostile. However desirable it might seem, a unified approach is simply not possible, given the present state of affairs of the study of theatrical movement and related areas. Still, it is not too much for us to seek a compatibility of approaches.

Because of their willingness to come together in such a project, to understand the strengths and weaknesses of each discipline or form--including one's own, the authors represented in this volume offer at least a hope of compatibility of approaches, and, ultimately, that is what this book is about.

It is all very human and natural to believe in some sort of knowledge tree, where facts of information and even understanding fall off the branches of scholarship like ripe fruit. But knowledge and understanding come with a certain loss of innocence, with some sweat and struggle, and with the pain of discipline. It is accompanied by the realization of how naked we stand in the middle of all we do not know. So while the contributors have provided us with their maps and guides through the literature of various areas of the garden, each of us must find a way to evaluate how specific information fits into the larger world of scholarship and not just how comfortably it meets a particular need. In so doing, each of us can find better ways to evaluate and understand our own discipline or form, and eventually, ourselves.

Bob Fleshman
1985

PART I
PRELIMINARY STUDIES

Chapter One

MEANING IN ARTISTIC MOVEMENT:
THE OBJECTIVE AND THE SUBJECTIVE

David Best

Introduction

This chapter will consider what I believe to be the most important single theoretical issue facing those of us who are concerned
with artistic movement, namely, the objective or subjective status
of artistic experience. Despite its importance, it is almost universally confused, often with seriously damaging practical consequences.
It is impossible to consider all aspects of the issue fully in one chapter. The intent here is to sketch the broad outlines of an argument,
and provide references to other publications for those who wish to
pursue further any aspects of the issue.

There is an important sense in which the artistic experience
of movement in dance and theatre, whether from the performer's or
spectator's perspective, is an objective matter. Very common subjectivist assumptions can be dangerously misconceived--dangerously,
because they destroy any hope of offering a justification of such
artistic experience. Nevertheless, such subjectivist assumptions
are by no means entirely misconceived. Far from it. They arise
from a recognition of, and insistence upon very important aspects
of artistic experience of movement. However, all too frequently
subjectivists tend to exaggerate and distort the valid and important insights which they wish to emphasize, and this can lead to
the disastrous misconceptions to which I refer.

The source of the trouble appears to be an equally common,
but equally misconceived notion of objectivity. It is because of a
prevalent, but much too narrow and rigid notion of what it is to
be objective, that so many people feel constrained to insist that
artistic experience of movement must be a subjective matter. It is
necessary to realize that the concept of objectivity is much more
subtle, flexible, and complex than is generally recognized. Hence,
in effect, a considerable proportion of this chapter will be devoted
to an exploration of the concept of objectivity, as it applies to the
artistic experience of movement in dance and theatre. Such an

3

exploration will show, I suggest, that there is no incompatibility between the more accurate account of objectivity which I shall offer, and the important aspects of artistic experience on which the subjectivist rightly wants to insist.

The terms "objective" and "subjective" can be highly misleading, and "objective" in particular, in the context of a discussion of the arts, can create emotive barriers. Hence, it might seem wiser to eschew the terms altogether, so as to avoid the difficulty of trying to overcome entrenched positions which are often defended with emotional fervor. But the issues can be confronted most clearly and directly in terms of the objective and the subjective, and it is therefore worth the risk. Perhaps I can appeal to readers not to make assumptions about the meanings of these terms before they have read the chapter. I think and hope that the main reasons for any immediate opposition to the suggestion that the performance and appreciation of artistic movement is a fully objective matter will prove to have been groundless. That is, again, the valid and important insights of subjectivism will have been shown to be part of a more adequate account of objectivity. At the same time, we shall have discarded the dangerously misleading, confused and extreme accounts of both objectivism and subjectivism.

It may be worth emphasizing at the outset a point to which I have already referred, and on which I am frequently misunderstood, that my argument in this chapter applies equally to the performer and to the spectator; to the actor and dancer as well as to the audience and critic. Too often it has been assumed by those who think they agree with my arguments on this issue, that whereas objectivity may apply to the judgments of the spectator, the experience of the performer must be a subjective matter. That very common confusion is based upon a fundamental misconception about the relation of body to mind.

One further point. When I refer to "education," "learning," "teaching," and cognate terms, I do not mean to restrict my account exclusively to what goes on in schools, colleges and universities. As many of us know to our considerable benefit, there is a great deal to be learned from the arts for the whole of one's life. Nevertheless, as I shall point out again, it is important to recognize that unless artistic experience can be shown to be open to objective assessment in some sense, then there can be no justification for including the arts in education, and accountability would be impossible.

1. Scientism and Subjectivism

A major underlying theme of much of this chapter can be indicated by the subtitle, "Scientism and Subjectivism: Two Sides of the Same Misleading Coin." For I want to expose as depending upon the same seriously mistaken presupposition (a) the common assumption

that the scientific is the only legitimate kind of objectivity (for simplicity of exposition I shall include the mathematical and logical
within this category); and (b) the supposed consequence that since
the artistic experience of performing and appreciating movement is
obviously not a scientific matter, then it must be purely subjective.
These assumptions are usually implicit in the kinds of views I shall
be criticizing, rather explicitly acknowledged.

There are several closely related and widely prevalent misconceptions which contribute to the confusion on this issue. I
shall offer a brief sketch of just four of them. These misconceptions can be roughly characterized as follows:

1. Artistic appreciation of movement cannot be objective because there can be radical and irreconcilable differences of
   opinion about the same performance. (We can call this the
   argument from disagreement.)
2. Involvement with movement, in dance or theatre, cannot be
   objective because personal, individual experience is essential for a full understanding of its meaning, whether as
   performer or spectator.
3. For complete freedom of expression, or for completely free
   judgment in appreciation, it is necessary to avoid the limitations imposed by having learned any techniques.
4. Artistic judgment depends ultimately upon intuition.

The concept of objectivity is very complex, but nevertheless
it is fairly easy to expose these as serious misconceptions. The
main difficulty in grasping the point is that of liberating oneself
from the overwhelming prejudice of our age towards an exaggerated
worship of the scientific method. I hope it is abundantly clear that
I do not in the least wish to undervalue the scientific method. My
aim is to show that it has its limitations, and that if we do not recognize these, we shall be liable to serious errors.

In order to confront the issue directly, let me state my theme
plainly: artistic judgments of movement in theatre and dance are
as fully objective as scientific judgments, and those who assume the
subjectivity of artistic judgments and experience, or that such judgments and experience are answerable solely to inner feeling or intuition, have been too much influenced by scientism, and have so far
failed to understand the nature not only of artistic appreciation and
expression, but also of all objectivity and knowledge.

It may be worth adding that, although I cannot directly discuss them here, the issue we are considering is of fundamental
general importance, in that it applies not only to the arts but to
such vital and largely ignored matters as the education of feeling,
creativity, personal relationships, and moral and personality development.

We can already begin to see why the prevalent misconceptions on this issue incur such seriously damaging consequences. On a subjectivist view no sense could be given to the notions of learning and teaching, and of progressively developing experience of the arts. I well recall offending a music lecturer in one Scottish university, who insisted on the subjectivity of artistic experience, by pointing out that if he were right he was not entitled to his salary. If an activity is not objective, then no standards can be applicable to it, since to set a standard necessarily implies the possibility of citing reasons which refer to objective phenomena. Without standards, no sense can be given to the notion of learning and teaching.

It should be said, since this contention so often arouses misguided opposition, that this is not to deny the importance of individuality in the arts. My insistence on objective standards should not be confused with an insistence on general or universal standards. When a tailor makes a suit to measure, his standards of what is objectively correct relate to the individual person for whom he is making the suit, not to people in general. Nevertheless, it is obvious that there are objective standards for what fits an individual. This already begins to expose a very common misconception, for it is too readily assumed that to insist on objectivity in the arts is to insist on the imposition of general standards which will inhibit or destroy the individuality and originality which is such an important part of involvement with the arts. We begin to see how it is that an oversimple and excessively rigid conception of objectivity can lead to a misguided, but understandable, resort to subjectivism. The subjectivist is right to insist on the vital importance of individuality in the arts, but he is wrong to assume that because of this, artistic experience cannot be objective.

The dilemma for a subjectivist teacher of the arts is that, as a teacher, it is incumbent on him or her to encourage standards, so that each individual student can develop to the maximum his or her artistic potential. Yet as a subjectivist, the teacher cannot do this, since a consequence of that view is that artistic meaning or value depends solely upon the private or individual feeling of each student.

As a brief initial guide, I shall take it, broadly from the Oxford Dictionary, that "subjective" means "belonging to the perceiving subject, i.e. to personal idiosyncrasy or purely private experience, as opposed to the objective, which depends upon real or external things." A more complete account will emerge, since this chapter is an exploration of the concept of objectivity.

In order to illustrate the common kind of assumption to which I want to draw attention as so seriously confused, let me quote just a few of those who adopt a subjective view, or whose views are naturally and commonly taken to be subjective.

David Hume captures this notion perfectly when he says:

"Beauty is no quality in things themselves; it exists merely in the mind which contemplates them."[1]

Louis Arnaud Reid writes of the feelings expressed in art that: "They belong, analytically and abstractly regarded, to the side of the subject and not of the object," and he adds that most philosophers would be ready to admit that.[2]

Philip Phenix writes of a dancer's movements: "They make visible the subjective life of persons by a series of symbolic gestures."[3] That is, artistic meaning is dependent not upon the objective movement, but upon the subjective life of persons of which the movement is a symbol.

T.S. Eliot has a similar view in his doctrine of the objective correlative,[4] i.e. the notion that the art object or performance is an objective correlate of the subjective feeling on which all artistic meaning ultimately depends.

Suzanne Langer writes that "felt life" is objectified in the work of art, and in this way: "The arts objectify subjective reality."[5]

There are many others one could cite who assume that artistic meaning is subjective. For instance, most theories of art which depend upon symbolism, i.e. a symbolic meaning for art, such as some theories of drama in education, and many writers on the meaning of movement, are also subjectivist. Examples can be found in the work of Laban, Eleanor Metheny, Margaret H'Doubler, but there are many more. (I consider the main fallacies of symbolism in Chapter 8 of my Philosophy and Human Movement.[6]) It is also significant of their resort to subjectivism that many such writers rely ultimately on intuition. But we shall return to that issue.

We need to dismiss immediately a contention which is commonly raised in support of a subjective position, and which may persistently cloud the issue. The argument for the contention goes something like this:

"The impression I have of the movement must come through my senses since I cannot perceive it through anyone else's sense-organs. Therefore my impression is, precisely, my impression, and no one else's, and therefore my judgment of the meaning of the movement must be purely subjective."

But such an argument would apply equally to such central cases of objectivity as mathematics and physical objects. For it is solely by the means of one's own faculties that one sees that $2+2=4$, and that the table is brown. Nevertheless, such judgments are objective. Hence the objectivity/subjectivity distinction has to come entirely within the platitude that one's impression is one's impression.

There is no support in the obvious fact of the reception of one's impression of the movement through one's faculties for the view that artistic meaning is a purely subjective matter. This issue is bedevilled by the common tendency to demand an incoherently ideal standard of objectivity as an area entirely beyond human powers of perception; in short, to confuse the objective with the absolute.

Now let us look at one of the strongest arguments for the contention that questions of the artistic meaning of movement in theatre and dance must be purely subjective. A scientist may adduce the commonly accepted assumption that if something is objective then it must be open to scientific examination. He will point out that all human actions, including for instance the movements of a dancer, are scientifically examinable in various ways, yet that these tell us nothing about their artistic meaning. Let us consider a thoroughgoing statement of this position in an article on dance.[7] The authors write: "Numerous claims for dance have been made, yet ... little published research is available to give substance to the claims. The position taken [here] is that dance is a form of behaviour, and as such, is open to scientific examination. That is, if something exists, it exists in quantity. The major method by which knowledge is developed in the behavioural sciences as well as in the physical sciences is by empirical investigation. Dance as a body of knowledge can be furthered in the same way." But none of these branches of science can discover anything in a dance to support statements made about artistic meaning. So the scientist who assumes the subjective status of questions of artistic meaning points out: "Since you concede that all human action is scientifically examinable, yet also that the artistic meaning of human action cannot be discovered scientifically, it must follow that the artistic meaning cannot be objectively there in the action, in which case, if any sense at all can be made of the notion of artistic meaning, it must be a purely subjective matter. Thus, it follows that statements made about artistic meaning in dance cannot be objectively substantiated."

This reveals the point of my proposed subtitle, "Scientism and Subjectivism: Two Sides of the Same Misleading Coin." For the subjectivist fully accepts this conclusion. He concedes without question that questions of artistic meaning cannot be objectively answered, since they are not open to scientific proofs, nor can they be given the definitive answers which he assumes to be characteristic of scientific inquiry. That is, the subjectivist accepts the doctrine of scientism that the only objectivity is scientific. Usually, he equally disastrously concedes that discussion of artistic meaning cannot be a rational activity. Small wonder that the literature on artistic meaning has been called the natural home of rapturous and soporific effusion. Small wonder, too, that the arts are so often accorded such a low status and priority in education. If those concerned with the arts themselves proclaim this subjectivist doctrine, then they can hardly expect others to take the arts seriously, and to recognize the enormously important contribution which the arts can make to people's lives.

The crucial point is that to concede that artistic meaning cannot be objective because it cannot be proven by scientific methods is already to have made the fatal mistake, which is to assume that the only objectivity is of a scientific kind. But there are numerous everyday examples which show conclusively how false that assumption is. For instance, the fundamental fallacy in the doctrine of scientism can be revealed by reference to the assertion, in the article quoted above, that if something exists it must exist in quantity and therefore be scientifically quantifiable. The misconception implicit in that assumption was neatly exposed in a cartoon I saw recently. A pair of ardent lovers were depicted embracing in the moonlight, and the young man was exclaiming ruefully: "I can't actually tell you how much I love you--I forgot my calculator."

Well, this reveals that there is something seriously amiss with the argument of any scientist who insists that if anything exists it must be scientifically measurable. But let us look closely at the argument.

It is true that all forms of behavior can be scientifically examined. It follows that the actions of a dancer can be scientifically examined. We have to concede the validity of that argument. Moreover, questions of artistic meaning and value obviously cannot be answered by scientific analysis. Hence. the conclusion seems inescapable that such questions are purely subjective.

But the argument for the conclusion that artistic meaning in movement cannot be objective is based upon a fundamental confusion. It confuses two quite distinct assertions: (a) all actions can be objectively explained scientifically; and (b) all objective explanations of actions are scientific.

Although it may be true that all actions can be explained scientifically, it does not follow, nor is it true, that all objective explanations of actions are scientific. Whereas it is true that we should demand objective substantiation for statements made about artistic meaning, not all objective substantiation is scientific. That is, we should not confuse the fact that all human behavior can be scientifically examined with the quite different, and false, supposition that scientific examination can tell us all we want to know about human behavior. The young man in the cartoon I quoted earlier could certainly provide objective proof of how much he loved the young lady, but not by scientific methods.

Objective Assessment Without Measurement

It is important to emphasize the crucial practical consequences of this issue. For instance, in many spheres of education, and in various countries, there is an increasing demand for accountability, which inevitably involves assessment. That is a demand which, in

principle, I entirely support. But, as a result of the misconception
we are now considering, there is a dangerously misconceived tendency to demand that all genuine educational progress and achievement should somehow be measurable, in scientific or quasi-scientific
terms. Where this is not possible, there tends to be a grave suspicion that no sense can be made of progress and achievement, and
therefore of learning and developing. That is, assessment tends to
be equated with measurement, and where something cannot be measured it is assumed that it cannot be objectively assessed.[6]

Again, we see the temptation toward subjectivism. The subjectivist is quite right to resist the notion that scientific tests and
measurements are the only ways of assessing progress. But it
would be a disastrous mistake to conclude that, therefore, such
progress cannot be an objective matter. To take an obvious case,
the validity of a reasoned argument can be objectively assessed, although it obviously cannot be measured. One can objectively assess
a student's progress in producing valid reasons to support his case,
but not by measurement. Moreover, anyone who disagreed with my
contention that objective assessment cannot be equated with measurement, could attempt to overcome this argument only by reasoned
argument, not by measurement. Hence, even the attempt would be
ironically self-defeating, since he or she would have to depend upon
our nonquantifiable assessment of the objective validity of his or her
reasons designed to show that there cannot be nonquantifiable objective assessment. It would be like pulling the rug from under
his or her own feet even to try to show that I am wrong.

To repeat, then, it is crucial to recognize that only some
kinds of progress can be measured. Moreover, the most important
ways in which we can progress, such as the ability to understand
people, moral and emotional development, our ability to understand
ourselves, cannot be measured, although they can certainly be objectively assessed. In short, many of the most important aspects
of human life require sensitive, informed, objective judgment.

Interpretative Reasoning

It is, then, important to recognize that there are different
but equally objective kinds of explanation. In this respect I particularly want to draw attention to explanations in terms of the kind
of reasoning which I call "interpretative," since it has been surprisingly overlooked by other philosophers, although it is central
not only to questions of artistic meaning, but also to all knowledge,
including the scientific.

We can begin to appreciate the significance of interpretative
reasoning when we recognize that there is a continuous scale between simply seeing a situation, and interpreting it; there can be
no sharp division between a plain fact and a situation which has

been interpreted. To illustrate the relation of perception to interpretation consider this drawing which can be seen as a duck or as a rabbit.

Each of two people, one seeing it as a duck, the other as a rabbit, could support his interpretation by citing, as reasons, objective features of the drawing, for example: "There are its ears." Moreover, anyone who could see it in either way would be able to choose how to see it. But it is important to notice that there is not an arbitrary, unlimited possibility here. It cannot be seen as a clock, for instance. Yet a subjectivist position does imply an unlimited possibility of equally intelligible or valid interpretation.

However, it may be that even when a particular interpretation is pointed out to someone, he or she cannot see it. He/she may be able to see the duck all right, but quite fail to understand how it can be seen as a rabbit. This sort of situation has important consequences not only for questions of artistic meaning, but also for scientific knowledge. It allows us to appreciate why the serious misconception has arisen that artistic judgments are merely subjective. For not everyone can see the same thing in a dance or theatrical performance, resulting in the possibility of arguments about interpretation which can become heated and irreconcilable.

Someone who cannot appreciate the meaning of a dance performance is not on that account suffering from defective eyesight. However carefully he or she scrutinizes it he or she may fail to appreciate its significance until someone points out how objective features of it should be interpreted. Suddenly it all makes sense, or a different sense. Yet, from a purely physical point of view, the viewer sees nothing which was not there before. That is, the significance of certain objective aspects which had been overlooked are pointed out.

Yet, there may not be a single correct interpretation of a work compared with which others necessarily reveal a lack of artistic insight and understanding. It is important to recognize that although a dance may be open to various interpretations, this does not imply that artistic meaning is purely subjective. There may be a wider range of correct or intelligible interpretation in the sphere of the arts but if one transgresses certain limits one can be wrong --objectively wrong--in artistic judgments just as in scientific judgments. An important characteristic of artistic meaning is that it allows for an <u>indefinite</u> but not <u>unlimited</u> possibility of valid interpretation. There has been a variety of interpretations of Shakespeare's play <u>King Lear</u>, but anyone who took that play to be a comedy would, quite obviously, be wrong.

What so often leads to confused thinking on this issue is a distortingly narrow conception of reasoning, so that people just cannot understand how reasoning <u>could</u> be relevant to meaning in the spheres of feeling and the arts. For instance, Witkin writes: "The arts stand in relation to the intelligence of feeling much as the sciences do in relation to logical reasoning." In fact, (and this has crucial educational implications), logical reasoning is <u>just</u> as relevant in the arts as in the sciences. It is largely the failure to appreciate the importance of interpretative reasoning which impels Witkin, and many others, to subjectivism.

There is a great deal more to be said about interpretative reasoning. In this chapter I can hope only to draw attention to how fundamental it is, not only to assessment of the arts, but also to scientific and other kinds of knowledge. (A further account of this issue and related issues can be found in my <u>Expression in Movement and the Arts.</u> [8]) To put the point baldly, my contention is not that the arts are like the sciences in yielding definitive and absolutely certain conclusions, but, on the contrary, that the sciences are like the arts in their ultimate answerability to new and different interpretation of objective features. There may be a greater tolerance of correct artistic judgment as compared with correct scientific judgment, but this is a difference of degree, not of kind. And by that I do not, of course, mean degree of objectivity or subjectivity. On the contrary, I insist that the arts are as fully objective as the sciences. What I mean is that there may usually be more scope for objective interpretation of the same dance or theatrical performance, than in the case of objective scientific interpretation of the same phenomenon. No matter how reliable and accurate the scientific instruments, scientific knowledge depends ultimately upon human perception, and, as I have tried briefly to show, perception cannot be coherently regarded as independent of interpretation.

Let me offer an illustration which brings out, in a particularly clear and practical way, the importance both of this point, and of interpretative reasoning. Near the island of Skomer, in Pembrokeshire, which is a sea-bird sanctuary, the West Wales Naturalists' Trust has provided a center known as the Lockley Lodge Interpretative Centre. The significance of the example is that the center tries to help visitors to interpret the sights and sounds which they encounter, so that they can understand and recognize what it is that they see and hear on Skomer. There is no distinction between correct interpretation and reality, or the facts. What counts as a fact depends upon interpretation. To interpret correctly is to know that this is, for instance, a Manx shearwater, rather than a puffin or a razorbill. You could not know this if you did not know how to interpret what you see and hear.

As Ben Shahn puts it: "The so-called 'innocent eye' does not exist. The eye at birth cannot perceive at all, and it is only through training that it learns to recognize what it sees."[9]

In complex cases, there is as much disagreement about scientific facts as there is about the meaning of a complex work of art. The argument from disagreement does nothing at all to show that questions of artistic meaning are purely subjective. What it does show is something crucially important about the character of objectivity, in the sciences as much as the arts.

It is crucial to recognize the full force of this point, for, contrary to what is commonly supposed, scientific verification, so far from being more "objective" and reliable than those disciplines which require interpretation, actually itself depends ultimately upon interpretation. Some scientists are under the misapprehension that they are dealing with indisputable facts, in contrast to those in the arts disciplines who, they suppose, indulge in mere vague speculation, and are therefore doomed to perpetual fruitless argument, with no possibility of final and decisive resolution. Indeed, the very suggestion that all science inevitably rests upon interpretation would probably be received by most people with derision, since it is commonly supposed that scientific discovery is far superior in decisive objectivity to such speculative uncertainty. Yet the most important aspect of science is not so much observation and experimentation, as interpretation. For, although the point is commonly overlooked, theoretical interpretation is a necessary precondition of any scientific fact or conclusion, and provides the substance of any observation. That is, as the theoretical interpretation changes, so will the character of the scientific facts and observations, since it is this theoretical structure which determines what can count as a fact. And since there is an indefinite possibility of theoretical change, the common assumption that the sciences provide indisputable certainties about the structure of a reality which is independent of human conception, is revealed as a myth. (Bronowski, in The Ascent of Man, brings out this point in a particularly clear and forceful way.)

The dependence of quantification upon interpretation is also, of course, the point of the aphorism: "Lies, damned lies, and statistics."

Perhaps it is largely the failure to recognize the ineliminable importance of interpretation to objective knowledge, and with it the common but fundamentally mistaken assumption that knowledge of reality is given only by scientific facts, which leads some theorists on the arts to the realm of pseudoscientific occult facts. That is, recognizing that the normal empirical method cannot account for some of the most important areas of human experience, and unaware that there are other equally objective methods of discovery, they are impelled towards a mysterious realm of supernatural facts, observable only by means of some archetypally metaphysical sense of feeling or intuition.

We can begin to appreciate that the major source of subjectivist theories of the arts is a deeply ingrained misconception about the nature of objectivity. This is the misleading coin of which scientism and subjectivism are the opposite sides. In relation to the first of the misconceptions to which I referred above, what I called the "argument from disagreement" is shown to be invalid because it depends upon a deeply mistaken notion of the objective. Roughly, the objective has been conflated with the absolute. Yet, as we have seen, despite the widespread misapprehension on the issue, it is as true of objectivity in any sphere as it is of artistic meaning, that it must allow for the indefinite but not unlimited possibility of valid or intelligible interpretation. But, in order forcefully to expose the common fallacies on this issue, it might be advisable to put the emphasis in different places, and to say of the sciences:

"The possibility of valid interpretation is indefinite."
And of the arts:
"The possibility of valid interpretation is not unlimited."

2. Objectivity, Interpretation, and Personal Experience of Movement

The second misconception, while correctly insisting on the central place of personal experience for a full understanding of artistic movement, distorts this important point by misguidedly concluding that therefore such understanding must be purely subjective. To consider this misconception will also allow me to refute an objection which is sometimes raised against some of my work, namely that I do not distinguish between the spectator and the performer, or that I concentrate too much on the spectator and do not adequately consider the experience of the performer.

It may well be that many readers will feel that so far I have been concerned exclusively or predominantly with the spectator. In the introduction, I laid emphasis on the fact that what I have to say in this chapter applies equally to the performer and the spectator; to the actor and dancer as well as the audience and critic. So far, we have been discussing interpretation, and it would be understandable if readers were to assume that this is a matter solely for spectators. In fact, such an assumption is fundamentally misconceived, since implicit in it is the notion that while the interpretation of objective movement may be important for the spectator, it is the experience itself which is important for the performer, and that this is a purely subjective matter which can be understood only by the performer. Such a notion reveals a fundamental confusion about mental concepts. Or, to put the point another way, it reveals a common but fatally confused failure to understand the relation between individual experience and objective criteria.

Perhaps the point can be appreciated most readily in the sphere of education. For, as I have earlier pointed out, subjectivists in this sphere inevitably incur severely embarrassing consequences, in that, on their own account, since individual meaning is purely private and inaccessible to anyone else, no sense could be made of learning and teaching.

But there are more fundamental problems which expose this prevalent but tempting subjectivist confusion, often revealed, for instance, in some phenomenological writing on dance and human movement. No sense can be given to the notion of meaning in terms of first-person, private experience, since there would be no way in which it could be identified. On this view nothing can be explained about these supposed experiences, since one cannot refer to them in a public language, neither can one identify them by reference to objective, observable criteria. It is important to remember that I am not in the least denying the importance of personal experience and individuality. The subjectivist is right to emphasize this, but he disastrously distorts his important insight.

The point is this. On a subjectivist account there is no logical relation between observable actions and personal experience. Whatever the movement, the experience is only contingently related to it--that is, the experience just happens to be related to the observable action, and it could have been related to a different action. Moreover, only the performer can know what is the meaning of his or her own movement experience. This kind of view is very common, but it is disastrously mistaken.

This point about answerability to observable criteria can, perhaps, be most clearly brought out by reference to kinesthetic awareness. There is a good deal of confused talk and literature on this topic, in which the tendency is to take the feeling as the ultimate or only arbiter--for instance, a dance is said to be right if it feels right. But, despite the prevalence of this view among many in the sphere of dance and movement, it is frequently controverted pragmatically, for instance, by the mirrors on the walls of dance studios. The crucial point, clearly conceded here, is that it is certainly not the dancer's kinesthetic feeling which is the final arbiter, but what he or she looks like (frequently confirmed by the use of mirrors). The dancer could not, initially and ultimately, know whether he or she were achieving the correct positions to express the meaning of the dance solely by reference to kinesthetic feeling. And neither could he or she know what it is he/she is feeling, except by reference to the objective criteria.

The same consideration applies, of course, to sporting activities, such as a tennis service, swimming, rowing and skiing. If one were to rely solely upon kinesthetic experience, one could not recognize where one was wrong.

But this is certainly not to denigrate the importance of kinesthetic experience and awareness. Too many modern philosophers seem to me to err in the opposite direction and fail to recognize the importance of the insight on which the subjectivist rightly insists, but which he exaggerates and distorts. For, quite apart from the enjoyment of kinesthetic and aesthetic feelings, it is a vitally important attribute of a good actor or dancer to develop reliable kinesthetic awareness, which will allow him or her to know what his or her movements look like. Thus, so far from belittling kinesthetic awareness, I would insist that it is essential. But it depends upon training, which is answerable to objective criteria.

It was interesting, in this respect, to hear Robert Cohan, in a radio program, commenting on Martha Graham's technique classes. He observed that these were not primarily to confer a greater range of movements on the dancer, but rather to give the dancer greater consciousness of bodily movements. Thus, through training the sensitivity of the kinesthetic feelings, the dancer can increasingly rely on the accuracy of her awareness of her observable movements. Moreover, she gains an increasing range of discrimination in her feelings as she gains an increased range of movements. Kinesthetic feelings are not quasi-mental objects, known only to the mover. On the contrary, without the overt movements the notion of kinesthetic experience would be unintelligible. The subjectivist notion of the experience itself, in isolation from its normal, perceivable context makes no sense. To take an obvious example, no experience could possibly count as that of serving an ace in isolation from the context of the rules and conventions of tennis. On the contrary, it is the characteristic objective circumstance of its occurrence which, as it were, tells me what experience I am having. It would be absurd, for instance, to say that one could have the experience of serving an ace while swimming, or if one had never played or even heard of tennis. Yet, on a subjectivist account this would be possible, since the experience is logically independent of the action.

To put it another way, if, while performing a movement, the mover should refer to the experience by saying: "It feels like this," there is no way of distinguishing the "it" from the "this." That is, the performer's experience is identified for him or her as well as the spectator, by the objectively perceivable movement in the context of its occurrence. It is for this reason that it is necessary to concentrate a philosophical examination of experience on such objective criteria. But to assume that this reveals a concern solely or predominantly with the spectator shows a fundamental failure to appreciate why it is necessary. I am equally concerned with the performer. To concentrate attention on objectively perceivable behavior is certainly not to denigrate the "experiencing" of it, but on the contrary, is the only intelligible way to provide an account of it.

It can now be understood why our consideration of the problem of objective interpretation is just as relevant to the performer as to the spectator. For the interpretation of the movement in a dramatic or dance performance identifies the experience which is being expressed by the performer.[10]

3. Free Expression Versus Learned Technique

I turn now to the third subjectivist misconception about movement in theatre and dance. It is closely related to the preceding issue. Again, it is commonly encountered, and again, although it is a serious misconception, it is based upon an important insight which, however, the subjectivist overemphasizes and distorts. The misconception is that there is a conflict between, on the one hand, freedom of expression, creativity and imagination, and on the other hand the teaching of techniques. The fallacy I want to expose as so damaging is expressed in the statement of one writer that freedom of expression to allow unrestricted development of individual feeling and creativity is inhibited by learned technique.

That this is a misconception can be clearly illustrated by considering the analogy with language learning. Roughly, in learning the techniques and practices of a language, a child is inevitably learning to understand the world in its terms. But it would be palpably absurd to suggest that this understanding is externally imposed and restrictive, and that consequently, for real freedom of expression and individual development each child should grow up alone on a desert island, where he or she can acquire his or her own concepts and understanding of the world. Clearly, so far from conferring greater freedom of thought, such a course of action would severely restrict the child's possible freedom of thought and individual development.

Nevertheless, I do not for a moment wish to suggest that the "free expression" school of thought should be dismissed as totally misconceived. It arose as a justifiable reaction against an educational policy which undoubtedly was restrictive in, for example, misguidedly elevating the ability to produce correct grammar to the status of an end in itself, rather than recognizing that it should be regarded as a means to the end of giving the child the possibility of greater freedom of expression. Thus, imagination and initiative were stifled in a mistaken overemphasis on stringent standards in modes of expression, at the expense of a concern for what was expressed. Hence, we see again that although this form of subjectivism is mistaken, it is by no means entirely mistaken. It is emphasizing, quite correctly, that too rigid and insensitive an imposition of technical skills is likely to destroy spontaneity, imagination, and capacity for free expression.

There are two major sources of this subjectivist misconception. The first is a failure to distinguish between the psychological and the philosophical issues. The important subjectivist insight is a psychological one, namely that there are attitudes to and methods of teaching which can stifle individuality, imagination and self-confidence. This is quite a different point from the philosophical or conceptual one for which I am arguing, namely that if certain techniques are not acquired, whether of language, the arts, or any other subject, an individual is not allowed, but rather de-prived of certain possibilities for freedom of expression.

Perhaps the misconception arises in this way. It is correctly recognized that some teaching of techniques leads to restrictions on freedom. From this, it is erroneously assumed, at least implicitly, that to remove all teaching of techniques is to remove all restrictions on freedom. Thus, a valid psychological insight is taken to such an invalid extreme that it becomes a conceptual confusion.

I suggest, then, that because of the confusion of the psychological with the conceptual issues, advocates of "free expression" assume that they are constrained to oppose notions of assessment, technical competence, and the learning of objective criteria. In fact, there is not necessarily any incompatibility here. Within limits, it is quite consistent to maintain that a "free" approach offers the most effective method of attaining technical competence without restricting individual creativity.

Individual Experience

The second source of this subjectivist misconception is much more complex. I can only sketch the outlines of an argument.

Central to this misconception is an oversimplified notion of individual personality as an entity logically distinct from its social context. In fact, on the contrary, no sense could be made of in-dividual thought, ideas, and experience, apart from the objective language and practices of a society. The educational consequences of this philosophical point are of a significance it would be impossible to exaggerate.

Now let me emphasize, because I am so often misunderstood on this point, that this is not in the least to deny the importance of the so-called "inner life," that is, thoughts, feelings and experiences which are not publicly expressed. It is to deny that any sense can be made of the notion that the mental experiences of an individual can be regarded as logically independent of the public practices, including the language and art forms, of a society.

Yet the enormous significance of this point is frequently unrecognized. Michael Argyle is a classic example of someone imbued with this very common misconception. For instance, in his book Bodily Communication,[11] Argyle writes:

> What is being expressed in music is an elaborate sequence of inner experiences including various emotions. It is because music can represent these experiences so well that it has been called "the language of the emotions."

This clearly implies that the "inner experiences" exist in the mind prior to and independently of any possible expression in a public medium, and that it just so happens that they can be expressed in music. On this conception the experiences are stored in the mind awaiting the availability of the most appropriate form of expression. Thus, such experiences might continue to exist indefinitely without ever being expressed since, for instance, their owner might never learn the requisite musical techniques. But in that case how could they be identified? Since, on this theory, their existence cannot be verified even in principle, how different is this from saying that they do not exist? Moreover, it would be a consequence of such a view that it could intelligibly be said that a dog could have such experiences but that he has not mastered the musical techniques necessary for the expression of them.

It can now be seen, then, that in sharp contrast to subjectivism, if, for instance, there were no art form of music, the respective experiences would not be merely inexpressible, but, much more importantly, they could not intelligibly be said to exist. And that is to say that the individual could not have such experiences unless he had acquired some grasp of the techniques and objective criteria of the art form of music. In this respect, the existence of the social practice, and the learning of its techniques and criteria, are necessary preconditions of the possibility of individual experience and development. And this applies equally, of course, to the experience of dance and theatrical movement.

This clearly exposes the fallacy that freedom for unrestricted personal development depends upon the avoidance of the teaching of techniques. On the contrary, the freedom of the individual to experience the relevant feelings necessarily depends upon and is conferred by his having learned those techniques.

Individual Feeling and Objective Criteria

This conceptual point, that freedom and creativity depend upon and are not restricted by technical competence, tends to arouse a hostile reaction from those subjectively committed to subjectivism. Let me illustrate from recent experience.

I have a love/hate relationship with skiing. I love it because it is exhilarating exercise, in lovely surroundings. I hate it because I can never get it right, except for tantalizingly brief moments. I struggle in vain to master parallel christies. On my last holiday, I awoke one morning to see that there had been a fresh fall of powder snow--which considerably flatters one's skiing. So I hurried out to my favorite practice slope and did several runs down which felt better each time. On my last run down I met a friend at the bottom of the slope and could not help exclaiming: "At last, I know what it feels like to do perfect parallels!" To which he replied "Oh no you don't. I saw you coming down."

Recently the Head of a Creative Arts Department responded to this example with hostility, accusing me of being "obsessed by technique." He said that if I had enjoyed my skiing even if it were not in perfect parallels, that should satisfy me. But, quite apart from his resort to emotive rhetoric in a supposed attempt to counter the philosophical point I was making, this is precisely the sort of misconception I want to expose. For, as I pointed out, I also enjoyed it the first time I ever went skiing--better described as when my skis went skiing, for I had no control.

Whether or not I enjoyed it is totally irrelevant to the philosophical point, as I hope is obvious. For, whatever my enjoyment, and whatever my feeling it certainly was not, logically could not have been, the feeling of skiing with perfect parallels. And there are objective criteria for that.

This is a classic case of the subjectivism to which I want to draw your attention, as being so harmful, educationally and artistically. The point is that there will be a whole range of feelings which one will be unable to experience unless one has learned the relevant techniques. I hope I shall not be misunderstood as being opposed to creativity, free expression, and the importance of feeling. On the contrary, I entirely support the encouragement of individual creativity. My point is that this is possible only if we have mastered the requisite techniques. Ironically, it is the subjectivist, who, by refusing to teach techniques, restricts the student's freedom of expression.

I want to have the feeling of parallel skiing. It is not enough to enjoy sloppy skiing. In that sense, I hate enjoying myself.

Does this mean that I am opposed to spontaneous feeling? On the contrary. There is a lot to be said about this common misunderstanding. But perhaps it is sufficient to quote Martha Graham, who once said that it takes at least five years of rigorous training to be spontaneous in dance.

It will be clear, again, how fundamentally opposed I am to the view that creativity is actually inhibited by learned technique. On the contrary, although of course technical competence does not necessarily give creative flair, it is a necessary precondition of such flair, and not only in dance and drama but also in the sciences, mathematics, philosophy, and any other discipline or activity.

As a further illustration of the point, in a recent radio interview the extraordinarily original jazz trumpeter, Dizzy Gillespie, was asked whether it was his lack of any tuition in techniques which had allowed him to develop his own highly individual style. He emphatically replied: "No, I should say not. A teacher is a shortcut." The interviewer pressed the point and asked: "But wouldn't a teacher, at least to some extent, have limited the development of your own particular style?" To which Dizzy Gillespie replied: "Not a good teacher."

Feelings

It may be worth pausing here to make the point that perhaps to most people, the importance of feelings in dance and drama seems to pose the biggest problem for my thesis on objectivity. For it is commonly assumed that the terms "feeling" and "objective" are almost contradictory. One can then understand the resort to subjectivism. For the feeling realm is commonly equated with the subjective. That is, roughly, it is taken that "subjective" is equated with, or at least entailed by "feeling." Now I hope it is clear that in that sense I do not in the least wish to deny subjectivity. For I insist on the crucial relevance of feeling and of individual, personal involvement in dance and drama. This, in my view, is one of the most important, yet one of the most widely neglected, contributions which the arts could make in education. The reason for my criticism of subjectivism is not because I am opposed to feelings, but because I am opposed to the harmful misconceptions about feelings which are entailed by subjectivist talk, and which are, disastrously, so commonly accepted. Examples of such misconceptions are that feeling and reason are opposed; that feeling and creativity are inhibited by learned technique; that feeling is a necessarily private matter beyond the objective sphere. All these very common misconceptions entail that feelings cannot be legitimately educational.

We should resist the radically mistaken, but prevalent myth that the arts are a matter of feeling rather than of reason and the intellect, and insist that the arts are a matter of feeling and of reason and the intellect. Indeed, we can go further, for it follows from my argument that the arts are a matter of feeling because they are also informed by reason and the intellect. That is the character of the feeling with which we are concerned in the arts. It is significant, and surely lends considerable support to my case, that an animal, because of its lack of rationality, cannot understand art;

and neither is an animal capable of the appropriate feeling-response to art. The feeling possibility depends upon the rational ability.

It is surely obvious just what substantial support this lends to our case for the educational credentials of the arts.

To return to the main thread, without the public, objective practices of dance and drama there could not be the appropriate "inner life of feeling." Moreover, the particular feeling is identified by what is objectively created. As Collingwood has put it: "Until a person has expressed his feeling, he does not yet know what feeling it is. The act of expressing it is therefore an exploration of his own feelings."

There are crucial educational consequences. For in teaching the art form, which necessarily involves assessment by objective criteria, the teacher is progressively extending the students' possibility of feeling-experiences. On a subjectivist view, even if it made any sense, this would be impossible, since, on that view, no sense can be made of assessment, and therefore of education. That is, where feelings are taken to be necessarily private, and logically separate from their possible expression in the objective medium of an art form, then no sense can be made of assessing what, if any, feelings students are having. Any work of art could be the expression of any feeling or none. Thus, there could be no place for learning and the progressive enrichment of both understanding and feeling.

We see again the absurdity of, and mortal damage to our case inflicted by, the pervasive myth that feeling and reason are totally separate, mutually exclusive and even conflicting faculties. It is high time we rid ourselves of the persistent and damaging fallacy that logical reasoning is predominantly or exclusively the province of the sciences, mathematics and the like. On the contrary, it is only by giving reasons that a teacher helps and encourages students to understand, appreciate and create art. Such reasons can progressively extend their capacity for feeling, imagination, creativity. In short, such extension of the possibilities of feeling is given only by an extension of understanding. (I consider this issue more fully in Expression in Movement and the Arts.)

4. Intuition

Given the background of our previous discussion, the question of intuition can be dealt with fairly briefly. However, it should be pointed out that my convictions on this issue are sharply opposed to many writers on artistic movement, such as, for instance, Suzanne Langer.

The most important aspect of the issue is very similar to the misconceptions we have just been considering. For where intuition is taken to be the only or ultimate ground of knowledge, then when one person intuits one thing, and another person another, they are in a position of incommunicable subjectivism. And since this would apply to everyone else, absolutely any or no meaning could be attributed to art.

Intuition makes sense only by reference to objective corroboration, i.e. to what can be observed to be the case. But, as in the parallel case of feeling we have just considered, this is not in the least to deny that intuition can be valuable and reliable. It is to insist that such value and reliability depends upon whether, in general, the intuition proves to be correct. And that depends upon whether what is intuited can be observed to occur, or to be the case. Thus, the intuition itself cannot coherently be regarded as the ultimate ground of knowledge, in any sphere.

To refer back to the example I used earlier, it is not intuition which justifies my saying that I can see the drawing as a rabbit. What justifies my seeing it in that way is the objective character of the drawing. Conversely, you would probably entertain grave doubts about my sanity if, in all seriousness, I were to insist that I know by intuition that it is neither a duck nor a rabbit but the Statue of Liberty.

Yet, to repeat the point since it is so often misunderstood, this is not in the least to denigrate the value and importance of intuition. On the contrary, it is only by means of educated intuitive leaps in, for example, philosophical and scientific inquiry, as much as the arts, that one can have any idea of the direction which the argument or experimentation should take. Nevertheless, even sound and fruitful intuitions depend for their soundness and fruitfulness upon whether one actually produces a valid philosophical argument or scientific theory. Similarly, the education of the vital creative vision and intuition of the artist is ultimately grounded in what he or she actually and objectively creates. You would soon become very sceptical of my persistent claims about the brilliant originality of my creative artistic vision and intuition if I never actually produced any art, or if the art I produced were banal and conventional.

In order to bring out clearly both the value of intuition, and also its ultimate grounding in objective criteria, let us consider the analogous case of a sense of direction. This is, as I have indicated, an appropriate parallel since intuition is very much what gives a sense of direction, not only to the artist, but to the philosopher, scientist and many other searchers after truth.

One's sense of direction obviously cannot itself be the grounds of knowledge, and its reliability is developed by progressively "getting it right," i.e. by objective corroboration. The parallel with an ultimate dependence on intuition, or "feeling" in this sense, would be to take the sense of direction as ultimately decisive. Thus, if I were the pilot of an airplane, and my sense of direction sends me to Alaska instead of California, it would have to be intelligible for me to insist that, despite the astonishingly cold weather, and despite what the oddly confused locals say, this must be California since my sense of direction is what ultimately justifies my claim to knowledge. It is important to be clear about this, and not to assume that I am taking an absurd and extreme example. For if the subjectivist does insist that artistic knowledge is ultimately grounded in feeling or intuition, these are the consequences of his position. Such a view would be like that of someone who, finding a discrepancy between his map and the landscape, insists that it is the landscape which must be inaccurate, and should be altered to fit the map.

It can be seen, then, why a resort to intuition is not genuinely explanatory at the fundamental level. When a theorist appeals to intuition as the basis of justification, that provides good grounds for the suspicion that something has gone seriously wrong with his argument. (For example, one of the principal grounds of my fundamental disagreement with Suzanne Langer is her ultimate appeal to intuition. I explain this issue more fully in Expression in Movement and the Arts.) For, as we see, at this level of explanation the notion of intuition does not work. It merely postpones, rather than explains, the fundamental problem. This is why Wittgenstein referred to it as an "unnecessary shuffle," since: "If intuition is an inner voice, how do I know how I am to obey it? And how do I know that it doesn't mislead me? For if it can guide me right, it can also guide me wrong."

In a perceptive article on this topic, Gilbert Ryle writes: [12]

> Some theorists who enjoy multiplying faculties, speak of Sense, Reason, and Intuition as different faculties, and part of what they have in mind when they speak of Intuition is such facts as that husbands sometimes feel that their wives are worried, connoisseurs feel that the shape of a Chinese bowl is just right, and generals feel that the moment for counter-attack has arrived.
> The inarticulateness of such feelings is, of course, just what is wanted to set apart the elevated and inscrutable findings of Intuition from the mundane and scrutinisable findings of Reason. Now this sort of talk is obviously silly. But it is true that some people's "noses" can be relied on in some sorts of matters; namely when they are intelligent people with a good deal of practice in matters of this sort.... If a wife feels that her husband is out of sorts, he probably is, unless she is very newly married or very silly; and if the dealer feels that the picture is genuine, while the collector feels that it is a fake, we had bet-

ter look up their records before taking sides.

Feeling, in this use, is not a magical way of getting the answers to questions, alternative to calculating, cross-examining, weighing pros and cons and so on. It is not a way of getting answers at all.... If we did not ride hunches, we should never move at all; though equally, if we merely rode hunches without doing any careful work as well, we should seldom get to a destination, and never get our hunches educated.

It is worth pointing out the ironic character of the difficulty which faces anyone who feels disposed to disagree with my argument about intuition. For, in order to try to produce a convincing case to show that artistic appreciation and experience is ultimately a matter not of objective reasons, but of intuition, he will be obliged to try to resort not to intuition, but to objective reasons.

Although it is a slight diversion, it may be worth reverting to our earlier discussion of feeling, in order to indicate, all too briefly, something of the enormous significance of the implications of the argument I am proposing. Erich Fromm has written a superb little book, carefully and significantly entitled The Art of Loving.[13] Fromm's important point is that people, generally, expect love simply to happen. It doesn't. But that expectation is the root cause of untold human misery, and the sad inability of so many people ever to achieve worthwhile human relationships. Contrary to the common view, such feelings, of love, friendship, and many others, have to be learned, as in the case of the arts. There is no easy shortcut. Some permissive, subjectivist views are most harmful because they deny this, and make a seductive appeal to laziness--to the idea that one needs only to wait for these feelings to happen, and that disciplined learning is restrictive and inhibiting. Thus, many people are permanently debarred from the freedom, the experiences, the creativity, which are possible only for those who have learned what is involved in loving, friendship, the arts.

Summary

The following summary may be helpful in providing an outline of the main points of the chapter, and their relationship with each other. I have tried, all too briefly, to argue: (1) That the scientific is by no means the only kind of objectivity; (2) That a crucial aspect of objectivity is interpretative reasoning. So far from being less objective than scientific proofs, it is necessarily presupposed in order to give sense to any scientific proof. (As Einstein has said: "In science imagination is more important than knowledge."); (3) That our conception of a thing logically determines our feeling about it. That is, the way we see something determines what we feel about it. For instance, my feeling about an object which I take to be a rope is likely to be very different

from my feeling if I take it to be a snake. This is what allows for
objective judgment of feeling, because feelings have such objective
criteria (consider my ski example). This is what gives sense to
the notion of the education of feelings through the arts. (I consider this issue more fully in a paper entitled "Accountability and
the Education of Feeling."[14]); (4) That therefore in giving interpretative reasons for the ways in which a drama or dance performance can be seen, we are giving reasons for ways of feeling about
it. There is no logical separation between feeling and reason, or
between feeling and objective criteria, as the subjectivist supposes;
(5) That such objective criteria are, ultimately, just as important
for the mover as for the spectator. The meaning of what the mover
is expressing is given, for him or her too, by the objective performance in the context of its occurrence; (6) That, nevertheless,
individual feeling, like intuition, is of considerable importance,
both for performer and spectator, as long as we recognize its ultimate dependence upon objective criteria; (7) That similarly, artistic freedom, and originality, depend upon, and are not restricted
by, the learning of techniques, with their objective criteria.

Conclusion

The objectivist is right to insist that there must be objective criteria for artistic meaning in drama and dance, and that
without them there could be no learning. But he is wrong if he
distorts this emphasis by assuming that there are general, definitive criteria, and that therefore there is no place for the importance of individual experience in the understanding of artistic
meaning.

The subjectivist is right to insist that individual experience
and involvement are central to understanding artistic meaning in
movement. But he is wrong if he distorts this emphasis by assuming
that therefore there can be no objective criteria for the artistic
meaning of movement.

What is required is to understand that the concept of objectivity is more complex and subtle than is recognized by either the
subjectivist or such an objectivist. A more adequate account reveals that there is no incompatibility between individual artistic
development, and the need for objective criteria. On the contrary,
without such objective criteria there is no sense at all to the notion
of learning, and of individual development.

For far too long there has been a disastrous failure to understand the nature of objective reasoning, with respect to the emotions generally, and to the arts in particular.[15] It has been gross-
ly misunderstood as irrelevant, or even inhibiting. This pernicious
misconception must be exposed for what it is. Objective reasoning
can be, and characteristically is, given in order to develop individual

potential for artistic experience of movement in dance and drama, both by oneself to oneself; and by good teachers to students.

It is solely by means of such reasoning, by reference to objective features of the movement, that individual development in the expression and appreciation of artistic movement is possible.

Notes

1. David Hume, Hume's Ethical Writings, MacIntyre, ed. (New York: Macmillan, 1965)

2. L.A. Reid, A Study in Aesthetics (New York: Macmillan, 1931)

3. P. Phenix, Realms of Meaning (New York: McGraw-Hill, 1964)

4. T.S. Eliot, The Use of Poetry and the Use of Criticism (London: Faber & Faber, 1933)

5. Suzanne Langer, Problems of Art (London: Routledge, 1957)

6. David Best, Philosophy and Human Movement (London: George Allen and Unwin, 1978)

7. L. Spencer and W. White, "Empirical Examination of Dance in Educational Institutions," British Journal of Physical Education, 3, 1 (1972)

8. David Best, Expression in Movement and the Arts (London: Lepus Books, Henry Kimpton Publishers, 1974)

9. B. Shahn, The Shape of Content (Cambridge: Harvard University Press, 1957)

10. For a further discussion of these issues see Expression in Movement and the Arts, especially section G, and Philosophy and Human Movement, Chapter 6.

11. M. Argyle, Bodily Communication (London: Methuen, 1975)

12. Gilbert Ryle, "Feelings," in Aesthetics and Language, Elton, ed. (Oxford: Blackwell, 1967)

13. Erich Fromm, The Art of Loving (London: George Allen and Unwin, 1957)

14. David Best, "Accountability and the Education of Feeling," Journal of Aesthetic Education (June 1981).

15. For a further discussion of this crucial issue, see Expression in Movement and the Arts, especially section F.

Addendum

A more extended discussion of these and related issues is contained in my Feeling and Reason in the Arts (London: George Allen and Unwin, 1985).

Chapter Two

CONTEMPORARY APPROACHES TO MOVEMENT TRAINING
FOR ACTORS IN THE U.S.

Craig Turner

Until this century, actors trained their bodies largely by observing and imitating the physical habits of older and more experienced professionals. The overwhelming concern usually revolved
around what was called "deportment" (i.e., technically open movement that could be easily seen) and included the proper way to
stand, sit, gesture, embrace, and so forth. In our own time, the
work of vaudeville, music hall and silent film comedy stars also reveals how physical skills were often a combination of God-given talent, ceaseless practice, and practical expediency.

However, the recent demands of new styles of plays, a larger
variety of stage-space configurations, the influence of television
and movies on a realistic acting style, as well as advances in understanding of how the body works, changed all of that. Now it is
difficult to find anyone who teaches deportment, except in its ves-
tigial form in classic opera. The bulk of movement training for actors, as well as the literature of the subject, addresses itself to
the variety of ways in which the body may be developed.

This essay is a brief attempt to provide an overview of the
current state of movement training for actors in the U.S. It is
not intended as a detailed analysis of all the systems--that is what
the bibliography is for--but only as a guide for those outside the
field. However, all of the systems have their limitations as well as
strengths and I have tried to make those clear where possible.

The annotated bibliography that is included within the text
gives the interested reader a start in investigating many of the
ideas shared in this article. I have included the more important
and comprehensive works with the expectation that the reader may
follow up on more specialized subjects by cross-checking references
in the books listed.

Also, I encourage the reader to consult other sections of this
book that further cover any of the topics discussed here.

Dance has been a popular subject for the actor wanting to train his body. From the classic Greek tragedy, rooted in the choric dithyramb, to the age of Louis XIV and the Restoration period with the emphasis on grace and style, dance has been considered integral to the theatrical experience. Even today, when the direct influence of dance for acting purposes has lessened-- except, of course, in the musical theatre--most young actors are encouraged to attend dance classes. Generally, jazz and modern dance have achieved popularity over the classic ballet style, but each can serve a specific purpose for the actor in training or for those who want to try a different movement experience.

Jazz and modern encourage impulsivity and spontaneity in the body, along with a stronger awareness of rhythm and variety in movement patterns. Ballet is particularly good for developing alignment, strength, and discipline in body form. Because each style has different strengths, it is better to encourage the young actor to try the one suited to his needs: Jazz is excellent for the tight, unsure actor who needs to try aggressive, expansive movement patterns while ballet gives a taller, stronger silhouette. Of course, any of these disciplines are valuable to the actor with dance ability and can be used specifically to train the musical theatre artist. In addition, the study of the theories of Laban and Labanotation can be helpful in developing an eye and sensibility for movement, although most actor movement specialists feel that the system is too cumbersome to be of direct use for the drama.

Although dance rightly can claim importance in movement training for the modern actor, it can also lead to artificial movement patterns that become so ingrained that they are difficult to remove. Most movement teachers have had experience with actors coming from a strong dance background; these students can seem relatively inflexible and unconsciously may carry over tensions inappropriate to an actor's needs. The great strength of dance--an awareness of what the body is doing--can seem mannered in the theatre. Of course, it is just as possible, if the dance teacher has some knowledge of the acting process and the needs of the actor, to develop, through dance, a relaxed, responsive, and aware body that will not hinder later training.

It is this last type of dance teacher that helped develop "stage movement" classes for acting programs, particularly in the 1950's and 1960's. Using techniques from dance, improvisation, and games, these classes were the first real attempt to deal with the actor's body in a unique format. Unfortunately, they were often little concerned with the subtleties of character movement and sometimes resulted in a kind of physical education for actors. The best of them, however, did provide real breakthroughs and insights for the actor willing to apply himself.

Cayon, Dolores. Modern Jazz Dance. Palo Alto, CA: National
Press Books, 1971.
A basic introduction to the jazz form.

Kirstein, Lincoln. Movement and Metaphor. New York: Praeger,
1970.
A broad historical and technical examination of the dance. Analyzes many different techniques, personalities, and theories.

Laban, Rudolf. The Mastery of Movement on the Stage. London:
MacDonald and Evans, Ltd., 1950, 2nd ed. 1960.
A required text for anyone in dance. The theoretical and
technical basis for Labanotation.

Litvinoff, Valentina. The Use of Stanislavsky Within Modern Dance.
New York: American Dance Guild Inc., 1972.
An attempt to answer the needs of a dominant acting method
through dance.

Penrod, James and Janice Plastino. The Dancer Prepares: Modern
Dance for Beginners. Palo Alto, CA: National Press Book,
1970.
A good, basic manual for the beginning student.

Smith, Ann. Stretch. New York: Simon & Schuster, 1969.
Lots of good, basic exercises.

Vaganova, Agrippina. Basic Principles of Classic Ballet. New
York: Dover Publications, 1969.

Fencing has long been a popular pastime for the actor. The
Elizabethan theatre featured fights that were integral to the action;
surely the actor of Shakespeare's time had to be at least competent
with various weapons. Sport fencing for actors continued to be
popular into this century and is still considered essential to the actor wishing to be proficient in the likely demands of classical plays.
There are few acting schools of any reputation which do not at
least encourage such study.

Stage fighting is a particular form of stage movement which
has developed its own specialists, theories, and history. It is a
practical skill which is also a significant training tool. The disciplines of empty-handed and weapon stage combat have developed
comparatively recently, but are growing in popularity as an expected part of a trained actor's repertoire. Although film fighting
has always been done by experts, and the slapstick of the silent
film era required a special kind of performer, the stage actor needs
to be able to handle all forms of theatrical violence in a predictable,
reproducible way, and various systems of combat are presently being taught. Weapon fighting takes a high degree of coordination,

commitment and stamina while the training involved in weaponless work often includes learning to fall, roll and use space in an aggressive way; both are valuable adjuncts to mainstream physical training.

Castle, Egerton. Schools and Masters of Fence from the Middle Ages to the 18th Century. New York: G. Shumway, 1969.

Gordon, Gilbert. Stage Fights: A Simple Handbook of Techniques. New York: Theatre Arts Books, 1973.
Interesting as an example of an early attempt to present fight techniques to a larger audience. Uses specific examples from plays, but otherwise lacking in detail.

Hobbs, William. Stage Fight: Swords, Firearms, Fisticuffs and Slapstick. New York: Theatre Arts Books, 1967.
A broad introduction to theory and practice by the best-known fight master in England. Although lacking specific detail, this is a particularly good book for fight theory and creation.

Katz, Samuel. Stage Violence: Techniques of Offense, Defense and Safety. New York: Richard Rosen Press, Inc., 1976.
Combination of armed and empty-handed techniques. The empty-handed explanations are sometimes misleading and some moves are simply dangerous. The armed combat descriptions are more sound.

Martinez, Joseph. Combat Mime: A Non-Violent Approach to Stage Violence. Chicago: Nelson-Hall Inc., 1982.

Nichols, Richard. "Empty-Handed Combat in the Actor Training Program." In Movement for the Actor, Edited by Lucille S. Rubin. New York: Drama Book Specialists, 1980.
A concise introduction to combat as a training tool.

Turner, Craig. "The Matrix of Stage Violence." The Fight Master No. 13: 6-8 and No. 14: 8-10, 1981.
An attempt to integrate fight training with the rest of actor training. Discusses stage fighting as an acting style.

Wise, Arthur, and Derek Ware. Stunting in the Cinema. New York: St. Martin's Press, 1973.
An excellent overview of fight and stunt techniques for films. Includes history, outstanding personalities and descriptions of various methods. Wise is an expert in theatrical weapons and Ware has wide stunt experience on stage and in films.

However, none of the areas of dance, stage movement, or fencing were entirely satisfactory in dealing with the development of character or in handling individual physical problems. Also, new plays and styles of theatre developing in the 1950's and 1960's seemed to demand new ways of training and using the actor's body; the work of Chaikin, Marowitz, the Living Theatre, the writings of Artaud, Spolin and The Improvisational Movement, The Theatre of the Absurd (to name only a few) all served to spur the exploration of different systems. Acting teachers and schools of acting, particularly in the early 1960's, began to cast about for new systems of movement analysis and development that would answer some of these questions. It is not incidental that these movements occurred as the modern theatre began demanding something beyond social-psychological realism and naturalism. New forms demanded new techniques.

The 1960's have already achieved a cultural mythic status as a time when great changes occurred in almost all aspects of American society. As a part of that dynamic scene, the American theatre was also tossed about as it underwent one new experiment after another. Movement training for actors followed this pattern of rapid change and experimentation. Theatrical styles of other cultures--particularly the Japanese and Chinese theatres--demonstrated traditions of theatre that have little or nothing to do with psychology in our Western sense or realistic character portrayal, and that have developed unique physical techniques and training methods. Research in various scientific disciplines began to question mind/body dualism and encouraged a new batch of systems which approached movement training as a gestalt of the body, mind, and imagination. The actor's body took on renewed importance not only in character expression but also in enlarging the actor's sensibilities.

Implied in all of this was the search for what has become known as the "balanced" or "neutral" or "centered" body--what Martha Graham called the "divine normal." Movement teachers suddenly saw that the basic alignment and energy patterns of the actor's body could be changed. The body and kinesthetic sense the actor had developed up to the moment of training was not unalterably set; the body could be adjusted and manipulated to give a more basic sense of balance, rhythm, alignment and motor patterns. In other words, instead of accepting the student's body as it was and adding layers of skill training on top of bad habits, there was a search for an idealized body structure through which the actor might achieve greater awareness and ease of expression.

The Alexander Technique, a system formulated by F.M. Alexander at the beginning of the century, was originally popularized by dancers as a way to overcome injury and stress. Now it is a common training tool in a number of actor training programs across the country. Involving gentle and subtle manipulation by the teacher, the technique encourages retraining the actor's kinesthetic awareness. Muscular habits of posture and movement are examined and more efficient patterns are substituted. The Alexander Technique is not a quick method of training; it does involve a patient and persistent association between the teacher and student. It is not specifically a theatrical technique and so must be used in conjunction with other performance specific methods, but those who have tried it claim greater ease, efficiency, and coordination.

Barker, Sarah. The Alexander Technique: The Revolutionary Way to Use Your body for Total Energy. New York: Bantam Books, Inc., 1978.
A practical handbook that deals with the how-to of the Alexander Technique. Noted for its clear presentation and good demonstration photos.

Barlow, Wilfred. The Alexander Technique. New York: Alfred A. Knopf, 1973.
An examination of the technique with medical implications.

Jones, Frank Pierce. Body Awareness in Action: A Study of the Alexander Technique. New York: Schocken Books, 1979.
A combination of Alexander's own writings and Jones's scientific experiments. Not light reading, but worth the effort.

Maisel, Edward., ed. The Resurrection of the Body: The Writings of F. Matthias Alexander. New York: Dell Publishing Co., 1974.
An excellent collection of articles.

Bioenergetics, originally a therapeutic system based on the work of Wilhelm Reich and developed largely by psychiatrists, especially Alexander Lowen, has attracted some specialists in theatre training. Based on the assumption that the actor's body is the result of mind and body interaction, an actor's lack of energy or chronic muscular tensions are frequently caused by the suppression of feelings that are revealed in posture and muscular imbalance. The body is seen as a feeling mechanism and it is through the body that feelings can be freed. Involving exercises and manipulations, bioenergetics requires training in psychology as well as physiology and must be approached carefully as it involves intimate feelings and discoveries about the actor's personal life--discoveries which may not reflect positively or at all in his acting.

Kurtz, Ron, and Hector Prestera. The Body Reveals. New York: Bantam Books, 1977.
A good introduction to bioenergetic analysis. Many pictures and diagrams.

Lowen, Alexander. The Betrayal of the Body. New York: Macmillan Co., 1972.

_____. Bioenergetics. New York: Penguin Books, 1976.

Lowen is the founder of Bioenergetics. These two books are the best of those he has written in explaining his theory and methodology.

Reich, Wilhelm. Character Analysis. New York: Noonday Press, 1972.

The Feldenkrais method, based upon the work of Moshe Feldenkrais, an Israeli scientist who has spent a lifetime studying physiology and psychology, attempts to retrain the nervous system which controls muscle. Basically, the method claims that faulty movement patterns and physical problems often result from the nervous system learning the wrong habits. To correct these bad habits, an actor must reestablish new motor patterns through simple, direct movements as well as integrated visualization techniques. The assumption is that patterns of thinking are reflected in the body, and vice versa; the actor's imagination is always involved in making the work more than a series of simple calisthenics. The teacher will not manipulate, but will only suggest simple movement patterns --many done lying on the floor--through which the student explores new sensations. Movements are slow, rhythmic, light, and graceful. The system necessitates quiet, personal self-work which may be too subtle for some training situations. The work of Feldenkrais, backed by years of scientific and clinical study, is seen as a valuable approach to basic body work by a number of movement training specialists.

Feldenkrais, Moshe. Awareness Through Movement: Health Exercises for Personal Growth. New York: Harper & Row, 1972.
The Introduction is a clear presentation of his theories. The bulk of the book includes sequential exercises that may be explored by the reader.

_____. Body and Mature Behavior: A Study of Anxiety, Sex, Gravitation and Learning. New York: International Universities Press, Inc., 1973.
Demands some knowledge of biology and kinesiology. A rewarding plea for reeducation of motor patterns with psychic reactions.

Linklater, Kristin. "On Moshe Feldenkrais." The Drama Review 16; No. 1 (1972), pp. 23-27.
An interesting personal account of the Feldenkrais experience by a noted American voice teacher.

Possibly the most startling of the new systems being touted by actor training specialists is Rolfing. Also called Structural Integration, this system of deep tissue manipulation was formulated by Ida Rolf as a way to relieve specific painful conditions. In the process, it was also discovered that Rolfing improved general functioning and psychological well-being. The system is administered in ten hour-long sessions during which the Rolfer, through manipulation, loosens and reorganizes the myofascia, the connecting tissue that surrounds the muscles. Supposedly through this process, habitual holding patterns of body structures may be released and reintegrated. There is some question as to how permanent these changes are; usually some method of repatterning is suggested so the body won't simply revert to old nervous-system "habits." Also, although Rolfers dispute the notion, some experts caution that this form of manipulation can involve severe pain. But there are many movement specialists who swear by what Rolfing has done for them and can do for others.

Feitis, Rosemary, ed. Ida Rolf Talks About Rolfing and Physical Reality. New York: Harper & Row, 1978.

Rolf, Ida P. Rolfing: The Integration of Human Structures. New York: Harper & Row, 1978.
An outstanding text that incorporates theory, technique and philosophy.

Schutz, Will, and Evelyn Turner. Body Fantasy. New York: Harper & Row, 1977.
An account of a series of Rolfing sessions, written by both the Rolfer (who is also a therapist) and his patient. Highly readable and informative.

Various forms of yoga have been incorporated widely into American actor training for many years. Some exercises have become so common that their Indian origins are largely ignored, but there is a wealth of technique available to anyone willing to take the time for further study and application. The term yoga actually refers to an incredibly extensive system of physical, mental and spiritual techniques meant to be applied to a wide range of human problems. Hatha-yoga is a form which concentrates on the development of physical health as a discipline for total well-being and spiritual awareness and, usually in a simplified version, is used in actor training. As it is most often practiced, yoga involves gentle, persistent stretching in various positions as well as breathing and meditation techniques. It is a very low-stress way to improve overall body flexibility and, to some slight degree, muscle tone. But yoga cannot, and does not claim to, solve severe alignment problems or widen the actor's sense of physical range. Yoga is done so slowly and under such relaxed conditions, that it can lead to dulled responses and rhythms. As a technique for slowing down, however, and getting actors to observe their movement carefully, it is quite valuable.

Simon, Ruth Bluestone. Relax and Stretch. New York: Collier Books, 1973.

Good, basic introduction to hatha-yoga with author's own variations included.

Vishnudevananda, Swami. The Complete Illustrated Book of Yoga.
New York: Bell Publishing Co., Inc., 1960.
The best, most complete book on hatha-yoga. Includes numer-
ous excellent photographs, discussions of philosophy and diet.

Various styles of massage, from Esalen to the Oriental
Shiatsu, are often used as a way of treating injury and lowering
muscular tension. Although they are clearly not movement systems
as such, and do not have top importance in movement training, they
are included.

Downing, George. The Massage Book. New York: Random House,
1972.

_____. Massage and Meditation. New York: Random House,
1974.
The first book is probably the best, concerning the style of
massage popularized through the Esalen Institute. Good, simple pictures with clear descriptions. The second volume is a
good companion book that explores massage as a meditative act.

Serizawa, Katsusuke. Massage: The Oriental Method. Tokyo:
Japan Publications, Inc., 1972.
A good introduction to Shiatsu or pressure-point massage.

Oriental martial arts--particularly judo, karate, aikido (Japanese) and T'ai Chi Ch'uan (Chinese)--have also been enthusiastically explored as a way to expand the actor's range of movement experiences. Ranging from the hard, aggressive partner contact of
judo and the strict exercise work (kata) or karate to the softer,
curvilinear essences of aikido and T'ai Chi Ch'uan, the martial arts
offer discipline, focus, strong connection between internal image and
physical technique, as well as respect and confidence in being able
to handle explosive, aggressive situations. But achieving such proficiency in the martial arts takes years, which actor training programs do not have. Also, unless the teacher has some familiarity
with actors' problems--and this is true for most of the movement
disciplines discussed here--it may be difficult for actors to apply
what is learned in class to a performance situation.

Egami, Shigeru. The Heart of Karate-Do. Tokyo: Kodansha International Ltd., 1980.
Fundamentals of karate in the Shoto-Kan style.

Huang, Wen-shan. Fundamentals of T'ai Chi Ch'uan: An Exposition
of its History, Philosophy, Technique, Practice and Application.
Hong Kong: South Sky Book Company, 1973.

The most complete book on T'ai Chi available, including classic texts and a thorough description of philosophy. The photos in the practice section are of poor quality and may be confusing, although no one can expect to learn any martial art from a book.

Kobayaski, Kiyoshi, and Harold E. Sharp. The Sport of Judo. Vermont: Charles E. Tuttle Co., 1980.

Westbrook, A. and O. Ratti. Aikido and the Dynamic Sphere. Vermont: Charles E. Tuttle Co., 1973.
A superb introduction to the philosophy and techniques of aikido.

The Lecoq system of movement training is fundamentally a method of analyzing movement through which the actor comes to a greater appreciation of his or her habits and mannerisms. Once the individual's style is isolated, then it is possible to subdue it enough to allow fresh, new impulses through. Although the work involves simple, natural exercise movements, breathing, and image work, it is the use of masks for which the system has become known. By denying the actor the most overused part of his or her body (the face), it is possible to see the expressive possibilities in the rest of the body. Neutral, character, and half-masks are all used and the student is continually called upon for new ideas and approaches in both scripted and improvised work. As a device to encourage a wider sense of physical truth and a method for identifying and dealing with movement problems, it is widely respected. However, what may at times seem to be a random, exploratory nature to the work can leave actors needing more guidance uneasy and frustrated. Though the work is fascinating in and of itself, the direct carry-over to acting may not always be readily apparent without a well-organized and articulate teacher.

Eldridge, Sears A. and Hollis W. Huston. "Actor Training in the Neutral Mask." Movement for the Actor edited by Lucille S. Rubin. New York: Drama Book Specialists, 1980, pp. 71-86.
An excellent introduction to the neutral mask in various styles with a theoretical discussion of its use and purposes.

Lecoq, Jacques. "Mime, Movement, Theatre." Yale/Theatre. Vol. IV #1, Winter 1973.
A brief description of his approach to movement training for the stage, with a brief look at masks.

Levy, Alan. "A Week Avec Lecoq." Mime, Mask and Marionette. Vol. 1, No. 1 (1978), pp. 45-62.
Includes interviews with Lecoq, other teachers at the school in Paris, and students.

Rolfe, Bari. Behind the Mask. Oakland, CA: Personabooks, 1977.
A fine introduction to mask technique with exercise suggestions.

_____. "The Mime of Jacques Lecoq." The Drama Review 16, No. 1 (1972), pp. 34-38.
A good, though brief, introduction to the Lecoq system.

At about the same time that the above systems were gaining popularity in actor training, there were reexaminations of traditional, theatrically related movement forms. The study of commedia dell'arte, mime and pantomime, and the circus arts have enriched many contemporary programs. All of these disciplines supply a format and style of performing. At the same time, their very nature reemphasizes the primacy of the actor at the hub of the performance experience; what the actor does through gesture and movement is the performance.

Commedia dell'arte techniques, based upon a historical style developed between the fifteenth and seventeenth centuries, have enjoyed some popularity recently, particularly as a performance style in such groups as San Francisco Mime Troupe and the Dell' Arte Players. The style is also used in training programs as a way to encourage greater range in style and physical expression. Predicated upon the use of half-masks which allow speech, most commedia training is a combination of improvised and scripted exercises. Since the character masks have a history and tradition, some explaining and demonstration is usually necessary to show the qualities of each mask.

There is some question about the value of re-creating such traditional characters that often have little meaning to a modern audience; most modern commedia performances involve more contemporary slapstick and topical humor than the pure stock characters of the Italian classic comedy. But as a training tool, it may have much wider value and, in addition, may be supplemented by half-mask work not based on any tradition. The use of half-mask, then, becomes a way to explore body motion further and is useful in showing body and voice as complementary elements in skills training.

Duchartre, Pierre Louis. The Italian Comedy: The Improvisations, Scenarios, Lives, Attributes, Portraits and Masks of the Illustrious Characters of the Commedia Dell'Arte. New York: Dover Publications, Inc., 1966.
A classic, basic source.

Oreglia, Giacomo. The Commedia Dell'Arte. New York: Hill and Wang, 1968.
Includes good descriptions of the characters and a number of scenerio selections.

Rolfe, Bari. Commedia Dell'Arte: A Scene Study Book. San Francisco: Persona Products, 1977.

A good basic text with lots of scenarios. Suitable as a text for class use.

Historically, mime and pantomime trace their antecedents back to the ancient Roman culture, but the modern impetus is really a twentieth-century product of such French influences as Jacques Copeau, Marcel Marceau, Jean-Louis Barrault, Jacques Lecoq and most important, Etienne Decroux. Although a number of other styles of mime have been developed, particularly in Europe, it is the French school which is usually the basis of American training in the art. Most mime taught today takes one of these forms: (a) the Decroux style of exercises which focus on the body as a subtle instrument of expression and which emphasize strict articulations, particularly in the torso; (b) the illusionistic style which encourages the re-creation of objects and forces outside the actor's body and is usually associated with the white-face art of Marceau; (c) a combination of the two preceding styles and the inclusion of improvisation and games.

The strict Decroux style is painstaking, deliberate physical work that encourages strict, precise, and controlled movement. Although invaluable for establishing an artistic unity and awareness of all parts of the body, it is, for the beginner at least, frequently tedious and difficult, involving a high degree of physical control that may be inappropriate at certain stages of training. The illusionistic style is the one most often thought of as "mime," due largely to Marcel Marceau's efforts in popularizing it. Because directors and producers share this view, the young actor is well advised to be familiar with it. Unfortunately, this style can lead to mugging, broad indicating, and a generalized use of gesture.

Kipnis, Claude. The Mime Book. New York: Harper & Row, 1974.
    Includes, history, terminology and basic techniques. Based on illusion style.

Shepard, Richmond. Mime: The Technique of Silence. New York: Drama Book Specialists, 1971.
    A sequential approach to mime based on simplified Decroux style with improvisational exercises.

Circus techniques have been incorporated in many training programs, particularly in the use of juggling and tumbling skills. A good teacher can provide the young actor with a series of movement experiences which develop coordination, balance, relaxation under pressure, timing, rhythm, and facing fears. Juggling is a clear adjunct to acting work; visualizing a ball pattern and doing it is equivalent to the image process involved in developing a character and is much more concrete with immediate feedback. The demand for skills such as juggling in some shows and styles of production makes an actor with this training more employable.

Burgess, Hovey. "Circus and the Actor." The Drama Review 16,
    No. 1 (1972), pp. 39-46.
    An interview with a well-known teacher of circus arts. Dis-
    cusses his work and philosophy in teaching circus skills to ac-
    tors.

_____. Circus Techniques: Juggling, Equilibristics, Vaulting.
    New York: Thomas Y. Crowell Company, 1977.
    Covers a vast amount of material and includes good, clear de-
    scriptions of techniques.

Carlo. The Juggling Book. New York: Random House, 1974.
    The most complete book for juggling. Includes ball, hoop, and
    pin skills. An ordered, sequential presentation of juggling
    technique.

Wiley, Jack. Basic Circus Skills. Harrisburg, Pa.: Stackpole
    Books, 1974.
    Covers the broadest range of circus acts, but not in great detail.

Theatre games and improvisation have been popular in acting
classes for many years and have often been explored more fully in
movement classes. Included in this category would be animal, character, and matter imitations, Spolin-based improvisational work, explorations based on sound or colors and the environmental/sense
memory work of the still-basic Actors' Studio-Stanislavski class.
All can be used to submerge the actor's imagination and body into
a shared reality. Particularly with animal or character work, it is
possible to develop a wider range of physical characterization than
the actor might come to on his or her own, and it provides an objective image to judge against. On the other hand, these exercises
do not provide an intensive or sophisticated approach to body work
and in some cases--in the animal work, for instance--the product
can be simple-minded and generalized.

Voice and speech teachers, in an effort to integrate their
work with the work of the body (again, a response to the new perception that mind and body are one) have also appeared with their
own body-emphasized systems. The two most famous systems--
those of Lessac and Linklater--take fundamentally different approaches
to their work. It is a noble effort, but is yet to be proved that
voice and body work can be done completely and efficiently through
one all-encompassing theory.

Lessac, Arthur. Body Wisdom: The Use and Training of the Hu-
    man Body. New York: Drama Book Specialists, 1980.

_____. The Use and Training of the Human Voice. New York:
    Drama Book Specialists, 1967.

Linklater, Kristin. Freeing the Natural Voice. New York: Drama
Book Specialists, 1976.

The dominant trend in American movement training at the
present is to use more than one of the above approaches. No one
system can answer all the different problems that actors may have.
Using multiple approaches also gives variety and rhythm to training.
The combinations possible using the systems mentioned are numerous, but there is usually an attempt to balance practical skills
(dance, mime, stage fighting) with more exploratory or retraining
methods (such as the Alexander Technique).

The proliferation of new movement systems in actor training
has resulted in some criticism of these systems. There is always a
tendency to explore the latest trend or to follow the latest messiah,
sometimes without thinking. A number of the leaders of the various systems are charismatic, unique individuals who inadvertently
encourage elitism and narrowness of understanding. It can become
fashionable to drop the name of the latest thing without encouraging a tough-minded analysis of what it actually does for the actor.

A number of movement specialists now recognize that the biggest task that lies ahead is the deliberate and precise incorporation
of only the best of these systems. The question now becomes, "How,
specifically, does this particular system relate to what an actor needs
to know?" Movement teachers are reexamining the acting process,
observing the actual physical requirements necessary for the task,
and making specific connections to the new work. It is too easy
for an actor to become preoccupied with mastering one of these new
disciplines (many of which were intended for lifetime application)
and missing its connection to the problems of acting.

As part of this concern, most responsible and informed movement specialists attempt to keep informed about the work being done
in acting and voice classes. Training programs are attempting to
integrate all the disciplines involved into a coherent whole. Specialists in all areas need to constantly reinforce their work as part
of a proposed unified technique. Also, that technique needs to be
flexible enough to allow the actor, years after training, to explore
other methods intelligently.

Bartal, Lea, and Nira Ne'eman. Movement, Awareness and Creativity. New York: Harper & Row, 1975.
The work is largely based on Feldenkrais and game-playing.

Dezseran, Louis John. The Student Actor's Handbook. California:
Mayfield Publishing Co., 1975.
A grab bag of body, voice, and inner process techniques.

King, Nancy. A Movement Approach to Acting. Englewood Cliffs,
N.J.: Prentice-Hall, Inc., 1981.

An excellent, informed sequence of movement techniques. Keyed
to be integrated into acting process work.

_____. Theatre Movement: The Actor and His Space. New
York: Drama Book Specialists, 1971.
A series of warm-ups, games, and improvisations.

Penrod, James. Movement for the Performing Artist. California:
Mayfield Publishing Co., 1974.
Another mixed collection of exercises and techniques. No real
viewpoint or attempt at organizing the process.

Pisk, Litz. The Actor and His Body. London: Harrap, 1975.
By a noted British teacher of movement. Although brief, the
book does explore breath, rhythm, and spinal articulations well.

Rubin, Lucille. Movement for the Actor. New York: Drama Book
Specialists, 1980.
Seven articles on various techniques: "The Alexander Technique
as a Basic Approach to Theatrical Training," by Aileen Crow;
"Successional Flow: An Approach to the Integration of Stage
Movement Training," by Jennifer Martin; "The Bodily Expression
of Emotional Experience," by Patricia Relph; "Image, Idea and
Expression: T'ai Chi and Actor Training," by Linda Conaway;
"Actor Training in the Neutral Mask," by Sears A. Eldredge and
Hollis Huston; "Emtpy-Handed Combat in the Actor Training Pro-
gram," by Richard Nichols; "The Natural and the Stylized: In
Conflict or Harmony?," by Valentina Litvinoff.

An exciting new area that is attracting theatre movement
specialists is the work of the social sciences in body motion communication. There has been a tremendous growth of interest in
body language, gestural variants, and power and status signs
(among many others) by anthropologists, psychologists and biolo-
gists. Analyses of body motion by these specialists in social situations within a cultural framework (i.e. "real life") should be of
great value to actor training, since modern Western theatre is
based primarily on our understanding of realism and the presentation of recognizable people on stage. It is also possible that
what we call stage movement is, at least partially, an extension or
variant of the human body motion that surrounds us all the time.

By analyzing some of the scientific material, the movement
specialist should find a considerable amount of data that will be
helpful in movement analysis of actors. The new approaches to
movement training cited before only go part way in dealing with
actors' problems; to release an actor from old patterns and habits
is not enough. This can lead to an overemphasis on what the actor is feeling rather than what the audience is understanding.
Movement data from the sciences might provide a logical and crucial step in tipping the balance back in favor of the audience's
interpretation of physical signs which the actor provides. Many

acting problems may boil down to finding the right cluster or sequence of movements to explain the character and his situation.

Of course, not all scientific systems of movement analysis
are appropriate, and the methodology of science should not substitute for artistic invention and truth. Although the work of
Birdwhistell, for example, is remarkably detailed and makes significant points about body motion as a product of context, his
system is probably too complicated to deal with practically for the
theatre artist. And the studies of anthropologists give us a wealth
of information concerning culturally identified gestures, but do
not help in developing the theatrical gesture with a meaning all its
own.

The work of ethology and biology, in particular, provides
elegant explanations for many of the realities of casting, typing
of actors, and the reaction of an audience to certain stock characters. The notions of territory, status, dominance and so forth
--seeing the body as an instrument that helps to shape social
behavior--is a dynamic way of analyzing almost any dramatic situation, as well as providing the individual actor with a way of
seeing himself or herself as the marketable commodity he or she is.

Birdwhistell, Ray L. Kinesics and Context: Essays on Body Mo-
    tion Communication. New York: Ballantine Books, 1972.
    A classic in the field. Difficult but rewarding reading.

Fisher, Seymour. Body Consciousness: You Are What You Feel.
    Englewood Cliffs, N.J.: Prentice-Hall, 1973.
    Analyzing the body and its motion as psychological expression.

Goffman, Erving. Gender Advertisements. New York: Harper
    Colophon Books, 1976.
    Includes theory and numerous examples from advertising.

Guthrie, R. Dale. Body Hot Spots. New York: Van Nostrand
    Reinhold Co., 1976.
    An approach based on biology and ethology. See especially his
    charts using various actors and actresses using a scale of
    "social organs."

Miller, Jonathan. "Plays and Players." Non-Verbal Communication,
    Robert A. Hinde, ed. London: Cambridge University Press,
    1977.
    Theatre and semiotics. Analyzing stage movement as sign.

Knapp, Mark L. Nonverbal Communication in Human Interaction.
    New York: Holt, Rinehart and Winston, 1972.
    A broad overview of the field with extensive bibliographies.

Laban, Rudolf. The Mastery of Movement on the Stage. London: MacDonald and Evans, Ltd., 1950. 2nd ed., 1960.
A good introduction to the developer of Labanotation.

Morris, Desmond. Manwatching: A Field Guide to Human Behavior. New York: Harry N. Abrams, Inc., 1977.
An extensive biological approach to movement. Many pictures and handy terminology.

Shawn, Ted. Every Little Movement: A Book About Delsarte. New York: Dance Horizons, 1974.
An authoritative work on Delsarte's little-known theories. Unfortunately, Delsarte's work has been widely misinterpreted and this is a useful remedy.

Todd, Mabel Elsworth. The Thinking Body. New York: Dance Horizons, 1972.
A classic that is clear and informative. An approach to kinesiology that discusses energy, muscle groups, and balance in a simple way.

Whatever scientific systems of movement we may ultimately find to be of most value, the goal should be to provide a movement system that the actor can rely on. In this regard, it is interesting to compare Western to traditional Oriental theatre forms. In our culture, the theatre has become an extension of everyday life, speech, and movement. In the traditional performance of many Eastern theatres, all events are codified. A Kabuki actor knows the rules and how he will be judged. The American actor is much less sure of what an audience expects or how it will measure stage events. (This insecurity is also true of the audition situation and may be a major element in the development of tension and stage fright.) This situation is exacerbated by the premium we place on the individuality of an actor's style; but at what point does the unique become indecipherable?

Perhaps we should leave psychology for a while as the emphasis in actor training and instead concentrate on the form and structure of the physical event called acting. Although we cannot simply invent a theatrical form ipso facto, we can attempt to investigate and codify theatrical movement with the help of some sciences.

Chapter Three

COMMEDIA DELL'ARTE AND MIME

Bari Rolfe

Commedia dell'Arte: Sit-Com of the Renaissance

It may seem surprising that an improvisational theatre form should enjoy a lavish amount of written material. But there it is. Few of the plays themselves are on record because they consisted of improvised or semi-improvised dialogue within a given scenario and were not set down in that form at the time. However, much has been published on its history, description, analysis, influence, characters, companies, plots, dealings, values, meanings and de-meanings. The scenarios, or plot outlines, were recorded and later led to the writing of many plays based upon them.

Antecedents to commedia dell'arte exist in the comedies of Plautus and Terence, the sketches and "come-ons" of charlatans selling wares, the wandering comics and acrobats of the village fairs, in Ariosto, Boccaccio, and in the rustic farces of itinerant companies; playwrights such as Angelo Beolco and Lope de Rueda eventually emerged from the general anonymity in the early 1500's.

The early commedia plays were still close to rustic farce, its characters being country people, playing simple, time-tested come-dies and with the innovative feature of women playing women's roles. Some rustic farces are Bilora, and Ruzzante Returns From the Wars by Beolco, the anonymous Master Pathelin, and the one-act comedies of Lope de Rueda. A number of non-commedia, writ-ten plays used many of commedia dell'arte elements, like George Gascoigne's The Supposes, and Giordano Bruno's The Candle Bearer.

As the itinerant companies carried improvised comedy through-out Europe, they began to include more sophisticated characters--society's middle class was also coming into being--such as merchants and doctors, and educated young lovers. But subject matter changed little except for slight toning down of the more outrageous vulgarities; love, lust, and lucre were still the motivating forces. Poems, songs, and literary conceits were then added for upper-class audiences; the young lovers themselves were often drawn from the educated classes.

As Italian commedia became popular in European countries, particularly France, England, and Spain in the second half of the sixteenth century, playwrights in those countries responded by composing dialogued plays on the traditional plots. Thus, Molière, who lived in Paris when the Italian comedians played there, wrote his early pieces as commedia plays. Among others were Bibbiena, Larrivey, Jean de la Taille, and Jacques Grevin. Typical of that period are the scenes and scenarios in the Gherardi collection.

Its popularity continued for a long time as theatre styles go. Playwrights well into the eighteenth century wrote commedialike farces, which dealt with similar themes, treated in a more literary fashion. Love and money were still the motives, but text became more important; scenes were wordy, more emphasis was placed on upper-class characters and witty, elegant delivery, and less on physical action (except for bedroom chases), which had been paramount in commedia dell'arte. Some of the playwrights were Jean-Francois Regnard, Pierre de Marivaux, Philippe de Destouches, Louis de Holberg, Ben Jonson, Giambatista della Porta, and Carlo Goldoni.

Commedia dell'arte (arte meaning "skill") was distinct from its contemporary written form, the commedia erudita. Many plays existed in both written and improvised form, and the dell'arte players often parodied the well-known literary pieces. Commedia's most popular, traditional, masked characters were: Arlecchino and Brighella, comic servants; the miser Pantalone; the pedant Dottore; and the Captain, a cowardly braggart. The perky servant Colombina and the young lovers Isabella and Lelio wore no masks. All names could be changed, and other characters such as innkeepers and magicians appeared as needed. To stage a production, a company of strolling players arrived in a town or village, set up a trestle stage in a square or fairground, and received from civic authorities permission to perform. The head player posted the scenario backstage and told the cast what play was to be done, making sure that everyone remembered the name of the town and topical references to be used. They memorized their entrances and exits and decided on what specific comic bits (lazzi) to include, for each actor had a store of rehearsed pieces of business that could be inserted into the play as desired. The professional actors were expert improvisers; they played only one character throughout their careers (the young lovers, grown older, might change to some older role), thus developing within a fixed character their own version with individual store of gags.

Staging was simple and flexible; a painted curtain upstage served for entrances and exits; signs or props denoted place; suggested disguises were accepted for reality. The atmosphere was earthy, with human foibles a fair target for trickery. Its shenanigans were aimed at idealistic resolutions; lovers joined, misers become generous either willingly or unwillingly, and everyone satisfyingly dealt with according to merit.

Commedia in our day has been re-created from drawings, description, and educated guess, for there has been no unbroken line of productions from then to now. Documentation is plentiful: accounts by travelers, historians and players; contracts, complaints, praise, theory, and iconography.

Long in abeyance, it is currently enjoying a new popularity. In his Paris school, Jacques Lecoq has been offering training in commedia dell'arte for the past twenty years. The Piccolo Theatre of Milan staged one commedia play, The Servant of Two Masters by Goldoni, which toured worldwide in 1959-60. The Tivoli Gardens in Copenhagen has featured performances of nineteenth-century ballet commedia since 1800. Jerry Blunt's class at Los Angeles City College wrote and performed Gap of Generations, published in 1970. Of the American companies, the San Francisco Mime Troupe played in parks and theatres in its early years from 1962; the Dell'Arte Players of Blue Lake, California, since 1977; and the Bond St. Players of New York, since the mid-70's. The first two troupes use commedia's farcical style for social-political statements about ecology, war, racism, monied interests, and similar issues. They write their own plays, although in its earlier period the Mime Troupe revised some written commedia plays for its special use. Bond St. Players emphasize topical material, and seek to evolve commedia to where it might have arrived today. All three companies use its elements of characterization, bold playing style, and sometimes masks, in their additional repertoires of non-commedia plays.

In this selected bibliography, the reader will find basic titles, listed alphabetically and including some foreign ones when English translations are not available. Those works containing significant bibliographies, notably Duchartre, Smith, Dick, and Nicoll, are marked with an asterisk. Collections of plays are indicated by "c." The number of foreign language titles is huge, and readers interested in additional references in several languages are referred to the bibliographies mentioned above. Duchartre's appendix contains titles of 760 scenarios; titles in French and Italian can be found in Smith, Appendix A. Smith also lists plays influenced by the Italian comedy in her Appendix B.

Allora, mai finita la commedia!

Adriani, Placido. La Commedia dell'Arte Vue à Travers le Zibaldone de Pérouse. Translated and edited by Suzanne Thérault. Paris: Editions du Centre National de la recherche scientifique, 1965. In French and Italian.
Includes some scenarios and lazzi.

Albert, Maurice. Les Théâtres de la Foire (1660-1789). Paris: Hachette, 1900. In French.

D'Ancona, Alessandro. Origini del Teatro Italiano. 2 vols.
    Florence: E. Loescher, 1877 and Turin, 1891. In Italian.

Andreini, Francesco. Le Bravure del Capitano Spavento (short
    title). Venice: 1607 and 1614; Paris: 1633. In Italian.
    Lazzi of the Captain.

Attinger, Gustave. L'Esprit de la Commedia dell'Arte dans le
    Théâtre Français. Paris: Librairie Théâtrale, 1950. In
    French.
    History of comic French theatre contains a key chapter on
    commedia; tracing of borrowed stories; "clandestine pantomime"
    1719.

c D'Auriac, Eugène. Théâtre de la Foire. Paris: Garnier Frères,
    1878. In French.
    Collection of plays presented at the Fairs of St. Germain and
    St. Laurent.

Beaumont, Cyril. The History of Harlequin. London: Beaumont,
    1926, 1967.
    Contains illustrations, scenes; Chacoon for Harlequin, drawings
    by F. le Rousseau.

c Bentley, Eric, ed. The Classic Theatre. Vol. 1. New York:
    Doubleday, 1958.
    Contains several commedia dell'arte plays.

c _____. The Genius of the Italian Theatre. New York: New
    American Library, 1964.
    Contains several commedia dell'arte plays.

Beolco, Angelo (Ruzzante). Bilora. In World Drama, edited by
    B. H. Clark. Vol. 2. New York: Appleton, 1933, pp. 1-9.
    One-act rustic comedy.

_____. Ruzzante Returns from the Wars. In The Classic Thea-
    tre, edited by Eric Bentley, vol. 1.
    One-act rustic comedy.

Bibbiena, Bernardo da. Follies of Calandro. In The Genius of the
    Italian Theatre, edited by Eric Bentley.

Bragaglia, Anton Giulio. "I Comici italiani maestri di teatro in
    Francia." In L'Esame 4 (April 1925). In Italian.

Compardon, Emile. Les Comédiens du Roi de la Troupe Italienne
    Pendant les Deux Derniers Siècles. Paris: Berger-Levrault,
    1880. In French.

Croce, Benedetto. "Commedia dell'Arte." In Theatre Arts 17 (De-
    cember 1933): 929-939.

Cunliffe, J. W. "The Influence of Italian on English Drama." In Modern Philology IV (1907).

Davis, R. G. The San Francisco Mime Troupe: The First Ten Years. Palo Alto: Ramparts Press, 1975.
History, 1962-1972.

The Deceived. In The Genius of the Italian Theatre, edited by Eric Bentley.
Full-length commedialike farce.

* Dick, Kay. Pierrot. London: Hutchison & Co., 1960.
The role, its history, poetics, etc.

c Drack, Maurice. Le Théâtre de la Foire, La Comédie Italienne et l'Opéra Comique. Paris: Librairie de Firmin-Didot et Cie., 1889.
Selected plays, end of seventeenth century to early nineteenth.

* Duchartre, Pierre Louis. The Italian Comedy. Translated by Randolph T. Weaver. New York: Dover, 1966. First published 1929.
One of the most complete treatments of history, characters; description of production; excerpts; illustrations; bibliography.

c Fournier, Edouard, ed. Le Théâtre Français au XVIe et XVIIe Siècles. 2 vols. Paris: Laplace, Sanchez, 1871. In French.
Comedies, illustrated. "Selection of the most remarkable comedies before Molière."

Garfein, Herschel and Gordon, Mel. "The Adriani Lazzi of the Commedia dell'Arte." In The Drama Review 22 (March 1978) T77: 3-12.

c Gherardi, Evaristo. Le Théâtre Italien (short title). 6 vols. Paris: Briasson, 1694 and 1791. In French.
Scenarios, scenes, illustrations, songs, notes.

Gilder, Rosamond. "Isabella Andreini--Europe's Prima Donna Innamorata." In Enter the Actress. New York: Theatre Arts Books, 1960.

Goldoni, Carlo. Memoirs of Carlo Goldoni. Translated by John Black. London: Knopf, 1926.

_____. The Servant of Two Masters. Translated by Edward J. Dent. Cambridge: Cambridge University Press, 1969.
Also in The Classic Theatre, edited by Eric Bentley.
Full-length late farce.

Gozzi, Carlo. <u>Memoirs of Count Carlo Gozzi</u>. Translated by J. A.
Symonds. London: Nimmo, 1890.

c Jeffery, Brian. <u>French Renaissance Comedy 1552-1630</u>. London:
Oxford University Press, 1969.
Discussion; synopsis of eleven comedies.

c Jones, Willis Knapp, tr. <u>Spanish One-Act Plays in English</u>. Dallas: Tardy Publishing Co., 1934.
Rustic farces.

Kott, Jan. "The Return of Harlequin." In <u>Theatre Notebook:
1947-1967</u>. Translated by Boleslaw Taborski. New York:
Doubleday, 1968.

Lanson, Gustave. "Molière and Farce." Translated by Ruby Cohen.
In <u>The Drama Review</u> 8 (Winter 1963) T22: 133-154. Written
1901.

Lea, Kathryn. <u>Italian Popular Comedy</u>. 2 vols. New York: Russell and Russell, 1962. First published 1934.
Vol. I: Its form, masks, and scenarios; development. Vol. II:
Contacts and comparisons with Elizabethan drama.

Littlewood, Samuel Robinson. <u>The Story of Pierrot</u>. London:
Herbert & Daniel, 1911.

Madden, David. <u>Harlequin's Stick--Charlie's Cane</u>. Bowling Green,
OH: Popular Press, 1975.
Brief, popular comparison of <u>commedia dell'arte</u> and silent slapstick comedy.

Malanga, Steve. "Send On the Clowns." In <u>Attenzione</u> (July 1980).
<u>Commedia</u> by Bond Street Players.

c Mas, Raoul. <u>Théâtre pour les Jeunes</u>, No. 2; <u>Parades et Farces
pour les Jeunes</u>, No. 15; <u>Nouvelles Parades et Farces pour
les Jeunes</u>, No. 20; <u>Quatre Grandes Parades</u>, No. 35. Cahiers
de l'Education Permanente. Paris: Ligue Française de
l'enseignement, 1959 to 1965. In French.
<u>Commedia</u> farces for young actors.

<u>The Mask</u>, a Quarterly Illustrated Journal of the Art of the Theatre. Edited by Edward Gordon Craig, Florence, 1909-1929.
Reissued 1966 by Benjamin Blom, Inc., New York. Volumes
3, 4, 5, 6 and 11 contain important articles and some scenarios.

Mazzone-Clementi, Carlo. "Commedia and the Actor." In <u>The Drama Review</u> 18 (March 1974) T61: 59-64.
His approach to teaching.

McDowell, J. H. "Some Pictorial Aspects of Early Commedia dell'
Arte Acting." In Studies in Philology 39 (January 1942).

Meyerhold, Vsevolod. "Farce." In Theatre in the Twentieth Cen-
tury, edited by Robert Corrigan. New York: Grove, 1963.
Also published as "The Fairground Booth." In Meyerhold on
Theatre, edited by Edward Braun. London: Methuen, 1969.

Miclashevski, Konstantin (Constant Mic). La Commedia dell'Arte,
Ou le Théâtre des Comédiens Italiens des XVIe, XVIIe, &
XVIIIe Siècles. Paris: J. Schiffren, 1927. In French.
Nicoll considers this to be the best.

c Molière (pseud. for J. B. Poquelin). Comedies. Translated by
Charles Mathew. London: Ward, Lock, 1890.

c _____. The Kiltartan Molière. Translated by Lady Gregory.
Dublin: Maunsel, 1910.

c _____. Four Molière Comedies. Translated by F. Anstey
(pseud.). London: Hodder & Stoughton, 1931.

c _____. Six Prose Comedies. Translated by George Gravely.
London: Oxford University Press, 1956.

c _____. Eight Plays. Translated by Morris Bishop. New York:
Random House, 1957.

c _____. Comedies. 2 vols. Translated by H. Baker & J. Miller, 1739. London: J. M. Dent and New York: Dutton,
1961-2.

c _____. One-Act Comedies of Molière. Translated by Albert
Bermel. 2d ed. New York: Ungar, 1975.

Moore, W. G. Molière, A New Criticism. Various editions 1949-
1968. Oxford: Clarendon Press, 1968.

Mortier, Alfred. Ruzzante. Paris: J. Peyronnet, 1925. In
French.

Murray, James Ross. The Influence of Italian upon English Literature During the 16th and 17th Centuries. Cambridge: Deigh-
ton, Bell & Co., 1886.

c Musard, M. Les Parades des Boulevards (short title). Paris:
Delaunay, 1810. In French.
Playhouse come-ons.

* Nicoll, Allardyce. Masks, Mimes and Miracles. New York: Cooper
Square, 1963. First published 1931.

Commedia section includes history, description, plays, players, illustrations.

* _____. The World of Harlequin. Cambridge: Cambridge University Press, 1963.
Analysis, relation to its time and place, ascendancy and decline.

Oreglia, Giacomo. The Commedia dell'Arte. Translated by Lovett F. Edwards. New York: Hill & Wang, 1968.
Describes characters; includes four scenarios.

Parfaict, C. and F. Histoire de l'Ancien Théâtre Italien (short title). Paris: Rozet, 1753 and 1767. In French.
From its origin in France to its suppression in 1697; excerpts and scenarios.

Poli, Giovanni. "Commedia dell'Arte: A Renewal of the Theatre." In Players Magazine 39 (January 1963): 102-103.

* Rasi, Luigi. I Comici Italiani. 3 vols. Florence: Lumachi, 1897-1905. In Italian.
Biography, bibliography, iconography.

Rolfe, Bari. Commedia dell'Arte, A Scene Study Book. Oakland: Personabooks, 1977.
Brief descriptions; scenes and lazzi.

c _____, tr. and ed. Farces, Italian Style. Oakland: Personabooks, 1978.

c Rueda, Lope de. Pasos Completos. Madrid: Taurus, 1967. In Spanish.
One-act farces.

Sand, Maurice. The History of the Harlequinade. 2 vols. London: Secker and New York: Benjamin Blom, 1915.

Scala, Flaminio. Scenarios of the Commedia dell'Arte. Translated by Henry F. Salerno. New York: New York University Press, 1967.
Fifty scenarios; appendix tracing borrowings by Elizabethan and French theatre.

Scherillo, Michele. La Commedia dell'Arte in Italia. Turin: E. Loescher, 1884. In Italian.

Schwartz, Isadore A. The Commedia dell'Arte and Its Influence on French Comedy in the 17th Century. Paris: H. Samuel, 1933.
Includes contents of the Gherardi collection.

Smith, Winifred. The Commedia dell'Arte. New York: Columbia

University Press, 1912 and Benjamin Blom, 1964.
History; influence; list of scenarios.

_____. Italian Actors of the Renaissance. New York: Coward-
MacCann, 1930.

_____. "Italian and Elizabethan Comedy." In Modern Philology
5 (April 1908).

Stiefel, A. L. "Lope de Rueda und das italienischen Lustspiel."
In Zeitschrift für Romanische Philologie XV (1897).

The Three Cuckolds. Text supplied by Leon Katz. In The Classic
Theatre, edited by Eric Bentley.

Uraneff, Vadim. "Commedia dell'Arte and the American Vaudeville."
In Theatre Arts 7 (1923).

Mime: Nor Sock Nor Buskin

Because this is a selected bibliography, and because mime is
such a large subject, an explanation of my guidelines will be useful.
The main thrust of the listed material, which covers history, theory,
commentary, analysis, and textbooks (both early and contemporary)
is that of mime for theatrical purposes: as an art form, as contributor to other art forms, and as a training technique. Related areas
are briefly touched on, some of them more fully dealt with in other
sections of this anthology: mime for recreation and in education;
masks; kinesiology as it applies to the stage; and weaponry (those
works intended for theatrical use). Clown and commedia dell'arte,
complete theatre forms in themselves, contain mime elements and
some basic titles are included herein. To find additional material
in these related areas readers might consult bibliographies listed
here and marked with an asterisk. Foreign titles are included when
they are significant and not available in English.

Within the subject of mime for theatre there is, obviously,
mime for mimes, also mime for actors, for singers and dancers and
puppeteers, in which the most important element might be the silent acting aspect of mime--body language, expressive movement,
physical characterization, choice and economy of gesture. Mime,
then, in its full sense touches many other areas, recalling the observation of Jacques Lecoq that "Mime is pre-eminently a research
art; all forms of art originate in its silent depths, for everything
moves, stirs, shifts, evolves, is transformed. It is in that common
mimetic source that the artist prepares for his choice of thrusts
toward the different forms of expression." That pool of mimetic
silence sends streams in various directions, and it is as difficult
to pin down an all-encompassing definition as it would be to demand that a stream cease moving. The circumstance presents both

a problem and a gift. The gift is of sight where there may not have been sight--the orchestra conductor whose hands and body are a visualization of the music; moving leaves and grasses tracing, miming, the dance of the winds; visceral muscles imitating the movement of music or dance; the onomatopoeic word; the athlete miming the mental play to come; the arrested motion of paintings, sculpture; the insight into the thousand mimic acts of everyday life. Much of this is not theatre, but is the stuff of theatre.

So, what is mime? Even we, the mimes, have trouble defining our art (as is true of poetry, dance, and what-have-you). Fortunately one can practice an art without defining it; it is also well to remember that analysis comes after the fact. The very word "mime" has changed in meaning through the years, from an actor in a spoken farce sketch in Roman theatre, to a generic term including pantomime, to tableaux vivants and dumb show, to Deburau's French period pantomime, to "le mime Marceau." Today a number of mime performers will no longer use that honorable term! And some European languages, despite their countries' mime artists, have no word for "mime," only for "pantomime."

A general concept serves me at the moment for a working premise: mime, including pantomime, employs primarily physical means of the body to communicate something other than the physical technique itself. Such a concept includes those mimes who are using props or illusions, sound or silence, story or abstraction, make-up or none. Deliberately broad, it includes rather than excludes, and is meant to encourage a broad physical approach to the body and its possibilities--a description, perhaps, rather than a definition.

For a nonverbal form it has spawned lots of verbosity. Those interested in an unselected bibliography may want to consult my 1978 Mime Directory Bibliography issued by the International Mimes and Pantomimists and containing everything I could find: 120 pages of titles, scripts, films, periodicals, and reference works. Two journals, Mime Journal and Mime, Mask and Marionette, both edited by Thomas Leabhart, are not indexed in this selected list, but all issues contain material of vital interest to mimes and other theatre people.

Here, then, is a selected bibliography of what a theater person can find about expressive bodies used in expressive ways.

Agel, Geneviève. Hulot Parmi Nous. Paris: Editions du Cerf, 1955. In French.
 Biography of Jacques Tati.

Alberts, David. Pantomime: Elements and Exercises. Lawrence, KS: University Press of Kansas, 1971.
 Textbook.

Alexander, F. Matthias. The Resurrection of the Body. New York: Dell, 1971.
Alexander Technique.

Aubert, Charles. The Art of Pantomime. New York: Benjamin Blom, Inc., 1970. From the French L'Art Mimique, Paris: Meuriot, 1901.
One of the earliest textbooks.

Baker, George P. Dramatic Technique. Boston and New York: Houghton Mifflin, 1919.
Includes effectiveness of silent acting in plays.

Banville, Théodore de. "Théodore de Banville and the Hanlon-Lees Troupe." Translated by Richard Southern from Preface to Mémoires et Pantomimes des Frères Hanlon-Lees, 1880. In Theatre Notebook 2 (July-September 1948): 70-75.

Barlanghy, Istvan. Mime: Training and Exercises. Translated from the Hungarian by Hugo Kerey; edited by Cyril Beaumont. London: Imperial Society of Teachers of Dancing, 1967.
Textbook.

Barrault, Jean-Louis. Reflections on the Theatre. Translated by Barbara Wall from the French Réflexions sur le Théâtre, Paris: J. Vautrain, 1949. London: Rockliff, 1951.
His education in theatre, including mime.

_____. The Theatre of Jean-Louis Barrault. Translated by Joseph Chiari from the French Nouvelles Réflexions sur le Théâtre, Paris: Flammarion, 1959. New York: Hill & Wang, 1961.
Further reflections; includes "Concerning Gestures," on excesses of mimes.

* Beaumont, Cyril W., comp., annot. A Bibliography of Dancing. New York: Benjamin Blom, Inc., 1963.
Books on dance in the British Museum Library.

Benedetti, Robert. "Acting is Moving." In ATA Stage Movement and Dance Bulletin, 1 (May 1972), #1.

Bentley, Eric. "Marcel Marceau." In What Is Theatre? New York: Atheneum, 1968.
Review essay.

_____. "Poet in New York." In New Republic 127 (December 1, 1952): 23.
Review essay of Barrault's Baptiste.

_____. "Pretensions of Pantomime." In Theatre Arts 35

(February 1951): 26-30. Reprinted as "The Purism of Etienne Decroux" in In Search of Theatre, New York: Knopf, 1953. Essay on Decroux.

* "Bibliography on Theatre Movement." Published periodically by the Theatre Movement Program of the American Theatre Association, 1000 Vermont N.W., Washington D.C. 20005.

Bieber, Margarete. The History of the Greek and Roman Theater. Princeton: Princeton University Press, 1961. Includes mime and pantomime.

* Birdwhistell, Ray L. Kinesics and Context: Essays on Body Motion Communication. New York: Ballantine, 1972.

Blackmur, R. P. Language as Gesture. New York: Harcourt Brace, 1952.

Blanchard, Olivier, ed. Mimes Suisses--Un Aperçu. Bern: Zahringer Verlag, 1975. In French and German. Interviews with eleven Swiss mimes, including Mummenschanz, Dimitri, Byland, and Quellet.

Bridge, William H. "Place of Pantomime in the School Curriculum." In Quarterly Journal of Speech Education 11 (November 1925): 350-359. To develop powers of observation and self-expression.

Broadbent, R. J. A History of Pantomime, 1901. Reprint New York: Citadel Press, 1965. Ancient Greece through eighteenth-century England.

Bulwer, John. Chirologia (short title), 1644. Reprint Carbondale: Southern Illinois University Press, 1974. Rhetorical gesture, the natural language of the hand.

Burgess, Hovey. Circus Techniques. New York: Drama Book Specialists, 1976. Juggling, equilibristics, vaulting.

Campbell, Douglas Gordon, M.D. "Posture, A Gesture Towards Life." In Physiotherapy Review 15 (1935): 43-47. Body language.

_____. "Your Actions Speak So Loudly." In Impulse, 1954, pp. 27-28.

Chaitanya. "The School of Silence." In Quest: A Quarterly of Inquiry, Criticism and Ideas 59 (1968): 48-51. Actor's pauses fill out the words.

Chaplin, Charles. My Autobiography. New York: Random House, 1960.

Charters, Ann. Nobody, The Story of Bert Williams. New York: Macmillan, 1970.
America's first famous vaudeville mime.

Chisman, Isabel and Wiles, G. Mimes and Miming. London: Nelson, 1934.
Textbook; plays.

Clark, Barrett H. "Last of the Pierrots." In Drama 13 (August-September 1923): 351-355.
Interview with Séverin.

Critchley, Macdonald. Silent Language. London: Butterworth, 1975.
Gesture of all kinds: theatre, dance, work, conversation, etc.

Curtis, Paul J. "Exploring Silent Acting." In Dramatics 44 (May 1973): 22.

Darwin, Charles. The Expression of the Emotions in Man and Animals, 1872. Reprint Chicago and London: University of Chicago Press, Phoenix Books, 1965.

Davis, R. G. The San Francisco Mime Troupe: The First Ten Years. Palo Alto, CA: Ramparts Press, 1975.
From 1962 to 1972.

Decroux, Etienne. Paroles sur le Mime. Paris: Gallimard, 1963.
In French.
The major work of this innovative teacher.

Dickens, Charles. Memoirs of Joseph Grimaldi. Edited by Richard Findlater. Illustrated by Cruikshank. New York: Stein & Day, 1968.
First published in 1838, edited by Boz, pseudonym for Dickens.

* Dictionary Catalog of the Dance Collection, 1974. Materials in the Dance Collection, Library and Museum of Performing Arts at Lincoln Center, New York Public Library.
Includes mime.

Dimitri. Dimitri Album. Bern: Bental Verlag, 1973. In French, Italian, and German.
Autobiography, mainly photographs.

Disher, M. Willson. Clowns and Pantomimes, 1925. Reprint New York: Benjamin Blom, Inc., 1968.

Dorcy, Jean. The Mime. Translated by Robert Speller, Jr. and
Pierre de Fontnouvelle from the French A la Rencontre de la
Mime et des Mimes, Paris: 1958. New York: Robert Speller
& Sons, 1961.
Includes essays by Decroux, Barrault, Marceau.

* Duchartre, Pierre Louis. The Italian Comedy. Translated by Ran-
dolph T. Weaver from the French La Commedia dell'Arte et ses
Enfants, Paris: Editions d'art et industrie, 1955. New York:
Dover, 1966.

Enters, Angna. Artist's Life. New York: Coward-McCann, 1958.
Includes abridged version of her First Person Plural, New
York: 1937.
Autobiography; description of mime pieces.

_____. On Mime. Middletown: Wesleyan University Press, 1965.
Log of twenty sessions teaching actors; description of her works.

_____. Silly Girl. Boston: Houghton, 1944. Illustrated by the
author.
Early autobiography.

Feldenkrais, Moshe. Awareness Through Movement. New York:
Harper & Row, 1972.
Feldenkrais technique.

Gestures. Monthly newsletter published through 1982 by The Mime
Guild, 1029 Harrison Avenue, Venice, CA 90291.

Graves, Russell. "The Nature of Mime." In Educational Theatre
Journal 10 (May 1958): 101-104.
On mimetic basis of speech; communicative effort.

Gordon, Gilbert. Stage Fights. New York: Theatre Arts, 1973.
Swordplay, mummers plays, fight sequences.

Gray, Vera and Rachel Percival. Music, Movement and Mime for
Children. London: Oxford University Press, 1962.
Lesson plans, imagery; based on Laban.

Hamblin, Kay. Mime: A Playbook of Silent Fantasy. New York:
Doubleday & Co. Dolphin Books, 1978.
A play- (rather than work-) book for nontheater groups.

Hausbrandt, Andrzej. Tomaszewski's Mime Theatre. Warsaw:
Interpress, 1975 and New York: Da Capo Press, 1977.
Photohistory.

Hobbs, William. Stage Combat "The Action to the Words." London:
Barrie & Jenkins, 1980.

_____. Stage Fight. New York: Theatre Arts, 1967.

Huston, Hollis. "Dimensions of Mime Space." In Educational Theatre Journal 30 (March 1978): 63-72.
Philosophical discussion.

Jaques-Dalcroze, Emile. Eurhythmics, Art, and Education. Translated from the French by Frederick Rothwell. New York: Barnes, 1930 and Benjamin Blom, 1972.
Rhythmic movement, its relation to teaching and the arts.

Karsavina, Tamara P. "Mimetic Action Old and New." In The Dancing Times 448 (January 1948): 185-187.
Comparison of mime in old and modern ballet.

Keaton, Buster. My Wonderful World of Slapstick. With Charles Samuels. New York: Doubleday, 1960.
Autobiography.

Kernodle, George. "Symbolic Action in the Greek Choral Odes." In Classical Journal 53 (October 1957): 106.
Choral pantomime in Greek drama.

Kerr, Walter. The Silent Clowns. New York: Knopf, 1975.
On Keaton, Chaplin, Lloyd, etc.

* Key, Mary Ritchie. Non-Verbal Communication: A Research Guide and Bibliography. Metuchen, NJ: Scarecrow Press, 1977.
Includes arts, performance, culture, daily life, notation, animals, etc.

Kipnis, Claude. The Mime Book. New York: Harper & Row, 1974.
Textbook.

Kirby, E. T. "Delsarte: Three Frontiers." In The Drama Review 16 (March 1972) T53: 55-69.
Delsarte's influence on American acting, oratory, dance, modern art, etc.

Laban, Rudolf. The Mastery of Movement, 1950. Third edition revised and enlarged by Lisa Ullman. London: Macdonald & Evans, Ltd.; and Boston: Plays, Inc., 1972.
Analysis of movement with orientation to mime; mime scenes.

Lawson, Joan. Mime. London and New York: Sir Isaac Pitman & Sons, 1957 and 1966.
History; meanings of ballet gesture.

Lecoq, Jacques. "Mime, Movement, Theatre." Translated from the French by Kat Foley and Julia Devlin. In Yale/Theatre 4 (Winter 1973): 117-120.
On his school.

Lewis, Arthur H. La Belle Otero. New York: Trident, 1967.
    Biography of Otero, 1868-1965.

Lowndes, Betty. Movement and Drama in the Primary Schools.
    London: Batsford, 1970.
    Perceptual-motor learning.

* Magriel, Paul David. A Bibliography of Dancing. New York:
    H. W. Wilson Co., 1936.
    Dance and related subjects, 229 pp.

Marceau, Marcel. "Language of the Heart." In Theatre Arts 42
    (March 1958): 58-59.
    Why he became a mime.

_____. "Silence Broken." In Los Angeles Times, August 18,
    1968, Calendar pp. 1, 30, 44.

Marlowe, Julia. "The Eloquence of Silence." In Actors on Acting,
    edited by Toby Cole and Helen Krich Chinoy. New York:
    Crown, 1st ed. 1949.
    Silent moments from plays.

Martin, Ben. Marcel Marceau, Master of Mime. New York: Gros-
    set & Dunlap and London: Paddington Press, 1978.
    Photobiography, onstage and off.

Mawer, Irene. The Art of Mime. London: Methuen, 1912 and 1949.
    History; technique; mime in education.

* Mayer, David III, comp. Annotated Bibliography of Pantomime and
    Guide to Study Sources. London: Commission for a British
    Theatre Institute, 1975.
    Brief, 12 pp., on English pantomime.

_____. Harlequin in his Element. Cambridge: Harvard Uni-
    versity Press, 1969.
    English pantomime 1806-1836.

McCabe, John. Mr. Laurel and Mr. Hardy., New York: Grosset
    & Dunlap, 1966.
    Biography; Foreword by Dick Van Dyke.

McKechnie, Samuel. Popular Entertainment Through the Ages,
    1931. Reprint New York: Benjamin Blom, 1969.

McMullan, Frank. "Pantomime in the Training of a Director."
    In Players Magazine 39 (January 1963): 114-115.
    Helps observation, control, and awareness of gesture language.

Mehl, Dieter, The Elizabethan Dumb Show. London: Methuen,
    1965.

Forms, uses, and contribution of pantomime in Elizabethan drama.

Mime Journal. Thomas Leabhart, ed. Pomona College, Theatre
    Department, Claremont, California 91711.
    Since 1974; one or two issues a year.

Mime, Mask and Marionette. Thomas Leabhart, ed. Marcel Dekker,
    Inc., Box 11305, Church St. Station, New York, NY 10249.
    Published two years, 1978-80.

Mime News. Diane Babel, ed. International Mimes and Pantomim-
    ists.
    Published from March 1976 to June 1979; bi-monthly newsletter.

Mime Times. Tony Montanaro, ed. South Paris, ME 04281.
    Newsletter, quarterly, 1976-1982.

Najac, Raoul de. Souvenirs d'un Mime. Paris: Emile-Paul, 1909.
    In French.
    Autobiography.

Nicoll, Allardyce. Masks, Mimes, and Miracles. 1931. Reprint
    New York: Cooper Square, 1963.
    History of mime, antiquity through commedia dell'arte.

Nobleman, Roberta. Mime and Masks. Rowayton, CT: New
    Plays, 1979.
    Exercises, projects, ideas, etc.; for children and adults.

North, Marion. Body Movement for Children. London: Macdonald
    & Evans, 1971 and Boston: Plays, Inc., 1972.
    Textbook.

Noverre, Jean-Georges. Letters on Dancing and Ballets. 1803.
    Translated by Cyril W. Beaumont, 1930. Reprint Brooklyn:
    Dance Horizons, 1968.
    Mime in ballet; action ballets.

Palffy-Alpar, Julius. Sword and Masque. Philadelphia: F. A.
    Davis, 1967.
    Stage fencing, with sword, foil, épée, saber.

Pardoe, T. Earl. Pantomimes for Stage and Study, 1931. Reprint
    New York: Benjamin Blom, 1971.
    History, technique, exercises.

Pennington, Jo. "Expression Through Movement.: In Dance Maga-
    zine, November 1926, pp. 18-19, 50-51.
    For singers, dancers, actors.

Pepler, H. D. C. <u>Mimes Sacred and Profane</u>. London: S. French,
 1932.
 Mime in ancient liturgy; some scripts.

Pickersgill, Mary Gertrude. "Stage Movement and Mime." In
 <u>Theatre and Stage</u> 2, edited by Harold Downs. London: Sir
 Isaac Pitman & Sons, 1951.
 Technique and exercises for actors.

Pisk, Litz. <u>The Actor and His Body</u>. London: Harrap and New
 York: Theatre Arts, 1975.
 Textbook; expressive bodies, theory, philosophy, poetry, and
 exercises.

Powers, Helen. <u>Signs of Silence</u>. New York: Dodd, Mead, 1972.
 Bernard Bragg and the National Theatre of the Deaf.

Rémy, Tristan. <u>Georges Wague, Mime de la Belle Epoque</u>. Paris:
 Girard, 1964. In French.
 Biography-history; includes other mimes of the period, expecial-
 ly women performers.

_____. Jean-Gaspard Deburau. Paris: L'Arche, 1954. In
 French.
 Biography.

* Rolfe, Bari, ed. <u>Mime Directory Bibliography</u>. International
 Mimes and Pantomimists, 1978.
 Books, articles, scripts, films, periodicals, reference.

_____. "The Mime of Jacques Lecoq." In <u>The Drama Review</u> 16
 (March 1972): 34-38.
 On his philosophy and methods.

_____ ed. <u>Mimes on Miming</u>. Los Angeles and San Francisco:
 Panjandrum Books, 1980.
 Some sixty mimes, antiquity to 1950.

_____. "Towards Speech in Every Limb." In <u>Educational Thea-</u>
 <u>tre Journal</u> 25 (March 1973): 112-119.
 Discussion review of some fifteen textbooks on mime and movement.

Sayre, Gwenda. <u>Creative Miming</u>. London: Jenkins, 1959.
 Textbook.

Schoop, Trudi. <u>Won't You Join the Dance?</u> With Peggy Mitchell.
 Palo Alto, CA: National Press Books, 1974.
 Brief autobiography as a dance-mime; her work as a dance/
 movement therapist.

Shawn, Ted. Every Little Movement, 1910. Reprint Brooklyn:
Dance Horizons, 1954 and 1963.
Delsarte philosophy of movement.

Shepard, Richmond. Mime, The Technique of Silence. New York:
Drama Book Specialists, 1971.

Source Monthly. Louise S. Jensen, ed. Mimesource, Inc., New
York, NY.
A monthly resource for mimes, clowns, jugglers, and puppeteers,
1982-83.

Symons, Arthur. "Pantomime and the Poetic Drama." In Studies
in Seven Arts, vol. 9 of his Collected works. New York:
E. P. Dutton, 1925.
The poetics of pantomime.

* Towsen, John. Clowns. New York: Hawthorn, 1976.
History, commedia dell'arte, etc.; illustrated.

Walker, Kathrine Sorley. Eyes on Mime. New York: John Day,
1969.
Mime in ballet.

Wallaschek, Richard. "Primitive Drama and Pantomime." In Primitive Music. London and New York: Longmans, Green & Co.,
1893.
Pantomime dance in early societies.

Wettach, Adrien (Grock). Life's a Lark, 1931. Translated from
the German by Madge Pemberton. Edited by Eduard Behrens.
Reprint New York: Benjamin Blom, 1969.
Autobiography.

Wiles, John. Leap to Life. London: Chatto & Windus, 1957.
Experiment with children, mostly boys, using movement and mime
with music.

Wilson, Albert E. The Story of Pantomime. London: Home & Van
Thal, 1949.
Eighteenth century to the present.

Winter, Marian Hannah. The Theatre of Marvels. Translated by
Charles Meldon from the French Le Théâtre du Merveilleux.
New York: Benjamin Blom, 1964. Preface by Marcel Marceau.
Spectacle theatre; illustrated.

Wise, Arthur. Weapons in the Theatre. London: Longmans, Green
& Co., 1968.
Stage violence for directors and actors; stage, film, and TV.

Workbook. The National Clown, Mime, Puppet, and Dance Minis-
tries. Box 24023, Nashville TN 37202.
Liturgical theatre. Annual workbook with articles, some bibliography; first issue 1979.

Chapter Four

ON THE MEANING OF MIME AND PANTOMIME

Annette Lust

Are there real differences between mime and pantomime? If so, what are these differences? And why should we even make distinctions between the two terms?

Differences in meaning between mime and pantomime have existed and still do. However, as these arts have evolved these differences have shifted and sometimes even disappeared. How have their meanings changed through the centuries? Both mime and pantomime stem from the word mimesis. This is an imitative process by which the primitive dancer or singer interpreted someone or something other than himself through animal, human, or superhuman disguises. In antiquity mime, the father of pantomime, was an imitative art par excellence which portrayed life in all its aspects.[1] This imitative meaning soon became subsidiary or was ignored.

Although among the ancients both mime and pantomime were essentially comprised of expressive movement, the general distinction was that in mime words could be combined to movement. Among the Greeks and Romans, mime, from the Greek mimos and the Latin mimus meaning imitator, was a short comedy written in prose which portrayed life (mimesis biou) and in which expressive gestures or dances, especially among the Romans, were more prevalent than the spoken text. It also referred to the mime actor who performed in such a play as well as to a buffoon who played in popular entertainments. (Among the Greeks it was extended to mean anyone who made grimaces.) Historian Margarete Bieber describes this dual meaning, "it was a play without masks imitating real life," but it was also "the performer in this simple drama."[2]

Pantomime was not always clearly distinguished from mime. In the Dictionary of Latin Literature, under pantomime, there is a referral to mime and both terms have the same definition.[3] We know, however, that pantomime, from the Greek pantos meaning "all" and mimos meaning "imitator," was born when recitation and song were separated from mimetic art. Among the Romans, where pantomime was especially popular, it denoted primarily the performer who imitated all characters and portrayed objects and animals by means of rhythmical movements and gestures while accompanied by a singer or a chorus. (The Greeks more commonly called this actor-dancer orchestes.) For drama historian Bieber, pantomime, contrary to other forms of theatre, was a "play given by a single actor who performs all roles with intense gesticulation and with different masks."[4]

The art of the ancient pantomimus included both acting and dancing. In his essay on pantomime Greek author Lucian describes the ancient pantomimus as a dancer who was, above all, an actor.[5] Since his movements were expressive and rhythmical the saltator (mime dancer) among the Romans was, in effect, a pantomimic performer. The functions of both dancer and actor were also implied in the term histrio, the Roman actor of tragedy and comedy which originated from the Etruscan hister meaning "a performer."[6] The first histriones from Etruria were pantomimic dancers who performed to flute music. Gradually the distinctions between histrio and mimus disappeared. During the Roman Empire "histrio," "mimus," "pantomimus" and "ludio" (actor) were often used synonymously.[7] These terms, allied to "saltator" and "joculator" or "jongleur," were retained until the late Middle Ages.[8]

During and after the Middle Ages, mime acquired several meanings. It meant not only the performer or his or her performance but the art of gesture practiced by all sorts of entertainers. By the ninth century "mimus" implied equally a singer, dancer and actor.[9] Like the joculatores or jongleurs, prestidigitators and puppet-showers of the Middle Ages, they were, broadly speaking, imitators of human things.[10] Similarly the masked commedia dell'arte players of the Renaissance, who mimed, sang, and performed acrobatics, were imitators of life.

From the sixteenth century on, these meanings were extended. Pantomime alluded (especially from the eighteenth century on) to the all-mute entertainment rather than to the performer. It also referred to the commedia dell'arte lazzis or short comic scenes in dumb show (for example, Harlequin catching flies and pulling off their wings), played by the Italian comedians who were masters in body expression. During the seventeenth and eighteenth centuries, allegorical and mythological pageant-type ballet pantomimes were performed at the courts of Europe and in the theatres. Among these were the Duchesse du Maine's ballet pantomimes at Sceaux and John Weaver's staging of The Loves of Mars and Venus at Drury Lane in 1717. The traditional-type dumb show in the eighteenth- and nineteenth-century French and English melodramas, as well as the Elizabethan dumb shows, were also called pantomimes. In France pantomimes with commedia dell'arte-type characters were played at the Théâtre de la Foire. When staged in the English music halls at Christmas, these were called Harlequinades. By the end of the nineteenth century, the English Christmas pantomimes such as Cinderella and Jack and the Beanstalk were comprised of spectacular scenic effects and popular music hall interludes with dialogue, acrobatics, singing and dancing in which Clown had replaced Harlequin and Pierrot. The Christmas pantomime had almost no mime or dumb show. Yet, even when dialogue, singing and dancing were more predominant in such entertainments as these, they were still called pantomimes or dumb shows because they contained some element, however remote, of the technique and art of miming. In nineteenth-century England and America, pantomime was incorporated into circus acts, as in clown George Fox's (1825-1877) Humpty Dumpty and in the performances of the Hannon Lees. Meanwhile in France, Deburau had immortalized the Pierrot pantomimes. From then on the term "pantomime" was associated with this type of mute entertainment. Today we call it pantomime blanche because of the whiteface worn by the mime artist.

Modern Meanings of Mime and Pantomime

Already in the mid-nineteenth century, François Delsarte's studies to render movement more natural and meaningful were to have repercussions on twentieth-century theatre and dance. Delsarte broadly described pantomimic movement as the "conveying realistically of emotions, dramatic episodes, human situations and activities without the use of words." Its aim is to express not only all possible bodily sensations, conditions, situations, all emotions possible to man. It also deals with space, the sense of space and direction.[11] Although today the principles of his sytem seem outdated, Delsarte's definition encompasses much of modern mime and pantomime.

At the turn of the century, French mime Georges Wague abandoned nineteenth-century classical pantomime, grown stereotyped by translating each word or idea literally into gestures, for a more spontaneous form which he called "modern pantomime."

Meanwhile, as the text in the theatre had become more important, movement training for the actor was neglected. Emphasis began to be placed on the particular techniques of the performer and mime became a more specialized art. Even today, although mime has retained much of the conventional nineteenth-century meaning of pantomime or acting without words, it is recognized as a non-literary silent entertainment in which the mime artist presents his or her own particular style. The mime, for example, of Marcel Marceau differs considerably from that of the Mummenschanz Theatre or from Tomaszewski's Polish Mime Theatre.

What are the meanings of mime and pantomime from midtwentieth century on? On the one hand, the terms "mime" and "pantomime" have continued to be used interchangeably. In Bowman's and Ball's Theatre Language Dictionary, under pantomime,

mime is given as a synonym.[12] Yet, greatly due to the impetus of
the twentieth-century French school of mime, as traditional nineteenth-
century pantomime evolved into modern whiteface pantomime and the
more imaginative form we now call mime evolved, there developed a
keener awareness of movement forms in all the theatre arts. Differences became more marked and similarities more precise. Today,
the art of mime has developed various codified expressions and techniques. Definitions vary according to school, practitioner and each
mime's personal expression. They are as divergent as the mimes
practicing them.

For Jean-Louis Barrault, both mime and pantomime refer to a
purely silent art which depicts actions through gestures and movements; they are in Barrault's words, "really the same thing--the
art of gesture. Barrault nevertheless distinguishes between popular, traditional-type pantomime of the second half of the nineteenth
century and twentieth-century mime. Popular, traditional-type nineteenth century mime is a "dumb or mute art" in which gestures are
substituted for words. Twentieth-century mime is a silent art which
does not, like the older, traditional type of pantomime, rely on a
limited gesture language--however eloquent. It is a lyrical and
spontaneous expression, forever seeking new movements, new gestures and aspiring to a more intense and poetic expressiveness.
Even twentieth-century pantomime often comments on the action
through a mute language which renders it naive and antiquated.
And while pantomime more often deals with comedy, mime has a
noble quality and excels in expressing the tragic.[13]

For mime teacher Jacques Lecoq, both mime and pantomime belong to the art of gesture. However, pantomime translates spoken
language into movement, as in the Deburau codes of the nineteenth
century. Traditional pantomime belongs to a particular period and
today has value mainly as a teaching technique. Mime is a silent
language. It precedes, accompanies, or follows the spoken word
when it is present.

Bob Fleshman of Loyola University finds more similarities than
differences between mime and pantomime. Whatever differences do
exist should not alienate mimes from one another. Fleshman compares theatrical movement to music of which there are many kinds--
serious and playful, commercial and artistic--but all are music.
However, "mime, potentially a more serious form than pantomime,
can express a greater view of life with more depth and subtlety.
Pantomime seems more audience oriented. Just as clowning, it is a
popular art form giving much joy but asking little. Some dramatic
art forms require an audience with a certain knowledge and special
sensitivity. Such is the case with mime."[14]

For Peter Bu, author of an essay in the periodical Mime Journal (1983), though mime, pantomime, theatre of gesture and theatre
of attitude have taken on particular meanings (pantomime refers to

nineteenth-century Deburau-type mime and mime, to Decroux-type
mime), they are all synonyms. He prefers the term "gestural theatre" to designate all mimed theatre as well as all theatre in which
actors express through their bodies, from Deburau to Decroux and
beyond. There should be no frontier between forms in which the
mimes utilize no other means except gestures, mimicry and attitudes,
and other kinds of gestural theatre. Why must mimes no longer be
mimes if at times they speak, sing, dance or perform with marionettes? However, when words, gestures and songs are utilized
equally, this is no longer called mimed, spoken or musical theatre
but total theatre. Bu's definition of mime under the broad category of gestural theatre breaches barriers between mime as a specialized art and multiple kinds of physical theatre.

Ronnie Davis of the San Francisco Mime Troupe compares the
pantomimist to the dancer and the mime to the actor. "The pantomimist, usually masked and mute, moves to music and deals with
nothing there. The mime, who may even speak or sing, moves to
act and uses tangible props, manipulating their symbolism to comment on the story. The pantomimist charms his spectator; he won-
ders, 'What does he have there?' Even if the mime works with
tangibles, he stimulates his spectator to ask himself, 'What does he
have there mean?' Pantomime is external while mime motivates external movement from an internal source."[15] Marceau is basically a
pantomimist who sometimes utilizes mime. Chaplin, who deals with
tangible objects, is a mime.

For David Alberts, author of Pantomime, Elements and Exercises, though the elements of pantomime may serve as a basis for
all mime forms, "pantomime depends upon accurately described objects, actions, situations and events to tell a story while mime, even
if it tells a story, depicts a theme more implicitly and abstractly....
Mime has a greater potential for diversity, for responsive imagination, and a broader range of subject matter."[16]

Mime clown Don Rieder adds that while pantomime replaces
words with gestures similar to signals, for mime, which is on a
deeper level and not as "talky," silence suffices and increases its
potential to express visual poetry.

For Thomas Leabhart, editor of the Mime Journal and founder
of the Corporeal Mime Theatre, who trained under Decroux, pantomime portrays a specific character in a specific situation (Marceau's
"Bip Chases The Butterfly"); the face and hands have more importance. The art form is individualized and charming; the typical
pose or posture is crouched, knees bent, moving backward with
small movements. Mime depicts universal man in a universal situation, or in one which is a symbol of a universal idea, as in Decroux's "Love Duet," "Carpenter," and "Combat." While pantomime
is personal and charming, mime is impersonal. The face is masked
or masklike and subordinated to the expression of the total body.[17]

Leabhart also differentiates between abstract mime and Decroux corporeal mime. Rather than depict a character or object concretely, the abstract mime artist evokes the dynamics of the inner spirit of the body. In corporeal mime, though he expresses a concrete situation with movements of his total body, the mime also evokes symbols of broader ideas and conflicts.

What of the relationship between mime and pantomime and acting, dancing and clowning? Rudolf Laban, the inventor of the Labanotation method, believes the stage arts developed from mime and that music in dance and speech in drama are movement forms which have become audible. Today, mime is sometimes used synonymously with acting. In the Theatre Language Dictionary, mime is defined first as "to act" and then as "especially to act in pantomime."[18] Pantomime is described as "expressive movement in acting ... sometimes called stage action or business."[19] Jacques Lecoq defines mime as an actor who moves better. Richard Shepard, author of Mime: The Technique of Silence, sees mime as acting in silent form. For Paul Curtis, mime is any kind of silent acting while pantomime is the art of creating an illusion of reality through imaginary objects and situations.

Today, due to the influence of Delsarte and Rudolf Laban on modern dance, there is a growing awareness of the importance of gestures and expressive movement in dance. In the early twentieth century, mime dancer Angna Enters pointed out that among the Greeks there was always a true union between pantomime, mime, and dance. Greek dance contained expressive movement which one could call mime.[20] Today, dancers such as Charles Weidman relate their gift as a dancer to their talent as a mime.

We often forget the role of miming in clowning. The clown is defined as a comic performer in a circus or theatrical production who wears an outlandish costume and make-up and entertains by pantomiming common situations or actions in exaggerated or ridiculous fashion as well as by juggling or tumbling.[21] Although clown pantomime contains more slapstick and farcelike gestures, it is still a form of physical theatre. Clowns today are more conscious of the importance of mime in clowning. A number of mime schools, as that of Jacques Lecoq, have incorporated clowning techniques into mime training. Even as early as the eighteenth century, Grimaldi, the father of today's circus clowns, utilized mime as well as speech in his art. Inspired by the commedia dell'arte, mime served to enhance a comical human quality in his clown. In the early twentieth-century, film comedians Chaplin and Keaton derived their comic effects through mimo-clownery. Among today's clowns who recognize the importance of mime in clowning is Hovey Burgess, author of Circus Techniques, who believes that most good clowns are natural or trained mimes. Avner the Eccentric, trained by Lecoq, combined miming and clowning in his clown shows. Clown-mime Ronlin Foreman feels that mime gives the clown more strength and a better understanding of how the body speaks.

From these varied definitions of the meanings of mime, pantomime, acting, dancing, and clowning we may reach a common understanding of basic terms which could generally apply to many forms
of modern mime. We could broadly describe all movement forms,
whether stylized and symbolic or natural and spontaneous, as expressive movement or gestural theatre brought into play by the
mime artist, actor, dancer, or clown. However, whenever mime or
pantomime is an autonomous form obeying only its own laws, it belongs to the art of the mime artist rather than to that of the actor,
dancer or clown who harmonizes it with a spoken text, dance steps
or clowning (while mime refers to the performer of mime or of pantomime, pantomimist or pantomime artist applies only to the performer of pantomime). Autonomous, concrete and occupational movement is today called pantomime. Nonliteral and universal movement
may be alluded to as corporeal or abstract mime. Abstract and
corporeal mime, like pantomime, utilize movements which are not
subsidiary to any other medium such as to a spoken text or to
dance movement. Abstract and corporeal mime differ from pantomime in that they depict not object illusions nor a specific character or anecdote, but nonliteral, unfamiliar yet meaningful emotions
and ideas by means of nontraditional, innovative and figurative
movement. And, although there may be no marked distinctions between abstract and corporeal mime, which are often inseparable
from one another, when mime conveys, through a plastic transfig-
uration of universal emotions and ideas, mainly intention and mood,
it is called abstract or nonrepresentational. And when it stresses
the movements of the body as a whole in a nontraditional manner,
refusing the conventional use of facial expression and movements,
it is called corporeal. (Examples of abstract and corporeal mime
are Decroux's Factory, Barrault's Sickness, Agony, Death and
Marceau's The Hands.) In direct contrast is the denotative expression of nineteenth-century traditional pantomime, in which familiar pantomimic conventions were transferred from father to son
or from mime to mime. A more recent example are Marceau's Bip
pantomimes in which occupational movements and gestures give the
illusion of the presence of concrete, specific, and familiar objects,
persons and action ("The Public Garden," "Bip at a Society Party").
Beyond these general distinctions there exist in the nineteenth- and
early twentieth-century traditional pantomime, as well as in twentieth-
century pantomime and mime, still more subtle and complex differences in technique and expression which are too extensive for the
purposes of this study.

Leonard Pitt, former assistant to Decroux, gives his view of
the differences between pantomime, based on conventional object
illusions; mime, which deals with real objects and specific characters; and abstract and corporeal mime which are nonrepresentational
and more universal forms.

"Pantomime is best defined by its use of the object illusion.
This is its essence, the primary element that distinguishes it from

mime. Without the object illusion there is no pantomime. The illusions created are of conventional objects we are all familiar with; rope, stairway, door. Because the objects are conventional and characters all have a specific identity, it follows that the expression of pantomime is literal rather than abstract. The anecdotes that make up the stories are easy to identify with as they are things that can happen to all of us. These elements are exemplified in Marceau's Bip pantomimes. The pantomimist ingeniously changes from one role to another, cleverly creating a world out of nothing. The audience delights in seeing something that isn't there and is more than willing to give itself up to this world of make-believe. This quality of magic and fantasy is pantomime's greatest appeal. People are easily charmed by it. Its very charm and magic make it more conducive to humour than to drama, and herein lie its greatest limits. A dramatic expression without romantic or sentimental notions is not the true realm of pantomime. The comic expression inherent to the pantomimic form in itself would diminish the weight of the dramatic content. When pantomime does attempt to become dramatic it inevitably turns toward sadness or pathos.

"Defining mime is more difficult because it is so broad and includes so many different types of performance. Generally speaking, however, there are two types of mime, literal and abstract. Two good examples of literal mime are Charlie Chaplin and Dimitri the Clown. Rather than creating the illusion of an object they use the actual object and relate to it only as long as it serves as a vehicle for the story. The object is never an end in itself. Rather than the spectators focusing on what is not there they are allowed to focus on what is being said.

"Abstract mime seeks to express the universals of human experience without referring to the specifics of character. plot or anecdote. This is true whether it be in Decroux's Corporeal Mime or in the work of Mummenschanz. Although the two differ vastly in many ways, the main thrust of their expression is abstract. In the case of a Corporeal Mime piece that does revolve around the illusion of an object there is no attempt to tell a story as in Decroux's piece The Carpenter, which explores the movements of the human body as it adapts to the weight and function of the objects. The movements are economized and heightened to reveal the dynamic relationship between the body and the object. In other pieces that do not revolve around an object illusion a theme is chosen and elaborated upon within the highly stylized movement of the Corporeal Mime. The emotional and psychological states of mind being expressed are real, but do not refer to specific individuals or situations. Whereas in pantomime the focus would be on the specific character and the events that surround his predicament; losing a job etc., the Corporeal mime would seek to articulate the inner dynamic rhythms of the emotion or state of mind as they are common to all. The abstract expression goes beyond the individual toward the universal, as in the Mummenschanz where, even though their work has none of the stylization or 'esprit classique' of the Corporeal Mime, nevertheless empnasizes the universals of human interaction without relying on the specifics of a given situation. In their pieces based on animal and insect movements they go beyond abstraction and express the very essence of organic intelligence: perception and response.

"When I see the wide variety of performances that fall under the heading of mime I wonder if there is any such thing as mime. Perhaps fifteen or twenty years ago it would have been easier to render definitions, but today where the boundaries between the various performance types have dissolved to give us mime-ballet, mime-theatre, dance-clown, clown-theatre etc. the task of drawing clear cut lines is difficult. I often tend to think that what we do have is physical theatre, a theatre rooted in the body and developed from improvisation rather than one that evolves from a written script.

"If there is such a thing that we can call mime, it is really a pool of physical skills from which evolves a vocabulary of expression that can be applied to any type of performance. Possessing this vocabulary consists in being able to tap one's own physical and psychological energy and knowing how to articulate this energy in every part of the body. Although the springboard for the mime is essentially physical, it is not only limited to the body. All the different aspects of theatre can be used, including the spoken word."[22]

We may more concretely understand the differences between mime and pantomime by imagining the same dramatic action in a pantomime, in the movement of a play or a film, and in corporeal or abstract mime. A pantomimist playing a given character and action, for instance, a prisoner desperately pounding against a prison wall, could create the illusion of an imaginary wall in space by means of conventional gestures and with a facial expression of despair and by closing and opening his hands against a flat surface. The stage or film actor miming this dramatic action would pound in despair on a real wall with nonstylized movement. Rather than play a given action and character, the performer of abstract and corporeal mime would depict a state of anguish through the movements of his whole body and a neutral facial expression. Also, rather than pound in anguish on an imaginary or a real prison wall, the latter would evoke a universal symbol of anguish, as man's fate to suffer on earth. Thus, the pantomimist, through stylized conventional movements, creates a specific illusion of objects and portrays a precise idea or emotion. The mime actor reacts to real objects with nonstylized movement. The performer of corporeal and abstract mime challenges the spectator's imagination to create a universal emotion or idea by means of unconventional and imaginative movements of his whole body. Otherwise, according to such mime masters as Decroux, the latter would "just be pantomime."[23]

Beyond referring to a specific technique or to movement used

by the mime, actor, dancer or artist in the theatrical arts, mime
may be envisaged as the basis of all art and every creative artist
as a "specialized mime"[24] who responds to exterior stimuli and chan-
nels his responses into some form of artistic expression. If, as the
ancients believed, the source of all emotion lies in the movements of
the soul which respond to the outer world, then these movements
translated into art are, broadly speaking, a form of mime expression.
The gestures of the mime, though still of the same reality, are a
more direct transposition than, for example, the words of the poet.
Before he created the psalm, David is said to have danced it in
front of the altar; the music of his soul was expressed first of all
in the rhythms of his body to which he later suited his psalms.[25]
A painting may also be a direct transposition of movement, those of
Giotto or Fra Angelico being examples of more life-like movements
while those of modern painters like Paul Klee are more abstract.
Each painter first creates an image drawn from life movement in
color, form, line and space or sound, releasing his or her particular vision into his art.[26]

In his Anthropology of Gesture Marcel Jousse describes "mimism" as a process by which we understand objects and human beings through the body's inner replaying or "gesturizing" of them.[27]
Mimism (opposed to "mimetism," which is an imitation of objects or
persons) is grasping the essence of, for example, a tree, its root-
ings, its vertical direction, or of a human being through his or
her rhythm and his or her internal space. In the same way the
artist transposes onto the canvas, not forms as they exist but what
he or she sees as their essence. For Jousse, man's thinking begins by corporeal reactions and his thoughts are the "intellection"
of these reactions. Language was developed when "mimism" became
vocalized or when gestures were made audible through words. Aristotle has said that man, the most miming of all animals, acquires
knowledge through mimism.[28]

Since mime, pantomime and other movement forms have regained popularity during the second half of the twentieth century
and now appear in the curricula of physical education, dance, actor training and therapy programs, differences in the interpretation of terms are continually growing. Definitions vary between
practitioners of mime and pantomime, between those of traditional
techniques and those of modern and abstract techniques, and those
who use mime autonomously and those who combine it with music,
dance, spoken text, or with other art forms.

Why is it important to continue to differentiate between mime
and pantomime? With the growing development of diverse mime
forms and the combining of this art with other theatre arts, mime
and pantomime are often loosely interchanged or characterized by
varied and ambiguous meanings. And though many mimes or
teachers of mime and pantomime may be able to describe and categorize their own particular art, they should also be sensitive to the

differences and similarities between other mime forms and their own and to the kinds of expressive movement which actors and dancers utilize. The purpose is not to create systems of formulas which isolate movement forms. By means of more precise terminology and the clarification of terms, elements in common as well as distinctions become more apparent. The techniques and expression particular to each school and style may then be more clearly formulated and each mime's own particular movement style better understood.

Although it may well resist having verbal limitations placed upon it, this art, as other art forms, is governed by laws and principles which should be made articulate, just as the discoveries of Freud, Jung and Adler have been incorporated into a coherent system which aids contemporary psychoanalysts. Today, the findings of mime masters such as Decroux (mime corporeal, statuaire du mime, etc.), Barrault (mime silencieux, mime muet), and Lecoq incorporated into a solid body of knowledge would aid mimes, actors, dancers, and those interested in corporeal expression to further explore the art. May these findings also bring about a realization of the need not only of each mime artist but of each actor and dancer to comprehend that form cannot exist without expressive content and that acting and dancing without expressivity are "soulless." For only with a deeper understanding of mime may the mime artist, actor, or dancer fully master his or her art as well as perpetuate the vital role of mime in all the theatre arts.

Notes

1. George E. Duckworth, The Nature of Roman Comedy (Princeton, NJ: Princeton University Press, 1952), p. 14.

2. The History of Greek and Roman Theatre (Princeton, NJ: Princeton University Press, 1961), p. xiii.

3. Dictionary of Latin Literature (New York: J. H. Mantinband Philosophical Library, 1956), p. 208.

4. The History of Greek and Roman Theatre, op. cit.

5. The Works of Lucian, II (Oxford: Clarendon Press, 1905), pp. 238, 256.

6. Duckworth, op. cit., p. 5.

7. A Dictionary of Greek and Roman Antiquities (New York: Harper & Brothers, c1855), p. 728.

8. B. Hunningher, The Origin of the Theatre (New York: Hill and Wang, 1961), pp. 67, 68.

9. Ibid., p. 72.

10. A. Nicoll, Masks, Mimes and Miracles (New York: Cooper Square Publishers, 1963), p. 152.

11. T. Shawn, Every Little Movement (Brooklyn, NY: Dance Horizons, 1963), pp. 71, 72.

12. W. P. Bowman and R. H. Ball, Theatre Language Dictionary (New York: Theatre Arts Books, 1961), p. 248.

13. Reflections on the Theatre (London: Rockliff, 1951), p. 157.

14. Robert Fleshman, letter to author, April 1977.

15. Arnie Passman, "Stop, Look, Listen, California Living," San Francisco Sunday Examiner and Chronicle (September 30, 1973), p. 40.

16. Pantomime: Elements and Exercises (Lawrence, KS: University of Kansas Press, 1971), pp. 54, 55.

17. Thomas Leabhart, letter to author, September 14, 1973.

18. W. P. Bowman and R. H. Ball, Theatre Language Dictionary (New York: Theatre Arts Books, 1961), p. 220.

19. Ibid., p. 248.

20. Angna Enters, "The Dance and Pantomime; Mimesis and Image," The Dance Has Many Faces, ed. Walter Sorell (Cleveland: World Publishing Co., 1951), p. 86.

21. The Random House Dictionary (New York: Random House, 1967), pp. 280-1.

22. Leonard Pitt, letter to author, July 1981.

23. Samuel Avital, "The Unique Art of Pantomime," The Rosicrucian Digest (1973), p. 21.

24. Jean d'Udine, L'Art et le Geste (Paris: F. Alcan, 1910), p. xvii, Lust trans.

25. Hilary Pepler, Mimes Sacred and Profound (London: S. French, 1932), p. 20.

26. Angna Enters, op. cit., p. 83.

27. Marcel Jousse, L'Anthropologie du Geste (Paris: Gallimard, 1974), p. 61, Lust trans.

28. Ibid., pp. 54, 55.

Chapter Five

BODY LANGUAGE AND NONVERBAL COMMUNICATION

Randall Harrison

Julius Fast's <u>Body Language</u> has sold more than two and one-half million copies. While many serious scholars consider Fast's book superficial--and even misleading--its enormous popularity attests to the growing public interest in communication through bodily movement. The actor steps on the stage today before an increasingly sophisticated and critical audience.

Basic Terminology

While the term "body language" has caught the public fancy, most scholars feel uncomfortable with that label. It suggests immediately that there is a close parallel between verbal language and the communication which takes place through bodily movement. It suggests that there should be a dictionary of movements, just as we have dictionaries of words. While it is true that certain hand gestures--those called "emblems"--have fairly precise meanings, the communication which comes through bodily movement is subtle, complex and often quite different from verbal language.

The more general term "nonverbal communication" is becoming entrenched in the scientific literature. Even this label, however, has its problems.

Some scholars object that it sounds essentially negative and residual. They argue that communication is a continuous, complex process, which, occasionally, also employs words. Some of these scholars would prefer more specific labels, such as "kinesics," for the study of communication through bodily movement; or "proxemics," for the study of space as communication. But in spite of these objections, the label "nonverbal communication" has grown in usage.

In 1956, Jurgen Ruesch and Weldon Kees published a book entitled <u>Nonverbal Communication</u>. While interest in this topic can be traced back to at least the time of Aristotle in the West, and to the days of Confucius in the East, Ruesch and Kees were apparently

79

the first to use the "nonverbal communication" label in a book title. Less than a quarter of a century later, in 1980, Frye published a book-length bibliography of nonverbal communication with more than 4,000 items.

While some scholars use the term "nonverbal communication" to mean specifically communication through bodily movement, others include a broader range of nonword communication, including the use of time, space, artifact, picture and music. Even those who focus primarily on bodily movement acknowledge the importance of the larger context. The appearance of a character, for example, may be as important as a particular movement. Similarly, staging, costume, props, and timing each contribute to the total impact.

Traditional Approaches

While dance and theatre have long studied movement, the early scientific literature emerged primarily out of psychology and anthropology. Recent contributions have also been made by social psychology, sociology, ethology, and communication research. The study of nonverbal communication has become increasingly interdisciplinary.

The early psychological approach focused on the individual. Researchers were curious, for instance, about the external nonverbal cues which correlated with inner states of emotion. Then, given certain cues, how accurate were observers in interpreting those stimuli? The anthroplogist, meanwhile, focused on culture. Language, for example, marches on, generation after generation, while the individual actors come and go. Anthropologists were interested in the continuing regularities in bodily movement, as well as cultural patterns in the use of space, time, and artifact.

By contrast, sociologist Erving Goffman (1959) took a roleplaying approach to nonverbal communication. In The Presentation of Self in Everyday Life, he explicitly uses a dramaturgical metaphor to explain social behavior. Meanwhile, social psychologist Albert Mehrabian (1981) examined human relationships in terms of three dimensions of "implicit communication": pleasure-displeasure, arousal-nonarousal and dominance-submissiveness.

Current Trends

Increasingly, both researchers and practitioners have called for a more holistic approach to verbal/nonverbal communication. Research has gone deeper, probing more and more dimensions of nonverbal communication. But at the same time, attempts have been made to reintegrate the total picture.

Today, the individual is recognized as a cognitive, affective, physical being. Information processing may be verbal (in the left hemisphere of the brain), but it may also be nonverbal (in the right hemisphere of the brain). Any given nonverbal cue may have origins at the physiological, biological, psychological, social, or cultural level. Certain emotions, such as happiness, sadness, surprise, fear, anger, and disgust, appear to be universal (Ekman and Friesen, 1975). At the same time, each individual may dampen, intensify, or mask these emotions, depending upon the individual's personality, social setting, and culture.

In sum, nonverbal communication provides the actor or dancer with a rich and complex repertoire of meaning, from the use of body, artifact, space, time, and even from specific nonverbal cues such as color or lighting.

The following selected, annotated bibliography gives a brief orientation to the massive and fast-growing literature on nonverbal communication.

Allport, G. W., and P. E. Vernon. Studies in Expressive Movements. New York: Hafner, 1967.
A reissue of the 1933 classic.

Altman, I. The Environment and Social Behavior: Privacy, Personal Space, Territory and Crowding. Monterey, CA: Brooks/Cole, 1975.

Andersen, P. A., J. P. Garrison, and J. F. Andersen. "Implications of a Neurophysiological Approach for the Study of Nonverbal Communication." Human Communication Research 6 (1979), pp. 74-89.
Argues for defining "nonverbal communication" in terms of right brain functions.

Andrews, R. J. "The Origins of Facial Expression." Scientific American 213 (1965) pp. 88-94.

Archer, D. How to Expand Your Social Intelligence Quotient. New York: M. Evans, 1980.
One researcher's approach to testing nonverbal sensitivity.

Argyle, M. Social Interaction. New York: Atherton, 1969.
The "new look" in social psychology; includes nonverbal communication.

_____. Bodily Communication. New York: International Universities Press, 1975.
Excellent introduction to nonverbal communication; includes origins in animal communication.

_____, and M. Cook. Gaze and Mutual Gaze. Cambridge: Cambridge University Press, 1976.
The role of eye behavior in social interaction.

Arnheim, R. Visual Thinking. Berkeley: University of California Press, 1969.
The conclusions of a famous perceptual psychologist.

Ashcraft, N., and A. E. Scheflen. People Space: The Making and Breaking of Human Boundaries. Garden City, NY: Doubleday/Anchor, 1976.

Baker, S. Visual Persuasion. New York: McGraw-Hill, 1961.
An ad man's well-illustrated argument for nonverbal communication.

Bauml, B., and F. H. Bauml. A Dictionary of Gestures. Metuchen, NJ: Scarecrow Press, 1975.

Bellman, B. L., and B. Jules-Rosette. A Paradigm for Looking: Cross-Cultural Research with Visual Media. Norwood, NJ: Ablex, 1977.

Benthall, J., and T. Polhemus. The Body as a Medium of Expression. New York: E. P. Dutton, 1975.

Berscheid, E., and E. H. Walster. Interpersonal Attraction. Reading, MA: Addison-Wesley, 1969.

Birdwhistell, R. L. Introduction to Kinesics. Louisville: University of Louisville Press, 1952.
Argues for a linguistic-type analysis of bodily movement.

_____. Kinesics and Context. Philadelphia: University of Pennsylvania Press, 1970.
Collected essays by the father of kinesics.

Blakeslee, T. R. The Right Brain. Garden City, NY: Doubleday/Anchor, 1980.
A popular introduction to right-mode thinking.

Bosmajian, H. The Rhetoric of Nonverbal Communication. Glenview, IL: Scott, Foresman, 1971.
A reader of popular essays.

Brannigan, C. R., and D. A. Humphries. "Human Non-verbal Behavior: A Means of Communication." Ethological Studies of Child Behavior, ed. N. Blurton-Jones. Cambridge: Cambridge University Press, 1972.
A classic example of the ethological approach.

Bruneau, T. J. "Chronemics and the Verbal-Nonverbal Interface."
The Relationship of Verbal and Nonverbal Communication, ed.
M. R. Key. The Hague: Mouton, 1980.
"Chronemics" is the study of time in communication.

Burgoon, J. "Nonverbal Communication Research in the 1970s: An
Overview." Communication Yearbook 4, ed. D. Nimmo. New
Brunswick, NJ: Transaction Books, 1980.

_____, and T. Saine. The Unspoken Dialogue: An Introduction
to Nonverbal Communication. Boston: Houghton Mifflin, 1978.
A basic text which takes a functional approach, examining the
uses of nonverbal communication.

Byrne, D. The Attraction Paradigm. New York: Academic Press,
1971.

Clynes, M. Sentics, the Touch of Emotions. New York: Doubleday, 1977.
An unusual theory about movement and emotion.

Darwin, C. The Expression of the Emotions in Man and Animals.
Chicago: The University of Chicago Press, 1965.
A reissue of the 1872 classic, which argues an evolutionary base
for facial expressions.

Davis, M. Understanding Body Movement: An Annotated Bibliography. New York: Arno Press, 1972.

_____. Nonverbal Communication Literature 1971-1980: An An-
notated Bibliography of Behavioral Study of Body Movement.
New York: Arno Press, 1981.

_____, ed. Interaction Rhythms: Periodicity in Communicative
Behavior. New York: Human Sciences Press, 1981.

Davitz, J. R. The Communication of Emotional Meaning. New
York: McGraw-Hill, 1964.

_____. The Language of Emotion. New York: Academic Press,
1969.

Dittman, A. T. Interpersonal Messages of Emotion. New York:
Springer, 1972.

Duncan, S. D. "Nonverbal Communication." Psychology Bulletin
72 pp. 118-137, 1969.

_____, and D. W. Fiske. Face-to-Face Interaction: Research,
Methods, and Theory. Hillsdale, NJ: Lawrence Erlbaum, 1977.

Edwards, B. Drawing on the Right Side of the Brain. Los Angeles: J. P. Tarcher, 1979.
A way to get in touch with right-brain processes by drawing.

Efron, D. Gesture, Race and Culture. The Hague: Mouton, 1972.
A reissue of the classic 1941 study.

Eibl-Eibesfeldt, I. Love and Hate: The Natural History of Behavior Patterns. New York: Schocken, 1974.

Eisenberg, A. M., and R. R. Smith. Nonverbal Communication. Indianapolis: Bobbs-Merrill, 1971.
A brief, introductory text.

Ekman, P. The Face of Man. New York: Garland, 1980.
Interesting photo study of cross-cultural universals.

_____, ed. Darwin and Facial Expression: A Century of Research in Review. New York: Academic Press, 1973.
Traces the influence of Charles Darwin and his once-controversial theory about facial expressions.

_____, and W. V. Friesen. "The Repertoire of Nonverbal Behavior: Categories, Origins, Usage, and Coding." Semiotica 1 (1969), pp. 49-98.
A major framework for understanding different types of gesture.

_____, and _____. Unmasking the Face: A Guide to Recognizing Emotions from Facial Cues. Englewood, NJ: Prentice-Hall, 1975.
Highly recommended for actors.

_____, _____, and P. Ellsworth. Emotion in the Human Face: Guidelines for Research and an Integration of Findings. New York: Pergamon Press, 1972.
A revised edition of this one is in the works.

Exline, R. V., S. L. Ellyson and B. Long. "Visual Behavior as an Aspect of Power Role Relationships." Nonverbal Communication of Aggression, 2, eds. P. Pliner, L. Krames, and T. Alloway. New York: Plenum, 1975.

Fast, J. Body Language. New York: M. Evans, 1970.
The most popular of the pop treatments; easy reading, but light, narrow and dated for the serious student.

Freedman, J. L. Crowding and Behavior. New York: Viking, 1975.

Frye, J. K. FIND: Frye's Index to Nonverbal Data. Duluth: University of Minnesota Computer Center, 1980.
Continuing updates are promised for this basic bibliography.

Goffman, E. Behavior in Public Places. New York: Free Press, 1963.

_____. Encounters. Indianapolis: Bobbs-Merrill, 1961.

_____. Frame Analysis. New York: Harper & Row, 1974.

_____. Gender Advertisements. New York: Harper/Colophon, 1979.
An interesting examination of role portrayals in the media.

_____. Interaction Ritual. Garden City, NY: Doubleday, 1967.

_____. The Presentation of Self in Everyday Life. Garden City, NY: Doubleday, 1959.
In his first of many books, Goffman used a dramaturgical metaphor.

_____. Relations in Public. New York: Basic Books, 1971.

Hall, E. T. Handbook for Proxemic Research. Washington, D.C.: American Anthropological Association, 1974.

_____. The Hidden Dimension. New York: Random House, 1966.

_____. The Silent Language. Garden City, NY: Doubleday, 1959.
An introduction to "proxemics," the use of space for communication.

Hanna, J. L. To Dance is Human: A Theory of Nonverbal Communication. Austin: University of Texas Press, 1979.
Not quite a theory, but an approach to studying the social significance of dance.

Harper, R. G., A. N. Wiens, and J. D. Matarazzo. Nonverbal Communication: The State of the Art. New York: John Wiley, 1978.
Good summary of the research literature on face-to-face interaction.

Harrison, R. P. Beyond Words: An Introduction to Nonverbal Communication. Englewood Cliffs, NJ: Prentice-Hall, 1974.

_____. The Cartoon: Communication to the Quick. Beverly Hills: Sage Publications, 1981.

_____. The Nonverbal Domain. Englewood Cliffs, NJ: Prentice-Hall, forthcoming.

Henley, N. M. Body Politics: Power, Sex, and Nonverbal Communication. Englewood Cliffs, NJ: Prentice-Hall, 1977.

Hess, E. H. The Tell-Tale Eye. New York: Van Nostrand Reinhold, 1975.
In addition to gaze direction, pupil dilation can be revealing.

Hinde, R. A., ed. Non-Verbal Communication. Cambridge: Cambridge University Press, 1972.
Excellent set of articles, mostly by British authors.

Izard, C. E. The Face of Emotion. New York: Appleton-Century-Crofts, 1971.

_____. Human Emotions. New York: Plenum Press, 1977.

Jourard, S. M. The Transparent Self. Princeton: Van Nostrand, 1964.

Kendon, A., R. M. Harris and M. R. Key. Organization of Behavior in Face-to-Face Interaction. Chicago: Aldine, 1975.

Key, M. R. Nonverbal Communication: A Research Guide and Bibliography. Metuchen, NJ: Scarecrow Press, 1977.

_____. Paralanguage and Kinesics (Nonverbal Communication). Metuchen, NJ: Scarecrow Press, 1975.

_____, ed. The Relationship of Verbal and Nonverbal Communication. The Hague: Mouton, 1980.

Kleinke, C. L. First Impressions. Englewood Cliffs, NJ: Prentice-Hall, 1975.

Knapp, M. L. Nonverbal Communication in Human Interaction. 2nd. ed. New York: Holt, Rinehart and Winston, 1978.
Probably the most widely used general text on the subject.

_____, J. M. Wieman and A. Daly. "Nonverbal Communication: Issues and Appraisal." Human Communications Resource 4(3) (1978) pp. 271-280.

Koivumaki, J. H. "Body Language Taught Here." Journal of Communication 25 (1975) pp. 26-30.
A critique of the "psychopornography" in many pop treatments of body language.

LaFrance, M., and C. Mayo. Moving Bodies. Monterey, CA: Brooks/Cole, 1978.
A readable, basic text.

Leathers, D. G. Nonverbal Communication Systems. Boston: Allyn and Bacon. 1976.
Another basic text, with a few offbeat topics, e.g., plastic surgery.

Leonard, G. The Silent Pulse. New York: E. P. Dutton, 1978.
A popular treatment of interaction rhythms.

Mehrabian, A. Nonverbal Communication. Chicago: Aldine-
Atherton, 1972.

_____. Public Places and Private Spaces. New York: Basic
Books, 1976.

_____. Silent Messages. 2nd. ed. Belmont, CA: Wadsworth,
1981.

Montagu, A. Touching: The Human Significance of the Skin.
New York: Harper & Row, 1978.

_____, and F. Matson. The Human Connection. New York:
McGraw-Hill, 1979.

Morris, D. Manwatching: A Field Guide to Human Behavior.
New York: Abrams, 1977.
An elegantly illustrated overview of nonverbal communication.

_____, P. Collett, P. Marsch, and M. O'Shaughnessy. Gestures.
New York: Stein and Day, 1979.
A study of twenty European gestures, but a rich background
to gestural communication generally.

Reich, W. Character Analysis. Translated by T. P. Wolfe. New
York: Orgone Institute, 1945.
Argues that life experiences become encased in a person's "body
armor."

Roach, M. E., and J. B. Eicher. Dress, Adornment, and the Social Order. New York: Wiley, 1965.

_____, and _____. The Visible Self: Perspectives on Dress.
Englewood Cliffs, NJ: Prentice-Hall, 1973.

Rosenfeld, L. B., and J. M. Civikly. With Words Unspoken: The
Nonverbal Experience. New York: Holt, Rinehart and Winston,
1976.
Illustrated and experiential, this one may be of particular interest to the student actor or dancer.

Rosenthal, R., ed. Skill in Nonverbal Communication: Individual
Differences. Cambridge, MA: Oelgeschlager, Gunn & Hain,
1979.
A report on the "PONS test" for measuring nonverbal sensitivity.

Ruesch, J., and W. Kees. Nonverbal Communication: Notes on the
Visual Perception of Human Relations. 2nd. ed. Berkeley:
University of California Press, 1971.

Ryan, M. S. Clothing: A Study in Human Behavior. New York: Holt, Rinehart and Winston, 1966.

Scheflen, A. E. Body Language and the Social Order. Englewood Cliffs, NJ: Prentice-Hall, 1972.

_____. How Behavior Means. New York: Anchor Books, 1974.

_____, and N. Ashcraft. 1976. Human Territories: How We Behave in Space-Time. Englewood Cliffs, NJ: Prentice-Hall, 1976.

Sebeok, T. A., A. S. Hayes, and M. C. Bateson, eds. Approaches to Semiotics. The Hague: Mouton, 1964.

Siegman, A. W., and S. Feldstein, eds. Nonverbal Behavior and Communication. Hillsdale, NJ: Lawrence Erlbaum, 1978.

Sommer, R. Design Awareness. San Francisco: Rinehart Press, 1972.

_____. Personal Space. Englewood Cliffs, NJ: Prentice-Hall, 1969.

Spiegel, J. P., and P. Machotka. Messages of the Body. New York: Free Press, 1974.

Watson, O. M. Proxemic Behavior: A Cross-Cultural Study. The Hague: Mouton, 1970.

Weitz, S., ed. Nonverbal Communication: Readings with Commentary. 2nd. ed. New York: Oxford University Press, 1979. An excellent reader, with a wide range of researchers.

Wiener, M., S. Devoe, S. Rubinow, and J. Geller. "Nonverbal Behavior and Nonverbal Communication." Psychological Review 79 (1972) pp. 185-214. A key attempt to distinguish "shared codes."

Wolfgang, A., ed. Nonverbal Behavior: Applications and Cultural Implications. New York: Academic Press, 1979.

Chapter Six

SYSTEMS OF DANCE/MOVEMENT NOTATION

Jill Beck

Historical Perspective on Dance Notation

Although it is possible that Egyptian hieroglyphics and the pictographs of primitive societies may have been used to capture dance movements, the oldest known manuscript which definitely employs a dance notation dates from the mid-fifteenth century. The earliest systems of dance notation, for example that shown in The Dance Book of Margaret of Austria of 1468, employed letter abbreviations in lieu of the full names of the social dance steps they described. A textual clarification of the steps indicated by the letters sometimes accompanied these notations. In general, however, the system of abbreviations assumed that the reader was already familiar with the basic style of the movements.

Thoinot Arbeau's Orchésographie, published in France in 1588, took dance notation a step further. Arbeau described the various steps and movements of several contemporary dances and added numerous illustrations. Movement phrases were notated by placing the step names next to the musical notes on which they occurred. Orchésographie is of special interest due to the information on manners and customs of the times it contains.

As social dances developed in the cultural centers of Europe, they began to include more complex floor patterns. Steps remained relatively simple, but the path of the dances became more involved and of increased importance. This change in the dances led to a new approach to dance notation. Track drawings of the spatial pattern of dance movements began to replace letter abbreviations of steps.

The most famous exponent of the track drawing type of notation was Raoul Feuillet, who, in 1700 published Chorégraphie, a system pioneered by Pierre Beauchamps. The Feuillet method combined track drawings with indications of the steps performed on that path. The system is highly respected today because it communicates a great deal of information in a simple way. Feuillet's notation is used widely in reconstructions of Baroque dance and Rudolf Laban credits Feuillet with the idea of a continuous center line marked off with strokes indicating timing. Cautions to bear in mind when using Feuillet notation are that timing is approximate (measures are shown but not count divisions) and information on movements of the upper body is limited.

Feuillet notation did not prove to be adaptable to the needs of the dances of subsequent eras, and the search for a universally applicable method continued. In the nineteenth century, faced with the greater use of arms, body and legs in developing theatre dance, notation turned toward pictorial representation. Arthur Saint-Léon, a well-known dancer and choreographer, published a system called La Sténochorégraphie in 1852 which was based on stick figures. Steps performed on the ground were notated on the lines of a five-line horizontal staff, while aerial steps were written between the lines. Movement notation was placed directly over corresponding music notation. Enrico Cecchetti was one of the prominent dance masters of the period who used Saint-Léon's system.

Saint-Léon's pictorial representations were, in effect, images of a series of positions found within a dance sequence. His system introduced a set of problems which notations based on stick figures have never been able to solve successfully: how to show exact transitions between separate moments in the notation; how to accurately portray the third dimension; and how to present precise timing information.

Frederick Zorn, German ballet master, proposed a system in 1887 which was similar to but more highly developed than that of Saint-Léon. Stick figure representations are highly stylized in the Zorn notation and the notation is placed under staves of music. The system did not remain in active use after the death of its inventor, but may be researched in Zorn's Grammar of the Art of Dancing.

At the end of the nineteenth century, experimentation began in Russia with dance notation based on music notation. The attraction of this approach was that timing indications are inherent in note values. Vladimir Stepanov developed his notation at the St. Petersburg Imperial Ballet and published it in Paris in 1892 in Alphabet des Mouvements du Corps Humain. In the same year Stepanov was invited to introduce his notation system to Moscow's Bolshoi Theatre. Later, in 1918, substantial amounts of choreography in Stepanov notation were taken from Russia by Nicholas Sergeyev, who transported volumes of notes with him to the West. The Harvard Library now houses a significant collection of classic Russian ballets preserved in Stepanov notation.

Stepanov's system shows direction and level of movement by the placement of notes on lines or spaces of the staff. Square notes signify supports and round notes, gestures. Stems of notes which point up indicate movement to the left and stems which point down, movement to the right. Leonide Massine adapted the Stepanov notation, adding to it and modifying it according to his own needs. Massine's system is explained in his book On Choreography.

Vaslav Nijinsky used a system of notation which closely resembles that of Stepanov to record portions of his choreography. The basis for Nijinsky's system is clearly musical notes, but his notation is not fully understood and is still being investigated. An article by Edward C. Mason, "Madame Nadine Nicolaeva Legat on the Nijinsky System of Notation" is one source of information on the subject.

Two other attempts to use music notation as a basis for dance notation were made by Pierre Conté (France 1931)) and Antonio Chiesa (Italy 1932). Conté used letter abbreviations in conjunction with his Ecriture de la Danse Théâtrale; Chiesa recorded army drill formations in a notation he called Motographia.

There have been diverse attempts in the twentieth century to develop a comprehensive system of notation. Richard Saunders (United States 1945) invented Dancescore, a collection of sheets listing common terms for steps in different dance styles. Notators circled appropriate words to capture the sequence of dance phrases. Space was left at the side of the Dancescore for indications of rhythm and floor pattern.

Famous modern dancers tried their hand at notation, including Doris Humphrey and Alwin Nikolais. Humphrey, together with Betty Joiner, used modified stick figures on scrolls which were unrolled as the dance progressed. Her ideas on notation are compiled in "The Dance Score: A Project for Dance Notation." Alwin Nikolais's system, called Choroscript, is discussed in his article "A New Method of Dance Notation." A modification of Labanotation which uses a five-line vertical staff which is read from the bottom up, Choroscript employs movement symbols based on musical notes.

Letitia Jay (Jay Notation, 1957) and Sol Babitz (Dance Writing, 1939) were two others who tried to develop a stick-figure-based system. Benesh notation and the Movement Shorthand of Valerie Sutton represent two contemporary efforts to adapt representational notation to the complexities of dance. (See following section.)

The latest development in dance notation has been the move to create sets of abstract symbols which can serve as a movement alphabet. The premise behind this approach is that different combinations of the symbols are capable of recording any type of human movement. Margaret Morris introduced a movement alphabet in England in 1928 in The Notation of Movement. Her system has been criticized for its choice of arbitrary symbols which are difficult to memorize. The other well-known abstract-symbols systems are Labanotation and Eshkol-Wachman Movement Notation.

Major Forms of Notation in Use Today

The major forms of notation in use today are Benesh notation and Labanotation. Labanotation, the system most widely used in North America, was invented by Rudolf Laban and first published in Schrifttanz in 1928. Laban's system is known in Europe as Kinetography.

Labanotation employs a three-line vertical staff which represents the human body, the center line of the staff dividing movements of the right from the left. Nine basic directional symbols form the basis of the system, and each symbol conveys four pieces of information: the shape of the symbol describes the direction of the movement; the length of the symbol shows how much time it takes to do the movement; the shading of the symbol tells whether the movement is on a low, middle, or high level; and the placement of the symbol on the staff determines which part of the body is in motion. The staff is read from the bottom up and timing is indicated by short strokes across the center line, marking off counts and lines across the entire staff marking off measures. Movement quality is described by effort symbols which clarify the dynamics of particular movement sequences. Phrasing can be shown by vertical bows which link specific movements together.

One of the strengths of the Laban system is its preoccupation with the flow of movement rather than with a series of positions present in a movement sequence. This allows Labanotation to render a more naturalistic account of dance than other notation forms. Additional positive features of the system are its rhythmic accuracy, precision in the recording of stylistic variations, and applicability to all forms of dance and human activity. These aspects of Labanotation have made it the most comprehensive system of notation in use today.

The center for Labanotation is the Dance Notation Bureau in New York City. Founded in 1940, the Dance Notation Bureau houses an extensive archive of dance scores as well as a research library and professional training center. A staff of certified notators adds twenty-five to thirty scores to the Bureau's archives each year. There are now more than 280 full-length scores available in Labanotation, including ballet, modern, musical comedy, and ethnic dance. The standard text used by the Dance Notation Bureau is Labanotation by Ann Hutchinson. Self-instruction is possible with the Study Guide for Elementary Labanotation by Hackney, Manno and Topaz.

Benesh notation was invented by Rudolf and Joan Benesh in England in 1955. The system is based on stick-figure representation of the human body, but is highly stylized and employs a number of nonpictorial symbols. Sections of a five-line horizontal staff are used to depict sequential images of the moving body. Lines drawn from one image to the next show the path of movement between the positions given. Timing is shown by the use of bar lines and by placing the dance notation below the corresponding measures of musical accompaniment.

Some of the positive aspects of the Benesh system are the speed with which it can record movement and the visual quality of the notation which suggests the general shape of the movement. However, the time value of movements can be only generally stated as can the relation of one movement to another.

The center for research and dissemination of the Benesh system is the Institute of Choreology in London. Benesh notation has been adopted by the Royal Ballet and is more popular in Europe than in North America. The two primary texts on this system are An Introduction to Benesh Movement-Notation by Rudolf and Joan Benesh and An Introduction to Benesh Movement Notation by Marguerite Causley. Self-instruction can begin with Benesh Movement Notation Beginner's Manual by Janet Wilks.

Two other systems of notation are attempting to offer competition to Labanotation and Benesh notation: Eshkol-Wachman Movement and Sutton Movement Shorthand. The Eshkol-Wachman method, invented by Noa Eshkol and Abraham Wachman in Israel in the 1950's and published in Movement Notation, sees movement as geometric patterns in space. The system is careful to label itself movement, as opposed to dance notation, since it is capable of recording the spatial patterns of any moving body, be it dancer, animal, or airplane. As regards dance, the basic premise of the Eshkol-Wachman notation is that each body part has an axis and that all movements of this axis (or "rod") occur within a sphere, known as the "system of reference." Numbers are assigned to points on the surface of the sphere within which the body part moves; the numbers are used to define the path of the body part as it moves from one area to another.

Eshkol-Wachman Movement Notation has been praised for its applicability to all forms of motion, and has the potential to be of significant service in scientific movement analysis. However, the staff is cumbersome in comparison with those of Labanotation and Benesh notation, and the plotting of movement with spatial coordinates has been criticized by dance artists who feel this captures only the most skeletal framework of a choreographic plan. Eshkol-Wachman notation is in use by The Chamber Dance Group in Israel, a group which engages in performance, research, and notation activities. It is on the curriculum of the University of Illinois and Tel-Aviv University.

Sutton Movement Shorthand, invented by Valerie Sutton, was first published in a book of the same title in c. 1973. Ms. Sutton acknowledges the influence of Zorn notation on her work. Sutton Movement Shorthand uses a horizontal staff with lines representing the shoulders, hips, knees, and feet, and records movement from the point of view of the audience, making it somewhat difficult for the dancer to reconstruct movement from the score. Round symbols below the staff show the facing of the performer and the relationship of limbs to the body. Boxes above the staff, called "information boxes," include further details such as the presence of physical contact. The merits of the system are that it is easy to learn and fast to write; one minute of solo dancing requires only two minutes of notation time. This advantage must be countered by the criticism that Sutton Movement Shorthand has difficulty capturing details of movement, such as the difference between a shoulder that is raised, rotated, or shifted. Sutton Movement Shorthand is taught in selected American dance programs (notably the Boston Conservatory of Music) and experimentation with the system is ongoing in Europe and South America.

Although Eshkol-Wachman Movement Notation and Sutton Movement Shorthand have certain positive features and are actively in use on a limited scale, the support of the international dance and movement research communities continues to fall behind Benesh notation and Labanotation. Labanotation maintains the position of the most universally accepted system for notating human movement.

Applications of Dance and Movement Notation

Now that the dance world has a library of more than 280 full-length dance scores in Labanotation alone (listed in Catalogue of Notated Dances, Dance Notation Bureau), questions are arising about the uses to which dance scores can and should be put. There are two principal schools of thought about this, one urging faithful reconstruction of original works and the other posing a more radical approach.

The more provocative attitude toward the use of dance scores contends that they should be open to individual interpretation. No one would dream of insisting that every performance of Hamlet be a carbon copy of the 1601 original. Each director who undertakes a production of Hamlet studies the script, analyzes it, and makes decisions about how best to express the ideas and emotions which seem most important in the play. The comparable point of view regarding dance scores is that they should be allowed to be used in restagings which reflect an individual director's insights and skills. Might not new interpretations of older choreographies make them more timely and/or of increased interest? Advocates of restaging would like dance directors to be permitted to exercise the same creativity in the reading of dance scores that music conductors and play directors

bring to their scores and scripts. They feel this is a natural progression in the developing field of dance.

The primary use to which notated scores have been put in
recent years involves attempts to faithfully reconstruct original
works. Reconstructions try to recreate a dance piece as it was
first performed. The value of reconstructions of dance works is
generally recognized, but dance notation is often criticized for
failing to provide all the information necessary for the detailed recovery of a choreography. When reconstructing a dance work, it
is always advisable to approach the dance score with prior knowledge
of the choreographer's place in dance history and his or her personal style. No musician expects each small detail of performance
information to be included in a music score. It may not be reason-
able for dancers to have different expectations from dance scores.
Essays on this and other philosophical and research issues in notation are printed in the Teacher's Bulletin (renamed Dance Notation
Journal in 1982), published twice-yearly by the Dance Notation
Bureau.

Apart from the applications of movement notation to the preservation and restaging of choreographies, notation presents the possibility of composing dance on paper. Advocates of this idea stress
that dancers have individual habits, preferences, and patterns of
movement which recur in their compositions. One means of breaking these patterns is to manipulate movement symbols on paper,
without planning the results in advance. Via this approach, dance
notation offers a new direction in choreographic experimentation.

Movement notation potentially may have an economic effect on
the field of dance by reducing the number of expensive rehearsal
hours of performance companies. If it becomes commonplace for
dancers to read and study their parts at home, just as musicians
do, they will learn to arrive at rehearsal already prepared for their
work. Limited rehearsal time will be needed for coaching and polish-
ing, and the long hours previously needed to teach dancers their
parts by imitation will be eliminated. The Hartford Ballet is design-
ing a prototype of a company training program in dance notation.

Notated dance scores are providing a new profession of dance
scholars with the primary source materials they require for research
purposes. For the first time, developments in dance are leaving
concrete and detailed history behind them, so that future generations will not have to rely on speculation about the nature of
twentieth-century movement. Scores prepared for documentation
purposes are generally accompanied by videotapes. Although videotape deteriorates and videotaped performances reflect only one interpretation of a piece under specific studio conditions, video is
considered a valuable supplement to notated scores. The emerging
videodisc technology will solve the problem of image degradation,
facilitate access to selected parts of dance works, and permit over-
lay of the dance notation on the picture.

Notated publications are beginning to serve to disseminate movement techniques to dancers and teachers far from the centers of dance activity. They allow subjects such as dance history to be taught using authentic examples, and offer dancers of different languages the possibility of communicating in a script which is universally understood.

All of the advantages which music notation brought to that art are now available to dance through movement notation. It is clear to what extent notation is preserving dance's past. What is unclear as yet is the impact dance notation will have on the future of the art.

Articles

Brock, Nancy. "The History of Dance Notation." Dance Observer (November 1941) pp. 116-117; (January 1942) pp. 8-9; (March 1942) pp. 36-38.

Cohen, Selma Jeanne. "A Language for Dancers." Dance Observer (April 1954) pp. 53-54.

_____. "Twenty-Year Growth of Dance Notation." New York Herald Tribune, May 22, 1960.

Field, John. "The Use of Benesh Notation in the Royal Ballet." The Dancing Times (August 1968) pp. 589, 596.

Humphrey, Doris. "The Dance Score: A Project for Dance Notation." Unpub. ms. 36p. Doris Humphrey Collection. Dance Collection, Library and Museum of Performing Arts at Lincoln Center, New York Public Library.

Hutchinson, Ann. "The Dance Notation Field Here and Abroad." Dance Magazine (November 1956) pp. 36-37, 55-59.

_____. "A Survey of Systems of Dance Notation." Laban Art of Movement Guild Magazine (May 1967) pp. 25-38.

Jay, Letitia. "A Stickman Notation." Dance Observer (January 1957) pp. 7-8.

Laban, Juana de. "Dance Notation." Dance Index (April-May 1946) pp. 89-132.

Martin, John Joseph. "A New Script: The Problem of Notation as Solved by Sol Babitz." New York Times, August 27, 1939.

Mason, Edward C. "Madame Nadine Nicolaeva Legat on the Nijinsky System of Notation." Dance and Dancers (August 1956) pp. 35-36.

Nikolais, Alwin. "A New Method of Dance Notation." In The Dance Experience, pp. 145-150. Edited by Myron Howard Nadel and Constance Nadel Miller. New York: Universe Books, 1978.

Rogers, Helen Priest. "Dance Notation." Dance Observer (April 1937) p. 39; (May 1937) p. 51.

Smith, Marion. "L'écriture de la Danse: Film of M. Conté's System." The Dancing Times (December 1949) pp. 142-143.

Woody, Regina Llewellyn Jones. "Introduction to Dance Notation." Dance Magazine (January 1959) p. 61; (February 1959) p. 61; (March 1959) p. 59; continued in subsequent issues through April 1960.

Books

Babitz, Sol. Dance Writing: Preliminary Outline of a Practical System of Movement Notation. Los Angeles: The author, 1939.

Benesh, Rudolf and Joan Benesh. Reading Dance: The Birth of Choreology. London: Souvenir Press, c.1977.

_____, and _____. An Introduction to Benesh Movement-Notation. Brooklyn, NY: Dance Horizons, 1969.

Canna, D. J. and Eugene Loring. Kineseography: The Loring System of Dance Notation. Hollywood, CA: Academy Press, 1955.

Causley, Marguerite. An Introduction to Benesh Movement Notation. New York: Arno Press, 1980.

Chiesa, Antonio. Motographia. serialized in Persio, March 15, 1934-1935.

Conté, Pierre. Ecriture de la Danse Théâtrale et de la Danse en Général. Niort: Progres, 1931.

Eshkol, Noa and Abraham Wachmann. Movement Notation. London: Weidenfeld and Nicolson, 1958.

_____ et al. Moving, Writing, Reading. Holon, Israel: Movement Notation Society, c. 1973.

Feuillet, Raoul Auger. For the Further Improvement of Dancing. Translated by John Essex. Farnborough, England and Brooklyn: Gregg International and Dance Horizons, 1970.

_____. Chorégraphie, Ou l'Art de Décrire la Dance. Paris: Michel Brunet, 1700.

_____. Recueil de Contredances. Paris: Michel Brunet, 1700.

Hackney, Peggy, S. Manno, and M. Topaz. Study Guide for Elementary Labanotation. New York: Dance Notation Bureau Press, 1979.

Hutchinson, Ann. Labanotation. New York: Theatre Arts, 1977.

Jackman, James L., ed. Fifteenth Century Basses Dances. Wellesley, Massachusetts: Wellesley College, 1964.

Jay, Letitia. Jay Notation. New York: n.p., 1957.

Laban, Rudolf von. Principles of Dance and Movement Notation. London: Macdonald and Evans, 1956.

_____. Schrifttanz. Wien: Universal-Edition, 1928.

Massine, Leonide. On Choreography. London: Faber and Faber, 1976.

Morris, Margaret. Creation in Dance and Life. London: Owen, 1972.

_____. The Notation of Movement. London: K. Paul, Trench, Trubner and Co., 1928.

Saint-Léon, Charles Victor Arthur Michel. La Sténochorégraphie; Ou, Art d'Ecrire Promptement la Danse. Paris: Chez l'auteur, 1852.

Stepanov, Vladimir Ivanovich. Alphabet des Mouvements du Corps Humain. Paris: M. Zouckermann, 1892.

_____. Alphabet of Movement of the Human Body. Translated by Raymond Lister, Cambridge, England: Golden Head Press, 1958.

Sutton, Valerie. Sutton Movement Shorthand. Irvine, California: Movement Shorthand Society, c. 1973.

Tabourot, Jehan [Thoinot Arbeau]. Orchesography. Translated by Mary Stewart Evans. New York: Dover Publications, 1967.

Wilks, Janet. Benesh Movement Notation Beginner's Manual. London: The Benesh Institute of Choreology, 1978.

Zorn, Friedrich Albert. Grammar of the Art of Dancing. Boston: n.p., 1905.

Catalogues and Bulletins

Catalogue of Notated Dances with addendum, available free of
charge from the Dance Notation Bureau, 505 Eighth Ave.,
New York City 10018.

Teacher's Bulletin (renamed Dance Notation Journal in 1982). New
York: Dance Notation Bureau, biannual publication.

Chapter Seven

BODY SYSTEMS*

Martha Myers, Margaret Pierpont, and Diana Schnitt

The human posture has fascinated observers for centuries. Whether the viewer is a street corner voyeur, a painter, or a doctor, people and how they carry themselves have been the subject for everything from clinical curiosity to sexual intrigue. During this past century, the interest in human posture as a field has grown, and most recently, it has become a specialty in its own right, with a focus on how best to accommodate postural change.

Body systems, body therapies, or body work? Practitioners come from a variety of backgrounds, and while no one quite agrees on what to call this new field, they do agree that the main task of the work is the recoordination of movement patterns. An underlying theme in this recoordination is that the changing of movement behavior often involves a psychological change. Either a psychological change will precede (and potentially cause) a change in movement behavior, or a change in movement behavior will precede a change in the psyche. The relationship is neither clearly understood nor well researched, but the observed phenomenon appears to reaffirm the theme of mind-body unity prevalent in the work as well as the emphasis on the experiential.

This field is interdisciplinary and, in many ways, this chapter of Part I overlaps quite directly with the chapter on Movement Analysis Systems and the chapter on Nonverbal Communication. One must first be able to observe movement accurately before attempting to recoordinate movement patterns. However, where the emphasis of movement analysis and nonverbal communication is on observation and interpretation respectively, the emphasis of this work is on movement change.

The first to gravitate toward this field seemed to be primarily

_____

*This essay is based on the series, "Body Therapies and the Modern Dancer" by Martha Myers, which appeared in Dance Magazine, February-July, 1980. MP

dancers, physical therapists, and dance therapists. Although the pioneers considered here were developing their ideas in the early to middle part of this century, they were still strongly influenced by residual nineteenth-century themes: self-reliance, strict codes of morality, self-control, authoritarian family-style living based upon rule and ritual, moré and folkway, and the work ethic reinforced an inhibition of many of man's internal feelings. Feelings concerning his carnality and experiential phenomena which contradicted familial and societal codes were submerged. Repression was at a peak and sophisticated thinkers rationalized that the Cartesian duality, with mind separate from body, was ultimately behind the repression. The pioneers in this field were aware of the incompleteness of this model and they felt the implications of its limitations.

When late nineteenth- and early twentieth-century advances in public health and developments in medicine and sexual hygiene allowed social and cultural attitudes to change, these pioneers were ready to participate. They looked to the radical intellectuals and artists of the day--from Freud to Renoir, Dalcroze, Delsarte, and Isadora Duncan, to D. H. Lawrence, Laban and the "Wandervogel" movement, with its emphasis on natural dress, body culture, and folk art to promote emergence of new aesthetic, cultural and political ideas. With World War I, transformations in dress codes and sexual roles were demanded and the body began a new liberation from its hidden role. One form this new liberation took was an interest in "correctives" which originated in German orthopedics and entailed postural exercises based upon mechanical principles.

While pioneers in twentieth-century movement studies embraced many of the social and cultural changes permitted by twentieth-century advances, many found industrialism--the realities of war and the growing fears of becoming a human cog in an organic machine--somewhat overwhelming. With the 1960's and 1970's--Vietnam, Eastern philosophies, natural dress, and the "me" generation--an environment similar to that of the "Wandervogel" movement was formed. The atmosphere was again conducive to the growth of holistic ideologies. And, as with most movements, the balance scales again tipped, with emphasis on the experiential often overriding analytical concern. The 1980's are seeing the number and range of people interested in movement change growing to include a variety of professionals: anthropologists, movement analysts, athletes, massage therapists, chiropractors, and some fairly traditional physicians and scientists. As this pattern of mix between the new and the traditional continues, we can look forward to a growing balance between the science and the art of man's changing movement patterns. Man is again wrestling to coexist with the machine, and this revived interest in the human posture and the "stress diseases" reflected within it, is one attempt to reconcile our coexistence.

Motivations of participants in body work vary from working

toward full recovery of muscle use after injury to alleviating vague
but annoying physical discomfort. Some wish to make specific improvements in posture and ease of movement, or achieve a general
sense of physical and mental well-being. The methods described
here are most commonly used among dancers, but are by no means
limited to people whose primary occupation involves intense physical activity.

After a series of lessons, students may become proficient
enough to incorporate what they have learned into their daily living. Whether learning is slow or occurs in an instantaneous breakthrough, it takes hours of practicing and developing one's capacity
to pay attention to subtle changes in movement in order to incorporate them into one's autonomic repertoire.

In the series of articles from which this essay is adapted,
four systems were covered in depth: Bartenieff Fundamentals^{tm},
the Alexander Technique, Feldenkrais Awareness Through Movement, and Todd-Sweigard Ideokinesis. They were chosen because
they are the oldest, most well-known, and most used among dancers, and because they all share the element of self-maintenance by
the student. There are many other related systems, and new ones
are cropping up every day. As well, practitioners are beginning to
become trained in more than one method, and they are creating their
own blends. Following is a summary of each of these four systems,
so that their roots and differences may be appreciated, followed by
an analysis of the elements that are essential and distinctive about
them as a group. In this way, those curious about the general
field may acquire both information about specific systems and a
frame of reference for looking at others they may encounter.

Irmgard Bartenieff, president of the Laban/Bartenieff Institute of Movement Studies in New York City, developed the body
system called Bartenieff Fundamentals^{tm}. It is an important component of the Certificate Program in Laban Movement Analysis at
the Institute. Bartenieff, who died in 1981, was also a physical
therapist, dance therapist, movement analyst, researcher, and
writer whose career spanned five decades.

Bartenieff received her dance training in the 1920's in Germany, where she also studied with Rudolf Laban, the inventor of
what is now called Laban Movement Analysis or Labananalysis. Included in this overall framework are Labanotation--the movement
recording system best known in the United States--Effort, Space
Harmony, and Fundamentals (Bartenieff's particular development of
Laban's theories). Dancers may be more familiar with the term
"effort/shape," which was used originally in this country to distinguish Laban's movement work from Labanotation. The terminology is changing as the theory evolves, but as a whole it deals
with analyzing movement through experience and observation.

The Laban framework identifies different aspects of movement: the mover's body sensations, the mover's feelings or attitudes towards such elements as weight, time, space, and flow, and the way the mover uses the space and the environment around him or her. These aspects, of course, are interrelated and of equal importance in movement.

Fundamentals both identifies principles basic to observing and performing movement and provides an evolving series of movement sequences which deal with mobilizing the body efficiently in its environment and preparing it to perform as wide a range of movement qualities and shapes as possible. Among concepts taken up in class are:

Dynamic alignment, a neuromuscular patterning or posture that responds accurately and sensitively to changes in standing, walking, and sitting and provides a flexible relationship with the environment. This concept is quite different from those notions of posture that base the way a person stands and moves on a fixed ideal or aesthetic model such as the shoulders-back, chest-out military posture and certain stylized alignments in ballet and modern dance.

Body attitude, the particular way in which a person's body reflects his or her internal feelings. In Laban theory, this is spoken of as the body's "accommodation" to space--convex, concave, or vertical, for example. Posture is more than a physical relationship between parts of the body; it is as personal as a signature and body therapists view it as a meaningful part of a person's life history.

Initiation of movement, how and in what part of the body a particular movement begins. In Fundamentals' sequences, close attention is paid to how a person initiates a movement. Proper initiation is essential to improving performance and preventing injury.

Weight transfer, how a person transfers weight, first from one part of the body to another, and then from one foot to another in moving through space. Weight can be transferred sequentially (one part following another), simultaneously (in a single unit), unilaterally (one whole side at a time), or bilaterally (the sides operating in opposition, i.e., the ordinary walk). The force an individual uses is also significant. Sequential movement has to do with how the movement goes through the body from joint to joint, and the term flow is used in Laban theory to describe this particular aspect of motion.

Besides specific sequences of movement that focus on initiation and shift of weight, there are sequences whose function is to connect the upper and lower parts of the body and the right and left halves of the body--with rotation as an important element--and to develop coordinated changing of levels. Beginning work takes place on the floor, because there the student doesn't have to cope with gravity, but mobilization to sitting and standing is emphasized. In her book, Body Movement: Coping with the Environment, Bartenieff explicitly describes all of these sequences.

The movement sequences of Fundamentals are not all new. They come from physical therapy, from Bartenieff's long years of investigation and teaching movement rehabilitation, and from developmental movement of infancy and childhood. Yet, Fundamentals approaches movement from a different point of view. The emphasis on how movement is done, with reference to the Laban elements of effort and space, distinguishes Fundamentals from a set of exercises. There is concern for the total body and for the quality and direction of the movement, a connection that leads to more fluent, efficient movement patterns and a richer movement experience.

One of the oldest body systems is the Alexander Technique. For three-quarters of a century, it has attracted students from all walks of life, among them Aldous Huxley, John Dewey, and Nicolas Tinbergen.

An injury inspired the discovery and development of the Alexander work. Frederick Matthias Alexander (1869-1955) loved to recite and act, and at nineteen, he was giving recitations of Shakespeare in Australian cities. His career was soon interrupted, however, by continuous bouts of hoarseness and loss of voice which resisted the best efforts of physicians. So the young actor decided to look for possible causes himself. With the aid of mirrors, he discovered that as he spoke, he pulled his head "backward and down," lifted his chest, and hollowed his back. In preparation for each speech, he repeated this pattern, which caused his breath to come in gasps by depressing his larynx and constricting his ribs.

The solution he discovered for these problems was to take him from the stage to a lifetime of teaching principles of healthful "self-use." The discoveries were startlingly simple, but their effect was profound. Alexander learned that by preventing the old stressful pattern of pulling the head down on his neck and instead, letting the head go forward and up, his whole body seemed to move upwards. His spine lengthened, his rib cage was freed, his breathing became less labored, and even his walking changed.

"Primary control," one of the key principles of Alexander's teaching, depends on a particular use of the head and neck in relation to the whole body. From his reading in physiology and neurophysiology, Alexander saw the head and neck as central to habitual misuse of the body and to its education towards efficient, pleasurable use. According to Alexander, the postural reflexes of the head and neck are central for orientation in the environment; reflexes let us know where we are in relation to our surroundings. Since the major sensory organs are located in the head, changing the orientation of the head and neck can alter the perceptions of self and the environment because of changes in the reflexive mechanism. Directing the head so it is poised lightly on the neck is one way the Alexander training counteracts the effects of gravity and corrects "kinesthetic errors" that have become habitual--and though comfortable, not useful--in a person's movement patterns.

Also important to the technique is the concept of "inhibition." Alexander believed that people can learn to deny or "inhibit" an inefficient movement pattern and consciously substitute one that produces more harmonious movement and feelings of ease and well-being. This "inhibition" is not a physical action but a mental decision. According to Alexander, people have a choice in response to stimuli, whether physical, mental, or emotional. They can choose not to respond at all, or they can select and learn new responses. For Alexander, the choosing must remain conscious, and choice is lost when response becomes automatic. When a posture becomes automatic and set, the muscles and joints have become locked into habitual movement responses, and thus, there are fewer movement choices the body is capable of making.

The three basic steps of the technique--awareness of a movement pattern, inhibition of the pattern, and substitution of a new one--are learned through the guidance of a trained teacher, usually in private sessions. By using a light and sensitive touch (acquired through years of training) and repetition of such key phrases as "head forward and up," "back lengthening into width," and "knees forward and out," the teacher helps the student establish more efficient movement patterns in simple actions such as sitting down, getting up, and walking.

Moshe Feldenkrais's method of body reeducation developed from such a wide range of disciplines that Feldenkrais has been called a Renaissance man. Feldenkrais, at seventy-eight, is the director of the Feldenkrais Institute in Tel Aviv, Israel, and a lecturer at Hebrew University. Of his sixteen published books, Awareness Through Movement and Body and Mature Behavior are the most widely known.

Feldenkrais has a doctorate in physics from the Sorbonne and was involved in a physics career until the age of fifty. An injury to Feldenkrais's knee (the result of avid soccer playing) was the catalyst for a new direction in his life. To many years of studying yoga and judo, he added systematic study of anatomy, neurophysiology, learning theory, and biochemistry. He successfully applied his knowledge to his own body and then to those of friends who came to him for advice. Gradually, a method evolved.

There are two branches to the work. Awareness Through

Movement is learned in group lessons. Functional Integration is practiced one-to-one with a trained practitioner who gently manipulates and readjusts the client's body parts. In group classes, the teacher does not demonstrate the movement or make physical corrections but instead gives verbal directions and descriptions. Each student works to achieve the goals of the lesson as fully as each body permits, following his or her time choices about how to best organize the limbs and the torso to do what the teacher describes.

The actions vary from a simple rolling over to the more complicated "arching the head to the back wall as the pelvis is tipped forward," or reaching with the left knee to the right elbow while lying on the floor. The class work is made up of very small actions, usually in one joint or two joints simultaneously. These actions focus on subtle interrelationships between joints and among major parts of the body--pelvis, ribs, legs, and shoulders. Often the student doesn't realize until he or she gets up that the joints have released to allow more pleasurable movement patterns to emerge.

Feldenkrais's approach to reeducation emphasizes: (1) drawing on early developmental patterns of human mobility; (2) providing more accurate data on spatial relationships of the parts of the body; (3) bringing habitual motor patterns to conscious attention; (4) developing a more articulate spine; and (5) establishing more organic breathing patterns, which make greater lung capacity available and free the rib cage and upper torso for more active involvement in the environment.

Feldenkrais's use of early childhood coordinations and reflexes involves such movements as "head foraging" (rolling the head from side to side); creeping; rolling over; sequences for developing the coordination between right and left sides, upper and lower halves of the body, and eye motions; and movements coordinating crawling and getting up and down from the floor. Feldenkrais's lessons also engage students in making a more accurate assessment of their bodies in space: how the limbs lie as they rest on the floor; whether the parts are symmetrical or asymmetrical, and how the energy flows between them. The goal is to help each individual establish a more complete body image or "schema" and more sensitive kinesthetic responses, all of which Feldenkrais sees as leading to a richer sense of self.

All of the body therapies are concerned with the relationship between the body and the mind as it affects body alignment and motion. In the early part of this century, Mabel Todd, a member of the faculty at Teachers College at Columbia University, developed a method of body reeducation based on the use of visualization, which she described as "psychophysical." The use of this term emphasized her sense of the importance of the interplay between physical stimulus and psychological response in the working of the neuromuscular system that produces movement. Todd's books, The Hidden You and The Thinking Body, have been rediscovered since the republication of the latter by Dance Horizons in 1968. Originally published in 1937, the ideas, insights, and practices discussed are still ahead of much contemporary practice in movement education.

Mabel Todd provided not just a dynamic theory of movement process, but postulated a new means for dealing with movement training and neuromuscular reeducation that would use the power of the imagination. She insisted, however, that the imagining be based on factual images. Her work was further developed by two of her students, Barbara Clark and Dr. Lulu Sweigard. Clark practiced primarily in her own studio, in private and group sessions. She also wrote several books, How to Live in Your Axis, Body Proportion Needs Depth, and How to Enjoy Sitting, Standing, and Walking.

Sweigard was responsible for the further development and promulgation of Todd's theory because she created a comprehensive body of movement material that could be practiced. The method of reeducation she formulated has been widely disseminated in her book, Human Movement Potential: Its Ideokinetic Facilitation, published in 1974. Because Sweigard taught for many years in the dance department of the Juilliard School, Ideokinesis, as her work came to be known, is probably the most familiar of the body therapies among dancers.

Ideokinesis is the word Sweigard coined to describe the work she did in muscular repatterning, which is aimed at improving dynamic alignment and movement patterns. The term links the two key processes of the method: "ideo," meaning idea or the stimulator of the movement, and "kinesis," meaning "the physical movement induced by the stimulation of the muscles." She described Ideokinesis as visualized movement without conscious voluntary direction. Movement patterns are learned through concentration on the desired effect of muscle action. Not imposing voluntary direction on the movement is the key concept of her method. She pointed out that subcortically, (unconsciously or automatically) patterned muscular action plays an essential role in all movement, and it "cannot be changed through voluntary effort." Therefore, the obvious way to make changes in bodily actions and skeletal alignment is through the cortex, which controls voluntary action. She proposed to do this by educating students in understanding how the body moves and how to change movement through the process of ideation (thought and visualization). The more we impose such voluntary controls on muscle coordination as holding, tightening, and "placing," the less hope we have of attaining efficiency.

Sweigard believed, based on her study and experience, that if you concentrate on the image of a movement, the central nervous system can "choose the most efficient neuromuscular coordination for its performance." Visualizing suffices to produce a proper initiation and pathway for the movement. But in order to achieve this effect in response to an image, the mover must: (1) "see" the exact location of the movement; (2) "see" the direction of the movement; and (3) have the desire to move. But the student must, above all, avoid interfering with this imagined movement by using voluntary muscle action.

In classes, students lie on the floor in the constructive rest position, knees bent at an easy angle, loosely tied together, with head and feet on small pillows and arms folded easily across the chest. With the aid of touch by the teacher, students visualize images that conform to nine "lines-of-action" that Sweigard designed to bring the skeleton into optimal operating efficiency. The extensive images she used in her lessons are metaphors to bring about the dynamic and differentiated relaxation that she believed would allow the giving up of habitual inefficient muscular habits and the substitution of better neuromuscular patterning in the body. Teachers have developed their own images and encourage students to do the same, since people respond differently to different words and images. The idea behind the image--such as widening across the lower back--is what is essential to the results.

There are a number of principles and attitudes these systems share. Efficiency of movement, based on sound physiological principles, is one goal shared by all. All the people who developed these systems had studied the body--anatomy, physical therapy, neurophysiology, biomechanics, and motor learning, among other disciplines. Training in these systems includes, at the very least, anatomy, and in Todd-Sweigard, for instance, knowledge of anatomy is essential for the student who wishes to use the system for his or her own development.

Body image can be a powerful force in the maintenance of established movement patterns that use excess strain and may even cause discomfort or pain. Much of our personal histories are carried in the body; memory is physical as well as mental. Unconsciously, we incorporate the movements of others with whom we associate into our own postures and actions. Our personal fantasies of our bodies sometimes can be more real and powerful than any physical training.

Each of these body systems emphasizes development of kinesthetic awareness and development of a more accurate picture of one's body, which leads to the capacity to develop new responses and a richer self-image. Almost imperceptible changes in the angle of the joints, or in the position of the head, and of the body segments to each other can dramatically alter mechanical and neuromuscular efficiency. Over a period of months or years, the body can be molded in a new image, with a different kinesthetic sensibility and relationship to the environment.

In childhood, basic movement patterns are established as babies learn to lift their heads, turn over, crawl, stand, and finally walk. Later, they learn hand-eye coordination and upper and lower body "connectedness" from throwing and catching a ball. The climbing, twisting, and falling, which are common to children's games, teach additional skills. For some children, for whatever reasons, these activities are limited or unsuccessful. Children may be urged to walk too soon before they have prepared for bipedal locomotion by creeping and crawling, which establish the neural patterns and muscular strength essential to full upright posture and coping with gravity. Traditional physical education contributes to establishment of faulty movement patterns by teaching children to copy postures and actions without giving attention to children's individual differences. Both Bartenieff and Feldenkrais use early childhood coordinations in their work, such as sequences for developing the coordination between right and left sides and upper and lower halves of the body, and getting up and down from the floor. They see establishment of these basic coordinations as key to fluent, efficient movement.

Since inadequate or disturbed breathing patterns are invariably associated with limited range of movement, the coordination of breathing with movement is an important component of the Feldenkrais and Bartenieff work. Todd-Sweigard uses the breathing to facilitate the release of muscles through visual images, while the Alexander teacher may draw the student's attention to the role of breathing in movement responses.

Touch is another important element in learning new movement patterns and possibilities. There are many ways to touch, from the slight pressure in Todd-Sweigard work that indicates location and direction of muscle release, to the actual guiding of the movement that can take place in Fundamentals, to the slightest touch in which the shared mental image of the student and teacher is of paramount importance. What all practitioners share is a finely tuned sense of touch. Touch can be powerful, therapeutically, and different kinds of touch affect the nervous system in different ways. It is an intriguing element in the way learning comes about in these body systems.

In all of these systems, the students lie down, a position that allows the force of gravity to release muscles that would otherwise contract to keep the body in a standing position. When the muscles are relaxed, new information is more readily available on the neuromuscular level.

Perhaps the distinguishing factor in all of these systems is how the learning takes place, which is integrally connected to the type of learning which results. The learning is what defines these systems as "body-mind."

Body therapists dislike the mechanistic approach to body movement that is typical of much physical education and sports. They disagree with the concept of single exercises for specific parts of the body such as abdomen, upper chest, and lower back. A mechanistic approach to movement, they contend, is not efficient and for most people, not enjoyable.

Rather than doing movement mindlessly, paying attention is crucial to the kind of learning these systems propose. In the Alexander Technique, the student's "self-use" is brought to his or her attention and through repetition, he or she learns to recognize restricting patterns and to substitute the appropriate changes. In Feldenkrais, movement is reduced to its smallest component and in Todd-Sweigard, to no conscious movement at all. By focusing on isolated motions that are on the smallest possible scale, the student is forced to focus on the smallest possible signals of bodily change.

Paying attention to sensation and intention is often encouraged through the use of sensory imagery, in Fundamentals, for example. Accurate and active visual images, as well as the words chosen to present them, are important in stimulating a desired kinesthetic response, and some of the most poetic are also right on target with some of the latest scientific thinking about how the neurological system works in motor learning. Through seeing the action performed accurately in one's mind, a new set of neuromuscular coordinations is established that produces greater motion in the joints, more efficient initiation of movement, and greater release of muscles. Visualization is a way of warming up the neurological pathways.

Feldenkrais, who is not metaphoric in his teaching, does ask for very precise imagination, such as imagining the movement six times before doing it, or leaving one part of the movement imagined. While imagery is important in the Todd-Sweigard work, learning to "think the thoughts without the images," in the words of one teacher, will trigger the experience and the student needs the image less and less. (Teachers need to have the motivating idea in mind as well when they do hands-on work.) In all the systems, the student learns to connect the process of his or her thoughts with the actions of his or her body, and these actions with moving through the environment. This connection is what attracts many followers and identifies these systems as something besides methods of physical training. The connection of the mind with the body also makes these systems relevant to psychological and behavioral change, although this is not an aspect that can be explored within the limits of this essay.

The bibliography that follows lists works relating to the specific systems and works that introduce related concepts and theories. Only books and articles in print and readily available were included. Your Body Works, edited by Gerald Kagan, is a wide-ranging introduction to methods not covered here such as Charlotte Selver's Sensory Awareness, Bioenergetics, Rolfing, and Reichian therapy, as well as other integrations of body-mind material with psychotherapy and some Eastern approaches to sensory awareness. Resource Directory: Specialists in Psychophysical Techniques for Dancers has a bibliography of interesting related material, not all of which is easily accessible but is at least available. In fact, many of the books mentioned here contain their own relevant bibliographies which, depending on the subject, cover everything from physics, to motor learning, to perception, to psychology, to rehabilitation. The Contact Quarterly is a magazine that offers a variety of interesting articles on uses of the body systems and interviews with different kinds of movement practitioners, such as Bonnie Cohen, whose work at the School for Body-Mind Centering is another aspect of this field about which little, as yet, has been written.

It is the nature of this field--whether it is called body therapy or body systems or body work--to connect with other fields which deal with the body and the psyche. It is hoped, within the confines of this essay, that those interested in the field will find some stabilizing ideas and means for pursuing the aspects that most interest them.

The Alexander Technique

Alexander, Frederick Matthias. The Resurrection of the Body. New York: Dell, 1974.

Barlow, Wilfred. The Alexander Technique. New York: Alfred A. Knopf, 1973.

Crow, Aileen. "The Alexander Technique as a Basic Approach to Theatrical Training." Movement for the Actor. New York: Drama Book Specialists, 1980.

Jones, Frank Pierce. Body Awareness in Action: A Study of the Alexander Technique. Schocken Books, Inc., 1979.

Leibowitz, Judith. "The Alexander Technique." Dance Scope Vol 4, No. 1.

Myers, Martha. "The Alexander Technique." Dance Magazine 54 (April 1980) pp. 90-94.

Stransky, Judith and Robert B. Stone. The Alexander Technique: Joy in the Life of the Body. New York: Beaufort Books, 1980.

Tinbergen, Nicolas. "Ethology and Stress Diseases." Nobel Prize lecture, 1973. Science 185 (1974) pp. 20-27.

Bartenieff Fundamentals^{tm}

Bartenieff, Irmgard. "Laban Space Harmony in Relation to Anatomical and Neurophysiological Concepts; Its Potential as a Functional Theory in Training and Retraining." Four Adaptations of Effort Theory in Research and Teaching. New York: Dance Notation Bureau, 1970.

_____. Notes on a Course in Correctives. New York: Dance Notation Bureau, 1977.

_____ and Martha Davis. "Effort-Shape Analysis of Movement: The Unity of Expression and Function." Research Approaches to Movement and Personality. New York: Arno Press, 1972.

_____, with Dori Lewis. Body Movement: Coping with the Environment. New York: Gordon and Breach, 1980.

Myers, Martha. "Irmgard Bartenieff's Fundamentals." Dance Magazine 54 (March 1980) pp. 88-91.

Youngerman, Suzanne. "Laban Movement Analysis: A Bibliography." New York: Laban Institute of Movement Studies, 1980.

Feldenkrais Awareness Through Movement

Feldenkrais, Moshe. Awareness Through Movement. New York: Harper & Row, 1977.

_____. Body and Mature Behaviour. International University Press, 1970.

_____. The Case of Nora. New York: Harper & Row, 1977.

Myers, Martha. "Moshe Feldenkrais's Awareness Through Movement." Dance Magazine 54 (May 1980) pp. 136-140.

Todd-Sweigard "Psychophysiology/Ideokinesis"

Clark, Barbara. Body Proportion Needs Depth. Tempe, AZ: Clark Manuals, 1975.

_____. How to Live in Your Axis. Tempe, AZ: Clark Manuals, 1968.

_____. Let's Enjoy Sitting, Standing, and Walking. Tempe, AZ: Clark Manuals, 1963.

Dowd, Irene. "Finding Your Center." Eddy Magazine (March 1977).

Myers, Martha. "Todd, Sweigard and Ideokinesis." Dance Magazine 54 (June 1980) pp. 90-94.

Sweigard, Lulu. "Better Dancing Through Better Body Balance." Journal of Health, Physical Education and Recreation 36 (May 1965) pp. 22-23, 56.

_____. Human Movement Potential: Its Ideokinetic Facilitation. New York: Dodd, Mead & Co., 1974.

Todd, Mabel Elsworth. Early Writings, 1929-1934. Brooklyn: Dance Horizons, 1977.

_____. The Hidden You. Brooklyn: Dance Horizons, 1953.

_____. The Thinking Body. Brooklyn: Dance Horizons, 1968.

Related Works

Benjamin, Ben. Are You Tense? The Benjamin System of Muscular Therapy. New York: Pantheon Books, 1978.

_____. "The Four Keys to Injury Prevention." Dance Magazine (October-January 1980).

Kagan, Gerald. Your Body Works: A Guide to Health, Energy, and Balance. Berkeley: Transformations Press, 1980.

Kern, Stephen. Anatomy and Destiny. New York: Bobbs-Merrill, 1975.

Levy, Deena. Resource Directory: Specialists in Psychophysical Techniques for Dancers. Oakland, 1980 (available from Psychophysical Education Book Service, 5267 Kicjsket Ave., Oakland, CA 94618, which also carries other books mentioned in the bibliography).

Masters, Robert and Gene Houston. Listening to the Body. New York: Delacorte, 1978.

Rabison, Samuel. "Muscle Tension, Body Structure and The Stress Diseases: The Place of Posture in Medicine." M.D. Dissertation, The University of Connecticut Health Center, 1976.

Rolf, Ida. Rolfing: The Integration of Human Structures. New York: Harper and Row, 1977.

Schilder, Paul. The Image and Appearance of the Human Body.
New York: International Universities Press, Inc., 1978.

Selver, Charlotte. "Sensory Awareness and Total Functioning."
General Semantics Bulletin, Nos. 20-21 (1957).

_____, with V. W. Brooks. "Report on Work in Sensory Aware-
ness and Total Functioning." Explorations in Human Potenti-
alities. Springfield: Charles C. Thomas, 1966.

Speads, Carola. Breathing: The ABC's. New York: Harper &
Row, 1978.

Publications

Contact Quarterly. Nancy Stark Smith and Lisa Nelson, Eds.
Box 603, Northampton, Massachusetts 01060.

"Kinesiology for Dance!" Dance Department. University of Water-
loo, Canada.

National Body Therapy Workshop

As part of the American Dance Festival, the National Body
Therapy Workshop has presented programs annually since 1980,
providing training and research for a national audience of dancers,
physical educators, physical and occupational therapists, fitness
directors, body therapy practitioners, and others interested in the
science and aesthetics of movement. The project is directed by
Martha Myers, Festival Dean and Director of its Center for Professional Training and Education. The workshop was conceived
to provide a forum for the exploration of different approaches to,
and views of, movement as a science and art affecting human health.

American Dance Festival
National Body Therapy Workshop
P.O. Box 6097, College Station
Durham, North Carolina 27708

Chapter Eight

TOWARD A COGNITIVE PSYCHOLOGY
OF HUMAN MOVEMENT

H. T. A. Whiting

That a subfield of psychology concerned with human movement
has not been clearly differentiated is all too clear. That such a
subfield is both necessary and possible, it is hoped in this chapter
to show.

Psychology is a field of study and not a discipline, in the
sense that its subject matter is not--as in say mathematics or physics
--logically cohesive. Its study does not "depend on one distinctive
mode of thinking or method of enquiry." Its knowledge is not "organised around a single system of interlocking principles, concepts
and definitions, designed to direct attention to a particular type of
question or way of looking at the world."* Rather, the events and
phenomena associated with psychology can be understood only through
several, interrelated, yet distinctive conceptual perspectives.

In any reductive model of biological organization, psychology
is focussed at the level of the individual although some of its sub-
fields have more commitment to the organic (physiological psychology) or the microsocietal level (social psychology). The position
of psychology with respect to the biological and social sciences was
sketched by Eysenck as long ago as 1957 (Fig. 1). Such a model
would still appear to be valid.

It is useful as a starting point to ask why psychologists
should pay attention to human movement and why, if it is so important,
no subfield of psychology exists which directs itself to an understanding of the significance of human movement?

In retrospect, it is always difficult to assign reasons for
particular lines of development. It is however somewhat surprising
that even the behaviorists were not unduly interested in movement

---

*This kind of argument was used by Renshaw (1975) in attempting
to demarcate human movement as a field of study.

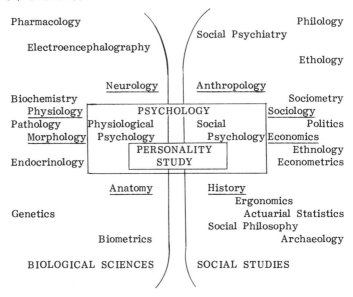

Fig. 1

The position of psychology with respect to the biological
sciences and social studies (Eysenck, 1957)

per se in spite of the fact that it would be difficult to think of
categories of behavior in which movement was not involved. For
various reasons, movement did not until comparatively recent years,
capture the imagination of psychologists--even those with more cognitive pretensions. One of the reasons is pointed out by Neisser
(1976) in discussing speech perception:

> It is far more natural to develop anticipations about articu-
> latory events in terms of their syntax and meaning than of
> their kinematics: so much more natural, in fact that it
> seems almost vulgar to mention the latter at all.

It will be necessary later in this chapter to return to this theme.

What Neisser is signaling here--albeit unconsciously--is the
dualistic thinking implicit in trying to separate out movement from
cognition. In point of fact, it is becoming difficult--other than in
overly simplistic terms--to state what is meant by cognition and
what is meant by movement. Weimer (1977) for example in a review article entitled "Motor Theories of the Mind" introduces a motor
metatheory in which he asserts:

... there is no sharp separation between sensory and motor components of the nervous system which can be made on functional grounds and that the mental or cognitive realm is intrinsically motoric, like all the nervous system.

From such a viewpoint, those classically designated "sensory" processes like perception, imagery, vision, memory, etc., are considered as motor processes (Weimer, 1977) or activities (Saugstad, 1977) and at the other extreme, recent interpretations of motor learning are being proposed in which cognitive parameters like intention and systems modeling are central (Whiting, 1980).

In as far as "the study of interactions between the human organism and its environment" has been suggested as a meaningful definition of the field of interest of psychologists (Saugstad, 1977) and in as far as a great deal of such interaction is mediated through movement, not only in an instrumental but also in an expressive and communicative way, it might have been expected that psychologists would have given movement more attention. The fact that this has usually been underplayed is implicit in the comments of Birdwhistell (1970) with respect to social interaction:

> It seems "natural" to believe that words or words plus grammar carry meaning in interaction and that all other behaviour is either modificatory, expressive of the individual personality differences of the particular participants (and thus nongeneralisable) or just incidental and accidental noise. It does "feel" as if communication is a stop-and-go intermittent process of action and reaction. To be asked to view communication as an altogether ordered and continuous system is anathemic to most of us. The suggestion that the idiosyncratic elements of the process are only to be detected after the isolation of structure comes as an insult for those of us who find our individuality most clearly demonstrated or proved by our communications. We think of communication as centrally verbal, centrally cognitive and centrally wilful and only laterally and by imperfection influenced by the other modalities of interaction. It is no surprise that our research designs will mirror this structure of conventional reality.

Ecological psychologists also draw attention to the fact that the animal and its environment are not logically separable or rather that in practice they are inseparable. A given species of animal is said to fit into a certain niche in the environment and, following Gibson (1979) a niche has been described as a set of "affordances" (Fitch & Turvey, 1978):

> The affordance of anything is a specific combination of the properties of its substance and its surfaces taken with reference to an animal.

As suggested above, it might be expected--at least to the layman--that behavioristic psychology at least would have made a considerable contribution towards an understanding of human movement since its dependent variable "behavior" includes "motor behavior." Such a viewpoint would be overly optimistic. As Alston (1974) states:

> ... whatever else it may include, the category of behaviour has from the beginning been designed to range over familiar examples of human action. The "science of behaviour" is explicitly intended to provide a theoretical understanding (explanation) of the things we do in daily life.... In view of these repeated protestations it comes as a shock to realise that comparatively little psychological research is concerned with hypotheses and theories, the dependent variables of which have to do with human action.

Already, in the above introduction, the terms movement, behavior and action have been introduced and it will be necessary to spend some time distinguishing between these terms, not only to avoid semantic confusion but because there are implications for the way in which the human brain controls what we do.

It should be noted for example from Alston's statement that there is an implicit distinction being made between human movement and human action. It is with overt actions (Fig. 2), defined by Alston as "actions that involve publicly observable bodily movements," that the student of human movement is particularly concerned.

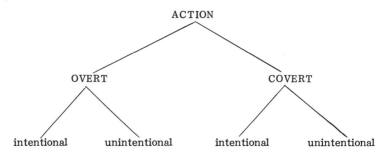

Fig. 2.
Action paradigm (Alston, 1974)

Not because they are necessarily of direct concern, but because they are the context for the dependent or independent variable with which he is concerned, i.e. human movement.

An action has an overall intention that can be brought about by a variety of different movements--starting from different postural conditions, i.e. it is "outcome" and not "movement" oriented. It will be necessary to return to the movement/outcome dichotomy later.

Reynolds (1980), in confirming that it is intended effects of movements which are normally called "goals," points out that movements are generally classed together if they produce similar external effects. "Pour," (for example) he suggests, is an action that empties a container by the force of gravity, but the movements could be as dissimilar as rotating a spade on its long axis, tipping a bucket by raising the bottom with one hand and holding the rim with the other or flexing the wrist while holding a pitcher.

Although as Ayer (1964) illustrates the inference from movement to intention lends itself to multiple interpretation, Reynolds (1980) confirms--with examples--that it is not as subjective as might be supposed. This viewpoint is reinforced by Tyldesley (1981) in his action-oriented studies of vision in sport. He draws attention to those information sources, such as preparatory movements of the opponent's body, which provide partial information about his planned actions. The fact that high-level sporting participants in particular are so good in their sport underwrites the efficacy of this method. It must also be emphasized that such people have extensive experience with a limited class of contextual cues.

Behavior and Movement

The distinction between behavior and movement is clarified by Hutt (1974) when she writes:

> Behaviour is not movement and to specify an action in terms of muscle activity or extension/flexion of the limbs is not a specification in terms of behaviour. Categories of behaviour are defined both morphologically and functionally i.e. in terms of their appearance as well as by their effects or context. In other words, it is reasonable to use "painting" as a behaviour category despite the fact that the motor patterns may vary over time and over individuals, whereas it is distinctly unhelpful to describe the activity in terms of discrete movement such as flexion of the digits or lateral displacement of the forearm. Identification of the motor constituents of a behaviour category is by no means the same as using these movements to reconstruct the behaviour.

But, this explanation still leaves the behavior/action dichotomy clouded.

Behavior and Action

One distinction made between behavior and action is in terms of the activities of animals and those of men. Reynolds (1976) for example draws extensively on the work of Max Weber (1864-1920) to illustrate such an approach. Weber proposes that if we describe what people or animals do, without inquiring into their subjective reasons for so doing, we are talking about their behavior. If we study the subjective aspects of what they do, the reasons and ideas underlying and guiding it, then we are concerned with the world of meaning. If we concern ourselves both with what people are, overtly and objectively, seen to do (or not do), and their reasons for so doing (or not doing), which relate to the world of meaning and understanding we then describe action.

> The characteristic which defines an action is intention, but intention is not a defining characteristic of muscle fibres. It is entirely reasonable for me to say that I intend to pick up an object. This is something which I choose to do, but I do not choose to transmit nerve impulses or contract a particular sub-set of extrafusal and intrafusal muscle fibres (Connolly, 1977).

Movement

Since the central focus of this chapter is on a psychology of human movement, it is necessary now to give more attention to the concept of movement. While its distinction from and relationship to behavior and action have been made, little has been said about movement per se. A start can be made by reference to the gestalt nature of an action as illustrated by the French philosopher Ricoeur (1966):

> The action is not a sum of movements; movement is a product of an analysis of a moving form by an outside observer who considers the body as an object.

The significance of this statement is exemplified by Hughlings-Jackson's comments earlier this century to the effect that the human brain thinks in terms of actions and not muscular movements.

The skilled person in particular does not concentrate attention on his or her movements. Attention demands decrease with proficiency. But, since there is a relationship between movement and outcome, it is possible to go back and analyze the movement from a subjective, an objective, or an affective point of view. There is of course a limit to such an analysis. Konorski (1966) for example gives a timely reminder:

> An illiterate man is unable to resolve the sound of a word into its phonemes and none of us can resolve a spoken word into its kinaesthetic elements.

The kind of definition of movement usually encountered would be "spatial displacement with respect to time," and, from the observer's point of view of course, this is what happens. But, such a definition would apply equally well to inanimate objects. In referring to distinctively human movements, it might be better to adjust this definition to "spatial displacement of the body or body parts over time brought about by an active brain." Only people and animals move. Objects may be in motion or they may be moved (Gibson, 1966).

Even with this kind of definition, problems occur when it is wished to progress from description to explanation. Pribram (1971) for example defines movements as:

> ... patterned muscular contractions which relates more to the underlying forces generated than to the observed spatial displacement. The distinction is an important one and is exemplified by an example quoted in an important position paper by Evarts (1973):

> ... suppose in one case you hold a tennis ball and move your arm up and down over a fixed distance and at a fixed speed. Then, you replace the tennis ball with a steel ball of the same size and repeat the arm motions in exactly the same manner. To an external observer there would be no difference between the arm movements with the two balls. Both movements would be over the same distance and at the same speed. The patterns of activity in your motor cortex would be quite different for the two movements however, because the muscular contractions required to lift the heavy steel ball are different from the contractions required to lift the lighter tennis ball.

This example is reiterating the fundamental point made by Bernstein (1967):

> ... the relationship between the result--for example the movement of a limb or one of its joints--and such commands as are delivered to the musculature from the brain through the effector nerves is very complex and non uni-vocal.

That is to say, the same (to an external observer) human movement may be produced by different neural commands on different occasions or different movements by the same neural commands. So much, for older ideas of "grooving in movements" in the sense of laying down a neural pathway:

> ... the older, naively materialistic concept of gradually "beaten" tracks or synaptic barriers in the central nervous system may already be considered to be relegated to the archives of science (Bernstein, 1967).

Psychology and Human Movement

If there has been a relative lack of interest in human movement

on the part of psychologists, to what can this be attributed?
Neisser's (1976) comments on speech perception have already been
given. They provide one of the reasons. Gallistel (1980), on the
other hand, attributes this lack to the excessive influence of the
information-processing viewpoint, pointing out that computers are
symbol-manipulating machines, taking symbols as inputs and producing symbols as outputs. The structure of overt computer action, he suggests, bears little resemblance to the structure of animal action. Thus, together with Turvey (1977) he notes the abun-
dance of theories of perception and the relative absence of theories
of action. Other reasons can no doubt be traced to the dichotomy
of human actions to which the physical antropologist Reynolds (1976)
refers:

> ... the practical or doing, making aspect and the logical,
> conceptual, thinking, rationalising aspect.

Reynolds prefers to see the emergence of conceptual awareness in
man as phylogenetically more significant than that of tool usage.
Whether the two should be polarized or whether his thesis should
prove to be the case, his arguments, based upon the relatively
unsophisticated skills of primitive man, are not altogether convincing:

> Tool-making could have evolved in a rather stereotyped
> "animal" way not involving symbolic thought. The frontal
> lobes, where most brain development has occurred in the
> evolution of man, is in any case not much concerned with
> the sensorimotor coordination involved in the manufacture
> of material things; people with damage in this area and
> people congenitally incapable of conceptual and abstract
> thought can often, nevertheless, do manual tasks involving
> the same thought processes as were involved in the con-
> struction of tools, fires and dwellings of early man.

To argue the similarities between nonnormal and primitive man carries little conviction. The problem of brain localization is notably
fraught with difficulty. Furthermore, Evarts (1973) for example
has recently pointed out that in regions of the cerebral cortex outside the motor cortex, neural activity is more dependent on the
context (intentions) in which the movement occurs than on muscular
activity per se. A person may become cognizant of the movements
themselves, but this is usually the result of analysis after the event
and is not normative.

With reference to Reynolds' statement, can it really be believed that even in a primitive community the skills to which he
refers were exercised outside a meaningful context and could it
reasonably be argued that a person incapable of conceptual and
abstract thought could learn to use such movements in an appropriate context? One is reminded of Ricoeur's (1966) critique of
such a narrow S-R interpretation:

The muscular contraction carried out, for example in a
laboratory and knowingly isolated from the history of the
individual, from the emotional and moral context of daily
professional and private life conceals all the civilising of an
intelligent adult's body.

However, the argument will not be pursued further, it is not central to the path being steered but enables some points of view to
be made. Suffice the comments on Reynolds' interesting and well-
argued thesis to indicate that in people's minds there is a meaningful distinction between the practical doing, making aspects and the
logical, conceptual, thinking, rationalizing aspects. While such a
distinction may be a useful categorization, it unfortunately leads to
value judgements being made which devalue the practical aspects in
comparison with those aspects which have come to be termed more
intellectual. Perhaps this has been most pointedly so where the
practical aspects are identified with those high-level skills encountered in physical education, dance and sport. Not only is this ex-
istentially the feeling of those involved in such practical fields, but
it is also well documented. It may be that such value judgements
are based more upon a misunderstanding of the nature of such activities than on prejudice, although the two are often confounded.
Certainly such a bias is not a recent innovation. Spiegel and
Machotka (1974) for example, in the context of social interaction,
draw attention to the comments of John Weaver (1712), one of the
principal dancers and choreographers of the early eighteenth century:

> ... a subject scarce ever before fully discussed in any lan-
> guage, that I know of. For while other Arts and Sciences
> have found learned patrons to recommend them to the
> World, by showing their Excellence, Use and Antiquity,
> dancing alone has been generally neglected or superficially
> handled by most authors; being thought perhaps too mean
> a subject for the ingenious labours of Men of Letters.

These authors point out that they have been able to discover only
one publication by a psychologist on the subject of dance (Sheets,
1965).

Not only are human actions dichotomized in the way suggested
by Reynolds, but so is the knowledge to which they are considered
to give rise. This may be the polarization of the "rational" and "intuitive" (Ornstein, 1977) or the epistemological distinction between
"knowing that" and "knowing how" (restated by Ryle, 1949). Both
the categorizations themselves, and the connotations attached to
them are questionable. Ornstein (1977), for example, indicates the
way in which we deemphasise and even devalue the arational, nonverbal modes of consciousness.

There are some activities of a practical nature to which the
bias being suggested is more prevalent. Peters (1966), a philosopher of education, for example, contrasts games as practical

activities with what he calls "serious" theoretical activities like science, history, philosophy etc., maintaining that games lack cognitive content and are "nonserious" in the sense that they do not illuminate other areas of life nor contribute much to the quality of living.

Perhaps neglect of the area of practical involvement by psychologists is determined less by a failure to appreciate the cognitive involvement characteristic of human actions or with its significance for other aspects of living and more with the difficulties involved in attempting to understand--to come to terms with--a phenomenon (human movement) with which we are all excessively familiar. While familiarity in this sense should not necessarily breed contempt, there are problems in focusing attention on something which one normally takes for granted without analysis and whose vocabulary is difficult to codify. Spiegel and Machotka (1974) also make the point about the methodological difficulties involved in trying to capture the expression of the body for observation and study:

> The phenomena are at once familiar and elusive--a nearly fatal combination.

Perhaps they suggest:

> ... the difficulty in finding a scientific method for dealing with ambiguity and illusiveness of movement tempts one to leave the topic within the realms of art and sensibility.

Ornstein's (1977) comments serve as a rider for Spiegel and Machotka's statement:

> The linear, rational mode is not the only way in which we gain knowledge, but it is a way in which we can clarify and communicate that which we understand.

Some of the difficulties raised probably arise because of the level at which skilled movement is defined. The restricted ecological validity of many laboratory experiments characteristic of research in the area of motor skill learning and performance tend to limit the concept of skill to relatively minor actions which quickly become autonomous in the sense that the performer need no longer reflect upon them. This is to be contrasted with the detailed attention which has been given by some developmental psychologists to early skilled behavior in which observational study in a natural setting lends itself to more cognitive interpretations.

Aspin (1977) in a well-reasoned philosophical article which attacks the dichotomy which is usually made between "bodily" and "intellectual" preoccupations, well appreciates the position being discussed. He refers to Entwhistle's (1969) distinction between complex and simple actions, the former being concerned with both

practical and theoretical activities. In distinguishing between overall performances of say a bowler in cricket, he points out that although the movements of both batter and bowler may have become
so routinized as to no longer require active attention in their performance, success in taking wickets involves the bowler in:

> ... taking into account, as a conscious act of theorising,
> such disparate factors as the state of the game, the plac-
> ing of the fielders, the conditions of the pitch etc....

Aspin comments:

> Knowing-how, in its turn, appears to depend crucially upon
> knowledge--that, at least in the sense of knowing what con-
> stitutes success in the action; while in the case of complex
> skills there is a dependence on knowledge of criteria and
> on contextual propositional knowledge, which may be explic-
> itly recognised, but which may also be the object of subsid-
> iary awareness as part of the general "Gestalt" of the whole
> action.

Skill

The prefix "skilled" in normal language usage can be used as
an adjective in conjunction with the nouns; action, behavior, and
movement. So that, it is normal to speak of skilled actions, skilled
behavior, skilled movements. It is necessary therefore to ask in
what sense such terms are different from one another or different
from their antonyms; unskilled actions, unskilled behavior, and unskilled movement. In so doing it is necessary to understand the
concept "skill."

The action/behavior distinction has already been made and
perhaps a distinction between skilled action and skilled behavior
can be exemplified by considering the "skill" demonstrated by animals and men. It might be argued for example that many high-
level skills can be taught to animals--as evidenced for example by
circus performers. It is not unusual for bears to ride bicycles or
sea lions to catch balls thrown towards them. It must be accepted, nevertheless, that there are differences in human skilled action
which distinguishes it from animal skilled behavior. Bronowski
(1973) comes to terms with this essential difference in comparing
an athlete and a gazelle in terms of the startle response and the
physiological demands of exercise. He makes the point:

> But there is a cardinal difference: the runner was not in
> flight. The shot that set him off was the starter's pistol,
> and what he was experiencing, deliberately, was not fear
> but exultation. The runner is like a child at play; his
> actions are an adventure in freedom and the only purpose

of this breathless chemistry was to explore the limits of his own strength ... the overriding difference, which is that the athlete is an adult whose behaviour is not driven by his immediate environment, as animal actions are. In themselves, his actions make no practical sense at all; they are an exercise that is not directed to the present. The athlete's mind is fixed ahead of him building up his skill and he vaults in imagination into the future.... The ability to plan actions for which the reward is a long way off is an elaboration of the delayed response, and sociologists call it "the postponement of gratification." It is a central gift that the human brain has to which there is no rudimentary match in animal brains until they become quite sophisticated, well-up in the evolutionary scale, like our cousins the monkeys and the apes.

Perhaps, the important key phrase in Bronowski's statement is that which talks about animal behavior in terms of its "being driven by its immediate environment" rather than being rationally derived. Carr (1980) picks up this point in suggesting that the extremely complex behavior of some animals (e.g. dam-building of beavers and "dancing" of bees) should not be taken as a model for the kinds of skill and know-how that are integral to human life, since the latter are informed by rationality and presuppose the existence of a complex and sophisticated social life of a kind that other animals do not possess. He points out further, that:

The teaching and learning of human skills involves the communication and transmission of complex rules, the grasp of which requires that capacity to perform mental acts which we call rationality.

The concept of intention as one of the criteria of skilled actions is an important one, because the instinctive behavior or "fixed action patterns" (Lorenz, 1937; Tinbergen, 1942) of animals often involves behavioral repertoires which are apparently quite complex but they are not generally looked upon as examples of skilled behavior. Such innately determined responses are elicited by appropriate environmental cues (releasers). As such they are to be distinguished from the intentional actions of man involved in the learning and performance of a skill.

The whole implication of the term "intention" and of actions being emitted is what might be termed "voluntary" behavior. The initiation of any skilled action is based in the first instance on the perception and necessary evaluation of the situation and the implications for the individual involved, i.e. the context in its widest sense.

Skilled actions which bring about a predetermined end result through the utilization of skilled movements are therefore on the above criteria, learned, they are complex in terms of the sequential and hierarchical ordering of simple response units and they are intentional.

It should be noted therefore that we do not observe skill directly, but infer its presence by the achievements of the person. A concept of this nature that does not directly refer to behavior but that is nevertheless closely tied to it, is known in the psychological literature as an intervening variable. The distinction is put in another helpful way by the philosopher Ryle (1969) in suggesting that skill is not an act, but a disposition, the power to act. What are observable and can be evaluated are movements and the outcome of such movements i.e. means and ends.

Activities

It is wished to make one further distinction—that between activities and movements—since with these two terms there has often been professional confusion. By physical activities is meant those insitutionalized forms of movement where the context is generally that of games, sports, dance, etc. While we may study (or appreciate) human movement in the context of an activity (e.g. the movements made in playing golf or the movements involved in a particular cultural dance) it is clearly also possible to study the activity itself independent of the movements involved (as happens for example in the so-called sociology of sport or history of dance). Activities are at a different organizational level from movements.

Movement and Its Outcome

Previously in this chapter it was maintained that actions are outcome-oriented. The sense in which this was implied was in terms of the intention being a predetermined end result e.g. performing a pas de deux, switching on the light, typing a letter. Such end results are achieved by means of movements, but generally speaking the focus of the person is not movement.

The simple difference can be emphasized by writing on a blackboard. The observable movements represent performance and the chalk marks on the blackboard the outcome of such movements. Such a dichotomy reflects back upon the definition of a skill as a predetermined end result. The difficulty in being precise in this respect is apparent from an examination of those complex activities often subsumed under the umbrella term physical education. In the activity of golf for example there are many skills with well-defined end results (e.g. putting the ball into the hole from a position on the green). There are other acts which are carried out in an attempt to achieve some end result which is less clearly defined—such as driving the ball up the fairway onto the green when it is known that the intention is not to hole the ball but to get it to come to rest in as favorable a position as possible. Sub-goals can consist of jumping the heights to which a bar is set. A number of different movement patterns may enable a performer to achieve such subgoals (e.g. Western roll, Eastern cut-off, Fosbury Flop). Such styles/techniques can be classified as skill, in which case, the end result is clearly different from those skills which can be defined independently of the movement. They are certainly examples of complex learned behavior intentionally carried out, but the end result is conformity to a movement pattern generally prescribed by a teacher or a coach. Thus, in jumping a predetermined height, the concern is with reproducing a prescribed movement pattern and success is judged not by the ability to jump a certain height, but by the ability to reproduce a relatively constrained movement pattern which because of individual differences in interpretation and physique cannot be absolutely defined. It is the performer's interpretation of a model that has been prescribed for him by demonstration, verbal mediation, film techniques etc. One of the major difficulties facing the teacher of such skills, is that of establishing for the learner an adequate model against which he may discriminate his own attempts. Furthermore, the success of the learner's attempts is subjectively assessed by the teacher in relation to the model which he or she has in mind. Thus, the skill of the teacher both in establishing such a model and in being able to compare such a model with the attempts made by the learner and providing adequate feedback which may aid such learning at various stages of development is continually called into question.

It would appear that the predetermined end result by which specific skills are defined may be: (a) independent of the way in which it is achieved--in the sense of a definitive movement pattern (for example, scoring a goal in soccer); (b) solely in terms of a prescribed movement pattern (for example, most dance actions); (c) a combination of both criteria (for example, ski-jumping). In terms of evaluation, a confusion of (a) and (b) can sometimes be unfortunate; when for example in the performance of skills for which category (a) is appropriate, teachers have laid undue emphasis on conformity to prescribed movement patterns notwithstanding that in many instances (of which games skills are good examples) the unconventional performer may have an advantage in that he not only confuses the display for the opposition but he has more opportunity to play against conventional opposition than the latter has to play against unconventional. In this case, naturally arising deception is being referred to, but it is worth noting that in the deliberate confusing of the display, it is the movements which are important, whether they be of the gross kind as involved in sidestepping, for example, or the more delicate facial expressions which are used as deception cues.

In most games (open?) skills, it is the outcome which is important (the goal scored, the opponent tackled, the defensive block etc.), not some prescribed movement patterns although the rules of such games may impose constraints on the latter. As Best (1975) illustrates:

> If we were to ask a hockey player, on the eve of an important match, "which would you prefer, to score three goals in a clumsy manner, or to miss them all with graceful movements?", there is little doubt what the answer would be, at least in most cases.

Reflection for a moment will confirm that for example in learning to play a game like badminton, improvement comes not so much from being taught new movements, as being made aware of possibilities—a process which might also be termed "social facilitation." The possible range of movements to exploit such possibilities are numerous. The psychologist Wright (1970) enlightens the topic:

> When the troopers of the Heavy Brigade charged the Russian cavalry at Balaclava, they had some difficulty in exchanging blows with them since they were unprepared for the Russians' less orthodox approach to mounted swordplay. The Heavy Brigade had been rigidly trained in their sword exercises and had been taught that each cut (specified by a number) had to be followed by a guard. After the engagement, a surgeon was treating a trooper for a sword wound in his scalp and asked how he came by it. "Well, I had just cut five (a body cut)," the man replied indignantly, "and the damned fool never guarded at all, but hit me over the head!"

In a similar way, Best (1975) confirms that there is another category of sports:

> ... in each of which the aim cannot be specified in isolation from the aesthetic, for example trampolining, gymnastics, figure-skating and diving .... [t]here is an intrinsic end, one which cannot be identified independently of the means.... It is not incidental, but central to those sports how one performs the appropriate movements.

Meaning in Movement

Implicit in the distinctions being made between movement, behavior and action is that of meaning. Specifically, in Weber's (1974) terms, actions are specified by the reasons for which they are being carried out, i.e. their interpretation involves consideration of meaning and understanding. Such meaning, it is maintained, arises out of the context in which the action arises. This distinction which separates movement and action is what Curl (1973) is striving for when he suggests that if we confine ourselves to definitions couched in the language of physical or mechanical laws, how would we make the distinction that the philosopher Ayer (1964) cogently makes in his classic illustration of the different meanings which can be ascribed to the act of raising an arm in order to drink a glass of wine? The single act Ayer suggests might be construed as:

> ... an act of self-indulgence, an expression of politeness, a proof of alcoholism, a manifestation of loyalty, a gesture of despair, an attempt at suicide etc.

Curl (1973) reminds us that any attempt to reduce the battery of different interpretations of simple arm movements to an objective mechanical formula would be to ignore some crucial factors in the determination of specifically human meaning. Human movement derives its meaning from its context.

The contextual frame of reference in which movement occurs is multidimensional. Perception of the meaning of movement depends upon the stance which it is decided to take. In Best's (1978) terms:

> ... the meaning and feeling of a movement in dance are quite different from the meaning and feeling of the same movement, from a purely physical point of view, as part of a service action in tennis.

So that, not only may the same physical movements be produced by different efferent outputs, but they may also have quite different meanings both to the person making the movements and to the observer of the movements. Moreover, the meanings attributed by the observer may not be the same as those intended by the mover. Therein lies one of the major problems in trying to understand posture and gesture in social interaction and in trying to make judgements about personality from movements.

Movement may be perceived in the context of different frames of reference--functional, scientific, aesthetic, moral etc.:

> For example, a bowler's action in cricket could be considered respectively, for its effectiveness in dismissing batsmen; as graceful; from a biomechanical view; or as fairly intimidating (Best, 1978).

Perhaps the most fundamental point to be made about meaning in movement is emphasized by Best (1978) when he points out that the range of possibilities of human movement provides a unique variety of experiences, because the feelings experienced while moving cannot be experienced in other ways.

The Concept of Hierarchy

Implicit in the concepts of action, behavior, movement, and motor elements is that of a hierarchical structuring. In a similar way, the cognitive representations of such systems are considered to be structured vertically into qualitatively different levels. During the course of development different motor elements are utilized. As a result of inherent predispositions or environmental experience, such elements become systematically serialized to produce modular units which subtend the motor elements comprising them. Such modules then become orchestrated into more complex units of behavior which may subserve the many human actions. This hierarchical idea is operationalized more meaningfully by Ricoeur (1966):

> I pass constantly from one point of view to another. For instance, I can say that I am hanging a picture, that I am holding a hammer, or that I am bending my fingers. Insofar as I have to learn to use tools and common objects (themselves products of human labour) my attention is ceaselessly led from the production of the work of pragma to the utilisation of the tool and the motions of the organ....

and by Koestler (1964):

> Learning to find the right key on the keyboard requires concentration, focal awareness, but when the latter habit has been acquired it becomes "instinctive," unconscious; attention is freed to concentrate on meaning and can "let the fingers take care of themselves": their control is relegated to lower levels of awareness and in all likelihood to lower levels of the nervous system.

Koestler points out that the concept of hierarchy is not simply that of "order or rank" but involves a special kind of organization in which the overall control is centralized at the apex of a kind of genealogical tree which branches out downwards with each sublevel (Fig. 3) retaining a degree of autonomy, the whole coordinated working being controlled by a superordinate system.

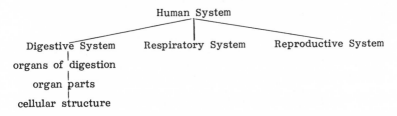

Fig. 3
Example of a hierarchical system

> A living organism or social body is not an aggregation of elementary parts of elementary processes; it is an integrated hierarchy of semi-autonomous sub-wholes, consisting of sub-sub-wholes and so on. Thus the functional units on every level of the hierarchy are double-faced as it were: they act as wholes when facing downwards, as parts when facing upwards (Koestler, 1964).

It is postulated that development involves the differentiation of such sub-systems in terms of both structure and function and their integration into a coordinated working unit. There is thus in Pew's (1966) terms a gradual shift in level of control from individual units to integrated sequences as a result of practice. Since "degrees of freedom" at joints, muscles, and tendons impose biological constraints on movement control, it is not surprising that there are systems which limit such degrees of freedom. Fowler & Turvey (1978) for example use the term "coordinative structures" to refer to "a group of muscles constrained to act as a unit." Such structures may be reflex in nature or may be built up over time through the medium of learning.

Cognitive Motor Systems

In discussing meaningful motor skills (i.e. those which occur outside the experimental laboratory), it has been found necessary to emphasize certain crucial concepts. In particular, the concepts of intention and meaning have been stressed from a number of different perspectives. It is useful for example to distinguish between:

> ... movements whose patterns form part of the genetically determined building plan of the CNS (which have little cognitive involvement)....

and those:

> ... which originate so as to attain consciously conceived outcomes (in which cognitive involvement is implicit).

In this connection, some critique was raised of Reynolds's conceptualization of skill development in primitive man which might be overly related to S-R considerations of human movement which in turn might be characteristic of only the simplest of actions. Additionally, the cognitive involvement implicit in normal skilled actions is reflected in the fact that such actions are the outcome of decision-making on the part of an active brain.

Human skilled actions then are contextually embedded. Such contexts have meaning for the mover and his actions are the outcome of consciously conceived decisions to respond in this way rather than that.

In these terms, it is perhaps not surprising that it is wished to postulate a cognitive-motor representation system as part of a more general cognitive representation system responsible for upper-level control of human physical actions. The general conception therefore of a cognitive motor system is in terms of a hierarchical organization, the various levels of which reflect a shift from representations of, at the lowest level, specific movement elements, to, at the highest level, motor plans or cognitions of more general operations. Following Shaffer (1980), a plan is looked upon as an abstract homomorphism of the performance representing its essential structure. All the details of the performance are not included in the plan, but they can be accessed as needed in the execution:

> The plan is executed in a continually renewing succession of higher-order units by a motor program, which may construct one or more intermediate representational actions leading to output, adding the details necessary to specify the movement sequence. This idea of using a hierarchy of abstract representations to construct performance from an intention is analogous to recent proposals in artificial intelligence for programs that solve problems.

Unfortunately, to date, very little conceptualization or empirical support for such a system exists. While for some cognitive theorists (e.g. Piaget, 1936, 1952; Bruner, 1964) motor activity and its representation is an early stage in and crucial to cognitive development of a more general kind, little concern has been shown by such workers in motor behavior after the sensorimotor period. This reflects the issue previously raised of the excessive involvement of psychologists to cognitive factors considered independent from their movement consequences. Nevertheless, the idea of a cognitive motor representational system is operationalized in Bernstein's (1967) statement:

> Over the course of ontogenesis each encounter of a particular individual with the surrounding environment, with conditions requiring the solution of a motor problem, results in a development (sometimes a very valuable one), in its nervous system of increasingly reliable and accurate objective representations of the external world, both in terms of the perception and comprehension of meeting the situation, and in terms of projecting and controlling the realisation of the movements adequate to this situation. Each meaningful motor directive demands not an arbitrarily coded, but an objective, quantitatively reliable representation of the surrounding environment in the brain. Such an action is also an active motor problem encountered during life and leads to a progressive filtering and cross-indexing of the evidence in the sensory synthesis mentioned above and in their components.

With the growth of cognitive psychology, such central representations as those implied by Bernstein, have become more acceptable. Schmidt's (1975, 1976) theory of motor learning for example involves the schema notion introduced earlier in the century by Head and utilized more extensively by Bartlett (1977) and by Piaget (1936, 1977). To Schmidt, the schema is an abstraction to which four sources of information contribute:

1. initial conditions
2. response specifications
3. sensory consequences
4. response outcome

This is but one of the current ideas available with respect to central representations of movement/acts. Pribram (1971) for example has reservations about Bernstein's (1967) interpretations of the nature of the representations to be found in the cortex. He maintains that in the motor cortex, it is not topological properties of space which are represented but the forces exciting muscle receptors. This "image of achievement"--in Pribram's (1971) terms-- is related to the field of external forces which it is necessary to overcome in order to successfully carry out an action.

The fact that the conceptualization of Pribram need not be incongruent with that of Bernstein is suggested by Den Brinker (1980) if--as suggested in the previously cited Shaffer (1980) quotation--it is accepted that representations of human motor actions can be conceived of at different levels. Den Brinker has coined the term "image of the act" to refer to the abstract representation of movement forms analogous to Bernstein's topological representations (see also, Whiting and Den Brinker, 1982). Eventually, if they are not to remain mere ideas, all such representations have to be translated into muscular activity, which to be successful must be finely tuned to the existing field of external forces to be overcome.

The implication of this kind of thinking is that during the course of development, the individual builds up a central representation of his or her environment and relationship to it which serves as a mediating mechanism in all later skill development. Such a representation is based upon perceptual and response information acquired during, as well as for the purpose of carrying out, actions by the individual. It is not difficult to understand in these terms the significance of movement for development or the implications of deprivation of experience and limited exposure to differential environments. Conversely, a high generalized skill level may be characteristic of the degree of comprehensiveness of such a cognitive motor system. The ability to formulate adequate working models of the future--a criterion for successful adaptation--is dependent upon the degree of differentiation and integration of information about past encounters and present conditions. The ability to successfully perform a novel skill is dependent upon the existing cognitive motor system and the extent to which it enables the person to understand the requirements of the new situation.

Although in this section, concern is with cognitive motor systems, in decision-making, the individual has access to more extensive cognitive systems. It would be expected that such an elaboration and extension would be a feature of development such that information obtained primarily by movement interactions with the environment at the sensorimotor stage would be extended and integrated by interrelating with other categories of stored information. For example, semantic information has relevance for skill learning and performance, for not only are names given to specific motor skills (e.g. waltzing, typewriting, sailing, etc.) and movement themes in educational gymnastics (e.g. twisting, turning, flight, curling, etc.) but also associations of the meaning of these names (and other words) have significance for motor actions through processes of dual or even multiple coding of information (Kohlberg, 1969).

While much skill is acquired fortuitously--in the sense that no formal teaching or teacher is involved--there is also a considerable amount of time given to more formal training in which language plays a definitive role. One of the advantages of language in this respect is the way in which it can short-circuit the learner's conceptualization of what is required of him or her, by helping to provide the learner with "an image of the future"--what is to be brought about. This obviates recourse to Skinnerian-type shaping programs such as would be required in animal skill training.

Movement and Cognitive Development

It will be clear from the discussion on cognitive motor systems, that a polarization of movement and cognition would be difficult to maintain. However, such polarization is not uncommon in the literature and is not restricted to movement/cognition. It is reflected--as Best (1979) has recently documented--in questions about movement and the intellect and movement and meaning. It would be well to recognize, with Best, the problems to which such thinking can give rise.

With respect to meaning in movement, it has been seen that Best stresses the influence of "context"--generally considered as "the whole set of circumstances in which it occurs." Best (1979) makes the further salient point:

> Thus, with certain minor exceptions, and excluding the symbolism which is possible in dance, human movement does not symbolise reality, it is reality. The experiences it provides are unique, they are not merely vicarious reflections of real-life experiences, through the medium of symbolism.

His comments on movement and the intellect take a different line of approach. While not denying that movements in subserving actions have cognitive involvement (i.e. that they are intelligently carried out), he points out that "intelligent" does not entail "intellectual." This is only to distinguish the essential nature of physical and intellectual activities.

If it is meaningless to ask questions about a supposed relationship between movement and cognitive systems, since changes in movement behavior imply changes in cognition and vice versa, perhaps a more interesting and informative approach would be to study the development of cognitive motor control systems and hence the implication that their development has for the way in which the individual operates in the world (i.e. for his level of competency). That major attention in this respect should be centered on infancy is not too surprising. It reflects to some extent a blurred distinction between earlier and later learning in the sense that the quality of the early experience in infancy determines the child's potential for skill learning of all kinds at later stages of development. The idea is reflected in Bower's (1977) comments:

> My concern throughout has been to show the importance of the psychological environment of the developing infant in speeding up or slowing down his attainment of fundamental cognitive skills. I believe that infancy is the critical period in cognitive development--the period when the greatest gains and the greatest losses can occur. Further, the gains and losses that occur here become harder to offset with increasing age.

Psychobiological Aspects of Movement

Two broad categories of motor acts were previously distinguished in this chapter: those movements whose patterns form part of the genetically determined structure of the CNS and those intentional movements utilized when man operates upon his environment. Thus, it is being emphasized that man's actions are a product of his biological nature and his cultural setting. They are the outcome of an interaction between maturational tendencies and environmental influences.

In the previous section, the unitary nature of cognitive motor systems was emphasized. The psychobiologist Trevarthen (1974) captures the spirit of this idea:

> ... coordination and regulation of all movements involves the brain in tasks so complex that it is absurd not to acknowledge that they are part of the mind, and they interact with all the rest of what is biological.... As a psychobiologist I turn to research on the brain to help obtain

understanding of how the mind works at all its levels. But I must be careful not to give you an exaggerated impression of what brain science can do to generate useful ideas in psychology. The goal is not to invent intelligent voluntary activity by looking at the brain. No one can do that. One has to look hard and long at the form and changes of form of what people do, when they run, or jump or catch, or throw, or dance to perceive underlying rules and structures. What brain science can do is provide a different line of evidence on which to interpret what one sees in the patterns of movement of people ... it is important to know that the brain grows amazingly elaborate new structures throughout life. It is the only organ of the body that continues true embryological differentiation of structure throughout the period after birth, and it does so in a big way.

In this respect, it is interesting to learn from Bernstein (1967) that even walking, which almost everyone does well, has a very slow development. The full skill of placing and alternating the limbs is not achieved until the early teens. The physiologist Sherrington (1940) coined the term "focal act" to distinguish between various grades of acts:

> We think of ourselves as engaged from moment to moment in doing this or that. This is a convenience of speech. At any given time, there is but one "focal doing" which presents the key piece of the performance to which all other motor events are subordinate. The crack pistol shot can hit his target whether he stands, sits or lies. Postures and movements that are but contributing to the focal act are called "satellite movements." Satellite movements fit into the total pattern of the act but they do not enter the level of awareness.

Kuypers (1973), on the basis of distinct neural mechanisms being present for the control of proximal and distal movements, distinguishes between what he terms proximal and distal motor systems. Trevarthen (1977) accepts a functional distinction between the mechanisms which orient specialized body parts by displacing proximal structures and trunk segments and those mechanisms which control distal segments to detailed elements of surroundings:

> Separate organisation in the brain of a proximal motor system and an array of distal motor systems is, it would seem, the basis for the development of voluntary control. Fine focal functions are differentiates of the orienting functions by which the whole body is moved. Developments in orientational control are vital to the production of integrations that bring focal functions together. Delicate processes of manipulation, for example, can only occur if the activities of the proximal segments of the arm and orientations of the head and eyes are stabilized to provide a foundation.

Trevarthen (1974) points out that under normal conditions of attention, the concentrated or focussed perception of fine detail and regulation of fine actions involves the stabilization of the main body parts as a base so that less regulation from the brain is necessary in their control. He maintains that almost perfectly predicted action by the body-support is necessary for any action at a distance whether it be seeing a small goal or shooting at it. The idea is similar to that discussed by Trevarthen (1977) in which he proposes two mechanisms of seeing:

1. Ambient vision--in the off-centre parts of the visual field --semiconscious but very sensitive to movement and change but not capable of resolving detail or colour clearly-- remarkably sensitive to the space structure in 3D of the surroundings. It is proposed that this kind of vision regulates large body movements and needs continuous shift of features in the eye.
2. Focal vision--in the foveal parts of the visual field-- requiring fixation or nearly still retinal images--used for controlling the fine movements of looking, or feeling or listening etc. that test for information in successive instants of contact.

A similar distinction is the outcome of studies of injuries to the brain. Two major categories of performance outcome result:

1. A deterioration in the regulation of whole-body adjustments normally brought about by large muscular forces moving heavy parts of the body.
2. The more refined movements of distal muscles moving light parts of the body in manipulative type tasks.

The two broad categories of motor acts described can be operationalized in the learning of a novel skill such as a dance step:

At the start, when the task is attempted without experience, the body becomes inactive with large parts locked so they do not generate large troublesome reactive forces and confuse the brain. Progress is steady, observant and hesitant on an artificially simplified base that is kept more or less wooden. But, this fixation has to be broken before proper fluidity of control can be achieved. Attention has to be spread from external, final goals to the necessary conditions in the body and in the whole action (Trevarthen, 1974).

The locking of the "large parts" of the body to which Trevarthen refers is important, in as far as it relates to the degrees of freedom in the moving limbs, the control of which gives rise to what are normally referred to as coordinated movements. In fact, Bernstein (1967) defines coordination in the following way:

The coordination of a movement is the process of mastering redundant degrees of freedom of the moving organ, in other words its conversion to a controllable system.

While the "woodenness" to which Trevarthen refers can be observed in many novel skill learning situations, Bernstein is at pains to point out that:

> ... fixation eliminating the redundant degrees of freedom ... is employed only as the most primitive and inconvenient method, and then only at the beginning of the mastery of the motor skill, being later displaced by more flexible, expedient and economic methods of overcoming this redundancy through the organization of the process as a whole.

The concept of "degrees of freedom" as a biological characteristic of man was raised earlier. The degrees of freedom of movement of a particular body segment are determined by the number of planes of movement through which it is able to be moved at a particular articulation, i.e. degrees of freedom may range from one at the elbow and knee to two at the wrist and ankle and to three at the hip and shoulder. For complex movements involving more than one joint articulation, the degrees of freedom increase. Higgins (1977) for example suggests that there are "seventeen degrees of freedom in the kinematic chain described by the articulations from the shoulder girdle to the fingers" and this is to consider only the refined movements of the throwing action. In addition, there are all the degrees of freedom associated with the "whole-body" adjustments involved in stabilizing the body for a standing throw or transporting the body for a throw while running. The situation is further complicated by the elastic muscles moving the body segments and introducing further degrees of freedom.

Language and Movement Behavior

Earlier reference was made to the use of speech as a regulator of movement behavior. It was also pointed out that speech may short-circuit the learning procedure by enabling a teacher to draw the attention of the learner to important information in the environment which might have a steering function or in telling the learner what particular movements to attempt (e.g. in learning the steps of the waltz, the teacher might suggest verbalizing slow, quick, quick, slow). Luria (1961), for example, in the context of speech and the regulation of behavior, comments:

> ... speaking to a child can in fact re-shape its significant perception of a compound stimulus and thus modify the "rule of force" and make the physically weaker component predominate. In optimum conditions this can be achieved in quite young children.

Zaporozhets (1957), in considering how competence develops with age, shows that improvement is paralleled by more effective use of imitation and of verbal instructions. Moreover, both imitation and verbal instruction are more effective if directed towards orienting responses as well as executive responses. Zaporozhets (1957) reports a direct relationship between the amount of spontaneous orienting behavior practiced by the child and the efficiency of the final performance; this would suggest that effective performance can be encouraged by participation in orienting behavior. Fellows (1968) has explained orienting behavior as that which serves to clarify the relevant aspects of the task or make them more distinctive. However, its main function as seen by Zaporozhets is to facilitate discrimination at a level which would be relatively low in an attention hierarchy:

> ... the main function is in the formation of the sensory part of the elaborated motor system in the preliminary analysis and synthesis of the afferent stimuli in the system.

An example of the procedure is given in a study by Neverovich Zaporozhets (1957) who was able to show that the efficiency with which tool operations were mastered and the actual standard of their execution were considerably higher when orientation to the method of performing the action could be produced in the child in the course of training; instead of the children's attention being directed towards the end product (i.e. getting a nail into a piece of wood), it was directed towards the feel of the movement by getting them to hammer on a table in which the end result was of less importance.

Implicit in the suggestions being made in the studies reported by Zaporozhets is that movements and their related parameters may have attached verbal labels which both teacher and learner understand. Obviously in developmental terms, the naming labels in themselves might be more meaningful with young children while the semantic content of more elaborate phrases and sentences might be utilized by older children.

It must also not be forgotten that language is not something which suddenly presents itself. The child is immersed in language from birth onwards and must be influenced by such language long before it is capable of uttering its first meaningful words. Numerous speculations and theories have been advanced about how language develops, but it is not intended to consider these issues here. However, in the context of language and movements, it is useful to note some recent comments of Neisser (1976). He points out the obvious relationship between the movements of certain parts of the body--known as the articulators (e.g. tongue, lips)--and the production of speech sounds:

> For this reason the movements of speech are sometimes called articulatory gestures.

While some of these production events are hidden from view, others --such as movements of the lips--are not only visible, but add additional information even to experienced listeners, particularly when noise constraints are present. Neisser also makes reference to the Tadoma system of speech perception by touch, in which speech information can be obtained tactilely by placing a hand over the speaker's lips and cheeks:

> To perceive speech, we must pick up information that specifies articulatory gestures. Any sense modality that can accomplish this may be employed for it.

Perhaps the most interesting speculation offered by Neisser and based on this proposition is that:

> Since articulatory events are motions of certain parts of the body, speech perception has something in common with perceiving other bodily motions, like those of dancers and athletes. In particular, the perception of facial expressions, nonverbal cues, "bodylanguage" and the like must be continuous with it. There is every reason to believe that speech perception begins as just one aspect of the general perception of other people's movements and does not become sharply differentiated for a child until he realises the denotative and propositional character of speech. That such evidence of prespeech is not confined to speech perception is implicit in the work of Trevarthen (1974). He refers to the lip and tongue movements of the infant child as "prespeech" because they have the outline form of speaking, and because they occur in the appropriate place in the exchange for the function of utterances. Trevarthen points out that such prespeech movements are frequently not voiced, although vocalisation is associated with them from the start.

The Russian Approach

Work stemming from Luria's (1961) laboratory and closely related to earlier theorizing of Vygotsky (1962) has, perhaps more than any other, focussed on empirical studies designed to obtain information about the role of speech in the control of movement. These studies and thinking were strongly influenced by Vygotsky's contention that the original function of language in the child is a social function. He uses language in the first place either to share something with others or to influence them. A synopsis of this thinking would suggest developmental progress from a stage at which the child allows his behavior to be directed by the speech of others to a stage at which he uses speech to direct his own behavior. The incorporation of the child's own speech into his movement activities would appear to develop through a series of stages terminating around the age of seven or eight. However, the work of Luria and Vygotsky shows that by special attention to the organization of the movement activity and particularly in relationship with adults, the time needed for the development to occur can be considerably reduced. Although the idea of stages is not emphasized in Luria's work, it is implicit. The concept of stage development has been discussed by Wozniak (1972):

> The organism is seen in stage theories as increasing in some attribute (e.g. in Piaget's theory, in the degree of equilibration existing in a given stage between assimilation and accommodation) in a relatively linear and continuous fashion until a critical point is reached (e.g. the full equilibration of accommodation and assimilation at a lower level) at which juncture there is a reasonably sudden transition to a new, higher, qualitatively distinct stage. This new stage is considered to be described by a new system of laws to which the previous stage did not conform.

An example from Vygotsky's work will serve to illustrate the change in language function with age. He presented children with a simple practical task (e.g. drawing or tracing a picture) and then complicated the procedure by, for example, removing the pencil, drawing pins, or tracing paper. Children of three to four years of age could not cope with the difficulty and appealed to adults for help. Children of five to seven years of age would try to solve the problem themselves, which usually produced an outburst of active speech not addressed to anyone in particular. (This has been referred to by Piaget as "egocentric speech" but it is worth noting that Vygotsky and Luria reject Piaget's interpretation that egocentric language is a functionless accompanying phenomenon but rather that it has a function in helping the child out of its difficulties. They support his contention by the observation that egocentric language increases when the child becomes faced with initially insoluble problems). Vygotsky suggests that such egocentric speech directs the child's orientation to its surroundings and it then extends to incorporate aspects of the child's previous experience in similar tasks as for example methods of approach to these kinds of problems. Later still, such speech precedes the activities inhibiting the child's direct attempts until it has verbally formulated how it is to approach the problem. The latter, it is suggested, represents a shift from accompanying speech to planning speech. Later still of course, speech as such disappears, although it might reappear even at the adult stage when particularly difficult problems ensue.

Movement Observation

In discussing the psychobiological aspects of movement it was proposed necessary to:

> ... look hard and long at the form and changes of form of what people do, when they run, or jump, or catch, or throw or dance to perceive underlying rules and structures (Trevarthen, 1974).

In terms of an understanding of brain function, this would be looked upon as a "top-down" rather than a "bottom-up" approach (in which an understanding of the structure of the brain is used as a basis for specifying what level of movements and behavior it is capable of producing).

While such an appeal does not necessarily mean the observation of movement per se, this is obviously a related consideration. Not only is movement observation a necessary methodological procedure for the research worker, but it is something which everyone utilizes in his normal social interaction where changes in posture and gesture have significance. Teachers of movement skills and judges of movement competitions (e.g. skating, diving, gymnastics) are perhaps even more critically involved in movement observation although as Best (1978) suggests, the reasons why people are observing the movement may differ:

> ... there may be various frames of reference from which the movement can be considered, such as the functional, scientific, aesthetic, and moral.

That there are problems in attempting to identify inner states by observation of external behavior has already been alluded to in Ayer's (1964) example of raising a glass. Best (1978) again clarifies this issue:

> It is unfortunate that a misconceived polarity has arisen about movement experience. As a crude characterisation the movement educationist concentrates on the experience, and regards the observable, quantifiable aspects of movement as relatively unimportant. On the other hand those of scientific inclination are perfectly happy about the perceivable, quantifiable physical movement, but sometimes tend to be suspicious of talk of the inner experience because it is not observable.
>
> In fact neither aspect alone is sufficient. To deny the inner experience is to deny the agent, without whom there would be no movement. Yet to deny the observable criteria is equally to deny the experience, since without the criteria the experience could not be identified.... So that perception of human movement is necessary in order to identify

the meaning of the experience. But without the experience there would be no human movement to perceive.

Observation of movement behavior seems to be based upon discrete structured events rather than continuous and undifferentiated movements. Persons are seen doing this and then that and then something else (e.g. a floor sequence in gymnastics--run, into arab spring followed by back somersault followed by backward roll to handstand, etc.). When asked what a person is doing, we do not normally describe it in terms of certain movement changes but in terms of certain behavioral changes. Newtson (1976) refers to this observational procedure as "parsing" of the stream of stimulus information presented by behavior. What Newtson did, was to have subjects:

> ... operate a continuous event recorder and to press the button when, in their judgement, one meaningful action ends and a different one beings (Newtson, 1973).

Using such a procedure, he was able to show that observers looking at common sequences showed a clear-cut patterning of marking in certain intervals (i.e. agreement between persons in segmenting is highly significant but not perfect). One source of disagreement was a difference in level of perceptual organization employed by perceivers. That is, persons varied in the degree to which they segmented a given sequence into its component parts e.g. over twenty seconds, or two actions over eight and twelve seconds. This level of perceptual analysis could be influenced by instruction:

> Human observers have a "range of analysis" in behaviour perception, from fine-unit segmentation to large unit segmentation within which they operate.

Newtson suggests that this is tapping a cognitive perceptual skill and is not related to personality characteristics per se. It might be thought of as one manifestation of a cognitive motor system and the interesting question would be that of a relationship between such a framework and the production of the movement itself. What effect for example do differences, in unit segmentation during the observation stage of a novel skill, have on the production of the movements involved in that skill?

Where in his range a given observer is operating at a given time is dependent upon the nature of the behavior sequence and the status of certain situational constraints. Predictability can also determine level (size of units) or perceptual analysis. Wilder (1974) for example showed that when beginning analysis of unfamiliar behavior, observers begin at fine unit levels and work their way up to larger units of organization. The principle is not unlike that already discussed in the hierarchical ordering of movement production.

Newton (1976) refers to the points of segmentation at which the behavior stream is broken up into its components as breakpoints. Observers were far more sensitive to deletions of the observed material at breakpoints (detecting them with fifty-four percent accuracy overall) than they were to deletions at nonbreakpoints (which were detected only twenty percent of the time):

> A series of breakpoints conveys an almost comicstrip quality in that it is easy to follow the course of the behaviour by viewing them alone. Some of the implications of a comicstrip analogy are related to caricatures--in terms of the essentially defining elements of a movement/action--and the kinds of "schema" that are cortically encoded.

It may be more accurate in these terms therefore to view ongoing behavior as a series of transitions between successive points of definition, with meaning a function of the nature of the transition:

> Persons viewing the breakpoint triads rated them as equally intelligible as persons viewing the continuous sequences themselves; both were rated as significantly more intelligible than comparably selected non-break points.

These studies support the view that the information defining the meaning of ongoing behavior is only intermittently available in the behavior stream. At some points in a sequence--the points of perceptual division--the actor passes through points of definition which may be used for perceptual organization by the observer.

As in any other area of skilled behavior, the performer has to learn which information is relevant and which redundant. Newtson (1973) refers to behavior observation as a feature monitoring process:

> The perceiver monitors some critical set of features (a subset of the available features) segmenting the behaviour into parts as one or more of the monitored features change state.

Thus, the skill of the observer may relate to his or her ability to select the relevant features for the particular appraisal that he or she is making, i.e. to learn which features are redundant and which have a high information load.

The Perception of Human Movement

A recent innovation in movement observation is that of determining what features are utilized by the observer in distinguishing between different categories of movement behavior (e.g. running, walking, skipping) or between the movements of say males and

females. In 1973 for example, Johansson attached miniature light
sources to the shoulder, elbow, wrist, hip, knee, and ankle joints
of his subjects and filmed them in motion in the dark. The moving
dot patterns so created gave a compelling impression of human location.

Kozlowski and Cutting (1977) have used similar techniques to
those of Johansson in an attempt to answer the question "Is it possible to recognize the sex of a walker from these dynamic displays?"
Instead of point light sources, they used reflective tapes, five centimeters in width, wrapped around wrists, arms above the elbows,
ankles and legs just above the knee. In addition, patches of tape
5 × 15 centimeters were attached to the belt at the hips and to the
shoulders as epaulets (half on shoulder, half on upper arm). Subjects were three male and three female undergraduates with normal
gait. After filming, each of the six walkers could be portrayed as
a cluster of four point-light configurations. Such facsimiles were
then presented to fifteen male and fifteen female undergraduate subjects whose task was to view the sixty possible configurations and
assign the label (as well as their confidence in their judgement on
a five-point scale) "male" or "female" to them.

The experiment was repeated using static displays. Not only
were the static configurations not recognized as people, but the
sex-typing was no better than chance. The results indicated that
while viewers of dynamic displays of light configurations of walkers
can recognize the sex of the walker, this cannot be done from viewing static displays abstracted from the dynamic sequence.

In further experiments, these workers demonstrated that manipulating some of the parameters associated with walking (e.g.
movements of hands and arms, speed of walking) disrupts the accuracy of sex identification. Furthermore, walking seems to be a
holistic act in that any of the cues available were sufficient e.g.
ankles alone yielded greater-than-chance performance.

More recently, Hoenkamp (1978) has extended the idea of
simulated movement and the way in which the parameters utilized
in the simulation can be adjusted to produce observers' impressions
of different movement categories. Utilizing similar techniques in
the initial stages to those of Johansson, Hoenkamp was able to analyze recordings of forty-five different movements (verbs performed
by an actress) and on the basis of these analyses, to isolate the
important parameters which were capable of producing distinctive
movement categories. Basically, he was able to demonstrate that
the movement of the lower part of the body could, by itself, provide the information necessary to distinguish between major gait
categories. The gait category seemed to be determined by the rate
of the time duration between the forward and return swings of the
lower leg. Hoenkamp proposes a simple model that gives a compelling impression of human gait in which the angles that the body

parts make with the vertical, change sinusoidally in time except for
the angle of the lower leg which changes in sawtoothlike manner.
Surprisingly, the parameters of speed of progression (since one
can run and walk at the same speed) and velocity of the individual
limbs do not in themselves enable the discrimination of movement
categories. The crucial parameter appears to be the breakpoint
(bp) of the sawtooth of the lower leg (Fig. 4).

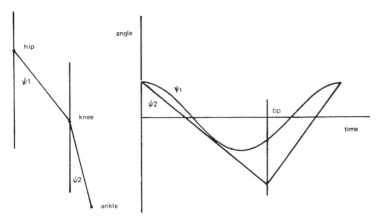

Fig. 4

Variation in time of the angular displacement of
the upper and lower leg, approximated as a sinusoid
and a sawtoothlike function (Hoenkamp, 1978)

For a bp of 0.6 it is easy to generate a movement labelled
"walking," but with such a bp it is hardly possible to arrive at a
compelling impression of "running." On the other hand for a bp
of 0.9 the reverse is true. Apparently, a bp value of 0.55 - 0.7
will generally be perceived as walking and higher values will do
for running. A bp of around 0.4 is usually interpreted as skating.

In one of his experiments, a pattern was generated for the
legs with a bp of 0.85. The pattern produced was shown to thirty
subjects only two of whom did not spontaneously assign it a "running" category word. Surprisingly, the figure simulated always
had one foot on the ground, i.e. aerial motion is not essential to
distinguish walking from running.

Personality Assessment Through Movement

The importance of movement observation in social interaction
was referred to in the previous section. The interpretations put
on movement in such situations are diverse in nature but one category of interest relates to the conveying of information about personality. As Vernon (1963) puts it:

> Our daily lives are largely made up of contact with other people, during which we are constantly making judgements of their personality and accommodating our behavior to them in accordance with these judgements.

The question which then arises is what features of the presented display of other people are utilized for these purposes. With respect to those aspects of nonverbal behavior included under the label kinesics (simply defined as body movements), Harper, Wiens and Matarazzo (1978) propose the following delimitation:

> ... movements of the head (excluding facial expressions and change in gaze direction or of eye contact), hands, feet and limbs (arms and legs) and body trunk. The most common physical actions representing these body areas probably include head-nods and head-turning, gestures (hands and arms) and postural shifts.

While all these categories of information are not at all times available, it seems clear that judgements are normally based on several of these categories in combination. With respect to personality, the question arises as to which if any of these combinations are reliable and stable indicators? How reliable and valid are the interpretations based on such information? Although people may orientate towards useful sources of movement information, subjective interpretation of these sources may cloud objectivity.

Early work on the expression of emotion in animals and man (Allport & Vernon, 1933) for example failed to find communalities in facial expressions but as Ekman and Friesen (1974) point out, such studies probably considered too wide a spread of emotions. They propose that movement characteristics can give fairly reliable information about emotional states:

> ... if you want to know what emotion someone is feeling you must watch the temporary changes in the face, because it is these rapid facial signals which give information about emotions.

Moreover, if constrained to the emotions of happiness, sadness, surprise, fear, anger, and disgust, not only can reliable appraisals be made, but they do not appear to be culture-specific. Making such appraisals is a skill which they propose can be taught.

The finding of a link between expressive behavior and personality in the Allport and Vernon (1933) study was, according to Lippa (1978), weak at best. In 1937, Allport was moved to state:

> The study of expressive behaviour requires the doctrine of traits, for the only secure interpretation of expression seems to be in terms of stable personal dispositions. Ex-

pressive behaviour, in brief, is the external aspect of inner
structural consistency!

Recent approaches to personality theory have been critical of
trait interpretation in terms of both their validity and utility. Mischel (1968), for example, hypothesized that expressive consistencies
in individuals might mistakenly be assumed to reflect behavioral consistencies in other domains. To Mischel then, no firm link between
expressive behavior and stable personality exists but rather expressive consistencies in persons incorrectly lead others to attribute
stable personality traits to them. Mischel prefers therefore to seek
situational interpretations of behavior rather than trait interpretations.

The question then remains which of these two extreme positions is most justified on available evidence? A compromise position
which further complicates the scene is provided by Bem and Allen
(1974) in an article appropriately entitled "On Predicting Some of
the People Some of the Time." They demonstrate that it is possible
to identify, on a priori grounds, those individuals who will be cross-
situationally consistent and those who will not. On this basis, they
suggest that personality assessment must give attention not only to
situations but to persons as well. This is reminiscent of more recent ecological psychological approaches. Kugler, Scott Kelso and
Turvey (1980) for example refer to Shaw and Turvey's concept of
"coalitional style" which claims that:

> ... any naturally evolved system is comprised of two logi-
> cally dependent components, the operational component (say,
> an organism) and its context of constraint (say, the eco-
> niche), and that any explication of systemic phenomena
> must be coordinated over four, mutually constrained and
> closed, end grains of analysis in the sense that no grain
> and neither component is disproportionally accredited with
> responsibility for the phenomena.

The work of Bem and Allen (1974) is extended by Lippa (1978) who
postulates:

> ... persons with high motivation and ability to control their
> expressive behaviour would demonstrate different patterns
> of consistency in their expressive behaviour from those dis-
> played by persons with low motivation with ability at expres-
> sive control.

i.e. "expressive control" as a moderator variable.

With respect to the motoric dimension, it is interesting to
note Ekman and Friesen's (1969) comment that the face is better
controlled than the arms and hands, which in turn are better controlled than the legs and feet. It would appear that the control of

expressive cues is more difficult for bodily expression than for facial (and perhaps vocal) expression.

Lippa (1978)--using the Snyder (1974) self-monitoring scale-- was able to show that:

1. High self-monitoring subjects demonstrated more expansive and "extraverted" expressive behavior than low self-monitoring.
2. High self-monitors were perceived by "raters" as more "friendly, outgoing and extraverted."
3. Assessed extraversion showed a weaker main effect than self-monitoring.
4. Hypothesis that persons high on expressive control show cross-situational consistency but gross-channel inconsistency was supported.

Overall, Lippa's (1978) findings confirm that:

1. Expressive control is an important moderator variable.
2. There are important differences in expressive display of extraversion and anxiety cues.
3. Bodily expressive behavior seems to be less controlled than facial or vocal expression.

With respect to personality assessment through movement, two further studies are worthy of comment--those of Lamb (1965) and North (1972). Lamb's (1965) initial contribution is documented in his book Posture and Gesture. In this text, he is clear that the purpose of the book is to show how details of movement behavior can be analyzed and recorded. There is no specific reference to personality but he does claim that insulting physical behavior will affect interpersonal communication and that a gesture merging into a posture communicates an attitude and this communication can be seen as "embodying something of the performer's personality." Lamb is not interested in posture as a "still physical position." It is necessary to know how the position was arrived at. That there are implications for personality assessment is implicit in his statement:

> ... subsequent sets of observation--no matter when or where taken, so long as they are an adequate sample, will always be analysed to an identical pattern.

These patterns he suggests can be used as a basis for a form of personality assessment. Lamb classifies three groups of people:

1. Communication types--broadly observant, exploratory, attentive, prepared to listen.
2. Presentation types--forceful, determined, confident, highly resolved, often dedicated.
3. Operation types--decisive, appearing always ready for action, facility in carrying out programs, systematic.

Within this classification Lamb maintains, one can fit a man to the most suitable work. However, the methods by which he reaches this conclusion seem rather obscure:

> Research along these lines supports the hypothesis that if a person is in a situation whose requirements he can meet through a physical application in line with the pattern of his posture/gesture merging, then he will have aptitude for taking action to deal with those requirements.

In other words, the matching of person's physical behavior to a particular job requirement is successful. He reports that several thousand individual studies on this basis have shown the hypothesis to be tenable but unfortunately, he does not give any details of the tests for validation or reliability. It should however be noted that more recently considerable attention has been given in the literature of nonverbal communication to both posture and gesture.

North's (1972) more recent book is concerned with the observation of movement behavior and is based on a considerable number of years of experience. According to her Introduction, she sets out with the following specific purpose:

> ... of validating the system of personality assessment through movement. The problem is that this method of observation and assessment, having been initiated by Rudolf Laban has been utilised by the few people to whom he taught the fundamental principles, and over the years, no one has systematically organised, clarified and published information about it in a form which others can use. This I have now undertaken to do.

She also claims that the objectivity of the observation can be and has been validated by the agreement of a team of observers. After such statements, it would be expected that a clearly set out record of personality testing and some indication of comparison to other accepted personality tests or proof of reliability and validity would be provided. But, as she states, she found difficulty in finding tests already acknowledged which cover the same or similar areas of personality assessment. Comparison of results was also a problem to her, as there seemed no common method of quantitative evaluation or scoring that could be used accurately.

Part III of the book is concerned with validation of assessment through movement as Carroll (1972) states in her critique of the book:

> The validity measures that North uses are the Stanford Binet Intelligence Scale (carefully standardised, but not a personality measure). The children's Apperception Test which is a projective test for which there is very conflicting

evidence and a teacher's rating scale which is inadequately explained in spite of the fact that rating scales are notoriously weak measures.

The observation of children's movement, which is referred to in the book, took place over two terms while she taught those being assessed. It is difficult therefore to see what the test really consisted of, and in fact whether the children's natural movements were conflicting or being reinforced by her teaching. It might also be expected that her observation might have been colored by whether or not the children were responding to her teaching in the way expected. In light of the evidence presented, it seems that the assessment was at the least subjective and there seems little evidence to support the reliability of the procedures. This is not in itself to deny that movement might be used for the assessment of personality on some more structured and scientifically validated system.

Allport, G. W. Personality: A Psychological Interpretation. New York: Holt, 1937.

_____, and P. E. Vernon. Studies in Expressive Movement. New York: Macmillan, 1933.

Alston, W. P. "Conceptual Prolegomena to a Psychological Theory of Intentional Action." S. C. Brown, ed., Philosophy of Psychology. London: Macmillan, 1974.

Aspin, D. N. "Kinds of Knowledge, Physical Education and the Curriculum." Journal of Human Movement Studies 3 (1977) pp. 21-37.

Ayer, A. J. Man as a Subject for Science. London: Athlone Press, 1964.

Bartlett, F. C. Remembering: A Study in Experimental and Social Psychology. Cambridge: Cambridge University Press, 1977.

Bem, D. J. and A. Allen. "On Predicting Some of the People Some of the Time." Psychological Review, 81 (1974) pp. 506-20.

Bernstein, N. The Coordination and Regulation of Movement. London: Pergamon, 1967.

Best, D. "The Aesthetic in Sport." Journal of Human Movement Studies 1 (1975) pp. 41-48.

_____. "Meaning in Movement." Journal of Human Movement Studies 4 (1978) pp. 211-33.

_____. Philosophy and Human Movement. London: George Allen & Unwin, 1979.

Birdwhistell, R. L. Kinesics and Context. Philadelphia: University of Pennsylvania Press, 1970.

Bower, T. G. R. A Primer of Infant Development. San Francisco: Freeman, 1977.

Bronowski, J. The Ascent of Man. London: BBC Publications, 1973.

Bruner, J. S. "The Course of Cognitive Growth." American Psychologist (1964) pp. 1-15.

Carr, D. "The Language of Action, Ability and Skill: Part II— The Language of Ability and Skill." Journal of Human Movement Studies 6 (1980) pp. 111-26.

Carroll, J. Book review, The Laban Art of Movement Guild Magazine (1972) p. 49.

Connolly, K. "The Nature of Motor Skill Development." Journal of Human Movement Studies 3 (1977) pp. 128-43.

Curl, G. "An Attempt to Justify Human Movement as a Field of Study." Human Movement—A Field of Study, J. D. Brooke & H. T. A. Whiting, eds. London: Kimpton, 1973.

Den Brinker, B. Internal paper, Department of Psychology, Interfaculty of Physical Education, The Free University, Amsterdam, 1980.

Ekman, P., and W. v. Friesen. "Non-verbal Leakage and Clues to Deception." Psychiatry 32 (1969) pp. 88-106.

_____, and _____. Unmasking the Face. Englewood Cliffs, NJ: Prentice-Hall, 1974.

Enwhistle, H. "Practical and Theoretical Learning." British Journal of Educational Studies 17 (1969) p. 117.

Evarts, E. V. "Brain Mechanisms in Movement." Scientific American 229 (1973) pp. 96-103.

Eysenck, H. J. The Dynamics of Anxiety and Hysteria. London: Routledge & Kegan Paul, 1957.

Fellows, B. J. The Discrimination Process and Development. London: Pergamon, 1968.

Fitch, H. L. and M. T. Turvey. "On the Control of Activity: Some Remarks from an Ecological Point of View." Psychology of Motor Behavior and Sport, D. M. Landers & R. W. Christina, eds. Champaign: Human Kinetics Publishers, 1978.

Fowler, C. A. and M. T. Turvey. "Skill Acquisition: An Event Approach with Special Reference to Searching for the Optimum of a Function of Several Variables." Information Processing in Motor Control and Learning, G. E. Stelmach, ed. New York: Academic Press, 1978.

Gallistel, G. R. The Organization of Action--A New Synthesis. Hillsdale, NJ: Erlbaum, 1980.

Gibson, J. J. The Ecological Approach to Visual Perception. Boston: Houghton Mifflin, 1979.

_____. The Senses Considered as Perceptual Systems. New York: George Allen & Unwin, 1966.

Harper, R. G., A. N. Wiens, and J. D. Matarazzo. Nonverbal Communication: The State of the Art. New York: Wiley, 1978.

Higgins, J. R. Human Movement: An Integrated Approach. St. Louis: Mosby, 1977.

Hoenkamp, E. "Perceptual Cues that Determine the Labelling of Human Gait." Journal of Human Movement Studies 2 (1978) pp. 59-69.

Hutt, C. Critique of "direct observation" by Cooper et al. Bulletin of the British Psychological Society 27 (1974) pp. 503-4.

Johansson, G. "Visual Perception of Biological Motion and a Model for Its Analysis." Perception and Psychophysics 14 (1973) pp. 201-11.

Koestler, A. The Act of Creation. London: Hutchinson, 1964.

Kohlberg, L. "Stage and Sequence: The Cognitive Developmental Approach to Socialisation." Handbook of Socialization Theory and Research, D. A. Goslin, ed. Chicago: Rand-McNally, 1969.

Konorski, J. Integrative Activity of the Brain. Chicago: University of Chicago Press, 1966.

Kozlowski, L. T. and J. E. Cutting. "Recognising the Sex of a Walker from a Dynamic Point-light Display." Perception and Psychophysics 21 (1977) pp. 575-80.

Kugler, P. N., J. A. Scott Kelso and M. T. Turvey. "On the Concept of Coordinative Structures as Dissipative Structures: I. Theoretical Lines of Convergence." Tutorials in Motor Behavior, G. E. Stelmach and J. Requin, eds. Amsterdam: North-Holland, 1980.

Kuypers, H. G. J. M. "The Anatomical Organisation of the Descending Pathways and Their Contribution to Motor Control, Especially in Primates." New Developments in E.M.G. and Clinical Neurophysiology, T. E. Desmedt, ed. Basel: Karger, 1973.

Lamb, W. Posture and Gesture. London: Duckworth, 1965.

Lippa, R. "Expressive Control, Expressive Consistency and the Correspondence Between Expressive Behaviour and Personality." Journal of Personality 46 (1978) pp. 439-73.

Lorenz, K. Studies in Animal Behaviour. London: Methuen, 1937.

Luria, A. R. The Role of Speech in the Regulation of Normal and Abnormal Behaviour. New York: Liveright, 1961.

Mischel, W. Personality and Assessment. New York: Wiley, 1968.

Neisser, U. Cognition and Reality. San Francisco: Freeman, 1976.

Newtson, D. "Attribution and the Unit of Perception of Ongoing Behavior." Journal of Personality and Social Psychology 28 (1976) pp. 28-38.

North, M. Personality Assessment Through Movement. London: MacDonald & Evans, 1972.

Ornstein, R. E. The Psychology of Consciousness. New York: Harcourt Brace Jovanovich, 1977.

Peters, R. S. Ethics and Education. London: George Allen & Unwin, 1966.

Pew, R. W. "Acquisition of Hierarchical Control over the Temporal Organisation of a Skill." Journal of Experimental Psychology 71 (1966) pp. 764-71.

Piaget, J. The Origins of Intelligence in the Child. Harmondsworth: Penguin, 1936, 1977.

_____. The Origins of Intelligence in Children. New York: International Universities Press, 1952.

Pribram, K. H. Languages of the Brain. Englewood Cliffs, NJ: Prentice-Hall, 1971.

Renshaw, P. "The Nature and Study of Human Movement: A Philosophical Examination." Journal of Human Movement Studies 1 (1975) pp. 5-12.

Reynolds, P. C. "The Programmatic Description of Simple Technologies." Journal of Human Movement Studies 6 (1980) pp. 38-74.

Reynolds, V. The Biology of Human Action. Reading: Freeman, 1976.

Ricoeur, P. Freedom and Nature; The Voluntary and the Involuntary. Illinois: Northwestern University Press, 1966.

Ryle, G. The Concept of Mind. London: Hutchinson, 1969.

Saugstad, P. A Theory of Communication and the Use of Language. Oxford: Global Book Resources, 1978.

Schaffer, L. H. "Analysing piano performance: A Study of Concert Pianists." Tutorials in Motor Behavior, G. E. Stelmach and J. Requin, eds. Amsterdam: North-Holland, 1980.

Schmidt, R. A. "The Schema as a Solution to Some Persistent Problems in Motor Learning Theory." Motor Control: Issues and Trends, G. E. Stelmach, ed. New York: Academic Press, 1976.

_____. "A Schema Theory of Discrete Motor Skill Learning." Psychological Bulletin 82 (1975) pp. 225-60.

Sheets, M. The Phenomenology of Dance. Madison: University of Wisconsin Press, 1965.

Sherrington, C. S. Man on His Nature. Cambridge: Cambridge University Press, 1940.

Snyder, M. "Self-Monitoring of Expressive Behavior." Journal of Personality and Social Psychology 30 (1974) pp. 526-37.

Spiegel, J. P. and P. Machotka. Messages of the Body. New York: Free Press, 1974.

Tinbergen, N. An Objective Study of the Innate Behavior of Animals. Bibliotheca Biotheoretica I, Rijksuniversiteit te Leiden, 1942.

Trevarthen, C. "Basic Patterns of Psychogenetic Changes in Infancy." Unpublished paper, Department of Psychology, University of Edinburgh, 1977.

_____. "Mechanisms of Skillful Movement and Their Growth." Unpublished paper, Department of Psychology, University of Edinburgh, 1974.

Turvey, M. T. "Preliminaries to a Theory of Action with Reference to Vision." Perceiving, Acting and Knowing: Towards an Ecological Psychology, R. Shaw and J. Bransford, eds. New York: Wiley, 1977.

Tyldesley, D. A. "Action-Oriented Studies of Vision in Sport." Vision and Sport. I. M. Cockerill and W. W. MacGillivary, eds. London: Stanley Thornes, 1981.

Vernon, P. E. Personality Assessment: A Critical Survey. London: Methuen, 1963.

Vygotsky, L. S. Thought and Language. Cambridge: MIT Press, 1962.

Weber, M. The Theory of Social and Economic Organisation. London: Free Press, 1974.

Weimer, B. "A Conceptual Framework for Cognitive Psychology: Motor Theories of the Mind." Perceiving, Acting and Knowing, R. Shaw and J. Bransford, eds. New York: Wiley, 1977.

Whiting, H. T. A. "Dimensions of Control in Motor Learning." Tutorials in Motor Behavior, G. E. Stelmach and J. Requin, eds. Amsterdam: North-Holland, 1980.

_____ and den Brinker, B. P. L. M. "Image of the Act." Theory and Research in Learning Disabilities, J. P. Das, R. Mulcahy and A. E. Wall, eds. New York: Plenum, 1982.

Wilder, D. "Units of Perception and Predictability of Behaviour." Unpublished manuscript, University of Wisconsin, 1974.

Wozniak, R. H. "Verbal Regulation of Motor Behaviour--Soviet Research and Non-Soviet Replications." Human Development 15 (1972) pp. 13-57.

Wright, D. S. Introducing Psychology. Harmondsworth: Penguin, 1967.

Zaporozhets, A. V. "The Development of Voluntary Movements." Psychology in the Soviet Union, B. Simon, ed. Stanford: University Press, 1957.

Chapter Nine

(NON) ANTHROPOLOGISTS, THE DANCE, AND HUMAN MOVEMENT

Drid Williams

Introductory

It is with mixed feelings that one approaches the task of writing a bibliographical essay designed to help American (or generally English-speaking) students of theatre, mime, music, dance, and "the arts" find their way around anthropological literature on the subject. For a start,

> It is commonplace to separate dance, along with music, from other forms of human behavior and label it "art." Once it has been so separated, it is often felt that it need not be dealt with. This ethnocentric view does not take into consideration the possibility that dance may not be "art" (whatever that is) to people of the culture concerned, or that there may not even be a cultural category comparable to what Westerners call "dance" (Kaeppler, 1978:46).

It is well known that the Hopi have no term for "art" in their language, for example, and this is not a "mere semantic problem."[1] Anthropologists hear nonanthropologists casually dismiss these matters all the time, knowing that even with the best of intentions, investigators who are anthropologically and linguistically naive will ride roughshod over the classifications and categories of another people. They are not aware that they are doing harm, yet

> ... there can be powerful and dissonant side-effects from the insistence of including art as an interface to dance. The manipulative attitudes of super-ordinate peoples can force adaptation by subordinate peoples that is not the same as an internally developed evolution. We may, for example, eventually force the Hopi kachinas onto the proscenium stage and Hopi "dance" may become an art. If this happens, the world will lose at least as much as it gains (Keali'inohomoku, 1980:42).

It is not my intention to polemicize the entire discussion to follow by starting with comments by concerned anthropologists that point to the dangers of superficial research. Nor do I wish for readers to make the error of assuming that the study of the body languages of another culture are best thought of in politicized, "minority" terms only. To reduce such complex issues solely to those realms of discourse is, to my mind, to remove the focus of our attention to secondary political, rather than to primary scholarly, concerns. Kaeppler states the case in the context of a people who, unlike the Hopi, are not "subordinate" to anyone:

> ... there is little anthropological reason for classing together the Japanese cultural form called mikagura performed in Shinto shrines, the cultural form called buyo performed within (or separated from) a Kabuki drama, and the cultural form commonly known as bon, performed to honor the dead. The only logical reason I can see for categorizing them together is that from an outsider's point of view, all three cultural forms use the body in ways that to Westerners would be considered dance. But from a [Japanese] cultural point of view either of movement or activity there is little reason to class them together. Indeed, as far as I have been able to discover, there is no Japanese word that will class these three cultural forms together that will not also include much of what from a Western point of view would not be considered "dance" (Kaeppler, 1978:46).

We would also be in error if we imagine that categorical and classificatory disparities exist only across language barriers in our present times or in relation to ethnicities other than our own. Baxandall (1972) clearly illustrates how the visual skills and habits evolved in the daily life of any society enter into its painters' style. Under a chapter heading, "Conditions of Trade," he tells us that

> ... a fifteenth century painting is the deposit of a social relationship. On one side there was a painter who made the picture, or at least supervised its making. On the other side there was somebody else who asked him to make it, provided funds for him to make it and, after he made it, reckoned on using it in some way or other. Both parties worked within institutions and conventions--commercial, religious, perceptual, in the widest sense social--that were different from ours and influenced the forms of what they together made (Baxandall, 1972:1, underline supplied).

Body languages, too, are "deposits of social relationships," especially with reference to dances, dramas and the like. On the one side, there are the choreographers and dancers, the directors and actors, who make the dance or drama. On the other, there are those who ask them to make it, and these works are used perhaps for entertainment, for edification or educational purposes or whatever, but all concerned work within commercial, social and perceptual conventions that influence what they make.

It is the anthropologist's unwillingness to sacrifice cultural diversity (as in the examples cited from our own or others' traditions) to the perhaps more satisfying conceptual closure of universal definitions of "art," "dance," "theatre" and such that prompts those of us in modern social and cultural anthropology to emphasize diversities of human symbolic expression. There is a noticeable lack of finality in the definitions of "art" and interpretations of artifacts, material or nonmaterial, in anthropological writings that may, in the end, arise from the nature of anthropological enquiry itself. See, for examples, Davenport (1968), Fernandez (1966), Forge (1965), Jopling (1971), Sieber (1971), Lewis (1980).

However rashly, from the discipline's inception, we have been committed to thinking from a worldwide data base. That aspect of our studies alone establishes clear parallels with the modern science of linguistics, where notions of worldwide cultural homogeneity are equally difficult to postulate. Chapman summarizes the point very well:

> There is not ... any serious popular conception that such things require "translation" from one culture to another. Most people, when faced with an unintelligible foreign language, will recognize the need for "translation"; non-verbal "language" gestures, and generally semantic use of the body, of the person, or of groups of people, are not usually granted the same status as language in this respect. Translation will not be thought necessary. In general, an "English-speaker" will interpret the gestures of, say, a "Breton-speaker," a "French-speaker" or a "Gaelic-speaker," according to an entirely "English" set of rules of interpretation, without feeling any need to go to the bother of "translating" (Chapman, 1982:13-14).

The mixed feelings that one has about guiding those working in theatre, dance, and related movement forms through anthropological literature on the subject derive explicitly from the anthropologists' viewpoints quoted above. On the one hand, one wants to stem the rising tide of naive universalism that expresses itself in a kind of artistic ecumenism among nonanthropologically trained writers. On the other hand, one wants to encourage serious scholars among nonanthropologists to--at the very least--acquaint themselves with the works of modern social and cultural anthropologists, some of whom have spent their lifetimes attempting to deal with the profound issues that studies of the dance and human movement entail.

It is because of this that this chapter is about anthropologists of the subjects of dance and human movement rather than about an anthropology of them,[2] because, in my view, it would be impossible to trace an assumed development of either subject through the discipline. The reasons for the impossibility are themselves instructive.

A Few Relevant Facts About Anthropology

Modern anthropology consists of several disciplines: prehistoric archeology as well as physical, social or sociological, cultural, linguistic and psychological anthropology, to cite only the broadest of nominal distinctions. These disciplines have separated out of a "general" anthropology which, in the second half of the nineteenth century and into the twentieth century, aimed to study humankind both as a biological and social being.[3] As a formal academic discipline, the subject did not appear until 1899 at Columbia University in the United States, where Franz Boas held the first chair, and until c. 1900 in Great Britain, where a chair was established at Liverpool University, occupied by Sir James Frazer. Prior to that, at Oxford, the subject was known as "Mr. Tylor's science";[4] the reference being to Edward Burnet Tylor, commonly considered on both sides of the Atlantic to be the father of modern social and cultural anthropology.[5]

The term "anthropology" had been long in existence, however, before Tylor was born, and was used by philosophers and theologians, among others, to denote a general preoccupation with studies of human nature--it still makes sense, for example, to speak of the "anthropology" of St. Peter, Plato, Aristotle or St. Paul, but to use the term in this way after the turn of the twentieth century is to use it differently from those who were to become professional anthropologists.

There are still some "general" anthropologists (i.e. those whose training included equal attention to, say, prehistoric archaeology, physical anthropology, and social or cultural anthropology)[6] mainly in the United States and in some European countries, but by the 1920's and 1930's, the different anthropological disciplines were beginning to separate from one another, although there are still scholars who are eminent in more than one. The sheer enormity of the discipline thus gives rise to confusions. For example, to identify oneself as an anthropologist in Great Britain today is to identify oneself as a social anthropologist (the other categories used are "physical anthropologist" or "archaeologist"); to identify oneself as an anthropologist in the United States is to evoke images, usually, of potsherds, skeletons, or chimpanzees. The systematic study of conventions, customs, codes of communication, or structured systems of human meaning does not, at least in popular interpretation, even compete.

The phrase "human movement" is, if anything, more problem-

atical (as in the statement, "I am an anthropologist of human movement"), because it is usually taken to mean "migrations"--or worse.
It is rarely associated with deaf-signing, the martial arts, rites and
ceremonies, dances, spatial oppositions, or with a notion of human
body languages that has a solid reality and that is taken seriously.
Students who wish to study this subject are very aware of these
problems.

They might be in a somewhat better position if they could
identify themselves from a theoretical standpoint: they could say
that they were studying kinesics,[7] proxemics,[8] semiotics,[9] but the
usefulness of terms such as these ends very quickly, because if
they say they are studying semasiology (the newest of the anthropological theoretical approaches), they are usually asked "what on
earth is that?"[10] In other words, to begin to inquire into the subject itself is to come up against social taxonomies, human categories,
and classificatory systems the hard way--not in the other cultural
contexts previously mentioned, but in the context of finding one's
way around the discipline itself.

For the student who does not want to study anthropology[11]
the problem is more extreme. Armed with little more, usually, than
the notion that anthropology is somehow connected with the study
of mankind the tendency is to go for the oldest names in the discipline. The usual result is that theories are revived that modern
anthropologists have long since abandoned[12] or, to go for whatever
happens to appeal to them, with the result that they generate curious scissors-and-paste collages of theory and method that are, in
the end, relatively useless to them or to anyone else--and that are,
on the whole, simply filed in the wastebaskets of practicing professional anthropologists--if they are ever seen by them.[13]

As each branch of the old general anthropology separated out,
its practitioners turned to other subjects, to other explanatory paradigms in the sciences, and to other techniques and modes of analysis that were more appropriate than were those of their erstwhile
colleagues. For example, modes of explanation in modern social
anthropology are often more closely allied to early French sociological theory or to contemporary linguistic theory than they are to
phylogenetic theories of evolution. Physical anthropology has stayed
very close to the biological sciences and emphasizes primate studies.
An example of more modern work that pertains to ethological studies
and human movement is that of Peng (1978). Hewes' work (1955,
1961) is an example of this tradition.

Psychological anthropologists, who studied the interaction of
culture and personality (e.g. Mead, 1931; Bateson, 1936; Benedict,
1934), and their students, came to depend heavily on psychology--
especially, as in Ray Birdwhistell's case, on depth psychology and
psychiatry. British social anthropologists moved closer to sociology,
history, political science, economics, kinship and law, and from

about 1950, there began to be a movement towards linguistics and structuralist preoccupations (see, for example, Needham, 1973, for British, and Dolgin, Kemnitzer and Schneider, 1977, for American developments). It is still the American curricula in most anthropology departments in the United States that continues to draw more or less equally on the biological and sociological sciences-- and to a much lesser extent, on psychology.

There are a few significant things that social and cultural anthropologists have in common: they are both cross-cultural disciplines in outlook and they advocate broadly comparative methods. Knowledge of ethnographies (that is, of anthropological writings about cultures of the world), of kinship structures, language and the history of the discipline are essential. Traditionally, both social and cultural anthropologists studied small-scale, tribal societies, although contemporary social and cultural anthropologists no longer confine themselves in this way.[14]

To my mind, Pocock describes the aims of social and many American cultural anthropologists briefly but well when he said:

> The anthropologist is concerned with a systematic understanding of what he sees going on around him. He learns the culture, as he learns the language of the people, on the assumption that action and belief are no more random than language. The first step is to find out by participation and identification the meaning which people themselves attach to what they do. He does not assume at the outset that phenomena may be labelled political, religious or economic because that is what initially they mean to him ... by not assuming that what he sees he immediately understands, he places himself "outside" the society he studies and to this extent approaches social facts "as though they were things" ... (Pocock, 1971:85).

Probably the greatest distinguishing features of a social and/ or cultural anthropological view of culture are the participant-observer method and fieldwork.

Participant-Observation

> The participant-observer method was first developed by anthropologists, though it is [now] also frequently used by sociologists, social psychologists, political scientists, and organization theorists. Its primary subject matter is a single, self-maintaining social system. The system may be a small community with its own culture, or a larger society with its culture, or a small and relatively isolated neighborhood, or a gang, clique, voluntary organization, or family, or a formal organization or institution, or a person (adap-

tation by clinical method), or a historical period. In each case the emphasis is on the individuality or uniqueness of the system, its wholeness or boundedness, and the ways it maintains its individuality. The primary objective is to describe the individual in its individuality, as a system of rules, goals, values, techniques, defense or boundary-maintaining mechanisms, exchange of boundary-crossing mechanisms, socialization procedures, and decision procedures. In one important variant, the primary interest is in recurring processes within or around such individual systems (Diesing, 1971:5-6).

This section begins with a quotation from Diesing's excellent book, because in it he offers the best overview of social scientific method and theory that I know of, and his work was used as a textbook for an advanced graduate course in theory and practice in the anthropology of human movement and dance at New York University towards completion of a master's degree.[15] For nonanthropologists who wish to gain a better understanding of what "holist" theory in the social sciences amounts to (Diesing, 1971: 203-234), of what "structural-functional" theory consists of (1971: 235-258) and "participant-observer" method (1971:2, 5-7, 17-21, 63), I can suggest no better source than this.

Indeed, if space permitted, I would simply quote this book at length, knowing full well that nonanthropologists are probably not going to consult the sources that Diesing cites, yet these are required beginning readings for those who eventually want to call themselves anthropologists of human movement: Beattie (1965, 1968); Eggan (1937, 1954); Epstein (1967); Evans-Pritchard (1940, 1962a, 1962b); Firth (1939, 1951, 1955, 1957); Fortes (1949) and Fortes and Evans-Pritchard (1940); Geertz (1967); Gluckman and Devons (1964); Goodenough (1968/1956); Harris (1968); Kaplan and Manners (1968); Kluckhohn (1944, 1949); Kluckhohn and Leighton (1946); Kroeber (1948); Leach (1951, 1954, 1957); Lévi-Strauss (1963); Malinowski (1922, 1944, 1954); Mandelbaum (1954); Maquet (1964); Mead (1955, 1956); Mitchell (1966); Murdock (1949); Nadel (1951); Radcliffe-Brown (1922, 1949, 1951a&b, 1952, 1957); Redfield (1953, 1962); Richards (1939 and 1956).

More to the point perhaps, even if these sources were consulted, the investigator into the dance, human movement, or theatre would require further guidance regarding the relation of "holist," "structural-functional," or "formalist" (Diesing, 1971:8-12, 29-32, 115-23) theory in descriptions of the dance or human movement. Of these, it is the "structural-functional" approach that has been used more widely by dance ethnologists (see Kurath, 1960; Hanna, 1965; Thompson, 1966; Singer, 1970).[16] A nonanthropologist can easily find him or herself afloat (or drowning) in a sea of theory and methodologies that can overwhelm.

Is it the case that theatre and dance seek academic integration with social and cultural anthropology? If so, it will be necessary for them to recognize that research in anthropology is not purely descriptive and that problems of interpretation and explanation are not ignored by anthropologists. They are, unfortunately, largely ignored by enthusiasts in the dance, photography, graphic arts, theatre, music and performing arts with the result that so far, no corpus of certified knowledge has emerged out of their collective efforts--and the Choreometrics project is only one example of an attempt to feed secondhand findings into a quasi-social scientific schema that remains unsatisfactory both to artists (see Bartenieff, 1967/1968), and to anthropologists (see Williams, 1974, Keali'inohomoku, 1974), but more of this later.

If it is true, as anthropological evidence indicates, that all human societies possess standards of excellence in connection with crafts, skills, art and symbolic expressions of all kinds, then the anthropologist would want to ask, "by what criteria other than those of the people who make them can we assess the merits of, say, an intricately carved Tlingit club,[17] a Japanese dance, a Hopi kachina figure, or a Mughal garden?"[18] Anthropologists grant the priority of indigenous meanings in these examples, just as they would do were the object under consideration a Scarlatti sonata, a raga played on an Indian sitar, a Yemeni wedding dance, a Brancusi sculpture, an Egyptian tomb effigy, or a disco-dance. And most anthropologists recognize too, that these indigenous meanings are only a part--however vital and essential--of the totality they try to explain.

This point can scarcely be overstressed, for on the whole, modern cognitive, semantic or symbolic anthropologists[19] regard their work as a highly complex act of translation in which they participate with native collaborators (whether inside or outside of their own culture) in an intricate process of theory building. A working anthropologist does not enter into dialogue with his or her informants in the same way that a teacher, journalist, businessman, government official, artist, missionary, representative from a grants foundation or tourist might do.

Elsewhere, I have given an account of the problems faced by the student of human movement and some of the attendant concerns regarding objectivity, preconceptions and the like; and I have done a public criticism of my own preanthropological essays (see Williams, 1976/7), so will not repeat them here. Suffice it to say that theory, method, and interpretation play dominant roles in social and cultural anthropology, such that even a critical bibliographical essay such as this cannot begin to give the novice all the help that is required, although it may serve to provide a simple, beginning map of an immense intellectual territory that possesses a fairly long and distinguished history.

The reason for this is simple: theory and method consist of actual procedures used by a scientific and/or scholarly community. These procedures, as Diesing rightly points out, have variations, and each of the methodologies is justified and explained by an ideology of scholarship and/or a philosophy of science which specifies the goals of the science, its limitations and boundaries.

> The conception of method is historically oriented and relativistic. Methods change slowly and continually: they develop, combine, and separate. They have no timeless essence--or any essence they may have does not become apparent in this approach--and are not separated by any fixed boundaries ..." (Diesing, 1971:18).

He further points out that:

> To find out what actually happens in science, direct observation is necessary in addition to reading. This means observation of work in progress, including the study of experimental apparatus, questionnaires, field notes and diaries, uncompleted models, and particularly the comparison of different stages in the development of an apparatus, questionnaire, or model. It means talking and listening, personally and in colloquia, about a scientist's own work and about the work of others, in order to discover not only actual procedures but also particular modes of thinking, approaches to problems, and critical standards. Direct participation in scientific work, experiencing at first hand the problems and the modes of solution in use, is indispensable if one is to infer the actual performance behind published work and to interpret the meaning of methodological discussions (Diesing, 1971:19).

All too often, however, what the nonanthropologist interested in the dance or human movement seems to want from anthropology is simple legitimation. That the dances, ceremonies, rituals and other nonvocalized sign systems of humanity represent an impressive data base is a proposition that few would deny. The theoretical and intellectual difficulties arise when one begins to consider how these data are to be handled. Merely having a data base and/or a loosely connected set of problems or ideas about it does not mean that one has adequate theoretical or methodological structures with which one can interpret the data or deal with the problems. There is a sense in which all of the social or human sciences deal with the same thing: people. They do not, however, set about explaining them in the same ways or for the same reasons.

Fieldwork

Nowhere is the lack of all of this more evident than it is in nonanthropological field writings. In Religion and Medicine of the Ga People, for example, the writer repeatedly refers to the dances of the Ga wɔyei (inadequately translated as priests) as "fits" or "hysterical fits." There are well-known difficulties involved in using terms such as "neurotic," "pathological," "paranoic," etc. with reference to persons in our own culture: the meanings of these terms (in the investigator's case, outside of the medical profession) are highly ambiguous. Are we to consent to their usage when they are superimposed on the actions of peoples of another culture, even though fieldwork has been done?

It is because of these illegitimate usages of terminology that an odd sense of disjunction pervades the experience of reading Field's accounts of Ga dances.[20] Underneath it all, one can sense some important facts that are treated as throwaway statements: the relation between types of dancing and the types of languages spoken during possession, for example, or the comments made about the lack of "any unbalance or hysteria in their everyday behaviour."

Following a description of a possession dance of the Kplekemɔ of Ogbame, a war divinity of the Alata group of the Ga, we are told:

> This goes on and on till the ethnographer, bored with understanding nothing of the Fanti, limp with the atmosphere of the room, and deaf with the noise, has gone home (Field, 1937:67).

Obviously, if the investigator understands nothing either of the spoken, far less the unspoken, language that such a dance represents, her reaction was probably the only possible one, but her conclusions are thereby rendered unconvincing:

> The wɔyo system is probably satisfactory from the western medical point of view, as well as having the social satisfactoriness of providing a dignified niche for the type of person who in Europe would be the misfit and plague of society (1937:109).

While there can be no doubt of the author's sincerity and one can only admire her honesty, one can justifiably reject most of her evidence as unreliable, even though it is, in this case, a result of field observation and participation.

Irresistibly, Evans-Pritchard's criticism of the Frazerian style of analysis of magic is brought to mind: that is, much more would have been known if Field had compared, in their completeness, the state of possession among the Ga wɔyei and hysterical fits which might occur in a New York or London hospital. At least this procedure might have determined whether the category "hysterical fit" is able to subsume both systems of actions, while at the same time doing justice to the realities of possession dances.

No amount of raw field data can make acceptable the sorts of crude categorization and classification that results from a separation of theory and description. The current popular dichotomy between theory and description masks a profound illusion: there is no such thing in modern social and cultural anthropology, anyway, of simply "telling like it is," as if the telling is either the same as, or can be divorced from, interpretation. Then too, it is often difficult, if not impossible, to infer meanings of body languages solely from the standpoint of having observed the movements that someone (or a group) has made. A contemporary philosopher makes the point this way:

> ... an intentional action is not the same as a physical movement since the latter can be described in various ways according to one's point of view and one's beliefs about the person performing it. One cannot specify an action, as opposed to a purely physical movement, without taking into account what the agent intended (Best, 1974:193).

Observation of behavior is usually nothing more than the apperception of gross physical movements, but this is not enough because the conceptual organization of the action is not given in the movement. A relevant ethnographic example is this:

> If one were to travel through various parts of West New Guinea, one might observe the following gestures by Papuans who notice you. They might put a hand to their navel, their breasts, or their armpit; they might also beckon you. If you are lured into approaching the beckoner, he will be quite surprised, for his hand simply said "hello." And so did the navel, and the breasts and the armpit, and so on. All of them are visible, observable signs of an invisible message which has to be inferred. Hence the vital role for social anthropologists of informants, and especially of key-informants (Pouwer, 1973:4).

To a linguistically naive investigator, these gestures might seem aberrant, perhaps exotic (i.e. "what a quaintly different manner of greeting these people have") and so on. The anthropological facts are quite different:

> ... the essence of life, called ipu is located in each of the jointing parts of the body separately, such as the knuckles, shoulder-blades and knee-caps. To these Papuans each individual person has a number of substantive ipu. English equivalents such as "spirit" or "principle of life" or for that matter mana hardly convey the meaning of ipu (Pouwer, 1973:3).

It is the concept of ipu that ties the Mimika gestures together, so to speak--that makes of them action signs (see Williams, 1979) and not merely movements--and it is the concept that makes sense, not only of their greeting gestures, but of other kinds of actions as well.

The registration of the gestures through visual means alone tells one nothing in the above case about ipu, nor much else. This problem is especially apparent in the writing of dances. Durr (1981) has written an excellent article discussing this and other related problems regarding the notation of human actions.

Psychologists use subjects in many of their experiments, and in a clinical, dyadic relationship, other persons are the subjects of diagnosis, treatment and such, and psychiatrists, in case studies, may describe these patients (or "clients"). Sociologists, using survey methods, use people as respondents, but anthropologists, having some aspect of culture as the object of research, use informants. This is, of course, a simplified picture, but one that states an important truth about the nature of anthropological fieldwork--a process that requires a minimum of one or two years--and if the anthropologist is working outside of his or her own native language, the fieldwork process can take much longer. A six-week jaunt, a summer's trip, or even six months' residence in another country simply does not qualify.

Dance in Anthropological Perspective[21]

Anthropologists, when studying their chosen community or subject, for the most part pay little serious attention to such things as dance or that aspect of human behavior loosely called the arts--relegating these esoterica in their classes to the never-reached end of a course, coupling them with "play," and considering them the frosting on the cake of the more important parts of culture. Occasionally, an anthropologist will make a tape recording of dance songs, photographs of costumes, or even motion pictures, thinking that he has done his duty as far as these aspects of culture are concerned. Although such recordings and photography may be of interest as far as the sound organization or movement patterns of a society are concerned, by themselves they can tell us little that is anthropologically significant. At least from the point of view of the "new ethnography" [see Sturtevant, 1974] an adequate description of a culture should place the same emphasis on dance as that given it by the members of that society--and in some parts of the world, this is indeed great. Anthropologists have been slow to recognize that a study and understanding of dance --which is sometimes a very conspicuous part of culture-- may actually assist in an understanding of the deep structures of a society and bring new insights into understanding other parts of culture (Kaeppler, 1978:32).

These statements are as true of British social, as they are of American cultural, anthropologists. Although Evans-Pritchard was years ago aware of its neglect, saying:

> In ethnological accounts the dance is usually given a place quite unworthy of its social importance. It is often viewed as an independent activity and is described without reference to its contextual setting in native life. Such treatment leaves out many problems as to the composition and organization of the dance (Evans-Pritchard, 1928: 446-462),

very little was subsequently written on the subject.

An example of the sort of thing Evans-Pritchard had in mind is to be found in Wolfson (1958), who reprinted an account of a dance witnessed in 1881 by an officer, Ellis, who was in the first West India regiment, who arrived on the then Gold Coast in 1874 and subsequently served as an administrative official there.

Although Evans-Pritchard hoped that anthropologists would recognize the importance of the dance, only a few Africanists actually published anything directly related to the subject, notably Lienhardt (1958), Mitchell (1956), Banton (1953). Again, I can do no better than to quote Kaeppler:

> The first publication about dance that had any real relevance to anthropology was Curt Sach's Eine Weltgeschichte des Tanzes, published in 1933 and translated into English in 1937 as World History of the Dance. This book has been widely used, and indeed is still used today, as a definitive anthropological study of dance. Although this book certainly has a place today in the study of the history of anthropological theory, it has no place in the study of dance in anthropological perspective [underline supplied]. Its theoretical stance is derived from the German Kulturkreis school of Schmidt and Graebner in which worldwide diffusion resulted in a form of unilineal evolution. But just as modern non-Western peoples do not represent earlier stages of Western cultural evolution, there is no reason to believe that non-Western dance represents earlier stages of Western dance. Yet some anthropologists find it possible to accept the latter without accepting the former [see Youngerman, 1974, for more detailed discussion, and Williams, 1976, for a review of Lange, 1976a, which is a modern version of Sachs' theories].
>
> Much more important for the study of dance in anthropological perspective, although he did not really address himself to the subject, was Franz Boas, whose orientation offers scope for analyzing dance as culture rather than using dance data to fit theories and generalizations. Boas felt

that man had a basic need for order and rhythm--a need
which Boas used to help explain the universal existence of
art. By refusing to accept sweeping generalizations that
did not account for cultural variability, he laid a foundation for the possibility of examining dance and responses
to it in terms of one's own culture rather than as a universal
language. In spite of Boas and others, however, the idea
that dance (or art) can be understood cross-culturally without understanding an individual dance tradition in terms of
the cultural background of which it is a part, is not yet
dead, especially among artists and dancers (Kaeppler, 1978:
33).

Just as Boas "did not really address himself to the subject,"
neither E. B. Tylor nor Sir James Frazer addressed themselves directly to the subject either. Modern students are sometimes offended
when they discover that Tylor referred to dancing as "frivolous and
meaningless" and they find it difficult to understand why he was
pessimistic about the future of dancing in modern civilization and
thought that what remnants there were in England of folk dancing
were dying out; that sportive dancing was falling off, and that although sacred music was flourishing, civilization had mostly cast off
sacred dance. "At low levels in civilization," he said, "dancing and
play-acting are one" (1898:15).

Tylor's real interest in symbolic movement did not lie in its
manifestations in dances, rather in the language of gestures used
in deaf signing. Tylor's work on gesture language is a rich and
original source of linguistically based movement theory in anthropology (see Henson, 1974, for fuller discussion). It requires much
more than superficial handling, then, to accommodate his theories
of gesture and movement to the dance as we understand it today
without risking distortion, either of Tylor's thought or of the dance.
But mention of Tylor's name carries with it a cautionary tale: his
thinking was in many ways a true reflection of the general evolutionary bias of nineteenth-century anthropology. Most of the writing about the dance during the period 1850-1900, whether contained
in works on other subjects or whether solely about the dance, begin with sections or whole chapters on early Greek, Roman, or
Egyptian dancing, or as in the case of Lilley Grove[22] (the wife of
Sir James Frazer), writing in 1895, the emphasis is on primitive
dancing.

For Frazer, dancing fitted into a scheme of stages of an assumed human intellectual development: at the lowest end of the
evolutionary continuum, the dance was placed as an exemplar of
magic. Frazer thought that primitives called on magic when their
capacity to deal with situations realistically was exhausted. Magic
thus provided a substitute reality: if a tribe could not really make
war on a neighboring village, then it could at least do a dance
about it. In the Frazerian scheme of things dancing was classified

as sympathetic magic, and magic was, of course, wrongheaded science. The point here is that in the intellectual battles that Frazer was really interested in fighting, he opposed both magic and science to religion. Although social anthropologists no longer accept Frazer's theory of stages of evolution or his assessments of dancing today, many artists, dancers, dance critics and others still use these ideas for--is it inspiration, legitimation, or for the general credibility of the subject?

Keali'inohomoku makes the latter point clearly, and in my view, once and for all, in an excellent article first published in 1969 and reprinted in 1980:

> Despite all [modern] anthropological evidence to the con-
> trary, however, Western dance scholars set themselves up
> as authorities on the characteristics of primitive dance.
> Sorell [1967] combines most of these so-called characteris-
> tics of the primitive stereotype. He tells us that primitive
> dancers have no technique, and no artistry, but that they
> are "unfailing masters of their bodies"! He states that
> their dances are disorganized and frenzied, but that they
> are able to translate all their feelings and emotions into
> movement. Primitive dances, he tells us, are serious but
> social. He claims that they have "complete freedom" but
> that men and women can't dance together. He qualifies
> this statement by saying that men and women dance to-
> gether after the dance degenerates into an orgy! Sorell
> also asserts that primitives cannot distinguish between the
> concrete and the symbolic, that they dance for every oc-
> casion, and that they stamp around a lot! Further, Sorell
> asserts that dance in primitive societies is a special pre-
> rogative of males, especially chieftains, shamans, and witch
> doctors. Kirstein also characterizes the dances of "natural
> unfettered societies" (whatever that means) (Keali'inohomoku,
> 1980:84).

Similar criticisms could be levelled at most of what we commonly call coffee-table books on the dance; cf. Haskell (1960), Kirstein (1924, 1935), DeMille (1963), Terry (1949, 1956, 1967),
Kinney (1924), Martin (1939, 1946, 1963), and the many
entries in dance encyclopedias under the headings "ethnic dance,"
"primitive dance," and "ethnologic dance."

If it is the case that anthropologists, taken as a whole, pay
very little serious attention to the dance[23] and dance scholars
seem consistently to produce either naive or unsound cultural anthropological theory about the dance, we may well ask, "just what
does an anthropology of the dance and/or human movement amount
to?" What, if anything, ensures an even minimal scholarly standing
for a would-be ethnological discipline within anthropology that possesses both intellectual and institutional connections?

Who are Anthropologists of Human Movement?

For a long time, Adrienne Kaeppler stood alone. Born in Wisconsin and having studied dancing since age five,[24] she lived in Hawaii for many years and was connected, first as a student and later as a faculty member, with the University of Hawaii and as a research anthropologist with the Bishop Museum. She first went to Tonga in 1964, but not to study dance. She went there to do an anthropological study of aesthetics, but her chief interest was in the relationship between social structure and the arts. As it happened, the arts of Tonga were dancing and bark cloth making. Her thesis on the structure of Tongan dance brought together her interests in anthropology and dance and her doctoral degree in anthropology was conferred in 1967 from the University of Hawaii.[25] Kaeppler is currently curator of oceanic ethnology at the Smithsonian Institution, Washington, D.C.

Joann Wheeler Kaeli'inohomoku (a native of Missouri) was also in Hawaii in the early 1960's, but she and Kaeppler were only casual acquaintances. Keali'inohomoku returned to the mainland to continue her master's degree at Northwestern University and subsequently did her doctoral work under the tutelage of Alan Merriam at the Indiana University. Although she had worked on the anthropology of dance before Kaeppler, her doctoral degree was not conferred until 1976--the same year as Williams and Hanna. Royce came to Indiana to teach there towards the end of Keali'inohomoku's doctoral career, having finished two years earlier. Keali'inohomoku taught modern dancing for several years and has studied the dances of Polynesia and Micronesia for six years. She carried out research on the religious and recreational dances of black Americans, and is currently studying and doing research among the Hopi, while teaching undergraduate anthropology at the University of Northern Arizona.

Anya Peterson Royce was born in California and did both master's and doctoral work in anthropology at the University of California, Berkeley. Her doctoral degree was conferred in 1974. She had met Keali'inohomoku (before she went to Indiana) in Tucson, Arizona at a CORD conference. She subsequently met Kaeppler and Hanna in 1974 at a conference, New Directions in the Anthropology of Dance that she convened in Bloomington, for which there exist no proceedings. The fact of the meeting is, however, recorded in Kaeppler (1978). Royce danced professionally in ballet in San Francisco and New York City. Her particular area of interest is in Latin America, particularly Mexico; at present, however, she is conducting research into mime and ballet in Poland, France and Italy. She has contributed a book (1977) on anthropology and dance. There is presently another book in press: "Movement and Meaning: Creativity and Interpretation in Ballet and Mime." Dr. Royce has been the director of the Latin American Area Study Program at the Indiana University, in Bloomington. At this writing, she is taking up a new administrative position as dean of faculties, continuing as a professor of anthropology academically.

Drid Williams, a native Oregonian, completed the Diploma, B. Litt. and D. Phil. degrees at the Institute of Social Anthropology, Oxford, after having resided in Ghana, West Africa, for three and a half years. She met Kaeppler, Keali'inohomoku, and Hanna for the first time in 1974 when she attended a combined CORD/SEM conference held in San Francisco, California. Williams was a professional modern dancer, had a company in New York City, and has taught and performed in the idioms of ballroom dancing, modern concert dance, Afro-Carribbean forms, North Indian Kathak dancing, and ballet. Her doctoral degree was conferred in June 1976. She is presently the director of a graduate program in the anthropology of human movement at New York University which will no longer exist after May 1984, and is faculty editor of the Journal for the Anthropological Study of Human Movement (JASHM), which will continue publication. Royce and Williams met at the International Summer Institute for Semiotic and Structural Studies (ISISSS '83) at the Indiana University in June 1983.

Judith Lynne Hanna (also a native of Missouri) received two master's degrees, one in political science at Michigan State University and one in anthropology at Columbia University. Her doctoral degree was conferred in 1976 at Columbia, and the fieldwork she did in Africa was carried out for thirteen months in 1962-1963. She studied dancing, mainly classical ballet, from age eight, although she has studied modern concert dance and was greatly inspired by the West African (Nigerian) dancer, Ukonu, at the Theatre Arts Department at U.C.L.A. She has written a book, To Dance Is Human, and is presently completing a book entitled, "The Performance-Audience Connection: Emotion and Metaphor in Dance and Society." She has received several grants and presently resides in Maryland. She has contributed a great deal of time to CORD, and is a dedicated promoter of the cause of dance studies.

These five women are, as it were, the first generation of those who had a strong interest in the dance and human movement who aspired, at the same time, to become fully qualified as professional anthropologists.[26] The next generation consisted of four people: Jill Sweet, Najwa Adra, Dianne Freedman, and Susanne Youngerman. Of these four, Sweet has recently completed her doctoral work at the University of New Mexico, and is now teaching at Skidmore College in upstate New York, Adra and Freedman have recently completed their doctoral work at Temple University, Philadelphia, Pennsylvania, and Youngerman has completed her doctoral work at Columbia University.

In fact, it is the case at this writing, that if the nine women mentioned above were to board the same aircraft to attend, say, a conference somewhere, and the aircraft were to crash, the field

would be catapulted (or nearly so) back to where it was when
Kaeppler started in 1962 in Hawaii, and where would that be?

Scattered Interests--Scattered People

Five students will complete master's degrees in the anthropology of human movement at New York University in 1983-84: Rajika
Puri, Edward K. Myers, Jr., Brenda Farnell, Dixie Durr and Diana
Hart-Johnson.[27] The recording of these names is meant only to
emphasize the fragility of the field, for many students (and others)
imagine that there is a subfield of the anthropology of the dance
and/or human movement out there somewhere: a library perhaps,
a university, a faculty of some kind that knows and teaches the
subject. In 1983, this is simply not the case. No department of
anthropology includes the subject in its curriculum, either in the
United States, England, Australia, Canada or France and only one
dance department has offered a degree in the subject that was affiliated with an anthropology department for five short years: 1979-
1984.

Kurath's work (see Kaeppler, 1978), and that of Alan Merriam
and other interested ethnomusicologists--the odd course here and
there in dance ethnology, such as those at the University of Hawaii,
the Indiana University, and U.C.L.A., the recent work of folklorists[28] and a few anthropologists, notably Blacking, as well as
Ekman, Rauget, Kubik and a few others--has not provided a con-
sensus on the scope, methods, or privileged topics of the field.

Kluckhohn's, LaBarre's, Firth's, Kristeva's, Hall's and Birdwhistell's works, valuable though they are, taken together really
do not provide an intellectual identity that is shared by a group of
practitioners, although Polhemus (1978) and Benthall (Kristeva's
translator, in Polhemus, 1978:264ff) would seem to have us believe
that they do.

Meaningful, significant periods of development in any field
are usually characterized by definable intellectual systems and by
faculties, societies, journals and groups of well-informed people
who are committed to them. Right now, it is possible, with a great
deal of effort, to identify certain intellectual systems that pertain
to human movement, e.g. "the summary of the Darwinian-universalist
tradition in Hinde's Non-Verbal Communication, a focus of the psychological literature dealing with the human body in Fisher's and
Cleveland's Body Image and Personality (1958) and a résumé of the
phenomenological-philosophical literature on the subject in Zaner's
The Problem of Embodiment (1971)" (Polhemus, 1978:10), but these
are of little assistance to those who seek an anthropological, rather
than a psychological viewpoint.

This is especially true of dancers, like myself, who over the years find themselves dissatisfied with positivistic, phenomenological, subjectivist, behaviorist, and Darwinian theories, especially of the dance. Perhaps there is a similarity here to the plight of third-world nationals who find themselves explained (and their activities subsumed) under the paradigms of nonnative speakers (whether of conventional, or body, languages).

The Body Reader (1978)

Only one-fourth of this book deals with movement (Part II, section B, entitled "Body 'Language' ") and my comments will therefore largely be concerned with pages 219-314. The section presents a strangely biased and inadequate view of the field, perhaps best explained in the words of one reviewer, quoted on the back cover of the volume:

> The authors are a constellation of the famous--Darwin, Mead, Kluckhohn, Kroeber, Birdwhistell, Barthes. A stimulating, challenging collection which leaves the reader free to make up his/her own mind.

But does it?

How can a reader "make up his/her mind" about, say, linguistic and sociolinguistic theories of bodily expression when many of these theories are left out? The five anthropologists of human movement mentioned earlier do not appear in this book--even in the list of "Further Readings" (p. 314ff). This means that ethnoscientific "emic-etic" theory was disregarded (and Kaeppler's work along with it), semasiology (and Williams' extensive linguistically tied theories), Stokoe's work with deaf-signing (see "Sign-Language Structure," 1980), and an important set of seminal articles, including Murray, Hallowell, Lee, and Turner (already cited), and Friedrich (1977), Witherspoon (1971), and Dolgin and Magdoff (1977).

Benthall devotes pages to an article (Kristeva, 1969), for which he is the translator, from a French journal, and ignores the work in human movement to be found in Semiotica (Ed. Thos. Sebeok, Bloomington, Indiana) that had several articles on movement by several authors that predated publication of this strictly limited anthology. If novice readers are already familiar enough with the field of human movement studies (see The Journal of Human Movement Studies, Vols. 1 through 6, published by Lepus Books, Henry Kimpton, Ltd., 106 Hampstead Rd., London NW1 2LS), they will be aware of Renshaw (1975), Williams (1976), and Best (1975; 1976a,b; 1978), and they will also be aware of a continuing attempt on the part of John Whiting,[29] editor of this series (now editor of Human Movement Sciences, emanating from Vrije University, Amsterdam) to develop an integrated approach to human movement studies. Often, however, novice readers are precisely

not aware of the many contributors, or the many intellectual streams
that flow through a notional map of this territory.

One simply wants to say that those authors who are represented in The Body Reader are handled in a scholarly and readable
fashion, but the value of the work is severely limited by its obvious creation of a muted group, i.e. the works of those authors
who are not mentioned. (For those interested in the theory of
muted groups, see Ardener, S. [1976]).

Another "Anthropology of the Body" (1977)

Preceding Polhemus' book by one year is a collection resulting from an Association of Social Anthropology conference by the
same name convened by Blacking in Belfast, Northern Ireland. Although four of us (Kaeppler, Keali'inohomoku, Williams, and Hanna)
were invited to the conference, only one attended. Hanna's presentation, which was published in this volume, is something that she
had written many times before, Kaeppler felt that attendance at this
conference was relatively unimportant, and Williams and Keali'inohomoku consciously boycotted it. Although Blacking remarks in his
Introduction that "What I mean by the anthropology of the body
probably differs considerably from the meanings assigned by other
contributors ..." (1977:1), his views dominate this volume. Blacking is considered, at least by some, to be the leading figure in
anthropological studies of human movement in Britain. There are
some who may have been willing to be published under the umbrella of the general paradigm he offers, but others were not.

Blacking's notions about movement are couched in a mixture
of paradigms, as are Sheets-Johnstone's.[30] His views of what society, culture, movement, and language consist of are diametrically
opposed to those offered by semasiology (see Williams, 1982), the
underlying premises of which differ as radically from those of
Blacking's anthropology of the body as does quantum mechanics
(the new physics of motion) from Newton's laws of motion (see Wolf,
1981). His views also differ radically from those of ethnoscientists.
One would want serious students to consult Kaeppler's recent contribution (1982) for the difference, for example, between using a
linguistic analogy for human movement, rather than linguistic models
for the analysis of human movement. As Kaeppler and Williams are
both theorists of human movement who use linguistic analogies, it is
important that this distinction not be overlooked, as it apparently
causes great confusion for several British colleagues.

One is tempted to enter into discussion of these matters
(something that hardly ever happens at a conference), however,
this essay is meant to be bibliographical; thus we will get on with
other references, advising students to read the many fine essays
that are included in the ASA volume, notably those of Ellen,

Sutherland, Strathern, and Arnold. Napier's review (1978) of this book is also useful, as is the viewpoint from taxonomies of the body, in Williams (1980).

The Performing Arts (1979)

Six of the essays in this volume, those by Petrosian, Mladenovic, Zhornitskaia, Sikharulidze, Anjelic, and Comişel were reviewed by Kürti (1980), whose conclusions about the volume are, on the whole, negative, as are my own. I was asked by the publishers to review the book, but did not want to do so until I had got to the source of the many contradictions, discrepancies and flat untruths it contains. In fact, the volume would be more accurately retitled, "The Tower of Babel Revisited: 24 Unconnected Essays on Music and Dancing."

Consultations with Keali'inohomoku provided me with answers,[31] and without going into detail, one or two assertions must be made to set the record straight for the benefit of serious students who sometimes tend to be somewhat naive about the vicissitudes of publication in the modern academic world: Keali'inohomoku had nothing to do with editing this volume and although John Blacking, in his Introduction, admits that he did not attend the conference, he says: "I have therefore had to rely upon the written versions of the papers and tape recordings of the meetings, in preparing this volume with Joann Keali'inohomoku ..." (1977:xiii).

Knowledge of this kind makes the reading of Blacking's Introduction and Sol Tax's somewhat pompous Editorial Preface of The Performing Arts problematical, to say the least, and very little else remains to be said, perhaps, except to point out that theory, method, analytical techniques, collections of papers and research findings in a field do not just establish or maintain philosophical, linguistic, social anthropological or historical perspectives disassociated from everyday life and the ongoing flux of events: they shape our various understandings of who we are and what we are right now. In particular this is true of a struggling new field of research. Thus, collections of this kind shape a certain view of the field, of ourselves and (because of its international character) of others.

If status-holders, editors, and publishing houses are going to abdicate scholarship, honesty and integrity for political acumen, superficiality and mass appeal, then serious students must (to protect themselves and the sanctity of their minds), eschew a certain naivete and incredulity. They must resign themselves, perhaps, to searching where possible for the facts of publication and take the trouble to find out something about the authors. They must make dedicated efforts towards looking at books and journals, not as if they miraculously appear out of nowhere, but look at them in the spirit of a search to understand the human realities (both positive and negative) that they represent. Regarding these matters, there is no more important passage in any book, nor one more relevant for the student of human movement in any field of interest than the section subtitled "The Importance of Independent, Critical Thinking" in David Best's book, Philosophy and Human Movement (1978: 22-25).

"Anthropological Perspectives" (1947)

Were I pressed into a position to suggest one (and only one) article written by an anthropologist to be read by students of Western theatre arts, I would probably direct them to Weston LaBarre's article, written in 1947, republished in Martha Davis' collection of reference materials in the Body Movement: Perspectives in Research series. The reason for my choice would be that he emphasizes over and over again, through the presentation of ethnographic materials, that there is no "natural" language of human emotional gesture. And he asks questions (e.g. "Is this instinctual reflex or mere motor habit?"; p. 58) of the kind that prompted my own preliminary examination of signs, symptoms and symbols (Williams, 1972).

There are details about Western forms of dance that are inaccurate (e.g. his statement that "... the motions of the classical ballet are highly stereotyped, they are semantically meaningless ..."; p. 61) but there is much valuable information to be gained from his work, and, indeed, from this collection that includes LaBarre (1947), Bailey (1942), Hewes (1955), Kurath (1960), Hall (1963), and Hayes (1957). Davis, in her capacity of advisory editor, has provided us with excellent reference materials in this collection. [32]

This is especially true of the Hayes contribution; probably the single most complete bibliography of gesture that we possess (and it is annotated, so that the student can at least make a crude division between writings that have been popularized and those that have not); however, such reference works as the Body Movement series pose important problems that, however obvious they might seem to social and cultural anthropologists reading this essay, are nevertheless of considerable importance regarding the future of the discipline. It is well known for example, that specialization was (and is) the intellectual equivalent of an economic division of labor in Western societies. As a systematic way of ordering our intellectual lives, it had its origins in the nineteenth century and its greatest development in the twentieth century. We live with and, (however ineptly) must try to cope with, the knowledge explosion, technology, and the increased speed of social change.

The problem with reference to human movement studies is that although more and more discipline-specific knowledge continues to be produced regarding gesture, dances, signing and all the rest, there seems to be less and less capability of understanding its relation to the other movement professions, to other sister disciplines' handling of the subject, or to the role that, whether we like it or not, we are being asked to assume in relation to them.

Some exceedingly strange anthropologies are in rapid process of development: anthropologies of the theatre, of dance, of drama and what you will. Current issues of The Drama Review[33] contain paradigm examples of the kind of thing to which I refer, as do a virtually endless stream of articles on dances throughout the world whose authors are uninformed by any alternative views of social organization or cosmology other than their own.

Davis' first collection of reprinted essays, excellent though it is, leaves a student entirely on his or her own with reference to the contents. It therefore conforms to a democratic ideal of education; that of factual knowledge that somehow stands alone,[34] based on an assumption that such reference materials will be used in a critical, judicious manner. It also seems to assume that any type of speculative theorizing by anyone at all about the subjects of dance and/or human movement is automatically a good thing.

The "Global Village" Syndrome

One of the most prevalent misconceptions about social and cultural anthropology today is to suppose that these disciplines consist of speculative theorizing of a quasi-philosophical or quasi-scientific kind about human nature. It seems to be believed by many that social-cultural anthropologists may be in possession of workable hypotheses or schemes for universal world order. Especially are anthropologists of human movement plagued by this, as we are thought to be experts (because we deal with the dance, liturgies, art, drama, symbols and such) in quasi-religious recommendations as to how life in an idealized unisexed global village might be conducted. Examples of such a conception of anthropology are to be found in any of the narratives accompanying the proliferation of television documentaries on the exotica of the world's peoples that have increased over the past two decades.

The German term "weltanschauung" best captures this kind of conception, which I interpret in this context as a kind of quasi-philosophical "anthropological view of life." To express this view is, usually, to make pious statements about the brotherhood of Man, the family of Man, or to utter clichés about the universality of movement and/or gesture. For example, a colleague recently sent a graduate student from the creative arts program into one of my classes to get an anthropological perspective and pick up enough methodology to enable her to do a photographic documentary on an Amazonian tribe in northern Brazil. My colleague believed that (1) a social scientific methodology could be grasped in fourteen weeks, (2) I would be interested, as an anthropologist, in a pictorial documentary produced by someone who cannot speak the language of the people in question, who is basically interested in producing a piece of Western photographic art about a strange and interesting subject. No prior questions were asked. It was assumed that I would be interested because her project concerned an alien people; however, any work produced in this manner would only interest me as example of Western art. It would be of no anthropological interest whatsoever regarding the subjects of the photographs, the Indians.

The confusion that is evident here becomes clearer when we consider just what an anthropologist of human movement is: while many of us may have been dancers, or may be able to communicate in signing dialects, or defend ourselves with martial arts techniques if attacked by muggers, we do not presume to tell those who are currently practicing artists how to choreograph a dance, take photographs, paint pictures, produce plays and the like. Nor as anthropologists do we expound on the attitudes, teaching methods, or practices of those who engage in dancing, sports, signing, the martial arts, liturgies, and so on. But, I find that there is very little understanding among artists about what social science really is; specifically, what anthropology is.

Many of my own students begin by reflecting upon the difference between, say, a novel about characters taken from a West African context and an anthropological account of the same cultural context. They read Bohannan's excellent article (1967) on her attempts to translate the story of Hamlet into a Nigerian language, Tiv. In the long process they must undergo to become anthropologists, they neither lose their love for, nor their appreciation of, art and artists, but neither do they confuse the two. They are encouraged, moreover, to refer to their writings as anthropology and as social science, not as novels, poetry or art, and I fail to see any good reason why persons writing from a general literary or humanistic point of view need refer to their work as anthropology. Surely, Michener does not now consider himself an anthropologist because of his writing on Hawaii, nor is Haley an anthropologist as a result of his writing Roots, nor would it be appropriate to subject either of these author's contributions to standard anthropological scrutiny.

Those who wish to create an anthropology of something out of a frustration, perhaps, with their own discipline's limitations, or out of a hunger to know more and experience more of the world, or out of a missionary-like zeal to promote world peace and understanding are responding quite naturally, perhaps, to some of the more unsettling and genuinely frightening features of the world we live in today, but it might be more profitable in the long run for them to find out just what the activity of learning to anthropologize consists of, because anthropology is not just a body of knowledge that can be acquired, like so many cases of tinned fruits and vegetables from the supermarket.

And of all people who might best understand this, one would have thought that artists--whatever their medium--might be the best qualified to do so. Just as one cannot learn to dance solely by listening to lectures or reading books about it, so one cannot learn anthropology simply by hearing or reading even what great anthropologists have to say. If students of the theatre, the dance, and the performing arts realize (and they do) that expert guidance is necessary in their own chosen fields of endeavour, why is it that they imagine that they do not need active participation in anthropology in order to understand what it is all about? In both cases, it is usually necessary to have expert guidance.

This is, again, another obvious point, but necessary to be made because another prevalent misconception about social anthropology is that it is what I shall call a history of mankind. Many are deceived by this notion, and it manifests itself in a belief on the part of nonanthropologists that all one has to do is to read what the great anthropologists (usually the works of Frazer, Tylor, Lang, Köhler, Darwin, Frobenius, and others) had to say.

Modern social anthropology should be regarded as the development of rigorous, critical, social scientific thinking that emphasizes, not simple description, but description that is informed by levels of interpretation, explanation, theory and metatheory. It should also be regarded as an ongoing, dynamic process, rather than as a reified body of dead knowledge, such that Tylor's theory of animism, say, which is thought to be just as valid now as when he conceived it, is seen in its proper historical perspective. It is not, as Evans-Pritchard so succinctly points out in a slim volume (1965) that one wishes that everyone interested in anthropology would read; especially his comments on page 100.

Conclusion

As I reflect upon what I have so far written, two things come to mind: first, one of the rather more trenchant remarks made by Ortega y Gasset:

> The same thing is happening in other orders, particularly in the intellectual. I may be mistaken, but the presentday writer, when he takes his pen in hand to treat a subject which he has studied deeply, has to bear in mind that the average reader, who has never concerned himself with this subject, if he reads, does so with the view, not of learning something from the writer, but rather, of pronouncing judgment on him when he is not in agreement with the commonplaces that the said reader carries in his head (1957/1930:18).

Those who have a penchant towards pronouncing judgments will be pleased that so many reasons for doing so have been provided in this essay, for very little of it conforms to commonplace notions about anthropologists, the dance or human movement, yet it is to be hoped that there are those among the readership who genuinely wish to learn--and it is for them that the writing has been done.

No one is more aware than I of the books that have not been mentioned, or the subject areas pertaining to human movement that are not addressed, for example, Oesterley (1923) on the sacred dance. The Vicar of St. Alban's treatment of the subject is a valuable documentation of references to dancing in the Old Testament and is a scholarly presentation of O.T. terms for dancing. It is also an excellent source of references to dance from the classics. Unfortunately, Oesterley did not allow his basic linguistic skills and materials and his considerable knowledge of biblical history to stand on its own merits: he chose to attempt an interpretation of his insights through the lens of Frazer's doctrine of sympathetic magic and (odd though the combination seems to an anthropologist) with reference to Marett's theories of primitive dancing (1932). Marett's theory was an activist one, and although he did not know this, his theory would more appropriately apply to many modern Western theories of dancing today than they did to the dances of traditional ethnicities.

Oesterley's interpretations of the origin and purpose of dancing were in agreement with other well-known writers of his time, some of whom were anthropologists and some not--Jevons, de Cahusac, Robertson Smith, Ridgeway, Harrison and others. [35] Oesterley's arguments (and others who subscribed to the religion side of the evolutionary controversy) [36] not unexpectedly shun humanity's real or putative connections with anthropoid apes and other primates and focus on imitation of supernatural powers as the origin of sacred dancing, which was thought to precede all forms of secular dancing. [37]

Robert Lowie (1925), an early American anthropologist best known for his theories of social organization, was concerned somewhat peripherally with North American Indian dances, ceremonies, and rituals, which he used as evidence of an aesthetic-cum-psychological theory that he was interested to promote. Students need to realize, however, that his interest in these dances was contextualized in his interest in his theory, thus, for example, we are given to understand that the Peyote and Ghost Dance cults merely illustrate the importance of psychological processes such as rationalization and secondary associations. Lowie says that any mental operations to be observed in relation to these dances will naturally be those described in textbooks of psychology.

The range of diverse peoples and dances he describes covers whole nations of Plains Indian and Pueblo peoples, with a few West

African and Polynesian ethnicities thrown into the bargain, yet his work raises an important theoretical issue: how far can textbook psychological theory, mainly developed in a social context of upper middle-class Viennese, really apply to any North American Indian dance, or to the concepts, mental operations and such that may have existed therein?

The point is this: adequately to comprehend any investigator's handling of data, it is necessary to understand the theory, interpretive strategies and assumptions that he or she has used to examine the data. Especially is this true of human movement, because human movement, like human culture, is not itself a material phenomenon. It is a cognitive and semantic organization of a material phenomenon, i.e. the human body (or bodies) and the spatial, physical environments in which it moves. Whether we look backwards, then, at what has been said about the subject or whether we look forward towards what might be written or studies in this field,[38] we might usefully consider that

> The relationship between dance and the sociocultural system in which it is embedded remains a central concern to anthropologists who have dealt with this cultural form--a form that results from creative processes which manipulate human bodies in time and space. Much of the anthropologically relevant work on dance that has been published to date views dance as a reflection of culture, that is, that dance is somehow separable from other parts of culture and of which it can be considered a mirror. For example, studies of the symbolic aspects of dance by Snyder (1972), and Hieb (1972), and the study of Keali'inohomoku of Hopi dance as a microcosm of Hopi culture (1972), take this stance. Although this view is perfectly acceptable both from the viewpoints of dance and of anthropology, it tends to mask the integral association of this cultural form with others (Kaeppler, 1978:45).

Kaeppler asks, "if only native categories can define what is dance in a particular society, then how can it be universal?" And she would defend the position, as I would, that the Western concept of dance may actually mask the importance and usefulness of analyzing human movement systems.

Postscript

Apart from those already mentioned, there is another valuable source for students to consult on contemporary writings on the subjects of dance, theatre, mime and the like in CORD (The Congress on Research in Dance). This is an international, interdisciplinary open membership organization whose purposes are: (1) to encourage research in all aspects of dance, including its related fields;

(2) to foster the exchange of ideas, resources and methodology through publications, international and regional conferences and workshops; (3) to promote the accessibility of research materials. The Dance Research Journal (DRJ) is edited and produced in Toronto and distributed by the New York office of CORD, which is housed in the Dance Department, Education Bldg., 684D, New York University, 35 W. 4th St., N.Y. 10003. Students must remember, however, that because of the open membership of CORD, the writings therein are extremely uneven and range from nonsense to the work of excellent authors.

Complete lists of the articles and reviews written by Kaeppler, Keali'inohomoku and Williams are, in the bibliographic section, published together for the first time, as is an index of articles that appear in the Journal for the Anthropological Study of Human Movement (JASHM), which is not, in its editorial policies, so academically egalitarian as is CORD. This journal is edited and produced by graduate students in the program of the Anthropology of Human Movement at New York University. Inquiries may be addressed to The Editors, JASHM, c/o SASHM, 21 Washington Place, N.Y.U., New York   10003.

I have attempted to discuss the literature presented in this essay in such a way that a reader who probably knows very little about anthropologists, the dance, and human movement can find his or her way about more readily in what may be unfamiliar territory. In order to do so, I have had to draw readers' attention to several prevalent misconceptions about social and cultural anthropology in general and about the anthropology of human movement in particular. In a survey article of this kind, it is impossible to do more for nonanthropologists and students than to issue warnings; however, there are those, I believe, who will accept what is offered here in the spirit in which it was intended--as an examination of the tip of the iceberg--realizing that the bulk of that which remains to be discovered (and discussed) lies below the surface, inaccessible to superficial or cursory treatment.

It is thus appropriate to conclude with a final warning: it seems to have become an article of faith among the movement professions, especially those of a behavioristic persuasion, that every movement has a meaning and that movement (in the context of a dichotomization of the verbal and the nonverbal)[39] is in general not only a more powerful means of human communication than is spoken language, it has the virtue of greater veracity. This is simply not the case, nor is the attempt to create a dichotomy between spoken language and movement a good intellectual position from which to begin, yet many influential writers (e.g. Argyle, 1975) proceed from this misconception, not only about movement, but about the human capacity for language-use itself (see Best, 1978:138-161 for fuller discussion).

The newer, linguistically tied theories of human action, i.e. the ethnoscientific approach (advocated by Kaeppler) and semasiology (Williams) offer alternative views: they represent scientific shifts of paradigm in the world of human movement studies, of which, at this writing, only a few dedicated students and fewer professional anthropologists are aware.

Notes

1. According to Keali'inohomoku, the Hopi do not consider tiihu (translated as dance) to be art. Their terms that we translate as forms of the word "dance" are tiihu (sing. noun) or tiitihu (plural; noun) that can be equally glossed "ceremony." The verb forms are wunima (sing.) and tiiva (plural).

2. We possess one book, entitled The Anthropology of Dance, published in 1977, by Anya Royce. It was reviewed by Williams (c1979) in Ethnomusicology.

3. The problems of terminology, the attitudes towards the history of social anthropology and the like, are well set out in the following general books about the subject: Beattie (1964), Bohannan (1969), Evans-Pritchard (1962), Lienhardt (1966).

4. Reference is made here to an excellent article by Lienhardt, in a collection of essays edited by Raison (1969), that is unfortunately now out of print. We hope to reprint Lienhardt's article on Tylor in JASHM in the near future.

5. It is a good idea for anyone trying to acquaint him/herself with some of the major figures in the discipline to consult the International Encyclopaedia of Social Sciences; volumes that are available in every good university library.

6. For a clear 'potted history' of the discipline of social anthropology, designed specifically for laymen, see Pocock (1975).

7. Only an inadequate summary of the kinesic approach to human movement studies can be given here. For complete discussion, the reader is referred to Birdwhistell (1970). The following points are relevant to the discussion: (1) as a term, "kinesics" refers to a body of knowledge that is prior to a field of study that would be called "Kinesiology"; (2) kinesics is based upon psychiatrically oriented interview material because body motion and gesture are important sources of information regarding personality and symptomology; (3) a diagnostic model of events is emphasized, as are diagnostic methods and values; (4) formalized gestures, theatrical performances and the like are only of collateral interest; and (5) the most important anthropological contributions to the

study of body motion as a communicational system are, in a
kinesist's view, the works of two exponents of the culture-
personality approach in American anthropology: Mead and
Bateson. Ray Birdwhistell was one of the first anthropologists to develop a full-fledged theory of human movement,
however, and he is still teaching at the Annenberg School
of Communications in Philadelphia. Unfortunately, he has
not published any further work on the development of kinesics, but his approach, from the outset, was what we have
called "psychological anthropology." Further comments about
kinesics may be found in Polemus (1978), and in Birdwhistell
(1952).

8. Proxemics may be the best known of extant anthropological
   theories and methods pertaining to the movement field.
   Started as a result of E. T. Hall's extended applied anthropological studies carried out for the American Foreign Service, the approach from proxemics deals with a theory of
   spatial interaction between two or more persons. The prox-
   imity of persons is of chief interest, for it is postulated that
   there are measurable zones (socially or culturally established)
   surrounding individuals that are generally out-of-awareness,
   but that influence daily interactions greatly. It is unfortunate that so much interesting and valuable work had to be
   tied to the notion of critical distance in animals. Untutored
   students should be wary of generalizing from these aspects
   of proxemics as a whole. For more thorough discussion, see
   Hall (1963, 1966 and 1966a) and Davis (1978).

9. A semiotic approach to the study of movement is not, like
   kinesics, proxemics or semasiology, a developed theory and
   methodology that is meant to treat human movement per se.
   A semiotic treatment of human actions simply means a scientific study of movement or behavior as signs. In Mead's
   definition (see Sebeok, et al., 1964), the term derives ultimately from John Locke's "semiotike": "the business where-
   of is to consider the nature of signs the mind makes use of
   for the understanding of things, or conveying its knowledge
   to others."

10. The term "semasiology" and its derivatives are from a Greek
    source and can be defined as "signification" in the sense of
    "meaning + logy." In the late nineteenth century, the word
    was used to refer to that branch of philology which dealt
    with the meanings of words. It seemed a particularly apt
    term for a theory and accompanying methodology that is de-
    signed to deal, ultimately, with the meanings of body lan-
    guages. In contrast to some semiological approaches, that
    purport to deal with the sign functions of machines and/or
    the movements of animals and the like, semasiology limits
    itself to the human domain, hence the different term.

Semasiology is based on an application of Saussurian ideas to human movement and the result is a theory of human actions that is linguistically tied, mathematically structured and empirically based. It is not behaviorally based. Semasiology is a form of semantic anthropology. For more thorough discussion, see Williams (1975 and 1982).

11. There are recent developments--e.g. an anthropology of the theatre, dance anthropology courses and such--that, although they use the term, are uninformed by members of the anthropological community. It is as if there is a revival of the period at the middle and end of the nineteenth century, when anthropology was still in its infancy, when it was "a happy hunting ground," as Evans-Pritchard so succinctly put it, "of men of letters and has been speculative and philosophical in a rather old-fashioned way" (1965: 5). On the whole, theory that was developed during this period in social anthropology's history has been abandoned --by anthropologists at least--and the revival that I have mentioned has little to offer except of negative value, judging from articles and books like those of Malm (1977), Schechner (1977), Blum (1973), Lange (1975).

12. Some examples of these are Hambly (1926), who expounded a theory of culture epochs, which suggests that "... history of juvenile development recapitulates the phases of mental progress through which the human race has toiled. The emotional life and want of foresight in children have a parallel in the career of primitive man." This work has long since passed into merciful oblivion in anthropological literature, such that it is disconcerting to see it resurrected in a study on the dance written in 1969 and quoted with approval. Hambly's theories neither enhance nor aid Frances Rust's contribution, Dance in Society. Since it was given a critical review by Williams (1974a), no more space will be devoted to it here.

13. It is necessary to mention the fact that some writings on the dance are so bad that it was necessary, in 1971, for me to photocopy some of them to prove to my B. Litt. supervisor at Oxford that I was in fact not indulging in overkill, but that I was accurately dealing with what the authors in question had said. Two examples of the kind of thing referred to are Segy (1953) and Jeffreys (1952).

14. There are many anthropologists now who work in their own cultures. I am one of these: my research was done in England on the ballet Checkmate and the Dominican post-Tridentine Mass. Although I spent three and a half years in Ghana, West Africa, I could not do my doctoral work on any of the research that I did there simply because I was

not fluent in any Ghanian language. The results of my stay there, and a criticism of my preanthropological essays are given in Williams (1976/77). It is important to note, however, that Judith Lynne Hanna, who was in West Africa for thirteen months in 1962-63, did do her doctoral work at Columbia University on the Ubakala Dance Plays in the mid-1970's, although she speaks no Ibo. This makes her work problematic for many of us.

15. The past tense is necessary because after the end of the spring term, 1984, the department of dance and dance education, SEHNAP, N.Y. University, will no longer have this program. Regrettably, the vicissitudes of economic constraints, plus the not inconsiderable influences of internal political infighting, have terminated all efforts towards positive growth of the subject in that particular academic context.

16. One of the best-known and most widely used references in dance ethnology is Franziska Boas' edited collection of articles entitled The Function of Dance in Human Society (1944). It is a useful collection because in it the functionalist approach to the study of dance and human movement is clearly set forth.

17. Lévi-Strauss uses this example, saying, "... we may ask whether it is in fact the case that works of art are always an integration of structure and event. This does not on the face of it seem to be true ... of the cedarwood Tlingit club, used to kill fish ... the artist who carved it in the form of a sea-monster intended the body of the implement to be fused with the body of the animal and the handle with its tail, and that the anatomical proportions, taken from a fabulous creature, should be such that the object could be the cruel animal slaying helpless victims, at the same time as an easily handled, balanced and efficient fishing utensil ..." (1966:26).

18. It is important to include the remarks of a critic, Arthur Wayley, who wrote the preface to Beryl de Zöete and Walter Spies' research monograph on Balinese dance (1938). Wayley draws attention in this passage to a writer, Ridgeway (1915), who believed that drama sprang from the dance and that Greek tragedy originated in primitive rites for the dead: "For example, Ridgeway ... makes only one casual mention of Bali, in connection with the shadow plays. His book indeed was written, not in order to discover the facts about oriental dance, but to prove a thesis about the origins of Greek Tragedy. Everywhere he assumes progress in a straight line from dance to relatively pure drama, whereas the facts in Indo-China as in Indonesia point to a circular process, in the course of which dance alternately links itself

to and detaches itself from drama. Nowhere can the contrast between the facts and Ridgeway's theory be better seen than in Burma. Here Ridgeway found a drama which 'had not advanced beyond the lyrical stage, consisting of dancing, singing and instruments of music,' though it had made 'distinct steps towards the true drama which Thespis in Greece and the forerunners of Marlowe and Shakespeare in England detached from the sacred shrines and lifted into a distinct artistic form [p. 256].' The facts, as recently shown by Maunting Htin Aung in his Burmese Drama are very different. The danced lyrical drama concerning which Ridgeway had information was the successor of a literary drama (dating from the first half of the nineteenth century) from which dance and song had been almost entirely eliminated. So far from having made 'distinct progress towards the true drama' the Burmese state was in Ridgeway's day in full flight from drama and embarked for the moment on the path of ballet and opera" (Wayley, in de Zöete and Spies, [1938] pp. xvii-xviii).

19. Tyler remarks that "The history of all scientific disciplines is marked by periods of intense theoretical innovation followed by relative quiescent periods of consolidation and refinement .... The very lexicon of anthropology reflects this ferment. The journals are full of articles on formal analysis, componential analysis, folk taxonomy, ethnoscience, ethnosemantics and socio-linguistics, to list but a few" (Tyler, 1969:1). Cognitive anthropology, then, marked one of the new orders in American anthropology, and the authors represented in this volume write from a different standpoint, i.e. Hymes, Gumperz, Conklin, Moerman, Frake, Haugen, Goodenough, Black, Metzger, Wallace, and Burling. Others, who might refer to themselves as "ethnoscientists" are Agar (1973), Basso (1970), Eckman, P. and Freisen, W. (1979), Joos (1962), Spradley (1972), and Goodenough (1970).

The volume entitled Symbolic Anthropology, edited by Dolgin, Kemnitzer, and Schneider (1977), is a useful guide to newer theoretical approaches in the discipline, and includes reprints of three very important early articles relating to the study of anthropology and human movement, i.e. Holliwell (1955), Lee (1950), and Turner (1972). Murray's paper (1977), written for the Symbolic Anthropology collection, is also significant as an example of the kind of developed theory of symbol and meaning that one would like to see in theatre and dance.

Finally, for the recent move toward theoretical innovation in British social anthropology, one would refer students to Crick (1976), Chapman (1982), Ardener (1971, 1973, 1975, 1978, 1982), Hastrup (1978, 1982), Nagata (1978), Wagner (1978), and Williams (1976, 1977, 1981, 1982).

20. The Ga are currently known as "the Accra people" because
    they have traditionally inhabited the coastal strip of land be-
    tween the Ewe, to the east, who settled around the mouth of
    the Volta River and the Fanti, to the west, who settled along
    the coast on the other side. Their tribal territory is bounded
    on the north by the Ashanti, and the national capital of
    Ghana, Accra, is situated on their land.

21. This is the title of Kaeppler's article in the Annual Review of
    Anthropology. My citations and use of her work have been
    with her knowledge and consent. Her article was the first
    to be published on the subject in the Annual Review, a pub-
    lication that has been in existence roughly ten years to date.
    There will probably not be another article published updat-
    ing this one until 1988-1989, thus readers may find the sec-
    tion entitled "Who Are Anthropologists of Human Movement?"
    helpful for an overview of developments after 1977-1978.

22. An interesting pair of historical works on the subject of danc-
    ing is that of Grove (1895) and Scott (1899). Scott was a
    dancing master who was fascinated by the origins and develop-
    ment of the dance and he attempted to trace stylistic and/or
    literary lines of antecedents to the then modern dancing (he
    means what we would now call social dancing). He believed
    that there was a uniform evolutionary development from the
    Paleolithic age, thence to Greece, and straight on to modern
    dancing and goes to some length to describe a Paleolithic
    man dancing. He criticized Mrs. Grove's book because it
    covered "a somewhat wide geographical range" and because
    little attention was paid by her to the dances of ancient
    Greece and Rome.
       Mrs. Grove had a slightly less narrow view than Scott's
    about the dances of non-Western peoples. She had access
    to, and freely used, the accounts of dances and savage
    tribes written or told to her by travellers, adventurers,
    missionaries and early anthropologists: Haddon, of the
    Torres Straits expedition, Andrew Lang, Catlin, Molina,
    Tennent, Capt. Cook and Chateaubriand find their way
    into her book. She was concerned that "the picturesque
    aspect of life was going to be weakened by the advance of
    civilization, reducing everything to smooth uniformity."
    Old rites were fast vanishing and when this applied to the
    dance of savage peoples, she thought that their disappearance
    was greatly to be deplored. She was mainly concerned be-
    cause these dances, in her view, were all connected with
    religion (1895:65-67).
       Although their approaches to the subject of dancing were
    very different, both authors were persons of excellent edu-
    cation and ability. It is difficult, perhaps, for students to
    understand how they could have produced such a collection

of baseless reconstruction, wild speculation, suppositions and nonsensical culture theory, yet, it may be that future generations will look upon more modern offerings one hundred years hence in much the same way.

23. There are always exceptions to a generalization such as this. We now possess a superb piece of work by an Oceanist, Edward ("Buck") Schieffelin (1976), who uses the Gisaro dance of the Kaluli of New Guinea as the basis for the cultural scenario of this people.

24. Kaeppler studied ballet, modern dance, tap dancing and acrobatic dancing throughout her childhood and teenage years. She became interested in Korean dancing in 1962, then branched out into Japanese, Chinese, Malaysian, Philippine, Balinese, Hawaiian, Javanese, and other Polynesian dancing. She has done detailed work on Tongan and Hawaiian dance.

25. Kaeppler's doctoral degree was not only the first degree given by the anthropology department at the University of Hawaii, it is (to date) the only doctoral degree that deals with the dance and human movement at that institution. Williams' degrees are the only ones that deal with the dance and human movement to have been done at the Institute of Social Anthropology at Oxford. Keali'inohomoku's doctoral work at Indiana, Royce's at Berkeley, Adra's and Freedman's at Temple and Sweet's at the University of New Mexico hold the same doubtful distinction; doubtful because it is virtually impossible to get these works published, because most of them are "too scholarly" or go against the usual fare of published dance materials.

26. It seemed appropriate, in other words, for some of us to try to bridge the gap between anthropology, the dance, and human movement. All of us have been aware of mainstream anthropologists' humility, reflected in such statements as "I didn't deal with the dance, because I don't know how to dance and it was too complicated to learn." Conversely, we have been equally aware that, as "practitioners" of the dance, we had little to contribute unless we could fully enter the discipline of social-cultural anthropology as qualified members of the profession.

27. The master's program in the School of Education at New York University was affiliated with the Department of Anthropology (Faculty of Arts and Sciences) there, and these students will continue their academic work at a doctoral level in the anthropology department. Farnell, among those listed, is English, Puri is a naturalized American, Durr, Myers, and Hart were born in the United States.

28. I refer here to students who have completed work in the new Department of Folklore Studies, started recently by Dell Hymes in the School of Education at University of Pennsylvania. Dr. Barbara Kirshonblatt-Gimblett, Jr., a graduate of this department, now heads the Department of Performance Studies in the Drama Department, School of the Arts, N.Y.U.

29. John Whiting is presently dean of the Inter-faculty for the study of human movement at Vrije (Free) University in Amsterdam, The Netherlands. For Polhemus to have ignored six volumes of publication in the field was a shocking oversight.

30. Maxine Sheets-Johnstone is the author of the only volume we possess on The Phenomenology of Dance. She has recently become interested in zoology, evolutionary biology and paleoanthropology. The result of her shift of emphasis is well explained in Sheets-Johnstone (1983). An excellent critique of the new position she has assumed is to be found in Varela (1983).

31. The following comments are based on an abridged version of an extended letter, written to Kürti and to me, that was accompanied by several conversations that took place around March 22, 1981.

32. Consultations with Martha Davis at the International Summer Institute of Structural and Semiotic Studies (ISISSS '83) at the Indiana University yielded the following information: Anthropological Perspectives of Movement, M. Davis (advisory editor), Arno Press, N.Y., 1975, is now available from the Ayer Company, Seeg Harbor, N.Y. Another bibliographic series by Davis, entitled Understanding Body Movement: An Annotated Bibliography (1972), has been reprinted by Indiana University Press, 1982. The sequel to that bibliography, by Davis and Skupien, entitled Nonverbal Communication and Body Movement: 1971-81, An Annotated Bibliography, has recently been published by Indiana University Press, Bloomington, 1982.

   It is unfortunate that the two recent bibliographies have created a muted group of authors who have published extensively in the field, notably Best, Kaeppler, Keali'inohomoku, Sweet, and others. Davis wishes to apologize for this, saying that the oversights were not intentional.

33. In a programmic statement about cultures, entitled "Intercultural Performance," Mr. Schechner makes several anthropologically naive statements--not unexpectedly, as he is not an anthropologist. But he loves anthropology, and one

detects an aura of distress about anthropologists because we
do not seem to be able to come simply and directly to the
point: the solution of world problems. Perhaps he wishes,
then, to speak for us? He leaps from "borrowing" to syn-
cretism without a blush. He pleads, not for the laborious
learning of other languages and cultures, but for "unlearn-
ing our own blockages" (whatever those may be). And he
exhorts us to "perform our own and other peoples' cultures"
projecting the notion that "All the world's a stage ..." with
a dimension of intended realism that is disconcerting, to say
the least. His ethnographic examples (e.g. spaghetti and
violins), although undiscussed, are interesting but problematical; are we to understand that these items in their
contexts have the same or a different status as, say, a
plate of chow mein? We hope not, but then how can we
tell? Any need for lengthy essays is swept off the board
at the outset--and we agree that these are often difficult.
Chow mein is a peculiarly American product, as is Mr.
Schechner's essay, unless he was performing some other
culture, of which, as one of his readers, I am unaware.

34. "Call the spectacles 'conditioning,' 'socialization' or what you will,
we all acquire at least one set of mental spectacles in virtue
of the fact of being born into a specific language, into a
given society and all the complex network of systems of communications which that implies. Then too, other sets of
spectacles may be acquired: the professional sets, as e.g.
physics, architecture, engineering, literature, anthropology,
music, psychology, etc. Here, too, the analogy applies: if
we fail to recognize the conceptual elements of the academic
discipline to which we are committed, we will fail to recognize
the true character of our ideas and our intellectual, or other
kinds of problems. This is equally true, of course, if we
consider the intellectual problems of our predecessors, many
of whom thought, felt and saw 'reality' and the world in very
different ways. They did not, nor do we, 'float free' as
Pocock puts it (1973) of their historical selves, or of their
personal anthropologies" (Williams, 1976/7:20).

35. I have not listed references for these authors here because
anyone interested may consult Evans-Pritchard (1965) and,
using his bibliography, follow up on the debates and issues
in which these authors were interested.

36. It is simply tedious to hear debates these days in newspapers
and on television programs regarding the recent controversy
over evolutionary vs. religious theories of creation and their
inclusion in school curricula. They are tedious because many
of them simply repeat, although in a far less knowledgeable
or scholarly fashion, the turn-of-the-century controversies
of science vs. religion. It is as if the protagonists of the

modern points of view imagine themselves to exist in a literary and historical vacuum or that they believe themselves
to be the generators of new insights. They are, however,
lamentably unaware of the metatheoretical developments in
modern intellectual attempts to know who we are in the
world that resulted in three identifiable metatheories: super-
naturalism, positivistic naturalism, and existential or her-
meneutic naturalism. (see Varela, 1983, for complete discussion.)

37. The opposition sacred/secular is used as a basis for one of
the few, if not the only, texts we possess written by a
theologian, Van der Leeuw (1963), that treats the dance.
Much could be said about this opposition and its usefulness
regarding studies of the dance, but spatial considerations
prevent any investigation here, as they prevent consideration of Nietzsche's opposition of Dionysian/Appollonian arts
(1895), in which the dance was classified as a paradigm example of the first term of the opposition. A social-scientific,
specifically Durkheimian, approach to the dance or to liturgy
can sometimes be recognized through an author's usage of
the opposition of sacred/profane, that stems from Durkheim's
usage of it in his famous work on religion (1915/1965).

38. I here append a list of those references used in Kaeppler
(1978) that are not well known, but that reflect more modern approaches to the study of dance in an anthropological
context: Harris (1976), Birdwhistell (1952), Jablonko (1968),
Keali'inohomoku (1972), Martin and Pesovar (1961), McLeod
(1974), Pike (1967), Proca-Ciortea (1971), Royce (1972,
1972a and 1973), Youngerman (1974), and Williams (1980).

39. In semasiology, we do not use the phrase "verbal/nonverbal"
because of its positivistic overtones. Instead, we use
"vocal/nonvocal," and we do this because of a major theoretical consideration, not because we wish to engage in petty
disagreement over words. If it is true that spatial points of
reference are points of application for linguistic predicates
in the human realm and if it is true that human language
use is the primary example of human logical and symbolic
complexification, then it is the case that a vocal/nonvocal
distinction is nearer the mark.

Agar, M. Ripping and Running. Seminar Press, New York, 1973.

Ardener, E. W. "Introductory Essay" Social Anthropology and
Language (ASA 10). London: Tavistock, 1971.

_____. "Behavior: A Social Anthropological Criticism."
Journal of the Anthropological Society of Oxford (JASO) 4 (3)
(1973) pp. 153-155.

_____. "The Voice of Prophecy: Further Problems in the Analysis of Events." Munro Lecture, Edinburgh, 1975.

_____. "Some Outstanding Problems in the Analysis of Events," The Yearbook of Symbolic Anthropology I, (1978). First given as Paper for Association of Social Anthropology (ASA) Conference in 1973.

_____. "Social Anthropology, Language and Reality." Paper for Association of Social Anthropology (ASA) Conference, Durham University, April 2, 1982.

Ardener, S., ed. "Introductory Essay" Perceiving Women. London: Malaby Press; New York: Halsted Press, 1976.

Argyle, M. Bodily Communication. London: Methuen, 1975.

Bailey, F. "Navaho Motor Habits" in Davis (1975). (Reprinted from American Anthropologist, 44, 1942.)

Banton, M. "The Dancing Compin." West Africa, (Nov. 7, 1953), pp. 43-44.

Bartenieff, I. "Research in Anthropology: A Study of Dance Styles in Primitive Cultures." CORD Dance Research Annual, I, 1968.

Basso, K. H. The Cibecue Apache. New York: Holt, Rinehart & Winston, 1970.

Bateson, G. Naven. 2nd ed. Stanford, CA: Stanford University Press, 1958; London: Cambridge University Press, 1936.

Baxandall, M. Painting and Experience in Fifteenth Century Italy. London: Oxford University Press, 1972.

Beattie, J. Other Cultures. London: Routledge & Kegan Paul, 1964.

_____. Understanding an African Kingdom: Bunyoro. New York: Holt, Rinehart & Winston, 1965.

_____. "Understanding and Explanation in Social Anthropology" in Manners and Kaplan (1968).

Benedict, R. Patterns of Culture. Boston: Houghton Mifflin, 1934.

Best, D. Expression in Movement and the Arts. London: Lepus Books, 1974.

_____. "The Aesthetic in Sport." JHMS, 1 (1) (1975) pp. 41-47.

_____. "Movement and the Intellect." JHMS, 2 (1) (1976) pp. 64-69.

_____. "The Slipperiness of Movement." JHMS, 2 (3) (1976) pp. 182-190.

_____. "Rhythm in Movement--A Plea for Clarity." JHMS, 2 (4) (1976) pp. 271-278.

_____. Philosophy and Human Movement. London: Allen Unwin, 1978.

_____. "Meaning in Movement." JHMS, 4 (4) (1978) pp. 211-222.

Birdwhistell, R. Introduction to Kinesics. Louisville, KY: Louis-ville University Press, 1952.

_____. Kinesics and Context. Essays on Body Motion Communi-cation. Philadelphia: University of Pennsylvania Press, 1970.

Blacking, J., ed. The Anthropology of the Body. New York: Academic Press, 1977.

_____. Introduction in The Performing Arts. New York: Academic Press, pp. v-vii.

Blum, O. "Dance in Ghana." Dance Perspectives, 56 (1973).

Boas, F., ed. The Function of Dance in Human Society. New York: Boas School, 1944. (Also Dance Horizons.)

Bohannan, P. "Miching Malleko: That Means Witchcraft" in J. Middleton, ed., Magic, Witchcraft and Curing. (American Museum Source), 1967.

_____. Social Anthropology. New York: Holt, Rinehart & Winston, 1969.

Chapman, M. "'Semantics' and the 'Celt.'" Paper given for Asso-ciation of Social Anthropologists (ASA) Conference, Durham University, April 2, 1982.

Crick, M. Exploration in Language and Meaning. Towards a Se-mantic Anthropology. London: Malaby, 1976.

Davenport, W. "Sculpture of the Eastern Solomons." Expedition. 10,2 (Winter 1968) pp. 4-25. (Also in Jopling, 1971.)

Davis, M., ed. Anthropological Perspectives of Movement. New

York: Arno Press, 1975. (Now available from Ayer, Co., Seeg Harbor, New York.)

_____. Understanding Body Movement: An Annotated Bibliography. Bloomington: Indiana University Press, 1972. Reprinted 1982.

_____. "An Interview with Edward T. Hall." Kinesis, 1 (1) (1978) pp. 6-15.

_____. Nonverbal Communication and Body Movement, (1971-81) An Annotated Bibliography. Bloomington: Indiana University Press, 1982.

Diesing, P. Patterns of Discovery in the Social Sciences. New York: Aldine, 1971.

Dolgin, J., et al., eds. Symbolic Anthropology. A Reader in the Study of Symbols and Meanings. New York: Columbia University Press, 1977.

_____, and J. Magdoff. "The Invisible Event." Symbolic Anthropology. New York: Columbia University Press, 1977.

Durkheim, E. The Elementary Forms of Religious Life. New York: Free Press, 1965; Macmillan, 1915.

Durr, D. "Labanotation: Language or Script?" JASHM, 1 (3) (1981) pp. 132-138.

Eggan, F., ed. Social Anthropology of North American Tribes. Chicago: University of Chicago Press, 1937.

_____. "Social Anthropology and the Method of Controlled Comparison." American Anthropologist, 56 (1954) pp. 743-763.

Ekman, P. and W. Firesen. "The Repertoire of Non-Verbal Behavior: Categories, Origins, Usage and Coding." Semiotica, 1 (1969) pp. 49-98.

Ellis, A. G. "West African Sketches" (1881) in Wolfson (1958), pp. 176-177.

Epstein, A. L., ed. The Craft of Social Anthropology. New York: Barnes & Noble, 1967.

Evans-Pritchard, E. E. 1928. "The Dance (Azande)." Africa, 1 (1958).

_____. The Nuer. Oxford: Clarendon Press, 1940.

_____. Social Anthropology and Other Essays. (Combining Social Anthropology and Essays in Social Anthropology), New York: Free Press, 1962.

_____. Essays in Social Anthropology. London: Faber, 1962.

_____. Social Anthropology and Other Essays. New York: Free Press, 1962.

_____. Theories of Primitive Religion. Oxford: Clarendon Press, 1965.

Fernandez, J. "Principles of Opposition and Vitality in Fang Aesthetics." Journal of Aesthetics and Art Criticism (JAAC), XXV, 1 (1966) pp. 53-64. (Also in Jopling, 1971.)

Field, M. Religion and Medicine of the Ga People. London and New York: Oxford University Press, 1937.

Firth, R. Primitive Polynesian Economy. London: Routledge & Kegan Paul, 1939.

_____. Elements of Social Organization. London: Watts, 1951.

_____. "Function" in W. Thomas ed., Yearbook of Anthropology. New York: Wenner-Gren Foundation, 1955.

_____. Man and Culture. London: Routledge & Kegan Paul, 1957.

Fisher, S. Body Consciousness. London: Calder & Boyers, 1973.

Forge, A. "Art and Environment in the Sepik." Proceedings of the Royal Anthropological Institute of Great Britain and Ireland, pp. 349-60, 1965. (Also in Jopling, 1971.)

Fortes, M. and E. E. Evans-Pritchard, eds. African Political Systems. London: Oxford University Press, 1940.

_____. The Web of Kinship Among the Tallensi. London: Oxford University Press, 1949.

Friedrich, P. "Shape in Grammar" in Dolgin, et al., (1977) pp. 381-393. (Reprinted from Linguistics, 75, Mouton, The Hague.)

Geertz, C. "Ritual and Social Change: A Javanese Example" in N. J. Demerath and W. A. Peterson eds., System, Change, and Conflict. New York: Free Press, 1967.

Gluckman, M. and E. Devons, eds. Closed Systems and Open Minds. Chicago: Aldine, 1964.

Goodenough, W. "Residence Rules" (1956) in Manners and Kaplan (1968).

_____. Description and Comparison in Cultural Anthropology. Chicago: Aldine, 1970.

Grove, L. Dancing. London: Longmans, Green & Co.,; Badminton Library, 1895.

Hall, E. T. The Silent Language. Garden City, NY: Doubleday & Co., 1966.

_____. The Hidden Dimension. Garden City, NY: Doubleday & Co., 1966.

_____. "A System for the Notation of Proxemic Behavior" in Davis (1975). (Reprinted from American Anthropologist, 65, 1963.)

Hambly, W. D. Tribal Dancing and Social Development. London: H. F. & G. Witherby, 1926.

Hanna, J. L. "Dance Plays of Ubakala." Presence Africaine, 65, First Quarter (1965) pp. 13-37.

_____. To Dance is Human: A Theory of Nonverbal Communication. Austin: University of Texas Press, 1979.

Harris, M. The Rise of Anthropological Theory. New York: Crowell, 1968.

_____. "History and Significance of the emic/etic Distinction." Annual Review of Anthropology, 5 (1968) pp. 329-50.

Hastrup, K. "The Post-Structuralist Position of Social Anthropology." The Yearbook of Symbolic Anthropology I (1978) pp. 123-148.

_____. "Establishing an Ethnicity: The Emergence of the 'Icelanders' in the Early Middle Ages." Paper for Association of Social Anthropology (ASA) Conference, April 2, 1982.

Hayes, F. 1975. "Gestures: A Working Bibliography" in Davis (1975). (Reprinted from Southern Folklore Quarterly, 21, 1957.)

Henson, H. British Social Anthropologists and Language: A History of Separate Development. Oxford: Clarendon Press, 1974.

Hewes, G. "World Distribution of Certain Postural Habits." American Anthropologist, 57 (2) (1955) pp. 231-244.

_____. "Food Transport and the Origin of Hominid Bi-pedalism." American Anthropologist, 63 (4) (1961) pp. 687-710.

Hieb, L. A. "Rhythms of Significance: Towards a Symbolic Analysis of Dance in Ritual." CORD Research Annual, VI (1972) pp. 225-32.

Hinde, R., ed. Non-Verbal Communication. (Non-Verbal Communication and Ethology of Body Behaviour.) Cambridge, Eng.: Cambridge University Press, 1972.

Holliwell, A. "Cultural Factors in Spatial Orientation" (1955) Culture and Experience. Philadelphia: University of Pennsylvania Press, pp. 184-202, (Reprinted in Dolgin, et al., 1977.)

Jablonko, A. "Dance and Daily Activities Among the Maring of New Guinea: A Cinematographic Analysis of Body Movement Style." Ph.D. thesis, Columbia University, New York, 1968.

Jeffreys, M. D. W. "African Tarantual or Dancing Mania." Eastern Anthropologist, Lucknow, 6 (2) (1952).

Joos, M. The Five Clocks. Indiana University Publications in Anthropology, Folklore, and Linguistics, 1962.

Jopling, C., ed. Art and Aesthetics in Primitive Societies. A Critical Anthology. New York: Dutton, 1971.

Kaeppler, A. "The Dance in Anthropological Perspective." Annual Review of Anthropology, 7 (1978) pp. 31-39.

_____. "Cultural Analysis, Linguistic Analysis and the Study of Dance in Anthropological Perspective." Festschrift for David McAllester. Publication forthcoming.

Keali'inohomoku, J. "Field Guides." New Directions in Dance Research: Anthropology and Dance--The American Indian. CORD Research Annual, VI (1972) pp. 245-60.

_____. "Caveat on Causes and Correlations." CORD News, 6 (2) (1976) pp. 20-24.

_____. "The Non-Art of the Dance." JASHM, 1 (2) (1980) pp. 38-44. (Introduction by Ruth Abrahams on pp. 36-37.)

_____. "An Anthropologist Looks at Ballet as an Ethnic Form of Dance." JASHM, 1 (2) (1980) pp. 83-97.

Kluckhohn, C. Navaho Witchcraft. Cambridge: Harvard University Press, 1944. (Beacon Press reprint.)

_____. and D. Leighton. The Navaho. Cambridge: Harvard University Press, 1946.

_____. "The Philosophy of the Navaho Indians" in F. Northrup ed., Ideological Differences and World Order. New Haven: Yale University Press, 1949.

Kristeva, J. (See Polhemus, T., 1978:264ff.) 1969.

Kroeber, A. Anthropology. New York: Harcourt, Brace, 1948.

Kurath, G. P. "Panorama of Dance Ethnology." Current Anthropology, 1 (3) (1960) pp. 233-254.

Kurti, L. Review of The Performing Arts. JASHM, 1 (2) (1980) pp. 123-28.

LaBarre, W. "The Cultural Basis of Emotions and Gestures" in Davis (1975). (Reprinted from Journal of Personality, 16, 1947.)

Lange, R. The Nature of Dance: An Anthropological Perspective. London: Macmillan, 1975.

Leach, E. R. "The Structural Implications of Matrilateral Cross-Cousin Marriage." Journal of the Royal Anthropological Institute, 81 (1951) pp. 23-56.

_____. Political Systems of Highland Burma. Boston: Beacon Press, 1954.

_____. "The Epistomological Background of Malinowski's Empiricism" in Firth (1957).

Lee, D. "Lineal and Nonlineal Codifications of Reality." Psychosomatic Medicine, 12 (1950) pp. 89-97. (Reprinted in Dolgin, et al., 1977.)

Leeuw, G. van der. Sacred and Profane Beauty. The Holy Art. (Translation-Green), London: Weidenfeld & Nicholson; New York: Holt, Rinehart & Winston, 1963.

Levi-Strauss, C. Structural Anthropology. New York: Basic Books, 1963.

_____. The Savage Mind. London: Weidenfeld & Nicholson, 1966.

Lewis, G. Day of Shining Red: An Essay on Understanding Ritual. Cambridge and New York: Cambridge University Press, 1980.

Lienhardt, G. "Anuak Village Headmen." Part 1: "Headmen and Village Culture," Africa, 27 (1957). Part 2: "Village Structure and Rebellion," Africa, 28 (1958).

_____. "Edward Taylor" in Raison (1969).

_____. Social Anthropology. London: Oxford University Press, 1966.

Lowie, R. Primitive Religion. London: George Routledge & Sons, 1925.

Malinowski, B. Argonauts of the Western Pacific. London: George Routledge & Sons, 1922.

_____. A Scientific Theory of Culture and Other Essays. Chapel Hill: University of North Carolina Press, 1944.

_____. Magic, Science and Religion. Garden City, NY: Doubleday/Anchor Books, 1954 (1948).

Malm, J. "The Legacy of Nihon Buyo." CORD Dance Research Journal, 9, 2 (1977) pp. 12-24.

Mandelbaum, D. "Form Variation and Meaning of a Ceremony" in R. Spencer ed., Method and Perspective in Anthropology. Minneapolis: Minnesota University Press, 1954.

Manners, R., and D. Kaplan, eds. Theory in Anthropology. Chicago: Aldine, 1968.

Martin, G. and E. Pesovar. "A Structural Analysis of the Hungarian Folk Dance." Acta Ethnographica (at the Academy of Science, Hungary), 10 (1961) pp. 1-2.

McLeod, N. "Ethnomusicological Research and Anthropology." Annual Review of Anthropology, 3 (1974) pp. 99-115.

Mead, M. Growing Up in New Guinea. London: George Routledge & Sons, 1981.

_____, ed. Cultural Patterns and Technical Change. New York: New American Library, 1955.

_____. New Lives For Old. New York: Morrow, 1956.

Mitchell, C. "The Kalela Dance." Manchester University Press (for the Rhodes-Livingstone Institute), No. 27, (1956).

Mitchell, J. C. The American Polity. Glencoe, IL: Free Press, 1966.

Murdock, G. Social Structure. New York: Macmillan, 1949.

Murray, D. "Ritual Communication: Some Considerations Regarding Meaning in Navajo Ceremonials" in Dolgin, et al. (1977), pp. 195-220.

Nadel, S. F. The Foundations of Social Anthropology. Glencoe, IL: Free Press, 1951.

Nagata, S. "Dan Kochhongva's Message: Myth, Ideology and Political Action Among the Contemporary Hopi." The Yearbook of Symbolic Anthropology I, (1978), pp. 73-88.

Napier, D. Review of The Anthropology of the Body. JASO, 9 (3) (1978), Michaelmas Term.

Needham, R., ed. Right and Left. Essays in Dual Symbolic Classification. Chicago: University of Chicago Press, 1973.

Nietzsche, F. Die Gebort der Tragodie. (The Birth of Tragedy.) Werke, Vol. a, Leipzig, 1895.

Osterly, W. O. E. The Sacred Dance. London: Cambridge University Press, 1923.

Ortega y Gassett, J. The Revolt of the Masses. New York: Norton and Co., 1957. (First published in 1930 as "La Rebelion de las Masas"--translation authorized, but anonymous.)

Peng, F. C. C. Sign Language and Language Acquisition in Man and Ape: New Dimensions in Comparative Pedolinguistics. For American Association for the Advancement of Science (A.A.A.S.), Selected Symposium, XVI. Boulder, CO: Westview Press, 1978.

Pike, K. Language in Relation to a Unified Theory of the Structures of Human Behavior. The Hague: Mouton, 1967.

Pocock, D. Social Anthropology. London: Sheed & Ward, 1971 (1961).

_____. "The Idea of a Personal Anthropology." Paper given at the Dicenniel Conference of the Association of Anthropologists, Oxford (available through JASHM editors) (1973).

_____. Understanding Social Anthropology. London: Hodder & Stoughton, 1975.

Polhemus, T., ed. The Body Reader. Social Aspects of the Human Body. New York: Pantheon Books, 1978.

Pouwer, J. "Field Work and Signification." Journal of Symbolic Anthropology, 1 (1973) The Hague: Mouton.

Proca-Ciortea, V. "Kinetic Language and Vocabulary." Yearbook of the International Folk Music Council for 1970, (1971) pp. 133-141.

Radcliffe Brown, A. R. The Andaman Islanders. Glencoe, IL: Free Press, 1922. (Reprinted 1948.)

_____. "Functionalism: A Protest." American Anthropologist, 51 (1949) pp. 320-323.

_____. "The Comparative Method in Social Anthropology." Journal of the Royal Anthropological Institute, 81 (1951) pp. 15-22.

_____. "Murngin Social Organization." American Anthropologist, 53 (1951) pp. 37-55.

_____. Structure and Function in Primitive Society. Glencoe, IL: Free Press, 1952.

_____. A Natural Science of Society. Glencoe, IL: Free Press, 1957.

Raison, T., ed. The Founding Fathers of Social Science. London: Penguin, 1969.

Redfield, R. The Primitive World and Its Transformations. Ithaca: Cornell University Press, 1953.

_____. Human Nature and the Study of Society. (Collected papers, Vol. a, M. P. Redfield, ed.) Chicago: University of Chicago Press, 1962.

Renshaw, P. "The Nature and Study of Human Movement: A Philosophical Examination." JHMS, 1 (1) (1975) pp. 5-11.

Richards, A. Land, Labor, and Diet in Northern Rhodesia. Oxford: Oxford University Press, 1939.

_____. Chisungu: A Girls' Initiation Ceremony Among the Bemba of Northern Rhodesia. London: Faber & Faber, 1956.

Ridgeway, W. Dramas and Dramatic Dances of Non-European Peoples.' Cambridge, Eng.: The University Press, 1915.

Royce, A. "Coreology Today: A Review of the Field." New Dimensions in Dance Research: Anthropology and Dance--The American Indian. CORD Research Annual, VI (1972) pp. 47-84.

_____. "Dance as an Indicator of Social Class and Identity in Juchitan Oaxaca." CORD Research Annual, VI (1972) pp. 285-97.

_____. "Social and Political Aspects of Dance Performance in Plural Societies." Paper presented at the Annual Meeting of the American Anthropological Association (1973).

_____. The Anthropology of Dance. Bloomington: Indiana University Press, 1977.

Rust, F. Dance in Society. London: Routledge & Kegan Paul, 1969.

Sachs, C. The World History of the Dance. (Translation-- Schoenberg). New York: Allen & Unwin, 1937.

Schechner, R. Essays on Performance Theory. New York: Drama Book Specialists, 1977.

_____. "Intercultural Performance." Drama Review, 26 (2T94) (1982) pp. 3-4.

Schieffelin, E. The Sorrow of the Lonely and the Burning of the Dancers. New York: St. Martin's Press, 1976.

Scott, E. Dancing in All Ages. London: Swan Sonneschein & Co., 1899.

Sebeok, T., et al. Approaches to Semiotics. The Hague: Mouton, 1964.

Segy, L. "The Mask in African Dance." Negro History Bulletin, 14 (1953).

Sheets-Johnstone, M. "Interdisciplinary Travel: From Dance to Philosophical Anthropology." JASHM, 2 (3) (1983).

Sieber, R. "The Aesthetic of Traditional African Art" in Jopling (1971) pp. 127-131.

Singer, A. "Holiday Dancing in a Greek-Macedonian Village." (Unpublished manuscript, 1970.)

Snyder, A. "The Dance Symbol." CORD Research Annual VI (1972) pp. 213-224.

Sorell, W. The Dance Through the Ages. New York: Grosset and Dunlap, 1967.

Spradley, J. Culture and Cognition. San Francisco: Chandler, 1970.

Stokoe, W. "Sign Language Structure." Annual Review of Anthropology, 9 (1980) pp. 365-390.

Sturtevant, W. "Studies in Ethnoscience." American Anthropologist, Special Issue on "Transcultural Studies in Cognition." 66 (2) (1964) pp. 99-131. (Reprinted in Manners & Kaplan [1968], pp. 475-500.)

Tax, S. General Editor's Preface in The Performing Arts. New York: Academic Press, 1977, pp. xiii-xxii.

Terry, W. "Dance, History of" in A. Chujoy and P. W. Manchester (comps. and eds.), The Dance Encyclopedia, New York: Simon and Schuster, 1967, pp. 255-259.

Thompson, R. F. "An Aesthetic of the Cool: West African Dance." African Forum II (2) (1966), American Society of African Studies (AMSAC), New York.

Turner, V. "Symbols in African Ritual." Science, 179 (Mar. 16, 1972) pp. 1100-5. (Reprinted in Dolgin, et al., 1977.)

Tyler, E. B. Anthropology. The Thinker's Library, Vol. 2, London: Watts & Co., 1895.

Tyler, S., ed. Cognitive Anthropology. New York: Holt, Rinehart & Winston, 1969.

Varela, C. "Cartesianism Re-visited: The Ghost in the Moving Machine." JASHM, 2 (3) (1983).

Wagner, R. "Ideology and Theory: The Problem of Reification" The Yearbook of Symbolic Anthropology I, (1978) pp. 203-210.

Whiting, J., ed. The Journal of Human Movement Studies, Vols. 1-6, London: Kimpton and Lepus Books, 1975-1980.

Williams, D. Review of Lomax (1968). CORD Dance Research Journal, 6 (2) (1974).

_____. Review of Dance in Society. CORD Dance Research Journal, 1 (2) (1974).

_____. "The Role of Movement in Selected Symbolic Systems." Ph.D. thesis, Oxford University, 1975.

_____. "Deep Structures of the Dance." JHMS, (Part I) 2 (1976) pp. 123-144, (Part II) 3 (1976) pp. 155-181.

_____. Review of The Nature of Dance: An Anthropological Perspective. CORD Dance Research Journal, 9 (1) (1976).

_____. "An Exercise in Applied Personal Anthropology." CORD Dance Research Journal 9 (1) (1976-77).

_____. "The Arms and Hands, With Special Reference to an Anglo-Saxon Sign System." Semiotica, 2 (1) (1977) pp. 23-73.

_____. "The Human Action Sign and Semasiology." CORD Dance Research Annual, X (1979).

_____. "Taxonomies of the Body, With Special Reference to the Ballet." (In two parts) JASHM, 1 (1) (1980) pp. 1-19 and 1 (2) (1980) pp. 98-131.

_____. Introductory essay of JASHM, Special Issue on Semasiology. JASHM, 1 (4) (1981).

_____. "Semasiology. A Semantic Anthropological Approach to Human Actions and Movement." Paper given at ASA Conference, Durham University, April 1, 1982.

Witherspoon, G. "Navajo Categories at Rest" in Dolgin, et al. (1977).

Wolf, F. A. Taking the Quantum Leap. New York: Harper & Row, 1981.

Wolfson, F. Pageant of Ghana. London: Oxford University Press, 1958.

Youngerman, S. "Curt Sachs and His Heritage: A Critical Review of World History of the Dance with a Survey of Recent Studies that Perpetuate His Ideas." CORD News 6 (2) (1974) pp. 6-19.

Zaner, R. The Problem of Embodiment: Some Contributions to a Phenomenology of the Body. The Hague: Martinus Nijoff, 1971.

Zoete, B. de and W. Spies. Dance and Drama in Bali. London: Faber & Faber, 1938.

The following is a complete bibliographical listing of the published works of Adrienne Kaeppler, Joann Keali'inohomoku, and Drid Williams, plus an index of Vols. I and II, Journal of the Anthropological Studies of Human Movement (JASHM), which is not as yet listed in major index sources.

Adrienne Kaeppler

In press:

"Structured Movement Systems in Tonga" in Paul Spencer, ed.,
    The Dance in Society. London: The Athlone Press.

"Tongan Music in the 19th Century" in Robert Günther, ed., Die
    Musikkulturen Asiens, Afrikas und Ozeaniens in 19 Jarhun-
    dert, Vol. 2.

"Oceanic Art" and "Bark Cloth" entries in Academic American En-
    cyclopedia.

The Significance of Cook's Third Voyage for the Study of Hawaiian
    Art and Society. Paper for the Conference "Captain James
    Cook and His Times" at Simon Fraser University, April
    1978.

The Performing Arts of Papua New Guinea.

In preparation:

Captain James Cook, Sir Ashton Lever, and Miss Sarah Stone: A
Study of Art and Artifacts of the 18th Century in the Leverian Museum.

1981a. Review of To Dance is Human: A Theory of Nonverbal
        Communication by Judith Lynne Hanna. American Ethnolo-
        gist 8 (1):218-219.
1981b. Record review of "Polynesian Dances of Bellona (Mungiki)
        Solomon Islands." Ethnomusicology 25 (2).
1980a. "Polynesian Music and Dance" in Elizabeth May, ed., Musics
        of Many Cultures, pp. 134-153. Berkeley: University of
        California Press.
1980b. "Pacific Islands: Dance" and "Tonga" in Grove's Dictionary
        of Music and Musicians. London: Macmillan.
1980c. Review of Master Mariner: Capt. James Cook and the Peo-
        ples of the Pacific by Daniel Conner and Lorraine Miller.
        Man, 15 (1):214-215.
1980d. Review of Introduction to Dance Literacy by Nadia Chilkov-
        sky Nahumck. Ethnomusicology, 24 (2):308-309.
1980e. "The Persistence of Tradition." Introductory Essay to
        Hawai'i: The Royal Isles, by Roger G. Rose, pp. 53-62.
        Bernice Pauahi Bishop Museum Special Publication 67.
1980f. Pahu and Pūniu: An Exhibition of Hawaiian Drums. Ber-
        nice Pauahi Bishop Museum, Department of Anthropology.
        40 pp.
1980g. Kapa: Hawaiian Bark Cloth. Hilo, Hawai'i: Bob Boom
        Books. 16 pp.
1980h. "Hawaiian Art: An Anthropological Perspective." Educa-
        tional Perspectives 19 (1):10-15.

1979a. Review of Pottery of Papua New Guinea and The Seized
Collections of the Papua New Guinea Museum. African
Arts 12 (4):87-88.
1979b. Review of An Annotated Bibliography of Oceanic Music and
Dance by Mervyn McLean. Ethnomusicology, 23 (1):142-143.
1979c. "Tracing the History of Hawaiian Cook Voyage Artifacts in
the Museum of Mankind." British Museum Yearbook 3, pp.
167-186.
1979d. "A Survey of Polynesian Art with Selected Reinterpreta-
tions" in S. M. Mead, ed., Exploring the Art of Oceania,
pp. 180-191.
1979e. Eleven Gods Assembled: An Exhibition of Hawaiian Wooden
Images. Bishop Museum Miscellaneous Publication. 20 pp.
1979f. "Aspects of Polynesian Aesthetic Traditions" in The Art of
the Pacific Islands, by J. Carter Brown, Douglas Newton,
Adrienne L. Kaeppler, and Peter Gathercole. Washington:
The National Gallery of Art, pp. 77-95 and 105-181.
1978a. Review of The Dance in the Pacific by W. H. Poort. American Anthropologist 80 (1):152.
1978b. "Polynesian Music, Captain Cook, and the Romantic Movement in Europe." Music Educators Journal 65 (3):55-60.
1978c. "Melody, Drone, and Decoration: Underlying Structures
and Surface Manifestations in Tongan Art and Society" in
Michael Greenhalgh, and Vincent Megaw, eds., Art in Society: Studies in Styles, Culture and Aesthetics. London:
Duckworth, pp. 261-274.
1978d. "Me'a Faka'eiki: Tongan Funerals in a Changing Society"
in Niel Gunson, ed., The Changing Pacific: Essays in
Honor of H. E. Maude. Melbourne: Oxford University
Press, pp. 174-202.
1978e. "Exchange Patterns in Goods and Spouses: Fiji, Tonga,
and Samoa." Mankind 11 (3):246-252.
1978f. "Dance in Anthropological Perspective." Annual Review of
Anthropology 7:31-49.
1978g. (Editor and Introductions) Cook Voyage Artifacts in Lenin-
grad, Berne, and Florence Museums. Bishop Museum Special Publication 66.
1978h. "Artificial Curiosities" Being an Exposition of Native Manu-
factures Collected On The Three Pacific Voyages of Captain
James Cook, R.N. Bishop Museum Special Publication 65,
xvi + 294 pp.
1978i. "L'Aigle and HMS Blonde: The Use of History in the Study
of Ethnography." The Hawaiian Journal of History 12:
28-44.
1977a. Foreword in Adrienne L. Kaeppler, Judy Van Zile, and Carl
Wolz, eds., Asian and Pacific Dance: Selected Papers from
the 1974 CORD Conference, CORD Annual VIII. New York:
Committee on Research in Dance, pp. iii-v.
1977b. "Polynesian Dance as 'Airport Art,'" in Asian and Pacific
Dance: Selected Papers from the 1974 CORD Conference,
CORD Annual VIII. New York: Committee on Research in
Dance, pp. 71-84.

1976a. Record review of "Traditional Music of Tonga" and "Tongan Festival Contingent: Vols. 1 and 2." Ethnomusicology 20 (3):612-615.

1976b. Review of Thor Heyerdahl, The Art of Easter Island. Times Literary Supplement, London.

1976c. "Tongans" in The Family of Man, 7 (90):2496-2498. London: Marshall Cavendish Ltd.

1976d. (Editor and Foreword) Reflections and Perspectives in Two Anthropological Studies of Dance: A Comparative Study of Dance as a Constellation of Motor Behaviors Among African and United States Negroes by Joann W. Kealiinohomoku and The Dance of Taos Pueblo by Donald N. Brown. CORD Research Annual VII. New York: Committee on Research in Dance.

1976e. "Dance in Tonga: The Communication of Social Values Through an Artistic Medium" in Daniel Lerner and Jim Richstad, eds., Communication in the Pacific. Honolulu: East-West Communication Institute, pp. 15-22.

1976f. (with H. Arlo Nimmo) Editors and Preface. Directions in Pacific Traditional Literature: Essays in Honor of Katharine Luomala. Bishop Museum Special Publication 62.

1976g. "Dance and Interpretation of Pacific Traditional Literature" in Adrienne L. Kaeppler and H. Arlo Nimmo, eds., Directions in Pacific Traditional Literature: Essays in Honor of Katharine Luomala. Bishop Museum Special Publication 62, pp. 195-216.

1976h. "Art," "Art of Oceania-Polynesia," "Bark Cloth," and "Dance" entries in David E. Hunter and Phillip Whitten, eds., Encyclopedia of Anthropology, New York: Harper and Row. pp. 20-21, 33-34, 53-54, and 113-114.

1975a. The Fabrics of Hawaii (Bark Cloth), Volume 14 of The World's Heritage of Woven Fabrics. Leigh-on-sea, Eng.: F. Lewis, Publishers, Limited. 16 pp. and 55 plates by Peter Gilpin.

1975b. "An Eighteenth Century Kāhili from Kaua'i." Archaeology on Kaua'i, 4 (2):3-9.

1974a. Record Review of "Musique de Guadalcanal: Solomon Islands." Ethnomusicology 18 (3):477-478.

1974b. "Tonga" in John Clammer, ed., Islands of the Pacific. Danbury Press. (Vol. 8 of Peoples of the World, E. E. Evans-Pritchard, editor.) pp. 54-61.

1974c. "A Study of Tongan Panpipes With a Speculative Interpretation." Ethnos 39 (1-4):102-128.

1974d. (with Dieter Christensen) "Oceanic Peoples, Art of (Dance and Music)" in Encyclopaedia Britannica. Fifteenth edition, Volume 13, pp. 456-461.

1974e. "Cook Voyage Provenance of the 'Artificial Curiosities' of Bullock's Museum." Man, The Journal of the Royal Anthropological Institute 9 (1):68-92.

1973a. Review of G. Kurath, Music and Dance of the Tewa Pueblos. American Anthropologist 75 (4):1065-1066.

1973b. Record Review of "Musique Polynesienne Traditionelle." *Ethnomusicology* 17 (1):146-147.

1973c. "Pottery Sherds from Tungua, Ha'apai; and Remarks on Pottery and Social Structure in Tonga." *Journal of the Polynesian Society* 82 (2):218-222.

1973d. "Music in Hawaii in the Nineteenth Century" in Robert Günther, ed., *Musikkulturen Asiens, Afrikas und Ozeaniens im 19. Jahrhundert*. Regensburg, Ger.: Gustav Bosse Verlag, pp. 311-338.

1973e. "A Comparative Note on Anutan Social Organization" in D. E. Yen and Janet Gordon, eds., *Anuta: A Polynesian Outlier in the Solomon Islands*. Pacific Anthropological Records, No. 21. Honolulu: Bishop Museum, Department of Anthropology, pp. 21-24.

1973f. "Acculturation in Hawaiian Dance." *Yearbook of the International Folk Music Council for 1972* 4:38-46.

1972a. "The Use of Documents in Identifying Ethnographic Specimens from the Voyages of Captain Cook." *Journal of Pacific History* 7:195-200.

1972b. "Method and Theory in Analyzing Dance Structure with an Analysis of Tongan Dance." *Ethnomusicology* 16 (2):173:217.

1971a. Review of S. M. Mead, *Traditional Maori Clothing*. *American Anthropologist* 73 (4):887-888.

1971b. "Rank in Tonga." *Ethnology* 10 (2):174-193.

1971c. "Hawaii" (Regional Survey) in *Meeting on Studies of Oceanic Cultures*. Canberra: Australian National University, pp. 87-111.

1971d. "Eighteenth Century Tonga: New Interpretations of Tongan Society and Material Culture at the Time of Captain Cook." *Man, the Journal of the Royal Anthropological Institute* 6 (2):204-220 and plates 1-6.

1971e. "Dance in the Pacific" (Subject Survey) in *Meeting on Studies of Oceanic Cultures*. Canberra: Australian National University, pp. 131-138.

1971f. "Aesthetics of Tongan Dance." *Ethnomusicology* 15 (2): 175-185.

1970a. "Feather Cloaks, Ship Captains and Lords." *Bishop Museum Occasional Papers* 24 (6):91-114.

1970b. "Tongan Dance: A Study in Cultural Change." *Ethnomusicology* 14 (2):266-277.

1969. (with W. H. Fitzgerald and Roland W. Force) *Dictionary of Asian-Pacific Museums*. Bishop Museum Press. 61 pp.

1968. "Coronation Week in Tonga." *Delphian Quarterly* 51 (1): 8-12.

1967a. *The Structure of Tongan Dance*. Unpublished Ph.D. dissertation, University of Hawaii. (Available from University Microfilms.)

1967b. "Preservation and Evolution of Form and Function in Two Types of Tongan Dance" in Genevieve A. Highland, et al., eds., *Polynesian Culture History: Essays in Honor of Kenneth P. Emory*. Bernice P. Bishop Museum Special Publication 56, pp. 503-536.

1967c. "Folklore as Expressed in the Dance in Tonga." Journal
of American Folklore 80 (316):160-168.

1966. "Sunday in Tonga." Delphian Quarterly 49 (4):8-11 and 15.

1965a. Record Review of "Music of the Magindanao in the Philippines." Ethnomusicology 9 (1):78-79.

1965b. "Preservation of the Arts in Hawaii." Delphian Quarterly
48 (3):1-7 and 36.

1965c. "Decorative Arts in the Marshall Islands" in E. H. Bryan,
Jr., Life in Micronesia. The Hour Glass, Kwajalein,
Marshall Islands. No. 16. Reprinted in Life in the Marshall Islands, 1972, pp. 164-172.

1964a. (with Robert N. Bowen) Pacific Anthropologists 1964.
Pacific Scientific Information Center, Bishop Museum. 71 pp.

1964b. "Papuan Gulf Masks from the Village of Muru." Baessler
Archiv. (Berlin) 11 (2):361-373.

1963a. Record Review of "Music of New Guinea: The Australian
Trust Territory, An Introduction." Ethnomusicology 7 (1):
60-61.

1963b. "Ceremonial Masks: A Melanesian Art Style." Journal of
the Polynesian Society 72 (2):118-138.

1962. (with Robert N. Bowen) Pacific Anthropologists 1962.
Pacific Scientific Information Center, Bishop Museum. 39 pp.

1961. Melanesian Masks in the Bishop Museum. Unpublished master's thesis, University of Hawaii.

Joann Keali'inohomoku

1981a. "Ethical Considerations for Choreographers, Ethnologists,
and White Knights," Journal of Association of Graduate
Dance Ethnologists, U.C.L.A. 5:10-23.

1981b. "Dance as a Rite of Transformation," Discourse in Ethnomusicology II: A Tribute to Alan P. Merriam, Caroline
Card, et al., eds. Bloomington: Ethnomusicology Publications Group, Indiana University, pp. 131-152.

1980a. (Reprint) "An Anthropologist Looks at Ballet as a Form
of Ethnic Dance," Journal for the Anthropological Study of
Human Movement (at New York University) 1, 2:83-97.

1980b. "Alan P. Merriam (1923-1980)," Dance Research Journal
13, 1:57-58.

1980c. "The Drama of the Hopi Ogres," Southwestern Indian Ritual
Drama. Charlotte J. Frisbie, ed. A School of American Research Book, Advanced Seminar Series. Albuquerque:
University of New Mexico Press, pp. 37-69.

1980d. Review of Ha'aku'i Pele I Hawai'i !, Hula Records.
Ethnomusicology 24:335-336.

1980e. Review of Flowers of the Wind: Papers on Ritual, Myth
and Symbolism in California and the Southwest, Thomas C.
Blackburn, ed. American Anthropologist 82, 3:653-654.

1980f. "The Non-Art of the Dance: An Essay," Journal for the
Anthropological Study of Human Movement (at New York
University) 1, 1:38-44.

1979a. "You Dance What You Wear, and You Wear Your Cultural Values," The Fabrics of Culture, Justine M. Cordwell and Ronald A. Schwarz, eds. World Anthropology Series. The Hague: Mouton, pp. 77-83.

1979b. (Co-Editor with John A. R. Blacking) The Performing Arts. World Anthropology Series. The Hague: Mouton.

1979c. "Culture Change: Functional and Dysfunctional Expressions of Dance, a Form of Affective Culture," The Performing Arts. Edited by John A. R. Blacking and Joann W. Keali'-inohomoku. World Anthropology Series. The Hague: Mouton, pp. 47-64.

1979d. Review of Gameel Gamal, a film by Gordon Inkeles. Journal of American Folklore 92:259-261.

1979e. Comments (response to "Anthropological Study of Dance," by Judith Lynne Hanna). Current Anthropology 20:327-328.

1979f. Review Essay of Dance and Human History, a film by Alan Lomax, Ethnomusicology 23:169-176.

1978. "Hopi Social Dance Events and How They Function," Discovery. Santa Fe: School of American Research, pp. 17-38.

1977a. "Ethnodance," The Religious Character of Native American Humanities. Department of Humanities and Religious Studies: Papers read at Interdisciplinary Conference 1977, Arizona State University, Tempe, AZ, pp. 144-154. (Article badly distorted by proofreader.)

1977b. Review of The Sorrow of the Lonely and the Burning of the Dancers by Edward L. Schieffelin, Dance Research Journal (formerly CORD News) 9/2:25-26.

1977c. Review of The Nature of Dance: An Anthropological Perspective by Roderyk Lange, American Anthropologist 79, 3:658-659.

1977d. Review of The Tree of Life, Flower Films. Journal of American Folklore: 90:377-378.

1977e. "Hopi Social Dance as a Means for Maintaining Homeostasis," Journal of Association of Graduate Dance Ethnologists, U.C.L.A. 1:1-11.

1976a. "A Comparative Study of Dance as a Constellation of Motor Behaviors Among African and United States Negroes," Reflections and Perspectives on Two Anthropological Studies of Dance. pp. 1-179. Edited by Adrienne L. Kaeppler. CORD Dance Research Annual VII.

1976b. Theory and Methods for an Anthropological Study of Dance. Ph.D. dissertation. Ann Arbor, Michigan: University Microfilms.

1975a. "Comments to the Editor," CORD Dance Research Journal 7, 2:55-56.

1975b. "Research Resources" ("American Indian Peoples, Arts of" by Gertrude Kurath, et al.), CORD Dance Research Journal 7, 2:26-27.

1975c. Review of "Lessons from the Dancing Ground to the Studio: Implications of Pueblo Indian Dance for Modern Dance" by Valentina Litvinoff, CORD Dance Research Journal 7, 1:33-34.

1974a. "Review Number One: Caveat on Causes and Correlations," (review of Folk Song Style and Culture by Alan Lomax). CORD News 6, 2:20-24.

1974b. "Field Guides," New Dimensions in Dance Research: Anthropology and Dance--The American Indian. CORD Research Annual VI, pp. 245-260.

1974c. "Dance Culture as a Microcosm of Holistic Culture," New Dimensions in Dance Research: Anthropology and Dance-- The American Indian. CORD Research Annual VI, pp. 99-106.

1972. "Folk Dance," Folklore and Folklife: An Introduction. Richard M. Dorson, ed. Chicago: University of Chicago Press, pp. 381-404.

1971. "Book Note" (Folklore of the North American Indians. Library of Congress), Journal of American Folklore 84:261-262.

1970a. Editor. Dance History Research: Perspectives from Related Arts and Disciplines. New York: Committee on Research in Dance (CORD).

1970b. "Perspective Five: Ethnic Historical Study," Dance History Research: Perspectives from Related Arts and Disciplines, Joan W. Kealiinohomoku, ed. New York: Committee on Research in Dance (CORD), pp. 86-97.

1970c. "An Anthropologist Looks at Ballet as a Form of Ethnic Dance," Impulse 1969-1970, Marian Van Tuyl, ed. San Francisco: Impulse Publications, pp. 24-33.

1970d. With Frank Gillis, "Special Bibliography: Gertrude Prokosch Kurath," Ethnomusicology 14:114-128.

1969a. Review of Africa Dances, film by United Nations, American Anthropologist 71:800-801.

1969b. Review of Michigan Indian Festivals by Gertrude Prokosch Kurath, Journal of American Folklore 82:176-177.

1967. "Hopi and Polynesian Dance: A Study in Cross-Cultural Comparison," Ethnomusicology 11:343-358.

1965a. Review of Flower in My Ear by Edwin G. Burrows, Anthropologica 7:158-160.

1965b. "Dance and Self-Accompaniment," Ethnomusicology 9:292-295.

1965c. Review of 'Ula Noweo and Filmstrip of Hawaiian Musical Instruments, Ethnomusicology 9:207-208.

1965d. Review of Folk Songs Hawaii Sings by John M. Kelly, Jr., Ethnomusicology 9:71-73.

1964. "A Court Dancer Disagrees with Emerson's Classic Book on the Hula," Ethnomusicology 8:161-164.

1963. Review of Sword Dance and Drama by Violet Alford, Journal of American Folklore 76:355-356.

1962-1964. Editor of News from the Pacific. Anthropological Society of Hawaii.

1961-1962. "Fa'a Samoa," News from the Pacific. Monthly column.

1960-1963. Dance reviewer for the Honolulu Star-Bulletin.

Drid Williams

In press: "A new paradigm in Movement Research." Keynote address
to Dance Ethnology Forum, UCLA on April 15, 1983. Publication forthcoming in Journal of the Association of Graduate
Dance Ethnologists 7.
Labanotation for Non-Dancers: An Ordinary Approach to
Movement Writing. S.E.M. Series, M. Herndon, ed. University of California, Berkeley: Norwood Press.
"Sacred Spaces: A Preliminary Enquiry into the Latin High
Mass." Publication forthcoming in Linguistics and the Humanities, R. Longacre, ed. University of Texas, Arlington,
and Linguisticum Forum.

1982. "Semasiology: A Semantic Anthropological View of Human
Movements and Actions" in ASA Monograph No. 22, Seman-
tic Anthropology, D. Parkin, ed. New York: Academic
Press, pp. 161-181.

1982a. "On the Dance: A Reply to Margolis' Ideas About the Auto-
graphic Nature of the Dance" in JASHM (Journal for the
Anthropological Study of Human Movement, at New York
University) 2 (2):54-70.

1982b. An Ethnographic Report, "On the Guardian Angels" in
JASHM 2 (1):1-53.

1981. "Introduction" in JASHM Special Issue "On Semasiology" 1
(4):207-225.

1980. "On Structures of Human Movement: A Reply to Gell" in
Journal of Human Movement Sciences 6 (4):303-322.

1980a. "Anthropology and Art" in a limited edition publication (D.
Ecker, ed.) by the Music Department, of essays that con-
stituted the SEHNAP Symposium on Qualitative Evaluation
of the Arts, July. New York University.

1980b. "Taxonomies of the Body, with Special Reference to the
Ballet" in JASHM 1 (1):1-17 & 1 (2):98-122.

1979. "Jargon: A Social Anthropological Comment on Labanotation"
in Momentum (A Journal of Human Movement Studies. Dun-
fermline College, Edinburgh University). 4 (1):40-51.

1979a. "The Human Action Sign and Semasiology" in CORD Research
Annual X:39-63.

1978. "Deep Structures of the Dance, With Additional Notes and
Comments for Anthropologists" in The Yearbook of Symbolic
Anthropology I, Schwimmer, ed. London: C. Hurst.

1977. "The Arms and Hands, With Special Reference to an Anglo-
Saxon Sign System" in Semiotica 21(1/2):23-73.

1976. "Deep Structures of the Dance: Part I, Constituent Syntag-
matic Analysis, and Part II, The Conceptual Space of the
Dance" in The Journal of Human Movement Studies, (J.
Whiting, ed.) 2 (2):123-144 & 2 (3):155-171. London:
Henry Kimpton & Co.

1976a. "An Exercise in Applied Personal Anthropology" in DRJ
(CORD Dance Research Journal) 9 (1):16-30.

1975. "The Brides of Christ" in Perceiving Women, S. Ardener, ed. London: Malaby Press; New York: Halsted Press, pp. 105-125.

1974. "A Note on Human Action and the Language Machine" in DRJ 7 (1)8-9.

1972. "Signs, Symptoms and Symbols" in JASO (Journal of the Anthropological Society of Oxford) 3 (1):24-32.

Reviews (in the capacity of consulting anthropology editor for CORD Dance Research Journal)

Lange, R. The Nature of Dance: An Anthropological Perspective. DRJ (1), 1976-77.

Best, D. Expression in Movement and the Arts. DRJ 7 (2), 1975.

Kaeppler, A. "Method and Theory in Analyzing Dance Structure with an Analysis of Tongan Dance." DRJ 7 (2), 1975.

Rust, F. Dance in Society: An Analysis of the Relationship Between the Social Dance and Society in England from the Middle Ages to the Present Day. DRJ 6 (2), 1974.

Lomax, A. et al. Choreometrics. DRJ 6 (2), 1974.

(In the capacity of Reviewer for the Journal of the Society for Ethnomusicology)

Best, D. Philosophy and Human Movement. Ethnomusicology 24 (2), 1980.

Royce, A. The Anthropology of Dance. Ethnomusicology 23 (3), 1979.

Journal for the Anthropological Study of Human Movement (JASHM)

Index to Volumes 1 and 2

Abrahams, R. K. "Dance Criticism and Anthropology" (Review Article). 1 (1):63-66 (1980).

Best, D. "Free Expression, or the Teaching Techniques?" 2 (2): 89-98. (Reprinted from British Journal of Educational Studies 27 (3)) (1982).

Douglas, M. and J. Gross. "Food and Culture: Measuring the Intricacy of Rule Systems." 1 (3):139-165 (1981).

Durr, D. "Labanotation: Language or Script?" 1 (3):132-138 (1981).

_____ and B. Farnell. "Spatial Orientation and the Notion of Constant Oppositions." 1 (4):226-245 (1981).

Fairbank, H. Review of M. Sheets-Johnstone (1983), "Thinking in Movement" (below). 2 (4) (1983).

Farnell, B. "Dance and Dance Education in England: A British Point of View." 1 (3):166-185 (1981).

_____. "Deep Structures of the Dance: A Reply to Zellinger's 'Directions For a Semiotics of Dance'" (Review Article). 2 (2):112-119 (1982).

_____. (See Durr and Farnell, above.)

Fellom-McGibboney, M. "Examples of Models Used in Data Presentation" (Review Article). 1 (1):67-69 (1980).

Ferrara, L. (See Varela and Ferrara, below.)

Frishberg, N. "Writing Systems and Sign Languages for the Deaf." 2 (4) (1983).

Green, J. "Computers in the Fine Arts." 1 (2):75-82 (1980). (Reprinted from Hancher Circle News, University of Iowa.)

Gross, J. (See Douglas and Gross, above.)

Hart, D. (See Puri and Hart, below.)

Hart-Johnson, D. Review of J. McConnell (1977), Ballet as Body Language. 2 (3):158-166 (1983).

_____. "On Structure in Martha Graham Technique with Comparison with American Sign Language." 2 (4) (1983).

Kaeppler, A. Review of J. Hanna (1979), To Dance is Human: A Theory of Non-Verbal Communication. 1 (3):186-188 (1981). (Reprinted from American Ethnologist 8 (1).)

_____. "Dance in Tonga: The Communication of Social Values through an Artistic Medium." 2 (3):122-128 (1983). (Reprinted from a Report on Communication in the Pacific--A Conference Held in Honolulu at the East-West Center, May 1975.)

Keali'inohomoku, J. W. "The Non-Art of the Dance." 1 (1):38-44 (1980).

_____. "An Anthropologist Looks at Ballet as a Form of Ethnic Dance." 1 (2):83-97 (1980). (Reprinted from Impulse 1969-70:24-33.)

Kürti, L. "The Structure of Hungarian Dance: A Linguistic Approach." 1 (1):45-62 (1980).

_____. Review of J. Blacking and J. W. Keali'inohomoku eds. (1979), The Performing Arts. 1 (2):123-128 (1980).

_____. Review of R. Patai's "Review of the Magyar Néprajzi Lexikon." 1 (3):201-206 (1981).

Martin, L. Review of A. Herman (1979), Ritual in the Celtic World. 1 (2):129-131 (1980).

Myers, E. A. "A Phrase-Structural Analysis of the Foxtrot, with Transformation Rules." 1 (4):246-268 (1981).

Puri, R. "The Family of Rama; Kinship Structures and the Dance." 1 (1):20-35 (1980).

_____. Review of D. Morris et al. (1979), Gestures: Their Origins and Distribution. 1 (3):189-194 (1981).

_____. "Polysemy and Homonmy, and the Mudra 'Shikhara': Multiple Meaning and the Use of Gesture." 1 (4):269-287 (1981).

_____. Review of J. W. Keali'inohomoku (1981), Dance as a Rite of Transformation. 2 (4) (1983).

_____. and D. Hart. "Thinking with Movement: Improvising vs Composing?" 2 (2):71-88 (1982).

Sealy, D. "Computerized Programs for Labanotation." 1 (2):70-75 (1980).

Sheets-Johnstone, M. "Interdisciplinary Travel: From Dance to Philosophical Anthropology." 2 (3):129-142 (1983).

Varela, C. "Cartesianism Revisited: The Ghost in the Moving Machine." 2 (3):143-157 (1983).
_____ and L. Ferrara. "The Nagel Critique and Langer's Critical Response." 2 (2):99-111 (1982).
Warshaw, R. Review of D. Williams (unpub. ms.) "Theories of the Dance: A Social Anthropological View." 1 (3):195-200 (1981).
Williams, D. "Taxonomies of the Body, with Special Reference to the Ballet." 1 (1):1-19; 1 (2):98-122 (1980).
_____. Introduction to Special Issue "On Semasiology." 1 (4):207-225 (1981).
_____. Review of L. Sweigard (1974), Human Movement Potential, Its Ideokinetic Facilitation. 1 (4):288-293 (1981).
_____ ed. Ethnographic Report "On the Guardian Angels." 2 (1):1-53 (1982).
_____. "On the Dance: A Reply to Margolis' Ideas about the Autographic Nature of the Dance." 2 (2):54-70 (1982).

PART II
MOVEMENT PERFORMANCE
OF OTHER CULTURES

Chapter Ten

ASIAN PERFORMANCE: GENERAL INTRODUCTION

Phillip Zarrilli and Rhea Lehman (Section Editors)

The Field of Traditional Asian Performance: An Overview

Asia is generally divided into three major geographical and cultural spheres or areas: South Asia, Southeast Asia, and East Asia. Collectively this region of the world is the most populous, includes some of the world's oldest civilizations, and has bred and/ or provided a home for many of the world's major religions (Hinduism, Buddhism, Confucianism, Islam, Christianity, Judaism). It should come as no surprise that the performance traditions of each Asian region are vast, complex, diverse, colorful, as well as intimate expressions of the stories, values, and beliefs of each individual culture. Within each major region exist a multiplicity of peoples, cultural traditions, languages, political states, and performance forms. In South Asia alone exist the modern states of Bangladesh, India, Nepal, Pakistan, Sri Lanka, and Tibet, each distinguished by its own linguistic, religious, and sociopolitical history. India alone boasts some fourteen major languages and the coexistence today of major populations following Hinduism, Islam, Christianity, and with smaller groups practicing Judaism, the legacy of Zoroastrianism, and a host of indigenous religious practices.

In spite of such diversity and complexity, it is possible to speak of Asian performance as a field in which individual forms of cultural performance from one region share general and common characteristics with other performance forms from other regions. These shared characteristics are a legacy of long periods of fruitful historical and cultural contact. The continuity of the general patterns shaping performance follow the same general contour as cultural assumptions shared by these highly diverse regions. A few of the major shared features or contours of Asian performance include the following:

1. Asian performance includes classical, folk, and ritual or religious forms between and among which there has always been a great deal of sharing.
2. Traditional Asian performance forms are characterized by

223

the joining of various arts; dance, acting, music, and narrative or text are enmeshed in one performance. For this reason Asian performance has often been called "total" performance. At least in classical forms. The various independent arts are not simply brought together; rather, they are interwoven in highly complex, densely packed systems.

3. So complex are many of the Asian forms that it literally takes a lifetime to become a master of the form. Training involves a meticulous process of transmission of detailed performance knowledge. Such transmission traditionally took place within families or lines or specialists, the neophyte beginning training in his youth.

4. The training involves a total education and reshaping of the body, and the implicit conjoining of the mind and body so that the individual performer is able in performance to "exist," "to become," or to "be" the role or character he is called upon to play.

5. The roles or characters the performer is called upon to play are set within prescribed artistic, aesthetic, emotional, and physical limits by the received performance tradition. Most often these roles or characters are archetypal, embodying widely recognized and shared assumptions about human nature in any individual character within a type.

6. These archetypal figures or roles are usually identifiable by characteristic external features of makeup, costume, and/ or mask. Each type is easily recognized by the audience.

7. As archetypes these "figures" display, fold out, and illustrate eternal values, principles, and beliefs of the culture. Such figures are most often drawn from myths, epics, and/ or important historical sources highly valued and popularly known to everyone in the culture.

8. Like costuming and makeup, the staging and use of the stage by the performers is governed by highly conventionalized and often formalized techniques.

9. Asian performance often assumes an audience educated in the conventions which guide and shape the performance form.

10. Asian performance is generally characterized by the coexistence of multiple functions, i.e., the same performance may simultaneously serve as a religious ritual or a means to a spiritual end or goal while entertaining its participants/ spectators.

These ten basic shared features of Asian performance display a unified, organic and decidedly non-Western view of man. There is no attempt in traditional forms of Asian theatre to create the illusion of reality. Reality is always present, but distilled, filtered, and colored by the religious/philosophical systems which shape the individual culture of origin, as well as by the conventions of the performance genre and aesthetic tradition. (Since the nineteenth century and the advent of close Occidental/Oriental contact, modern

Western performance styles, especially realism, have become an important part of an urban, Western-educated and informed art community. Such Western-based forms of performance as modern theatre and dance were at first merely attempts to copy Western plays and styles of performance. More recently contemporary Asian theatre movements have been reexamining their own cultural and performance roots so that such performance now serves as a mediator between traditional and modern modes of performance.)

While these are undeniably shared features of Asian performance, one cannot but be struck by the vast differences which separate an individual Asian culture's mode of shaping these general features. The reserved, contemplative, slow, and what appear to the novice to be irregular rhythmic patterns of the Japanese Noh makes it seem at best a distant cousin to the flamboyant, vigorous, masculine, often fast-paced, and consistently cyclical, repetitive Indian Kathakali dance-drama. The Noh actor outwardly at first appears passive--the face, if not covered by a mask, is itself a mask. Both actual mask and facial mask serve as one part of the Noh performer's modes of expression of the figure that he is presenting. The apparent impassivity is a vehicle for subtle, inner expression. How different that "impassive" face appears from the constant gesticulation, movement, and vibrancy in the independent articulation of each individual muscle in the Kathakali actor's face! All these highly codified and articulated movements of the facial and eye muscles, however, are but a part of the conventionalized system of creation of the Kathakali "figure." For the individual able to go beyond the surface differences, able to probe into the inner processes which inform the performer's art, it is at the substrata beneath the external form that the unity of Asian performance lies hidden. While the Noh and Kathakali actors perform within the constraints of their own highly evolved and articulated aesthetic and performative systems, they share an undeniable link.

The very diversity and complexity of the field of Asian performance has precluded publication of many works which address either the common features of Asian performance, or the individual expressions of each cultural area. Such cross- and pancultural study demands years of field experience and an intimate knowledge of a number of Asian cultures. Without a doubt the most important individual in the field who has provided an overview in his writings is A. C. Scott. In The Theatre in Asia, (New York: Macmillan Publishing Co., Inc., 1972) Scott makes available one of the few comprehensive overviews of the field. The volume includes specific chapters on India, the Islamic world, China, and Japan. The introductory chapter, "The Framework of Asian Theatre," is an excellent place to begin a study of Asian performance, including Asian movement. Scott's wide-ranging discussion covers sources of Asian performance in storytelling and puppetry, and then goes on to discuss the main ingredients of Asian performance including primacy of the performer, pantomime and gesture, form in movement, combat, masking, music, mood, and the contemporary situation of the meeting of West with East. This otherwise excellent and readable introduction to the vast range of Asian performance relegates much important information to footnotes and does not devote an equal amount of attention to the theatre of Southeast Asia.

Of his other writings, one of the most important is Scott's "Reflections on the Aesthetic Background of the Performing Arts of East Asia," (Asian Music, 6, 1-2, 1975, pp. 207-216). This article is one of the few attempts at a pan-Asian understanding of principles and practices of movement through an examination of both movement itself and principles which guide cultural systems of movement. Scott draws on Indian, Japanese, and Chinese examples in his discussion of Asian approaches to movement through controlled gesture, which by its brilliance of performance technique carries an immediate power of suggestion and communication to an audience. He goes on to discuss general movement, hand gestures, dance, and one of the most significant sources of the Asian actor's evolved art of movement --combat systems. Throughout, principles and practices of Zen Buddhism are used as a composite Asian (India-China-Japan) nexus of practice/principle to illuminate examples and observations in contrast to Western theatre movement and practice. While by Scott's admission these are "fragmentary" comments, the article is an exciting provocation for further research, observation and cross-cultural comparison of Asian principles and techniques of movement. Like his other work, this article is suffused with Scott's own empathetic understanding of Asian systems of movement gained from his years of practical (in Chinese martial art T'ai Chi Ch'uan) as well as academic study of Asian forms.

In addition to Scott's work, the reader can turn to several edited collections of materials which provide a rich invitation to many forms and features of Asian performance from the classical and traditional to the modern. These cross-cultural sourcebooks include James Brandon, ed., The Performing Arts in Asia (Paris: Unesco, 1971); Eliot Deutsch, Studies in Comparative Aesthetics (Honolulu: University Press of Hawaii, 1975), "Theatre in Asia," (special issue of The Drama Review, 15, 3, 1971); Adrienne Kaeppler, Judy Van Zile, and Carl Wolz, eds., Asian and Pacific Dance: Selected Papers from the 1974 Cord-Sem Conference (CORD Dance Research Annual, VIII, 1977). Each collection contains important contributions on a variety of individual Asian performance forms and/or on comparative aesthetic principles and traditions which inform performance in an Asian culture.

Given the conjoining of the arts in Asia, a helpful additional introductory text to the field of Asian performance is William Malm's Music Cultures of the Pacific, the Near East and Asia (Englewood Cliffs, N.J.: Prentice-Hall, Inc., 1977). Malm's text is a solid introduction to Asian musical styles and instruments.

A few other publications on Asian theatre approach cross-cultural performance thematically and historically. For example, several authors have researched the important historical links between performance in India and Southeast Asia through the transmission of Indian epics. Suresh Awasthi's "The Ramayana Theatre Tradition in India and South-East Asia" (Quarterly Journal of the National Centre for the Performing Arts, 1, 1, 1972, pp. 47-60) is a general comparative survey of the stylization and conventions of the Rama saga in traditional theatre, puppet theatre, and modern dance-dramas in these countries. S. Singaravelu treats the same topic in his, "The Ramayana and Its Influence in the Literature, Drama and Art of South and Southeast Asia," (Tamil Culture, 12, 1966, pp. 303-14).

Mention should also be made of those works which treat Asian performance as part of a total field of performance. For example, E. T. Kirby uses a number of examples of Asian performance in his Ur-Drama (New York: New York University Press, 1975) which reopens the question of the origins of theatre and presents the hypothesis that the origins of performance are found in shamanism and trance dance. Kirby takes examples from Indian demon dancing, Chinese mediums, Japanese Noh, as well as Western forms such as the Greek theatre and European folk and mummers' plays. Andrea Lommel's Masks: Their Meaning and Function (London: Paul Elek Books, 1972) describes and analyzes the role of masked ceremony and drama through the world and in this context includes several sections on Asia.

The Interface: Asian and Western Performance

The influence of Asian theatre on modern and postmodern performance and performance theory reads like a who's who in the world of playwriting as well as performance: Yeats, Wilder, Miller, St. Denis, Craig, Claudel, Eisenstein, Barrault, Artaud, Brecht, Meyerhold, Grotowski, Schechner, Brook, Kei Takei, Monk ... the list could go on. Nearly every major figure of twentieth-century performance has considered, reflected upon, and often been inspired by Asian performance. The two most important general sources which provide a background for a study of the interface in modern theory and practice of performance are Leonard C. Pronko's well-known Theater East and West: Perspectives Toward a Total Theater (Berkeley: University of California Press, 1967) and Part V of E. T. Kirby's anthology, Total Theatre, entitled, "The Oriental Stage: Hieroglyphic Form," (N.Y.: Dutton, 1969). Pronko's book invites the reader to a discovery of the feast of Asian theatre by examining some of the major forms of Asian theatre and the influence they have had on many major figures in contemporary Western theatre. He covers Balinese performance, Chinese Opera, Noh, and Kabuki. Kirby's edited collection of essays is preceded by a brief three-page introduction in which he draws parallels between Asian

and Occidental performance and introduces each of the essays
(authored by Eisenstein, Pronko, Claudel, Barrault, Artaud, and
the modern dancer, Sophia Delza).

For the individual interested in pursuing the topic of the history of the influence of Asian performance on modern Western performance, a few of many possible sources are suggested here as a
beginning guide. An important early secondary source is Earl
Miner's The Japanese Tradition in British and American Literature
(Princeton: Princeton University Press, 1958) which traces the
historical relationship between and influence of Japanese literature
upon British and American authors. While Miner's volume concentrates on literary influences, he includes one chapter on "Kabuki
and Noh as Dramatic Criteria" and another on form and the Noh in
Yeats' plays. Another secondary source of importance on Yeats'
relationship to the Noh stage is Akhtar Qamber's Yeats and the Noh,
With Two Plays for Dancers by Yeats (New York: Weatherhill,
1974).

Major primary sources for the study of a few of the major
twentieth-century theatrical theorists/practitioners influenced by
Asian theatre include the following. Edward Braun's translation,
Meyerhold on Theatre (New York: Hill and Wang, 1969), includes
several brief commentaries on Asian performance, especially Japanese. Arnold Rood's Gordon Craig on Movement and Dance (New
York: Dance Horizons, 1977) has a number of entries in which
the topic is Craig's ruminations on Oriental theatre. John Willett's
edited collection on Brecht, Brecht on Theatre (New York: Hill
and Wang, 1957) includes Brecht's essay, "Alienation Effects in
Chinese Acting." Antonin Artaud's The Theatre and Its Double
(New York: Grove Press, 1958) contains several important essays on Asian performance, "On the Balinese Theater," and "Oriental and Occidental Theater." Sergei Eisenstein's Film Form (New
York: Harcourt Brace Jovanovich, 1949) includes his most important essays on Asian form, "The Unexpected," and "The Cinematographic Principle and the Ideogram."

While many other primary and secondary sources exist, the
sources cited above may serve as a beginning point for a study of
the history of East/West theatrical interface. More specialized studies abound, mostly in the form of journal articles such as Maria P.
Alter's "Bertolt Brecht and the Noh Drama," (Modern Drama, 11, 1,
1961, pp. 130-136).

Among the most important stimuli which perked interest in
Asian theatre in this century have been the search for inspiration
in myth and ritual, the search for artistic inspiration and "new"
aesthetic forms, and finally the search for "new" techniques of
performance and performer training. As Western directors and
performers searched for responses to the mainstream of Euro-
American theatre, Asian theatrical forms and techniques presented

the explorer with models of total theatrical forms where the actor appeared to be a consummate and selfless performer whose sheer physical/technical virtuosity could dazzle the most innocent bystander. The simple staging means and methods, the acceptance of highly conventionalized techniques of stage deportment, the minimal means of theatrical realization, and the archetypal representation of characters offered the Western theatre artist an exciting panorama of possibilities for infusion of new life into his stale theatre world at home.

From the early experiments in dramatic form of William Butler Yeats, based on his limited understanding of the Noh theatre of Japan to the relatively recent techniques which Jerzy Grotowski borrowed from Kathakali; from the inspiration provided Bertolt Brecht by Mei Lan-fang, the famous female impersonator of the Chinese Peking Opera stage, to the flights of fancy created by Antonin Artaud's experience with Balinese dance in Paris, Asian theatre has influenced most of the major theatre practitioners and theoreticians of the twentieth century. All such influences might best be understood as falling into two general categories. First of all, Asian performance techniques have often served as the stimulus for the creation of expressive performance models.

One example of many is that of Bertolt Brecht. Brecht's critique of Mei Lan-fang's performance techniques, observed in Moscow in the spring of 1935, led to his first recorded conceptualization of Verfremdungseffekt, in "Alienation Effects in Chinese Acting." Brecht's experience gave him an expressive model for the conceptualization of his own approach to acting. In much the same way Brecht himself drew upon Japanese and Chinese scenographic models in his productions, most often using the suggestive and sparse constructions which could provide the types of image juxtaposition he wished in his total productions.

A second decisive way in which Asian performance techniques have influenced Western acting and actor training is direct adaptation of specific techniques. This type of influence comes from a much more intimate knowledge of actual performance techniques than does the expressive model. Brecht did not need to learn Peking Opera acting in order to receive inspiration for the crystallization of his ideas--he merely had the experience of observing one performance demonstration.

The single most important example in the Western theatre world of the potential value of adaptations and integration of Asian techniques and insights into performer training is found in Grotowski's use of Kathakali, documented in Towards A Poor Theatre. It was in this book that Grotowski discussed his training techniques, so sought after as a means of psychophysical work during the 1960's. Grotowski's "plastiques" demanded of the Western performer the same type of fluidity and elasticity of body needed by the Kathakali performer. Drawing on an eclectic number of sources, Grotowski constructed his own exercises. Grotowski stated the purpose for his exercises:

> To discover those resistances and obstacles which hinder him (the actor) in his creative task. Thus the exercises become a means of overcoming these personal impediments. The actor no longer asks himself: "How can I do this?" Instead, he must know what not to do, what obstructs him. By a personal adaptation of the exercises, a solution must be found for the elimination of these obstacles which vary for each individual actor (p. 133).

In his exercises for the "facial mask," Eugenio Barba (who recorded these exercises for Grotowski) included those based on both Delsarte and Kathakali.

> The reactions of the face correspond closely with the reactions of the entire body. This does not, however, exempt the actor from executing facial exercises. In this respect, in addition to Delsarte's prescriptions, the type of training for the facial musculature used by the actor from the classical Indian theatre, Kathakali, is appropriate and useful.
> This training aims to control every muscle of the face, thus transcending stereotyped mimicry. It involves a consciousness and use of every single one of the actor's facial muscles. It is very important to be able to set in motion simultaneously, but at different rhythms, the various muscles of the face. For example, make the eyebrows quiver very fast while the cheek muscles tremble slowly, or the left side of the face react vivaciously while the right side is sluggish (pp. 145-6).

Eugenio Barba related in correspondence the story of how these Kathakali exercises came to be included in Grotowski's exercises. While Grotowski had traveled to India several times, he probably only saw Kathakali in Europe. It was Barba himself who went to the Kerala Kalamandalam in 1963 for a short three-week stay. During his stay he observed Kathakali training, but did not take classes. On his return to Europe in February, 1964, Barba went to Opole, Poland where he explained "the exercises and other impressions I had gathered to Grotowski and his collaborators. Some of the exercises I had explained, especially the eye ones, were adapted to the training the Laboratory's actors were following at that time." Grotowski's use of such selected techniques, along with his other contacts with Indian theatre, have been well documented and discussed by M. Christopher Byrski in "Grotowski and the Indian Tradition," (Sangeet Natak, 23, 1972, pp. 16-25).

In his own work after leaving the Polish Laboratory Theatre, Eugenio Barba also introduced specific Kathakali exercises into his system of actor training. Writing of the use of his India experiences, Barba notes in "Words or Presence," (The Drama Review, 16, 1, 1972, pp. 47-54):

> At the very beginning (of my own work in Scandinavia), I tried to introduce into the training some elements from Kathakali--eye training, leg-training. But very soon we abandoned this attempt since our work took a completely different course.

While he abandoned as counterproductive to his goals the use of such specific Asian theatre techniques, Barba discusses how Kathakali has continued to inspire his vision of the type of theatre he wished to create:

> What has remained within me is the sort of suggestive power which I felt the Kathakali actor had in spite of the conditions in which he was performing. This sort of suggestivity has become a reference point in my speeches to my collaborators and others. But of course, it could not be achieved by imitating or adapting the superficial outer layer of a technique which originated within a different cultural context, with a very different aesthetic from our European one. How could we Europeans--as actors--become as suggestive as the Kathakali or other Oriental actors? How could we reach a suggestivity which did not put a layer on the personal and historical experiences the actor had undergone? This has been the preoccupation in my work. But the Kathakali actor stands for me as a distant, glittering star helping me to find my way to some other galaxy.

Barba traces his group's transition from an initial "program of set exercises that we taught everybody and that everybody had to follow" termed "bio-mechanics" (after Meyerhold's work) to a "process of self-definition, far removed from any utilitarian justification and guided by individual subjectivity." The initial set of exercises, in addition to the Kathakali adaptations, were developed eclectically from "ballet, mime, pure gymnastics, Hatha-Yoga, and acrobatics." Barba feels that his own performance group, shedding adherence to such specific techniques, broke the "myth of technique."

> In the beginning of our activity we too believed in the "myth of technique," something which it was possible to acquire, to possess, and which would have allowed the actor to master his own body, to become conscious of it. So, at this stage, we practiced exercises to develop the dilation of the eyes in order to increase our expressiveness. They were exercises which I had taken from India while studying the training of Kathakali actors. The expressiveness of the eyes is essential in Kathakali, and the control of their musculature demands several hours of hard

training daily for many years. The different nuances each have a precise significance; the way of frowning, the direction of a glance, the degree of opening or closing the lids are codified by tradition and are in fact concepts and images which are immediately comprehensible to the spectator. Such control in a European actor would only restrain the organic reactions of the face and transform it into a lifeless mask.

Barba's use of Kathakali passed from his original adaptation of specific techniques for Grotowski's Polish Lab, and then his own work, to an expressive model in which the Kathakali actor continues to hold for Barba a vision of what can be achieved through his new approach of self-definition. Barba concluded that it is

meaningless to go to Japan or India and take exercises from Kabuki or Kathakali in order to adapt them passively to the European pedagogical tradition, in the hope that our actors too might become "virtuosi" like their Oriental colleagues. Let me repeat, it is not the exercises in themselves that are decisive, but one's personal attitude, that inner necessity which incites and justifies on an emotional level and with a logic that will not allow itself to be trapped by words, the choice of one's own profession.

This rejection of pure Kathakali techniques for the Western actor is an important historical documentation of Barba's own artistic evolution and the change in attitudes among some members of the theatre community since the 1960's.

Out of Eugenio Barba's years of experimental work in Western theatre and intimate contact with Asian performance comes one of the most important reflections on the interface between theatre of various cultures in his recent article, "Theatre Anthropology," (The Drama Review 26, 2, 1982, pp. 5-32). Barba's version of "theatre anthropology ... studies the sociocultural and physiological behavior of man in a performance situation" in order to attempt to find out "how to construct the material bases of his art." The first task is to attempt to trace "recurrent principles" discoverable across styles and cultures of performance. Barba seeks such principles, not to discover universal laws, but rather as a practical assistance to the performer concerned with the practice of theatre. He seeks to discover what is common and shared in performance, rather than what makes performance within culture unique (as would the scholar of Asian theatre or anthropology). In the Introduction to his extended article, Barba differentiates between the Occidental and Oriental actor. The substance of the article is then devoted to an examination of different performance traditions and principals of a number of different Asian cultures. Barba's search for principles at his Odin Teatret institute has joined together a collection of individuals from a variety of disciplines, including scientists, scholars

of both Asian and European theatres, and practicing artists of a
wide range of performance traditions. The remainder of the article
documents Barba and his collaborators' search for principles-in-
practice, always raising the question of the interface between West
and East, Occident and Orient. Each of the principles that Barba
examines is of great interest and importance for all those who study
movement. For example, the first principle that Barba explores is
the difference between the use of the body in daily life and the use
of the body in performance. After examining a number of examples
from Asian performance, he concludes that there are three types of
body use: (1) daily use in which "techniques have communication
as their aim"; (2) virtuostic techniques in which they "aim for
amazement and the transformation of the body"; and (3) extradaily
techniques in which the aim is "information; they literally put the
body in-form." The remainder of the article builds from these basic notions of body use. Barba's process of reflection is provocative, stimulating, and revealing. Without a doubt this is the most
important single source written in recent years on the interface between Western and Asian performance. In the course of the article
Barba brings into his discussion of principles many of the most important forms of classical Asian theatre including Peking Opera, Noh,
Kabuki, Kathakali, Balinese dance, and Kyogen.

In addition to Barba's recent article, several of the most important other general discussions of the use of techniques and principles in the training and performance of Western actors are Robert
Benedetti's "What We Need to Learn from the Asian Actor," (Educational Theatre Journal, 25, 1973, pp. 463-68), and Lee Worley's discussion of the principles and techniques of the theatre program at
Naropa Institute entitled, "On Acting," (Performing Arts Journal,
3, 2, 1978, pp. 53-60). In addition, the work of one individual scholar, Mark Nearman, is making available to the performance community
translations and commentaries on Zeami's treatises. The significance
of Nearman's work (see "Zeami's Kyui," Monumenta Nipponica, 33, 3,
1978, pp. 299-332; and "Kyakuraika: Zeami's Final Legacy for the
Master Actor," Monumenta Nipponica, 35, 2, 1980, pp. 153-198),
is that his commentaries speak in terms that performers can understand. And it is precisely these principles which Barba, Benedetti,
and Worley, each in his own manner, are groping toward and addressing.

While Barba rejected the passive use of specific Asian techniques in training, others have used such techniques creatively and
not just as panaceas for the lack of established, disciplined sets of
received Western body techniques. Not just techniques, but techniques and the principles embodied in the Asian theatre form are
sources for others working from Asian theatre back to the West.
One such individual who has studied Kathakali intensively is Julie
Portman. Although Ms. Portman's work is relatively unknown, it
is representative of a growing number of practitioners and per-
former/scholars who have studied specific forms of Asian performance

in depth with masters and applied the techniques and insights of such studies to Western performance. Julie Portman was first introduced to Asian theatre by A. C. Scott who was directing the University of Wisconsin-Madison Asian Theatre Program. Ms. Portman, after receiving M.A. and M.F.A. degrees in theatre and theatre direction, began her professional career in Boston where she was founder and artistic director of Theatre Workshop, Boston. For Ms. Portman, work and experimentation in new forms of theatre led to a revival of interest in the past; to the basic principles of dance-drama at work in the oldest and most traditional forms of theatre still existing today, particularly as found in Asian theatre. In 1970, Ms. Portman was awarded a Fulbright grant to travel to India where she studied Kathakali dance-drama as a private student of V. P. Ramakrishnan. In 1972 she made her debut in Kerala, India, as a Kathakali actor, playing the role of Lord Krishna at Guruvayur, Kerala. Since her return Ms. Portman first developed a group of "small theatre pieces for solo performer inspired by my own work in Kathakali and influenced as well by my studies in classical voice" and then pursued her "interest in the fusion of Eastern and Western forms of classical dance-drama" ("Agamemnon at Tufts University," Asian Theatre Bulletin, 5, 2, 1979, p. 10). Ms. Portman's performance of "Inspirations from the East" included in 1979 a two-part program. Part I consisted of "Techniques of Kathakali-dance-drama" while Part II included three poems "interpreted in mime, movement, gesture, sound and song."

After joining the faculty of Tufts University as artist-in-residence, Ms. Portman staged a production of Aeschylus' Agamemnon adapted from Gilbert Murray's translation. In a brief article explaining her approach to the production, Ms. Portman discusses the fusion of Kathakali techniques and inspiration with the Greek materials:

> The production will incorporate the use of symbolic gesture, archetypal characterization and expression of emotion, dance as ornamentation and several dramatic conventions inspired by my experience as a student of Kathakali. The objective of this production is a retranslation of the Agamemnon into an artistically meaningful ritual form.

For Julie Portman, Kathakali has provided a specific experience of a highly stylized form of theatre whose techniques and principles of stylization serve as an inspiration for her own creative work as a performer and director. Certainly her period of intensive Kathakali training in Kerala provided her with sufficient immersion in Kathakali's basic techniques to have the singular ability to transform both the techniques and principles knowledgeably in her own creative work. This is one of the major factors which differentiates the work of individuals like Julie Portman from Eugenio Barba and others. Her work is colored by her personal immersion and intimate knowledge of the form as learned and practiced in the indigenous culture.

Among the many other young performer/scholars two have published several important contributions on Balinese mask theatre (topeng) and their own experience and transformation of the form to the Western context. Ron Jenkins has authored two important articles including "Topeng: Balinese Dance Drama" (Performing Arts Journal, 3, 2, 1978, pp. 39-52) and "Becoming a Clown in Bali," (The Drama Review, 23, 2, 1979, pp. 40-56). John Emigh's excellent introduction to topeng, "Playing With the Past: Visitation and Illusion in the Mask Theatre of Bali," (The Drama Review, 23, 2, 1979, pp. 11-36), along with the accompanying translation by I Nyoman Kakul, of "Jelantik Goes to Blambangan," (pp. 37-48) may serve as a prelude to the two outstanding video documents which Emigh created for Farley Richmond's Michigan State series on "Asian Acting Techniques for Western Actors and Directors." Emigh's companion video pieces, "Acting Techniques of Topeng, Masked Theatre of Bali," and "Adopting Topeng, The Masked Theatre of Bali," are a delight as he introduces the various Balinese masks as guides to character interpretation, movement, and vocalization. The highlight of Emigh's work are the excerpts from Little Red Riding Shawl which incorporate the topeng masks, movement, training, and performance structure in the Western context.

Julie Portman's Agamemnon and John Emigh's Little Red Riding Shawl are both examples of "translations and transformations" of Asian techniques and principles to produce new Western works for a Western audience. Other Westerners working in Asian theatre have also produced "recreations or reproductions" of traditional Asian plays in the indigenous style. Two of the most important documents discussing the history and practical problems of producing traditional plays in translation with Westerners are James Brandon's, "Kabuki in English: Toward Authenticity," (in Japanese Tradition: Search and Research, edited by Judith Mitoma Susilo, Los Angeles: University of California, Los Angeles, 1981, pp. 73-91), and Leonard Pronko's videotape, "Kabuki for Western Actors and Directors" (Michigan State University series). Brandon's article presents the history of Kabuki productions at the University of Hawaii over many years and projects a possible future for authentic Kabuki in America. Pronko's videotape includes filmed illustrations of productions and slides of his transformation of The Revenger's Tragedy to Kabuki style.

A most important resource in the area of performance interface at the production and training level has been Asian Theatre Bulletin, and more recently Asian Theatre Journal. Asian Theatre Bulletin contains reviews of Western reproductions of traditional Asian plays, as well as documentation of experiments in application of Asian form and technique to Western plays. Although articles are brief and succinct, some important commentary on performer training has appeared in recent issues. Of particular interest are Kathy Foley's "Thoughts on Learning Another Culture's Performance Art," (Asian Theatre Bulletin, 8, 1, 1982, p. 1); Farley Richmond's "Why Reinvent the Wheel?" (Asian Theatre Bulletin, 5, 2,

1979, pp. 9-10); and Leonard Pronko's note on "Western Influence on Traditional Asian Performance," (Asian Theatre Bulletin, 5, 1, 1979, p. 8). Craig Turner offers an important and provocative note on masked acting and training in "Experimenting with Japanese Noh Masks in Western Actor Training," (Asian Theatre Bulletin, 6, 2, 1980, p. 29).

The interface between Asian and Western performance is a constant process. Each year new Western experiments, plays, productions are fertilized by Asian insights or techniques. David Henry Hwang's The Dance and the Railroad draws heavily on the Peking Opera (produced in New York in 1981). The recent history of the Time and Space Limited Theatre Company under the direction of Linda Mussman has been to focus on Japanese theatre in their productions of The Bandit Princess and Katana (1980) by contemporary female Japanese playwright, Kikue Tashiro.

One of the longest and most fertile areas of interface in performance training and body work has been the use of Asian martial arts in Western actor training. The "Asian Martial Arts" chapter is a further and more specific development of the long-term and rich process of interface between East and West.

Audio-Visual Sources for Asian Performance: A Guide to Major Collections

The most important resources available for study of Asian movement are films and videotapes. Within the limitations of the media, raw footage of the film or videotape, regardless of the narration, camera angle, point of view, etc. still presents the student with a moving image in space. While each of the specific sections of the bibliography which follow contain recommended audiovisual resources, what follows here is a cataloguing of major collections and series of resources available on Asian performance. Individual films and videotapes are listed and annotated under the appropriate geographical area.

The Asia Society, Asian Performing Arts Resources, (725 Park Avenue, New York, New York 10021.

The Asia Society Performing Arts Department makes available the most extensive set of Asian performance and audiovisual materials in existence. Resources include videotapes, films, slides, publications, and records. The series of videotapes has been made in New York studios whenever the Society sponsors a group of performing artists from Asia. While the introductory commentary is at times distracting, the videotapes are an invaluable resource for at least brief glimpses of Asian movement systems. The monographs on many of the forms presented in video format, written by leading Asian performance scholars, are an important introductory resource

which should be used in conjunction with videotape viewing. A
catalogue of complete resources is available on request.

Asian Theatre Program, "Asian Film Lending Library":
(Film Service, 746 Massachusetts, Lawrence, Kansas 60044).

Established as a project of the Asian Theatre Program of the American Theatre Association, the Asian Film Lending Library includes
films and videotapes of a variety of Asian performances. Some
films and tapes are of indigenous Asian performances produced on
location in Asia. Other tapes and films are productions of Asian
plays in translation and have been produced in the United States.

Institute for the Advanced Study of Theatre Arts (IASTA):
(310 West 56th Street, New York, New York 10019).

IASTA was an early pioneer in producing traditional Asian plays
by matching guest Asian professionals with American professional
actors. Five of IASTA's film resources are on Asian topics. Although the production quality of the films is generally poor, they
provide brief if inadequate glimpses into some early experiments in
East/West interface.

Japan Foundation/Mitsu Productions: "Asian Traditional
Dance and Musics" (#602 Nishi-Azabu Condominium, Nishi-
Azabu 3-8-11, Minato-ku, Tokyo, 106, Japan).

The series to date includes five 16mm color sound films made on
location in various parts of India. Much of the footage shown includes lengthy shots of performances.

Lincoln Center for Performing Arts Library: Dance Film
Collection.

The Dance Film Collection at the Lincoln Center Library in New
York represents a major repository for the archival collection of
films and videotapes of dance and dance-drama forms from Asia.
Not only do the holdings include many of the major film and video
documents available for general distribution, more importantly the
collection houses rare and often "one only" copies of many unique
videotapes. The collection includes both materials made on location
in Asia, and also documentation of performances and training sessions of Asian performers while in the United States, or of experiments and adaptations of Asian techniques in the Western setting.
One example of the entries describing works in the collection follows:

Mala nrtta [and] Symphony #6 in G Major (Videotape) 1978.
26 min. sound. b. & 2. E1A-J. 1/2 in. 1 reel.
Videotapes in performance on June 2, 1978 at the High
School Printing Auditorium, N.Y. Performed by dancers

of the class of 1978, School of Performing Arts, N.Y.
Contents: Mala Nrtta. Choreography: Matteo. Music:
traditional South Indian (first movement) and Joseph
Haydn. In 3 movements: Ranga Puga, danced by Rox-
anne Artesone; Chanda Lasya; Namste. (The two last
movements danced by the company, are a synthesis of
Western music with Bharata Natyam dance techniques).

The range of materials is far reaching. Included in the following
list are just a few selections which serve as a representative sample of the holdings:

> Mohiniyattam. 13 min. sd. color 1978. Videotape of
> performance at University of Hawaii by Betty Jones and
> Sandra Hurlong.
> The Red Detachment of Women. 1972. 120 min. Telecast
> NBC, 1972. China Ballet Troupe of Peking.
> Dances of Bali. 1973. 30 min.
> Indrani and Her Classical Dancers of India. 1975. 55 min.
> WGBH Boston.
> Music and Dance of Pakistan. 1973. 30 min. WCBS-TV.
> "Camera Three." Performance by members of the National
> Folk Ensemble of Pakistan.
> Ram Thai: Dance Art of Thailand. 1978. 30 min.
> WCBS-TV. "Camera Three."
> Religious and Ceremonial Dances from Tibet. 1977. 50
> min. Videotaped at Brooklyn College 1975. Performed
> by Tibetan Lhama Society.
> Miyabi Ichikowa. Japanese Traditional Dances. Videotapes.
> 23 min.

(All of the holdings in the collection are noncirculating. Appoint-
ments for viewing are required.)

> Michigan State University Instructional Media Center: "Asian
> Theatre, Techniques and Application" (Marketing Division,
> Michigan State University, East Lansing, MI 48824).

An extremely important new addition to audiovisual materials on
Asian theatre, this recent series concentrates on both traditional
forms of Asian performance as well as the interface between East
and West. Under the guidance of Professor Farley Richmond, the
series includes three major sets of tapes categorized under the
following general titles: Part I: Techniques, Part II: Application,
and Part III: Performances. Each tape features a guest expert on
a particular aspect of Asian performance. Guests include both
Asians as well as Western scholar/practitioners. Tapes in Part I
explore basic performance techniques of specific forms, while those
in Part II stress application of Asian techniques to the training of
Western performers.

There are numerous bibliographies covering Asia generally, and there are many highly specialized reference works, all of which could provide guidance to useful, related information. However, those bibliographies cited here deal exclusively with theatre, or else offer substantial theatre listings within their broader content.

Bibliographic Guide to Dance. Boston: G. K. Hall and Co., 1976- .
Annual bibliographical supplement to the Dictionary Catalog of the Dance Collection.

Bibliography of Asian Studies. Association for Asian Studies, Inc., University of Michigan, 1956- .
A periodic publication, with comprehensive coverage of Western language scholarly monographs and articles concerning East, South and Southeast Asia. Arranged by region, country, and subjects including dance and theatre.

Brandon, James R. ed. "Asian Theatre: A Study Guide and Annotated Bibliography." Theatre Perspectives, No. 1, University and College Theatre Association (1980).
A very good general guide with brief annotations, covering history, theory, practice, plays, audiovisual materials and reference works.

Dictionary Catalog of the Dance Collection. Boston: G. K. Hall and Company, 1974. 10 vols.
Author, title and subject listing of multimedia materials in the Performing Arts Research Center of the N.Y. Public Library. An excellent comprehensive source with many pertinent citations.

Richmond, Farley. "Asian Theatre Materials: A Selected Bibliography." The Drama Review, 15, 3 (Spring 1971), pp. 312-23.
A good, general resource.

General Works

Awasthi, Suresh. "The Ramayana Theatre Tradition in India and South-East Asia (The First International Ramayana Festival)." Quarterly Journal of the National Centre for the Performing Arts, 1, 1 (Sept. 1972), pp. 47-60.
A general comparative survey of the stylization and conventions of the Rama saga in traditional theatre, puppet theatre and modern dance-dramas in these countries.

Benedetti, Robert L. "What We Need to Learn from the Asian Actor." Educational Theatre Journal, 25 (1973), pp. 463-68.
Discusses a "sense of the centre," "relaxation," and discipline of the Asian actor in performance based on observations of performance demonstrations.

Bennett, Isadora. "A Primer on Asian Dance." Ballet Review, IV, 5 (1973), pp. 71-100.
A simplified, potentially misleading introduction to the music and dance of Asia, particularly focusing on India, Japan, Thailand, and Korea. The article also attempts to relate dance forms to religious roots.

Bowers, Faubion. Theatre in The East: A Survey of Asian Dance and Drama. New York: Grove Press, 1960.
A general introduction to forms in South, Southeast and East Asia.

Brandon, James R. Brandon's Guide to Theater in Asia. Honolulu: The University Press of Hawaii, 1976.
A handy and useful practical guide for theatregoing throughout Asia listed by country.

_____, ed. The Performing Arts in Asia. Paris: Unesco, 1971.
A collection of papers delivered at the 1969 Beirut Round Table focusing on the relationship between indigenous performing arts and the new mass arts of radio, television, and film. The contributions are arranged in four parts and include: (1) an overview of two of the main theories of Asian performance found in the Indian Natyasastra and Zeami's theory of Noh; (2) a description of the contemporary state of theatre in seven Asian countries introduced by a "View from the West"; (3) accounts of the technological media in various Asian countries; and (4) summaries of major discussion topics.

Brockett, Oscar. History of the Theatre, 4th ed. Boston: Allyn and Bacon, 1982.
Chapter 10, "The Theatre of the Orient," is a general introduction with emphasis on the theatre of China and Japan.

Deutsch, Eliot. Studies in Comparative Aesthetics. Honolulu: University Press of Hawaii, 1975.
Includes very good essays on the concept of rasa in Indian theatre and of yugen in Japanese theatre.

The Drama Review. 15, 3 (Spring 1971), "Theatre in Asia" (special issue).
A rich collection of articles and interviews on traditional and modern theatre in Burma, Indonesia, Malaysia, Korea, China, India, and Japan.

Frost, Helen. Oriental and Character Dances. New York: A. S. Barnes and Co., 1930.
A Western version of choreography for selected dances of India, Burma, Tibet, and Ceylon. Accompanying musical scores, based on Indian melodies, composed by Lily Strickland.

Ghosh, Manomohan. Contributions to the History of the Hindu Drama: Its Origin, Development and Diffusion. Calcutta: K. L. Mukhopadhyay, 1958.
A collection of essays on Indian and Southeast Asian traditional theatre.

Graham-White, Anthony. "The Characteristics of Traditional Drama." Yale Theatre, 8, 1 (Fall 1976), pp. 11-24.
Considers nine common characteristics of traditional dramatic forms around the world, including Asian traditional theatre forms.

Gunawardana, A. J. "From Ritual to Rationality: Notes on the Changing Asian Theatre." The Drama Review, 15, 3 (Spring 1971), pp. 48-62.
Examines the nature of exchange between East and West in an insightful article that traces modern developments in Asian theatre.

Hall, F. "Noh, Kabuki, Kathakali." Sangeet Natak 7 (1968), pp. 33-75.
This comparative article discusses the three forms in relation to their common basis in Indian religion, their similarities and differences in theme and character, in acting styles and physicalization, the structure of performance and the role of improvisation, and other aspects which link these three very distinct dramatic forms.

Hartnoll, Phyllis, ed. The Oxford Companion to the Theatre. London: Oxford University Press, 1967.
Includes entries on the drama of China, Japan, India, Malaya, and Java.

Kaeppler, Adrienne L., Judy Van Zile, Carl Wolz, eds. "Asian and Pacific Dance: Selected Papers from the 1974 CORD-SEM Conference." C.O.R.D. Dance Research Annual VIII, 1977.
Excellent articles covering Kutiyattam, ballet in China, Noh, and forms in Polynesia and Java. Also includes a performance chronology of Asian dance in New York City, 1906-1976.

Kirby, E. T. Ur-Drama. New York: New York University Press, 1975.
Reopens the question of the origins of theatre. Presents hypothesis of origins in shamanism and trance dance as "ur-drama." Examples are taken from Indian demon dancing, Chinese mediums, Japanese Noh, Greece, and European folk and mummers' plays.

Lessley, Merrill J. "A Comprehensive Study of Oriental and Occidental Acting." Ph.D. diss. University of Utah, 1969.

Lommel, Andrea. Masks: Their Meaning and Function. London: Paul Elek Books, 1972.
Describes and analyzes the role of masked ceremony and drama throughout the world. Includes several sections on Asia.

Malm, William. Music Cultures of the Pacific, The Near East and Asia. Englewood Cliffs, N.J.: Prentice-Hall, Inc., 1977.
A very good introduction to Asian musical styles and instruments.

Mantzius, Karl. A History of Theatrical Art in Ancient and Modern Times. Trans. Louise von Lossel. New York: Peter Smith, 1937. Six vols.
Contains a number of chapters on Chinese, Indian and Japanese theatre.

Pronko, Leonard. "Oriental Theatre for the West: Problems of Authenticity and Communication." Educational Theatre Journal, 20, 3 (October 1968), pp. 425-46.
Offers practical solutions to the problems in producing Asian plays in the West. Considers such difficulties as language and duration of performance, and the abstract nature of Asian theatre forms.

Ridgeway, William. The Dramas and Dramatic Dances of Non-European Races in Special Reference to the Origin of Greek Tragedy with an Appendix on the Origin of Greek Comedy. Cambridge: Cambridge University Press, 1915.
An attempt to trace the origins of theatre in India, Java, Burma, Cambodia, China, and Japan. Much of the work is now out of date.

Scott, A. C. "Reflections on the Aesthetic Background of the Performing Arts of East Asia." Asian Music, 6, 1-2, (1975), pp. 207-216.
One of the few attempts at an all-Asian understanding of principles and practices of movement through an examination of both movement and principles of movement. Draws on Indian, Japanese, and Chinese examples in discussion of Asian approaches to movement through controlled gesture, which by its brilliance of performance technique carries an immediate power of suggestion and communication to an audience. Goes on to discuss general movement, hand gestures, dance, and one of the most significant sources of the Asian actor's evolved art of movement combat systems. Throughout, principles and practices of Zen are used as a composite Asian (India-China-Japan) nexus of practice/principle to illuminate examples and observations in contrast to Western theatre movement and practice. While by Scott's admission these are "fragmentary" comments, the article is an exciting provocation for further research, observation and cross-cultural comparison. Scott is, indeed, a master of Asian performance who also practices such systems of movement and whose commentary is enhanced by his empathetic and personal assimilation of an insider's understanding of the techniques and qualities of Asian movement.

_____. The Theatre in Asia. New York: Macmillan Publishing Co., Inc. 1972.

One of the few available general overviews of Asian theatre, offering specific chapters on India, the Islamic world, China, and Japan. The introductory chapter, "The Framework of Asian Theatre," is an excellent place to begin a study of Asian performance. Scott's wide-ranging discussion covers sources of Asian performance in storytelling and puppetry, and then goes on to discuss the key ingredients of Asian performance including the primacy of the performer, pantomime and gesture, form in movement, combat, masking, music, mood, and the contemporary situation of the meeting of West and East. This otherwise excellent and readable introduction to the vast range of Asian performance relegates much important information to the footnotes and does not devote an equal amount of attention to the theatre of Southeast Asia.

Shawn, Ted. Gods Who Dance. New York: E. P. Dutton, 1929.
A personal account of dance in most of Asia, as Shawn experienced it while on tour.

Singaravelu, S. "The Ramayana and Its Influence in the Literature, Drama and Art of South and Southeast Asia." Tamil Culture, 12 (October-December 1966), pp. 303-14.
Briefly reviews the role of the Rama epic in the art, architecture, shadow plays and dance-dramas of India, Thailand, and Indonesia. Theatrical forms mentioned are the Wayang Kulit, Wayang Wong, RomLila, and Khon.

Sivaramamurti, C. Nataraja in Art, Thought and Literature.
New Delhi: National Museum, 1974.
A superb study of the theme and symbolism of Nataraja-Siva, Lord of the Dance, as it appears in Indian art and culture, and elsewhere in Asia. The focus on dance is consistent throughout the work. Beautifully illustrated.

Southern, Richard. The Seven Ages of the Theatre. London: Faber and Faber, 1962.
Relates a variety of Asian theatre forms to developments in European and African theatre at various points of theatrical evolution.

Thokur, N. C. "The Open Stage and Its Conventions." Sangeet Natak, 49 (July-September 1978), pp. 5-27.
A cross-cultural comparison of the nature and use of the open stage, as contrasted to proscenium staging. Considers the nature of stylized theatre forms as necessitated by the stage, and also examines the symbolic function of props, the establishment of multiple locales via description or actors' movements, the facilitation of subplots through stage flexibility, the use of "invisible" stage attendants, and other staging conventions.

Vatsyayan, Kapila. "Some Dance Sculptures from Champa." Quarterly Journal of the National Centre for the Performing Arts, 7, 4 (December 1978), pp. 1-19.

One of several articles by this author which traces the history of dance movement patterns in South and Southeast Asia through the sculpture of various periods. By concentrating on Champa sculptures from Vietnam, Vatsyayan points out the pan-Asian dance style which can be traced to the Natyashastra system of India.

_____. "The Dance Sculptures of Lara-Djonggrang (Prambanan)." Quarterly Journal of the National Centre for the Performing Arts, 6, 1 (March 1977), pp. 1-14.

An analysis of the dance sculptures from this Indonesian temple, comparing them to similar sculptures in India and Southeast Asia. By comparative study of the poses and dance styles, the author concludes that these sculptures are not an imitation of Indian models, but that they are evidence of an active dialogue between these countries.

_____. "Some Evidence of Dance in Pagan." Quarterly Journal of the National Centre for the Performing Arts, 6, 4 (December 1977), pp. 1-22.

This well-illustrated article supplements Vatsyayan's earlier article on the dance sculptures of Lara-Djonggrang. Here, the author focuses on bronze, terra cotta figures, wood carvings and paintings in Pagan, Burma, as evidence of an affinity of approach towards dance movement patterns in India, Sri Lanka, and Burma.

Wells, Henry W. "Asian Classical Drama Today." Literature East and West, 10, 3 (September 1966), pp. 220-34.

Discusses the cultural roots and aesthetics of the classical dramas of India, China, and Japan.

Withey, J. A. "Research in Asian Theatre: An Indian Model." Educational Theater Journal, 23, 2 (1971), pp. 127-134.

Dated overview of state of research and materials for study of Indian theatre.

Zarina, Xenia. Classical Dances of the Orient. New York: Crown, 1967.

A general, introductory work.

Chapter Eleven

SOUTH ASIAN PERFORMANCE

Phillip Zarrilli and Rhea Lehman

Introduction: The Organization of the Materials

The South Asia region consists of a number of modern states
including Bangladesh, India, Nepal, Pakistan, Sri Lanka, and Tibet.
While each specific country, its culture, and its cultural performances are equally important, the dominant tradition in the performing arts has historically been Indian. This predominance is manifest
in historical terms, as well as in the sheer volume of materials on
South Asian performance and aesthetic principles. The focus, then,
of the following chapter is on India. The nature, forms, and literature on Indian performance are discussed in the essay portion of
this chapter, which is followed by the specific bibliographical entries
on Indian performance. Following the Indian materials, the literature on performance in the remaining South Asian countries is presented by country, arranged alphabetically.

The Nature of Indian Performance

In India, as in other Asian cultures, the traditional concept
of theatre is often one in which music, dance, and drama converge.
This is clearly delineated in the classical foundation of Indian theatre, the Natyasastra, the encyclopaedic work on Indian theatre compiled by 200 A.D. This ancient Sanskrit treatise distinguishes
three facets of performing which are essential to understanding the
nature of movement in many Indian performance forms. These facets are: nrtta, which is pure, abstract or decorative dance; nrtya,
which is dance with thematic or narrative content; and natya, which
combines language with movement. A given performance form usually involves a combination of these facets in a complex structure.
Similarly, this blending of the elements of dance, music, and drama
is prevalent in folk and ritual forms, as well as in the classical
forms, though the structure and function of the elements may be
quite different. Because of such complex structures, the reader
may encounter some inconsistent use of terminology; some writers
may view a particular form primarily as dance, and rely on dance

245

terminology, while other writers may regard the same form in the terminology of the theatre. The term "dance-drama" is often applied as an acknowledgement of such complexity.

Besides the total nature of Indian performance, there are other general characteristics of traditional forms. The traditional theatres of India rely on common sources for their content. The stories and characters of these forms are drawn from Vedic sources and from the Indian epics, the Mahabharata and the Ramayana. Although the specific conventions of performance traditions may be quite different, the characters are archetypal, exhibiting clearly recognizable traits, in well-known episodes. Audience interest, therefore, is often focused on the performer's technical skill in physicalizing (and in some cases vocalizing) the character within the conventions of the particular tradition. Understanding the performer's training process thus also becomes important in appreciating each tradition.

Another characteristic common to many forms of traditional Indian performance is the distinction between two styles or types of movement, the Tandava style and the Lasya style. Tandava encompasses movement which is vigorous, strong, or typically masculine in nature. Lasya is that movement which is graceful, lyrical, or typically feminine. Although these two styles are prescribed in classical treatises, they are rooted in mythology: the God Siva originated the Tandava style and his consort Parvati originated the Lasya style. With this mythological basis, the understanding of these two distinctive types or qualities of movement pervades most traditional forms.

Western influence and modernization introduced new dimensions in Indian performance. While many of the characteristics of traditional forms are still evident in modern forms, contact with the West has brought new theatres, new plays (Western and native), new choreography, and new production methods. The advent of commercial theatre and the competitive dictates of popular demand have wrought many changes. India's prolific film industry has also had an influence. Major dramatic innovations by Indian playwrights and a new theatre movement resulted as a protest against the trends of commercial theatre. The content of new plays has increasingly involved realistic and secular themes of contemporary social or political relevance. New forms have evolved, and some traditional forms have been adapted, to varying degrees, to meet the needs of cultural change.

India is a nation of vast linguistic and cultural diversity, with an equally vast spectrum of performance forms. And the nature of movement in these many forms is equally diverse. For example, gestures may variously function decoratively, mimetically, naturalistically, or linguistically (as a highly codified sign language). In order to more specifically understand the nature and function of movement in this broad range of Indian performance forms, the three major formal categories used here and by many authors should be clarified. These categories of the classical, folk/regional, and ritual/religious forms should provide the reader with at least a beginning framework for study of Indian performance.

The Forms of Indian Performance

The field of Indian performance is a dynamic, ever-changing panorama. The complexity, volume, and variety of genres and forms is matched by a remarkably high degree of historical continuity and similarity of structure across geographically and linguistically diverse regions. The complexities of the field defy clear categorization in comfortable, easily explainable categories. Yet, in order to describe this field and to differentiate, compare, contrast, and define particular performance forms and to illustrate both their unique, as well as common characteristics, some broadly descriptive categories, or spheres of influence and definition, are necessary. These three broadly descriptive spheres of influence include the classical sphere, the ritual/religious sphere, and the folk/regional sphere.

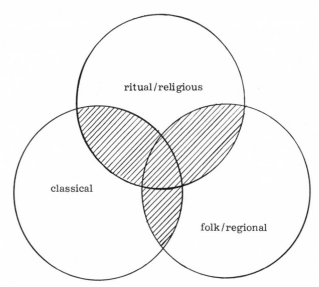

These three spheres interface. The areas of interface and commonality are those of dynamic interplay between and among performance techniques, aesthetic principles, performance styles, languages, texts, socioeconomic groups, and castes. The degree of interface between defining characteristics of each sphere depends upon historical circumstance as well as local/regional developments.

The classical sphere of performance is characterized by a high degree of refinement in performance technique. Refinements are usually made possible by inheritance, preservation, and the strength of tradition to keep changes to those in nuance of expression. Forms which fall primarily within the classical sphere are those which usually follow well-articulated aesthetic principles, most often with reference to the Natyasastra. Classical forms assume a relatively high degree of audience knowledge and education so that the elaborations, refinements, and embellishments presented in performance can be appreciated. Classical forms are usually those for which there has historically been some constant form of traditional patronage, allowing the performers freedom to develop and refine their performance arts. Finally, classical forms tend toward self-conscious recognition among performers as well as patrons of the articulated aesthetic principles which shape the form. Such self-conscious reflexivity of form keeps the performance system relatively closed. Adaptation, change, etc. are protected by the received tradition and aesthetic principles of the form. Those who control the tradition and admissibility of change are usually the senior masters of the form and/or powerful patrons.

In contrast to the classical sphere, the folk/regional sphere is characterized by its immediate accessibility, by its vitality and exuberance, and by its readily communicable modes and message of performance. While the classical sphere of performance embraces refinement in nuance of technique, folk/regional forms tend toward broader expressive gesture and statement. This does not mean that folk performance techniques are easily acquired. On the contrary, many folk performance forms and techniques are as complex and difficult to master as classical forms. While artistic mastery may take years, folk/regional forms do not require an educated or elite audience to appreciate that artistry. Folk/regional performances speak more directly to the people, and there is less mediation by refined aesthetic principles. Indeed, the operative aesthetic principles of folk forms usually include means of achieving immediate communication and rapport with the audience. This concern with immediacy is often reflected in a more open performance structure, with less attention given to guarding performance techniques and traditions. The traditions and techniques of folk forms are there, not to protect or guard a received aesthetic system, but rather to serve the end of accessibility and communication. The operative aesthetic principles are not ends themselves. There is comparatively little self-conscious awareness, adherence to, and appreciation of those principles and their realization. Performers of folk/regional forms may be full-time professionals, but historically they have seldom received patronage from higher castes. Although there are exceptions, if professional, most folk troupes will be dependent on the vicissitudes of the market (i.e., they must keep and hold their

audiences to make their living). On the other hand, many folk/
regional performances are seasonal, and performers are employed
in other occupations in the nonperformance season.

The third major sphere of performance is the ritual/religious.
There are two major types within this broad category: ritual performance and devotional performance, each of which has its own set
of distinguishing features. What is shared by ritual and devotional
performances is the major emphasis given in both to the function of
the performance in its specific context. The overriding concern in
a ritual and/or devotional performance is the achievement of the religious or ritual end--the fulfillment of a vow, the granting of a
boon, or the transportation of the individual into a devotional state
(bhakti).

Ritual performances are first of all religious rituals in which
the primary goal is an efficacious end or purpose. They are organized at the center around the achievement of the desired goal
of the particular ritual, i.e., propitiation of a single deity or group
of deities. The organizational impetus for the performance has a
different center from that found in the folk or classical spheres of
performance. Here the locus and center is the specific function
the ritual serves. However, in India the ritual may and often does
have highly complex and colorful performances which are a part of
the ritual event. Such performance elements may include makeup
and/or masks, elaborate and colorful costuming, properties used
either literally or symbolically to convey appropriate action or to
represent a deity, a wide variety of dance and/or movement patterns set to musical/rhythmic accompaniment, and often the conveying of a story (perhaps a myth or epic) associated with the
deity, deified ancestor, etc. Some ritual performances even include mini-dramas in which there is a more literal enactment of
cosmic and highly dramatic events in the story of the deity, such
as a battle. In ritual performances the performance elements,
while extremely important, serve to highlight and emphasize the
achievement of the ritual. While there is often the use of artifice
in costuming and makeup, it is used to assist in achieving a real
end and goal, often the transformation of the performer into the
deity. According to popular belief, this is an actual transformation of the performer into the deity who may then be worshipped
by the spectator/participants. Once established, ritual performances are often relatively closed systems in which the received
ritual structure must be precisely performed in order for the
efficacy of the ritual to be attained. The priest and/or ritual
specialist is usually the overseer of the received tradition and
responsible for the maintenance of the form.

While a devotional performance also sets out to achieve a desired goal or end, the goal is the transportation and transformation
of the audience/spectators/participants into a state of devotion
(bhakti). In devotional performances people usually come to get

at least a glimpse or a vision of the god (darsan). In the Raslila the object is "to transport the worshiper behind the encrustations of this world to a state of loving simplicity." (John Stratton Hawley, At Play With Krishna. Princeton: Princeton University Press, 1981, p. 50). The direct accessibility and communicability of devotional forms link them closely with the folk/regional sphere of performance. It is in the display and play of the well-known and obvious manifestations of the gods; it is in the revealing of the familiar tableaux; it is in the familiarity of the stories and rhythms of the devotional songs that the emotional effect and transportation of the devotee occurs in such performances.

The three major spheres of Indian performance form a dynamic field where there is constant interplay among and between forms and traditions of performance. No form is in the exclusive domain of one sphere of performance. The classical Sanskrit drama tradition, as well as such extant regional variations as the Kutiyattam style of staging acts of dramas in Kerala, are replete with rituals. While Kutiyattam was nurtured within the confines of the temple and was performed as a visual sacrifice to the presiding deity of the temple, nevertheless it existed historically and is performed today as primarily a classical form of theatre for an elite and educated audience. In all forms of Indian performance multiple functions coexist simultaneously without contradiction.

While classical and folk/regional forms have rituals which are a part of the total structure of the performance event (perhaps including opening prayers for the success of the performance and a closing benediction), the performance may exist as an end in itself. That end may be the union of audience and performers in the creation and realization of sentiments (rasa), or in folk performance, simply the entertainment and delight of the gathered audience. On the other hand, ritual and devotional performances are means to an end other than that contained within the means, techniques, and interactions of performance itself. At times ritual performances may be absorbing, fascinating, even entertaining, but these modes of involvement of the audience/participants will be momentary steps along the path to the ultimate and larger goal of the performance.

Classical, folk, and ritual performances may all use similar means to create their performances. For example, each may use patterning or repetition. However, they will differ in the purpose and degree of self-conscious design used to articulate those patterns and sequences. Repetition may exist in a ritual performance to create a magical/ritual effect. For example being thrown onto a bed of white-hot coals 100 rather than fifty times will double the likelihood the ritual will achieve its efficacious end. On the other hand, classical performance may use repetition to create an aesthetic or stylistic effect through appreciation of and articulation of an intricate design. The intrinsic interest of the spectator/participant in each sphere of performance will likewise differ. For the audience/

participant at a devotional performance, absorption into a state of devotion may be the goal. For the educated elite at a classical performance, absorption in the performance may come in response to cycles of rhythmic patterns so familiar that they awake responses to the moments of congruence in the patterning, or in his or her excitement over a particular performer's interpretation and realization of a role at a specific performance. For the audience member at a folk performance, the intrinsic interest might be in the sexual suggestiveness of a particular actress' or actor's evocative dance, or the sharing of a good laugh as he or she unmistakenly recognizes him or herself or a neighbor in the guise of a broadly caricatured character type appearing onstage. These spheres of performance, then, provide us with windows into Indian performance so that it can be better described and understood. But they are merely windows where the view and scenery are constantly shifting, altering, and changing.

The Literature on Indian Performance

Attempting to work one's way through the dense and diverse forest of literature on Indian performance is a difficult task. For the individual most interested in performance, and more particularly in the use of the body in theatrical traditions, one must contend with a mass of material which may not, at first glance, appear directly relevant to understanding movement or the place of movement in performance. The literature on the subject is not one unified body of work; rather, there simultaneously exist a number of different and diverse "literatures," (and even subliteratures within one category) that make the task more difficult. Indeed, there exist extensive and substantive literatures in the following major areas, all of which are of either historical and/or immediate contemporary importance in understanding the development and current state of movement in Indian performance: the literature concerned with Sanskrit drama, aesthetics, and performance (including the history and origins of theatre in India); the literature exclusively devoted to one or more genres or forms of Indian dance; the literature dealing with one or more forms or styles of Indian theatre; and the growing body of work on Indian performance written from a social science point of view, examining the wider cultural context of Indian performance. As we shall see, each of these four major literatures has many subdivisions or subliteratures.

If this multiplicity of literatures is not enough to confound the neophyte, equally perplexing are the multiple points of view offered by writers in English since the nineteenth century in works written on some aspect of Indian performance, or a related topic of aesthetics and/or drama. When approaching any work on Indian performance, the reader should attempt to keep in mind the author's point of view as well as the type of book authored.

Perhaps the best way of considering the broad scope of literature in English on Indian performance is as a field in which there are two interlocking matrices or grids which, when taken together, describe that field. The first matrix consists of the type of publication, i.e. the specific literature to which it belongs. The second interlocking matrix is the author's point of view. In order to unpack the dense warp and weft which constitutes this field of literature, a representative sample of works are described below so that the reader can begin to identify the various points of view and types of literature which constitute the field.

Beginning with the point of view, there exist at least eight identifiable points of view in English works on Indian performance. The eight points of view in their pure form address a single audience and are written for a specific purpose. These eight points of view (with examples of each type) include the following:

1. Picture or art books showing a form of performance for an appreciative audience, i.e. coffee-table books. [A good example of such publications are those which appear in Marg, the highly polished art magazine or those appearing in The Times of India Annual. The accompanying descriptions are often substantive and reliable, however, the major purpose of the publications is pictorial presentation of forms of performance.]

2. Critical reviews or works written by Indians on Indian performances using a received set of aesthetic assumptions as the means for expression of the review of a performance or of a particular performer's work. [The most notable examples in this category are the commentaries of K. P. S. Menon on Kathakali dance-drama of Kerala. Menon's reviews, such as "Chengannur Raman Pillai," (Kalamandalam Annual, 1968, pp. 9-11) or "Guru Kunju Kurup," (Quarterly Journal of the National Centre for the Performing Arts, 2, 1, 1973, pp. 18-24) are not "critical" in the Western sense, but rather are knowledgeable and often sympathetic abstracts on the life and art of great Kathakali artists written by an individual steeped in the performance traditions and accepted as an "inside appreciator" by the artists themselves. The task of the "critic" is not that of a modern, Western critic, but rather to serve as an embodiment of tastefully presented reflections on the individual artist's lifework. Menon, and others like him, possess a high degree of self-conscious awareness of history, and of the received aesthetic principles which guide the form they discuss.]

3. Panegyrics written in praise of "things Indian," usually subjective in nature but written without the same intimate knowledge of a form and the artists possessed by individuals like Menon. [An excellent example of this type of uncritical praise is that found in K. R. Pisharoti's "Kerala Theatre," reviewed in greater detail below.]

4. Publications written by practicing artists (usually dancers) which document specific forms of performance through narrative and visual images in order to give a basic understanding of a form, and often to serve the purpose of giving an introductory history to the form. [Of the many books that fall into this category, two major examples are Ernakshi Bhavnani's The Dance in India (Bombay: Taraporevala House of Books, 1965) and Ragini Devi's Dance Dialects of India (Delhi: Vikas, 1972). Bhavnani's volume in more oriented toward technique, while Devi's book consists of general, introductory descriptions written sympathetically by an individual who has studied a number of the forms as a dancer.]

5. Works written by performance scholars and/or scholar/ practitioners which are intentionally historical, descriptive, documentary, and objective. [The works of many individuals can be included here, but those of a number of Indian and Western scholars are of particular note, including Mohan Kokhar, Suresh Awasthi, Kapila Vatsyayan, Martha Ashton, and Clifford and Betty Jones. Kapila Vatsyayan's recent volume, Traditional Indian Theatre: Multiple Streams (New Delhi, National Book Trust, 1980) is a complex scholarly work ranging broadly across diverse genres. Perhaps the model study of performance-as-performance in terms of documentation is Martha Ashton's carefully researched article, "Of Music, Bells, and Rhythmic Feet: The Dance of Yakshagana," (Anima, 1, 1, 1974, pp. 40-55).]

6. Scholarly works written from an historical and/or literary orientation, usually including translations, commentaries, and historical studies and most often devoted to Sanskrit dramas or Sanskrit treatises, and written by Sanskrit scholars. Early works in this category were often concerned with questions of the origin of Indian theatre. [The seminal early scholarly study was A. Berriedale Keith's The Sanskrit Drama (London: Oxford, 1924).]

7. Recently authored works which take a performance approach to the history of Sanskrit drama, including in their work insights from the history and current practices of regional forms of performance. These may be authored by Sanskritists, or non-Sanskritists, but always involve the author in questions of practical production. [The work of V. Raghavan is a pioneering effort in the reconstruction of the performance of Sanskrit dramas in the past and in techniques and principles for the staging of Sanskrit dramas today.]

8. The scholarly point of view of social scientists who consider performance as one part of Indian culture, and therefore take a wider sociocultural approach, emphasizing the context of the performance and/or the social systems which produce the art, rather than looking exclusively at the performance itself. [Milton Singer's When a Great Tradition Modernizes

(New York: Praeger, 1972) is the most important beginning resource in understanding Indian performances as forms of cultural performance.]

While each of these eight points of view may be clearly defined and identified in specific examples, it is often the case that a specific publication will possess multiple points of view. When multiple points of view exist, there is often a skewing of information, and a resulting tension between points of view in the materials, which makes it unclear whether the writer is presenting the information objectively or presenting the information to fit a preconceived idea of what is proper to present. For example, this "crisis in point of view" is present in M. L. Varadpande's recent Krishna Theatre in India (Atlantic Highlands, N.J.: Humanities Press, 1982) which is caught somewhere between a coffee-table picture book and a critical, scholarly approach to the history, literature, and performances of Krishna materials. While Varadpande's book is attempting to be objective and scholarly, other volumes present an ideal, uncritical image of a performance genre or form. Many works on Indian performance do not possess a self-reflexive and clearly defined point of view (admittedly a Western notion in the first place, but important for the reader to understand). It is not that there is anything "wrong" with any of the above eight points of view; rather, it is when there is no self-conscious articulation of that point of view for the reader that the reader may then suffer from "double vision" and not immediately recognize what is often ambiguity in the work.

The confusion over point of view is a result of a number of complex factors, but two of the most important are the hold of tradition on Indian performance and the implicit position the writer takes as "insider" or "outsider." In India, being a part of a correct tradition gives an individual power. One of the most important legitimizing factors in one's relative position within any group or subgroup is how close one is to the source or to the traditional manner of doing things. In the struggle for legitimization, nearly everyone makes a claim to be a part of a tradition or the traditional way of doing things. For a long time, it was assumed by many writers that there actually existed a single, legitimate tradition. Such a point of view was naive and never took into account the realities of social discourse. That reality is quite simply the fact that any specific performance style is a dynamic field of social interaction in which tradition is always in constant flux and change, even if such changes are largely in the nuance of technique within a form or style. The reader needs, then, to be aware that works which present a performance form as "the style of ..." may be oversimplifying complex social, cultural, and historical circumstances in order to present an ideal picture of the performance genre.

A second important facet of point of view is the difference between "insider/outsider," or "subjective/objective." However, these dichotomies are not simple sets of oppositions. The "insider" in a picture book is an appreciator. The "insider" in the "panegyric in praise," is an Indian steeped in a particular region, or style of performance (perhaps from a traditional family which has patronized a form) and who by legitimacy of birth, heritage, and experience is an "insider" to the form about which he writes. The "outsider" is clearly seen when the scholarly point of view is taken (either by an Indian or a Westerner) and when that objective point of view is kept constant through a work. These are clear-cut examples of "insider/outsider" points of view. Confusion arises, however, when a scholar is also an appreciator, and allows such appreciation to skew the materials presented. It is difficult to draw the line between presenting objectively what one researches, and presenting materials so that the reader appreciates the form in the same way that the writer grew to appreciate that form. This is a constant dilemma to any author of materials on Indian performance. Perhaps an historical example will clarify.

During the period of British hegemony in India and with the growth of a newly British-educated class, many of those wielding political and social power within India in the late nineteenth and early twentieth century came to disparage "things Indian." In the early twentieth century, a reaction against the British-dominated point of view of Indian culture and art attempted to reverse the negative attitude which had been taken by the educated toward their own artistic traditions. This reversal led many leaders to attempt a cultural revival which would preserve those traditional arts which had been disparaged, and nearly allowed to die. For example, in the world of Kathakali the poet Vallathol emerged as the leader of a movement to maintain this classical dance-drama in the traditional mold. Vallathol and other visionaries were seeking to arouse public sympathy as well as money to provide new means of patronage and appreciation which would replace the breakdown in the old patronage system for the arts. Many of the early works of the twentieth century were authored from an appreciator's point of view and had a programmatic concern with eliciting a positive response to a movement for preservation of art forms. Many works written on Kathakali take this point of view of appreciation; there is no critical edge to such works. The lack of a critical and objective edge is a reflection of the historical period during which many of these earlier works were written. In some cases these early works helped to draw attention to neglected forms and produced specific public reactions in support of forms and their preservation, thus serving a specific social, political, and economic end. However, the lack of a critical perspective became commonplace.

One of the earliest writers to identify the problems with point of view and to criticize the lack of perspective in many early works of the twentieth century was the well-known scholar, V. Raghavan. He wrote as early as 1933 ("Kathakali and Other Forms of Bharata

Natya," Triveni: Journal of Indian Renaissance, 6, 2, 1933, pp.
148-169) about the dangers of Indian writers delivering "panegyrics of praise" to indigenous arts.

> It appears to me that the greatest danger awaiting the fu-
> ture of art in India is provincial superiority complex. It
> seems that even in the realm of art there is little possibil-
> ity of all provinces federating into one unity of Indian Art.
> It has become very common now for one province to abuse
> another, each trying to show up to the Western world that,
> in respect of cultural advancement, art, literature, etc.,
> it alone stands supreme in the whole of India. Each prov-
> ince says, as the Upanishadic seer said of the Brahman:
> "It alone existed at first; nought else winked": Nanyat
> kinchanamishat. This kind of feeling permeates the writ-
> ings of those who write about the forms flourishing in their
> own provinces. (p. 149)

Raghavan's observation is a summary warning to those who would
study Indian performing arts. Each work must be judged against
others so that purely hyperbolic statements can be sorted out from
more objective accounts. Once hyperbole and panegyric are recognized for what they are, and this is a very "Indian" method of approaching "things Indian" especially arts relating to an individual's
own regional culture and history, then the reader can wield his
own critical knife in cutting through the maze of sources available.

We have not selected in this bibliography to wield that knife
for the reader. We have purposely included many such sources.
V. Raghavan's discriminating review (1933) of the early literature
on Kathakali dance-drama as it was in the process of being rediscovered follows the overstatements made by K. R. Pisharoti in his
article, "Kerala Theatre." Raghavan points out Pisharoti's biased
claim that in Kerala, theatre is

> "truer and nearer to the ideals of the ancient Hindu stage
> traditions." He concludes his paper with the statement
> that in the Kathakali "may be seen almost the highest per-
> fection of the arts of acting and dancing, the perfect
> realization as yet known of the technique so scientifically
> elaborated and described by Bharata in his Natya Sastra.
> Such vanity results from a vicious provincial patriotism.
> It is a pity that writers do not care to do sufficient re-
> search and compare the forms of art of their provinces
> with those available in their neighbourhood and all over
> India. (pp. 148-149)

For the individual attempting to study Indian performing arts, a
discriminating and critical faculty must be developed early on in
reading to sort out the wheat from the chaff.

Another important warning in readings on Indian performance is to be aware not only of those who would make any art "hoary and ancient," but also those who would render the arts suffused with a religious "awe or mysticism." A companion piece to Rag-havan's is Phillip Zarrilli's "Demystifying Kathakali," (Sangeet Natak, 43, 1977, pp. 48-59) which is a critical review of publications on Kathakali since the 1950's and how such publications have created a "Kathakali mystique." Zarrilli proceeds to illustrate how this mystique has taken on a life of its own, even influencing the context and presentation of Kathakali for tourists in Kerala.

Hopefully this outline of the multiple literatures and multiple points of view which constitute the warp and weft of the field of publications on Indian performance will give the reader a self-conscious awareness of what to expect in approaching the field. With these markers and warnings in mind, a guide through the literature follows.

Guide Through the Literature

The following guide corresponds to the organization and content of the bibliographical entries which follow. This guide is suggestive and selective, and simply attempts to direct the reader to the most important representative works to be found in each of the subject areas of the bibliography itself. The literatures are so extensive on the host of performance forms that we have selected a few examples of representative forms in each major category (classical, folk/regional, and ritual/religious) which are well-written guideposts for further reading in the field.

1. Bibliographies

Those two bibliographies which are devoted exclusively to theatre and dance in India, and which offer the most comprehensive coverage, are Farley Richmond's "Indian Theatre Materials" in the Journal of South Asian Literature (X, 2, Winter 1975, pp. 327-76), and Judy Van Zile's Dance in India: Annotated Guide to Source Materials (Providence, R.I.: Asian Music Publications, 1973). Used together, these two works provide for the reader a very extensive list of sources.

2. General Works on Indian Performance

Given the complexity of even a simple description of the field of Indian performance, it is not surprising that few good general introductions exist on the subject. Aside from the complexities of describing the field, equally difficult is constructing a reasonably accurate chronology of the history of Indian performance. Most works which attempt a comprehensive historical and descriptive overview suffer from the problems endemic to the field. The publications suggested here are those which are least likely to mislead the reader in the least number of areas of Indian performance. Som Benegal's A Panorama of Theatre in India (Bombay: Popular Prakashan, 1968) concentrates on the contemporary theatre since the nineteenth century, but includes a brief introduction and overview of Sanskrit drama and theory, as well as a summary of traditional theatrical forms. Balwant Gargi's Theatre in India (New York: Theatre Arts, 1962) also slights the classical Sanskrit theatre in emphasizing the modern theatre. Indian Drama (published by the Publications Division, Government of India, 1956) includes a collection of essays (largely historical in viewpoint) covering the Sanskrit drama, and the regional modern dramas of most modern Indian states. Adya Rangacharya's The Indian Theatre (New Delhi: National Book Trust, India, 1971) is one of the most straightforward, brief, and dependable general surveys of Indian theatre covering the origin, development, and staging of Sanskrit dramas, traditional forms, as well as modern regional theatre and drama. An important work, currently in press, which deserves mention is the jointly authored work by Farley Richmond, Darius Swann, and Phillip Zarrilli (with contributions by several other Indian theatre specialists), Indian Theatre. The authors attempt a substantive, comprehensive survey which gives equal attention to each major era and a representative sample of each major form of Indian performance. The volume includes a major chapter on Sanskrit drama and theatre, focusing on the theatrical aspects of the Natyasastra; an in-depth survey of ritual and religious theatrical forms through specific studies of Teyyam, Raslila, and Ramlila; presentation of the popular folk theatre traditions of north and south India through studies of Nautanki, Tamasha, Jatra, Cavittu Natakam and Yakshagana; a chapter on classical dance-dramas with emphasis on Kathakali and Chhau; and finally, a closing chapter on the modern and contemporary theatre of India. Farley Richmond also edited an important special edition of the Journal of South Asian Literature exclusively devoted to "Theatre in India," (10, 1975, pp. 2-4). This special issue includes a variety of important resources on a wide range of topics including articles on the shadow theatre, Raslila, Jatra, Kathakali, Yakshagana, and Krishnattam, and translations of a wide range of plays.

In addition to these general works and sources on Indian performance, the reader should consult research, field reports, and descriptions of Indian and South Asian performance in a number of current periodicals. Two of the most important, published four times a year in India, are Sangeet Natak and the Quarterly Journal of the National Centre for the Performing Arts. Both publish substantive scholarly articles on a wide variety of performance forms. QJNCPA also includes news and notes on current, important performances. Other important Indian journals to consult include: Natya, the glossy, highly polished art publication; Marg, which occasionally includes major layouts on performing arts; and more recent publications like Kalakshetra, the journal of the arts academy in Madras. Contemporary theatre is reported in Enact, although seldom do the articles cover performance techniques or reports on movement. Outside of India the most important publications on Indian performance in English appear in such journals as The Drama Review, Performing Arts Journal, C.O.R.D., or Ethnomusicology. Most directly concerned with Asian performance is Asian Theatre Journal (replacing the older Asian Theatre Bulletin). Indeed, the appearance of Asian Theatre Journal should be a boon to current information, scholarly publications, and performance reports on all of Asian theatre.

3. The Cultural Context: Anthropological Studies of Indian Performance and Culture

The anthroplogical study of performance in India has been led by the pioneering work of Milton Singer of the University of Chicago. In three major works edited or authored by Singer, his notion of "cultural performances" as encapsulations of Indian culture find expression in his own work and that of a variety of other scholars. For the serious student of performance studies and/or Indian performance, familiarity with all three of Singer's works is essential (in chronological order: Milton Singer, ed., Traditional India: Structure and Change. Philadelphia, American Folklore Society, 1959; Milton Singer, ed., Krishna: Myths, Rites, and Attitudes. Chicago: University of Chicago Press, 1968; Milton Singer, When a Great Tradition Modernizes. New York: Praeger Publishers, 1972.). While the student of Indian performance may at first be most interested in the techniques, forms, and structure of performance itself, a full understanding of any performance can only be gained through a study of the context, nesting, meaning, and significance of that performance as an expression of its own culture. Singer's work concentrates on the context of discrete performances and on the performances as events encoding complex expressions of the culture. With a few exceptions it will remain for future research and writing to join the close description of the event and its process of creation with the contextual studies of cultural anthropologists.

Perhaps the best example of a work which draws a total picture of theatrical performance in India is the work of Norvin Hein (The Miracle Plays of Mathura. New Haven: Yale University Press, 1972). In this work Hein presents complete descriptions of performances of the five types of religious drama (Jhanki, Kathak, plays of the Bhaktamal Natak Mandali troupe, Ramlila, and Raslila) found in Mathura, a district of North India famous as a center of pilgrimage. In Hein's work the structural and contextual aspects of performance are brought together in descriptions of these vibrant and lively devotional forms of drama.

While Hein's study is important for its inclusion of the wider social context, many of the anthropological studies of Indian performance have focused on music and oral performance rather than theatrical forms. While beyond the scope of this bibliography, mention of a few of the most important studies will serve as a guide to some of the most recent methods being used in the study of Indian performance. The most important beginning place is Daniel M. Neuman's The Life of Music in North India (Detroit: Wayne State University, 1980) which interprets the music of North India as a cultural phenomenon. Following Neuman, the reader should turn to the following: Stuart Blackburn's work on the Tamil Bow Song Tradition (see "Performance as Paradigm: The Tamil Bow Song Tradition," Ph.D. dissertation, University of California, Berkely, 1980; and "Oral Performance: Narrative and Ritual in a Tamil Tradition," Journal of American Folklore, 94, 372, 1981, pp. 207-227; Joan Erdman's publications on patronage in Jaipur (see "The Maharaja's Musicians: The Organization of Cultural Performance at Jaipur in the 19th Century," American Studies in the Anthropology of India, edited by Sylvia Vatuk, New Delhi: Manohar Publications, and "The Artist in Indian Society: Patrons and Performers in Rajasthan," Ph.D. dissertation, University of Chicago, 1980); and Jon Higgins' parallel work on patronage (see "From Prince to Populace: Patronage as a Determinant of Change in South Indian (Karnatak) Music," Asian Music, 7, 2, 1976, pp. 20-26). For the individual most interested in studying movement and theatrical forms in the wider context of Indian culture, further attention should be given to recent specialized academic journals in anthropology, South Asian studies, performance, folklore, and ethnomusicology.

4. Studies in Early Indian Performance

The touchstone against which all Indian performance has been judged since its appearance is the Natyasastra, the encyclopaedia manual of performance theory and practice written between 200 B.C. and 200 A.D. and ascribed to the sage Bharata. So vast is the scope of the Natyasastra compared to Aristotle's Poetics that it covers everything from the origins of theatre, how to write a play, and how to articulate each specific limb in creating a character for performance, to the delineation of a complete aesthetic theory centering around the concept of rasa ("flavor," or often translated "sentiment"). When written, the Natyasastra reflected the theatrical practice and theory of a living, healthy, vibrant theatrical tradition for the staging of dramas written primarily in Sanskrit, the court language of the time but also including Prakrits, or local languages. While Sanskrit dramas continued to be produced through the tenth century A.D., the most important period of literary activity and dramatic production of Sanskrit classics was between approximately 350 and 750 A.D. By the tenth century Sanskrit theatre and drama were on the decline due to complex socioeconomic, literary, and artistic reasons. But even with this decline in Sanskrit dramatic activity, further treatises on the drama and commentaries on aesthetic theory (especially focusing on the rasa concept) continued to be written. For example, Dhanamjaya's Dasarupa (translated by George C. O. Hass, Delhi: Motilal, 1962) was written in the last quarter of the tenth century A.D.

As the vitality of Sanskrit theatre waned, there was a gradual increase in the importance of regional forms of dramatic production whether in Sanskrit, or in regional languages. Sanskrit is still the language of several forms in different parts of India, including Ankia Nat of Assam, Kuchipudi of Andra Pradesh, and most importantly in the Kutiyattam theatre of Kerala. The legacy of the Sanskrit theatre tradition suffuses many types and styles of Indian performance throughout the subcontinent. It is the Sanskrit dramatic tradition which provides the central force in the continuity of what has been defined as the "classical" performance tradition of India. Many forms of extant Indian performance can only be fully understood in terms of history, technique, and conventions, by studying the Sanskrit theatre tradition. In addition many publications on extant forms of Indian performance often use concepts or make reference to the Sanskrit classical tradition.

The complex history of Sanskrit drama, aesthetics, and production has produced a number of subliteratures, each of which is important in understanding the history of Sanskrit theatre, its legacy in Indian performance, the current status of Sanskrit drama in production, and the link between the Sanskrit stage and contemporary performance. The best place to begin a study of ancient Sanskrit drama, aesthetics, and theatrical practice is with the general works on the topic. Most of the earlier secondary sources on the Sanskrit theatre took little if any notice of the extant forms of Sanskrit and regional language theatres, even those where an obvious link exists with the conventions and techniques of the Natyasastra. Of the general works on the topic of Sanskrit theatre, S. C. Bhatt's Drama in Ancient India (New Delhi: Amrit Book Company, 1961) is a simple introduction. A. Berriedale Keith's The Sanskrit Drama in Its Origin, Development, Theory and Practice (London: Oxford Univ. Press, 1924) has for years served as the beginning sourcebook in English for the study of Sanskrit drama, theatrical practice, and aesthetics. The other important, early twentieth-century Western look at the Sanskrit theatre is Sylvain Levi's recently translated, The Theatre of India, Vols. I and II (Calcutta: Writers Workshop Publication, 1978, translated by Narayan Mukherji from the French). Volume I covers various aspects of dramatic art, a history of Indian dramatic literature, and aesthetics. Volume II discusses the origins of drama, possible Greek influences, dramatic practice (hall, stage, preliminaries, troupes, actors, direction, management), and gives passing notice to modern

and contemporary theatre. More recently I. Shekhar's Sanskrit
Drama: Its Origin and Decline (New Delhi: Munshiram Manoharlal,
1977, 2nd ed. Originally published in 1960 by E. J. Brill) focuses
on the non-Aryan elements that might have influenced the development of Sanskrit drama. Shekhar also draws on dance and drama
traditions from South India in his arguments, including early Tamil
evidence in poetry, Bharatanatyam and the Devadasi tradition, etc.
He suggests that the cause of the decline of Sanskrit drama was
linked to class conflicts. M. Christopher Byrski's work (see "Can
Sanskrit Drama Tell Us Anything More?" Educational Theatre Journal, 27, 4, 1975, pp. 445-452) suggests a new approach to the
study of Sanskrit drama based on Indian aesthetics and ethical
criteria rather than "impressionism" which he feels has plagued
earlier scholarship.

In addition to the general works on the subject of Sanskrit
drama and theatre, a number of more specialized subliteratures exist, consisting of both primary and secondary materials. The first
subliterature is of course the canon of extant Sanskrit plays. While
a complete review and cataloguing of translations of Sanskrit dramas
is beyond the scope of this work, a good recent translation of several Sanskrit plays which also contains a brief but informative overview of the history of Sanskrit drama is Michael Coulson's Three
Sanskrit Plays (Middlesex: Penguin, 1981).

A second major subliterature created by the development of
Sanskrit drama were the treatises on dramaturgy, theatrical practice, and aesthetics of the drama, and later commentaries on the
commentaries. If the Natyasastra is the touchstone of Sanskrit
drama and theatrical practice, it would seem a logical place to begin. However, there are difficulties with simply attempting to read
this encyclopaedic work. To date, only one translation has appeared (Manomohan Ghosh, ed. and translator, The Natyasastra
Ascribed to Bharata-Muni. Calcutta: The Royal Asiatic Society of
Bengal, 1950, 1961, 2 vols. Revised 2nd ed. of Vol. 1, Calcutta:
Granthalaya Private, Ltd., 1967). While all agree that Ghosh's
translation was a monumental undertaking, the translation has many
difficulties, especially from a theatrical point of view. For the individual approaching the Natyasastra through the performing arts
and not through Indian literature and aesthetic theory, Pramad
Kale's The Theatric Universe (Bombay: Popular Prakashan, 1974)
may serve as a helpful companion volume. Kale is conversant with
both Western and Asian theatre, and presents the Natyasastra in
terms of communication processes and theory. His translations of a
number of important passages of the Natyasastra provide new theatrical insights into the work.

Consulting a few other secondary sources written from a
variety of scholarly points of view will assist in further clarifying
many facets of the Natyasastra and Indian aesthetics. Darius L.
Swann's "Indian and Greek Drama: Two Definitions" (Comparative

Drama, 3, 2, 1969, pp. 110-120) provides an informative comparative discussion of Aristotle's Poetics and the Natyasastra. Swann
clearly and understandably differentiates between Greek and Indian
types of action and imitation, catharsis and rasa, and cultural notions of time and history. Edwin Gerow's Indian Poetics (Vol. V of
A History of Indian Literature, edited by Jan Gonda. Wiesbaden:
Otto Harrassowitz, 1977) is an overview of the entire field of Indian
poetics, and places the Natyasastra in the larger historical context
of similar treatises and commentaries devoted to the subject of Indian
poetics. A good comparative analysis of the views of four medieval
Indian aestheticians on the nature of the aesthetic experience in the
theatre is contained in Sucharita Gamlath's "Indian Aesthetics and
the Nature of Dramatic Emotions" (British Journal of Aesthetics, 9,
4, 1969, pp. 372-386). Finally, one of the most important secondary
sourcebooks for the individual interested in movement is Kapila
Vatsyayan's Classical Indian Dance in Literature and the Arts (Delhi:
Sangeet Natak Akademi, 1968). Vatsyayan's study is a detailed,
technical analysis of dance as treated in the Natyasastra and other
treatises. Her wide-ranging study compares the dance with classical sculpture, painting, and literature. This complex and dense
work is the best study of classical movement and dance in terms
of India's own aesthetic expressions of performance; however, reading the work requires at least a preliminary knowledge of the history and substance of classical Sanskrit drama, aesthetics, and
practice.

A more recent subliterature of the classical Sanskrit theatre
is the growing body of work concerned with both the historical and
contemporary staging of ancient Sanskrit dramas. The acknowledged
pioneer and expert in the field was V. Raghavan. His prolific career included not only the highest quality of scholarly research, but
also practical attempts to produce Sanskrit dramas using his research
findings. It was the happy marriage between his practical attempts
at staging and his keen scholarly mind which produced such an
abundant body of work whose insights are founded on an insider's
understanding of the practical necessities of the stage. The
Samskrita Ranga Annual, first published in 1958, was a forum for
substantive articles on current research on regional theatre forms
and on Sanskrit drama and performance. Some of the most important articles appearing in the Annual include Raghavan's "Production of Kalidasa's Plays in Ancient India," Samskrita Ranga Annual, 1, 1958-59; three articles from Samskrita Ranga Annual, 5,
1967: "Kutiyattam--Its Form and Significance as Sanskrit Drama," "Indian Classical Concept of Total Theatre," and "Kalidasa,
Sanskrit Drama and Indian Theatre." One of Raghavan's most important and useful general overviews of Sanskrit drama in performance may be found in his article, "Sanskrit Drama: Theory
and Performance," (Comparative Drama, 1, 1, 1967, pp. 36-48).

The most important source to appear in recent years on the
production and performance of Sanskrit drama is Sanskrit Drama in

Performance, edited by Rachel Van M. Baumer and James R. Brandon (Honolulu: The University Press of Hawaii, 1981). The volume is a collection of papers presented at a conference on "Sanskrit Drama in Performance," by a cross-disciplinary group of international scholars concerned with the history, aesthetics, and performance of Sanskrit and/or regional Indian theatre. The volume specifically addresses the "performing tradition of the Sanskrit theatre." The two major questions addressed in the volume are how Sanskrit plays were performed in ancient India and how Sanskrit plays can be staged today. The two opening essays deal with performance in ancient India. V. Raghavan's paper on "Sanskrit Drama in Performance," is an extension of his earlier research in the field. This is a wide-ranging and excellent overview of the topic from an historical point of view. He organizes much of the diffuse Natyasastra which related to performance and summarizes and distills that detailed information for the reader. Kapila Vatsyayan's "Dance Techniques of Sanskrit Theatre" is a suggestive and creative review of movement in ancient Sanskrit theatre. The remainder of the volume is equally important and makes this collection of essays the single most important primer and source for those interested in the production and performance of Sanskrit drama in ancient India, or in the contemporary theatre world. An excellent follow-up resource on earlier productions of Sanskrit plays is Farley Richmond's well-illustrated "Sanskrit Plays Abroad," (Times of India Annual, 1971, pp. 39-48) which traces the history of a variety of adaptations of classical Indian dramas in England, Europe, Russia, China, and America. Phillip Zarrilli's "Kalidasa's Sakuntala in Performance," (Sangeet Natak, 55, 1980, pp. 17-40), is a complete illustrated review of the decision-making process concerning questions of translation, order of performance, set and costume design, music, and acting style, and movement in the contemporary staging of Kalidasa's Sanskrit classic.

5. Descriptive, General, and Comparative Studies of Multiple Forms of Performance

In addition to publications which attempt a comprehensive survey of the history and major types of Indian performance, there are a number of works with a more limited objective. These works include a diverse body of literature on performance and range from those written as general introductions to extant regional forms of performance, to those taking a thematic or topical approach to an historical or comparative study of specific forms of performance. A few reliable general introductions to a broad range of extant performance forms include Ragini Devi's Dance Dialects of India (Delhi: Vikas Publications, 1972) which covers a wide variety of forms from the classical Bharatanatyam and Kathakali, to the ritual Bhagavati performances of Kerala, to a number of folk performances. More focused on technique than Devi's study is Enakshi Bhavnani's The Dance in India (Bombay: Taraporevala's Treasure House of Books,

1965) which surveys major features of classical, folk, and tribal dances of India.

Examples of publications which take a thematic or topical approach to multiple forms of performances are such widely diverse works as Ram Dhamija's illustrated pictorial overview of a wide variety of masks and their use in various theatrical forms in India in "Masks of India," (Times of India Annual, 1967, pp. 73-80) to the very important recent publication by Kapila Vatsyayan, Traditional Indian Theatre: Multiple Streams. (New Delhi: National Book Trust, 1980). Vatsyayan's volume is explicitly written to provide both a substantive overview of a variety of theatrical forms as well as to display the "underlying unity" discernible in the various regional language forms of Indian performance. Although technical in its assumed vocabulary, this is the most important and comprehensive overview and comparison of Indian theatre forms to appear in recent years. It includes major chapters on a wide variety of performance traditions including Kutiyattam, Yaksagana, Bhagavatamela and Kuchipudi, the three forms of Chhau, Ankia Nat and Bhaona, Ramlila, Raslila and Krishnalila, Yatra, Bhavai, Svanga, Khyala, Nautanki, and Tamasha. While each chapter includes sections devoted to staging and movement techniques in a particular form, the overriding concern of the text is with the thematic development of the topic of "underlying unity" of various Indian forms of performance.

A large body of publications focus more specifically on forms of classical dance. Some standard introductory works describing classical Indian dance include Faubion Bowers', The Dance in India (New York: AMS Press, 1967) which is a balanced overview of the basic features of four of the major classical Indian dance styles (Bharata Natyam, Kathakali, Kathak and Manipuri) based on personal observations of the training and performance in India. The straightforward introductory commentary on the difficulties of modern Indian dance are perceptive and timely today. The Dance in India offers good general descriptions of basic positions and movements in the four forms covered. Mohan Khokar's Traditions of Indian Classical Dance (Delhi: Clarion Books, 1979) devotes a brief chapter to a number of forms including Bharata Natyam, Kathakali, Kathak, Kuchipudi, Orissi, Chhau, Manipuri, and Yakshagana. One of the most authoritative yet straightforward studies of the four major classical dance forms is Kapila Vatsyayan's Indian Classical Dance (New Delhi: Publication Division, Ministry of Information and Broadcasting, 1974).

In the folk/regional category of Indian performance, Balwant Gargi's Folk Theatre of India (Seattle: University of Washington Press, 1966) has long served as the primary introduction to a wide variety of Indian folk performance forms, from Jatra and Nautanki to Yaksagana and Raslila. Kapila Vatsyayan's regional/geographical survey, Traditions of Indian Folk Dance (New Delhi: Indian Book

Company, 1976) is the best introductory source covering multiple forms.

Most of the published studies of ritual/reglious performance are focused on specific forms of ritual or devotional drama. The most significant and important scholarly study which covers multiple types of devotional drama is Norvin Hein's The Miracle Plays of Mathura (New Haven: Yale University Press, 1972), which focuses on Ramlila and Raslila.

6. Specific Forms of Performance

In sheer volume, the largest number of publications on Indian performance cover a specific form. The bibliographical entries on specific forms have been arranged alphabetically under the appropriate major category of performance to which an individual form belongs. In this brief guide through the literature, we can do no more than suggest a few examples of the best available literatures. Examples will include suggested readings on Kathakali dance-drama and Mohiniattam female dance from the classical sphere of performance, Yaksagana from the folk/regional sphere, and the closely related Teyyam and Bhuta ritual performances of Kerala and Karnataka respectively in the ritual/reglious sphere.

While there exist more publications on the well-known Kathakali dance-drama of Kerala than on any other specific form of Indian theatre, what is striking about the plethora of publications is that so little has been said until recently that sheds new light on the history, performance, and context of the form. The most concise, straightforward, brief introduction to the form in existence is Clifford Jones' "Kathakali: Epic Dance-Drama of India" (Monographs on Music, Dance and Theater in Asia, Vol. VII, 1980. New York: The Asia Society). Three of the most striking visual presentations of Kathakali have appeared in the last few years (see Joseph H. Mazo, "Dance from the Edge of India," Geo, 5, 3, June 1981, pp. 40-60; Madhur Jaffrey, "A Total Theater Filled with Dance, Music, and Myth," Smithsonian, 9, 12, March 1979, pp. 68-75; and Clifford R. Jones, "The Fireworks of India's Kathakali Theater," Asia, 3, 6, March/April 1981, pp. 36-41). Each of these articles appeared in publications for a more general public. Mazo's article and the accompanying photographs capture best the life of the student and professional in training and in performance.

Several recent publications are beginning to offer new insights into the structure, techniques, and context of Kathakali. L. S. Rajagopalan and V. Subramanya Iyer's "Aids to the Appreciation of Kathakali," and the accompanying translation by Iyer of the play, Nala Caritam Attakatha from the Kathakali repertory (Journal of South Asian Literature, X, 2-4, 1975, pp. 205-248) together give an inside understanding of some of the main features of the performance structure of a Kathakali performance. M. P. Sankaran Namboodiri's "Bhava as Expressed in the Vacikam and Angikam aspects of Abhinaya in Kathakali," (C.O.R.D. Dance Research Annual, XIV, in press) is a major contribution given by a practicing Kathakali actor of the actor's art of expression in the dance-drama. Finally, Phillip Zarrilli's recent The Kathakali Complex: Actor, Performance, Structure (New Delhi: Abhinav, 1984) is the most detailed work on Kathakali published to date. The volume unfolds the shaping of a Kathakali actor from selection through training to the night of performance, using both narrative and visual documentation of training and performance techniques, including movement and dance. In addition, the book contains a close, detailed microanalysis of the structure of a Kathakali performance score broken down into its smallest component parts. The influence of Kathakali on contemporary Indian and Western performance is also covered in the final chapter of the book.

The best individual publications on Kerala's form of classical female dance include Betty Jones' article, "Mohiniyattam: A Dance Tradition of Kerala, South India," (C.O.R.D. Dance Research Monograph One, 1971-72, pp. 7-47), and a special issue on "Mohnini Attam" (Marg, 26, 2, March 1973). Jones' article is an excellent, well-documented study, assessing various forces which shaped the development of the form. The article also offers specific accounts of training and production elements. The Marg special issue gives a very good overview of the form, highlighted by excellent photographs. A short article "Mohiniattam--The Dance of the Enchantress," (Marg, 32, 2, 1978-79, pp. 75-80) is also of value for descriptions of basic movements and technique.

Yakshagana, the folk/regional language dance-drama of Karnataka state, is best introduced through Martha Ashton's brief article, "Yakshagana: A South Indian Folk Theatre," (The Drama Review, 8, 3, 1969, pp. 148-155) which could be followed by a reading of Ashton's and Bruce Christie's Yakshagana (New Delhi: Abhinav Publications, 1977). The book-length study, written for a general audience, is a solid overview of the northern style of the form, and appeals to the senses of the reader in its graphic presentation. More substantive are Ashton's other works on Yakshagana. Ashton's thesis ("Yakshagana Badagatittu Bayalata as Indian Dance Drama," Mighigan State University, 1972) is a carefully researched, close study of the northern style of Yakshagana which provides detailed and specific information on all aspects of the traditional training and performance of this form of dance-drama. Her subsequent publication of the short article, "Of Music, Bells and Rhythmic Feet: The Dance of Yakshagana," (Anima, 1, 1, 1974, pp. 40-56) is a fine example of careful visual and narrative documentation of theatrical movement well-communicated to either a general reader or specialist. Equal in importance to the article on dancing is Ashton's "A Structural Analysis of Costume and Makeup in Yaksagana Badagatittu Bayalata," (in Structural

Approaches to South India Studies, Harry Buck and Glen Yocum, eds. Chambersburg, PA: Wilson Books, 1974, pp. 115-136). While the body of Ashton's work represents an outstanding contribution to the documentation of this traditional form of folk/ regional performance, little exists on the breakdown of the traditional form of performance under current socioeconomic pressures and the changes wrought on the form by these pressures.

In the area of ritual/religious performance, in addition to Hein's work already mentioned (The Miracle Plays of Mathura), several examples of relatively recent research may serve as beginning places for readings in the literature. Clifford Jones' two articles, "Dhulicitra: Historical Perspectives on Art and Ritual" (in Kaladarsana: Studies in the Art of India. New Delhi: Oxford & IBH Publ., 1981, pp. 69-75) and "Kalam Eluttu: Art and Ritual in Kerala," (in Religious Festivals in South India and Sri Lanka, Guy R. Weldon and Glen E. Yocum, eds. Delhi: Manohar, 1982, pp. 267-294) are superb examples of careful scholarship on ritual performance. Other articles which may introduce the reader to the field include Martha Ashton's "Spirit Cult Festivals in South Kanara," and Wayne Ashley's "Teyyam Kettu of Northern Kerala," (The Drama Review, 23, 2, 1979, pp. 91-98 and 99-112) which provide introductory descriptions of these forms. A later article by Ashley and Regina Holloman, "From Ritual to Theatre in Kerala," (The Drama Review, 26, 2, 1982, pp. 59-72) is an important contribution to an understanding of the social processes surrounding the life of traditional ritual forms in modern India today.

7. Modern and Contemporary Dance

The interchange between India and the West over the last 150 years has effected rich developments and experimentation in the dance forms of both India and Western nations. One of the best attempts at an overview of this exchange is Mohan Khokar's article, "Western Interest in, and its Impact on, Indian Dance," (Bulletin of the Institute of Traditional Cultures, Madras, Part II, 1961, pp. 203-217.) The article covers the period between the 1830's and 1960, particularly emphasizing the work of Ruth St. Denis and Uday Shankar. F. Hall's article, "Influence of Indian Dance on the West," (Sangeet Natak, 28, 1973, pp. 30-49), also gives an historical view of the incorporation of Indian dance themes in Western ballet. Of particular interest is the fact that Hall focuses on style of movement.

A special issue of Natya, ("Dance, Drama and Ballet," 7, 4, December 1963) is devoted primarily to modern developments in Indian dance. The issue also includes some articles on traditional forms, which are helpful when read in conjunction with the articles which discuss the new choreography.

More recently, Sangeet Natak published a special issue devoted to the life and the career of Uday Shankar (Sangeet Natak,
48, April-June 1978). Shankar's choreography was a major influence in the development of modern Indian ballet, and the items in
this collection describe Shankar's rediscovery of his native artistic
traditions as well as his experimental process.

8. Modern and Contemporary Theatre

The East-West interchange and the modernization of India has
also engendered a broad and complex new range of dramatic offerings in India, including translations and adaptations of modern Western plays, innovations and experimentation in new, indigenous plays
and productions, and the adaptations and syntheses of traditional
forms with new forms. Indeed, the coexistence of traditional and
modern forms has raised many questions about the relationship of
such seemingly diverse forms and their respective roles in social,
political and cultural terms in an evolving India.

Two special issues of Sangeet Natak offer solid overviews of
contemporary trends. The first, "Roundtable on the Contemporary
Relevance of Traditional Theatre" (Sangeet Natak, 21, July-September
1971) records the findings of a panel which confronted the so-called
"gulf" between the traditional and the modern heritage in Indian
theatre. The panel covered a variety of traditional forms, discussing issues of viability and processes of assimilating such traditions
in contemporary activity. The next issue, "Theatre Today" (Sangeet
Natak, 22, October-December 1971) includes articles by and interviews with major playwrights and directors about the development
and changes in folk forms, and about specific dramatic experiments
by these practitioners. The reader most concerned with movement
in contemporary Indian theatre will also find some valuable commentary on the influence of the cinema on staging and acting styles.

Since modernization in Indian theatre has often meant a shift
away from traditional dramas with mythological content in favor of
Western or new plays with themes of social and political relevance,
it is important to understand the role of theatre in India as an instrument of social change. Farley Richmond's article, "The Social
Role of Theatre in India" (Sangeet Natak, 25, 1972, pp. 64-83) is a
good introduction to this subject. Richmond's article examines several periods of social protest and political propaganda as manifested
in Indian drama in the nineteenth and twentieth centuries. "Theatre
In Asia" (The Drama Review, 15, 3, 1971) also includes a series of
articles which specifically address the relationship of theatre and
politics in India.

Modern developments in theatre have followed different directions in the different regions of India. "Indian Drama and Stage

Today" (Indian Literature, 1, 2, April-September 1958, pp. 75-150) is one of few sources which provides a cross-regional survey of these developments. Though the publication is somewhat dated, it does include brief, primarily historical articles on the Assamese, Bengali, Gujerati, Hindi, Kannada, Kashmiri, Malayalam, Marathi, Oriya, Punjabi, Tamil, Telugu, and Urdu dramas.

There are also numerous studies which treat the theatre of a single language region. Two publications devoted to Bengali theatre and drama are mentioned here, as good examples. Prabhurcharan Guha-Thakurta's work The Bengali Drama: Its Origin and Development (London: Kegan Paul, Trench, Trubner, 1930), is a very good critical history, with extensive coverage of the Jatra, and of the evolution of modern spoken drama from the eighteenth century on. The author also discusses the theatres and aspects of staging and acting. A more recent publication, Bengali Theatre, by Kironmoy Raha (New Delhi: National Book Trust, India, 1978) is another very good history. Raha considers the influences of Jatra and British drama on the development of Bengali drama, the formation of private and professional theatres, the transition to commercial theatre, the New Drama movement, and contemporary commercial theatre. The work of several of the dominant practitioners is described, including methods of acting and production.

India Bibliographies

Awasthi, Suresh. "Theatre Collections and Museums in India." Theatre Research, 7, 1-2 (1956), pp. 73-76.

Jain, Sushil Kumar. Indian Literature in English. 3 vols. Regina, Saskatchewan: University of Saskatchewan, 1965-67.
    Vol. 2 covers drama, including those materials in English from the British Museum and India Office Libraries.

Patterson, Maureen L. P., and William J. Alspaugh, eds. South Asian Civilizations: A Bibliographic Synthesis. Chicago: The University of Chicago Press, 1981.
    A comprehensive resource that includes very specific theatre and drama subject headings.

Renou, Louis. "Research on the Indian Theatre since 1890." Samskrita Ranga Annual, 4 (1966), pp. 67-91.
    A very useful, annotated guide covering Sanskrit drama and theatre.

Richmond, Farley. "Indian Theatre Materials." Journal of South Asian Literature, X, 2 (Winter 1975), pp. 327-76.
    An excellent resource with annotations. Includes classical and folk dance, Sanskrit drama and theatre, traditional drama and theatre, and regional-language drama and theatre.

Schuyler, Montgomery. A Bibliography of the Sanskrit Drama.
New York: Columbia University Press, 1906.

Van Zile, Judy. Dance in India: An Annotated Guide to Source
Materials. Providence, RI: Asian Music Publications, 1973.
An excellent, detailed bibliography with brief annotations. Includes reference works, history and theory, major classical dance
forms, folk and tribal dance forms, audiovisual materials, a guide
to Labanotation scores, and a list of resource organizations.

General Works on Indian Performance

Benegal, Som. A Panorama of Theatre in India. Bombay: Popular
Prakashan, 1968.
Overview and introduction to the Indian theatre, covering the
Sanskrit drama and theory, a summary of other traditional forms,
and the development of modern drama.

Chattopadhyaya, Kamaladevi. "National Theatre." Natya, 1, 1
(October 1956), pp. 7-10.
Considers the role of traditional theatre in historic India, and
the role of modern drama in contemporary India.

Coomaraswamy, A. K. The Dance of Siva. New York: Farrar
Straus, 1957.
The title essay in this collection of essays on Indian art and
society deals with the cosmic manifestation of Shiva's dance.

Da Cunha, Gerson. "Theatre in India" in International Theatre
Annual, 3. New York: Doubleday, 1958, pp. 128-39.

Das Nirmal. "The Hindu Dance." Theatre Arts Monthly, 22, 12
(December 1938), pp. 899-905, 907.
Brief comments about the origin and development of dance
forms in India.

Dasgupta, Hemendranath. The Indian Stage. 4 vols. Calcutta:
Metropolitan Printing and Pub. House, 1944.
An exhaustive history of the theatre in Bengal, beginning with
chapters on classical Sanskrit drama through the development of
modern Bengali theatre and drama to 1944.

Emroch, Edna. "Dance of the Orient." American Dancer, 10, 3
(January 1937), pp. 24, 46.
Brief comparison of dance East and West.

Ganguly, Anil Baran. Fine Arts in Ancient India. New Delhi:
Abhinav Publications, 1979.
Categorization and short description of sixty-four branches of
Indian fine arts, with chapters on dance, music, drama, and other

arts such as magic, cooking, horticulture, gambling, etc. The work is based on sources from ancient Indian literature, notably the Kama Sutra. This edition is a slight elaboration on the earlier book.

_____. Sixty-four Arts in Ancient India. New Delhi: English Bookstore, 1962.

Gargi, Balwant. Theatre in India. New York: Theatre Arts, 1962.
A good introduction, covering classical, traditional, and regional forms, and especially emphasizing modern theatre.

Government of India. Indian Drama. Delhi: Publication Division, 1956.
A good, cross-sectional introduction to Indian theatre, this collection of essays covers the Sanskrit drama and the regional modern dramas of the Hindi, Assamese, Bengali, Gujarati, Kannada, Kashmiri, Malayalam, Marathi, Oriya, Punjabi, Tamil, Telugu, and Urdu theatres. The viewpoint is primarily historical.

Gupta, Chandra Bhan. The Indian Theatre, Its Origin and Development Up to the Present Day. Banaras: Motilal Banarasidass, 1954.
A general survey of theatre with some limited references to dance.

Ramaswami Sastri, K. S. Indian Dance as a Spiritual Art. Madras: Author, 1961.

Ramdass, P. Raja. "A Study of the Theory of Acting in India." M.A. thesis, University of Utah, 1960.

Ranade, Ashok. "Voice Culture and Dramatic Speech." Quarterly Journal of the National Centre for the Performing Arts, 7, 4 (December 1978), pp. 23-48.
Using the Marathi drama as a point of reference, this article analyzes the nature of speech in drama. Speech types are defined, such as conversation, dialogue, monologue, soliloquy. Styles of speech are discussed, such as prose, verse, colloquial and poetic, and the dramatic potential of each style is evaluated. The principles of speech set forth in the Natyashastra are also reviewed. There are direct and implied references to the corresponding role of gesture and action.

Rangacharya, Adya. The Indian Theatre. New Delhi: National Book Trust, 1971.
Brief historical survey of Indian theatre from its origins through Sanskrit drama to the modern search for a new theatre. Includes a chapter on regional forms of traditional theatre. Simple, straightforward, well-illustrated overview.

Richmond, Farley, ed. "Theater in India." Journal of South Asian
    Literature, X, 2-4, (1975).
    Special issue on "Theatre in India." This collection of essays
and translations is one of the most valuable contributions to Indian
theatre available. Included in the volume are important articles on
the "Shadow Theatre in Andhra Pradesh"; "The Braj Ras Lila";
Jatra (including a translation of a modern play, Hitler); an excellent technical introduction to appreciating Kathakali accompanying a
translation of one part of the famous play, Nala Caritam Attakatha;
"The Rituals of Yaksagana"; and Krsnattam dance-drama.

_____, Darius Swann and Phillip Zarrilli. Indian Theatre
    In press.
    Comprehensive survey and overview of Indian theatre written
and organized on the basis of chronology as well as genre. Covers
all aspects of Indian theatre from the classical Sanskrit stage
through a wide variety of regional forms extant today, to the
modern and contemporary theatre of India.

Somasundaram Pillai, J. M. Siva-Nataraja, The Cosmic Dancer in
    Chidambaram. Annamalainagar: Author, 1970.
    An excellent study of the symbolism and the iconography of
Nataraja--the image of Siva, the Cosmic Dancer.

Yajnik, Ramanlal Kanaiyalal. The Indian Theatre: Its Origin and
    Its Later Developments Under European Influence, with Special
    Reference to Western India. New York: George Allen and Un-
    win, 1934.
    Part One serves as a general introduction to Sanskrit dramatic
theory, including aspects of staging, and to the contact between
Indian and European drama. Part Two is devoted to the rise of
the modern vernacular theatres in India, emphasizing the influence
of Shakespeare. This part also surveys various productions.

The Cultural Context: Anthropological Studies of Indian
    Performance and Culture

Hein, Norvin. The Miracle Plays of Mathura. New Haven: Yale,
    1972. See complete entry under Ritual/Religious Forms.

Singer, Milton, ed. Krishna: Myths, Rites, and Attitudes.
    Chicago: University of Chicago Press, 1968 (first published
    1966, East-West Center Press, University of Hawaii).
    An interdisciplinary work, this series of essays examines cultural
expressions and performances of the Krishna legend.

_____, ed. Traditional India: Structure and Change. Phila-
    delphia: American Folklore Society, 1959.
    Part of a larger work on the structure of Indian civilization and

problems and processes of culture change. Part II of the work is devoted to "Cultural Performances and Cultural Media." In this section important studies by major scholars are collected and focus on a variety of cultural performances from Ram Lila to the methods of religious instruction imbedded in a variety of South Indian performances.

_____. When a Great Tradition Modernizes. New York: Praeger Publishers, 1972.
A classic work in the anthropological approach to the study of performance, the volume introduces the concept of "cultural performances" which encapsulate, in discrete performances, Indian culture.

Sanskrit Drama, Aesthetics, and Performance

Appa Rao, P. S. R. Bharata's Naatya Saastra: Indian Dramatology. P. S. R. Appa Rao and P. Sri Rama Sastry, trans. Hyderabad: Naatya Maalaa Pub., 1967.
A good commentary on the Natyasastra.

Baumer, Rachel Van M. and James R. Brandon. Sanskrit Drama in Performance. Honolulu: The University Press of Hawaii, 1981.
A collection of essays including V. Raghavan's "Sanskrit Drama in Performance," which organizes much of the diffuse Natyasastra relating specifically to performance. Kapila Vatsyayan's "Dance Techniques of Sanskrit Theater" draws specific examples from Sanskrit plays and applies descriptions from the NS to a close reading of stage directions and then reviews movement types required for a production of The Vision of Vasavadatta. Pragna Thakkar Enros' chapter on "Producing Sanskrit Plays in the Tradition of Kutiyattam," is an excellent introduction to the form. Other important essays combine to make this volume a primer for those interested in practical production of Sanskrit dramas. [NS=Natyasastra]

Beer. Roland. "Kalidas and Brecht." Sangeet Natak, 38 (October-December 1975), pp. 11-20.
Assesses dramatic structure and dramatic content of verses in an essay comparing Brecht's and Kalidasa's plays. The analysis offers several implications for movement.

Bharata. Natya Sastra. Manomohan Ghosh, trans. and ed. Calcutta: The Royal Asiatic Society of Bengal, 1950, 1961. 2 vols. Revised 2nd ed. of vol. I, Calcutta: Granthalaya Private Limited, 1967.
The encyclopedia of Sanskrit drama and theatre composed between 200 B.C. and 200 A.D. The work covers a host of topics including theatre architecture, acting, costuming, dance, gestures of all parts of the body, makeup, properties, how to write plays, music, rituals of performance, types of dramatic roles, and many others.

Bharata. Tandava Laksanam, Or The Fundamentals of Ancient Hindu
Dancing. B. V. Narayanaswami Naidu, P. S. Naidu and O. V.
R. Pantulu, trans. Madras: G. S. Press, 1936.
A translation of the fourth chapter of the Natyasastra, on dance,
with a glossary of technical dance terms taken from other chapters.
Good introduction provided by the translator.

Bhat, G. K. "Natya and Nrtya: An Aspect of Dramatic Representation." Journal of the Bombay Branch of the Royal Asiatic Society. XXXIX, 40 (1964-65), pp. 143-155.
Speculation as to the extent and nature of dance within performances of ancient Sanskrit drama.

_____. The Vidusaka. Ahmedabad: New Order Book Co.,
1959.
An excellent and thorough study of the origins, development and
function of this clown character in the Sanskrit drama. Also includes an analysis of several examples of the character as he appears in selected dramas.

Bhatt, S. C. Drama In Ancient India. New Delhi: Amrit Book
Co., 1961.
A good introduction to the Sanskrit drama, including origins,
elements of staging, society as reflected in the drama, the theoretical background, and several of the major dramatists.

Bhise, Usha. "The Technique of Medieval Sanskrit Drama."
Quarterly Journal of the National Centre for the Performing
Arts, 8, 4 (December 1979), pp. 15-24.
Examines the role of dance in medieval Sanskrit drama. Based
on the precepts of classical treatises, and on specific examples from
the drama, the article explores the ways in which the written drama
dictated performance technique, and how technique later affected
dramatic structure, imagery, and rhythms.

Byrski, M. Christopher. "Can Sanskrit Drama Tell Us Anything
More?" Educational Theatre Journal, 27, 4 (1975), pp. 445-452.
Suggestions for a new approach to the study of Sanskrit drama
based on Indian aesthetic and ethnical criteria rather than "impressionism."

_____. "Theatre and Sacrifice: Natya and Yajna." Prajna, IX,
1 (October 1963), pp. 63-70.
Reexamines the first chapter of the Natyasastra in the light of
the central focus of the Vedas, i.e. yajna or the sacrifice symbolizing the function of creation. Theatrical performance is seen as a
form of sacrifice.

Chaudhury, Pravas Jivan. "The Theory of Rasa." Journal of
Aesthetics and Art Criticism, XI, 2 (December 1952), pp. 147-
150.

Though this article is written in terms of poetry, it provides a good, short analysis of rasa. Includes some comparisons to Western aesthetics.

Coomaraswamy, Ananda and Gopala Kristnayya Duggirala. The Mirror of Gesture Being the Abhinaya Darpana of Nandikesvara. New Delhi: Munshiram Manoharlal Publishers Pvt. Ltd., 1977 (Originally published 1917, Cambridge: Harvard University Press).
First English translation of Nandikesvara's classical text on gesture in Indian performance. Coomaraswamy provides an introductory essay on the nature of Indian acting.

Dace, Wallace. "The Concept of Rasa in Sanskrit Dramatic Theory." Educational Theatre Journal, 15 (1963), pp. 249-54.
Explains rasa as the audience's "tasting" an emotion as opposed to experiencing it in real life. Clarifies this aesthetic experience with explanations from various classical treatises, and with comparisons to Western theoretical writings.

Dalal, Minakshi L. Conflict in Sanskrit Drama. Bombay: Somaiya, 1973.
An examination of Sanskrit dramatic theory and practice in terms of the Western notion of dramatic conflict.

Dhananjaya. The Dasarupa: A Treatise on Hindu Dramaturgy. George C. O. Haas, trans. Delhi: Motilal Banarsidass, 1962 (First published N.Y.: Columbia University Press, 1912).
Tenth-century Sanskrit text presenting a set of rules governing theatre and drama. Includes an extensive introduction and translation.

Dwivedi, Swaranlata. "Sudraka's Mricchakatika in Nai Nautanki." Natya (Winter 1958-59), pp. 25-28, 63.
A review of a current production, which essentially addresses the difficulties in producing a Sanskrit play in contemporary India.

Enros, Pragna Thakkar. "A Reconstruction of the Style of Producing Plays in the Ancient Indian Theatre." Ph.D. diss., Toronto, 1979.
Intended as an aid in reconstructing the authentic style of producing Sanskrit plays, this thesis relies on evidence from theoretical treatises on dramaturgy, on plays from the classical period, and on the existing form of play production for Kutiyattam.

Gamlath, Sucharita. "Indian Aesthetics and the Nature of Dramatic Emotions." British Journal of Aesthetics, 9, 4 (1969), pp. 372-386.
A good, comparative analysis of the views of four medieval Indian aestheticians on the nature of the aesthetic experience in the theatre.

_____. "A Philosophical Investigation into the Nature and Role of Emotion in Drama with Reference to Classical Indian Aesthetics." Ph.D. diss., University of London, 1969.

Gargi, Balwant. "Production of The Little Clay Cart." Sangeet Natak, 5 (July-September 1967), pp. 37-44.
Gargi describes his staging choices and methods for production of this Sanskrit play at the University of Washington. General references to movement.

Gerow, Edwin. "Indian Poetics" in A History of Indian Literature, Vol. V, Jan Gonda, ed. Wiesbaden: Otto Harrassowitz, 1977, pp. 217-301.
Valuable current scholarly overview of the history and development of Indian poetics from prehistory to the late theorists. Gerow includes short, succinct, scholarly, yet readable sections on all the major figures and works in Indian poetics from the Natyasastra to Rajasekhara to Abhinavagupta. An important resource for the serious student of Indian theatre aesthetics.

Gnoli, Raniero. The Aesthetic Experience According to Abhinavagupta. Rome: Instituto Italiano Per Il Medio Ed Estreme Oriente, 1956.
A translation of Abhinavagupta's commentary on the Natyasastra. The introduction to this edition provides valuable explanation of Abhinavagupta's theory.

Gopinath, Natanakalanidhi. Abhinaya Prakasika. Madras: Natana Niketan Publications, 1957.
A selection of translated verses from various Sanskrit texts, concerning fundamentals of Indian dancing.

Jha, Bechan. Concept of Poetic Blemishes in Sanskrit Poetics. Varanasi: Chowkhamba Sanskrit Series Office, 1965.
An analysis of literary "defects" as treated in the Natyasastra and other theoretical works pertaining to Sanskrit drama.

Kale, Pramod Keshav. "The Natyasastra of Bharata: A Selective Critical Exposition for the Western Theatre Scholar." Ph.D. diss., University of Wisconsin, 1967.

_____. The Theatric Universe. Bombay: Popular Prakashan, 1974.
The best introduction to the Natyasastra written from a decidedly performance perspective which makes intelligible to the Western student of performance many of the concepts and processes of classical Indian aesthetics of performance. It places in the total aesthetic context of the NS the use and training of the body.

Kangle, R. P. "Abhinavagupta." Quarterly Journal of the National Centre for the Performing Arts, 9, 2 (June 1980), pp. 13-19.

Some biographical information about this Sanskrit writer is included, but most of the article is an exposition of parts of the Natyasastra, with particular attention given to Abhinavagupta's interpretation.

Keith, Arthur Berriedale. The Sanskrit Drama in Its Origin, Development, Theory and Practice. London: Oxford University Press, 1924.
Standard work in the field for years. More recent works have challenged many of the assumptions as well as historical developments outlined in Keith's text.

Konow, Sten. The Indian Drama. Trans. S. N. Ghosal. Calcutta: General Printers and Publishers, 1969.
A scholarly historical analysis of the Sanskrit drama, considering origins and theoretical foundations, the structure and types of dramas, and the major dramatists and their works. There are also introductory remarks about performance methods.

Levi, Sylvain. The Theatre of India. 2 vols. Narayan Mukherji, trans. Calcutta: Writers Workshop Publication, 1978.
This is the long-awaited English translation of Levi's classic work on the history of Indian theatre, and Sanskrit drama and theatre in particular. Volume One covers various aspects of dramatic art, a history of Indian dramatic literature, and aesthetics. Volume Two discusses the origins of drama, possible Greek influences, dramatic practice (hall, stage, preliminaries, troupes, actors, direction, management), and modern and contemporary theatre.

Mankad, Dolarray R. The Types of Sanskrit Drama. Karachi: Urmi Prakashan Mandir, 1936.
A critical analysis of Sanskrit dramatic theory as it influenced the development of different types of drama.

Masson, J. L. and M. V. Patwardhan. Aesthetic Rapture: The Rasadhyaya of the Natyasastra. 2 Vols. Poona: Deccan College, 1970.
A translation of the chapter on rasa from the Natyasastra, and of major passages from the commentary by Abhinavagupta. The authors' introductory chapter provides helpful analysis of Sanskrit theory of aesthetic experience.

Mayo, Donald S. "Indian Drama, Its Theory, Development and Practice in Relation to Hindu Philosophy." M.A. thesis, University of Hawaii, 1952.

Mukerjee, Radhakamal. "'Rasas' as Springs of Art in Indian Aesthetics." Journal of Aesthetics and Art Criticism, XXIV, 1 (Fall 1965), pp. 91-96.
Discusses rasa as it functions in all the fine arts in India, with particular emphasis on painting and drama. The arousal of rasa

through gesture, posture, movements and glances is analyzed briefly.

Mukherji, Ramaranjan. Literary Criticism in Ancient India. Calcutta: Sanskrit Pustak Bhandar, 1966, Chaps. 4, 5, 6.
A highly technical study of Sanskrit poetics and criticism. Chapter 4 is devoted to the theory of rasa.

Nandikesvara. Abhinayadarpanam. Manomohan Ghosh, trans. and ed. Calcutta: Manisha Granthalaya Private Ltd., 1975 (3rd ed.).
Next to the Natyasastra, the most important text treating gestures used in Indian performance. Includes an extended set of introductory materials on the manuscript, abhinaya, and the work itself. Accompanied by illustrations of basic hand gestures.

Nath, R. "A Study of the Sanskrit Texts on the Inter-relationship of the Performing and the Plastic Arts (With Special Reference to the Devangana of Khajuroho)." Quarterly Journal of the National Centre for the Performing Arts, 8, 2 (June 1979), pp. 1-22.
Examines passages from the Natyasastra, the Vishnudharmottara-Purana, the Aparajitaprchchha, the Samarangana-Sutradhara, and Kshirarnava. Emphasis is on the theoretical roots linking the rhythmic qualities of the dance to temple sculpture. Excellent illustrations and explanation.

Nehru, Jawaharlal. "The Old Indian Theatre." Natya, 1, 4 (December 1957), pp. 23-27.
A brief, historical review of Sanskrit drama, with some comparison to Greek tragedy.

Neog, Maheswar. "Mudras in the Kalika-Purana." Sangeet Natak, 45 (July-September 1977), pp. 5-7.
Treats comparatively the development of mudras and histrionic hastas. Concentrates on four hands, including description of hand and finger placement.

Panchal, Goverdhan. "Bharata's Stage in Action." Sangeet Natak, 34 (October-December 1974), pp. 64-80.
Detailed description of size, shape and design of a middle-sized rectangular theatre as proposed in the Natyasastra. Also considers use of the space in terms of staging problems and movements of the actors in specific situations in various dramas.

_____. "The Curtain in Abhijnana Sakuntala." Sangeet Natak, 41 (July-September 1976), pp. 5-12.
Explores the use of three different types of stage curtain, as suggested by stage directions in Sakuntala. Interprets the quality of movement and mood created by use of these stage devices.

_____. "The Curtain in Classical Sanskrit Drama." Sangeet Natak, 25 (July-September 1972), pp. 23-38.
Article traces a number of historical references to use of the curtain in Sanskrit theatre, and explores the variety of uses of the curtain. By examining these stage directions, the author discusses the quality and mood of entrances and exits, and various staging conventions employing the hand-held curtain.

Raghavan, V. "The Aesthetics of Ancient Indian Drama." Indian Literature, I, 2 (April-September 1958), pp. 67-74.
Explains rasa as the emotional states in the themes of plays, as the aesthetic response of the audience, and as the attainment of complete absorption when inner spirit is "dis-covered"; thus character and plot serve or are vehicles of rasa. Discusses staging technique in terms of the ideal of refinement; some reference to movement.

_____. "Sanskrit Drama: Theory and Performance." Comparative Drama, I, 1 (Spring 1967), pp. 36-48.
A very good introduction to the art of Sanskrit drama, covering some of the early literary references to it, and theoretical aspects such as modes of dramatic expression, dramatic structure, elements of character and action, rasa, and occasions of performance. Production technique is discussed, including the functions of music, gesture and movement. Raghavan also suggests several reasons for the decline of Sanskrit drama.

_____. "Uparupakas and Nritya-Prabandhas." Sangeet Natak, 2 (April 1966), pp. 5-25.
Theoretical discussion of two dramatic classifications based on classical treatises.

Ramachandran, K. V. "Music and Dance in Kalidasa." Journal of Oriental Research, (1948-49, 1950-51), pp. 116-135.
Discusses dance as found in the works of this Sanskrit dramatist.

Rangacharya, Adya. Drama in Sanskrit Literature. Bombay: Popular Prakashan, 1967.
A very good study of Sanskrit drama, considering its relation to other Sanskrit literary forms, its origin, development of the form in terms of plot and characters, and an examination of plays and playwrights. The author also gives attention to stage conditions and aspects of performance.

_____. Introduction to Bharata's Natya-Sastra. Bombay. Popular Prakashan, 1966.
A short, simplified version of the classical treatise, with very helpful interpretation. An excellent introduction.

Rao, D. Subba. "A Critical Survey of the Ancient Indian Theatre in Accordance with the Bharata Natyasastra and Its Commenta-

---

tors." <u>Journal of the Oriental Institute</u>, 2, 2 (October 1959),
pp. 188-208.

Richmond, Farley. "Sanskrit Plays Abroad." <u>Times of India Annual</u>,
1971, pp. 39-50.
A survey of productions of Sanskrit drama in Germany, England,
America, China and Russia. Richmond describes the adaptations of
the scripts, as well as the staging techniques used in these productions of <u>Shakuntala</u>, <u>The Little Clay Cart</u>, <u>The Vision of Vasavadatta</u>
and <u>Bhagavad-Ajjukiya</u> (<u>The Priest and the Prostitute</u>).

Shah, Priyabala. "Ancient Indian Drama." <u>Natya</u>, 1, 1 (October
1956) 19-20, 40.
Describes the ten or twelve types of play, as defined in the
<u>Natyasastra</u> and in the <u>Visnudharmottara</u>.

————. "Costume and Make-up in Ancient Texts." <u>Natya</u>
(Winter 1958-59), pp. 5-7, 60.
Describes the four categories of costume, makeup, decoration
and symbolic set pieces established in classical treatises.

Shastri, Surendra Nath. <u>The Laws and Practices of Sanskrit Drama</u>.
Varanasi: Chowkhamba Sanskrit Series Office, 1961.
A comprehensive explication of the canons of Sanskrit drama.
This exhaustive study covers all elements of the drama and also
examines the application of these dramatic laws by the playwrights.

Shekhar, I. <u>Sanskrit Drama: Its Origin and Decline</u> (2nd ed.).
New Delhi: Munshiram Manoharlal, 1977. (Originally published
in 1960 by E. J. Brill).
Focuses on the non-Aryan elements that might have influenced
the development of Sanskrit drama. Shekhar also draws on dance
and drama traditions from South India in his arguments, including
early Tamil evidence in poetry, Bharatantyam/Devadasis. Suggests
that the cause of the decline of Sanskrit drama was linked to class
conflicts.

Sundaram, C. S. "Drama, Dance and Music in the Works of Bana
and Harsa." <u>Samskrita Ranga Annual</u> (1958-59), pp. 17-23.
Scholarly analysis of these elements in the works of two Sanskrit
dramatists.

Swann, Darius L. "Indian and Greek Drama: Two Definitions."
<u>Comparative Drama</u>, 3, 2 (1969), pp. 110-120.
Enlightening comparison for the Western student of Greek drama
and Sanskrit drama as informed by Aristotle's <u>Poetics</u> and Bharata's
<u>Natyasastra</u>. Differentiates between types of action and imitation,
as well as catharsis and rasa. Finally the two traditions are differentiated according to understandings of time and history.

Unni, N. P. <u>Nala Episode in Sanskrit Literature</u>. Trivandrum:
College Book House, 1977.

An examination of this episode and theme from the Mahabharata. The work surveys other poetry and drama which also incorporate the Nala theme.

_____, ed. Sanskrit Plays of V. Krishnan Tampy. Trivandrum: College Book House, 1977.
Collection of eight Sanskrit plays authored by the late V. Krishnan Tampy, Sanskrit scholar of Kerala, for performance during annual Sanskrit College Day Celebrations. The English preface and introduction present some basic information on the status of the production of Sanskrit plays in the twentieth century.

Uresekar, H. S. "Music in Sanskrit Drama." Journal of the Bombay Branch of the Royal Asiatic Society, 41-42 (1966-67), pp. 124-144.

Vatsyayan, Kapila. Classical Indian Dance in Literature and the Arts. Sangeet Natak Akademi, 1968.
Detailed and technical analysis of dance, as treated in Natyasastra and other treatises, in comparison with sculpture, painting, and literature. Excellent study of dance movement.

Verma, K. M. Natya, Nrtta and Nrtya: Their Meaning and Relation. Bombay: Orient Longmans, 1957.
Explains origin and development of these terms, and the relationship of "pure" and "mimetic" dance and acting in drama.

Winternitz, M. History of Indian Literature. Subhadra Jha, trans. Delhi: Motilal Banarsidass, 1963.
The most important chapter is that on "Dramatic Poetry," pp. 178-301.

Zarrilli, Phillip B. "Kalidasa's Sakuntala in Performance." Sangeet Natak, 55 (January-March 1980), pp. 17-40.
Description of the process of adaptation, rehearsal, and performance of Kalidasa's Sakuntala. Includes brief section on acting and movement styles selected, with accompanying photographs.

Miscellaneous Studies in the History of Early Indian Performance

Basu, Jogiraj. "Music, Dance and Drama in the Vedic Age." Prabuddha Bharata, 66 (May 1961), pp. 223-227.

Byrski, M. Christopher. Concept of Ancient Indian Theatre. New Delhi: Munshiram Manoharlal, 1974.
Exploration of the earliest philosophical concept of theatre in India.

Chandra, Abinash. "References to Dancing in the Vedas." Natya, 8, 4 (1965), pp. 22-23.

A variety of examples from the Vedas are quoted which articulate philosophical concepts and describe dance as an expression of divine glory.

Chitre, P. A. "The Drama in India: The Beginnings." Natya, 9, 1 (1966), pp. 2-4.
The etymology and mythic origins of natya are reviewed. Author emphasizes the idea that drama developed from the existing art of dance. The notion that Indian drama is derived from the Greek drama is rejected, and early indigenous examples of drama are discussed.

Goswamy, B. N. "Those Moon-Faced Singers; Music and Dance at the Royal Courts in the Panjab." Quarterly Journal of the National Centre for the Performing Arts, 7, 1 (March 1978), pp. 1-10.
By reviewing pictoral and written accounts, the author assesses the extent and nature of the nautch performances (a combination of singing and dancing) at the court of Balwant Singh in the eighteenth century.

Jain, Jyotindra. "New Evidence of Wall Paintings with Rasa Dance and Other Themes." Quarterly Journal of the National Centre for the Performing Arts, 10, 4 (December 1981), pp. 14-19.
Illustration and description of wall paintings, apparently from the eighteenth century, in Hafeshvara Mahadeva temple. The paintings are of the incarnations of Vishnu in narrative form, of rasa dance (stick dance), and of scenes from the epics and Puranas.

Narayanan, M. G. S. "Devadasi System in Kerala." Kalamandalam Annual (1969), pp. 31-35.
Close historical study, including dance training described in the early south Indian epic poems.

Naidu, B. V. N., and P. S. Naidu and O. V. R. Pantulu. Tandava Laksanam or The Fundamentals of Ancient Hindu Dancing (reprint). New Delhi: Munshiram Manoharlal, 1971.
Primarily sets forth definitions of the Karanas (fundamental poses). Includes a glossary of technical terms.

Neubauer, Jutta Jain. "The Stepwell of Sathamba (Gujarat) and Its Sculptured Scenes of Dance and Music." Quarterly Journal of the National Centre for the Performing Arts, 10, 2 (1981), pp. 1-16.
Examines Gujarat stepwell sculptures as expressive of classical movement and bodily action in the dance.

Ramachandran, Nirmala. "Classical Dance of the Ancient Tamils." Tamil Culture (Madras), XII, 1-2 (1966), pp. 171-180.
Briefly outlines some of the precepts of the Silappadikaram, and suggests that this treatise might have predated the Natya Sastra.

The article refers to aspects of the dance such as hand gestures, the eleven types of dance and a brief description of their contents, and the legendary origin of dance.

Ramachandran, P. "The Devadasis of Travancore," Journal of Kerala Studies, 6, 3-4 (1979), pp. 385-429.
Historical study of the devadasi (dancing-girls employed in temples) system in the southern region of modern Kerala. Includes a discussion of recruitment, duties (including the study and performance of dance), and social status.

Srinivasa Iyengar, C. R. Indian Dance. Madras: Blaze Pub., 1948.
Outlines characteristics and themes of music and dance, based on ancient literature and treatises, such as the Ramayana, Geeta Govinda, padams, and Sanskrit dramas.

Varadpande, M. L. Ancient Indian and Indo-Greek Theatre. Atlantic Highlands, NJ: Humanities Press, Inc., 1981.
Examines the historical connections between the theatre and drama of ancient India and Greece.

_____. "Nagarjunakonda Amphitheatre." Sangeet Natak, 30 (October-December 1973), pp. 26-37.
Focuses on the excavation of this enclosure which offers evidence of dramatic art performances, though no classical treatise describes such a rectangular theatre space as this one. Good description of the space.

_____. "Theatrical Arts in Jataka Tales." Sangeet Natak, 38 (October-December 1975), pp. 29-34.
Stories from Jataka are explored for their references to popular entertainments from ancient India. Actors, dancers, singers, musicians, tumblers, wrestlers, magicians, and bards appear in these stories. Information on the entertainer's status, on types of theatres, patronage and festivals is extracted. Some mention of acrobatic stunts and dancing feats is included.

Vatsyayan, Kapila. "The Classical Indian Dance and Sculpture." Diogenes, 45 (Spring 1964), pp. 24-36.
Briefly discusses rasa as a theory for aesthetics and technique in the Indian arts, concentrating on the relationship between sculpture and dancing. Assesses the dance in terms of its spatial and temporal qualities. Argues for the correspondence between dance and sculpture throughout Indian history, and that a study of Indian dance in a given period may be made through the study of sculptural representations.

_____. "Some Dance Sculptures from Assam." Quarterly Journal of the National Centre for the Performing Arts, 10, 3 (1981), pp. 19-35.

Reevaluation of some Assamese sculptural figures as they relate to dance motifs. An expansion in light of new explorations by the author of her basic arguments in Classical Indian Dance in Literature and the Arts.

General Studies of Multiple Forms of Performance

Baruah, Gojen. "Classical and Folk Dances of Assam." Kala Vikash Kendra (Cuttack), (1963), pp. 31-35.
Very brief remarks on a few forms.

Bhavnani, Enakshi. The Dance of India. Bombay: D. S. Taraporewala Sons and Co., 1972.
Written from a dancer's point of view, this general work is a valuable overview of major forms of Indian dance and dance-drama. It describes all of the main schools of classical dance, and then devotes specific chapters to technical descriptions with line drawings and photographs of techniques including hand gestures, face, head, eyes, eyebrows, and neck; the feet, timing, and rhythm; Indian music and instruments; and finally, design, costume, and jewelry of dance forms. The author concludes this general study with surveys of folk and tribal dances of various regions of India, as well as the "revival of dance" in modern India.

Chattopadhyay, Kamaladevi. "Some Dance-Dramas of South India." Natya (Winter 1958-59), pp. 46-48.
General comments about the dance-drama forms Kudiyattam, Kathakali, Krishnattam, Yakshagana, Kuchipudi, and Bhagavata Mela Nataka.

Cousins, J. H. "Dance-Drama and Shadow-Play" in The Arts and Crafts of Kerala, by Stella Kramrisch, J. H. Cousins, and Vasudeva Poduval. Cochin: Paico Pub. House, 1970.
Overview of development and types of performance in Kerala.

Devi, Ragini. Dance Dialects of India. Delhi: Vikas Pub., 1972.
General introduction to a variety of specific dance and dance-drama forms of India including short chapters on Bharata Natya, Kathakali, Krishnattam, Mohiniattam, Kuchipudi, Bhagavata Mela, Kuttiyattam, ritual performances to Bhagavati, Yakshagana, Orissa dance, Chhau of Seraikella, Kathak, Manipuri, and folk performances. Includes personal accounts of this early modern Indian dance pioneer's own career and performances. Excellent photographs make this a valuable basic, introductory source from an artist's point of view.

_____. Dances of India. Calcutta: Susil Gupta, 1962.
Short introductory study of dance, covering Bhagavata Mela, Bharatanatyam, Kathakali, Kathak, Chhau of Seraikella, and Maniprui.

Devi, Sri Ragini. Nritanjali: An Introduction to Hindu Dancing.
New York: Hari G. Govil, 1928.
A simplified introduction to the traditional conventions and motifs
of Indian dance, including the symbolism of gesture and movement.

De Zoete, Beryl. The Other Mind: Dance and Life in South India.
London: Victor Gollancz, 1953.
Personal account of travels, and description of many perform-
ances. Excellent photographs.

Dhamija, Ram. "Masks of India." Times of India Annual (1967),
pp. 73-80.
Illustrated overview of the wide variety of masks and their use
in India.

Gaston, Anne-Marie. "Encounter with Indian Dance." Sangeet
Natak, 19 (January-March 1971), pp. 24-33.
Comparison of ballet and modern dance with Bharata Natyam
and Orissi.

Ghose, Rajeshwari, "The Martial Element in the Dance of India."
Festival of Asian Arts. Souvenir Program. (5th ed.) Hong
Kong (1980), pp. 125-127.
Substantive though brief overview of the relationship between
martial arts, combat, and performance forms throughout India.

Khokar, Mohan. "The Geeta Govinda in Dance." Natya, 9, 4
(1966-67), pp. 32-35.
Analyzes the incorporation of the Geeta Govinda, the earliest
possible songbook of the Hindus, in the repertoires of Orissi,
Krishnattam, Manipuri and Bharata Natyam.

Kuppuswamy, Gowrie and M. Hariharan. Readings on Indian Music.
Trivandrum: College Book House, 1979.
Includes several very brief and cursory articles on the relation-
ship between music and dance including, "Krishna Theme in Music
and Dance," "A History of Indian Opera," "Kathakali and Dance
Drama in India," and "Music in Sanskrit Drama."

Marg. Vol. 19, 2 (March 1966) Special Issue: Invitation to Dance.
The articles cover a range of dance forms, including Bhagavata
Mela, Therukoothu, Yakshagana, Kuchipudi, and Krishnattam.

Menon, C. A. "The Histrionic Art of Malabar." Journal of Indian
Society of Oriental Art, IX (1941), pp. 105-132.
Surveys Kerala Society and performance forms of each strata of
society from ritual to classical arts. Most emphasis on description
of Kathakali.

Menon, V. K. Narayana. "The Place of Music in Indian Dance-
Dramas" in Theatre India, National Drama Festival Cochin,

<u>1977</u>. Trichur: Kerala Sangeetha Nataka Akademi, 1977.
The role of music in a wide variety of dance-dramas.

Mukhopadhyay, D. D., ed. <u>Lesser Known Forms of Performing</u>
<u>Arts in India</u>. New Delhi: Sterling, 1978.
Collection of twenty-two brief articles on a wide variety of
forms of Indian performance from the relatively well-known Kutiyattam to little-known forms like Yathrakkali.

Narasimhacharya, V. V. "Contribution to the Telugu Region to the
Dance Art." <u>Journal of the Music Academy</u> (Madras), 45
(1974), pp. 192-210.

Narayana Menon, Vatakke Kurupath. "Music of India and Its Role
in Indian Dance." <u>Atlantic Monthly</u>, 192, 4 (October 1953),
pp. 152-57.

Nawab, V. S. <u>419 Illustrations of Indian Music and Dance in</u>
<u>Western Indian Style</u>. Ahmedabad: Sarabhai Manilal Nawab,
1964.

Pani, Jiwan. "The Female Impersonator in Traditional Indian
Theatre." <u>Sangeet Natak</u>, 45 (July-September 1977), pp.
37-42.
Briefly considers the historical impetus for female impersonation.
Discusses the female impersonator's functions in stylized convention. Describes, with illustrations, the major traditional theatre
forms incorporating female impersonation, in terms of costume,
makeup, and background of the performers.

_____. "Hanuman and Traditional Indian Theatre." <u>Sangeet</u>
<u>Natak</u>, 35 (January-March 1975), pp. 5-16.
Surveys the various interpretations of Hanuman's characteristics, based on the <u>Ramayana</u>. The lack of consistent interpretation
is explained by examining the delineation of the character in various forms of theatre. Brief comments on movement, costume, and
makeup.

Panikkar, Kavalam Narayana. "Thouryathrikam on the Traditional
Stage in Kerala" in <u>Theatre India, National Drama Festival</u>
<u>Cochin, 1977</u>. Trichur: Kerala Sangeetha Nataka Akademi,
1977.
Discusses three basic elements of the composite drama in traditional performance in Kerala including vocal music, dance, and
instrumental music.

Patil, Vimla and Sunil Kothari. "Radha in Indian Song and Dance."
<u>Times of India Annual</u> (1972), pp. 19-28.
The article describes the attributes of Radha, consort of Krishna, as she appears in poetry, music, painting, and dance.

Poduval, R. V. "The Malabar Drama." Madras Christian College Magazine Quarterly Series, 8 (April 1928), pp. 101-107.

Raghavan, V. "Kathakali and Other Forms of Bharatanatya." Triveni: Journal of Indian Renaissance (Madras), 6, 2 (1933), pp. 148-169.
Corrective to mistaken panegyrics in blind praise of Kathakali, the article places Kathakali in the comparative context of other forms making use of essential features of the Natyasastra, especially the Tamil Terukkoottu.

Rainer, Yvonne. "From an Indian Journal." The Drama Review, 15, 3 (Spring 1971), pp. 132-138.
Impressionistic descriptions of a variety of dance and theatre forms.

Ramanathan, Bhushabam S. "A Survey of the Traditions of Music, Dance and Drama in Madras State." Bulletin of the Institute of Traditional Culture, (Part 2) (1960), pp. 214-221.

Ranganath, H. K. The Karnatak Theatre. Dharwar: Karnatak University, 1960.
Briefly considers classical and traditional forms, with major emphasis on contemporary developments, in Mysore State.

Renouf, Renee. "Visit to India." Dance Magazine, 42, 1 (January 1968), pp. 48-51.
Firsthand account of several dance schools.

Richmond, Farley. "Selected Crafts of Traditional Indian Theatre." Times of India Annual (1972), pp. 29-36.
In a comparative survey, Richmond describes the design, construction, and use of masks, makeup, and costumes in a variety of traditional theatre forms.

_____. "Some Religious Aspects of Indian Traditional Theatre." The Drama Review, 15, 3 (Spring 1971), pp. 122-131.
A description of the ritual components in a variety of traditional forms, including Kathakali, Kutiyattam, Yakshagana, Prahlada Charitam, Ramlila, Krishnattam, and Therukoothu.

Sarabhai, M. The Sacred Dance of India. Bombay: BVB, 1979.
A short, general introduction to a variety of classical and folk forms. Along with cultural and historical background, there are some brief comments on training and technique.

Schramm, H. "Musical Theatre in India." Asian Music 1, 1 (1968-69), pp. 31-40.
Views India's dance-dramas as musical theatre. Explains the theoretical basis (from classical treatises) and historical development of "musical drama" in India. This emphasis on music is the

author's viewpoint in outlining the modern forms, both classical and folk, which have evolved today. Little reference to movement.

Sitaram, K. N. "Dramatic Representations in South India, with Special Reference to Travancore and Tinnevelly District." Journal of the Royal Asiatic Society of Great Britain and Ireland (1924), pp. 229-237.

Tagore, Pratima. "The Dance in India." Theatre Arts Monthly, 20, 1 (January 1936), pp. 54-58.
A brief, introductory statement about dance forms in India.

Varadpande, M. L. "Dashavatar." Sangeet Natak, 50 (October-December 1978), pp. 37-44.
Discussion of the mythic and historical development of Krishna dramas. Specific reference to the hand gestures which indicate the various incarnations of Vishnu. Mentions a variety of forms which incorporate this tradition and briefly enumerates some performance distinctions among them.

_____. Krishna Theatre in India. Atlantic Highlands, NJ: Humanities Press, 1982.
Traces the history, continuity, and various manifestations of Krishna performance from the earliest times through the present. Includes chapters on specific forms of Krishna theatre such as Ras Leela, Ankia Nat, Krishna Attam, Kala, as well as general chapters on Krishna performance in folk theatre and classical dance. The discussion of each form includes a brief description of techniques and staging.

_____. "Religion and Theatre." Sangeet Natak, 53-54 (July-December 1979), pp. 5-13.
Assesses the influence of Buddhism, Jainism and the Shaiva and Vaishnava cults on Indian dance and theatre. Excellent background reading but little direct reference to movement.

_____. Traditions of Indian Theatre. New Delhi: D.K., 1978.
Collection of essays on various topics of Indian theatre history and practice. The three concluding chapters on "Ganesha," "Vidusaka," and "Sutradhara" include general comparative reviews of historical and extant practice relating to each topic.

_____ and Sunil Subhedar, eds. The Critique of Indian Theatre. Atlantic Highlands, NJ: Humanities Press, 1982.
Collection of scholarly research papers and essays, many published early in the twentieth century and not readily available today, on the history of Indian theatre and drama. Of most importance is Pisharoti's early article (1922) on "Acting in Kerala" which concentrates mainly on the various Kuthu forms of Kerala, especially Kutiyattam.

Vatsyayan, Kapila. "The Tradition of the Performing Arts."
Quarterly Journal of the National Centre for the Performing
Arts, 4, 1 (March 1975), pp. 32-40.
Discusses the artistic manifestations of different social groups in
India. Addresses the nature of movement as an impersonal vehicle
of communication.

_____. Traditional Indian Theatre: Multiple Streams. New
Delhi: National Book Trust, 1980.
Although somewhat technical in its assumed vocabulary, this is
the most important comprehensive, recent overview of Indian theatre traditions. It includes major chapters on a wide variety of
theatrical traditions including Kutiyattam, Yaksagana, Bhagavatamela
and Kuchipudi, the three forms of Chhau, Ankia-Nata and Bhaona,
Ramlila, Raslila and Krishnalila, Yatra, Bhavai, Svanga, Khyala,
Nautanki, and Tamasa. Each chapter includes sections devoted to
staging and movement techniques of the theatrical form, understood
within the context of the literary, historical, and performative circumstances of its growth and development. The author explicitly
is writing with two purposes in mind: (1) to provide substantive
overviews of specific theatrical forms, and (2) to display the "underlying unity" discernible in the various regional language forms.

Wilson, H. H., V. Raghavan, K. R. Pisharoti, and Amulya Charan
Vidyabhusan. The Theatre of the Hindus. Calcutta: Susil
Gupta, 1955.
One of the most valuable collections of articles on a wide variety
of Indian theatre topics including origins of early drama and the
dance-theatre at Ramgarh, architecture, various types of plays,
scenic methods, language of plays, rasa, characterization, and
plots. K. R. Pisharoti's chapter on "South Indian Theatre" is an
overview of a wide variety of theatrical forms in Kerala.

Zarrilli, P. B. "Kalarippayatt and the Performing Artist East and
West: Past, Present, and Future." Ph.D. diss., University
of Minnesota, 1978.
Traces the history, development and relationship of kalarippayatt,
martial art of Kerala, to a wide variety of performance forms. Includes specific documentation of martial techniques, stances, movements, and compares basic movement features of performance forms
to the martial art.

Classical Forms

Ambrose, Kay. Classical Dances and Costumes of India. London:
A. and C. Black, 1957.
A short, general description of the four major classical schools.
Includes illustrations of movement sequences.

Balakrishna Menon, K. C. Indian Classical Dances. Calcutta:
Rabindra Bharati, 1967.

A standard introduction to Bharata Natyam, Kathakali, Kathak, and Manipuri. Includes discussion of technique.

Benesh, R., J. Benesh, and M. Balchin. "Notating Indian Dance." Sangeet Natak, 9 (1968), pp. 5-24.
Though the transmission of dance heritage in India has been successful even without a notation system, due to extensive oral tradition and guru-pupil relationship, the authors stress the current need for accurate notation due to rapid changes in teaching, in audiences and in performers. Much of the article is devoted to the development and use of the Benesh system in general, and also its specific application to the four classical dance styles of India. Illustrations of the notation itself help clarify its use for both solo and group performance.

Bose, Mandrankranta. Classical Indian Dancing. Calcutta: General Printers and Pub., 1970.
A highly detailed explanation of the technique of classical dancing, based on a number of Sanskrit treatises.

Bowers, Faubion. The Dance of India. New York: AMS Press, 1967.
A balanced overview of the basic features of four of the major classical Indian dance styles based on personal observations of the training and forms in India. His straightforward introductory commentary on the difficulties of modern Indian dance are perceptive and still timely today. Bowers offers good general descriptions of basic positions and movements in the dance and dance-drama forms.

"The Classical Performing Arts of Kerala." Malayalam Literary Survey, I, 3-4 (1977), pp. 153-165.
General cursory introduction to Koothu, Kutiyattam, Mohiniattam, Krishnattam, and Kathakali.

Devi, Ragini. "Living Traditions of the Hindu Dance." American Dancer, 14, 8 (June 1941), pp. 14, 32.
Brief remarks on classical dance theory.

Gopinath. Natanakalanidhi. The Classical Dance Poses of India. Madras: Natana Niketan Pub., 1955.

Government of India. The Dance in India. New Delhi: Pub. Division, 1964.
A brief introductory work, primarily focused on the four classical schools, Kathakali, Bharata Natyam, Kathak, and Manipuri. Well-illustrated.

Ikegami, Y. "A Stratification Analysis of the Hand Gestures in Indian Classical Dancing." Semiotica, 4, 4 (1971), pp. 365-391.
Although the article is highly technical in places, it is useful for its codification of hand gestures, their formation and meaning, and their relationship to the language of the performers. Gestures are

also analyzed for their abstract and pantomimic qualities, and for their efficiency as a communication system.

Khokar, M. Traditions of Indian Classical Dance. Delhi: Clarion Books, 1979.
A good general description of Bharata Natyam, Kathakali, Kathak, Kuchipudi, Orissi, Yakshagana, with a brief chapter also devoted to modern forms. Khokar also considers the historical and mythical sources for the classical forms.

La Meri (R. M. Hughes). The Gesture Language of the Hindu Dance. New York: Benjamin Blom, 1964.
A short, general introduction which includes illustrations of 200 hand gestures and their meanings.

Ram Gopal and Serozh Dadanchanji. Indian Dancing. London: Phoenix House, 1951.
A general introduction to Indian dance, with historical background and explanation of the tradition, and brief chapters on Bharata Natyam, Kathakali, Kathak, and Manipuri.

Sangeet Natak, 29 (July-September 1973).
A tribute to four great teachers, including Guru Amubi Singh (Manipuri dance) and Guru Kunju Kurup (Kathakalai). Articles offer biographical information and some accounts of performance technique and style.

Singha, Rina and Reginald Massey. Indian Dances: Their History and Growth. London: Faber and Faber, 1967.
A standard introductory work covering Bharata Natyam, Kathakali, Kathak, Manipuri and Odissi, with brief chapters on other forms. Aspects of training, technique, and repertoire are included along with cultural and historical background.

Vatsyayan, Kapila. Indian Classical Dance. New Delhi: Publications Division, Ministry of Information and Broadcasting, 1974.
A good, basic study of the four classical dance forms. Authoritative yet not overly technical.

_____. "Indian Classical Dance--A Pointer and a Provocater." Natya, 9, 3 (1966), pp. 8-9.
Discusses the Indian dance tradition as one of total theatre, and the role of improvisation in keeping the dance a vital part of the culture.

_____. "The 108 Karanas." Sangeet Natak, 3 (October 1966), pp. 51-62.
Discussion of the 108 classical dance poses, based on the Natya Sastra.

Venkatachalam, G. Dance in India. Bombay: Nalanda Pub., 1945.

Contains highly subjective, "enthusiastic appreciations" of several Indian dancers, as well as brief chapters on Bharata Natyam, Kathakali, Mohini Attam, Kathak, and Manipuri.

Folk/Regional Forms

Agarkar, A. J. Folk-Dance of Maharashtra. Bombay: Rajabhau Joshi, 1950.
Analysis of different social groups, castes and tribes, and the folk dances of each, within Maharashtra. Covers occasions and motifs for dances, as well as movements, formations, and music.

Anand, M. R. The Dancing Foot, Delhi: Publications Division, 1967.
A very brief introduction to a few of the major folk dance forms in India. The photographs are helpful but text contains little description or analysis of movement.

Banerji, Projesh. The Folk-Dance of India. Allahabad: Kitabistan, 1944.
Covers the major folk forms of the major regions in general description. Some information on origins of tradition.

Bhanawat, Mahendra. "Overview of the Folk Theatre of Rajasthan." Sangeet Natak, 53-54 (July-December 1979), pp. 26-32.
Historical and legendary origins of the variety of folk forms in this state. Some description of performances but only general references to movement.

Choondal, Chummar. "Some Folk Arts of Kerala." Malayalam Literary Survey, V, 3-4 (1981), pp. 44-51.
Cursory description of Paavakkuthu (shadow play), Cavittunatakam, and the folk play, Kummaatti.

_____. "The Folk Arts of Kerala." Malayalam Literary Survey, I, 3-4 (1977), pp. 177-185.
Brief listing of numerous Kerala folk arts.

_____. Studies in Folklore of Kerala. Trivandrum: College Book House, 1978.
Brief introductions to a variety of forms.

Das Gupta, S. P. "A Short Introduction to the Variety of Folk Dances in India." Folk-Lore, 4 (1963), pp. 163-191.
A comprehensive, state-by-state catalogue of folk dances. There are brief descriptions of each dance, including some general descriptions of movement and formations.

Dutt, G. S. "Folk Dances and Folk Songs of Bengal." Modern
    Review, 52, 1 (July 1932), pp. 44-52.
Mentions Raibeshe, Kathi, Dhali, Jari, Baul, Kirtan, Avatar.

Ezekiel, Nissam. "The Folk Dances of India." Times of India An-
    nual, 1960, pp. 22-33.
Brief introduction to several dances.

"Fairs and Festivals of Kerala." Census of India 1961. VII B(i),
    1966.
Comprehensive catalogue with descriptions of Kerala festivals
including a list of performances associated with each festival. Includes a few brief descriptions of selected games and performances.

Folk Arts Directory (Nadodi Drissyakala Soochika). Trichur:
    Kerala Sangeetha Nataka, 1978.
A catalogue of Kerala's numerous folk arts; entries include a
brief description of each form including content, music, costumes,
purpose, and a list of artists.

Gandhi, S. "Experiments in Folk Drama." Sangeet Natak, 11 (1969),
    pp. 52-68.
Author focuses on the Bhavai and Nautanki plays, discussing
textual changes made in order to alter or clarify various rasas.
The author's reinterpretation of several texts is also discussed in
terms of the changes necessary in acting style and choreography.

Gargi, Balwant. Folk Theater of India. Seattle: University of
    Washington Press, 1966.
General overview of many of the important folk theater forms
of India including Jatra, Nautanki, Bhavai, Tamasha, Ramlila,
Raslila, Therukoothu, Yakshagana, Chhau, and brief comments on
a number of lesser-known forms. Excellent photographs and line
drawings make this a valuable introduction to the variety of forms.

Kurup, K. K. N. Aryan and Dravidian Elements in Malabar Folk-
    lore. Trivandrum: Kerala Historical Society, 1977.
Description of the grand festival of Ramavilliam celebrated every
twenty-five years in Kerala. Little attention paid to movement.

Marg. Vol. 13, 1 (December 1959) Special Issue: Folk Dances of
    India.
This issue considers folk dances in the following regions:
Andhra, Assam, Bengal, Bihar, Gujarat, Himachal Pradesh, Kanara,
Kerala, Kashmir, Maharashtra and Konkan, Madya Pradesh, Orissa,
Punjab, Rajasthan, Saurashtra, and Uttar Pradesh. Treatment of
so many forms is necessarily brief and simply descriptive in most
cases, but, as usual, the issue is profusely illustrated. An appendix categorizes each form according to its adherence to social, ceremonial, religious, or war motifs.

Mathur, Jagdish Chanra. Drama in Rural India. New York: Asia
Pub. House, 1964.
This excellent introduction surveys a variety of folk forms. The
author stresses ties between folk and classical traditions, and covers performance space and aspects of staging, costumes, makeup,
ritual components, common themes, acting conventions, the functions
of dance and music, and puppet drama.

Mukhopadhyay, Durgadas, ed. Lesser Known Forms of Performing
Arts in India. New Delhi: Sterling Publishers, 1978.
A collection of short essays, each devoted to a different tradi-
tional form. The book provides a good cross-sectional introduction,
covering forms such as Mahari, Karama, Dalkhai, Ankiya Naat,
Yakshagana, Mohiniattam, Tamasha, and several musical forms.

Natya. Folk Theatre Number. VI, 4 (1962).
Special folk theatre issue examines a variety of forms from
Kashmir, Rajasthan, Gujarat, Andhra Pradesh, Bihar, Punjab, and
Sri Lanka, and includes short articles covering Yakshagana, Bhagat,
Therukkoothu, Maanch, and Yatra.

Patnaik, D. N. "Folk Plays of Orissa." Sangeet Natak, 32 (April-
June 1974), pp. 26-33.
Brief treatment of Chadaya Nata, Ramleela Suanga, and Yatra,
covering dramatic content, staging, role of music, characters and
social significance. Little direct reference to movement.

_____. "Some Folk Dances of Orissa." Sangeet Natak, 23
(January-April 1972), pp. 42-52.
Historical and descriptive coverage of Paika Nritya (a battle
dance) and several ritual dances. Includes some descriptions of
dance movements.

Raghavan, M. D. Folk Plays and Dances of Kerala. Trichur:
Mangalodayam Press, 1947 (published by Rama Varma Archeo-
logical Society).
Most complete and perceptive short study of Kerala's many folk
forms, divided into religious, martial, and recreational dances. The
concluding chapter is a movement analysis of the collective forms.

Shukla, H. Folk Dances of Gujarat. Ahmedabad: Director of
Information and Tourism, 1966.
Surveys a variety of dances, considering function and social
context.

Spreen, H. L. and R. Ramani. Folk Dances of South India. (2nd
ed.) London: Oxford University Press, 1948.
Includes a table of terms, illustrations of and explanations for
steps and movements in executing Kummi and Kolattam folk dances.
Melodies and lyrics are also notated and translated in this collection
of South-Indian folk dances.

Swann, Darius. "Three Forms of Traditional Theatre of Uttar Pradesh, North India." Ph.D. diss., University of Hawaii, 1974.
Analysis and description of Ras Lila, Ram Lila and Svang.

Varadpande, M. L. "Ganesh in Indian Folk Theatre." Sangeet
Natak, 27 (January-March 1973), pp. 64-75.
Assesses the attributes and iconography of Ganesh as dancer
and supreme actor. Mentions folk forms which invoke or include
aspects of Ganesh in performance as a character or as presiding
deity.

_____. "Vidusaka in Indian Folk Theatre." Sangeet Natak, 33
(July-September 1974), pp. 56-65.
Argues for the traditional importance of humor in the Indian
theatre, based on the connection between "mimicry" and "imitation,"
and based on its emphasis in classical treatises. Speculates that
the comic Nata figure of folk theatre was the model for the Vidusaka
of Sanskrit drama. Briefly describes the distinctive characteristics
of the comic figure as he appears in a variety of folk theatre forms.
Includes some description of physical action.

Vatsyayan, K. M. Traditions of Indian Folk Dance. New Delhi:
Indian Book Co., 1976.
Knowledgeable survey of major forms of folk dance of each region and state in India. Following a basic description of the geog-
raphy and culture of each area of India, the work focuses on specific dances of each region and often includes specific descriptions
of movement patterns shown in line drawings and/or accompanying
photographs. An excellent beginning place for the student of Indian
folk dance.

Ritual/Religious Forms

Ashton, Martha Bush. "Spirit Cult Festivals in South Kanara."
The Drama Review, 23, 2 (1979), pp. 91-98.
Well-illustrated introduction to spirit dances of Kanara.

Bhagvat, Durga. "The Karma Festival and Its Songs." Quarterly
Journal of the National Centre of the Performing Arts, 3, 2
(June 1974), pp. 18-36.
This harvest festival includes ritual, songs, and dance. The
article covers the participating tribal groups, and two legends concerning the origin and practices of the ritual dances. Gives detailed description of the movements and style of the dance which
accompanies the ritual, as well as variant forms of the dance. Lyrics of accompanying songs are also included.

Hein, Norvin. The Miracle Plays of Mathura. New Haven: Yale
University Press, 1972.
Comprehensive study of five forms of religious drama (Jhankik,

Kathak, plays of the Bhaktamal Natak Mandali troupe, Ramlila, and Raslila) found in Mathura, a famous North Indian center of pilgrimage. A complete work which includes both specific descriptions of performance structure and techniques (including excellent photographs) as well as translations of examples of text-in-performance. Particularly effective are Hein's descriptions of the ras dances of the Raslila.

Jones, Clifford. "Dhulicitra: Historical Perspectives on Art and Ritual" in Kaladarsana: American Studies in the Art of India, Joanan G. Williams, ed. New Delhi: Oxford and IBH Pub., 1981, pp. 69-75.

_____. "A Kerala Village Temple Festival: Ritual and Folk Art Forms as Communicators of Traditional Culture." Annals of Oriental Research, Silver Jubilee Volume, 1975, pp. 399-420.
Deals mainly with the Puram Vela festival in honor of Bhagavati in one small village in Kerala. Describes in great detail each component part of the festival including processions, pujas, music performances, the Ramayana puppet performance, and the performance of the Bhagavati Pattu ritual.

Khokar, Mohan. "Serpent Dance of Malabar." Kalamandalam Annual (1968), pp. 13-15.

Panikkar, Kavalam Narayana. "Ecstasy of the Folk Dance--The Mystical Rhythms of the Village Community." Marg, 32, 2 (1978-79), pp. 81-84.
Brief descriptions of five Kerala folk-ritual performances.

Stache-Rosen, Valentina. Bhutas and Teyyams: Spiritworship and Ritual Dances in South Kanara and North Malabar. Bangalore: W. Q. Judge Press (prepared by Max Mueller Bhavan), 1978.
Catalogue for exhibit includes an introduction to spirit worship, numerous photographs and short commentaries on specific deities.

Varma, L. A. Ravi. "Yatrakali and Bhadrakali-Pattu" Bulletin of the Rama Varma Research Institute, 9, 1 (1971), pp. 13-32.
Two forms of semireligious performance/entertainment are briefly described.

Vatsyayan, Kapila. "Workshop on Masks and Mask-Like Makeup in Traditional Theatre: Their Relevance in Education." Quarterly Journal of the National Centre for the Performing Arts, 9, 1 (March 1982), pp. 42-46.
Review of 1981 workshop which includes descriptions of Mudiyettu, Padayani, and Teyyam.

Welbon, Guy R. and Glenn E. Yocum. Religious Festivals in South India and Sri Lanka. Delhi: Manohar, 1982.
Collection of scholarly articles on a wide variety of festivals, many with performance elements.

Specific Classical Forms

1. Bharata Natyam

Anderson, Jack. "Indian Rasa for U.S. Students." Dance Maga-
zine, 44, 2 (February 1967), pp. 28-30.
Assesses Bharata Natyam technique as taught at the N.Y.
School of Performing Arts.

Balasaraswati, T. "Bharata Natyam." Quarterly Journal of the
National Centre for the Performing Arts, 5, 4 (December
1976), pp. 1-8.
This artist argues against contemporary efforts to "purify" or
add novelty to the Bharata Natyam recital. She offers theoretical
justification for maintaining the traditional sequence of the recital,
and for traditional discipline in training. She compares the art of
the dancer to the serenity of the yogi.

_____. "Music and the Dance." Quarterly Journal of the Na-
tional Centre for the Performing Arts, 2, 4 (December 1973),
pp. 41-45.
Briefly discusses the interrelationship of bhava, raga and tala,
and stresses the need for dance students to achieve an equal mastery of dance and music. Most of the article relates Balasaraswati's
own training and development as a Bharata Natyam artist.

Bhide, Sucheta. "King Shahaji's Prabandha." Quarterly Journal
of the National Centre for the Performing Arts, 6, 2 (June
1977), pp. 28-41.
Author analyzes the seventeenth-century writer's work as a form
of dance recital, relating the present-day repertoire of Bharata
Natyam to the Prabandha. Provides good evidence that the adavus
practiced in Shahaji's period were essentially the same as those of
current Bharata Natyam practice.

Dayal, Leela (Row). Nritta Manjari: The 62 Fundamental Sequences of Bharata Natyam. Calcutta: Indian Society of
Oriental Art, 1948.
Very good illustrations and discussion of author's concept of
basic movement sequences.

Ghurye, Govind Sadasiv. Bharatanatya and Its Costume. Bombay:
Popular Book Depot, 1958.
A very good study, which traces the history of the dance in
legend, literature and aesthetics, in painting and sculpture. These
sources are also examined for exact details about all aspects of
costuming.

Haskell, Arnold. "The Meaning of Classical Dancing." British
Journal of Aesthetics, 2, 1 (1962), pp. 55-58.
A very brief analysis of classical ballet and Bharata Natyam, in
terms of their impact and meaning as classical forms.

Iyer, E. Krishna. Bharata Natyam and Other Dances of Tamil Nad.
Baroda: M. S. University of Baroda Press, 1957.
A descriptive, introductory work.

Khokar, Mohan. "Bharata Natyam and Kuchipudi." Asia Society
Monographs on Music, Dance and Theatre, III, 1976.
Brief discussion of the development of these two forms, elements
of technique, and description of items of the repertoire.

_____. Dancing Bharata Natyam: A Manual on Adavus, the
Basic Dance-Units of the Art. New Delhi: National Printing
Works, 1979.
With a helpful introduction, this book is a very good technical
manual. The adavus are clearly explained through step-by-step
description, a series of photos, and a chart relating each photo,
time beat and dance syllable. A supplementary cassette tape is
also available.

Marg. Vol. 10, 4 (September 1957) Special Issue: Bharata Natyam.
The first articles cover the devotional and historical tradition of
Bharata Natyam, followed by an introduction to the musical forms.
The section on Nritta illustrates the twenty-eight single hand gestures, describes and illustrates fifteen basic adavus (dance units),
and gives brief consideration to the 108 Karanas or sculptured
dance poses of the Chidambaram temple. The Nrittya section illustrates the double hand poses, and gives examples of the poetry
of Padams, Sabdas and Slokas, along with their accompanying ragas
and talas. The dance-drama forms of Bhagavata Mela and Kuchipudi
are examined. There is also a brief explanation of the different
parts of the repertoire, and a geneology of gurus. Notes and
photos on major contemporary artists complete this issue.

_____. Vol. 32, 3 (1978-79) Special Issue: Bharata Natyam.
This more recent issue devoted to Bharata Natyam contains some
of the same subjects and information included in the 1957 issue. In
addition, there is information on the theoretical and technical aspects
of the different modes of expression (abhinaya). Two dance-drama
forms, Bhagavata Mela Nataka and Kuravanji are treated extensively, and a section on the Mysore school of Bharata Natyam has been
added. The last section, on contemporary artists, has also been
greatly expanded.

Naidu, P. Srinivasulu. "Bharata Natya Sastra: The 108 Karanas."
Marg, 5, 2 (1951), pp. 51-71.
With a brief introduction, the article lists, illustrates and de-
scribes all the dance poses of the Natya Sastra, as sculpted in the
Chidambaram temple.

"Problems Facing Bharata Natyam Today: Report of a Seminar."
Bulletin of the Institute of Traditional Culture (1967), pp.
253-307.

Ranganathan, Edwina. "Kuravanji Nattiya Nadagam: A Dance
    Drama from Madras State." Comparative Drama, IV, 2
    (Summer 1970), pp. 110-119.
    A good introduction to these dance-dramas, performed in Bharata
Natyam technique. The article covers history, thematic content,
plot summaries, and elements of staging and performance, including
comparison between traditional and current staging practices.

Sarabhai, Mrinalini. "The Eight Nayikas: Heroines of the Classi-
    cal Dance of India." Dance Perspectives, 24, (1965).
    A very good introduction; this article provides historical, cul-
tural and philosophical background to the art of Bharata Natyam.
As well as evoking the spiritual quality of the dance, the article
explores the dominant sentiment of love, and its accessory emotions. Certain aspects of the repertoire and technique are also
discussed. And the author has translated eight songs which delineate the different sentiments of love expressed by the eight
basic heroine-types referred to in the Natya Shastra.

_____. Understanding Bharata Natyam. Baroda: University of
    Baroda, 1965.

Sathyanarayana, R. Bharatanatya: A Critical Study. Mysore:
    Sri Varalakshmi Academies of Fine Arts, 1969.
    A scholarly, comprehensive analysis of theory, practice, his-
tory and current conditions of this classical form. Of special
interest are Chapters 3-5, which cover theory of movement, technique and teaching, and items of performance.

Scripps, Luise. "A System of Ethnic Dance Notation." Ethno-
    musicology, 9, 2 (May 1965), pp. 145-149.
    Explanation and examples of the author's system, devised for
Bharata Natyam.

Subramaniam, P. V. Bharata Natyam. New Delhi: Samkaleen
    Prakashan, 1980.

Vatsyayan, Kapila. "Bharatanatyam, Its Origin, and Recent
    Development." World Theatre (Brussels), 5, 2 (Spring 1956),
    pp. 142-53.

_____. "Notes on the Relationship of Music and Dance in India."
    Ethnomusicology, 7, 1 (January 1963), pp. 33-38.
    Excellent discussion of the interrelationship of music and dance
in Bharata Natyam.

2. Kathak

Kalyanpurkar, Mohanrao. "Shambhu Maharaj." Quarterly Journal
    of the National Centre for the Performing Arts, 2, 4 (Decem-
    ber 1973), pp. 11-20.

Biographical tribute to this great exponent of Kathak dance. Contains excellent, explicit descriptions of his abhinaya (especially the use of head, neck, face, and hand gestures) for expressing various texts. Good assessment of his style.

Kothari, Sunil. "Kathak: North Indian Dance." Asia Society Monographs on Music, Dance, and Theater, (1974).
Concise history, development of performance styles and schools, and a typical performance are reviewed. Also covers pure and expressional aspects of Kathak, rhythmic structure and performance of dance, as well as dance improvisations. Finally, reviews and praises the dance of Birju Maharaj.

Marg. Vol. 12, 4 (September 1959) Special Issue: Kathak.
This issue varies somewhat from the usual format. There are articles which cover general historical background, technique, music and costume. In addition, other articles deal with the traditions of the three major schools of Kathak, the historical role of the nautch-girls, and the contributions to the art of Kathak by Raigarth Raja and Menaka, patron and artist, respectively.

Pratnaik, Prabodh Kumar. "Historical Background and Evolution of Kathak Dance." Kala Vikash Kendra Journal (1962), pp. 24-28.
Includes an historical view of the Lucknow and Jaipur styles.

Rao, Maya. "Kathak and Its Relation to Ballet." Natya, 7, 4 (December 1963), pp. 64-72.

Saxena, S. K. "Kathak, Some Terms and Distinctions." Sangeet Natak, 51 (January-March 1979), pp. 5-14.
A technical argument for use of the term "intra-form" to describe various movement components within a Kathak recital. There are also technical references to aspects of dance composition.

_____. "Towards an Aesthetics of Kathak-Dance." Sangeet Natak, 43 (January-March 1977), pp. 5-47.
Scholarly aesthetic analysis of the dance form with a focus toward clarifying categories and aesthetic predicates for critical analysis of performance. Directly addresses the nature and meaning of movement.

Vatsyayan, Kapila. "Kathak." Journal of the Madras Music Academy, 27 (1956), pp. 74-88.
A good, general survey.

3. Kathakali

Barba, Eugenio. "The Kathakali Theatre." The Drama Review, 11, 4 (1967), pp. 37-50.
While a somewhat exaggerated oversimplification and romanticization

of the Kathakali actor, the article includes some very good specific descriptions of the Kerala Kalamandalam training in the mid 1960's, including physical gesture and expression, as well as design and function of costume and makeup.

Bolland, David. Enjoy Your Kathakali. Somerset, England: Bolland, 1975.
Earlier personal limited edition publication of A Guide to Kathakali.

_____. A Guide to Kathakali. New Delhi: National Book Trust, 1980.
A handy reference tool for quick review of the major plays in the Kathakali repertory.

Boner, Alice. "Kathakali." Journal of the Indian Society of Oriental Art, (Calcutta), 3 (1935), pp. 61-74.
Valuable as one of the earliest records of Kathakali training at the Kerala Kalamandalam. Sensitively written overview with some excellent photographs of early productions in lamp light before electricity and with the smaller rice-paste cuttis. Also includes detailed descriptions of the performance of selected Kathakali scenes including the well-known Kunjan Kurup performing the role of Kucela, the poor Brahmin.

Chaitanya, Krishna. "The Aesthetics of Kathakali." Sangeet Natak, 15 (January-March 1970), pp. 5-10.
Sets forth Kathakali's aesthetic emphasis on "presentation" as opposed to "identification," stressing the mimetic performance. Considers the relationship of the gesture system to connotation and denotation, and levels of metaphor and simile. Contrasts these and other elements with Sanskrit drama.

_____. A History of Malayalam Literature. New Delhi: Orient Longman, 1971.
Chapter Five covers the "Evolution of the Dance-Drama," in Kerala focusing on Kathakali and Thullal.

"Costumes and Accessories in Kathakali" in Census of India: 1961, VIIA, Selected Crafts of Kerala, pp. 26-74.
A brief history and introduction to the dance-drama is followed by a comprehensive description of Kathakali's characters, makeup types, costuming, and the processes and places of creation of Kathakali's properties and costumes. A detailed appendix of individual characters and specific costume items and accessories along with photographs completes this exhaustive catalogue of the topic.

George, K. M. A Survey of Malayalam Literature. London: Asia Publishing House, 1968.
Includes short introductory chapters on the plays of Kathakali and Thullal.

Gopinath, Guru. "Kathakali." Malayalam Literary Survey, V, 3-4
    (1981).
    Cursory overview.

Gopinath, Mohan. "Kathakali Music--An Appraisal." Malayalam
    Literary Survey, II, 1 (1978), pp. 55-62.
    Origins and change in Kathakali music today.

Hatch, Emily G. "Kathakali: The Indigenous Drama of Malabar."
    Ph.D. diss., Cornell University, 1934.
    One of the earliest comprehensive studies of Kathakali, includ-
ing extensive descriptions of training, massage, and Kathakali
dance.

Iyer, K. Bharatha. Kathakali: The Sacred Dance-Drama of Mala-
    bar. London: Luzac and Company, 1955.
    An introductory survey of Kathakali. Chapter IX, covering
mudras, is well illustrated and gives precise examples. Chapter
XI gives some good basic descriptions of selected scenes noting
the quality and dynamic movement and their relation to rasa.
There is a short general section on Kathakali dance.

Jaffrey, Madhur. "A Total Theater Filled with Dance, Music, and
    Myth." Smithsonian, 9, 12 (March 1979), pp. 68-75.
    General performance description accompanied by excellent black-
and-white and color photographs.

Jones, Clifford R. "The Fireworks of India's Kathakali Theater."
    Asia 3, 6 (March/April 1981), pp. 36-41.
    Brief introduction with superb photographs.

_____. "Kathakali: Epic Dance-Drama of India." New York:
    Asia Society Monograph, 197?
    An excellent short summary and introduction to Kathakali in-
cluding precise and specific descriptions of some of the basic
movement patterns.

_____ and Betty True. Kathakali. New York: Theatre Arts
    Books, 1970.
    An introduction to Kathakali, Chapters VI-IX provide specific
performance-related information including choreography, musical
accompaniment, the integration of music in the dance-drama, and
acting techniques.

Kothari, Sunil. "Kathakali--The Sacred Dance-Drama of Kerala."
    Marg, 32, 2 (1978-79), pp. 55-65.
    Overview with excellent photographs. The note on the actor's
performance of textual interpretations is helpful, especially the
paragraph relating Kathakali performance to Kutiyattam's enactment of Toranayudham.

Kurup, C. G. R. "The International Centre for Kathakali."
  Kalamandalam Annual, (1968), pp. 21-25.
  History, purpose, teaching, and new productions of Delhi centre.

_____. "Kathakali on the Modern Stage." Natya, 9, 4 (1966-67),
  pp. 25-31.
  Looks at possible changes involved in the transition of Kathakali
from traditional to modern stage. Discusses the stage, lighting,
orchestra, and repertoire.

Kurup, Guru Kunju. "The Art of Kathakali." Kathakali (April-
  June 1968), pp. 8-10.

Marar, Kuttikrishna. "The Hand-Symbols in Kathakali." Modern
  Review (Allahabad), 61 (June 1937), pp. 680-685.
  Brief, illustrated, somewhat confused reconstruction of origins
of Kathakali gesture language.

Marg. Vol. 11, 1 (December 1957) Special Issue: Kathakali.
  An introductory article on historical tradition is followed by aspects of the physical discipline, including the movement of the
eyes, the physical exercises and massage, and an illustrated dictionary of the hand gestures and facial expression. Other articles
discuss the costumes, headdresses and makeup of the major character types, the general style and rhythms of Kathakali music, the
literary aspects of Kathakali with examples from several plays, and
brief biographies of the major contemporary exponents. A short,
introductory article on Ottan Thullal, the "poor man's Kathakali,"
is also included.

Mazo, Joseph H. "Dance from the Edge of India," GEO, V, 3 (June
  1981), pp. 40-60.
  Dilip Mehta's excellent photographs capture the onstage and
behind-the-scenes atmosphere of Kathakali. The article is a straightforward and balanced introduction to the form and to the atmosphere
of a traditional performance.

Menon, K. P. S. "Chengannur Raman Pillai." Kalamandalam Annual
  (1968), pp. 9-11.
  Life, personality, and roles of a well-known southern-style
Kathakali actor.

_____. A Dictionary of Kathakali. Bombay: Orient Longman,
  1979.
  A valuable reference guide to Kathakali's technical terms.

_____. "Guru Kunju Kurup," Quarterly Journal of the National
  Centre for the Performing Arts, II, 1 (1973), pp. 18-24.
  Biographical account of the life and acting technique of one of
the great Kathakali actors.

_____. "Kurichi Kunhan Panikker." Kalamandalam Annual
(1969), pp. 17-19.
Kathakali actor known for humorous and comic roles.

Miller, Barbara Stoler. "Moving Designs of Masked Emotion."
Parabola, VI, 3 (Summer 1981), pp. 85-89.
A short review of the Kerala Kalamandalam's United States per-
formances of Dakshagyagam.

Misra, Susheela. "Kabuki and Kathakali--Some Impressions."
Sangeet Natak, 14 (October-December 1979), pp. 40-49.
A short, comparative survey concerning the male actor tradition, the training methods, characters and makeup, stage devices,
musical accompaniment, and elements of acting style (mime and
gesture) in both forms.

Nair, M. K. K. "Traditional Disciplines in Training." Sangeet
Natak, 24 (1972), pp. 50-56.
Review of purpose, training, and influence of Kerala Kalaman-
dalam.

Nair, P. K. Parameswaran. "Kathakali in India and Abroad."
Kalamandalam Annual (1968), pp. 17-20.

_____. "Nalacharitam--the Attakkatha par Excellence."
Kalamandalam Annual (1970), pp. 13-15.
An article written in appreciation of Warrier's well-rounded
characters in this best-loved Kathakali play.

Nair, V. Madhaven. "Innovations in Kathakali." Sangeet Natak,
2 (April 1966), pp. 86-92.
Suggests changes in Kathakali plays and performances in the
future.

_____. "Towards a Better Appreciation of Kathakali."
Sangeet Natak, 24 (April-June 1972), pp. 57-60.
Author argues for more translation of Kathakali texts, especially
the padas (songs), and a concurrent effort to widely publicize
the meanings of the mudras (hand gestures).

Namboodiri, M. P. Sankaran. "Bhava as Expressed in the Vacikam
and Angikam Aspects of Abhinaya in Kathakali." Dance as
Cultural Heritage, Selected Papers from the ADG/CORD Conference, 1978.
A clear, concise, and well-written explanation of the importance
of bhava (feelings, moods) in Kathakali acting. The author speaks
with the authority of the practical actor as he gives numerous
specific examples which illuminate the actor's approach to movement
and characterization. The explanation of the Kathakali text and
the use of vocal sounds to express emotion is the first of its kind

in English. As an actor, the author is able to clarify through specific examples how even the change in direction of a movement can give a completely different feeling to the same action.

Nayar, M. K. K. "Kathakali: Origin, Growth and Content." Kathakali (January-March 1968), pp. 6-11.
A short, general introduction.

_____. "Krishnan Nayar, Marvel of Kathakali Stage." Kalamandalam Annual (1970), pp. 29-32.
The life and art of another well-known Kathakali actor.

Nayar, P. Krishnan. Attakkatha or Kathakali. Madras: University of Madras, 1958.
An English introduction by C. Achyuta Menon contends that Kathakali comes under nrtya and not natya. Outlines gesture language. Traces much of the background of the form from the martial origins of the Nairs.

Omchery, Leela. "The Music of Kerala--A Study." Kalamandalam Annual (1969), pp. 7-15.
Best existing study of Kathakali music and the relationship between vocalists, orchestra, and actor/dancer.

Pandeya, Gayanacharya Avinash C. The Art of Kathakali. Allahabad: Kitabistan, 1961.
A general introduction to Kathakali which introduces Natya Sastra materials in an ambiguous manner. The most important parts of the book are those reviewing some of Uday Shankar's and Guru Gopinath's work and adaptations.

Poduval, Vasudeva. Diagrams of Hand Poses in Kathakali. Trivandrum: Government Press, 1930.
A brief, introductory guide.

Premakumar. The Language of Kathakali: A Guide to Mudras. Allhabad: Kitabistan, 1948.
Basic catalogue of the twenty-four root mudras with line drawings of single hand positions, and a list of double and single hand gestures used with each mudra. As a catalogue it is a handy reference, but has little value for understanding the dynamic movement in space required to create full mudras. (Based on the Hastalakshana-Dipika).

Raja, M. K. "Kathakali: Its Historical and Histrionic Background." Malayalam Literary Survey, I, 2 (1977), pp. 41-54.
Focuses on Kathakali's history.

Rajagopalan, L. S. "Damayanti In Nalacharitham Attakatha." Sangeet Natak, 14 (October-December 1969), pp. 30-39.
The article deals with the issue of characterization in Kathakali,

focusing on a single character. Though the emphasis is literary, much is implied about depiction of character through movement.

Rea, Kenneth. "Theatre in India: The Old and the New, Part 1." *Theatre Quarterly*, VIII, 30 (Summer 1978), pp. 9-23.
The first in a four-part series covering traditional and modern forms of Indian performance, this article focuses on Kathakali as a "preserved art." It specifically covers training at the Kerala Kalamandalam, a step-by-step performance description, and an interview with a senior Kathakali actor.

Shankar, Ragenara. "The Mime of Kathakali." *Modern Review* (Calcutta), 57 (March 1935), pp. 354-358.
General overview of the history, makeup types, performance, and training.

Siegel, Marcia. "Ritual as Life." *Dance Magazine* (January 1974), pp. 76-78.
A comparative review of performances by the Kathakali company of the Kerala Kalamandalam, the National Chinese Opera Theater, and Meredith Monk. The review is valuable for its specific descriptions of movement and performance technique by the Kathakali troupe.

Tampy, K. P. Padmanabhan. *Kathakali*. Calcutta: Indian Publications, 1963.
A brief, generalized, somewhat misleading overview of Kathakali.

Varma, Ambalapuzha Rama. "Mankulam Vishnu Namboodiri." *Kalamandalam Annual* (1971), pp. 31-33.
Review of life and diverse roles played by this well-known actor.

Varma, Prince Kerala. "The Appurtenances of Kathakali." *Bulletin of the Rama Varma Research Institute*, V, 2 (1937), pp. 131-136, continued in VI (1938), pp. 31-37.
The first part of the article traces the history of Kathakali. In the second part, the author asserts a different hypothesis for the origins of Kathakali in a Dravidian dance, probably "martial dances." Evidence from costume and daily dress of Nairs is presented.

Vatsyayan, Kapila. "Kathakali-Dance Theatre of India." *The World of Music*, 10, 1 (1968), pp. 22-35.
Good general description of the use of the "curtain look," the nature of the characters and thematic content, interplay of song and dance, movement patterns, abstract and expressive qualities of the dance, and the makeup and costume types.

"Vazhenkata Kunchu Nair is Sixty." *Kalamandalam Annual* (1969), pp. 4-5.
Biographical sketch of a Kathakali actor and his approach to character portrayal.

Venu, G. Kathakaliyile Kaimudrakal. (The Hand Gestures in
Kathakali). (Malayalam). Trichur: Kerala Sangeetha Nataka
Akademi, 1977.
The best attempt to date at developing a systematic notation
method for recording Kathakali hand gestures (mudras) in performance. Signs are developed for the twenty-four basic single-
hand alphabet and selected examples of single and combination
hands are recorded showing hand positions, dynamic movement,
and facial movement accompanying the hands. (Based on the
Hastalakshana-Dipika).

Warrier, Unnayi. Nalacharitham. V. Subramania Iyer, trans.
Trichur: Kerala Sahitya Akademi, 1977.
A complete translation of Warrier's Nalacharitham, Parts I-IV,
Iyer includes an informative introduction to Kathakali and to the
play's place in the Kathakali canon. The rather technical discussion of slokas and padams, and Iyer's appreciation of the poet's
skill in constructing the dance-drama illustrate a strong sense of
indigenous aesthetic appreciation of the play. The plot summary
and comments, and especially the inclusion of attaprakaram ("stage
directions, or how to act") give a basic idea of the performance of
the play, and make this the most important translation of a Kathakali play to date.

Zarrilli, Phillip. "A Microanalysis of Performance Structure and
Time in Kathakali Dance-Drama." Studies in Visual Anthropology, 1983.
A close, detailed study of the "micro" structure of a Kathakali
performance and the aesthetic and cultural significance of that
structure.

_____. "De-Mystifying Kathakali." Sangeet Natak, 43 (January-
March 1977), pp. 48-59.
Attacks the Western attitude of mystique attached to Kathakali
by analysis of five facets of the stereotyped image: Kathakali as
"ritual," the "transformed" actor, the "transported" audience, the
"dreamlike" world, and the ancient "tradition." Assesses movement
and gesture, and the actor's training and method from this objective viewpoint.

_____. The Kathakali Complex: Actor Performance, Structure.
New Delhi: Abhinav, 1984.
Especially valuable are the chapters on Kathakali training,
Kathakali in performance, and performance structure. The per-
formance structure chapter includes word-by-word descriptions/
illustrations of the acting process for each component part of a
Kathakali performance.

4. Kuchipudi and Bhagavata Mela Natakam

Acharyalu, C. Rama. "Costume and Make-up in Bhagavata Mela
     Natakam." Natya, 4, 2 (1960), pp. 4-7.
   Brief description of make-up and costume for various character
types.

Iyer, Krishna E. "Bhagavata Mela; Dance-Drama of Bharata Natya."
     Sangeet Natak, 13 (1969), pp. 46-56.
   A good introductory article which briefly describes the events of
a performance, the characteristics which distinguish this form from
Kathakali, and the current status of the form. Some historical information and analysis of movement are also included.

Jones, Clifford. "Bhagavata Mela Natakam, A Traditional Dance-
     Drama Form." Journal of Asian Studies, 22, 2 (February
     1963), pp. 193-200.
   Excellent overview of the history, techniques, and staging of
this form of dance-drama performed in Tanjore District. This form
of dance-drama is compared to aspects of the Sanskrit drama and
theatre. The lengthy description of the staging of Prahlada Charitam provides a narrative account of the dramatic action and staging
of the most important play in the repertory.

Kothari, Sunil. "Bhagavata Mela Nataka." Quarterly Journal of
     the National Centre for the Performing Arts, 8, 2 (June 1979),
     pp. 33-45.
   This article traces the classical roots and historical development
of this dance-drama form. There is also some description of performance events.

Kuchipudi Natyam. Hyderabad: Indian Art Theatre, 1966.
   Very good historical study, including description of elements of
performance.

Naidu, M. A. Kuchipudi Classical Dance. Hyderabad: Andhara
     Pradesh Sangeeta Nataka Akademi, 1975.
   A concise history of the form, with description of aspects of
the repertoire.

Raghavan, V. "The Bhagavata Mela Nataka." Journal of the Indian
     Society of Oriental Art, (June-December 1937).

_____. "The Veethi Bhagavatam of Andhra." Sangeet Natak,
     11 (January-March 1969), pp. 33-36.
   A short consideration of this form which is derived from Kuchipudi. Mentions dramatic content, role of Vidushaka, music and
dance elements.

Rao, S. V. Joga. "The Dance Dramas of Mellattur." Aryan Path,
     35, 7 (July 1964), pp. 310-15.

An introduction to the Bhagavata Mela Nataka form, which resembles Kuchipudi. Brief remarks cover the performance circumstances, the sequence of performance events, and historical development.

Rao, Vissa Appa. "Kuchipudi School of Dancing." Sangeet Natak Akademi Bulletin, 11-12 (April 1959), pp. 1-8.
Discusses origins and influences, items of the repertoire, and some examples of dances.

Sastry, P. Sri Rama. "The Kuchipudi: A Classical Style of Indian Dance." Natya, 9, 2 (1966), pp. 12-14.
A general introduction, briefly mentioning origins, particularly the development from Yakshagana, and the characteristics of the dance style.

Souvenir on Kuchipudi Natya Seminar. Hyderabad: Andhra Pradesh Sangeeta Nataka Akademi, 1959.

5. Kutiyattam

Byrski, Maria C. "Is Kudiyattam a Museumpiece?" Sangeet Natak, 5 (July-September 1967), pp. 45-54.

Free, Katharine B. "Greek Drama and the Kutiyattam." Theatre Journal, 33, 1 (1981), pp. 80-89.
Cursory and often hypothetical comparison of features of, and possible influences on, the Kutiyattam Sanskrit theater of Kerala, India and the classical Greek theatre.

Iyer, K. Bharatha. "Kutiyattam The Sanskrit Drama of Kerala." Times of India Annual (1962), pp. 19-26.
Short, standard introduction to this form, describing performance sequence and technique of the actors, origins of the form, the stage, role of music, and dramatic structure.

Jones, Betty True. "Kuttiyattam Sanskrit Drama: Changing Criteria of Excellence" in Asian and Pacific Dance: Selected Papers from the 1974 CORD-SEM Conference. CORD Dance Research Annual VIII (1977), pp. 1-17.
In this article, Jones concentrates on the Kutiyattam actor. She assesses the actor's training in terms of angikabhinaya (physical movement) and vacikabhinaya (use of voice), and relates these factors to performance structure. Finally, by examining cultural changes, the author analyses concurrent changes in the actor's technique.

Jones, Clifford R. "Notes on the Restoration of a Temple Theatre for Sanskrit Drama." Quarterly Journal of the National Centre for the Performing Arts, IV, 1 (March 1975), pp. 25-31.

Describes the reconstruction undertaken at the Vatakkunnathan temple in Kerala, and briefly mentions the traditional significance of such temple theatres.

_____. "The Temple Theatre of Kerala: Its History and Description." Ph.D. diss., University of Pennsylvania, 1967.
Authoritative discussion of the physical theatres (Kuttambalam) of Kerala's Kutiyattam. Includes chapters on the history, origins, and status of the actors.

_____. "Temple Theatre in Kerala: Kuttampalam." Kalamandalam Annual (1968), pp. 45-49.
Short technical description with photographs of Kutiyattam's temple theatre stage.

_____. "Temple Theatres and the Sanskrit Tradition in Kerala." Samskrita Ranga Annual, 6 (1972), pp. 101-110.

Mathur, J. C. "Inside a Temple Theatre: A Personal Account of Kootiyattam." Sangeet Natak, 26 (October-December 1972), pp. 20-32.
A good description of Koothambalam stage in Vatakkunnathan Temple in terms of the performance, auditorium and other spaces. Describes the progression of performance, from preparatory actions and invocation, to plot summary, use of props and curtain, and poses incorporated. Provides an analysis of acting: the interplay of gesture and language; use of pada and shloka; the single character playing multiple roles; and other conventions of performance such as intonation and the mixture of Sanskrit and Malayalam.

Menon, Devaki. "The 'Kuttu' of the Kerala Theatre." Journal of the Music Academy (Madras), 25, 1-4 (1954), pp. 122-129.

Nair, D. Appukuttan. "Abhinaya in Kutiyattam." Theatre India, National Drama Festival Cochin, 1977. Trichur: Kerala Sangeetha Nataka Akademi, 1977, pp. 32-39.
Outlines the process of textual elaboration and augmentation in performance of specific passages of Kutiyattam plays.

_____. "Kutiyattam--Fantasy and Poetry in Dance." Marg, 32, 2 (1978-79), pp. 66-74.
In addition to serving as a clear and concise introduction to the form, this article focuses on selected structural elements of the performance of the script. A clear step-by-step tracing of the complex unfolding of a Kutiyattam performance is presented. There is also an effective description of the performance of grammatical variations on the root of a word in the text.

Oleksin, Susan. "Mantrankam at Peruvanam." Sangeet Natak, 45 (July-September 1977), pp. 43-46.
A description of a Koodiyattam performance from July 7 to

August 16, 1976. Includes a plot summary, description of the
stage and preliminary rituals, costume and makeup, and curtain
conventions. Concentrates on the role of the Vidusaka, his performance style and interplay with dialogue, music and gesture.

Panchal, Goverdhan. "Koottampalam Sanskrit Stage of Kerala."
Sangeet Natak, 8 (April-June 1968), pp. 17-30.
A detailed description and analysis of a temple theatre. Brief
references to an actor's use of the stage space.

_____. "Kuttambalam and Its Links with Bharata's Stage."
Quarterly Journal of the National Centre for the Performing
Arts, 6, 1 (March 1977), pp. 27-44.
A well-illustrated investigation of the correlation between the
Kuttambalam (the temple stage of Kutiyattam) and the vikrshta
madhya (rectangular middle-sized theatre) described in the
Natyashastra. Through detailed description and illustration of
both stages, the author concludes that the Kuttambalam is directly
linked to the classical stage. The article also includes references
to staging and the changes necessitated by the evolution of the
Kutiyattam.

Portman, Julie A. "What Was It Like? You Ask..." Kalamandalam
Annual (1971), pp. 23-30.
Illustrated description of four evenings of Kutiyattam performance outside the temple including the premiere performance of the
second act of Kalidasa's Sakunthalam as restaged by one of the
noted Kutiyattam actors.

Raghavan, V. "Koodiyattam." Natya, 6, 3 (1962), pp. 21-22.
Brief introductory comments covering the hereditary tradition of
the actors, the repertoire, the distinguishing technique of rasa and
bhava (the expression of the eye, recitation of verse, and then the
hand gestures), dramatic structure and improvisations, the role of
the Vidushaka, and the music.

_____. "Kudiyattam: Its Form and Significance as Sanskrit
Drama." Samskrita Ranga Annual, 5 (1964-65, 1966-67), pp.
77-87.
Technical discussion of Kutiyattam and its relationship to earlier
and contemporary treatises on theatrical performance and the light
Kutiyattam sheds on production of Sanskrit dramas.

Raja, K. Kunjunni. "Kootiyattam (A General Survey)." Quarterly
Journal of the National Centre for the Performing Arts, 3, 2
(June 1974), pp. 1-12.
Contains historical information with an emphasis on the development of the Vidushaka role. General description of the Kootham-
palam stage and auditorium, the stage manuals, musical instruments,
the four aspects of abhinaya as employed in Kootiyattam, and the
talas or rhythmic patterns.

_____. Kutiyattam, An Introduction. New Delhi: Sangeet
    Natak Akademi, 1964.
A detailed technical introduction to Kutiyattam, this brief text
(38pp.) includes a clear description of the acting and interpretation of the Sanskrit texts as well as a few brief descriptions of
some of the staging. Due to lack of illustrations and translation of
Sanskrit verses, the pamphlet is best read as an intermediate or advanced study.

Rajagopalan, L. S. "Music in Kootiyattam." Sangeet Natak, 10
    (October-December 1968), pp. 12-25.
Good analysis of songs, chants, instrumentation and structure
of the music used in this form.

Richmond, Farley. "The Rites of Passage and Kutiyattam."
    Sangeet Natak, 50 (October-December 1978), pp. 27-36.
Richmond interprets the performance events of Kutiyattam in
terms of rite of passage, based on the work of Victor Turner and
Arnold Van Gennep. The article includes specific description of
performance space, costume and makeup, ritual actions and actors'
movements, the roles of the clown and "stage manager," and the
tradition of Kerala's actor families.

Tarlekar, G. H. "Vidusaka in the Kuttiyattam." Indian Antiqui-
    ties, II, 4 (October 1967), pp. 21-28.

Unni, N. P. "Kulasekhara and the Kerala Stage." Journal of Indi-
    an History, 54, 2 (1976), pp. 320-349.
Reviews the basic features of Kutiyattam staging of Sanskrit
dramas, compares Ankia Nat to Kutiyattam, discusses, with examples, the interpolations in texts performed in Kutiyattam, and
traces the importance of the indigenous dramatist, Kulasekhara,
for the Kerala stage.

_____. "Mattavilasa on the Kerala Stage." Journal of Kerala
    Studies I, 1 (1973), pp. 81-90.
Description of the Kutiyattam form of staging Mattavilasa of the
Pallava king Mahendravikramavarman.

_____. Sanskrit Dramas of Kulasekhara, A Study. Trivandrum:
    Kerala Historical Society, 1977. (First published in the Jour-
    nal of Kerala Studies in two parts under the title, "Kulashek-
    hara Varman, The Royal Dramatist of Kerala," III, 2 (1976),
    pp. 239-316; III, 3-4 (1976), pp. 325-406).
Comprehensive study of the author, his plays, the influence of
classical dramas on the author, and the role of Kulasekhara and his
plays in Kutiyattam staging of Sanskrit plays.

6. Manipuri

Dayal, Leela Row. Manipuri Dances. London: Oxford University
 Press, 1951.
 This book contains a catalogue of forty-three dance movement
sequences, with illustrations, instructions, and the corresponding
bols (rhythmic syllables). Choreography and instructions for several dances are also included.

Khokar, Mohan. "Dance and Ritual in Manipur." Sangeet Natak,
 10 (October-December 1968), pp. 35-47.
 Largely a photographic essay with very brief comments on the
dances.

Lightfoot, L. Dance Rituals of Manipur, India; An Introduction to
 Meitei Jagoi. Hong Kong: Standard Press, 1958.
 Personal account of the Lai Harouba and other rituals of the
Meiteis. Although Lightfoot concentrates on cultural and historical
background, there are photos and scattered references to the
dances.

Marg. Vol. 14, 4 (September 1961) Special Issue: Manipuri.
 The major dance forms of Manipur are the subject of this issue,
with a variety of articles. The interplay of myth, legend, and
history is explored in terms of impact on the development of dance
in this area. Two articles are devoted to technique. The festival
of Lai Haraboa, Rasleela, Sankirtan and Cholom are covered.

Singh, E. Nilakanta. "Classical Tradition of Nata Movements."
 Sangeet Natak, 10 (October-December 1968), pp. 26-34.
 Technical analysis of various components of dance movements,
costumes, and music in Manipuri dance in light of classical treatises.

7. Mohiniattam

Jones, Betty True. "Mohiniyattam: A Dance Tradition of Kerala,
 South India." CORD Dance Research Monograph One (1971-
 1972), pp. 7-27.
 An excellent, scholarly account of this dance form. Jones provides an historical view, covering the traditions and mythology,
and the social-political context which shaped the development of the
form. In particular, aspects of training, music, makeup, costumes,
stage arrangements, and items of the performance are considered.
Some elements of technique are also briefly mentioned. The documentation provides valuable references for the reader.

Marg. Vol. 26, 2 (March 1973) Special Issue: Mohini Attam.
 The issue includes a solid consideration of the mythic and historic origins of the form. Elements of the technique are also

discussed, both in terms of theory and physical practice. Different aspects and examples of the repertoire are examined. The usual sections on music, costume and the artists of the form also appear.

Nayar, M. K. K. "Mohiniattam." Kalamandalam Annual (1969), pp. 25-29.
Introductory history and description.

Radhakrishna, Geetha. "Mohiniattam and Its Choreographic Poten-tialities." Malayalam Literary Survey, V 1 (1981), pp. 46-50.
Personal account of involvement in the dance and sources/ inspiration for choreography.

_____. "Mohiniattam--The Dance of the Enchantress." Marg, 32, 2 (1978-79), pp. 75-80.
Brief overview including clear descriptions of basic movements and quality of movement, supplemented by excellent photographs.

8. Odissi

Kothari, S. "Gotipua Dancers of Orissa." Sangeet Natak, 8 (1968), pp. 31-43.
Introductory comments on the mythic and historic origins of this dance tradition, the physical training of the selected boys, some unique acrobatic feats which distinguish this form from Odissi dance, the festival occasions for performance, costume and makeup, and brief mention of the tradition of patronage.

Kothari, Sunil. "Odissi Dance." Quarterly Journal of the National Centre for the Performing Arts, 3, 2 (June 1974), pp. 37-49.
Traces the history of this form through discussion of various dance sculptures in Orissan temples. Briefly relates the history of patronage and training traditions. Discusses technique as de-lineated by palm leaf manuscripts, some of which are illustrated. Considers aspects of movement which distinguish this style from other classical forms.

Marg. Vol. 13, 2 (March 1960) Special Issue: Orissi.
After a general introduction, an historical overview is presented, including an examination of dance sculptures from Orissan temples, mythic sources, and the historical development of the form. There are also articles covering technique, and the traditional items of the repertoire. Songs and instruments, costumes, ornaments, and makeup are briefly touched on. The issue concludes with the men-tion of the contemporary exponents of this form.

Patnaik, Dhirendranath. Odissi Dance. Bhubaneswar, Orissa: Sangeet Natak Akademi, 1971.
With very good historical and cultural background, this book provides description of technique and items of the repertoire,

costume and makeup, and also briefly introduces the various treatises on music and dance in Orissa.

Folk/Regional Forms

1. Bhavai

Chandarvaker, Pushkar. "Bhavai: A Type of Folk Drama of
    Gujarat." Folk-lore (Calcutta), 14, 6 (June 1973), pp. 217-23.
    As a short introduction, the article discusses the origin of the
form, some performance practices, dramatic themes, and explains
some technical terminology.

Desai, S. R. Bhavai: A Medieval Form of Ancient Indian Dramatic
    Art (Natya) as Prevalent in Gujarat. Ahmedabad: Gujarat
    University, 1972.
    A study of the Bhavai, folk-theatre of Gujarat, covering its
religious origins, music and dance, costumes and makeup, and its
similarities to ancient dramatic types. The work also contains
translations of many vesas (scenes) with stage directions.

Richmond, F. P. "Bhavai: Village Theatre of West India."
    Papers in International and World Affairs, Michigan State
    University, 1969 Series, 2, pp. 13-28.

2. Cavittunatakam

Choondal, Chummar. "Christian Theatrical Arts in Kerala."
    Souvenir Program, XXXVII, Indian History Congress. De-
    partment of History, Calicut University, 1976, pp. 78-80.
    Emphasis on Cavittunatakam with brief mention of staging and
choreography.

_____. "Medieval Religious Drama of Europe and Chavittuna-
    takam of Kerala." Malayalam Literary Survey, II, 3 (1978),
    pp. 76-85.
    Origins of Christian dance-drama.

Chummar, C. T. "Foreign Influence of Theatrical Arts of Kerala
    with Special Reference to Cavittu Natakam." Ph.D. diss.,
    University of Kerala, 1976.

Raphy, Sabeena. "Chavittu-Natakam, Dramatic Opera of Kerala."
    Sangeet Natak, 12 (April-June 1969), pp. 56-73.
    This Kerala folk dance-drama form is considered by the author
to be a Christian counterpart to Kathakali. The historical basis of
this East-West blend is examined. The article also outlines briefly
the music, dance steps, acting style, instruments, costume and
makeup, sources of texts, actor training, performance preliminaries,
and some typical scenes from a performance.

3. Chhau

Arden, John. "The Chhau Dancers of Purulia." The Drama Review,
15, 3 (Spring 1971), pp. 65-75.
Description of a performance with some cultural background provided.

Awasthi, Suresh. "Chhau Dance Festival and Seminar Organised
by Anamika Kala Sangam (Feb. 4-6, 1977, Calcutta)." Quarterly
Journal of the National Centre for the Performing Arts, 6,
2 (June 1977), pp. 42-47.
Illustrated report on first major festival of the three forms of
Chhau dance.

_____. "Seraikella Chhau." The Drama Review, 23, 2 (June
1979), pp. 77-90.
Suresh Awasthi interviews the master of Seraikella Chhau, Guru
Kedar Nath Sahoo. The section on the creation of new dances and
choreography is particularly informative as is the discussion of the
grammar of Chhau movement.

Bhattacharyya, Asutosh. Chhau Dance of Purulia. Calcutta:
Rabindra Bharati University, 1972.
The most authoritative, comprehensive study of the Purulian
form. Provides anthropological background, extensive description
of repertoire, performance, costumes and masks, music, technique
of the dance, and comparisons to Kathakali, the dances of Bali,
and the Seraikella and Mayurbhanj forms.

_____. "The Chhau Masked Dance of West Bengal: A General
Survey." Quarterly Journal of the National Centre for the
Performing Arts, 5, 2 (June 1976), pp. 16-28.
Offers an etymological consideration of the origins of the Purulian style of Chhau. The cultural and historical background of the
area are discussed in relation to the development of the form. Performance space and thematic content are mentioned. Good description of costumes, mask-making process, instruments, and of several
of the unique movement patterns.

Blank, Judith. "The History, Cultural Context, and Religious
Meaning of the Chou Dance, Theatre of the Ex-state of
Mayurbhanj, Orissa." Ph.D. diss., University of Chicago,
1972.

Bowers, Faubion. "The Great Discovery of the Royal Chhau."
Dance Magazine, 38, 3 (March 1964), pp. 40-41, 52.
Brief coverage of the Seraikella form.

Chaudhuri, D., ed. Chho Dance: A Socio-Cultural Profile.
Calcutta: Akademi of Folklore, 1977.
A monograph with very brief articles, including information about
the life and conditions of the artists and mask makers.

Gargi, Balwant. "The Chhau Dance Drama." Times of India Annual (1967), pp. 63-72.
This description of the Seraikella form covers such aspects as the construction and function of the masks, thematic content of dances, the expressive qualities of the dance movements, specific steps and gaits, the interplay of dancers and musicians.

Khokar, Mohan. "Chhau: Dance of Masks and Moods." Natya, 10, 1 (1967), pp. 34-37.
The article focuses on the Chhau mask in terms of its mimetic potential through animation by the body.

_____. "Chhau, Mask Dance of Seraikella." Pushpanjali V, 1 (1969), pp. 77-92.
Well-illustrated description of the Seraikella form, including comments about the current status of the art.

_____. "The Seraikella Chhau Dance." Quarterly Journal of the National Centre for the Performing Arts, 2, 2 (June 1973), pp. 25-32.
A short, introductory article which mentions the physical training of the dancers, the thematic content of the dances, and gives a few brief descriptions of specific dances.

Kothari, S. "The Chhau Dance." Sangeet Kala Vihar, 1, 2 (1970), pp. 25-28.
Good commentary on the Seraikella form that assesses the role of the mask and the nature of movement and physical expression in relation to the mask. Also discusses training exercises, gaits, footwork and dance units.

_____. "The Chhau Dances." World of Music, 11, 4 (1969), pp. 38-55.
A general introduction primarily concerned with the Seraikella form, with some comparative references to the Chhau of Mayurbhanj. Discusses interpretations of the name "Chhau," the art of mask making, the symbolic nature of movements, function of the music, and the current status of the art form.

Mahapatra, Sitakant. "Chhow Dance of Mayurbhanj: The Tasks Ahead." Quarterly Journal of the National Centre for the Performing Arts, 7, 3 (September 1978), pp. 31-44.
Careful analysis of possible origin and influences in the development of Chhow dance. Author questions the accepted view of martial origins, pointing out similarities with Santali dances and with other ritual and folk traditions. Argues for a better method of formal codification of the dance and for a systematic compilation of the accompanying lyrics.

Marg. Vol. 22, 1 (Dec. 1968) Special issue: Chhau.
The issue is divided into two parts, the first covering the

Seraikella form, and the second covering the Mayurbhanj form. The origins and ritual nature of Seraikella Chhau are discussed. Other sections cover the physical exercises and dance units, the thematic content of the repertoire, the art of mask making, with a concluding piece on the music. The part devoted to the Mayurbhanj form also begins with historical background, then considers basic steps and gaits of the technique, and the choreographic and rhythmic patterns in performance.

Pani, Jiwan. "Chhau--A Comparative Study of Sareikela and Mayurbhanj Forms." Sangeet Natak, 13 (July-September 1969), pp.
35-45.
Examines the similarities in these two apparently different forms, in terms of the dance steps and gaits, the symbolic and expressive qualities exhibited in the dance units, the rituals and context of performance, and the music and rhythmic patterns involved.

Reck, D. "The Music of Matha Chhau." Asian Music, 3, 2 (1972),
pp. 8-14.
Provides general background on Chhau: the festival context, etymology and meanings of the name, the performance circumstances, the events of a performance in the Puruliau form, various themes in the dances, and the structure of the accompanying music. Good introductory overview.

Richmond, Farley. "The Chhau Dance of Purulia." Asia Society
Monographs on Music, Dance, and Theatre, I, 2 (1974).
Traces origins. Compares Purulia Chhau with other Chhau forms. Also covered are patronage, performance space, description of dance with characteristic examples of the tandava (masculine) style of performance. Two basic character types and their respective gaits are described as well as the performance structure, preliminaries in honor of Ganapadi, character entrances, combat with specific exam- ples of staging and movement. Finally, music, masks, and costumes and their effect on movement are presented.

_____. "Purulia Chhau: An Introduction." Keli (Cochin), 8
(1971), pp. 15-21.
Introductory survey of the characteristics of the Purulian form.

Sharma, S. P. "The Chhau Dance of Seraikella." Modern Review,
69, 1 (January 1941), pp. 97-101.

Singh Deo, J. B. Chhau, Mask Dance of Seraikela. Cuttack:
Jayashree Devi, 1973.

Vatsyayan, K. M. "A Study of Mayurbhanj Chhau in Relation to
Other Dance Forms in Orissa." Journal of the Music Academy
45, 1-4 (1974), pp. 118-130.

_____. "The Chhau Dance of Mayurbhanj." Quarterly

Journal of the National Centre for the Performing Arts, IV, 4
(December 1975), pp. 1-13.
Addresses the problem of classifying this form, as either classical or folk. Bases the analysis on examination of cultural milieu
and environment, of physical technique (steps, gaits, units of
movement) and dramatic structure.

Vestal, Theodore M. The Chhau Dance of India. New Delhi:
Educational Resources Center, 1970.
An introductory, descriptive guide to all three forms of Chhau.

4. Gambhira

Ghosh, Pradyot. "Gambhira: Traditional Masked Dance of Bengal."
Sangeet Natak, 53-54 (July-December 1979), pp. 53-77.
Traces etymology of "Gambhira" to establish cultural context of
the dance worship. Discusses the general anthropological and historical function of the mask, and compares its use in Gambhira to
other mask forms. Traces other cultural influences on the development of the form. Classifies specific dance types of the form and
generally describes movement. Lists the rhythmic sounds employed
in principal dances.

5. Jatra

Bhattacharyya, A. "Yatra of Bengal" Sangeet Natak, 12 (1969),
pp. 29-39.
Historical survey of the development of Yatra in Bengal. Some
reference to staging and movement, particularly for modern practices.

Chowdhuri, Alindra. "Changing Forms of Jatra." Natya, 6, 3
(1962), pp. 26-27.
Traces the origin of Jatra, the popular folk drama of Bengal.
Argues that the changes in style and presentation over centuries
have left contemporary Jatra without its original folk-art soul.

Chowdhury, Santi P. "Jatra: Bengals Theatre-in-the-Round."
Times of India Annual (1978), pp. 43-48.
A good general introduction, covering the development of the
form, elements of staging, routine and management of the company,
current status, and dramatic content.

Dash, Dhiren. "Jatra, People's Theatre of Orissa." Sangeet Natak,
52 (April-June 1979), pp. 11-26.
Explains the complex meaning and application of term "Jatra."
Looks briefly at historical tradition and surveys the variety of
theatre forms which may fall under this heading, including Chhau,
Chaiti Ghoda Nata, Pala, Dandanata, Rasa Lila, Krishna Lila, Patua
Jatra, Bandi Nata, Rama Lila and others.

Farber, C. "Problems of Studying Urban Specialists: 'Jatra' in
    Calcutta." Journal of the Indian Anthropological Society 10,
    2 (1975), pp. 117-32.

Farber, Carole Marie. "Prolegomenon to an Understanding of the
    Jatra of India: The Traveling Popular Theatre of the State of
    West Bengal." Ph.D. diss., University of British Columbia,
    1979.
An ethnographic study of this popular professional theatrical
form, assessing the Jatra for its commentary on Bengali social and
cultural life.

Husain, Syed Sajjad. "Jatra or Bengali Folk Drama." Pakistan
    Quarterly, 5, 1 (Spring 1955), pp. 59-60.
Brief account of the popular music-drama of Bengal in Bangladesh.

6. Nautanki

Awasthi, Suresh. "Nautanki--An Operatic Theatre." Quarterly
    Journal of the National Centre for the Performing Arts, 6, 4
    (December 1977), pp. 23-36.
A good introduction to this operatic form. The article covers
recent productions which introduced elements of the modern theatre, the origin and development of the form, and brief discussion
of dramatic structure, conventions of staging, thematic content,
metrical forms in the verse dialogue, the influence of the Parsi
theatre movement, and the musical style.

7. Tamasha

Abrams, Tevia. "Folk Theatre in Maharashtrian Social Development
    Programs." Educational Theatre Journal, 27, 3 (1975), pp.
    395-407.
Tamasha presented as an example of a traditional Asian form of
folk performance serving as a vital, mass entertainment as well as
for propaganda purposes in the hands of the government.

_____. "Tamasha: People's Theatre of Maharashtra State,
    India." Ph.D. diss., Michigan State University, 1974.
Comprehensive study of Tamasha which focuses most attention
on the use of Tamasha by social and political groups for propaganda
purposes. Chapter 1 includes descriptions of the stage, structure
of performances, acting styles, song, dance, and musical accompaniment.

"Dadu Indurikar." Quarterly Journal of the National Centre for
    Performing Arts, 2, 4 (December 1973), pp. 21-40.
An interview with this renowned Tamasha artist, covering a
broad variety of his experiences, including such aspects as the

training of performers, performance circumstances, company management practices, the improvisational nature of performances, the function of various characters, and the hardships of touring.

Khanapurkar, D. P. "Tamasha." Eastern Anthropologist, 7 (1953), pp. 19-36.
A very brief introduction, followed by translations of typical songs from a Tamasha performance.

Nadkarni, D. G. "Marathi Tamasha Yesterday and Today." Sangeet Natak, 12 (1969), pp. 19-28.
The evolution of Tamasha, with emphasis on the dramatic content of the form. Scattered references to staging.

Rea, Kenneth. "Theatre in India: The Old and the New, Part IV." Theatre Quarterly, 9, 34 (1979), pp. 53-65.
Briefly reports on Tamasha, Marathi theatre in Bombay, and the National School of Drama in New Delhi.

8. Thullal

Chaitanya, Krishna. A History of Malayalam Literature. New Delhi: Orient Longman, 1971.
Chapter Five covers the "Evolution of the Dance-Drama," in Kerala, focusing on Kathakali and Thullal.

————. "The Thullal of Kerala." Sangeet Natak, 27 (January-March 1973), pp. 49-53.
This satiric form of dance narration is considered in terms of diction, rhyme, aesthetic action, costume, makeup, and gesture. Includes comments comparing this style to various styles of Western writers. Focuses on the works of eighteenth-century writer Kunchan Nambiar.

George, K. M. A Survey of Malayalam Literature. London: Asia Publishing House, 1968.
See entry under Kathakali.

Khokar, Mohan. "Thullal Koran: Dance-Raconteur of Krala." Natya, 9, 3 (1966), pp. 13-15.
General treatment of origin, costume, makeup, and sequence of the performance of this form.

Pillai, P. K. Sivasankara. "Origin and Development of Thullal." Kalamandalam Annual (1970), pp. 17-21.
General overview of types of Thullal, solo performance of Kerala.

Sharma, V. S. "Evolution of Thullal." Sangeet Natak, 52 (April-June 1979), pp. 5-10.
Historical discussion of this form as a blend of prior classical and folk forms. Brief references to movement quality of the dance.

9. Yakshagana

Ashton, Martha Bush. "Of Music, Bells and Rhythmic Feet: The
Dance of Yakshagana." Anima I, 1 (1974), pp. 40-55.
An excellent and thorough review of all the basic features of
Yakshagana dance, accompanied by diagrams, floor patterns, and
illustrative photographs. A model of good writing on Indian dance
which communicates the techniques as well as the spirit and context
of the performances.

_____. "The Rituals of Yaksagana Badagatittu Bayalata."
Journal of South Asian Literature, 10, 2-4 (Winter-Summer,
1975), pp. 249-274.

_____ and Bruce Christie. Yaksagana: A Dance Drama of India.
New Delhi: Abhinav Publications, 1077.
Rewrite of Ashton's more detailed Ph.D. thesis for a general
audience. The best well-illustrated general introduction to Yaksagana available. The work includes chapters on the creation and
delivery of the prose sections of the plays, training, music, dance,
and staging. Bibliography, glossary, and excellent color and black-
and-white photographs.

_____. "Yakshagana Badagatittu Bayalata." Asia Society Mono-
graphs on Music, Dance and Theatre, V, (1978).
Best overall introduction to the traditional Yakshagana Bayalata
available, covering performance area, five constituent parts of a
performance, troupes, music, literature, dialogue/acting, makeup
and costumes, props, and a complete though brief, section on dance
and troupe competitions.

_____. "Yakshagana Badagatittu Bayalata: A South Indian Dance
Drama." Ph.D. diss., Michigan State University, 1972.
The most comprehensive and thorough study of Yaksagana Badagatittu Bayalata available, the thesis includes extensive documentation of dance steps and patterns as well as staging. The thesis
can serve as a model of thoroughness of documentation of an Indian
dance-drama form. A shorter, more condensed version of the work
is Yaksagana: A Dance Drama of India by Martha Bush Ashton and
Bruce Christie.

_____. "Yakshagana: A South Indian Folk Theatre." The
Drama Review, XIII, 3 (Spring 1969), pp. 148-155.
A good introduction, covering history and development of the
form, performance structure and sequence, character types and
their costumes and makeup, performance occasion, and preliminary
rituals.

Jaffrey, Madhur. "Yakshagana: Karnataka's Lively Folk Theatre."
Asia, 1, 6 (March-April 1979), pp. 8-15.
Excellent color photographs illustrate this general introduction to
Yakshagana. Includes a performance description.

Karanth, K. Shivarama. "The Yakshagana of Karnataka." Quarterly
   Journal of the National Centre for the Performing Arts, 3, 3
   (September 1974), pp. 1-8.
With some mention of historical development, and of the costumes
and makeup used, the article focuses on the operatic nature of the
form, its musical composition and the function of dance.

_____. "Costume and Make-Up in Yakshagana Dance-Drama."
   Natya (Autumn 1959), pp. 5-6, 49.
Discusses the function of costume and makeup in Yakshagana,
and briefly describes their types.

_____. Yaksagana. Mysore: Institute of Kannada Studies,
   University of Mysore, 1974.
The first complete study of Yaksagana, the chapter on dance is
marred by the author's programmatic concern with improving
Yaksagana. As such, the chapter is an excellent documentary of
the forces of change on a traditional folk dance-drama form.

_____. "Yakshagana: A Musical Dance-Drama." Sangeet Natak
   (October 10, 1958), pp. 13-20.
General introduction to the bayalata style.

Rea, Kenneth. "Theatre in India: The Old and the New, Part
   II." Theatre Quarterly, 8, 31 (1978), pp. 45-60.
A well-rounded overview of Yaksagana in the modern world from
training and performance through its modern variant forms and innovations. Includes a concise history of the new style Yaksha-
Ranga, as well as an interview with K. Shivarama Karanth, founder
of the new Yaksha-Ranga style.

"Shree Dharmasthala Yakshagana Sabha." Quarterly Journal of the
   National Centre for the Performing Arts, 2, 3 (September
   1973), pp. 25-30.
Description of a Yakshagana performance by this troupe. Also
compares traditional practices with some current trends.

Upadhyaya, K. S. "Yakshagana Bayalata." Sangeet Natak, 11
   (January-March 1969), pp. 37-51.
A general consideration of historical origins of the form and
its distinctions from other dance and drama forms. Analyzes the
unique aspects of its music, drama and dance content, of the
makeup tradition, and the preliminary dances given at each performance.

Ritual/Religious Forms

1. Ankiya Nat

Richmond, Farley. "The Vaisnava Drama of Assam." Educational

Theatre Journal, 26, 2 (May 1974), pp. 145-163.
Discusses Vaisnavism and the impact of its philosophical principles on theatre, as a vehicle to propagate the faith. Among the
variety of forms created for this purpose, Ankiya Nat, established
by Sankaradeva, is the focus of this article. Describes performance circumstances and techniques.

2. Kaisika Purana

Welbon, Guy Richard. "The Enactment of the Kaisika Purana at
Tirukkurunkuti--A Surviving Temple Drama in South India."
Samskrita Ranga Annual, 6 (1972), pp. 113-134.
A valuable description of the setting, actors, preparations, au-
dience, and mechanics of the only surviving performance of the
Kaisika Purana in the Visnu temple at Tirukkurunkuti in Tamil
Nadu. Includes a translation of the text.

3. Krishna Lila

Kinsley, David. The Divine Player: A Study of Krsna Lila. Delhi:
Motilal Banarsidass, 1979.
An analysis of the relationship between play (lila) and religion in
the Hindu context. For devotees of Lord Krsna, life becomes a
dramatic display of devotionalism through role playing and identification with Krsna or Radha. Provocative for its suggestive comments on the state of consciousness of performance and performance as life.

Razdan, Inder. "Stage, Decor and Costume in Krishna Leela."
Natya, 6, 2 (1962), pp. 28-29.

4. Mudiettu

Vidyarthi, Govind. "Mudiettu: Rare Ritual Theatre of Kerala."
Sangeet Natak, 42 (1976), pp. 51-63.
Overview of the ritual theatre form including a step-by-step account of ritual structure and basic dramatic dynamics from the opening floor drawings and rituals/songs through the appearance of various characters, culminating in the battle between Darika and Kali.

5. Ramlila

Awasthi, Induja. "Ramlila: Tradition and Styles." Quarterly
Journal of the National Centre for the Performing Arts, 8, 3
(September 1979), pp. 23-36.
A good, general introduction. Covers the origins, the literary
basis of the form, and some of the common elements of staging

shared by regional variations. Four main styles of traditional
Ramlilas are also defined.

Awasthi, Suresh. "Ramacharitamanas of Tulsidas--An Appreciation."
    Quarterly Journal of the National Centre for the Performing
    Arts, 2, 3 (September 1973), pp. 1-8.
    Discusses the Ramaleela as a theatrical form which evolved from
the recitation of the epic poem Ramacharitamanas, with general
comments about several Ramaleela forms.

Gargi, Balwant. "Ramlila in Ramnagar." Sangeet Natak, 13 (July-
    September 1969), pp. 27-34.
    A short, very general description of an annual Ramlila. Little
specific reference to movement.

Schechner, Richard. "Theatre-Experience: Ramlila of Ramnagar."
    Sangeet Natak, 49 (July-September 1978), pp. 28-32.
    In this interview, Ramlila is considered in terms of its cultural
context.

_____ and Linda Hess. "The Ramlila of Ramnagar." The Drama
    Review, 21, 3 (September 1977), pp. 51-82.
    Comprehensive overview of the thirty-one-day major Ramlila of
Ramnagar. Excellent photographs, maps and charts provide a visual
panorama of the processional cycle play's major events.

6. Raslila

Hawley, John Stratton. At Play with Krishna: Pilgrimage Dramas
    from Brindavan. Princeton: Princeton University Press, 1981.
    A collection of four plays from the ras lila cycles performed by
one company in Brindavan; the translations include selected staging
descriptions which give some idea of the use of the stage and limited
movement in the lilas. The theological explanation of the significance
of the beginning ras dance is a clear and revealing exposition. Especially important is the description of the ras dance in the context
of "The Great Circle Dance."

Samar, D. L. "Rasdhari, Folk Theatre of Rajasthan." Sangeet Natak,
    20 (April-June 1971), pp. 50-56.
    The historical development of the Rasleela of Rajasthan. Consid-
ers the performers and the changes from professional to nonprofessional staging, various performance spaces, thematic content, and
brief mention of music and dance.

Singh, Guru Bipin. "The Rasleela of Manipur." Quarterly Journal
    of the National Centre for the Performing Arts, 3, 3 (Septem-
    ber 1974), pp. 27-36.
    The article surveys this Rasleela primarily as a dance form, de-
scribing the location and occasions of performance, the participants,

musical and dramatic structure, the sequence of events in performance, with general descriptions of dance movements.

7. Krishnattam

Iyer, K. Bharatha. "Krishnattam." Times of India Annual (1966),
pp. 71-80.
Beautifully illustrated general introduction to the devotional
dance-drama of Lord Krishna performed at Guruvayur Temple.

Panikkar. Kavalam Narayana. "Krishnanattom." Malayalam Literary
Survey, I, 1 (1977), pp. 33-41.
Concentrates on history, relation to Kathakali, with brief mention
of choreography and current status of the form.

8. Teyyam

Ashley, Wayne. "The Teyyam Kettu of Northern Kerala." The
Drama Review, 23, 2 (1979), pp. 99-112.
Best short introduction to this ritual form of Kerala, the article
concentrates on the ritual context and significance of the performance.

_____ and Regina Holloman. "From Ritual to Theatre in Kerala."
The Drama Review, 26, 2 (1982), pp. 59-72.
Study of social processes and change in the life of the traditional
ritual performance Teyyam of Kerala.

Kurup, K. K. N. The Cult of Teyyam and Hero Worship in Kerala.
Calcutta: Indian Pub., 1973.
Introduction to the cult of Teyyam, including history and brief
descriptions of individual deities propitiated.

_____. "Teyyam of Kerala." Sangeet Natak, 53-54 (July-
December 1979), pp. 45-52.
A general introduction to this ritual dance of Kerala. Some discussion of origins and influences on development, social positions of
performers and their training, performance activities, costumes and
makeup, and evidence of classical elements in this form.

Mencher, J. P. "Possession, Dance and Religion in North Malabar,
Kerala, India." International Congress of Anthropological and
Ethnological Sciences, 9 (1964), pp. 340-345.
Study of Teyyam with emphasis on caste, possession, and social
control.

Modern and Contemporary Dance

Crowder, Linsley. "Namaste: Matteo and the Indo-American Dance

Co." Dance Magazine (February 1972), pp. 32-37.
Short article with background information on Matteo and his
training, and the formation of his company in New York. Mentions
his innovation of using Western ballet barre as training tool for
Bharata Natyam.

Ferragello, Nancy. "Ethos of Movement." Natya, 9, 3 (1966),
pp. 10-12.
Examines American modern dance forms and their capacity for
capturing and communicating vital emotions, as part of an argument
for Indian choreographers to investigate authentic folk and tribal
dances as sources for developing new forms.

Franda, Marcus. "Two Dancers from Madras." Hanover, N.J.:
American University Field Staff Reports, #24 Asia (1981).
The major focus of the article is on V. P. and Shanta Dhanan-
jayan who run a small dance academy in Madras. Tracing the social, economic and cultural pressures facing dancers today, the article offers a helpful differentiation between traditional Bharata
Natyam and modern film versions as well as giving short descriptions of new innovations created in contemporary choreography.

Hall, F. "Influence of Indian Dance on the West." Sangeet Natak,
28 (1973), pp. 30-49.
Historical consideration of Indian dance themes and style of
movement as employed by Western artists of the ballet.

_____. "Nritya Darpana: A Study in Modern Choreography."
Marg, 6, 4 (1953), pp. 47-52.
An historical view of the modern developments in "ballet" choreography, which blends Western models with elements of the four
classical Indian styles.

Kagal, Carmen. "Indian Interlude in Modern Dance." Span
(March 1966), pp. 33-39.
Detailed review of the "Indian" dances of St. Denis and Shawn
with excellent photographs.

Khokar, Mohan. "Western Interest in, and Its Impact on, Indian
Dance." Bulletin of the Institute of Traditional Cultures
(Madras), Part II (1961), pp. 203-217.
Overview of the relationship between Western and Indian dance
from the 1830's to the 1960's. An especially good summary of the
early work of St. Denis and Uday Shankar.

Natya (New Delhi), 7, 4 (December 1963) Special Issue: Dance
Drama, and Ballet.
Special dance, drama and ballet issue, with primary emphasis
on modern developments. Includes a series of articles covering
various aspects of the Indian ballet, as well as short articles on
Kuchipudi, Seraikella Chhau, Manipur Rasleela, Kathak, and new
choreography in classical traditions.

Sangeet Natak, 48 (April-June, 1978), Special Uday Shankar Issue.
A special issue devoted entirely to the life and work of Uday
Shankar, perhaps the most influential choreographer of modern
eclectic Indian ballet. While varying widely in the quality of contributions, collectively the issue gives a clear picture of Uday Shankar's "rediscovery" of his own artistic traditions which inspired his
early choreographic style. The experimental process used in the
creation of Shankar's dance pieces is clearly presented, as is the
training process used at his school.

Sondhi, Krishanlal. "The First Institute of Choreography in India."
Natya, 8, 2 (1965), pp. 12-16.

Modern and Contemporary Theatre

Alkazi, E. "Resurgence of the Theatre in India." Times of India
Annual (1967), pp. 53-60.
Author briefly explores a number of problems inhibiting the
theatre in contemporary India, such as the inadequacy of dramatic
criticism, the lack of trained personnel, poor productions, and linguistic barriers among regions. Several modern writers and plays
are also discussed.

Anand, Mulk Raj. The Indian Theatre. New York: Roy Pub.,
1951.
A short, critical history and description of recent dance and
drama in the Andhra, Bengali, Marhatti, Gujerati and Hindustani
theatres, and an assessment of traditional or folk forms, which the
author feels should be adapted in order to revitalize the theatre
today, and in order to create a new, indigenous tradition.

Ashley, Wayne and Regina Holloman. "From Ritual to Theatre in
Kerala." The Drama Review, 26, 2 (1982), pp. 59-72.
Recent anthropological/performance research on a "new drama"
production making use of an actual traditional Teyyam ritual performance in a new dramatic context. An important study in the
power of performance as agent, and mediator of cultural change.

Bandyopadhyay, S. K. "Trends in Modern Bengali Drama."
Indian Writing Today, 4, 3 (1970), pp. 149-55.
A brief historical view of the trends in Bengali drama since the
early 1940's.

Banerjee, Branjendra Nath. Bengali Stage: 1795-1873. Calcutta:
Ranjan Publishing House, 1943.

Barua, Birnichi Kumar. Modern Assamese Literature. (Chap. 3).
Gauhati: Lawyer's Book Stall, 1957.
Analyzes four types of drama--mythical, social, historical and
romantic--and the major playwrights for the modern Assamese
theatre.

Becker, Ann. "Rabindranath Tagore as a Theatre Artist." M.A.
thesis, University of Oregon, 1958.

Bhalla, M. M. A Handful of Dreams: Essays and Reviews in Search
of Indian Theatre. Alok Bhalla, ed. Delhi: Kailash Book Co.,
1970.
A collection of short, critical articles, dealing with issues of the
contemporary theatre in India. Some are performance reviews. Two
consider the state of the art and its future directions. There are
also brief commentaries on Nautanki, folk-theatre and opera, and
East-West views of the concept of total theatre.

_____. "Post Independence Theatre in India." Natya, 5, 3
(1961), pp. 10-12.
Discusses the diverse values of classical, folk and Western forms
of theatre in India today, and their mutual impact and potential for
theatre in the future.

Bhattacharyya, D. H. Origin and Development of the Assamese
Drama and the Stage. Gauhati: Barua Agency, 1964.
An extensive history of theatre and drama in Assam, covering
early Sanskrit drama, folk plays and Bhavanas, and emphasizing
the dramas, stages and staging from the nineteenth to early twentieth centuries.

Bhole, Keshevarao and N. V. Joshi. "The Marathi Sangeet."
Sangeet Natak, 15 (January-March 1970), pp. 41-56.
Two authors discuss the contribution of Marathi drama to Indian
music. They offer some important insight into the historical and
formal interplay of drama and music on the Marathi stage.

Biswas, A. R. "Shakespeare and the Indian Theatre and Drama."
Calcutta Review, 175, 3 (June 1965), pp. 195-239.
A comparative view which assesses the influence of the Shake-
spearean stage and drama on the development of Indian theatre,
primarily in the nineteenth century. Although the Bengali theatre
is the major source for comparison, other language theatres in India
are also considered.

Byrski, M. Christopher. "Grotowski and the Indian Tradition."
Sangeet Natak, 23 (1972), pp. 16-25.
Traces similarities and parallels between Grotowski's early
theatre work and Indian thought, exercises (including Yoga), and
performances.

Chowdhuri, Ahindra. "The Theatre (1858-1919)" in Studies in
Bengal Renaissance. Atul Chandra Gupta, ed. Jadavpur:
National Council of Education, Bengal, 1958.
A short, historical account of the theatre and drama in this
period of development in the Bengali theatre.

Cousins, James H. The Plays of Brahma: An Essay on the Drama in National Revival. Bangalore: Amateur Dramatic Assoc., 1921.
An argument to revive native drama, and to include selected influences from European and Japanese theatre.

De Cuhna, Gerson. "Language Theatre in India." Natya, 1, 1 (October 1956) pp. 21-26, 41.
Assesses the current status of the Assamese, Bihari, Bengali, Gujerati, Hindi, Kannada, Marathi, Malayalam, and Manipuri language theatres.

"East West Theatre Seminar on Total Theatre." Natya, 9, 4 (1966-67), pp. 6-21.

Fabri, Charles. "Dance Dramas of Tagore." Natya, Tagore Centenary Number (1962), pp. 10-15.
Analysis of Tagore's dance dramas.

Futehally, Laeeq. "The Theatres We Played In ... Uzra Begum Interviewed." Natya, 4, 2 (1960), pp. 40-42.
An interview with the leading actress of Prithvi Theatres, in which she recalls performance circumstances while touring.

Gargi, Balwant. "The Pulse of the Indian Theatre." Times of India Annual, 1975, pp. 43-51.
Reviews contemporary plays in the Hindi, Marathi, Kannada, Bengali and Punjabi theatres. Although the emphasis is on dramatic content, there are some references to staging.

Gilbert, Eddie Reid. "The National School of Drama Contributes Significantly to Theatre Training in India." Ph.D. diss., University of Wisconsin, 1971.
History of modern theatre training in India, and in particular the creation of the National School of Drama.

Guhi-Thakurta, Prabhurcharan. The Bengali Drama: Its Origin and Development. London: Kegan Paul, Trench, Trubner, 1930.
A very good critical history of Bengali drama with extensive coverage of the Yatra, as well as the development of the modern spoken drama, from the eighteenth century on. This study also considers the theatres, and some aspects of staging, including acting styles.

Gunawardana. A. J. "The Uses of Tradition: An Interview with E. R. Sarachchandra." The Drama Review, 15, 3 (Spring 1971), pp. 193-200.
Sarachchandra discusses many of the essential conventions of traditional Asian theatre forms, and explains why and how he adapts them in his plays.

"Indian Drama and Stage Today." Indian Literature, I, 2 (April-
September 1958), pp. 75-150.
This section includes a series of articles covering the historical
development of the Assamese, Bengali, Gujurati, Hindi, Kannada,
Kashmiri, Malayalam, Marathi, Oriya, Punjabi, Tamil, Telugu, and
Urdu dramas.

Kale, K. Narayan. Theatre in Maharashtra. New Delhi: Maharashtra Information Centre, 1967.
A short, general history of theatre and drama in the region of
Maharashtra, from mid-nineteenth century to the 1960's. Includes
occasional references to staging.

Kale, Pramod. "Epic to Polemic--Social Change in Marathi Drama,
1843-79." Sangeet Natak, 23 (January-March 1972), pp. 31-43.
Thorough study of development and influences in Marathi drama
during this vital period. Includes references to performance structure, improvisation, and the "epic" or presentational nature of the
performance which characterized the style of the playwright Bhave's
company.

Khanolkar, C. J. "The Dashavatara Traditional of the Konkan."
Quarterly Journal of the National Centre for the Performing
Arts, 3, 1 (March 1974), pp. 13-22.
A good introduction to this form. Describes the dramatic content and structure, several typical scenes, costumes, musical accompaniment, acting style, masks and makeup, with brief mention
of dance steps.

Krishnamurti, S. R. "Future of the Amateur Stage." Bulletin of
the Institute of Traditional Culture, 2 (1962), pp. 215-224.
Emphasis is on the status of contemporary theatre in Madras.

Machwe, P. "The Drama in Modern India." Natya, 1, 1 (October
1956), pp. 11-18, 42.
After a brief review of dramatic tradition in India, this article
considers the modern developments in the drama of various regions
of India.

Marathi Natya Parishad. The Marathi Theatre: 1843-1960. Bombay:
Marathi Natya Parishad, 1961.

Mathur, J. C. "Theatre and Theatre Architecture in India Today."
Natya, 4, 1 (1960), pp. 7-11.
A general description of a variety of types of stages used in
rural and professional theatre forms, with recommendations for
future construction of composite theatre houses which could accommodate all these forms.

Medhi, Kaliram. "Origins of the Assamese Drama" in Aspects of
Early Assamese Literature. Banikanta Kakati, ed. Gauhati:
Gauhati Univ. Dept. of Pub. 1953.

An historical account, covering origins in the 16th century, relationship to the Sanskrit drama, and pre-modern plays and playwrights.

Mehta, Kumud. "Bombay's Theatre World: 1860-1880." Journal of the Asiatic Society of Bombay, 43/44 (1968-69), pp. 251-278.

_____ and Vijay Tendulkar. "Utpal Dutt." Quarterly Journal of the National Centre for the Performing Arts, 2, 2 (June 1973), pp. 11-24.
An interview with Utpal Dutt, in which the celebrated theatre personality discusses recent developments in Bengali theatre. Although the emphasis is on the dramatic offerings of various theatre groups, there are scattered references to staging. Much of the commentary is directed to the Jatra.

"Modern Trends in Indian Theatre." Bulletin of the Institute of Traditional Culture, Part 2 (1962), pp. 169-174.

Mookerhee, S. P. "The Bengali Theatre." Calcutta Review, 10 (1924), pp. 109-36.
Early history of Bengali theatre and dramatic literature, emphasizing the period 1857-1873.

Mukerji, Amar. "Bengali Drama and Theatre." Calcutta Review, 140 (September 1956), pp. 214-224.
Primarily an historical overview of Bengali drama, with some references to staging and acting style.

Nadkarni, Jnaneshvar. "The Temperament of Marathi Drama." Sangeet Natak, 2 (April 1966), pp. 63-73.
Briefly recounts the history of Marathi theatre, focusing on dramatic content and the role of music as a distinctive feature of this drama. Little direct reference to movement.

_____. New Directions in the Marathi Theatre. New Delhi: Maharashtra Information Centre, 1967.
An excellent historical survey of modern Marathi theatre and drama, with primary emphasis on post-1943 activities.

Naik, Bapurao. Origins of the Marathi Theatre. New Delhi: Maharashtra Information Centre, 1967.
Traces the history of Marathi theatre prior to 1900.

Raha, Kironmoy. Bengali Theatre. New Delhi: National Book Trust, 1978.
A good historical study, this work considers the influences of Jatra and the English theatre on the development of the Bengali theatre, the formation of private and professional theatres, the transition to commercial theatre, the New Drama movement and the "other theatre," and the contemporary commercial theatre. Special consideration is given to several of the dominant figures (producers,

playwrights and actors), and descriptions of acting styles and staging are also included.

_____. "The Bengali Theatre." Natya, 9, 4 (1966-67), pp. 65-67.
Historical view of Bengali theatre, with particular attention to dramatists and producers. Notes the transition in popular appeal from commercial theatre to the avant garde movement of nonprofessionals, and the overall effect of these changes. Assesses the current status of the theatre with speculation about its future. No reference to movement.

Rangacharya, Adya. "The Kannada Stage--Then and Now." Quarterly Journal of the National Centre for the Performing Arts, 2, 4 (December 1973), pp. 1-10.
Personal reminiscences and critical reactions to a variety of Kannada and Marathi plays. The comments mainly address dramatic content, with a few references to acting.

Ray, Nihar Ranjan. "Tagore's Influence on Indian Dramatic Literature and the Stage." Natya, 5, 3 (1961), pp. 4-8.
Argues that Tagore's dramatic works, particularly his symbolical plays and dance-dramas, have been inadequately understood and produced.

Rea, Kenneth. "Theatre in India: The Old and the New, Part III." Theatre Quarterly, 8, 32 (1979), pp. 47-66.
Focus on modern attempts at synthesis between indigenous traditions and Western approaches/sensibilities. Although only limited attention is given to movement, important as an overview of the work of three major figures including Utpal Dutt, Bodal Sircar, and Habib Tanvir. The brief description of a Jatra performance and the interview with Tanvir are particularly valuable.

Richmond, Farley. "Contemporary English-Language Theatre in India." Ph.D. diss., Michigan State University, 1966.

_____. "Indian Theatre at Michigan State University." Sangeet Natak, 32 (1974), pp. 40-47.
Reviews a cultural/educational/theatrical approach to the study of Indian theatre as a part of Indian culture and attempts to translate the Indian performance milieu to a Western audience and environment.

_____. "The Political Role of Theatre in India." Educational Theatre Journal, 25, 3 (October 1973), pp. 318-334.
Also in Marxist Influences and South Asian Literature, Vol. II, Asian Studies Center, Michigan State University, 165-186. Essentially the same text as "The Social Role of Theatre in India," Sangeet Natak.

_____. "The Social Role of Theatre in India." Sangeet Natak, 25 (1972), pp. 64-83.
View of theatre in India as an instrument of social change, examining several periods of social protest and political propaganda manifested in the drama in the nineteenth and twentieth centuries. Little direct reference to movement.

"Roundtable on the Contemporary Relevance of Traditional Theatre." Sangeet Natak, 21 (July-September 1971).
A special issue devoted to the so-called "gulf" between the traditional and the modern heritage in Indian theatre. The panel addresses the problem of how to assimilate tradition in contemporary activity. A variety of traditional theatre forms are discussed in terms of their viability, their developing and synthetic forms, and their place in contemporary society. A useful issue that provides a good overview.

Samar, Devi Lal. "Folk Drama for the Contemporary Stage." Sangeet Natak, 26 (October-December 1972), pp. 5-14.
General traditions in folk drama are contrasted with various elements of modern drama in India, such as the performer's relationship with audience, female roles, character, themes, staging devices.

Schechner, Richard. "Intersections: Indian Traditional, American Experimental Theatre." Fulbright Newsletter, New Delhi (Winter 1976), pp. 8-17.
Explores five areas of intersection between traditional Indian and American experimental theatre including staging, extended performances, dominance of contextual material, audience participation, and nonacting or display.

Segal, Zohra. "The Last Curtain; The End of the Prithvi Theatres." Natya, 4, 2 (1960), pp. 31-39.
Short biographical and historical account of Prithviraj and the establishment of his touring theatre company.

Sengupta, Rudraprasad. "Bengali Theatre: Quo Vadis?" Sangeet Natak, 39 (January-March 1976), pp. 30-37.
Examines the history and developments in Bengali theatre from the 1940's on, and poses several causes for the changes in troupes and repertoires.

Shaw, Denis. "Ester Leach, 'The Mrs. Siddons of Bengal.'" Educational Theatre Journal, 10 (1958), pp. 304-310.
Historical view of British efforts, in early eighteenth century, to establish theatre in Calcutta. Focuses on the highly successful career of this professional actress, including her impetus in establishing the Sans Souci Theatre. Good anecdotes but no reference to acting style or movement.

Subramanyam, Ka Naa. "Traditional Tamil Drama and the Present
Impasse." Sangeet Natak, 4 (March-April 1967), pp. 27-36.
An historical view which surveys the dramatic antecedents of
modern Tamil drama. Makes only general references to staging and
performance.

Swaminathan, Mina. "Creative Drama for Young Adults." Quarterly Journal of the National Centre for the Performing Arts, 4,
4 (December 1975), pp. 14-24.
Description of a social services program for children of working
mothers, in Delhi. References to therapeutic value of movement.

Tanvir, Habib. "The Indian Experiment." Theatre India, National
Drama Festival Cochin. Trichur: Kerala Sangeetha Nataka
Akademi, 1977, pp. 5-10.
Examines the current status of contemporary Indian theatre and
its relationship to and use of folk theatre as a process of rediscover-
ing India's own theatrical traditions.

"Theatre in Transition." United Asia, X, 1 (1958), pp. 100-126.
A series of articles concerning modern theatre and drama in
India, including topics such as actor-producer Prithviraj Kapoor
and his contribution, modern Gujerati and Marathi drama, and modern theatre in Kerala. Although the articles emphasize history,
dramatic style, and content, there are references to staging and
acting styles.

"Theatre Today." Sangeet Natak, 22 (October-December 1971).
This issue is entirely devoted to "Theatre Today" and includes
a variety of articles and interviews covering issues in the contemporary Indian theatre, such as the influence of cinema on staging
and acting style, the changes in folk forms of theatre, contemporary dramatic experiments by several playwrights. Little direct
reference to movement.

"Theatres, Indian and Western: Their Mutual Impacts. Reports of
Seminars." Bulletin of the Institute of Traditional Culture,
Part 1 (1962), pp. 41-105.

Warekar, Mama. "Development of Marathi Theatre." Orient Review
(September 1957), pp. 267-274.
Historical survey of Marathi theatre since mid-nineteenth century,
with commentary on the social significance of theatre.

Audio-Visual Materials

1. Videotapes

Acting Techniques of Kutiyattam, Sanskrit Theatre of India.
Michigan State Asian Theatre Series. Color, sound, 55 minutes.

Farley Richmond gives a brief introduction. In Part I he demonstrates the basic body posture for male and female characters and explains a few simple physical movements. Part II examines the use of gestures as language and contains a filmed excerpt of a professional actor. In Part III, Indian instructors demonstrate the eye exercises and facial expressions used to convey the emotions and sentiments of the characters. The section concludes with a masterteacher demonstrating how various facial expressions are combined with one symbolic gesture to produce a variety of different effects.

Chhau: Masked Dance of Bengal. Asia Society. Color, sound, 30
    minutes.
The Purulian form is featured, as performers execute a dancedrama in costume and makeup, and a single dancer also demonstrates basic dance patterns and steps used in the form. These technical aspects are performed without mask or costume.

From India to East Lansing--Surpanakha--Producing a Sanskrit
    Drama. Michigan State Asian Theatre Series. Color, sound,
    31 minutes.
Graphically describes the research, preparation and rehearsal process which led to performance of an Indian play by American theatre students.

Heen Baba and His Dance and Drum Ensemble. Asia Society.
    Color, sound, 30 minutes.
Presents Heen Baba of Sri Lanka with his versions of the following dances: cobra dance, elephant dance, drum duet, butterfly dance, peacock dance, and a closing dance.

Indrani and Her Classical Dancers and Musicians of India. Dance
    Workshop, WGBH, Boston. (Produced for Jerome Robbins
    Film Archive). Color, sound, 55 minutes, 1975.
An important document of Indrani's work in Indian dance, the tape includes, among other pieces, "Manduka Shabdom" (The Conticum of the Frog) in Kuchipudi style danced by Indrani; and "Vana Varnanam" (In the Forest) in Kathakali style danced by V. P. Ramakrishnan.

Kathak: North Indian Dance. Asia Society. Color, sound, 30
    minutes.
A series of solos, duets, and a trio are performed by Indian artists, demonstrating both elements of pure, abstract dance, and narrative dance. The dancers' interplay with the musicians is emphasized in the final dance.

Kathakali Classical Dance. Lincoln Center. Black and white, sound,
    25 minutes.
Recording of a workshop by Krishnan Namboodiri including exercises and movements.

Kathakali Dances from India. Lincoln Center. Videotape. Color,
  sound, 53 minutes.
Performance and demonstration by Krishnan Namboodiri.

Kathakali, Indian Dance-Drama, Featuring M. P. Sankaran Namboodiri. UCLA Office of Instructional Development. Color,
  sound, 40 minutes.
An award-winning videotape of a performance of selections from
"The Killing of the Demon Narakasure" by M. P. Sankaran Namboodiri of the Kerala Kalamandalam. A brief introduction provides
a summary of the story, and an introduction to Kathakali dance-
drama with excellent close-ups of makeup in process. The performance tape is recorded on two audio tracks, one providing narrative commentary and a "translation" of the hand gesture language
to assist the viewer in understanding the conventions of performance. The scene selected includes the well-known peacock dance,
a highly accomplished piece of Kathakali set choreography and a
favorite of connoisseurs.

Kathakali: South Indian Dance-Drama from the Kerala Kalamandalam.
  Asia Society. Color, sound, 30 minutes.
Selections from the Kerala Kalmandalam performance of Daksaya-
gam while on tour in the United States.

Masked Dance-Drama of Bhutan. Asia Society. Color, sound, 30
  minutes.
One of two videotapes devoted to this group of royal dancers
and musicians from the kingdom of Bhutan. They perform a scene,
with chanting and spoken dialogue, which are translated by a narrator. A very short excerpt from a folk dance is also performed.

The Royal Dancers and Musicians from the Kingdom of Bhutan.
  Asia Society. Color, sound, 30 minutes.
This videotape of a film includes footage taken in Bhutan, and
shows the opening-day performances in a three-day festival. There
is coverage of ritual ceremonies, a variety of dances, the antics of
clowns, scenes from a dance-drama, and the concluding dance. The
performers are also shown in rehearsals.

Seraikella Chhau, The Masked Dance of India. Michigan State Asian
  Theatre Series. Color, sound, 39 minutes.
Kedar Nath Sahoo, director of the state government training
center and chief exponent of Seraikella Chhau, performs excerpts
from choreographed pieces. Interspersed are demonstrations of
many of the basic movement patterns adapted from the martial arts
tradition of the region. He performs exercises, dances the gaits
appropriate to birds, and does movements which depict the daily
chores of housewives. The tape begins with a short introduction
to the art, illustrated with photographs, and is highlighted by Mr.
Sahoo's masked performance of the peacock dance.

Sitara In Kathak. Asia Society. Color, sound, 30 minutes.
This Kathak artist performs four different dances, in costume, with accompaniment by tabla and harmonium. Several of these dances emphasize the fast and intricate rhythms executed in the dancer's footwork.

Surpanakha (The Amorous Demoness). Michigan State Asian
Theatre Series. Color, sound, 90 minutes.
A fascinating and colorful English-language dramatization of incidents drawn from the Ramayana. A lovesick demoness disguised as a beautiful woman attempts to seduce the unwilling victim. After gentle persuasion fails, the demoness assumes her true form and attempts to terrorize her beloved into submission. Her boasts of sexual prowess serve as a humorous highlight of the production. In a spectacular conclusion, the demoness is disfigured and vows to seek revenge.

Thovil: Ritual Chanting, Dance and Drumming of Exorcism. Asia
Society. Color, sound, 30 minutes.
A variety of exorcistic dances (torch, ceremony, Devol, fire, and shawl) from Sri Lanka.

Yakshagana: Ritual Dance Theatre from South Kanara, India.
Asia Society. Color, sound, 30 minutes.
Selections from the tour performance of a Yaksagana Bayalata company on tour, the tape focuses on a wide variety of movement, including footwork, jumping and whirling, and battle scenes.

Yamini Krishnamurti: South Indian Dance. Asia Society. Color,
sound, 30 minutes.
Selection of performances in two classical styles. Pieces include "Navarasa Slokam" (depicting the nine basic classical sentiments) in Bharatanayam style, "The Frog Who Became a Queen," in Kuchipudi style, the "Tillana," a pure abstract Bharatanatyam selection, and finally a Kuchipudi excerpt showing Krishna's early youth.

2. Films

Ajuba Dance and Drama Company. Contemporary South Asia Film
Series, South Asian Area Center, University of Wisconsin-
Madison. Color, sound, 20 minutes.
Excellent introductory film on the popular Nautanki theatre of North India. The film focuses on one specific company of performers under the leadership of Bhaggal, the director. Footage includes the life of performers, rehearsals, travel, setup, and the performance itself.

Bharatanatyam. Cinema 16 Film Library, Inc., New York. Black
and white, sound, 10 minutes.
Dances of Indrani and Shanta.

Chhau Dance of Bengal. Films Orientalia. Color, sound, 17
   minutes, 1969.
Film of Chhau in a village in Bengal, includes excerpts from the
Ramayana in performance.

Chhau, the Masked Dance of Bengal. Bureau Mass Communication,
   New York State Education Dept., Albany. Color, sound, 30
   minutes.

Dances of India. Bailey Films. Black and white, 12 minutes.
Folk dances from various geographical regions of India.

Dances of India: Bharatanatyam. Information Service of India,
   Washington, D.C. 10 minutes.

Divine Dances of India. Folklore Film, Stockholm. Color, sound,
   37 1/2 minutes, 1976.
Filmed at the February 1976 Festival of Indian Dances in New
Delhi, Udaipur, and Bombay, the collage includes short segments
of Kathakali, Kathak, Bharatanatyam, Odissi, Kuchipudi, Chhau,
Manipuri, and a few tribal and folk dances.

Floating in the Air Followed by the Wind. Indiana University,
   Bloomington. Color, sound, 34 minutes.
Documentation of Hindu Festival of Tamil Indians now located
north of Kuala Lumpur in Malaysia. Devotees of Murugan are depicted performing sacrifices to the deity. The film focuses on
several devotees under the guidance of Guru Kurup who assists
them in attaining a trance state. Footage includes training/prac-
tice in entering trance and closely follows the use of dance and
rhythmic movement in entering the ecstatic state when Murugan
takes over the individual. The fairlike atmosphere of festival is
captured, providing insight into the wider context of the event for
devotees/performers.

God With a Green Face. American Society for Eastern Arts, San
   Francisco, CA. Color, sound, 25 minutes.
Opening of the film on Kathakali includes footage of makeup,
and actors' commentary on early experience of the form. Kunju
Nair, one of the famous Kathakali actors, is featured playing Rama
in a scene with Sita from the Ramayana. Other cuttings from this
performance of the Ramayana include Ravanna disguised as a holy
man, Ravanna killing Jatayu, the battle between Bali and Sugriva,
Hanuman meeting Ravanna, and Rama and Ravanna in a final con-
frontation.

The Goddess Durga--Durga Puja--Festival of Calcutta. Japan
   Foundation/Mitsu Productions Series. 16 mm., color, sound,
   43 minutes.

Guru Kunju Kurup. Films Division, Government of India. 16 mm,
   black and white, sound, 9 minutes, 1970.

Documentary of this great actor including excerpts from a performance of Hala Caritam and an interview with the actor at the age of ninety.

An Introduction to Yakshagana Bayalata. Michigan State University
    Asian Studies Center. 16 mm., sound, color, 38 minutes,
    1975.
Performed and presented by Dr. Martha Ashton, Yakshagana specialist, and her teacher from India, the film is an excellent introduction to the Yakshagana of Karnatak including history, make-up, costuming, basic gestures, culminating in a performance of the female role of Radha in costume.

Kathakali. Information Service of India, Washington D.C. Color,
    sound, 22 minutes.
A short introductory film produced in a studio.

Kuchipudi Dance, Part I: Ancient and Modern. Lincoln Center.
    Color, sound, 21 1/2 minutes, 1973.
Documentary of Kuchipudi including solo dances as well as excerpts from dance-dramas.

Kuchipudi Dance, Part II: Bhama Kalapam. Lincoln Center.
    Color, sound, 1973.
Discusses the origin of Kuchipudi and the performance of the dance-drama, Bhama Kalapam.

Kutiyattam: Sanskrit Temple-Drama. Asian Theatre Film Lending
    Service. 16 mm., color, sound, 27 minutes.
An excellent introduction to the only existing form of regional Sanskrit drama in India which dates from approximately the ninth century. The film includes an introduction to temple-theatre architecture, an overview of actor training, and production excerpts. The first performance sequence includes the opening dance of the Sutradhara (stage manager). Next is a passage from the combined acting portion of the play Subhadradananjayam showing a love scene between Subhadra and Arjuna, as well as excerpts of the Vidusaka or Sanskrit drama clown. The Vidusaka's opening conventionalized gestures and comic action are shown, as well as his "playing" with Arjuna. Finally, a selection is taken from a dramatization of the Ramayana. This selection includes a scene with Ravanna, his Charioteer, and the captured Sita. Jatayu, hearing Sita's cries, performs his opening dance/entrance, miming the actions of a bird. He then challenges Ravanna. The film concludes with the battle between Ravanna and Jatayu.

Lord Shiva Danced. Asiatic Petroleum Corp., N.Y. Black and
    white, sound, 20 minutes.
1948 film of Ram Gopal and his dancers. Includes cuttings of Bharanatyam, Manipuri, Kathakali (without makeup or traditional costumes), Kathak, and new dances out of old traditions.

Mahakali Pyakhan--Masked Dance of Nepal. Japan Foundation/Mitsu
    Productions Series. 16 mm., color, sound, 30 minutes.

Masque of Malabar: A Study of Kathakali. Produced by David
    Bolland ("Malabar," Brent Knoll, Somerset TA 9 4EH, Eng-
    land). Color, sound, 42 minutes.
The best documentary available to date, the film includes description and commentary on training, makeup, and costuming made
at both the famous Kerala Kalamandalam as well as the FACT Kathakali School. Also included are two excellent cuttings from full performances on location. A shorter version (20 minutes) is also
available under the title, Malabar Masque.

Oraons of Bihar. Asiatic Petroleum Corp., N.Y. Color, sound,
    17 minutes.
Introduces Oraon village life, with good footage of the tribal
dance form.

Purulia Chhau--Masked Dance of East India. Japan Foundation/
    Mitsu Productions Series. 16 mm., color, sound, 30 minutes.

Sanskrit Drama: The Vision of Vasavadatta. IASTA. 16 mm.,
    color, sound, 15 minutes.
Brief film documenting Mrinalini Sarabhai's production of this
Sanskrit classic with American professional actors. Footage includes student/actor training, and commentary on the attempt to
reconstruct the style of classic Sanskrit plays based on Bharata
Natyam and other forms of classical Indian theatre. Footage of
dubious quality.

Seraikella Chhau--Masked Dance of East India. Japan Foundation/
    Mitsu Productions Series. 16 mm., color, sound, 30 minutes.

Tanjore: A Centre of Art and Culture. Asiatic Petroleum Corp.,
    N.Y. Black and white, sound, 13 minutes.
Documents temple sculpture and uses Bharatnatyam dance in
juxtaposition to sculptures to illustrate temple architecture.

O Tempora O Mores. Asian Film Lending Library. 16 mm., black
    and white, sound, 20 minutes.
Sound track is difficult to understand and not of great quality,
nor is the film footage, but it does show a few extended scenes.

Therayattam. Radim Films, Inc., N.Y. Black and white, sound,
    18 minutes.
The "dance of the gods" of Kerala State in Southwest India, this
early film contains valuable footage of a variety of Teyyam ritual
performances. Deities enacted include Pataviran, a deified fighter
skilled in martial arts; Chamundi; Kali, an aspect of Durga worshipped for smallpox protection; Kuttichattan, a manifestation of
Ganapati; Kantakarnan, as aspect of Shiva controlling diseases who

dances with torches around his waist to destroy disease; and Gulu-
gan in a hand-painted mask.

Wedding of the Goddess. 2 parts. South Asian Studies Film Dis-
        tribution, University of Wisconsin-Madison. 16 mm., color,
        sound, 76 minutes.
    Covers possession as a part of the ritual process. Illustrates
the movement of one who becomes possessed.

Yakshagana--Dance-Drama of South India. Japan Foundation/Mitsu
        Productions Series. 16 mm., color, sound, 38 minutes.

3. Filmstrip

Traditional Theatre of South India. 2 parts. Olesen Films, 1535
        Ivar, Hollywood, CA. 52 frame filmstrip written and photo-
        graphed by Professor Farley Richmond.

4. Slide Collection

Asian Dance and Drama, Vol. I, South Asia. Asia Society, New
        York. Collection of slides.

Other South Asian Countries

1. Bangladesh

Husain, Syed Sajjad. "Jatra or Bengali Folk Drama." Pakistan
        Quarterly, 5, 1 (Spring 1955), pp. 59-60.
    Brief account of the popular music-drama of Bengal in Bangla-
desh.

2. Nepal

Dayal, Leela Row. "Sanskrit Plays in Kathmandu." Indian PEN,
        27 (December 1961), pp. 375-77.

Fantin, Mario. Mani Rimdu, Nepal. New Delhi: The English Book
        Store, 1976.
    A photo study of the Mani Rimdu with minimal accompanying ex-
planation of the plates.

Jerstad, L. G. Mani-Rimdu; Sherpa Dance-Drama. Seattle: Uni-
        versity of Washington Press, 1969.
    Comprehensive study of Mani-rimdu, the Nepalese form of Cham,
performed in monasteries by Buddhist monks. The study includes
the religious and historical context of the performance, and detailed

descriptions of the physical setting, musical instruments, costumes, masks, actor training, and the conveyance of meaning through various aspects of performance. The excellent accompanying photographs, glossary and bibliography makes this an especially valuable study.

3. Pakistan

Azuri, Madame. "The Folk Dances of West Pakistan." Pakistan Quarterly, 10, 4 (1962), pp. 41-45.
    Discusses a variety of forms, including Khatak, Lughthi, Luddi, Bhangra, Shedhi Lava, Jhoomer, Bargha, Mogarman.

Enayetullah, Anwar. "Theatre in Pakistan." Pakistan Quarterly, 12, 4 (Autumn 1964), pp. 54-59.
    Brief coverage of the history and current trends in the drama of Pakistan.

Ishaq, S. Evolution of Classical Dancing in Pakistan; A Study. Karachi: Printers Combine, 1969.
    A short, historical study which also briefly discusses Kathak.

Jasimuddin. "The Drama of the People: East Pakistan's Soul in Action." Pakistan Quarterly, 9 (Autumn 1959), pp. 36-39.
    Briefly covers jatra, tamasha, and alkaf.

Mohyeddin, Zia. "The Urdu Theatre." Pakistan Quarterly, 7, 4 (Winter 1957), pp. 30-35.
    A statement about the status of modern theatre in Pakistan, with some historical background.

Rukh, Lala. "Folk Dances of Pakistan." Pakistan Miscellany, 2 (March 1958), pp. 105-111.
    A general introduction with cursory descriptions of several dances.

Zaman, Hameed. "Karachi Causerie." Pakistan Quarterly, 13, 1 (Spring 1965), pp. 70-79.
    An assessment of dance and theatrical activities in Karachi, in 1964-1965.

4. Sri Lanka

Ames, Michael M. "Tovil: The Ritual Chanting, Dance, and Drumming of Exorcism in Sri Lanka." Asia Society Monographs on Music, Dance, and Theater, IV (1977).
    Explains three types of ceremonial arts, the status of priests/performers, the world of demons, and focuses on the five main demons propitiated through Tovil. A Tovil ceremony is described

including basic movement of priest/performer and possessed patients, and the conclusion of the ceremony in laughter.

De Zoete, B. Dance and Magic Drama in Ceylon. London: Faber and Faber, 1957.
Travelogue in diary form describing the author's encounter with ceremonial dance and drama in Sri Lanka.

_____. "Some Souvenirs from Kandyan Dances." Marg, 5, 3 (1951), pp. 78-85.
With some background information about the dance tradition of Ceylon, the author gives descriptive accounts of the dancers, dances, and the dance school in Kandy.

Godakumbura, C. E. Sinhalese Literature. Colombo: Colombo Apothecaries, 1955.
Chapter 24 covers folk drama.

Goonatilleka. M. H. Masks and Mask Systems of Sri Lanka. Colombo: Tamarind Books, 1978.
This profusely illustrated work considers the ritual dances of Tovil and Sanni, and the dance dramas of Kolan and Sokari. While the emphasis is on the construction of masks and description of mask types, there is also much attention given to the cultural context of the masked dances, to the ritual and dramatic content, and to performance description. An extensive bibliography is also very useful.

_____. "Mime, Mask and Satire in Kolan of Ceylon." Folklore, 81 (Autumn 1970), pp. 161-76.
Excellent description and analysis of this folk drama form.

Gunasinghe, Siri. Masks of Ceylon. Colombo: Department of Cultural Affairs, 1962.

Gunawardana, A. J. Theatre in Sri Lanka. Colombo: Department of Cultural Affairs, 1976.
A very good introduction to folk, ritual and modern forms, including some description of performance.

Jayewardene, E. D. W. Sinhala Masks. Kandy: T. B. S. Godamunne and Sons, 1970.

Kambar, Chandrashekhar. "Ritual in Kannada Folk Theatre." Sangeet Natak, 25 (July-September 1972), pp. 5-22.
Details the extent to which Kannada folk drama has taken its form from religious ritual. Specific examples of each are described. Emphasis is given to thematic content, and to elements of dance and music. Descriptions of the stage, the audience, makeup, staging conventions and dramatic structure are also included.

Kandiah, T. "Tamil Drama in Ceylon: A Tradition Usurped."
South Asian Review, 5, 1 (1971), pp. 29-40.
An indictment of the dramatic offerings on the modern Tamil
theatre, criticizing a variety of types of plays, for their senti-
mentality and irrelevance. Author considers the lack of a vital,
critical tradition as the cause.

Kotelawala, Sicille. "The Classical Dance of Sri Lanka: The
Kandyan Dance." Asia Society Monographs on Music, Dance
and Theatre, I (1974).
Considers evolution of the dances, costumes, musical instruments, and includes performance descriptions.

Makulloluwa, W. B. Dances of Sri Lanka. Sri Lanka: Department
of Cultural Affairs, n.d.
This monograph is intended as an introductory overview of the
dance traditions of Sri Lanka. A generalized discussion of origins
precedes a comparative view of the four prevalent dance forms:
Kandyan, Sabaragamuwa, Ruhunu, and Bharata Natyam. Specific
items of performance in Sinhalese dances are described, with general references to movement. Four types of folk dance are briefly
mentioned. Color plates also help illustrate these dances.

Obeyesekere, Gananath. "The Ritual Drama of the Sanni Demons:
Collective Representations of Disease in Ceylon." Comparative
Studies in Society and History, 11, 2 (April 1969), pp. 174-
226.
An interpretation of the symbolism and social functions of these
ritual dramas. Includes extensive description of ritual proceedings.

Obeyesekere, Ranjini and Gananath. "Comic Ritual Dramas in Sri
Lanka." The Drama Review, 20, 1 (1976), pp. 5-19.
Interprets irreverence and satire in religious ritual as a form of
catharsis or purification. Examines this notion specifically in light
of Sinhalese comic ritual drama. Three examples from dramas illustrate comic catharsis (via theme of castration anxiety) or psychological release. Description and quoted stage directions clarify
physical action.

Pertold, O. "The Ceremonial Dances of the Sinhalese." Archiv
Orientalni (Prague), 2 (1930), pp. 108-38, 201-54, 385-426.
An excellent, thorough survey of masked, and nonmasked ceremonial dance forms in Sri Lanka. Includes an extensive, though
dated, bibliography.

Raghavan, M. D. "Kandyan Dancing." Bulletin of the Institute of
Traditional Cultures (1961), pp. 1-8.

_____. Sinhala Natum; Dances of the Sinhalese. Colombo:
M. D. Gunasena, 1967.
This comprehensive, descriptive study of dance in Sri Lanka

covers a diversity of forms, from court dance to folk dance, including Kolam, Li-Keli, Raban, Kandyan dance, and others. Lyrics from accompanying songs are also translated.

Sarathchandra, E. R. Folk Drama of Ceylon. Colombo: Department of Cultural Affairs, 1966.
First published in 1952, the work is a valuable description and analysis of Sinhalese folk and ritual dramatic and quasi-dramatic forms. Forms discussed include folk-religious ceremonies such as the Rata Yakuma performed for ensuring safe delivery for pregnant women, dramatic interludes attached to religious rituals such as the ritual of the God Kohomba, the Kolam or masked plays, Sokari, the Nadagama or folk opera, the puppet plays and the Roman Catholic Passion play.

_____. The Sinhalese Folk Play and the Modern Stage. Colombo: Ceylon University Press, 1953.
A very good study covering ritual and cultural background, and offering detailed descriptions of Kolam, Sokari, Nadagama, puppet plays, the Catholic Passion play, and various examples of modern drama.

Seneviratna, Anuradha. "Kandyan Dance: A Traditional Dance Form in Sri Lanka." Sangeet Natak, 32 (April-June 1974), pp. 5-25.
An excellent introductory article. Includes discussion of legends and ritualistic origins of the form, adavus and forms of the dance, training method and exercises. Compares performance and techniques with Kathakali and Bharata Natyam. Describes the relationship of the dance to music, and briefly looks at the development of two traditions, as well as several related forms.

Vithiananthan, S. "Tamil Folk Drama in Ceylon." Tamil Culture, 11 (1964), pp. 165-72.
Aspects of staging and some general descriptions of movement and dance are included, but the article primarily presents the author's view of the necessary steps for invigorating the Tamil folk drama, such as incorporating new themes, emphasizing the dramatic content, and modernizing the lighting and makeup.

5. Tibet

"Allegorical Lama Dance." China Reconstructs, 7, 2 (February 1958), pp. 17-19.
A discussion of the dance-drama Bujak.

Burang. "Strange Theatre in Tibet." Theatre Arts, 32, 2 (February 1948), pp. 72-73.

Hummel, Siegbert. "Boy Dances at the New Year's Festival in

Lhasa." East and West, 15 (January 1964-March 1965), pp. 50-52.

Kolmas, J. "Ch'am, the Miming Dances of Tibet." New Orient, 3 (October 1962), p. 145.

"Revival of Tibetan Opera." Peking Review, 43 (October 25, 1960), p. 18.

Tanvir, Habib. "The Buddhist Theatre of Tibet." Natya, 9, 3 (1966), pp. 22-26.
  Very good introduction, which also relates these plays to Indian drama.

Chapter Twelve

SOUTHEAST ASIAN PERFORMANCE

Kathy Foley

If an analysis of western drama starts with the statement that in the beginning there was the word, those who have studied Southeast Asian forms know that in the beginning there was the dance. A stylized system of movement is the filter through which character is expressed. Plays often move toward their climax in danced battles. Trance dance and martial arts dances may be a part of performances. Sometimes the drama seems merely to be a setting for the long, essentially nondramatic dances that shine like jewels, the highlights of the performance.

Categories of Performance

This chapter contains a bibliography which uses three categories for classifying performance: traditional, popular, and modern. Within the traditional theatre, court, folk, and ritual forms are not really separate. The art of the people has fed the tradition of the ruler, which, in turn, has affected the art of the people. Ritual forms are practiced by king and commoner alike. A performance form that is in one context ritual may be nonritual in other contexts.

The social changes of the last hundred years have resulted in the inception of new forms that cater to the semiliterate, urban audiences. These new performance forms have generally borrowed elements from the traditional theatre. But significant differences have led scholars to view this theatre as a separate category-- popular theatre. Movement is still important in this theatre, but to a lesser degree than in the traditional theatre.

The final form of theatre that is considered a category in the bibliography is termed "modern." Modern is a term used to discuss the performance forms of the urban elite. Since it is the work of artists who are usually the products of Western-influenced education, modern theatre in Southeast Asia is comparable to the theatre seen in any major city of the world. Dance and drama are often

349

looked upon as separate categories. For drama, the word becomes
the thing. For dance, the choreographer, rather than tradition,
sets the step.

The eyes of the many authors listed in this bibliography have
focused on the intricate dance and theatre of Southeast Asia. For
some the hand has proved to be quicker than the eye. Others have
trained themselves first to see, then to record, and finally to comprehend. These authors have managed with intelligence and ele-
gance to translate the dance of gestures into a dance of words.
The following books are useful resources for visualizing and understanding the theatrical movement of Southeast Asia.

Bibliographies

Recent years have brought the publication of significant bibliographic works that include Southeast Asian drama. Two were
invaluable in drawing up this listing, and a number of the annotations given are based on information provided in them. The first
is James R. Brandon and Elizabeth Wichmann's Asian Theatre: A
Study Guide and [Annotated] Bibliography. This source covers the
Southeast Asian area with intelligence and excellence, but due to
the authors' focus on drama, books that deal more exclusively with
dance and annotations of significant articles from dance and ethnomusicological journals are sometimes excluded.

A second major resource is the New York Public Library's
Dictionary Catalogue of the Dance Collection, Performing Arts Research Center published in 1974 and its annual update, Bibliographic Guide to Dance, 1975- , both published by G. K. Hall in Boston.
That source catalogues the best collection of books, photos, and
films on Southeast Asian dance in the country, and perhaps in the
world. There are a number of foreign language sources and much
visual documentation in its unique collection that I have not included
in this listing, especially when I felt sufficient English language
materials were available and commercially obtainable visual materials
were more accessible.

Two other sources are useful in keeping up with the continuing scholarship. The reader should consult the thrice yearly listing in the journal Ethnomusicology and the annual Bibliography of
Asian Studies, put out by the Association for Asian Studies.

All Southeast Asia

There is no one source to go to for general information on
theatre movement throughout the Southeast Asian area. But Faubion
Bower's Theatre in the East: A Survey of Asian Dance and Drama
and James Brandon's Theatre in Southeast Asia can each be useful

in a different way. Although Bower's work is now nearly thirty years old and was written for a popular audience, it remains a useful tool because it concretely describes performances viewed. For areas like Burma and Laos, where movement description has not been a focus of other writers, this remains a relatively informative source. For other areas, which have merited more in-depth descriptions by later scholars, Bower's descriptions are still useful in that they document a specific point in time that can be used for comparison with more current material.

Brandon's work is less useful for movement description than for the wealth of information on a variety of forms that he manages to incorporate into a useful theoretical frame. His categories of traditional (folk and court), popular, and modern, have been adapted for this bibliography. His comments on the greater significance of dance in the Indian-influenced area of Southeast Asia, as opposed to the Chinese-influenced area, remain evocative. Though other scholars have dealt in greater depth, the breadth of Brandon's discussion remains impressive. The book is a useful reference tool, but will not help the reader visualize the movement.

One other book that spans a number of countries is worthy of note. Xenia Zarina's Classical Dances of the Orient is the only work on a variety of Southeast Asian traditions which begins from a dancer's perspective. It describes her experience of studying dance in Thailand, Cambodia, Java, Bali, Japan, and India before World War II. To master any of these traditions is, of course, a lifetime of work. The book has serious faults. The author often uses pictures of herself to illustrate positions and gestures. Her lack of training is immediately apparent. An alert reader will not take her photos as an accurate representation of the tradition. She uses ballet terminology to discuss positions and technique. Although this allows the author to communicate with her chosen reader--the Western dancer--it sometimes communicates falsely. Scholars who have striven to create more precise terminologies for Southeast Asian forms, using language that indicates weight and energy usage, avoid some of the leaping to conclusions that Miss Zarina's work might prompt. And, after saying all this, I still recommend that the reader look at this book. Read it with caution, realize that it speaks almost exclusively of court variants, which are only a segment of the traditions, but realize too that the chapter on Cambodia is perhaps the best description of Cambodian movement written in English. The sections on Java, Bali, and Thailand can be useful if the reader reads them in conjunction with the more comprehensive works on these traditions that are noted in the country listings below.

Books which limit their discussion by area and/or genre tend to yield more precise information, and where a dancer has studied with intensity and then written with passion, the results have been remarkable. Indonesian dance and drama have most successfully evoked this combination of talents. For Java and Bali the resources are rich.

Indonesia

Bali has already merited two generations of excellent writing on theatrical movement. The rubbing of elbows and minds of foreign anthropologists, artists, and dancers in the 1930's led to an explosion of writing about dance and drama that incorporated good movement description. The best of much fine scholarship on movement that came from that period is Beryl de Zoete and Walter Spies' Dance and Drama in Bali. Although it is not easy reading, it ultimately encompasses everything one could ask to know. Clear descriptions of movement, precise descriptions of genres with indications of variations within each genre from area to area, excellent photo documentation--all are provided. Although the multiplicity of forms can, initially, overwhelm the reader, continued attention to the book clarifies the unity in the endless diversity. The book is a time machine to pre-World War II Bali.

Though it long seemed that no act could follow the breathtaking tour-de-force of de Zoete and Spies, a forthcoming work by I Made Bandem and Fredrik deBoer has done so. What Dance and Drama in Bali was to the 1930's, Kaja and Kelod: Balinese Dance in Transition is to today. It chronicles the latest chapter in Balinese dance history. The panorama is still vast, but the vista from kaja (mountain--holy) to kelod (sea--dangerous, profane) has widened to include mass-tourism, overseas tours of Balinese dancers, national dance academies, and the discotheques of Kuta Beach. The authors provide perspective on all of these phenomena within a general framework which divides performance into three categories: (1) ritual, (2) connected to a religious ceremony but not ritual, and (3) entertainment. These are the categories that Balinese artists and scholars have established. The authors correlate the categories of movement with the space in which dances are performed, from inner temple, to second temple courtyard, to secular space. The architectonics of Balinese dance emerge. Precise movement description by Bandem, a major Balinese dancer, is indicative of the trend of the current generation of scholarship: Southeast Asian scholars are taking the lead in writing about their traditions. The results are rich.

Claire Holt has done for other areas of Indonesia what de Zoete and Spies did for Bali. Everything she wrote contains precise movement description, though much of the material remains in the form of field reports, rather than fully worked analyses. Her Art in Indonesia: Continuities and Change, however, is outstanding for both its careful description and perceptive analysis, especially of Central Javanese dance and drama. The flowing movement and contemplative nature of the court dance have inspired flowing prose, and fact is correlated with fact to reach scholarly conclusions that resonate with the rightness of a gamelan phrase ending on a gong.

Holt did most of her work in the 1930's, so her writing reflects a world that is already modified. The author whose work provides a useful counterpoint to Holt's is Soedarsono, the Javanese scholar-artist. He has produced an impressive corpus of work, including Dances in Indonesia and Living Traditional Theatres in Indonesia: Nine Selected Papers. The former briefly describes dances from all areas of Indonesia. The section dealing with Soedarsono's own Javanese tradition is, indubitably, the strongest, but other sections give a sense of the scope of dance in the archipelago. In the second book, Soedarsono allows himself to focus on particular topics, hence the depth of his analysis is increased.

An understanding of the movement used in popular theatre is harder to obtain from the literature. James Peacock's Rites of Modernization: Symbolic and Social Aspects of Indonesian Proletarian Drama is clearly the best source, but movement description is not a focus of the text. This is, however, a fascinating look into a representative popular theatre form. Some scholars have disputed Peacock's contention that ludruk, a theatre form found in Surabaya, is, via changes in its plots, facilitating the transition of audience members from rural, traditional values to urban, modern values. But no one would argue that the anthropologist's idea of going to theatre to test the pulse of Indonesia is inappropriate.

Movement in modern dance and drama is not well documented. Indonesian magazines like Horizon, Budaya Jaya, and Basis occasionally carry articles and pictures. One English-language article, however, that gives a sense of the experimentation that is going on is Julie Taymor's "Teatr Loh, Indonesia, 1977-8" in The Drama Review. Rendra is the artist whose work has been most evocative, and one wishes a good description of the staging and movement in his productions were available in English, but content, not movement description, has been the focus of writing on his experiments.

Other short articles on various Indonesian forms that should be looked at are Enoch Atmadibrata's "Indonesia: West Java: Dance" in New Grove Dictionary of Music and Musicians, one of the few sources on Sundanese and Cirebonese performance; John Emigh's excellent article on topeng "Playing with the Past: Visitation and Illusion in the Mask Theatre of Bali" in The Drama Review; Colin McPhee's "Dance in Bali," a 1948 issue of Dance Index which covers most major genres; and Miriam Morrison's "The Bedaya-Serimpi Dances of Java" in Dance Chronicle. These short inscapes into a few of the traditions of Indonesia will help the reader orient himself, and appreciate the richness of Indonesian theatrical movement.

Malaysia and Singapore

Materials on Malay performing arts are increasing steadily, but no book that represents the arts of the total population, Malay, Chinese, and Indian, has yet been written. For information on Malay drama and dancing, Taman Indera by Mubin Sheppard is a good introduction. It is excellently illustrated and the author has spent a lifetime studying traditional Malay performing arts. A dissertation (available through University Microfilms) is also worth noting: Mohamed G. Nasaruddin's "Dance and Music of the Desa Performing Arts of Malaysia" was accepted in 1979 by Indiana University. Its attempt to discuss all the performing arts of the Malay villages makes its focus sometimes diffuse, but the clear attention to movement makes it unique among the Malay materials.

The best source on popular theatre is in Malay: Rahmah Bujang's Sejarah Perkembangan Drama Bangsawan di Tanah Melayu dan Singapura (History of the Development of Bangsawan in Malaya and Singapore). There is no readily accessible source that contains much movement description. For modern theatre the reader should consult the weekly drama column "Talking Drama with Utih" published from 1972-1979 in the New Sunday Times, a major Malaysian newspaper. Utih is the pen name of Krishen Jit, an important scholar and critic. A selection of his articles is being prepared for publication in a bilingual edition to be published in 1983. Malay language magazines which have chronicled the current dance and theatre scene are Dewan Sastra, Dewan Budaya and early issues of Dewan Masyarakat. All are published in Kuala Lumpur by Dewan Bahasa dan Pustaka.

Philippines

Reynaldo Alejandro has written two very useful works on dance in the Philippines. "Sayaw Silangan: The Dance of the Philippines," (Dance Perspectives 51) was put out in 1972. A survey of dance in the islands from prehistory to the present, it manages to present a wealth of information in a cogent fashion and includes excellent illustrations. Philippine Dance: Mainstream and Crosscurrents published in the Philippines has received some criticism from dance ethnologists because of its strong focus on current theatrical dance. Many of the beautiful pictures of the folk genres discussed in the text are interpretations of these dances by modern troupes that specialize in theatrical versions of folk material. But for the author, a choreographer of modern theatrical dance, the blossoming world of dance theatre in the Philippines is clearly the mainstream. The book should be read with this consciousness, and appreciated for the information that it contains on companies and choreographers of today who are using the past to create current statements.

For material on specific dramatic forms, the choices are dis-
appointing. Authors tend to mention movement only in passing,
and the reader is forced to go to many sources to gain only bits
and pieces on gesture. Still, some sources are more communicative
than others. Teresa Muoz's "Notes on Theatre: Pre-Hispanic
Philippines (Religion, Myth, Religious Ritual)" in Brown Heritage,
edited by Antonio Manuud, draws together material from many ethnographic sources. Liwayway Mendoza's "Lenten Rites and Practices: The Philippines" in The Drama Review is a field report on
holy week theatricals and processions. Felicidad Mendoza's The
Comedia (Moro-Moro) Rediscovered is the best source on the traditional theatre form which throws Moorish princesses into the arms
of Christian princes. Pictures, it should be noted, are of current
productions and the author is a director of "improved" comedia,
which may affect her interpretations.

Information on movement in the popular theatre of the Philippines, the operatic zarzuela, is also scattered, but background is
in Tomas Hernandez's The Emergence of Modern Drama in the Philippines (1898-1930). The section on the staging of plays, though
very brief and not focused on movement, attempts to reconstruct
what a performance was like. For learning about movement in modern productions follow articles in current journals such as Archipelago and Solidarity, which sometimes include pictures, as well as
some description of staging.

Thailand

Thai traditional forms have received considerable treatment.
For description of movement and depiction of positions, training
exercises, hand gestures, the reader should look at the work of
Dhanit Yupho, who has put out a series of pamphlets and books
as part of his work at the Department of Fine Arts in Bangkok.
The most comprehensive work by this author is Classical Siamese
Theatre which has been translated by P. S. Sastri. It provides
an overview of Thai forms including martial dances, theatrical
dances, folk dances, and contains information on movement training, costumes, and other matters pertaining to performance.

Mattani Rutnin's The Siamese Theatre is a collection of reprints from the Journal of the Siam Society. It is rich in information about Thai theatre, but unfortunately the authors tend to
describe movement only tangentially. A 1980 dissertation for the
University of Hawaii by Surapone Virulrak is the best source on
Thai popular drama, likay, as it contains a clear description of the
types of dance used and movement conventions of this theatre form.
The title is "Likay: A Popular Theatre of Thailand."

Other Southeast Asian Countries

The performing arts of other Southeast Asian cultures are, indubitably, rich. Anyone who has seen a performance, a film, or talked with someone who knows that tradition will understand this. But the literature easily available in English does not give an adequate sense of movement in the form. The reasons for this are partially the vagaries of history. For areas like Vietnam and Cambodia where the French maintained colonial rule, the major literature is in French. And clearly the political instability that has been a fact of life, in the northern part of Indochina has resulted in a dearth of literature on art forms of countries in that area in recent years. In some areas the continued existence of the arts has been questioned--Cambodia under the Khmer Rouge is a case in point.

Brief suggestions for reading on the dance and drama of these countries are as follows:

Burma. A standard reference for information on theatre is Kenneth Sein and Joseph A. Withey's The Great Po Sein: A Chronicle of Burmese Theatre. Unfortunately the text gives little sense of the virtuosic dance, though it does give insight into the wonderful world of theatre in Burma. They say that seeing is believing: the reader might do best by viewing the videotape, Dancers and Musicians of the Burmese National Theatre.

Cambodia. Xenia Zarina's Classical Dances of the Orient has already been suggested as a source on classical Khmer ballet. The Royal Cambodian Ballet (Phnom Penh: Information Department, 1963) is another useful source, but it is the rare library which has a copy. In French, Adhémard Leclère's Le Théâtre cambodgien and Samdach Chaufea Thiounn's Danses cambodgiennes have good discussions of gesture. Leclère's work may be more accessible since it was published in a number of places (see the full citation in the Cambodia listing).

Laos. I know of no strong source.

Vietnam. Huynh Krac Dung discusses gesture in the traditional opera of Vietnam in Hat Boi, Théâtre traditionnel du Viet Nam. Song-Ban's The Vietnamese Theatre reflects the thought of a communist writer on traditional and popular theatre. Two academic works by Duane Hauch contain brief information on movement. The first is his M.A. thesis, "Descriptive Study of Hat Boi: Classical Theatre of Vietnam," and the second is "The Cai Luong Theatre of Vietnam, 1919-1970," a Ph.D. dissertation for Southern Illinois University, accepted in 1972. The latter discusses the popular theatre form of the Southern region.

Conclusion

The arts of dance and drama have traditionally flourished throughout Southeast Asia, but documentation in books rather than bodies is largely a phenomena of this century. That Southeast Asian artists themselves are increasingly entering into the literary discourse, describing what it is they do and how they do it, researching the performances of the past, via records by foreign observers, as well as undertaking research in areas that have been less affected by economic and social change, is a significant development. The result of this development is yet to be assessed, and time will be needed to understand the impact. It may be that certain "moved" traditions (i.e. communicated only by the doing) will be replaced by notated traditions, and it may be that certain forms will be preserved only in the documents, until they find some artist-reader-viewer who uses the documents to reconstruct or create something new. But for those interested in understanding the performing arts of this area, it is an auspicious time to undertake study. The documentation of the past is still available in the minds and bodies of older artists. The excitement of the present is apparent in the performances to be seen daily in places like Jakarta, Manila, Kuala Lumpur. Though much may change, one suspects that the need for theatrical expression will remain strong in these cultures. As long as that is the case, there is a need for people with eyes trained to see the movement, ears tuned to hear the music, with sense to apprehend the meaning, and sensitivity to communicate their knowledge to others in writing. This compiler* invites the reader to continue the work of the authors listed here.

Southeast Asia

1. Bibliographies

Association for Asian Studies. Bibliography of Asian Studies.
     1955- . Annual.
   The most comprehensive listing of books, articles, dissertations available. Look under "Art" and "Literature" for entries on dance, theatre, and drama.

Brandon, James R., and Elizabeth Wichmann. Asian Theatre: A
     Study Guide and Annotated Bibliography. Theatre Perspectives 1. Edited by Anthony Graham-White. American Theatre Association, 1980.

---

*The compiler wishes to acknowledge the University of California at Santa Cruz and the National Endowment for the Humanities for grants which partially supported the preparation of this work. Among the many who gave suggestions of materials which should be included are the following individuals who deserve special thanks: Nancy Nanney, Rachel Cooper, Rucina Ballinger, and Stephanie Krebs.

Excellent coverage of the Southeast Asian area. Sections devoted to Burma, Cambodia, Indonesia, Laos, Malaysia and Singapore, the Philippines, Thailand, and Vietnam. Because of theatre emphasis, significant dance materials are not always included.

"Current Bibliography and Discography." Ethnomusicology. 1- . Triannually.
Books, articles, and dissertations that reflect current scholarship. Look under "Dance."

New York Public Library, Research Libraries. Dictionary Catalogue of the Dance Collection, Performing Arts Research Center. 10 vol. Boston: G. K. Hall, 1974; and Bibliographic Guide to Dance. Boston: G. K. Hall, 1975- . Annual.
Excellent resources in dance ethnology. Annotated resources of one of the major dance collections in the country.

_____. Catalogue of the Theatre and Drama Collections. Boston: G. K. Hall, 1967-1976.
Includes Part 1, No. 1, a listing by cultural origins; Part 1, No. 2, a listing by author; Part 2, books on theatre; and Part 3, nonbook collection.

Withey, Joseph. "An Annotated Bibliography of the Theatre of Southeast Asia to 1971." Educational Theatre Journal, 26 (May 1974), pp. 209-220.
More recent bibliographies now replace this early work, except for a few citations.

2. General

Bourguignon, Erika. "Trance Dance." Dance Perspectives, 35 (1968), pp. 1-60.
Touches on trance dance in Bali, hobby horse dance in Java, and female spirit-medium trance in Vietnam, as well as the phenomena of chant and rhythmic movement in Islamic mystic communities. Notes that dance is used to change breathing patterns, whirling movements alter balance, and expectation and suggestion are significant factors in trance performances. A significant article.

Bowers, Faubion. Theatre in the East: A Survey of Asian Dance and Drama. New York: Grove Press, 1956.
Descriptions of performances viewed contain some movement information. Includes sections on Burma, Thailand, Cambodia, Laos, Malaysia, Indonesia, the Philippines, and Vietnam. Illustrations augment text.

Brandon, James R. Theatre in Southeast Asia. Cambridge: Harvard University Press, 1967.
General survey of traditional and modern theatre in Southeast

Asia. Cultural and social aspects receive considerable attention. Brandon divides dance of the area into two categories: Indian influenced and Chinese influenced. Dance is more significant in the Indian-influenced area which includes all of Southeast Asia except Vietnam and Cambodia. Pictures throughout.

Chakravarti, N. P. "Indian Dance Forms in Southeast Asia." France-Asie 17 (1960), pp. 194-98.
Thai, Cambodian, and Indonesian forms are compared to Indian prototypes as set forth in the Natyasastra, Sanskrit treatise on performing arts.

Cogniat, Raymond. Danses d'Indochine. Paris: Editions des Chroniques du Jour. 1932.
Cambodian, Vietnamese, and hill tribe dances of Indochina are excellently illustrated. The very general text in French is synopsized in English.

Cuisinier, Jeanne. La Danse sacrée en Indochine et en Indonésie. Paris: Presses Universitaires de France, 1951.
A general description of ritual folk and court dance in Indonesia (Sumatra, Java, Bali) and Indochina. Notes female dance is more stationary than male. Contrasts Hindu- and Chinese-based dances. Only abbreviated movement descriptions of forms discussed.

_____. "The Indian Influence Upon the Dances in the Far East." Indian Arts and Letters, New series, 3 (1929), pp. 101-05.
With reference to Southeast Asia.

Draeger, Donn F., and Robert W. Smith. Comprehensive Asian Fighting Arts. Tokyo: Kodansha International, 1981.
Best source on martial arts of Burma, Thailand, Malaysia and Indonesia, and the Philippines. Martial training has deeply affected theatrical movement throughout area.

The Drama Review, 15, 3 (1971), pp. 83-121. Special issue. "Theatre in Asia."
Includes articles on Burma, Indonesia, and Malaysia. While movement is not a focus, pictures give some insight.

Jones, Betty True, editor-in-chief. Dance as Cultural Heritage: Selected Papers from the ADG/CORD Conference 1978. CORD Research Annual XIV. Forthcoming.
Volume I contains I Made Bandem's "The Evolution of Legong from Sacred to Secular Dance of Bali," Sal Murgiyanto's "Basic Principle of the Javanese Court Dance," Hilary Olsin-Windecker's "Characterization in Classical Yogyanese Dance," and Volume II includes articles on Javanese dance by Jan Hostetler and Ben Suharto, an article on dance in Irian Jaya by Soedarsono, one on bird imagery in Philippine dance by Reynaldo Alejandro, one on Balinese dance by Rucina Ballinger, and a consideration of social

context as a determinant of style and structure in Asian dance by Robert Garfias.

Mitchell, John D. "The Theatre of India and Southeast Asia," In Asia and the Humanities. Horst Frenz, ed. Bloomington: Indiana University Press, 1959.
With special reference to Thailand.

Monographs on Music, Dance and Theatre in Asia, Vol. 1- . New York: Asia Society, 1974- .
Prepared in conjunction with U.S. tours of Asian groups. Includes essays on Burmese theatre (Vol. 2 and Vol. 6), and martial arts and masked dance from Sunda, West Java (Vol. 4).

The New Encyclopaedia Britannica. Chicago, 1974.
The Micropaedia contains short articles on specific theatre topics, with references to longer articles found in the Macropaedia, including "Southeast Asian Peoples, Arts of, Performing Arts," and "Drama in East and West."

New Grove Dictionary of Music and Musicians. Edited by Sadie Stanley. London: Macmillan, 1980.
Contains excellent articles on "Indonesia" and "Southeast Asian Theatre." "Laos," "Malaysia," and "Vietnam" articles contain more limited information on movement.

Osman, Mohd. Taib, ed. Traditional Drama and Music of Southeast Asia. Kuala Lumpur: Dewan Bahasa dan Pustaka, 1974.
Useful background material, but movement is mentioned only tangentially in Mubin Sheppard's "Ma'yong--The Malay Dance Drama" (pp. 133-42), Mustapha Kamil Yassin's "The Malay Bangsawan" (pp. 143-53), A. L. Becker's "Journey Through the Night: Some Reflections on Burmese Traditional Theatre" (pp. 154-64), Chua Sariman's "Traditional Dance Drama in Thailand" (pp. 165-171), and J. Roces "The Traditional Theatre of the Philippines" (pp. 172-84).

Ridgeway, William. The Dramas and Dramatic Dances of Non-European Races: In Special Reference to the Origin of Greek Tragedy, with an Appendix on the Origin of Greek Comedy. 1915. Reprint. New York: Benjamin Blom, 1964.
Information on Burmese, Cambodian, and Malayan theatre. More recent information makes much of this work obsolete.

Shawn, Ted. Gods Who Dance. New York: E. P. Dutton, 1929.
Covers dance in most of Asia.

Zarina, Xenia. Classical Dances of the Orient. New York: Crown, 1967.
Insights of a Westerner studying dance in Thailand, Java, Bali, and Cambodia prior to WW II. Though information is fragmentary, anecdotes touch on important aspects of dance in these cultures. Illustrations supplement author's movement descriptions.

3. Audiovisual Materials

Alejandro, Reynaldo; James Brandon; Robert Garfias; and Roger
Long. "Asian Dance and Drama: Slide Library Developed by
VRI and the Asia Society," Vol. 2 (Southeast Asia). New
York: Asia Society, n.d.
Prepared by experts on Southeast Asian performance.

Burma

1. Terms

Anyein pwe: comic song and dance pieces. Nat pwe: dance
drama for the invocation of animistic spirits. Zat pwe: night-long
performance involving traditional dramatic performance along with
other song, dance, and dramatic pieces.

2. Bibliographies

Jenner, Philip N. Southeast Asian Literatures in Translation: A
Preliminary Bibliography, Asian Studies at Hawaii, 9. Honolulu: University Press of Hawaii, 1973.

Trager, Frank N. Annotated Bibliography of Burma. New Haven:
New York University Burma Research Project, Human Relations
Area Files Press, 1956.

Wang, Janelle, et al. Burma: A Selected and Annotated Bibliography. New Haven: Human Relations Area Files Press, 1973.

3. Traditional

"The Animal Dancers of the Shans." The Dancing Times (November
1935), pp. 191-92.

Ba Han. "The Evolution of Burmese Dramatic Performance and
Festal Occasions." The Guardian, 13, 9 (September 1966),
pp. 18-24.
Description of religious celebrations and the accompanying dramatic performances. Notes dancers were attached to pagodas in
temple city of Pagan.

Beaumont, Cyril W. A Burmese Pwe at Wembley: Some Impressions
of Burmese Dancing. London: n.p., 1924.
Reaction to a performance given at British Empire Exhibition.
Illustrated.

Brown, R. Grant. Burma As I Saw It, 1889-1917, with a Chapter
on Recent Events. New York: Fredrick A. Stokes, 1925.

A chapter on drama (pp. 118-30) gives accounts of theatrical presentations at the turn of the century by an intelligent observer.

Chen, T. D. "Music and Dance in Burma." Eastern Horizons, 1,5 (1960), pp. 44-46.
     Reactions of a critic in the People's Republic of China to Burmese music and dance.

"The Cultural Needs of Burma." The Ninth Anniversary Burma, 7 (1957), pp. 55-78.
     A pictoral survey of Burma's cultural treasures including dancers from the cultural mission to the U.S.S.R., and classes at the school of music and dance.

Frost, Helen. Oriental and Character Dances. Music by Lily Strickland. New York: A. S. Barnes, 1927.
     Includes illustrations, background information, music, and choreography of dances from Burma as well as other Asian countries.

Garfias, Robert. "Burmese Hsaing and Anyein," 6, 3 (1979); and "Burmese Music and Dance," 2 (1975). Monographs on Music, Dance and Theatre in Asia. New York: Asia Society.
     Brief, but useful background by an expert on music.

Gosh, Manomohan. "The Dances of Burma and the Indian Natya." Indo-Asian Culture, 1 (1953), pp. 266-272.
     On the similarity of Burmese and Indian dances.

Gyi, J. A. M. "At the Play in Burma." Blackwood's Magazine, 171 (April 1902), pp. 562-71.
     Description of zat pwe performance.

Htin Aung, Maung. Burmese Drama: A Study with Translations of Burmese Plays. London: Oxford University Press, 1957.
     Although one of the most authoritative books on Burmese drama, the focus is on literature rather than performance aspects. Useful for background.

Khin Maung Lat. "Tekkatho: Burmese Dance." Forward, 14, 2 (1975), pp. 12-17.

King, Eleanor. "Transcendent Dance." Korea Journal (Seoul), 19, 9 (1979), pp. 49-54.
     An account of a zat pwe performance and Korean Buddhist and shamanic dance.

Lewis, Norman. Golden Earth: Travels in Burma. New York: Scribner's, 1952.
     "Dramatic Entertainment" (pp. 27-34) gives a description of dance at an anyein pwe. The chapter on "The Buffalo Dance"

(pp. 251-260) describes the convulsive trance dance of the <u>nat-ka-daw</u> (women married to animistic spirits), and the attack of the buffalo-masked priest on the onlookers.

Maung, E. "The Burmese Drama." <u>Journal of the Burma Research Society</u>, 8 (1918), pp. 33-38.
Sees three major points of origin for the drama: (1) gestures of story tellers, (2) religious dramas relating to the Buddha, and (3) dances of sacrifice to the thirty seven nat spirits, in which the priestess becomes a spirit-medium.

Mydans, Shelly. "The Ancient Dance of Burma Comes to Dazzle American Audiences." <u>Smithsonian</u> (October 1975), pp. 70-79.
A brief description of Burmese culture and of a zat pwe. Excellent color photos.

Myo Min, U. "Traditional Dances of Burma." <u>The Atlantic Monthly</u> (Supplement), 201 (February 1958), pp. 166-67.
Includes action drawings of theatre dance, recording costume and gesture, in an issue devoted to Burma.

Pilcher, Velona. "Dancing from Burma." <u>Theatre Arts</u>, 8 (October 1924), p. 673.
Review of dancing at British Empire Exhibition.

Ramasubramaniam, Sri V. "The Mediaeval and the Pre-Modern Burmese Theatres." <u>Bulletin of the Institute of Traditional Cultures</u> (Madras) (January-June 1974), pp. 106-17.
General account of a zat pwe.

Scott, James G. (Shway Yoe). <u>The Burman, His Life and Notions</u>. 1895; New York: Norton, 1963.
Brief chapters on plays, dancing, and music by a major scholar. Recounts acrobatic abilities of performers, noting unusual muscle isolations enable dancers to move a single muscle.

Sein, Kenneth, and Joseph A. Withey. <u>The Great Po Sein: A Chronicle of the Burmese Theatre</u>. Bloomington: University of Indiana Press, 1966.
A novelistic recreation of the Burmese theatre in the early twentieth century. Focuses on the Sein family, an innovative troupe. Information on movement is given only in passing, but important aspects of cultural context are clarified. Sketches of dancers are included.

Shawn, Ted. "Dancers of Burma." <u>Dance Magazine</u> (June 1926), p. 32.

Stewart, John, A. "The Burmese Drama." <u>Journal of the Burma Research Society</u>, 2 (1912), pp. 30-37.
Description of a zat pwe. Notes that song and dance frequently

overshadow strict dramatic gesture. Interlude scene occurs in each performance after "prince" and "princess" meet. Story pauses for two hours of singing and dancing. Princess may perform six kinds of dance in a half hour as clown critiques her.

_____. "The Burmese Stage." Journal of the Royal Society of Arts (London), 87, 4516 (June 9, 1939), pp. 761-75.
Gives history of Burmese theatre and describes a zat pwe performance.

Vatsyayan, Kapila. "Some Evidence of Dance in Pagan." National Center for the Performing Arts, Bombay, Quarterly Journal, 6,4 (1977), pp. 1-22.
Compares sculptural evidence of dance in Burma to Indian and Sri Lankan sculptures.

Withey, J. A. "The Burmese Pwe Through Western Eyes." The Guardian, 8, 3 (March 1961), pp. 39-40.
Reactions of a Westerner to zat pwe. Similarities to and differences from Western theatre are noted.

4. Audiovisual Materials

The Dancers and Musicians of the Burmese National Theatre. (60 min.) Bureau of Mass Communications, New York State Education Department, Albany, New York. 3/4" or 2" Videotape, color.
Made during the 1975 tour of Burmese National Theatre. Also available from Asia Society in New York.

Cambodia

1. Traditional

Cardi, Felix. "Danses sacrées au Cambodge." La Revue musicale (Paris) (November 1920), pp. 34-43.

Casey, Robert. "The Four Faces of Siva." National Geographic Magazine, 54 (September 1928), pp. 303-332.
Pictures of court dancers show training and performance.

Cravath, Paul. "The Classical Dance-Drama of Cambodia: A Historical and Descriptive Study." Ph.D. diss., University of Hawaii, 1982(?).
Based on field research.

Cogniat, Raymond. Danses d'Indochine. Paris: Editions des Chroniques du Jour, 1932.
Excellent illustrations of classical dance.

Cuisinier, Jeanne. "The Gestures in the Cambodian Ballet: Their Traditional and Symbolic Significance." Indian Arts and Letters, New series, 1, 2 (1927), pp. 92-103.
A useful article.

Groslier, George. "Avêc les danseuses royales du Cambodge." Mercure de France, 203 (May 1928), pp. 536-65.
By a major authority.

_____. Danseuses cambodgiennes. Paris: Augustin Challamel, 1913.
Includes sixteen plates.

_____. "Le Théâtre et la danse au Cambodge." Journal asiatique, 214 (1929), pp. 125-43.
Description of performance and training.

Leclère, Adhémard. Le Théâtre cambodgien. Paris: Ernest Leroux, 1911. (Also in Revue ethnographique et de sociologie, 11-12 [1910]; and in Human Relations Area Files: Indo-China, Source No. 178).
Compares Cambodian and Siamese dance claiming that the Cambodian model is the elder. Explores the impact of Indian dance. Illustrations included.

Ly Sing Ko. "Lakhon and the Chinese Theatre." Eastern Horizon (Hong Kong), 4, 6 (1965), pp. 25-29.
Argues that Chinese theatre has developed under the influence of Khmer models. Compares movements indicating numerous similarities. Clowns and terminology also point to Southeast Asian origins.

Marechal, Sappho. Costumes et parures khmers. Paris: Editions G. Van Oest, 1927.

_____. Danses cambodigiennes. Saigon: Editions de la Revue Extreme Asie, 1926.

Pastore, Louise. "Classical Khmer Ballet of Cambodia, Brooklyn Academy of Music, N.Y. City, Oct. 19-24, 1971." Dance Magazine, 45 (December 1971), p. 88.
Performance review.

"Ramker (Ramayana Khmer)," Kambuja (October, November, and December 1969).
Illustrations of this Khmer version of the Ramayana are scenes from puppet genre (nang sbek) and masked plays (kawl).

Royal Cambodian Ballet. Phnom Penh: Information Department, 1963.
This useful but brief pamphlet relates the effects of social change on the royal dance troupe.

Recounts that Cambodian dance, after a period of decay, was reborn in the nineteenth century. At this time Siamese dance was used as a model and a "softer" movement style was introduced. Males who continued to "dance with their eyebrows raised" were relegated to clown and demon roles. States that gestures in the dance are to be expressive of situation and emotion. Special musical accompaniment is used for each movement or phrase.

Strickland, Lily. "The Cambodian Ballet." Musical Quarterly, 12, 2 (1926), pp. 266-74.
A traveler's effusive praises, some pictures.

Thierry, Solange. "Les Danses sacrées au Cambodge" in Les Danses sacrées. Paris: Editions du Seuil (1963), pp. 343-73.
Discussion of ritual dance includes animal dances of the popular tradition, religious processions, and classical dance.

Thiounn, Samdach Chaufea. Danses cambodgiennes. Phnom Penh: Institut Bouddhique, 1956.
Discusses the mythical origins of the dance, explains the importance of temple reliefs as documentation of dance in former periods, recounts the training of royal dancers, and explicates specific gestures of the dance in detail, with illustrations.

Zarina, Xenia. "Royal Cambodian Dances." In Classical Dances of the Orient. New York: Crown, 1967, pp. 59-88.
An excellent introduction to Cambodian movement. Describes training exercises, costume, music, and performance in the royal palace.
Though all roles except for clowns are played by women, dancers playing male roles or giants are distinguished by the arrogant carriage of the head. Plie positions and an inverted elbow joint are characteristic. Sample dance exercises, and explanation of how gestures become a sign mime of the text and/or representation of the dramatic action are included.

2. Audiovisual Materials

Goddess Dancers of Cambodia. (30 min.) Camera Three telecast December 12, 1971. Produced and directed by Merrill Brockway. Commentary by Faubion Bowers. Videotape, color.
Several dances by Classical Khmer Ballet. Interviews, demonstration of daily exercises and explanation of meaning of gestures. Dances shown are Sita's abduction, the queen of apsaras, and the legend of the goddess of the waters. (In Dance Collection of the N.Y. Public Library.)

The Royal Ballet of Cambodia. (82 min.) Directed by Hang Thun Hak. 16 mm. film, color, sound. Three reels.
Reel 1 shows dance-drama on legendary origin of Angkor. Reel

2 is visit to School of Royal Cambodian Ballet. Reel 3 shows school's graduation ceremony. (In Dance Collection of N.Y. Public Library.)

Indonesia

1. Terms

BALI: Arja: a popular drama in which performers sing and dance. Baris: a martial dance done by males. Barong-rangda: a masked dance drama in which a mythical protective creature called a barong struggles with a witch (rangda). The characters may appear in other contexts but their natures are constant. Gabor and mendet: temple offering dances. Gambuh: archaic dance drama of Javanese origin. Kris dance: dancers stab themselves while in trance. Legong: stylized dance drama done by prepubescent girls. Topeng: mask dance drama. Sanghyang: trance dance in which spirit possesses performer.

CELEBES: Ma'bugi: Group trance dance to prevent disease.

JAVA: Bed(h)aya and S(e)rimpi: sacred female court dances. Beksa(n): martial dance done by males. Dabus: dance in which performers stab selves with awls, eat hot coals, etc. while in trance. Golek: lively, female dance of Central Java. Ketoprak: popular theatre form of Central Java. Kuda kepang, kuda lumping, and jaran kepang: trance dances of different areas in which hobby horse dancers go into trance. Langendrian: a dance drama in which dialogue is sung, performed by female cast. Lenong: popular theatre form of Malay speakers in West Java. Ludruk: popular theatre form in Surabaya, East Java. Penca silat: martial arts dance. Sandiwara: popular theatre form of Sunda, West Java. Sintren: female trance dance. Topeng: literally "mask," used to identify a variety of mask dance forms. Wayang golek: rod puppet theatre. Wayang kulit: shadow play. Wayang orang or wayang wong: dance drama in the style of puppet theatre.

SUMATRA: Randai (rendai): a drama form derived from dramatic circle dance. Silé: martial arts dance.

2. General

Atmadibrata, Enoch. "Indonesia, West Java: Dance" in New Grove Dictionary of Music and Musicians. Vol. 9. Sadie Stanley, ed. London: Macmillan, 1980, pp. 211-215.
    Concise information on Sundanese and Cirebonese dances of West Java. One of few English sources.

Bandem, I Made, and Fredrik deBoer. Kaja and Kelod: Balinese

<u>Dance in Transition</u>. Kuala Lumpur: Oxford University Press, 1982.
Most thorough and accessible source on current Balinese performance with precise descriptions of movement.
Explores the range of Balinese dance from sacred to secular noting the correlation between the type of dance and the space used.

Black, Star, ed. <u>Guide to Bali</u>. Singapore: Times Printers, 1973.
Valuable for its 146 color photos by Hans Hoefer, many of theatre performances.

Brandon, James R. "Play Production in the Indonesian Professional Theatre," <u>Asian Culture</u>, 2, 1 (1960), pp. 74-87.
Gives background on costuming, makeup, rehearsal, and performance procedures.

_____. "Types of Indonesian Professional Theatre." <u>Quarterly Journal of Speech</u>, 45 (February 1959), pp. 51-58.
Description of wayang orang dance drama, and regional popular drama forms (ketoprak--Central Java, ludruk--East Java, and sandiwara--Sunda.)

Cartier-Bresson, Henri. <u>Les Danses à Bali</u>. Text by Antoinin Artaud and Beryl de Zoete. France: Collection Huit, 1954.
Excellent pictures of young girls dancing legong, and of dancers in the rangda-barong drama.

Cooper, Rachel. "Structure and Function of Academi Seni Tari Indonesia, Bali." M.A. thesis, UCLA, 1982 (?).
Dance ethnology thesis.

Covarrubias, Miguel. <u>Island of Bali</u>. New York: Alfred A. Knopf, 1937.
Information on Balinese drama is accurate and photographs and sketches capture the dynamism of the dance.

_____. "The Theatre in Bali." <u>Theatre Arts Monthly</u>, 20, 8 (1936), pp. 575-659.
Discusses many forms briefly, with excellent illustrations.

de Zoete, Beryl, and Walter Spies. <u>Dance and Drama in Bali</u>. London: Faber and Faber, 1938; Kuala Lumpur: Oxford University Press, 1973.
The most detailed study of theatre in Bali reflects the state of the art prior to WW II. The wealth of detail may overwhelm the uninitiated, but the detailed descriptions of movement, costume, variations within a specific dramatic genre, etc. are a bonanza for the dedicated researcher. Excellent photos.

Hoefer, Hans J. <u>Java: Official Guide to the Island of Java</u>. 3rd ed. Singapore: APA, 1978.

Discussion of performing arts (pp. 79-93) is general but outstanding photos of dramatic forms from all parts of Java make this
a useful book.

Holt, Claire. Art in Indonesia: Continuities and Change. Ithaca:
    Cornell University Press, 1967.
    Chapters on the dance and dance drama are excellent. Move-
ment quality is discussed and historical background given. Excellent photos.
    Notes Indian influence. Movement is earth oriented, and plié or
kneeling positions are common. Spatial use is limited. Focus of
movement is on use of hands, feet, head. Contrasts Javanese and
Balinese dance, noting the flowing quality of the former and the
hypertense nature of the latter. Notes that both Java and Bali
prefer row or file formations in group dances, in contrast to the
outer islands, which often use circular or serpentine shapes. Describes all major forms of Central Java and Bali and gives some
attention to other areas.

Kaudern, Walter. Ethnographical Studies in Celebes. Vol. 4.
    Games and Dances in Celebes. Goteborg: Elanders Boktryckeri,
    1929.
    Discusses circle dances, ritual, and professional dance.

Lendra, I Wayan, and Leslie Scoren. "A Glance at Balinese Dance
    from Classical to Contemporary." Journal of Association of
    Graduate Dance Ethnologists, 5 (Spring 1981), pp. 24-28.

McPhee, Colin. "Dance in Bali." Dance Index, 7, 7-8 (1948).
    An issue devoted to Bali. Excellent introduction to major forms
by a musician with a clear eye. Gives history, describes dance
clubs, music, audiences, plays. Characterization is established by
movement. Refined (alus) and coarse (kras) from the two poles on
the character scale. Notes major types of dance including baris,
barong, gambuh, and topeng. Floor patterns for dances are noted.

_____. A House in Bali. Kuala Lumpur: Oxford University
    Press, 1979.
    Personal account of author's experiences in Bali with attention
to arts.

_____. Music in Bali: A Study in Form and Instrumental Or-
    ganization in Balinese Orchestral Music. New Haven: Yale
    University Press, 1966.
    Although the focus remains clearly on music, the section "Plays
and Dances" (pp. 16-19) gives brief information on movement, and
references to specific dramatic genres occur throughout the text,
with sixteen photos of dance.

Moerdowo, Dr. Reflections on Indonesian Arts and Culture.
    Surabaya: Permata, 1963.

Clear concise chapters on Javanese dance and music, and Bali (including theatre).

Natapradja, Iwan. "Sundanese Dances" in Selected Reports in Ethnomusicology, 2 (1975), pp. 103-108.
One of few English sources on dances of the Sundanese of West Java. Includes description of characteristic movements.

Pigeaud, Th. Javaanse Volksvertoningen: Bijdrage tot de Beschrijving van Land en Volk. Batavia: Volkslectuur, 1938.
A monumental work that discusses dance in all parts of Java, with focus on Central Java. Notes that the palace arts of Central Java affected the villages there, and influence spread to Sunda, East Java, and Madura. Explores in detail the mask-dance drama. Notes that a refined character in the beginning and a rough character entering later are recurring features of mask-dance genres in a variety of areas. Pigeaud begins from this clue to hypothesize about the ur-form of the mask dance which may be the source of all the traditional dramatic genres. Discussion of many genres, but movement analysis is minimal.

Poort, W. A. The Dance in the Pacific: A Comparative and Critical Comparison of Dancing in Polynesia, Micronesia, and Melanesia. Katwijk, Netherlands: Van der Lee, 1975.
Draws attention to comparable features of Indonesian and Oceanic dance. Categories used are too broad to achieve useful comparison, but the attempt is interesting for those with background in the traditions discussed.

Pronko, Leonard C. Theater East and West: Perspectives Toward a Total Theater. Berkeley: University of California Press, 1974.
In discussion of how theatre in the East can inspire theatre in the West, the author gives eyewitness accounts of many Balinese forms. See "Artaud and Bali" (pp. 1-33).

Ramseyer, Urs. The Art and Culture of Bali. Oxford: Oxford University Press, 1977.
In this excellent examination of Balinese culture, selected drama and music forms are discussed. Especially good on ritual forms. Outstanding illustrations.

Wagner, F. A. Indonesia: The Art of an Island Group. New York and London: Methuen, 1959.
Includes comments on various dramatic forms. Background is useful; movement description is minimal.

3. Traditional

Achjadi, Judi. "The Dance in Indonesia." Folklore (Calcutta), 17, 2, 181 (1975), pp. 70-73.

Arnis Md. Nor, Mohd. "Rendai Dance Among the Minangkabau in West Sumatra." M.A. thesis, University of Hawaii, 1982 (?). Dance ethnology thesis.

Artaud, Antoinin. The Theatre and Its Double. Mary Caroline Richards, trans. New York: Grove Press, 1958.
Two essays discuss Balinese theatre. Artaud's intuitive reactions to the dance drama of Bali help him define the nonliterary theatre he wishes to initiate. Powerful description of Balinese performance.

Ballinger, Rucina. "The Tradition of Dance in Bali" in Dance as Cultural Heritage: Selected Papers from the ADG/CORD Conference 1978. CORD Research Annual XIV. Forthcoming.

Bandem, I Made. "The Baris Dance." Ethnomusicology, 19 (1975), pp. 259-26. (Also in Dance in Africa, Asia and the Pacific: Selected Readings, Judy Van Zile, ed. New York: MSS Information Corporation, 1976.)
Baris is a warrior drill dance that shows physical maturity and prowess with weapons. Dramatic baris (baris melamphan) tell stories from the Mahabhrata or Ramayana. The characteristic moves, stances, and sectional divisions of the dance are noted. Trembling fingers and bulging eyes convey the strength of the character.

_____. "The Barong Dance." World of Music, 18, 3 (1976), pp. 45-52.
Notes different types of barong masks, discusses musical accompaniment, with illustrations.

_____. "Pandji Characterization in the Gambuh Dance Drama." Master's thesis, UCLA, 1972.
Pandji is a refined male character. A thesis in dance ethnology.

_____. "Wayang Wong in Contemporary Bali." Ph.D. diss., Wesleyan University, 1980.
Discusses wayang wong dance drama as an example in the evolution of Balinese dance. Attention to dance, history, and social function of the form in addition to play translation.

_____, and Fredrik deBoer. "Gambuh: A Classical Balinese Dance Drama" Asian Music, 10, 1 (1978), pp. 115-127.
Gambuh is the oldest and most formal variety of dance drama in Bali. It represents the aesthetic of the exiled Javanese of the Majapahit court. The posture, walks, gestures of the form seem archaic to modern audiences, and the choreography is more fixed than in contemporary forms.

Bateson, Gregory, and Margaret Mead. Balinese Character: A Photographic Analysis. Special Publication, 2. New York: Academy of Sciences, 1942.
Photos of barong dance drama. Text analyzes the witch figure

(rangda) as an image of the threatening mother and sees the barong as an image of the nuturing father.

Baudish, R. A. "Javanese Dance." Indo-Asian Culture, 5, 2 (1956), pp. 206-215.
A comparison of ballet, wayang wong, and wayang kulit. Notes the relationship between human wayang wong dancer and the wayang kulit puppet.

Belo, Jane. Bali: Rangda and Barong. Monographs of the American Ethnological Society, 16. Seattle: University of Washington Press, 1949; reprinted in 1966.
Excellent study of the barong-rangda drama, including description of movement of the characters in performance. Examines interpretations of rangda as the Indian goddess Durga, and as the threatening mother figure, as suggested by Bateson and Mead. Contrasts these trance performances with those of children who become incarnations of the gods.

_____. Bali: Temple Festival. Monographs of the American Ethnological Society, 22. Seattle: University of Washington Press, 1953.
Description of odalan (anniversary) festival of temple, describing dances (gabor, mendet, legong) which serve as entertainment for gods and men. Gives understanding of cultural context of traditional dance.

_____, ed. Traditional Balinese Culture. New York: Columbia University Press, 1970.
Excellent information on Balinese arts by major writers. "'Bandit Island,' A Short Exploration Trip to Nusa Penida," (pp. 67-84) by Claire Holt, "Dance and Drama in Bali" (pp. 260-289) by Beryl de Zoete and Walter Spies, "Dance in Bali" (pp. 290-321) by Colin McPhee, and "Form and Function of the Dance in Bali" (pp. 322-330) by Claire Holt and Gregory Bateson contain precise movement description. Margaret Mead's "Strolling Players in the Mountains of Bali" (pp. 137-146) reports on a barong performance. Many of these essays are extracted from other works by these authors.

_____. Trance in Bali. New York: Columbia University Press, 1960.
Most comprehensive report on trance performance in Bali. Describes a variety of performances of each genre in the 1930's. Field notes of different researchers are included allowing different perspectives to come into play. Typical movement characteristics of trance dance that emerge include "unitary movement" (whole body section moves as a unit), and "economy of movement" (only the part of the body necessary to the action is engaged). Compares movement of dancers with puppets (pp. 11-13). Puppets represent spirits. Child dancers are considered the best since

their movement is most puppetlike. Trancers act childishly, which by association is godlike. Sanghyang dedari (trance dance of young girls who become incarnations of gods); barong-rangda; kris dancers who stab themselves in trance; and folk trancers who become a monkey, pig, snake, etc. are described.

Bloch, Stella, and Ananda Coomarswamy. "The Javanese Theatre." Asia (July 1929), pp. 536-39.

Brakel, Clara. "The Court Dances of Central Java and Their Relationship to Classical Indian Dancing." Archipel. (Paris), 11 (1976), pp. 155-66.
Notes the impact of Indian dance on Java has been overstressed by some researchers. The refined (alus)/strong (gagah) dichotomy in Javanese dance does not fully correspond with the female (lasya)/ male (tandava) split of Indian dance.

Brakel-Papenhuyzen, Clara. "Manuscripts of Javanese Court Dances." Bijdragen tot de Taal-, Land-, en Volkenkunde. (The Hague), 131, 2 (1975), pp. 344-346.
Calls attention to the existence of manuscripts of court dances dating from the early decades of this century in palace libraries of Java. Notes the movements of one dancer are generally given in chronological sequence, musical instruments that determine the length of movement are noted, and simple floor patterns given.

Coast, John. Dancers of Bali. New York: G. P. Putnam, 1953.
Personal account of Balinese dancers at home and on tour. Minimal descriptions of dancing lessons and movement, but interesting background material.

Cuisinier, Jeanne. "Les Danses sacrées à Bali et à Java." In Les Danses sacrées. Paris: Editions du Seuil, 1963.
Brief information on many forms.

Daniel, Ana. Bali: Behind the Mask. New York: Alfred A. Knopf, 1981.
Anecdotal account of author's experience in studying with Kakul, a major topeng dancer. Excellent photos.

de Kleen, Tyra. Mudras: The Ritual Hand-Poses of the Buddha Priests and Shiva Priests of Bali. Reprint. New York: University Books, 1970.
Hand poses are also used in the theatrical dance.

_____. Temple Dances in Bali. Stockholm: Ethnological Museum of Sweden, 1936.
Illustrated.

_____. Wayang: Javanese Theatre. Stockholm: Ethnological Museum of Sweden, 1947.

Text is brief and sometimes misleading. Watercolor illustrations of court dancers are unusual.

de Zoete, Beryl. "Dances in Bali and Indian Influences." Indian Arts and Letters, 17 (1943), pp. 53-58.

Dunn, Deborah. "Topeng Pajegan." Ph.D. diss., Union Graduate West, 1983 (?).

Emigh, John. "Playing with the Past: Visitation and Illusion in the Mask Theatre of Bali." The Drama Review, 23, 2 (1979), pp. 1-36.
Excellent introduction to topeng. Describes performance, movement of various masks. Maintains topeng is a theatrical form drawing on tradition of spirit visitation.

Foley, Mary Kathleen. "The Sundanese Wayang Golek: The Rod Puppet Theatre of West Java." Ph.D. diss., University of Hawaii, 1979.
"Movement" (pp. 159-172) describes Sundanese classical and social dance that the puppet theatre draws upon. Ngibing is movement regulated by the constraints of classical dance: its various walks, abstract movements, and dramatic gestures are described. The importance of martial arts dance and social dance for lower-class characters' movement is noted. Information applies to human theatre as well as puppet theatre.

_____. "The Dancer and the Danced: Trance and Dance in Sunda." Paper presented at the American Theatre Association Convention, 1982.
Describes sintren, a female spirit-medium form in West Java, noting the use of slow, flowing movement. Contrasts this with strong movement of male trancers who become possessed by animals (kuda kepang) or who stab themselves with awls (dabus), comparing these dances with strong style in dramatic dance.

Goris, Roelf. Bali: Atlas Kebubajaan: Cults and Customs. [Jakarta]: Pemerintah Republic Indonesia, 1950.
Excellent photos of performance forms.

_____. The Island of Bali: Its Religion and Ceremonies. Photos by W. Spies. Batavia: Royal Packet Navagation, 1931. Chiefly photos.

Hadiwijojo, KGPH. Bedoyo Ketawang. Surakarto: Radja Pustaka, n.d.
In Indonesian. An excellent discussion of this ritual court dance.

Harrell, Max. "Penca, the Art of Self Defense, and Topeng Babakan, Masked Dance, from Sunda, West Java." Monographs on

<u>Music, Dance and Theatre in Asia</u> Vol. 4. New York: Asia
Society, 1977.
Lists masks used in topeng babakan, discusses music.

Herbst, Ed. "Aesthetics in Balinese Artistic and Spiritual Practice." <u>Asian Music</u>, 13, 1 (1981), pp. 43-53.
A 1971 conference in Bali set up a gradation of performances as
<u>wali</u> (sacred), <u>bebali</u> (connected to religious ceremony but not rit-
ual), and <u>balibalihan</u> (for entertainment). The author argues that
these categories are not functional because trance can intrude into
the most secular performance and commercialism continues to en-
croach on the most sacred.

Hiss, Philip. <u>Bali</u>. London: Robert Hale, 1941.
Chapters on music, dance and drama give simple, accurate introduction and describe actual performances. Beautiful illustrations.

Holt, Claire. "Batak Dances." <u>Indonesia</u>, 12 (October 1971), pp.
65-84.
Describes performances of a variety of masked and unmasked
dances. Hornbill funeral dance in which two performers play birds
and <u>hoda-hoda</u>, in which a horse dancer careens about while two
masked dancers slowly weave around, are particularly interesting.

_____. "The Dance in Java." <u>Asia</u>, 37 (December 1939), pp.
943-46.
Nontechnical Introduction by a Western expert.

_____. <u>Dance Quest in the Celebes</u>. Paris: Archives Inter-
nationales de la Danse, 1939.
Dances of Macassars, Buginese, and Toraja. Excellent pictures.
Floor patterns and description of movement characteristics of about
twenty dances are given. A number of trance and some animal-
impersonation dances are included. The trance dance of the
Buginese <u>bissu</u> (priests), leading to self-stabbing, and the <u>ma'bugi</u>,
a circle dance which wards off illness, are particularly interesting.

_____. "Dances of Minangkabau: Notes by Claire Holt."
<u>Indonesia</u>, 14 (October 1972), pp. 73-88.
The use of martial arts movement is pervasive in the dance of
this Indonesian ethnic group. Mock combat dance (sile), randai--
a dramatic circle dance which recounts local epics, and ecstatic
dance in which performers pierce themselves with awls are described.

_____. "Dances of Sumatra and Nias: Notes by Claire Holt."
<u>Indonesia</u>, 11 (April 1971), pp. 1-20.
Describes a variety of dances viewed. Imitative dances include
the dance of the hawk and the dance of the cat. The former is
done on tables and performer hops and flaps arms. The latter is

distinguished by a clawlike use of the hand. Film documentation of
many Indonesian dances studied by Holt prior to WW II is in Dance
Museum of the Royal Opera in Stockholm. Photo documentation is
in Drottningholm Theatre Library.

_____. "The Development of the Art of Dancing in the Mang-
koenagaran" in Het Triwindoe Gedenkboek Mangkoenagoro VII.
Surakarta, 1939.

_____. Théâtre et danses aux Index Néerlandaises. Paris: Les
Archives Internationales de la Danse, 1939.

_____. "Two Dance Worlds: A Contemplation." Impulse (San
Francisco) (1958), pp. 17-28.
Compares Martha Graham's work with Javanese dance-drama.

_____, and Gregory Bateson. "Form and Function of the Dance
in Bali" in The Function of the Dance in Human Society.
Franziska Boas, ed. Reprint. New York: Dance Horizons,
1972.
Interrelationship between movement characteristics and cultural
causes is explored. Angularity and sudden changes in direction
may be related to belief that spirits (who need to be avoided)
travel in straight lines. Trance dance is an important mode of
releasing frustration.

Hood, Mantle. "The Enduring Tradition: Music and Theatre in
Java and Bali" in Indonesia. Ruth McVey, ed. New Haven:
Human Relations Area Files Press, 1963.
Contains general comments on dance-dramas by a major scholar.

Hostetler, Jan. "Bedaya Semang: Problems in a Reconstruction
Project" in Dance as Cultural Heritage: Selected Papers from
the ADG/CORD Conference 1978, forthcoming.
Discusses a major Javanese dance work of the court of Yogyakarta
that has not been performed for sixty years, chronicling difficulties
involved in contemporary efforts to reconstruct it for performance.

_____. "Bedhaya Semang: Sacred Dance of Yogyakarta."
Archipel, in press.
By examining literary references and comparing this sacred
women's dance to the bedhaya ketawang, its counterpart in the
Surakarta court, an attempt is made to understand the role of this
dance in the Javanese court of Yogyakarta.

Hudson, Judith. "Some Observations on Dance in Kalimantan."
Indonesia, 12 (October 1971), pp. 133-150.
Describes variety of dances, including mock battle dances, trance
dance at the conclusion of death rites, and shaman's dances. Comments on recent trend to separate art from ritual. Compares movement of scarf in shaman's trance dance to scarf manipulation in
Javanese dance. Good introduction.

Jenkins, Ron. "Bali: The Dance Drama Chalonarong." The
    Drama Review, 22, 2 (1978), pp. 84-88.
Brief account of a barong-rangda performance.

_____. "Becoming a Clown in Bali." The Drama Review, 23, 2
    (1979), pp. 49-57.
Author describes personal experiences studying topeng.

_____. "The Holy Humor of Bali's Clowns." Asia, 3, 2 (1980),
    pp. 9-35.
Describes the clown characters in the topeng. Clowns entertain
the gods and teach the people through humor and dance.

Kakul, I Nyoman. "Jelantik Goes to Blambangan." I Made Bandem
    and John Emigh, trans. The Drama Review, 23, 2 (1979), pp.
    35-48.
Stage directions indicate movement in this translation of a topeng
performance by a major Balinese performer.

Kartomi, Margaret. "Jaran Kepang and Kuda Lumping: Trance
    Dancing in Java." Hemisphere (Sydney), 17, 6 (1973), pp.
    20-27.

_____. "Music and Trance in Java." Ethnomusicology, 17, 2
    (1973), pp. 163-208.
Trance dances are collective experiences which induce feelings
of security, as well as modes of venting otherwise unacceptable
emotions. Discusses horse dance and the tjowongan, a custom in
which entranced women animate a doll, in examining the music of
these trance dances.

_____. "Performance, Music and Meaning of Reyog Ponorogo."
    Indonesia, 22 (October 1976), pp. 85-130.
Account of a 1971 performance of horse dance gives some movement description. Performance includes dramatic struggle of a
barong and a coarse character.

Koentjaraningrat. "Javanese Court Dances." Asian and Pacific
    Quarterly of Cultural and Social Affairs 8, 2 (1976), pp. 8-18.

_____, ed. Tari dan Kesusasteraan di Djawa: Dance and Litera-
    ture in Java. Published in connection with the eighth anni-
    versary of Javanese Dance Institute. Yogyakarta: Taman
    Siswa, 1959.
"Javanese Court Dances" by Koentjaraningrat is in English.
Other articles discussing methods of teaching dance, topeng, and
ketoprak are in Indonesian, but summarized in English.
    Koentjaraningrat divides dance according to function as religious
(bedaya and serimpi), martial (including beksan lawang of Yogyakarta and beksa bandabaya, a word dance of the Paku Alam court),
and dramatic (including wayang, langendrian and topeng). He discusses the relation of movement, character, and music for the main

character types: female, refined, strong, coarse, and monkey. Slow music and low placement of elbows in relation to shoulder, and feet in relation to knees characterizes female and refined technique.

Kullman, Colby, and William Young, eds. Theatre Companies of the World: Selected Reports. Westport, Conn.: Greenwood Press, forthcoming.
The "Indonesia" section contains excellent information on major theatre troupes in the country. Information on the individual troupe gives insight into the particular genre the group represents. Movement is not a focus, but some information is given in Deena Burton's "Panji Asmara" on a mask-dance form of Cirebon, and Jan Hostetler's "K. P. H. Krida Mardawa" on the performing arts bureau of the court of Yogyakarta. Other articles are useful for background, including Marianne Ariyanto's, "Kokar and Asti" on the dance high school and academy in Bali, and her "Peliatan and Teges," which examines Balinese villages as performing units. R. Anderson Sutton and Peggy Ann Choy's articles "Wayang Orang Negesti Pandowo" and "Wayang Orang Sri Wedari" give the history of two of the major dance drama troupes of Central Java.

Kunst, Jaap. Een en Ander over de Muziek en den Dans op de Kei-Eilenden. Konikljige Vereeniging Indisch Instituut Meldedeeling, 64, Volkenkunde, no. 18. Amsterdam: DeBussy, 1945.
Music and dance in the Kai Islands. Illustrated.

Lansing, John Stephan. Evil in the Morning of the World: Phenomenological Approaches to a Balinese Community. Michigan Papers on South and Southeast Asia 6. Ann Arbor: Center for South and Southeast Asia Studies, University of Michigan, 1974.
Chapter 4 on the "trance-dance play" identifies the barong figure with innocence. Description of performance including movement is given.

_____. "Rama's Kingdoms: Social Supportive Mechanisms for the Arts in Bali." Ph.D. diss., University of Michigan, 1977.
Anthropologist on the function of the arts in different Balinese communities, ritual villages to court-influenced communities.

Lelyveld, Th. B. van. La Danse dans le théâtre javanais. Paris: Librairie Floury, 1931.
Fine pictures of Javanese dance. Text tends to look for Indian parallels that are not always applicable. Author uses Indian names for hand gestures, although they are not used by Javanese.

_____. "The Dances of the Javanese Theatre." Indian Art and Letters, 9 (1935), pp. 126-39.

_____. De Javaansche Danskunst. Amsterdam: Van Holkema en Warendorf, 1931.

Levinson, Andre. "Javanese Dancing." Theatre Arts Monthly, 14
    (December 1930), pp. 1056-65.
Fundamental character of Javanese dance is discussed and relation to puppet movement is emphasized.

Lucas, Heinz. Java-Masken: Der Tanz auf Einem Bein. Kassel:
    Erich Roeth, n.d.
Text is marred by the author's need to prove his thesis that the
mask dances derive from a pan-Asian ritual of life through death.
Over a hundred masks are pictured, but rarely on the dancer. Information is fragmentary.

Ludwig, Ruby Ornstein. "Wayang Wong: The Javanese Classical
    Theatre." World of Music, 18, 1 (1976), pp. 15-22.
A general introduction.

Mead, Margaret. "The Arts in Bali." Yale Review, 30, 2 (1940),
    pp. 335-347.
Notes Balinese are exposed from childhood to a gesture, posture
system that makes them capable of assimilating the more complicated
patterns of dance. Balinese culture breeds into its members a need
for a rich artistic life to cope with the tensions that are part of
that society. An evocative article.

Morrison, Miriam. "The Bedaya-Serimpi Dances of Java." Dance
    Chronicle, 2, 3 (1978), pp. 188-212.
Excellent overview of female court dances. They are a demonstration in movement of the Javanese ideal of refinement. Though now
most often presented as theatre art they retain the court aesthetic.
Contemporary artists choreograph within the constraints of the
movement repertoire of these dances and they are the source of
other styles of male and female dance.

_____. "The Expression of Emotion in the Court Dances of
    Yogjakarta." Asian Music, 7, 1 (1975), pp. 33-38.
The facial expression of each character type is a reflection of
the "eternal condition of the character," and therefore remains
constant though the actions of the drama change.

_____. "Woman's Dance and Tradition in Jogyakarta." Dance
    Research Annual, VIII: Asian and Pacific Dances. Selected
    Papers from the 1974 CORD/SEM Conference. Adrienne
    Kaeppler, Judy Van Zile, and Carl Wolz, eds. 1977.
Contrasts the sacred woman's classical dance with the dancing
girl tradition of the popular culture to emphasize dissimilarities.

Nio Joe Lan. "Chinese Songs and Plays in Batavia." China Jour-
    nal (of Science and Art), 23, 1 (1935), pp. 198-200.
Illustrations enhance concise information.

Ogden, Joan. "Dances of Java." Arts Asiatique, 6 (1976), pp.
    29-34.

Olsin-Windecker, Hilary. "A Study in Transition: Jaya Budaya, Javanese Dance in Jakarta." M.A. thesis, UCLA, 1981.
A dance ethnology thesis discussing continuities and change in Javanese dance drama in Jakarta.

Onghokham. "The Wayang Topeng World of Malang." Indonesia, 14 (October 1972), pp. 111-24.
Report on masked dance-drama in East Java. Discussion focuses on masks and the place of the art in a changing social order. Minimal information on movement is included.

Ornstein, Ruby. "Topeng: Masked Dance of Bali." Essays on Asian Theatre and Dance. New York: Asia Society, 1972.
Brief introduction.

Owensby, J. "A Notation of Golek Asmadano." Journal of the Association of Graduate Dance Ethnologists, 5 (Spring 1981),pp. 37-46.
Labanotation.

Raffles, Sir Thomas Stamford. The History of Java. 2 vols., 1830. London: Black, Parburg, and Allen, 1917. Reprint.
Some of the earliest information available on Javanese performing arts. Interesting material on dancing girl tradition. Information and illustrations are not totally reliable, but remains an important historical document.

Resink-Wilkens, A. J. "De Kalana-dans." Djawa, 4 (1924), pp. 99-104.
Includes twenty photos of typical movements and text describing them.

Revel-MacDonald, Nicole. "La Danse des hudoq (Kalimantan Timur)" Objets et mondes, 18, 1-2 (1978), pp. 31-44.

Rickner, Robert. "Theatre as Ritual: Artaud's Theatre of Cruelty and the Balinese Barong." Ph.D. diss., University of Hawaii, 1972.
Extended descriptions of the barong-rangda dance drama based on field study. Special attention to elements of trance, ritual, possession, and the metaphysical function of performance. Compares ritual function with audience-focused function intended by Artaud.

Rogers, Pamela. "Topeng Babakan as a Transmitter of Cultural and Ethical Values in the Village of Slangit." M.A. thesis, UCLA, 1982 (?).
Dance ethnology thesis on Cirebonese mask dance.

Scoren, Leslie. "Legong Keraton of Bali: An Analysis of Style and Structure in Relation to Social Environment." M.A. thesis, UCLA, 1981 (?).
A thesis in dance ethnology.

Simatupang, R. O. Dances in Indonesia. Jakarta: Jajasan
Prapantja, n.d.
Detailed information on movement, but most useful to someone
who is acquainted with indigenous terminology. Javanese material
is most complete.

Soedarsono. "Classical Javanese Dance: History and Characterization." Ethnomusicology 13, 3 (1969), pp. 498-506. (Also in
Dance in Africa, Asia and the Pacific: Selected Readings.
Judy Van Zile, ed. New York: MSS Information, 1976.)
Dance-drama wayang wong is derived from the old masked dance-
drama and the characterizations it uses are taken from the shadow
play. Other dance-drama forms have drawn from it in turn. Before
WW II dancers were trained for a specific role and had to possess
the physical and mental qualities of that role. Specific physical requirements of major character types are listed. Other dance-drama
forms are derived from wayang wong, and have adopted its characterization system.

_____. Dances in Indonesia. Jakarta: Gunung Agung, 1974.
Dance in Java, Sunda, Bali, Sumatra, Kalimantan (Borneo) and
Sulawesi (the Celebes) is briefly described. Bibliography contains
additional Indonesian and Dutch sources. A general introduction
to the scope of Indonesian dance by an expert.

_____. Java dan Bali: Dua Pusat Perkembangan Drama Tari
Tradisionil di Indonesia. (Java and Bali: Two Centers of De-
velopment for the Traditional Dance Drama.) Yogyakarta:
Gadjah Mada, 1972.

_____. Living Traditional Theatres in Indonesia: Nine Selected
Papers. Yogyakarta: Gadjah Mada (Academi Seni Tari In-
donesia), 1974.
Collection of papers on Javanese and Balinese theatre by a
Javanese expert.

_____. Tari-Tarian Indonesia. (Dances of Indonesia) Bagian,
1. Jakarta: Projek Pengembangan Media Kebudayaan, 1976.

_____. Tari-Tarian Rakyat di Daerah Istimewa Yogyakarta.
(Dances of the People in the Area of Yogyakarta.) Yogyakarta: Academi Seni Tari Indonesia, 1976.
Unique data. Reports on popular performing arts found in each
village noting movement, costume used, instrumentation, who participates, length of performance, cost.

Soepandi, Atik, and Enoch Atmadibrata. Khasanah Kesenian
Daerah Jawa Barat. (Characteristic Arts of West Java.)
Bandung: Pelita Masa, 1977.
Best source on Sundanese dance. Discusses penca silat martial
dance, wayang style dances, topeng as well as other forms, giving
names of typical movements and describing them.

De Srimpi- en Badajadansen aan het Soerakartasche Hof. (The
    Serimpi and Bedaya Dances at the Court of Surakarta). Illus-
    trated by Tyra de Kleen. Weltevreden: (Dutch East Indies)
    Topografische Dienst, 1925.
Describes training of the Bedaya dancers in the early part of
the century. Watercolor paintings of the female court dances capture a sense of the movement and atmosphere. In Dutch and English.

Suanda, Endo. "The Social Context of Cirebonese Performing Art-
    ists." Asian Music, 13, 1 (1981), pp. 27-42.
Unique background on Cirebon performers, although no actual
movement description is contained.

Surjobrongto, B. P. H. The Classical Yogyanese Dance. Moh.
    Harun Wijono and Mudjanattistomo, trans. Yogyakarta: Lem-
    baga Bahasa National Tjabag II, 1970.
A blend of information and metaphysical commentary.

Surjodiningrat, Wasisto, Raden Mas. Gamelan, Dance, and Wayang
    in Jogjakarta. 2nd ed. Yogyakarta: Gadjah Mada University
    Press, 1971.
Although movement is described in terms that communicate only
to those trained in the style, this pamphlet contains, in compact
form, important information on the history of all the major Javanese
classical dance and dance-drama genres.

Susilo, Hardja. "The Javanese Court Dance." World of Music, 21,
    1 (1979), pp. 90-102.
General introduction by an authority.

Tirtaamidjaja, N. "A Bedaja Ketawang Dance Performance at the
    Court of Surakarta." Indonesia 1 (1966), pp. 31-61.
Unique data on sacred woman's dance. Discusses rehearsal and
performance, giving diagrams of dance formations, text of song.

Vatsyayan, Kapila. "The Dance Sculptures of Lara Djanggrang
    Prambanan: A Comparative Study." National Centre for the
    Performing Arts, Bombay, Quarterly Journal, 6, 1 (1977),
    pp. 1-14.

Vredenbregt, J. "Dabus in West Java." Bidjragen tot de Taal-,
    Land-, en Volkenkunde, 129 (1973), pp. 302-320.
Describes dance in which performers pierce selves with awls.
Pictures and descriptions of performances by three groups give
some information on movement. Emphasizes that the aim of the
performance is not to go into trance but to remain in conscious
control. This contention differs from standard interpretations of
the form.

Woodward, Stephanie. "Evidence for a Grammatical Structure in

Javanese Dance: Examination of a Passage from Golek Lam-
bangsari." Dance Research Journal, 8 (1976), pp. 10-17.
Unusual in its precise analysis of movement and choreography.

_____. "Dance Training East and West: Setting the Mind and
Body in Motion." Eddy, 8 (Spring-Summer 1976), pp. 59-65.

Wahyono, M. "Masks and Men: Topeng: A Regional Javanese
Dance Form." Hemisphere (Sydney), 22, 1 (1978), pp. 2-5.

Young, Elizabeth. "Topeng in Bali: Change and Continuity in a
Traditional Drama Genre." Ph.D. diss., University of
California-San Diego, 1980.
Fieldwork for this anthropology dissertation included extensive
videotaping of performances, followed by playback to elicit viewer
comment. Minimal movement description is included, but background
on the form and its current state is useful.

4. Popular

Hatley, Barbara. "Ludruk and Ketoprak: Popular Theatre and
Society in Java." Review of Indonesian and Malayan Affairs,
7, 1 (1973), pp. 38-58.
A general description based on 1970-72 fieldwork.

_____. "Wayang and Ludruk: Polarities in Java." The Drama
Review, 15, 3 (1971), pp. 88-101.
Illustrations of clowns and female impersonators onstage give
sense of form. Text argues that ludruk, like traditional shadow
theatre, pictures a two-class society. But ludruk more accurately
reflects current Indonesian society in that its elite is not one of
aristocratic birth, but of doctors, government officials and soldiers.

Grijns, C. D. "Lenong in the Environs of Jakarta: A Report."
Archipel, 12 (1976), pp. 175-202.
Describes popular theatre of Malay-speaking areas near Jakarta.
Notes the use of martial arts movement for male characters. Focus
of article is on description of troupe operation, rather than move-
ment. Finds lenong stories support the status quo rather than
promoting social change. Contrasts with ludruk as interpreted by
Peacock.

Peacock, James. "Anti-Dutch, Anti-Muslim Drama Among Surabaja
Proletarians: A Description of Performances and Responses."
Indonesia, 4 (October 1967), pp. 44-73.
Synopses of four ludruk plays and audience reaction.

_____. Rites of Modernization: Symbolic and Social Aspects of
Indonesian Proletarian Drama. Chicago: University of Chicago
Press, 1968.

An anthropological study of ludruk in Surabaya which argues plots promote modernization by inculcating nontraditional ideals. Although focused on sociocultural aspects of theatre, insights into the stylized movement of the singer and its relation to the wayang ideal is discussed and contrasted with the actions of the clown (pp. 168-173).

Vanickova, E. "A Study of the Javanese Ketoprak." Archiv Orientalni. (Prague), 33, 3 (1965), pp. 397-450.
Treats the popular theatre form in its history and relation to classical theatre.

5. Modern

Rendra. The Struggle of the Naga People. Max Lane, trans. New York: St. Martin's Press, 1979.
Introduction discusses work of Rendra, major dramatist and political activist. Text of play and reviews. Little movement description is included.

Taymor, Julie. "Teatr Loh, Indonesia, 1977-78." The Drama Review, 23, 2 (1979), pp. 63-76.
Description of training and rehearsal process of a modern drama company composed of Americans, Indonesians, and Europeans in Bali. Pictures and process are representative of modern experiments in Indonesia.

6. Miscellaneous

Anderson, Benedict. Mythology and Tolerance of the Javanese. Modern Indonesia Project Monograph Series. Ithaca: Southeast Asian Program, Cornell University, 1965.
Gives deep insight into the meaning of the wayang characters to the Javanese viewer.

Kunst, Jaap. Music in Java: Its History, Its Theory, and Its Technique. E. L. Heins, ed. 3rd ed. 2 vol. The Hague: Martinus Nijhoff, 1949.
Indispensable background to study of dance and drama forms.

Mangkunagoro VII of Surakarta. On the Wayang Kulit (Purwa) and Its Symbolic and Mystical Elements. Southeast Asia Program Data Paper, 27. Claire Holt, trans. Ithaca: Cornell University, 1957.
An impressive contemplation of the symbolic meaning of the wayang by a Javanese.

7. Audiovisual Materials

The Light of Many Masks (60 min.). By Wayne Lockwood and
Karen Goodman. 16mm. film, color, sound.
Gives context of topeng performance as well as performance
excerpts.

Miracle of Bali: Night (60 min.), Recital of Music and Dance (60
min.), and Midday Sun (30 min.). Xerox Corporation. 16mm
film, color, sound.
Excellent excerpts from a variety of dances and dance dramas.

Penca and Topeng Babakan from Sunda, Indonesia (30 min). Asia
Society. 3/4" videotape, color.
The first part of the tape shows martial arts dance. The second
part shows a premier performer of the masked dance of the Cirebon area. Taped in U.S.

The Topeng Dance Theatre of Bali (30 min.) Asia Society. 3/4"
videotape, black and white.
Djimat, a major topeng performer, dances. Taped in U.S.

Traditional Dances of Indonesia. By Film Forms International, San
Francisco. 16mm. color, sound.
A series of fine films of Balinese, Javanese, and Sumatran dance.
Balinese dances are Legong Kraton (20 min.), Baris Jago & Kebyar
Duduk (20 min.), and Barong (32 min.); Surakarta dances are
Bedoyo Elo Elo (23 min.), Bedoyo Pangkur (23 min.), Srimpi Gon-
dokusomo (19 min.), Srimpi Anglir Mendung (19 min.), Menak
Konchar (11 min.); and Yogyakarta dances are Beksan Menak (19
min.), Lawung Ageng (40 min.), and Langen Mondro Wonoro (32
min.). Sumartan dances are Tari Piring and Tari Alang (20 min.).

Trance and Dance in Bali (20 min). 16mm film, black and white,
sound.
Film by Gregory Bateson and Margaret Mead shows a barong-
rangda play in Bali in the 1930's.

Laos

1. General

Bowers, Faubion. Theatre in the East: A Survey of Asian Dance
and Drama. New York: Thomas Nelson & Sons, 1956.
Chapter on Laos (pp. 183-86) is brief but contains some movement information. Notes the impact of Thai culture on Laos. Describes three female dances. All dances contain four fundamental
features: salutation, making-up, flower taking, and walking.

Compton, Carol Jean. "Mohlam: A Social and Linguistic Analysis

of a Form of Laotian Folk-Singing." Ph.D. diss., University of Michigan, 1977.
Discusses form of singing which is used in the popular theatre of Laos. In addition to content analysis author gives accounts by seven performers of how they learned the distinctive dance, poetry, and singing style of the form.

de Berval, Rene, ed. Kingdom of Laos. Saigon: France-Asia, 1959.
Short accounts of spirit medium dance are found on pp. 158-9 and 166-9.

Nginn, Pierre S. "Laotian Songs and Dances." Hemisphere (Sydney), 14, 1 (1970), pp. 11-13.

"Review of the Presentation of the Lao Theatre at That Luang." Friendship: Quarterly Magazine of the Lao American Association, 1, 1 (1965).
Describes improvised comic skits involving three characters and a good deal of audience participation, which author compares to commedia dell'arte.

2. Audiovisual Materials

La Fête des eaux à Vientiane. (20 min.) Produced by the Comite du Film Ethnographique, Musée de l'Homme, Paris, with assistance of Centre National de la Recherche Scientifique. Directed by Michèle Cognany and Jacques Lemoine. 16mm. film, color, sound.
Documentary on Water festival with street processions, ritual offerings at temples, dancing, and boat races. (In the Dance Collection of the New York Public Library.)

Malaysia and Singapore

1. Terms

Bangsawan: a popular theatre form. Barongan: animal mask which is danced. Dabus: dancers pierce selves with awls. Ketoprak: popular theatre form, Javanese-influenced. Kuda kepang: horse trance dance. Manora: Thai-influenced dance drama. Ma'yong (mak yong): dance drama developed at Malay courts, all-female troupe except for clowns. Silat: Malay martial art with dance stylization.

2. General

Beamish, Tony. Arts of Malaya. Malayan Heritage Series 2. Singapore: Donald Moore, 1954.
Chapter 7 emphasizes the multiracial nature of Malayan theatre.

Camoens, Cantius Leo. "History and Development of Malay Theatre." M.A. thesis, University of Malaya, 1981.
Discusses traditional theatre, (bangsawan,) and modern theatre
to 1970.

Shahrum Bin Yub. "Mah-Meri Masks." Federation Museums Journal, 8 (1963), pp. 18-23.
Discusses aboriginal masks used in ceremonial dances. With
photos.

Sheppard, Mubin. Taman Indera: Malay Decorative Arts and
Pastimes. Kuala Lumpur: Oxford University Press, 1972.
Discussion of ma'yong dance drama (pp. 58-67) and Malay dancing (pp. 82-93) is included. See section on silat and trance performance (pp. 190-203) also. Excellent photos and general remarks
on Malay performing and plastic arts and culture.

3. Traditional

Banks, David. "Trance and Dance in Malaya: The Hindu Buddhist
Complex" in Northwest Malay Folk Religion. Special Studies
74, Buffalo: Council on International Studies, 1976.

Burridge, K. O. L. "Kuda Kepang in Batu Pahat, Johore." Man,
61 (1961), pp. 33-36.
Horse trance dance.

Cuisinier, Jeanne. Danses magiques de Kelantan. Paris: Institut
d'enthnologie, 1936.
Though the focus is on ritual rather than theatrical aspects of
the dance, important information on a variety of forms is included.
Gives general characteristics and symbolic value of five Malay and
some Siamese forms found in the Kelantan area. Includes good
movement description and pictures of typical movements of one
dance.

Daugharty, Angela. "Wayang Adjusts to Changing Times and the
Show Goes On." Straits Times Annual (1975), pp. 45-52.
Chinese opera in Singapore.

D'Cruz, Marion. "Joget Gamelan: A Study of Its Contemporary
Practice." M.A. thesis, Universiti Sains Malaysia, 1978 (?).
On Malay classical court dance with detailed photos of gestures.

Firth, Raymond. "Ritual and Drama in Malay Spirit Mediumship."
Comparative Studies in Society and History, 9 (1967), pp.
190-207.
Excellent descriptions of movement and good theoretical discussion.

Kassim bin Haji Ali, Mohammed. "Kuda Kepang: Dance Perform-
    ance in Batu Pahat, Johor." Federation Museums Journal 19
    (1974), pp. 1-20.
    Horse trance dance performance.

Ly Sing Ko. "Chinese Drama in Malaysia." France-Asie, 20
    (1965-66), pp. 157-71.
    Description of Chinese theatrical technique with comment on the
decline in standards in Malaysia.

Malm, William. "Malaysian Ma'yong Theatre." The Drama Review,
    15, 3 (1971), pp. 108-14.
    Text introduces form, but does not discuss movement. Pictures
show female dancers and clowns in action.

_____. "Music in Malaysia." World of Music, 21, 3 (1979),
    pp. 6-14.
    Brief description of various dances is included in this general
survey of Malaysian music. Three clear photos of trance form,
martial dance, and ma'yong.

Nasaruddin, Mohamed G. "Dance and Music of the Desa Performing
    Arts of Malaysia." Ph.D. diss., Indiana University, 1979.
    Comprehensive introduction to traditional performing arts. Music
and dance are the core elements of the performing arts in Malay villages and certain features of the dance recur in form after form.
Dance is used to open and close most performances, character type
is delineated by dance. Brisk movements indicate rough characters;
flowing movements, refined ones; and crude movements, clowns.
Thai and Indonesian dance have influenced the dance of Malay
forms.
    In addition to the many dance-drama forms, there are dances
with some dramatic content, such as kuda kepang and barongan.
These two with dabus are characterized by repetition and emphasize leg movement. They contrast with the dance-drama forms
where more movement focus is on the hands. Core movements of
ma'yong are described.

Ong Cheng Lian. The Teochew Opera Troupes: A Study of the
    Business and Social Organization of Opera Players. Singapore:
    University of Malaya, Department of Social Studies, n.d.
    History of Teochew opera in China and Singapore with attention
to music, costumes, movement, makeup, troupe organization, training, and magico-religious beliefs.

Sheppard, Mubin. "Joget Gamelan Trengganu." Journal of the
    Malaysian Branch Royal Asiatic Society, 40 (1967), pp. 149-
    152.
    This court dance tells stories of the Indonesian prince, Panji.
It was imported from Rhiau in the seventeenth century. Instruments and costumes are discussed, little on movement.

_____. "Manora in Kelantan." Journal of the Malaysian Branch Royal Asiatic Society, 46, 1 (1973), pp. 161-73.
Information on Thai-influenced form.

_____. "Ma'yong--The Malay Dance Drama." World of Music, 15, 3 (1973), pp. 21-33.
Brief introduction to all aspects of Ma'yong.

_____. "The Trengganu Roget." Journal of Malaysian Branch Royal Asiatic Society, 14 (1938), pp. 109-114.
Deals primarily with history of this dance form which originated among Achenese in Sumatra and came to Malaysia via Borneo.

_____. "A Recording of the Ma'yong Dance Drama of Kelantan," Federation Museums Journal New Series, 12 (1967), pp. 55-103.
Describes videotaping of eleven plays. With eleven pages of black-and-white photos.

Soong, Charles. "Sabah's Traditional Dances." Sarawak Gazette, 100, 1402 (1974), pp. 264-270.

Swettenham, Frank A. "The Malay Nautch." Journal of the Singapore Branch Royal Asiatic Society, 2 (1878), pp. 163-67.

Wright, Barbara. "Dance is the Cure: The Arts as Metaphor for Healing in Kelantanese Malay Spirit Exorcism." Dance Research Journal, 12, 2 (1980), pp. 3-10.
Pictures and description give sense of structure of performance and movement used in trance dance in Kelantan. Curing performances are done for patients, who may often be women who are experiencing a divorce. A medium goes into trance. If possessed by a female spirit, movement is refined, and ma'yong dance style is apt to be used. If the possessing spirit is male or animal, more robust movements, sometimes drawn from silat, the martial art, are used.

Yousof, Ghulam-Sarwar. "The Kelantan Mak Yong Dance Theatre: A Study of the Performance Structure." Ph.D. diss., University of Hawaii, 1976.
This is the most in-depth description and analysis of this major dance-drama form, but movement is only briefly described (pp. 128-33).
Female dances show little variety and are basically slow, circular dances. Male performers, who always play clown roles, have more complicated and stylized dances. Hand gestures, arm, foot and body position combine to identify the specific character or role type. The exception to the rule is the elaborate opening dance done by the women, which is described in some detail.

4. Popular

Bujang, Rahmah. Sejarah Perkembangan Drama Bangsawan di

Tanah Melayu dan Singapura. (History of the Development of Bangsawan in Malaysia and Singapore). Kuala Lumpur: Dewan Bahasa dan Pustaka, 1975.

Hussain, Sufian; Mohd. Thani Ahmad; and Johan Jaaffar, eds. "Drama: Bangsawan Sebagi Drama Transisi." (Drama: Bangsawan as a Transitional Drama) in Sejarah Kesusasteraan Melayu. (History of Malay Literature). Vol. 1. Kuala Lumpur: Dewan Bahasa dan Pustaka, 1981.

Yassin, Mustapha Kamil. "The Malay Bangsawan" in Traditional Drama and Music of Southeast Asia. Moh. Taib Osman, ed. Kuala Lumpur: Dewan Bahasa dan Pustaka, 1974.
Good background on this century-old popular theatre form, but little attention to movement. Bangsawan is the commedia dell'arte of the East. Character types included heroes, heroines, genies, and clowns. Although the form adopted the proscenium stage and scenery system from the West, most other elements were derived from local tradition.

_____. "Theatre in Malaysia." Interview by A. J. Gunawardana. The Drama Review, 15, 3 (1971), pp. 102-107.
Little movement description and pictures are of Thai rather than Malay dancers, but useful background on bangsawan.

5. Modern

Alwi, Syed, "Amateur Dramatics in Malaya." News Bulletin of the Institute of International Education, 30 (December 1954), pp. 40-43.

Ang, Tian Se. "Modern Chinese Drama in Malaysia and Singapore." Tenggara, 6 (1973), pp. 140-53.

Ariffin, Zakaria, ed. Drama Melayu Dalam Esei. Kuala Lumpur: Dewan Bahasa dan Pustaka, 1981.
Articles by leading theatre people and critics written in last twenty years.

Jit, Krishen. "Talking with Utih." New Sunday Times (weekly), 1972-1979.
Column by major critic and scholar of Malaysian theatre. A bilingual collection of these articles is being prepared for publication.

Lim, Shirley. "Theatre in Malaysia." The Malaysian, 1, 3 (1968), pp. 15-18.

Nanaff, Abdullah. "Modern Malaysian Theatre." Asian Pacific Quarterly, 6, 4 (1975), pp. 64-67.

Nanney, Nancy. "An Analysis of Modern Malaysian Drama." Ph.D.
    diss., University of Hawaii, 1983 (?).
    Based on fieldwork. Three periods of modern Malay-language
drama are discussed with some reference to theme, character,
structure, and some performance aspects.

6. Audiovisual Materials

Tari-Tarian Malaysia (23 min.) by Filem Negara Malaysia. Black
    and white, sound, 1968.
    Ma'yong and other dances.

Philippines

1. Bibliographies

Dizon, Fe S. "Seventy Years of the Philippine Theatre: An Anno-
    tated Bibliography of Critical Works, 1900-1970." Select
    (January 1973), pp. 3-27.

Saito, Shiro. Philippine Ethnography: A Critically Annotated and
    Selected Bibliography. Honolulu, University Press of Hawaii,
    1972.

2. General

Alejandro, Reynaldo G. "Contemporary Dance in the Philippines."
    Dance Magazine, 51 (July 1977), p. 99.
    Reports on active companies.

_____. Philippine Dance: Mainstream and Crosscurrents.
    Philippines: Vera-Reyes, 1978.
    Contemporary choreographer explores the varied roots and cur-
rent realities of Philippine dance. Modern theatrical dance receives fullest treatment, and many of the pictures of the folk forms
discussed are actually interpretations of these dances by modern
artists. Beautiful illustrations and extensive bibliography enhance
text. Best source on modern dance.

_____. "Sayaw Silangan: The Dance in the Philippines."
    Dance Perspectives, 51 (1972).
    Best introduction to all variants of dance in the Philippines.
Sections on tribal dances, Muslim dances, hispanic and indigenous
folk dances of Christians, and current dance. Good movement description and excellent photos throughout.

Banas, Raymundo C. Philipino Music and Theater. Quezon City:
    Manlapaz, 1969.

Factual, historical, and biographical information on all types of Philippine theatre and dance. See section on songs and dances (p. 79) and chapters on theatre (p. 172). Almost no analysis, but useful.

Chaffee, Fredric H., et al. Area Handbook for the Philippines. Washington: U.S. Government Printing Office, 1969, pp. 135-37, 141-46.
Catalogues the various dramatic forms.

Cruz, Isagani R., ed. A Short History of Theatre in the Philippines. Manila: Philippines Educational Theatre Association, 1971.
Excellent background on Philippine theatre. Essays on all periods with a bibliography of 385 entries. Movement is not a focus.

Edades, Jean. "Filipino Drama of the Past and Present." Theatre Annual (1947), pp. 18-36.
Numerous forms of theatre are described and examples given.

Goquingco, Leonor. "Dance in the Philippines." Dance Magazine, 29 (December 1955), p. 12.
Overview of many dances with brief descriptions and some analysis of movement. Notes flowing, mystic quality of moro dancing, and the differing rates of various body parts; the arms, hands, and head moving languorously while feet seem to move more quickly and vigorously.

_____. "Dances of the Emerald Isles." Arts Asiatique, 2 (March-April 1972), pp. 13-18.

Hernandez, Tomas C. The Emergence of Modern Drama in the Philippines (1898-1912) and Its Social, Political, Cultural, Dramatic and Theatrical Background. Ph.D. diss., University of Hawaii, 1975. (Also available as The Emergence of Modern Drama in the Philippines (1898-1930). Philippine Studies Working Paper 1. Honolulu: Asian Studies Program, University of Hawaii, 1976.)
Excellent source on traditional as well as popular theatre in the Philippines. See information on ritual dance of pre-Christian priestesses (pp. 16-17), discussion of the stylized, melodramatic performance of comedia (p. 33), report on use of can-can in zarzuela performance (p. 72), in addition to discussion of the staging of early modern plays with six early photos.

Pimentel, Narciso Jr. "The Philippine Theatre: From Karangatan to Neorealism." Theatre Arts, 38 (1954), p. 66.
Summary of history and present state of Philippine theatre with some production photos.

Rentana, Wenceslao Emilio. El Teatro En Filipinas. Madrid:
    Libreria General De Victoriano Suarez, 1909.
    An old but standard work.

Shawn, Ted. "Dancing on the Isles of Fear." The Dance (Febru-
    ary 1927), p. 34.
    Describes dances viewed.

Vreeland, Nena, et al. Area Handbook for the Philippines. 2nd
    ed. Washington: U.S. Government Printing Office, 1976,
    pp. 148-53.
    General overview of music and dance up to the 1970's.

3. Traditional

Aquino, Francisca Reyes. Fundamental Dance Steps and Music.
    Manila: n.p., 1954.
    Instructions by an expert who has devoted a career to studying
Philippine dances and adapting them to present to modern audiences.

_____. Philippine Folk Dances. 5 vol. Manila: n.p., 1950-
    1966.
    Instructions for each dance with illustrations. By an expert.

_____. "Philippine Folk Dances." The Journal of the American
    Association for Health, Physical Education and Recreation
    (December 1952), pp. 11-12.

Benedict, Laura Watson. "A Study of the Bagobo Ceremonial Magic
    and Myth." Annals of the New York Academy of Sciences, 25
    (May 1916), p. 15.
    Brief description of dancing at ginum festival.

Bernal, Rafael. "The Moro-Moro: Possibility for Folkloric Thea-
    tre." Comment (Manila), 15 (1962), pp. 115-23 (Also in Unitas
    [Manila] 35 [December 1962], pp. 545-53).

Brillantes, Gregorio. "The Play was not the Only Thing: Three
    Centuries of the Ateneo Stage." Manila Review 3, 4 (1977),
    pp. 103-08.

Cole, Fay Cooper. Traditions of the Tingguians: A Study in
    Philippine Folklore. Field Museum of Natural History Anthro-
    pological Series 14. Chicago: Field Museum, 1915, p. 440.
    Describes a sacred dance, the da-eng and a couple dance in
which couples use a cloth as dance accessory.

Cole, Mabel Cook. Savage Gentlemen. London: G. Harap, 1929.
    Describes potato dance of Negritos--a pantomimed search for

sweet potatoes (p. 166), and moro dancing in which the musicians dance between strokes on instruments (p. 223).

Fajardo, Libertad. Visayan Folk Dances. 3 vol. Manila: Solidaridad, 1961-1975.

Jara, Josefa. "Music of the Philippine Islands." National Education Association Journal of Proceedings and Addresses, (1915), pp. 879-882.
Dance of Negrito, Igorot, Mohammedans of Mindano is mentioned briefly. Describes in some detail a Bicol dance performed at street intersections when the Southern Cross constellation appears at the height of house eaves. Chorus sings love songs while boys woo girls with a birdlike swooping dance.

Jenks, Albert Ernest. "The Bontoc Igorot." Philippine Islands Bureau of Science, Division of Ethnology Publications, 1 (1905).

MacTavish, Shona. "Tribal Dance in Mindano." Silliman Journal, 20 (1973), pp. 217-225.
Report on field study seeking to validate thesis that religious symbolism lies behind indigenous dance. Gives information on five dances of Manobo and Badjaos, without clarifying how they fit into total dance repertory. Facts are useful, but article is self-validating.

Mercada, Monina A. "Countryside Festivals." Archipelago, 5 (1978), pp. 22-26.
Nine pictures of various dances.

Mendoza, Felicidad. The Comedia (Moro-Moro) Rediscovered. Manila: Society of St. Paul Makati, 1976.
Discussion of this romantic, traditional theatre by a reviewer of the form who seeks to create "improved" comedia. Illustrations are of current productions. Though information may reflect author's current interpretations of the style, this is the most comprehensive discussion of movement in the comedia. The stylized gestures of battle included sword waving and the stomp of a foot as the death blow was delivered (p. 34). More information on battle dances and different movement choices for Christians and Moors is given (pp. 54-64).

Mendoza, Liwayway. "Lenten Rites and Practices: The Philippines." The Drama Review, 21, 3 (1977), pp. 21-32.
Pictures and field report on holy week processions and theatrical presentations of the life of Christ. Flagellation is common in processions and crucifixions are enacted. Photos included.

Molina, Antonio. "Forum on Filipino Music: Filipino Musical Heritage in Folk Dances." Comment (Manila), 19 (1963), pp. 29-35.

Eastern European and German forms have affected Filipino dance as well as Spanish forms.

Muoz, Teresa. "Notes on Theatre: Pre-Hispanic Philippines (Religion, Myth, Religious Ritual)" in Brown Heritage: Essays on Philippine Cultural Traditions and Literature. Antonio G. Manuud, ed. Quezon City: Ateneo de Manila, 1967.
Describes variety of quasi-dramatic dances reported by early missionaries and visitors and examines indigenous customs that point toward ritual roots for the drama. Concisely pulls together much ethnographic material.

Orosa, Rosalinda. "The Filipino Dances in Character." ASEAN Journal, 3, 1 (1978), pp. 19-26.

Panizo, Alfredo, and Rodolfo Cortez. "Introduction to the Pampango Theatre." Unitas, (Manila), 41 (March 1968), pp. 124-37.
Briefly describes many traditional dramatic forms.

Pigafetta, Antonio. The Voyage of Magellan: The Journal of Antonio Pigafetta. Trans. by Paula S. Paige from the Edition in the William L. Clement's Library, University of Michigan, Ann Arbor. Englewood Cliffs, NJ: Prentice-Hall, 1969.
Earliest European account of music and dance in Philippines-- brief passages.

Realubit, Maria. "The Bicol Dramatic Tradition." Philippine Social Science and Humanities Review, 41, 1-2 (1976), pp. 1-203.

Reed, William Allan. "Negritos of Zambales." Philippine Islands, Division of Ethnology Publication, 2, 1 (1904).
Report based on field study describes briefly potato, bee, torture, lovers, and weapons dances.

Riggs, Arthur. "Seditious Drama in the Philippines." Current History, 20 (1951), pp. 202-07.
A political conservative's account, notes that in one play actors could move into position so that their seemingly innocuous costumes formed composite image of revolutionary flag. Little on movement otherwise.

Rosal, Maria. "Some Dramatic Ur-forms in Iloco Folk Tradition." Mindano Journal, 4, 1-4 (1977-78), pp. 409-42.

Rosario, Elaine del. "Philippine Life, Legend and Lore in Dance." Kalinangan (April-June 1975), pp. 24-27.

Santiago, Francisco. "The Development of Music in the Philippine Islands" in Encyclopedia of the Philippines. Zoilo M. Galang, ed. Vol. 8. Manila: Philippine Educational, 1936.
Short descriptions of a variety of dances (pp. 137-39).

Tolentino, Francisca Reyes (Aquino). Philippine Folk Dances and
Games. New York: Silver Burdett, 1935.
Basic handbook with diagrams of steps, and hand and arm movements, by an expert. Though steps are from folk sources, author
has revised some choreography to suit modern audiences.

_____. Philippine National Dances. New York: Silver Burdett,
1946.
Music, information on the dance, and illustrations of dance and
costume for fifty-four dances. Intended for school use.

Worcester, Dean C. "Head Hunters of Northern Luzon." National
Geographic Magazine, 40 (July-December 1912), pp. 855-97.
Tribal dances of Ilongot, Kalinga, and Ifugao are described and
illustrated. Dances are associated with war and head-hunting.

4. Popular

Fernandez, Doreen. The Iloilo Zarzuela, 1903-1930. Quezon City:
Ateneo de Manila University Press, 1978.
Excellent background on history, socioeconomic context, authors,
plays, staging; but movement descriptions are minimal. Contains
two playscripts in Hiligayon vernacular, and music transcriptions
for songs.

Lapena-Bonifacio, Amelia. The Seditious Tagalog Playwrights:
Early American Occupation. Manila: Zarzuela Foundation of
the Philippines, 1972.
Historical background on zarzuela as a political tool.

Mojares, Resil. "Theatre and Audience in Cebu 1890-1930."
Manila Review, 3, 1 (1977), pp. 74-80.

Orosa, Rosalinda. "The Philippine Zarzuela (Notes and Footnotes)."
Asian Pacific Quarterly, 6, 1 (Summer 1974), pp. 34-46.

5. Modern

Bayanihan Philippine Dance Company. Our First Five Years.
Manila: n.p., n.d.
About the major company using folk material as inspiration for
their highly theatrical dance presentations.

Cadar, Usopay H. "The Bayanihan: How Authentic is its Repertoire?" Solidarity, 5 (December 1970), pp. 45-51.
Bayanihan misrepresents its material by claiming it authentically
presents the dances of different ethnic groups. Examples of how
three dances diverge from their prototypes, especially in terms of
music.

Carpio, Rustica C. "The Plight of the Philippine Theatre." Solidarity, 2 (September-October 1967), pp. 9-14. Assesses condition of modern Philippine theatre.

_____. "Trends in Contemporary Philippine Drama and Theatre." Asian Culture Quarterly, 6, 2 (1978), pp. 33-51.

Cohen, Selma Jeanne. "Working Together." New York State Theatre Program (1964), p. 18.

Edades, Jean Garret. "Looking Toward a Philippine National Theatre." Journal of East Asiatic Studies, 7, 2 (April 1958), pp. 248-51. Suggests playwrights use indigenous materials.

Fernandez, Doreen G. "Theatre Today: Going Home Again." Archipelago, 2, A-22 (1975), pp. 10-14. Modern drama developed on university campuses as an English language theatre. PETA, Babaylan, and other groups have guided it back toward a vernacular theatre. Pictures of two modern productions.

Fitch, Joseph. "The Filipinos' Search for Cultural Identity through Theatre" in Search for Identity: Modern Literature and the Performing Arts in Asia: Papers presented to the 28th International Congress of Orientalists under the Governorship of A. R. Davis International Congress of Orientalists, 28th, Canberra, 1971. Sydney: Angus & Robertson, 1974.

"Forum on the Filipino Theatre." Comment (Manila), 12 (1961), pp. 42-65. (Also in Literature at the Crossroads. Manila: Florentino, 1965.) Brief reports on modern theatre and its problems by Rodrigo Perez III, Rosalinda Orosa, Severino Montano, Leonor Goquingco, Wilfrido Guerrero, and Lamberto Avellana.

Guillermo, Lourdes E. "The Bayanihan." Music Journal, 22 (1964), pp. 23-25. History of Bayanihan dance company with four black-and-white photos.

Hering, Doris. "Bayanihan Philippine Dance Company." Dance Magazine, 33 (December 1959), pp. 26-27.

Joaquin, Nick. "Popcorn and Gaslight." Philippine Quarterly (September 1953). Joaquin writes knowingly of the rise and fall of the moro-moro and zarzuela, and of their successor, the Tagalog movie, while advocating a return to traditional forms in order to reinstate a popular theatre.

Montano, Severino. The Arena Theatre of the Philippines. Manila: Arena Theatre, 1955.
Describes the community-based Arena Theatre, its achievements and aims.

Villaruz, Basilio Esteban, ed. Sayaw Silanganan ng 1976-77: The Philippine Dance Annual and Guide to the National Ballet Festival. Manila: Folk Arts Theatre and Ballet Federation of the Philippines, 1977.

_____. "The State of Dance in the Philippines Today." Eddy, 9 (Winter 1977), pp. 31-38.

5. Audiovisual Materials

Bayanihan. (55 min.) Produced and distributed by Robert Snyder. Directed and written by Allegra F. Snyder. 16 mm film, color, sound.
Interpretations of various Filipino dances by a major company. Bayanihan's interpretation of folk materials has significantly affected the style of many other troupes.

Ilocano Music and Dance from the Northern Philippines (19 min.) black and white, sound; Music and Dance from Mindanao, the Philippines (19 1/2 min.) black and white, sound; Music and Dance from Sulu Islands, the Philippines (17 min.) black and white, sound; Music and Dance of Bagobo and Manobo Peoples on Mindanao, the Philippines (12 min.) color, sound; Music and Dance of the Hill Peoples of the Northern Philippines Part 1 (29 min.), color, sound; Part 2 (11 1/2 min.) black and white, sound; Music and Dance of Yakon Peoples of Basilan Island, the Philippines (11 min.), color, sound; Samal Dances from Taluksangay, the Philippines (12 1/2 min.), color, sound, 16mm films. By Robert Garfias and Harold Schultz, 1969. Released by University of Washington Press.
Ethnic dances and music ensembles filmed under direction of a noted ethnomusicologist.

Thailand

1. Terms

Khon: classical mask dance drama, done by a predominantly male cast. La(h)kon or lakon nai: classical female dance drama. Lakon jatri (chatri) or manora: southern form which dramatizes the Manora story. Likay: Thai popular theatre.

2. General

De La Loubere, Simon. "Concerning the Shows, and Other Diver-
     sions of the Siamese" in The Kingdom of Siam, Part 2. 1963;
     London: Oxford in Asia Historical Reprints, Oxford University
     Press, 1969, pp. 44-50.

Rangthong Jaivid. A Souvenir of Siam. Bangkok: Hatha Dhip
     Press, 1954.
     Collection of articles on Thai theatre, music, and art, including
150 pages on "Classical Siamese Theatre" by Dhanit Yupho, and
many photographs.

Redwood, John Ekert. "The Siamese Classical Theatre." Educa-
     tional Theatre Journal, 5 (1952), pp. 100-05.
     A traveler's account.

Roosman, R. S. "Cross-Cultural Aspects of Thai Drama." Journal
     of Oriental Literature, 8 (January 1967), pp. 43-51.
     Interrelationships with theatre forms of other countries.

Rutnin, Mattani, ed. The Siamese Theatre: A Collection of Re-
     prints from the Journals of the Siam Society. Bangkok: Siam
     Society, 1975.
     Contains excellent background articles on masked (khon) and
unmasked (lakhon) classical dance drama, on the folk form lakhon
jatri, and on the popular likay theatre. Photographs are useful
for understanding movement, but text contains minimal movement
description.

Simmonds, E. H. S. "Mahorasop in a Thai Manora Manuscript."
     Bulletin of the School of Oriental and African Studies, 30, 2
     (1967), pp. 391-403.
     Nineteenth-century description of khon, lakon, Chinese drama,
and puppet performances at competitive festivals.

Tramot, Montri. Kanlalen Khong Thai (Thai Entertainments).
     Bangkok: Department of Fine Arts, 1954.
     By an expert on music. Discussion of likay (pp. 66-87) de-
scribes the use of gestures, which have been modified from the
classical dance repertoire. Notes the importance of dance has been
diminishing as stories become more contemporary.

3. Traditional

Allsop, K. "Siam Dance Lives Again." Dance Magazine, 29
     (October 1955), pp. 35-39.
     Describes training in classical dance drama in Bangkok, with
photos of costuming.

Coedes, Georges. "Origine et évolution des diverses forms du théâtre en Thailand." Bulletin de la Société des Etudes Indochinoises (Saigon), 38, 3-4 (1963), pp. 489-506.
The origins and development of major forms of Thai drama by a major scholar, with illustrations.

Cuisinier, Jeanne. "Le Manora." Journal de la Société des Oceanistes (Paris), 2 (1946), pp. 55-77.

Damrong, Prince. History (of the Dance Drama) of Inao. Bangkok: Pracand Press, 1963.
Deals mostly with lakon nai, female classical dance drama.

_____. Pictoral Figures Depicting Basic Postures of Thai Dancing. Bangkok: Department of Fine Arts, 1959.
Excellent illustrations.

Dhaninivat, Prince. "Pagentry of the Siamese Stage." National Geographic Magazine, 91 (1947), pp. 209-12.
Includes descriptions of movement, costumes, music for dance-drama forms.

_____. "The Shadow Play as the Possible Origin of the Masked Play." Journal of the Siam Society, 37 (1948), pp. 26-32.
Sees the khon as derivative from puppet play.

_____. and Dhanit Yupho. The Khon. Bangkok: National Culture Institute, 1962.
Good introduction to masked dance-drama. Illustrated, with discussion of training.

Different Postures of Thai Classical Dance, from Treatise on Dancing. Bangkok: Soma Nimit, 1968(?).
Mostly illustrations.

Education and the Ceremony of Paying Respect to the Teachers at the School of Dramatic Art and Recent Thai Classical Dance-Dramas Presented by the Department of Fine Arts. Bangkok: Department of Fine Arts, 1962.
Description of School of Dramatic Art. Scenarios for a khon and a lakon jatri.

Fraser, Thomas. Rusembilan: A Malay Fishing Village in Southern Thailand. Ithaca, NY: Cornell University Press, 1970.
Describes curing performances which use trance, martial arts dance and other forms briefly. See "Amusements."

Ginsburg, Henry. "The Manora Dance-Drama: An Introduction." Journal of the Siam Society, 60 (1972), pp. 169-81. (Also in Rutnin--see Thailand--General.)
Most concise introduction to Manora, a folk genre done at temple

fairs. Describes performance structure: musical prelude leads to dance solos by all members of the troupe, the clown jokes and skits sometimes replace stories. Little movement description.

Graham, Walter Armstrong. Siam, 3rd ed. Vol. 2 London: Moring, 1924.
Lengthy discussion of music and dance.

Krebs, Stephanie. "The Film Elicitation Technique: Using Film to Elicit Conceptual Categories of Culture" in Principles of Visual Anthropology, Paul Hockings, ed. The Hague: Mouton, 1975.
All examples are drawn from Thai dance.

_____. "Nonverbal Communication in Khon Dance-Drama: Thai Society Onstage." Ph.D. diss., Harvard University, 1975.
Appendix contains fifty basic gestures of Thai classical dance and gives their meaning, although no movement description is attempted.

Miller, Terry. "Kaen Playing and Mawlum Singing in Northeast Thailand." Ph.D. diss., Indiana University, 1975.
Discusses the dramatic contexts in which this singing is used.

Montrisart, Chaturong. "Thai Classical Dance." Journal of the Music Academy (Madras), 32 (1961), pp. 126-43.
Illustrated.

Nicolas, Rene. "Le Lakhon Nora, ou Lakhon Chatri et les origines du theatre classique siamois." Journal of the Siam Society, 18, Part 2 (1924), pp. 85-110. (Also in Rutnin--see Thailand--General).
Description of troupe, role types, music, modes of teaching and initiation of actors follows a discussion of history. Little actual movement description.

Sterling, Adeline. "Drama and Music in Siam." Inter-Ocean, 13 (1932), pp. 139-44.

Strickland, L. "Music and Dancing in Siam." Etude, 56 (1938), p. 440.

Subhadradis Diskul, M. C. "The Siamese Dance." Arts and Letters, 28 (1954), pp. 30-31.
Considers extent to which Thai dance dramas are derived from Indian sources.

Yupho, Dhanit. Classical Siamese Theatre. P. S. Sastri, trans. Bangkok: Hatha Dhip, 1952.
Provides valuable overview of important forms. Describes and illustrates fifty-two dances including martial dances, folk dances, theatre dances from the khon and lakhon repertoire. The alphabet

dance, the training dance which contains the ma-bot, the rudimentary figures of Siamese dance, is discussed (pp. 73-74) and the
names of nineteen figures are given.

_____. The Custom and Rite of Paying Homage to Teachers of
Khon, Lakhon, and Piphat. L. Lauhabandhu, trans. Bang-
kok: Fine Arts Department, 1961.
Artists show reverence to teachers through dancing this cere-
mony, and the skill they have gained in training is made manifest.
Illustrated.

_____. The Khon and Lakon: Dance Dramas Presented by the
Department of Fine Arts. Bangkok: Department of Fine Arts,
1963.
Programs of thirty-two performances presented 1945-62 at the
National Theatre, including plot outlines, historical background,
and notes on theatre technique, with many illustrations.

_____. Khon Masks. L. Lauhabandhu, trans. Bangkok: Fine
Arts Department, 1960.
Contains little on movement. Primarily useful as a guide for
identifying characters by their masks. Many illustrations.

_____. The Preliminary Course of Training in Thai Theatrical
Art. Bangkok: National Culture Institute, 1955.
A valuable tool. Outlines basics of lakon dance technique.
Gives sixty-eight positions that make up the alphabet of dance.
Notes dancers are taught a single role.

_____, ed. Sinlapa Lakhon Ram Ru Kumu Nattasin Thai (Dance
Drama Arts or Thai Performing Arts Handbook). Bangkok:
Siwaphon, 1973.
Articles by experts on drama.

Zarina, Xenia. "The Royal Thai Ballet" in Classic Dances of the
Orient. New York: Crown, 1967, pp. 35-58.
Useful introduction.

4. Popular

Bowers, Faubion. "Twins of Siamese Theatre: Likay." Saturday
Review, 38 (June 11, 1955), pp. 31-32.
Brief description.

Smithies, Michael. "Likay: A Note on the Origin, Form and Future
of Siamese Folk Opera." Journal of the Siam Society, 59,
Part 1 (1971), pp. 33-63. (Also in Rutnin--see Thailand--
General.)
Compact introduction to improvised popular form's history, story
content, audience, and music. Little movement description. Dance

is of secondary importance and borrows gestures from the classical tradition.

Virulrak, Surapone. "Likay: A Popular Theatre in Thailand." Ph.D. diss., University of Hawaii, 1980.
Excellent description of all aspects of genre, with most extensive movement description available. "Dance" (pp. 179-88) discusses three types used: (1) ones derived from classical lakhon tradition; (2) rock and roll dances; and (3) pseudo-Indian dances. Dramatic gestures to indicate specific emotions or symbolize actions are borrowed from the classical tradition, but are executed in a more casual manner, at the actor's discretion. This contrasts with the strict rules of the lakhon. Movement conventions (pp. 227-232) include following a semi-circular floor pattern on entrances and exits, assuming position onstage according to social position, and giving certain gestures to cue the orchestra.

5. Modern

Mallakul, M. L. "Dramatic Achievement of King Rama VI." Journal of the Siam Society, 63, Part 2 (1975), pp. 260-78.
Pictures accompany lecture on king's contributions to spoken drama.

6. Audiovisual Materials

Dawadungs: A Dance of the Second Heaven. (12 min.) Cornell University Southeast Asia Program, 1956. 16mm. film, color, sound.
A Thai classical dance performed by Yibbhan Xoomsai.

The Diamond Finger. (28 min.) Produced by the Government of Thailand, 1957. Distributed by NYU Film Library, 26 Washington Plaza, New York. 16mm film, color, sound.
Fine example of classical dancing. Set and lighting show influence of Western theatre technique.

Vietnam

1. Terms

Cai luong: popular operetta form of south. Hat boi: classical theatre which shows similarity to Chinese opera. Hat cheo: improvised folk form of the north.

2. Traditional, Popular, and Modern

"Classical and Reformed Theatre." Vietnam Magazine, 5, 10 (1972), pp. 4-7.
Brief account of hat boi and cai luong.

Cogniat, Raymond. Danses d'Indochine. Paris: Editions des Chroniques du Jour, 1932.
Excellent illustrations of Vietnamese dancers.

Coulet, Georges. Le Théâtre annamite classique. Toulon: 1928.
On hat boi. Largely a personal reaction, but some attention to performance elements.

Gras, E. "Une Soirée au théâtre annamite." Bulletin des Amis du Vieux Hué (Hanoi) (1916), pp. 99-106.

Hauch, Duane E. "The Cai Luong Theatre of Vietnam, 1915-1970." Ph.D. diss., Southern Illinois University, 1972.
The most detailed study of this popular musical theatre form of South Vietnam. A description of all aspects.

_____. "A Descriptive Study of Hai Boi, the Classical Theatre of Viet Nam." M.A. thesis, University of Hawaii, 1970.
The most detailed study in English. Description of all aspects. Gestures (pp. 32-38) may enhance the feeling of the songs in this opera theatre form, or may be used to express ideas not included in the dialogue. The author divides gestures into three types: (1) ones that describe action (i.e. stylized modes of giving birth, riding, drinking are described); (2) ones that symbolize character (i.e. bearded characters may stroke length of beard with both hands to indicate thoughtfulness); and (3) ones that symbolize emotions (i.e. to express sadness, the actor looks at the ground, then sits as he lifts his gaze). With useful illustrations and extensive bibliography of foreign language sources.

Huynh, Khac Dung. Hat Boi, théâtre traditionnel du Viet Nam. Saigon: Kim Lai an Quan, 1970.
The major book on classical theatre in Vietnam. Movement and gesture are discussed in detail (pp. 93-100), and illustrations are included, as well as translations of two plays.

Knosp, M. Gaston. "Le Theatre en Indochine." Anthropos, 3 (1908), pp. 280-293.
Discusses hat boi and contrasts it with classical Khmer drama, finding it more popular and "lascivious."

Lelière, M. "Le Théâtre annamite." Extreme-Asie, 5; 56, 57, 59 (1931), pp. 127-42, 183-202, 281-98; 6, 60 (1932), pp. 329-38.
Theatre's development in Vietnam as given in Chinese documents.

Nguyen-Phuoc Thein. "Cai-luong and the Vietnamese Theatre." Viet-My, 8, 4 (1963), pp. 2-10.
On the history of popular theatre.

_____. "Vietnamese Theatre: The Show Must Go On." Vietnam Magazine, 7, 5 (1974), pp. 12-15.
Status of classical and popular theatre in South Vietnam in early 1970's.

Pham Duy. Musics of Vietnam. Dale R. Whiteside, ed. Carbondale: Southern Illinois University Press, 1975.
A useful source due to wealth of information rather than depth of analysis. Bits of information on movement can be gleaned. Sections on cult music (pp. 89-93) and songstresses (pp. 95-110) refer to but do not describe gestures. Chapter on theatre gives history of different forms. Names of specific gestures of classical theatre are cited (pp. 123-24). Importance of dance in the popular hat cheo theatre is discussed (p. 136).

Shen Hua. "Vietnam's Brilliant Hat Cheo Opera." Chinese Literature, 12 (1960), pp. 195-97.
Review of performance given in China of popular theatre form.

Song-Ban. The Vietnamese Theatre. Hanoi: Foreign Languages Publishing House, 1960.
Brief, clear accounts of classical, popular, and modern drama. Modifications of traditional forms by communist ideology are evident. Section on classical theatre has short commentary on use of movement.

Tran Van Khe. "Le Theatre vietnamien" in Les Théâtres d'Asie. Jean Jacquot, ed. Paris: Centre National de la Recherche Scientifique, 1961, pp. 203-19.
Classical and popular theatre described by an expert.

Van Giang. The Vietnamese Traditional Music in Brief. n.p.: Ministry of State in charge of Cultural Affairs, n.d.
Pictures (black and white) of folk dances and hat boi, little analysis or explanation.

"Vietnam." The Drama Review, 13, 4 (1969), pp. 146-53.
Propagandistic performances in north and south during the Vietnamese War are discussed.

Vietnamese Theatre. Saigon: Review Horizons, n.d.
Brief remarks, some illustrations.

Young, E. P. "Theatre in the Democratic Republic of Vietnam." New Orient, 1, 6 (1960), pp. 1-4.
Descriptions of four types of theatre then performed.

3. Audiovisual Materials

Vietnamesen: Hinterindien, Sud Vietnam; Kulttänze in einer
    Buddistischen Pagode bei Hue (20 min.). By R. Kaufman,
    1963. 16mm. film, color, sound. Released by Institute fur
    den Wissenschaftlichen Film, Gottingen.
    Ceremonies of Mahayana Buddhism. Ecstatic dances of women
who swing attributes (knives, clubs, swords) to indicate what ghost
they incarnate.

Chapter Thirteen

EAST ASIAN PERFORMANCE: JAPAN

Leonard Pronko

Overview

The origins of Japanese theatre are recounted in a myth which
blends humor with seriousness, sex with metaphysics, and drama
with dance. To draw the Sun Goddess out of a cave in which she
had hidden herself in a fit of pique, the deity Heaven-Alarming-
Female turned over a bucket and danced upon it, stamping reso-
nantly. "Then she became possessed, exposed her breasts, and
pushed her skirt-band down to her genitals. Then Takamo-nö-para
[the heavenly plane] shook as the eight-hundred myriad deities
laughed at once." Needless to say, the Sun Goddess, curious at
the uproar, emerged from her cave, bringing sunlight back to the
world.

This tale, effectively translated with plentiful commentary in
the recent edition of Kojiki by Donald Philippi (University of Tokyo
Press, 1969), delineates the significant aspects of Japanese performing arts as they were to develop in the following two thousand
years. While all of them do not contain all the elements of the prototypical performance, they usually blend two or more. Whatever
the form, drama and dance are closely woven together. In most
performing arts in Japan, words and music are wedded, so that the
movement patterns are often an interpretation of the text. Such,
at least, was the case in early traditional forms. As they evolved,
however, some became more abstract, divorcing themselves gradually from the text, or from any specific referential qualities. This is
what happened with Bugaku, the court dance which originated in
India, China and Korea, and, during the Heian period (794-1185),
became highly refined, attenuated, and totally Japanese. Today,
not even the performers are aware of the meanings in most of their
gestures.

The Nō drama likewise, in its heyday under Kannami (1333-
1384) and his son, Zeami (1363-1443), contained more mimetic movement than it does today. Under the impact of protection, first by
the refined court of the Ashikaga shoguns, and in the seventeenth

and eighteenth centuries by the Tokugawa, it became ever more refined and ceremonial, losing its original earthiness and most of its
imitative movement.

Kabuki, a popular form patronized by the rising merchant
class from the seventeenth through the nineteenth centuries, remained more realistic and earthy. Under the influence of the puppet theatre, which delighted in making inhuman dolls behave as
though they were living beings, the Kabuki actors introduced more
mimetic movement into their performances, and particularly into their
dance pieces. Responding to an expert audience of connoisseurs,
they refined their movements and evolved a rich language of gestures and mime, suggesting character and emotion. In the twentieth century, many such gestures lost their meaningfulness for audiences unacquainted with the old ways of living, unaccustomed to
smoking long pipes or dealing with the traditions of the pleasure
quarters. As a result, while movement in the older Kabuki pieces
remains somewhat fixed in its classic modes, new Kabuki plays and
particularly the new dances, show a moving away from mimetic gesture, a tendency towards abstraction.

The world of Kabuki dance, often called simply Japanese
Dance (Nihonbuyō), has become a separate world since the early
twentieth century. Related to the world of Kabuki by its origins
and by a large portion of its repertoire, Nihonbuyō today is seeking its own path, blending folk dance, Kabuki, modern dance, ballet, and avant-garde techniques.

The Japanese are conservative, yet highly curious and eager
to try the new. In their performing arts they have clung tena-
ciously to the old while experimenting with the novel and exotic.
Whereas most nations have discarded old forms as they adopted
new ones, Japan has kept the old along with the more recent.
This leads to a striking richness in Japanese performing arts and
an incredible complexity when one attempts to determine the various influences, relationships, and overlays. The amazing abun-
dance of folk performances is a case in point. Some of them are
thought to preserve elements of the Nō as it was performed in the
thirteenth and fourteenth centuries, some show us what Kabuki
may have been like in its origins in the early seventeenth century
or in its flourishing days of the nineteenth century. Shamanic
dances in faraway hamlets are perhaps a throwback to the tub-
thumping performance of Heaven-Alarming-Female, without, however, the more racy elements of that prototypical dance. In a
thousand shrines across Japan, chaste maidens dance ceremoniously
in movements unchanged for fifteen hundred years or more, while
festival Kagura performances mix such ceremoniousness with comic
antics or heroic stances obviously imitated from Kabuki. In several shrines and in the Imperial Household, on special occasions,
one can witness Gagaku/Bagaku performances that rehearse movements brought to Japan in the seventh century, and which have

persisted unchanged since their zenith in the eleventh century, although they disappeared long ago on the Asian mainland.

What characterizes all Japanese movement, whether in life or in the performing arts, is a certain ceremoniousness. Ceremony is important in all phases of Japanese life, and this is reflected in the dance and theatre. Theatre movement is rarely casual. Normally, it is careful, precise, formal, weighty, dignified, and often slow, breaking into rapid or staccato movements only for comic or dramatic effect. Even the folk dances, like the Bon Odori, are quite regular and elegant in their simplicity and control. If there is some sense of abandon in certain folk dances performed under authentic conditions by true folk participating in a ritual act, that abandon is carefully disciplined when these same folk elements become part of a true performing art, presented by practiced dancers before an audience. The earthiness of the folk performance has been carefully hidden by refinement and sophistication which threaten, at times, to devitalize the performance.

Fortunately, an equally important characteristic of the Japanese, both in and out of performing arts, is a deep-seated vitality. This electrifying energy is often kept hidden, but in moments of stress or tension it emerges. In theatrical performances where it is not felt, we have the impression that art has stifled life. But in the finest performances, beneath the subtlety and finesse, one senses a focus and a solidity that are deeply satisfying and help the spectator to experience kinesthetically the movements and emotions of the performer.

Such an experience derives in part from the centered movement in most performing arts. Perhaps because the Japanese have lived traditionally close to the ground, sitting upon the floor rather than on chairs, they have learned in their performing arts to find quite naturally the center of their own gravity, emotion, and energy at that focal point just below the navel. Lowering the hips to achieve this feeling of centeredness is typical of most Japanese movement, including, of course, that used in the martial arts where such grounding is essential. Bugaku appears to use the hips in a higher position, yet even here they are often lowered for certain stances, and as a preparation for stretching.

Within the framework of ceremonious movement with a strong centered base, a large variety of movements are used: from the bold virility of Bugaku or Nō to the willowy gentleness of women's dance in Kabuki; from the smooth flow of Bugaku and Nō to the explosive stamping of Kabuki's bravura aragoto style.

Three major components used separately or blending in various manners, give rise to the fundamental ways of moving in Japanese performing arts: mai, odori, furi. Before attempting to define them, it should be pointed out that technical terms in Japanese aesthetics often change meaning from one writer to another. In-deed, many of them have a number of accepted meanings, some-times one of a general nature and the other more specialized.

Mai refers to the elegant, usually slow movements used in Bugaku and Nō. It is generally considered the oldest form of Japanese dance, and is characterized by simplicity, a use of broad circular movements, and the capacity to convey some kind of mean-ing, however abstractly. The word mai also implies an artistic movement performed by a specialist for spectators. Odori, on the contrary, implies a folk type dance engaged in for the pleasure of the movements but not as a spectator performance. It is charac-terized by a more rapid tempo than mai, by a strong rhythmic ele-ment, and such movements as stamping and jumping. The hands tend to be used in a more decorative fashion than in mai, and the dancing carries no meaning.

Originally Kabuki dance as presented by Okuni in the early seventeenth century was largely made up of odori. But Okuni and her epigones soon added elements of mai, taken from the Nō, which was the dominant theatre of the day. By the time Kabuki reached maturity it used a complex mixture of mai and odori, plus the mi-metic element of furi. Furi has the fundamental meaning of pos-tures, that is to say the poses used in a dance, its choreography. The specialized meaning of furi, however, is imitative gestures. According to some critics such furi in Kabuki dance derive from the puppet theatre, but surely many of them were simply borrowed from life. Since many performing arts in Japan are closely tied to storytelling, and perhaps originated in the efforts of a storyteller to dramatize his tales by gesturing meaningfully or dramatically, it is only natural that such mimetic gestures should be found on stages everywhere in Japan. Sometimes attenuated and only vague-ly suggestive, they are often illustrations of words in the accompa-nying text, and are readily understood--or at least may be guessed at--when one understands the text.

Whatever the performance may be, patterns derived from mai, odori, or furi form an important part of the presentation, for Japa-nese traditional theatre never deviated from the almost universal practice of considering performing arts an amalgam of text, music, and movement. It was only toward the end of the nineteenth cen-tury, under the impact of newly discovered Western realism and naturalism, that the Japanese theatre embraced the heresy of a theatre of words alone. That, too, under the name of Shingeki (new theatre), has become part of the current theatrical scene in Japan, but it does not interest us here, for movement in Shingeki is no different from movement in realistic theatre throughout the world.

Studies of Multiple Forms

A good deal has been written on Japanese theatre, most of it devoted to the two major dramatic forms, Nō and Kabuki. The student interested in understanding the use of movement in these and other Japanese performing arts will find few books or articles devoted exclusively to the subject. But many of the works on specific genres contain sections describing or analyzing movement, and several books focus in some detail on gestures, poses, or dance elements.

Overviews of Japanese theatre are scarce. The best is Peter Arnott's The Theatres of Japan. Although there is not much detail on movement, the book is rich in descriptions of specific performances. Arnott has a solid understanding of world theatre, and is able to make significant comparisons for the novice. He is objective in his judgments, and takes a penetratingly analytic attitude, seeing things in new and stimulating ways. The Theatres of Japan covers effectively the major traditional theatrical forms, and in a final chapter, describes a number of modern productions, some purely western, some blending East and West.

The Traditional Theater of Japan by Inoura Yoshinobu and Kawatake Toshio is a one-volume version of an earlier publication in two volumes. The second half, devoted to Kabuki and Bunraku, is not particularly enlightening, containing as it does a number of vague generalizations, poor translations, and nonsequiturs. The first half, however, will be of immense interest to anyone pursuing a study of the dance and theatre that led up to the development of Nō. Nowhere in English is that period covered so thoroughly, so clearly, and so vividly as in the chapters where Inoura evokes early performances of Kagura, Bugaku, Gigaki, New Sarugaku, Ennen, Dengaku, Sarugaku and Shūgen Nō.

Another excellent treatment of similar materials will be found in The Ballad-Drama of Medieval Japan by James T. Araki. Ostensibly a study of the Kowaka form which is related obliquely to Nō, about half of The Ballad-Drama is devoted to an admirable delineation of the forms that contributed to the glory of Nō. It includes vivid descriptions of a number of performances, and read in combination with one of the books listed below on Kabuki, would give the student a good introductory view of Japanese traditional theatre. For those with more background, and interested in delving in more detail into the forms that immediately preceded Nō, P. G. O'Neill's Early Nō Drama (Lund Humphries, 1958) is the standard work. Scholarly and quite thorough, it may be more confusing than helpful to the beginner, since it amasses a good deal of meticulous detail in its 150 pages of text.

Japanese sacred dance, Kagura, rehearses, in ways as varied

and ancient as Japan itself, the original performance of Heaven-Alarming-Female before the cave of heaven. A single slim volume is devoted to Kagura, fortunately written by a dancer and a poet. Eleanor King's Kagura recalls with the practiced eye of a dancer the many details of a dozen different Kagura performances, and evokes them eloquently with a poet's pen. The author almost goes beyond the limits of words in bringing before the mind's eye the movements of shamanesses and priestesses, now delicate and attenuated, now strong and bold.

A major contribution to our understanding of Japan's rich heritage of dances and dramatic performances in the countryside has been made by Frank Hoff. His Song, Dance, Storytelling: Aspects of the Performing Arts in Japan contains an enlightening discussion of Kagura and other folk performances, seen in a broad perspective. His article, "Dance to Song in Japan" in Dance Research Journal, includes a suggestive discussion of the relationship between word and gesture in shamanistic and religious dance. Hoff has also been instrumental in disseminating in the United States knowledge of material written by the critic who is the grand old man of countryside performances in Japan, Honda Yasuji. Honda's article, "Yamabushi kagura and bangaku: Performance in the Japanese Middle Ages and Contemporary Folk Performances," in Educational Theatre Journal, translated and edited by Hoff, is a carefully documented study of movement in two kinds of folk performance. Drawing on long years of scholarship, Honda places these forms in a broad context, dealing with both religious and performance elements.

Specific Forms

1. Bugaku

The early court dance, Bugaku, noble, elegant and virile, is again evoked with a dancer's sensitivity and an artist's control of words by Eleanor King in her short study, Bugaku. The author describes with loving detail performances she witnessed at Tennoji Temple in Osaka, and supplements words with impressionistic color drawings.

For a scholarly approach to Bugaku, with meticulous attention to every detail of movement, one should turn to Carl Wolz's Bugaku: Japanese Court Dance, with the Notation of Basic Movements and of 'Nasori'. As the title indicates, Wolz has recorded with the accuracy of Labanotation the fundamental patterns and ways of moving in Bugaku, along with the entire Labanotation score of a major piece.

The charming, personal account of Bugaku and its accompanying music in Gagaku (Weatherhill/Tankosha, 1971) by a lifelong practitioner of the form, Togi Masatarō, gives little precise information regarding movement. It will be useful largely for the many splendid photographs in black and white and in brilliant color.

2. Nō

When the effete, overrefined Heian period ended, and the power fell into the hands of the military caste, Bugaku froze into museumlike perfection. The military adopted a new theatrical form, but one with roots deep in the past, the Nō. At first popular, with a variety-show format, the ancestors of Nō, Dengaku and Sarugaku, slowly developed a more dramatic center, lost their circuslike elements, and gradually became more noble, dignified and inner-turned. Finally by the late seventeenth or eighteenth centuries the Nō too had become a museumlike entertainment, or rather a ceremony: slower and more studied than in its brilliant period of development in the thirteenth and fourteenth centuries. The vicissitudes of this history and the particulars of performance style are outlined in numerous fine studies, for Nō is one of the supreme achievements of the Japanese, both for its texts and for the profundity of its performing style. Most books devoted to Nō, however, have little to say regarding details of movement, and texts in English are often published in a format which suggests that Nō exists to be read rather than to be experienced in the theatre.

Nakamura Yasuo's Noh: The Classical Theater adds a little to our understanding of Nō movement, but its major contribution is through its dazzling array of photographs. The major introduction to Nō in English is Donald Keene's Nō: The Classical Theater of Japan, which has almost 200 pages of photographs. Among these are details of movement, walking styles, and gestures in Nō and Kyōgen, accompanied by ample explanations. Other series of pictures illustrate a complete program of Nō and Kyōgen.

While the Keene volume offers the best introductory text, there is a recent work which studies with discipline and precision the performing techniques of Nō: Nō as Performance: An Analysis of the Kuse Scene of 'Yamamba' by Monica Bethe and Karen Brazell. The kuse is normally the central scene of a Nō play, in which the major preoccupation of the main character (shite) is presented through dance and song. Bethe and Brazell for the first time in English have undertaken to analyze every aspect of this scene in Yamamba, presenting separate studies of each element, and finally putting them together in a "scenario" showing how all work together to achieve the total meaning of the scene. Nō as Performance is an immense contribution to our understanding of the Nō experience, and will hopefully lead to other studies, both more general and equally as precise. Two videotapes are available to accompany this book (see Audiovisual listings), making the set, without a doubt, the most valuable instructional work in English available to the would-be performer of any of Japan's theatrical arts.

While collections of plays normally consist chiefly of a text, several of the Nō collections give added information which helps us to visualize the performance. The Noh Drama: Ten Plays From the Japanese has an excellent Introduction, some stage directions, and--best of all--contains tiny line drawings of the stances taken by actors at important moments of the play. This volume was originally published in 1955, but has been reprinted. Unfortunately, two other volumes in the same series have not been republished and are difficult to find.

Two recent volumes are the first in a new series, The Noh by Shimazaki Chifumi, publishing Nō plays of each category in volumes together. Volumes I and III have so far appeared, the first featuring god plays and the other, woman plays. They are notable for their thorough and lucid Introductions which treat painstakingly the question of movement, dance, and gesture in Nō.

A great step forward in the translation of Nō texts is taken in Royall Tyler's two volumes, each containing four or five Kyōgen and eight or nine Nō plays: Pining Wind: A Cycle of Nō Plays and Granny Mountains: A Second Cycle of Nō Plays. Instead of attempting to make a beautiful literary work easily comprehensible to the English-language reader, Tyler remains as faithful as possible to the ambiguities and vagueness of the Japanese, thus allowing us to experience something similar to that of the original text. Normally translators make choices for the reader, taking one of a number of possible meanings, whereas in Japanese the text most often possesses the polyvalence of a Symbolist text. The reader interested in studying the differences in the two approaches might well read the beautiful version of Yashima in the skillfully executed volume by Makoto Ueda, The Old Pine Tree and Other Noh Plays (University of Nebraska Press, 1962), then compare it with Tyler's close translation.

Tyler includes all stage directions, with a glossary of movement terminology, and indicates the various subdivisions of the text and the vocal modes used in chanting or singing. These enlightened and enlightening translations open up many new possibilities and perspectives to the reader who can only approach Nō through English.

Among articles, there are two of particular interest. Carl Wolz's "The Spirit of Zen in Noh Dance" in Dance Research Annual, goes to the heart of Nō movement by discussing its spiritual basis, and how such spirit is translated into minimal gestural language. Mark J. Nearman, in two brilliant translations and interpretations of the treatises of Zeami has made a breakthrough in Nō theory equivalent to those of Tyler in Nō texts and Bethe and Brazel in Nō performance techniques. In "Zeami's Kyūi: A Pedagogical Guide for Teachers of Acting," (Monumenta Nipponica, Autumn 1978) and "Kyakuraika: Zeami's Final Legacy for the Master Actor,"

(Monumenta Nipponica, Summer 1980), Nearman brings meticulous scholarly understanding of the Japanese language to bear on these supremely important texts discussing the artistic training and levels of attainment of the Nō actor. But Nearman brings much more to his task: artistic sensibility, spiritual and psychological understanding, and thorough grounding in theatrical practice. This all adds up to a dazzling presentation of insights never yet suspected into the works of Zeami, and a meaningfulness for modern western actors which reaffirms the universality of Zeami's vision.

3. Kabuki

From the end of the seventeenth century until the end of the nineteenth century, the popular theatre, Kabuki, so dominated Japanese drama that when people said "play" or "shibai," they were referring to Kabuki. Since the end of the Second World War, when Kabuki troupes began to visit the West more frequently than before, and Westerners began to see performances in Japan, this highly theatrical drama has become increasingly better known in the West. A number of books present an overview of Kabuki. Generally considered the finest treatment of the subject in English is Earle Ernst's The Kabuki Theatre. Written from a broad background of world theatre, and with a deep knowledge of Kabuki, descriptive and analytic. Pages 165 to 180 deal in particular with movement. Ernst traces the history of Kabuki dance, its various components and styles. His brief treatment of mie is perceptive and illuminating, stressing the balance, self-containment and dynamic tension of this focal moment in Kabuki performance. It is in these pages, too, that Ernst succinctly points out that rhythm and design "are the essential qualities of Kabuki movement." Although there is no detailed study of specific movements, beyond a brief description of a number of mie, Ernst's discussion goes beneath the surface to discover the principles at work in this most visual of theatre forms.

Ernst's book was first published in 1956. Predating it by four years was Faubion Bowers' Japanese Theatre, which, despite its title, deals mostly with Kabuki. Introductory chapters treat Nō and other forms preceding Kabuki, and the book might well serve as a general introduction to Japanese theatre by a writer who knows Japan intimately and lived there even before the Second World War. A few factual errors are offset by the lively, highly readable style and a wealth of information, including brief translations of some pieces as yet unavailable in English. Mime, dance, and gesture are discussed in appropriate places, and related to the aesthetics of Kabuki.

A. C. Scott's The Kabuki Theatre of Japan offers another good introduction to Kabuki, including a short chapter on Nō, some discussion of the puppets, and a number of details on movement in Kabuki dance and in the nondance plays as well. Kabuki by

Hamamura Yonezo and others is more partial in its view. Rather than a panoramic look at Kabuki, this book offers several essays on various facets of the art. The authors stress the visual splendor of Kabuki, including the excitement generated by the stylized movement. Gunji Masakatsu's Kabuki is a rapid survey of Kabuki's history and performance techniques. Like the Keene volume on Nō in the same series, it contains almost two hundred pages of photographs, which are a rich source of understanding Kabuki's visual splendor, including poses characteristic of role types. Samuel Leiter's Kabuki Encyclopedia, in convenient alphabetical order, offers a listing of almost any term connected with Kabuki, including names of movement patterns and styles.

The Actors' Analects, translated and edited by Charles J. Dunn and Bunzo Torigoe is a translation of Yakusha Rongo (the original text is also included), a series of essays by Kabuki actors at the end of the seventeenth and in the early eighteenth centuries. It will help the reader grasp the historical importance of certain kinds of movement, and the attitudes toward dance, roppō exits, and other such techniques in this formative period of Kabuki.

The major study to date of movement in Kabuki is contained in a fascinating book which is the joint work of three outstanding American Kabuki scholars. Studies in Kabuki by James R. Brandon, William P. Malm and Donald H. Shively contains three enlightening essays on Kabuki acting, music and historical context. Brandon's contribution is important to our understanding of Kabuki patterns or kata, and this is indeed the title of his essay: "Form in Kabuki Acting." The well-organized chapter discusses kata as performance style, as specific techniques, and as individual interpretation. The student interested in understanding the details of Kabuki movement should turn to this work both for an introduction to the subject and for an elucidation of movement patterns which he has perhaps witnessed in performance or on film but not thoroughly understood.

Translations of Kabuki texts have become more sophisticated and useful in the last ten years or so. Even before that, A. C. Scott, as early as 1953, had published translations of two important plays with detailed descriptions of movements, enabling the reader to envision, at least to some degree, the performance of the play. Genyadana is a nineteenth-century kizewamono or "raw" domestic play featuring a handsome rake turned thief as its hero. Kanjinchō, often considered the finest of Kabuki plays, is derived from Nō and belongs to the famous collection of eighteen plays of the Ichikawa family, the Jūhachiban. Containing a good deal of dance, it depends heavily for its effects upon the movement.

In 1966 James R. Brandon brought out a second translation of Kanjinchō with even more thorough stage directions, since he made the translation with Tamako Niwa in view of an English language performance. Along with it his group performed The Zen

Substitute, a hilarious Kabuki adaptation of the Kyōgen piece,
Hanago. Kanjinchō and The Zen Substitute (published as Kabuki
Plays) set a new standard for translations of Kabuki, making it
clear that considerations of performance were equally important as
the words. Records of the music for these plays are available
from Samuel French, and the scripts indicate the music cue numbers. Although it is, of course, impossible to perform authentic
Kabuki movement without having studied for many years, the
Brandon scripts give sufficient detail so that an imaginative choreographer might approach the plays in a creative spirit and
achieve something artistically viable although very different from
the Kabuki presentation.

In his Kabuki: Five Classic Plays, Brandon again applies
his thorough understanding of Kabuki performance to his translations of five masterworks of the repertoire. He has clearly watched
these plays time and again in performance and on tape, recording
in minute detail the particulars of movement, music, set, and costumes. These are indeed acting scripts, and two portions, Narukami (Thundergod) and Sukeroku, are available from the American
Theatre Association Library in versions filmed or taped when Brandon produced them at the University of Hawaii. (See Audiovisual
listings.)

Samuel L. Leiter has made an outstanding contribution to the
study of Kabuki movement with his collection of plays entitled The
Art of Kabuki: Famous Plays in Performance. As the title indicates, the popular plays included here are approached as performance pieces, not as literary works. Leiter gives full production
notes in his texts, but the main contribution is contained in his
carefully researched introductions where he describes the movement
patterns (kata) for major moments in each play, and compares those
of one actor with another. Since there is a good deal more freedom in kata than many people realize, Leiter is able to bring under
discussion the attitudes of dozens of important actors throughout
Kabuki's history. In the case of Shunkan he documents meticulous-
ly performances by the unorthodox Zenshinza and compares them to
those by more traditional Kabuki troupes.

If the student desirous of understanding Kabuki movement
had time (or money) for only two books, he should without hesita-
tion turn immediately to Leiter's Art of Kabuki and Brandon's essay
in Studies in Kabuki. Brandon has recently developed his ideas
regarding performance of Kabuki in English in a paper published by
the College of Fine Arts at the University of California at Los Angeles: "Kabuki in English: Toward Authenticity," (Japanese Tradition: Search and Research). Leiter, too, has pursued his interest in Kabuki movement through a number of articles. "The Frozen
Moment: A Kabuki Technique" (Drama Survey) looks at the climac-
tic pose known as mie, featured in many kinds of Kabuki performances. "Keren: Spectacle and Trickery in Kabuki Acting"

(Educational Theatre Journal) describes some of the special trick effects used in Kabuki, including quick changes and flying.

Several articles by Leonard Pronko in Educational Theatre Journal contribute details on movement in Kabuki as well. In "Freedom and Tradition in the Kabuki Actor's Art," he points out the margin of liberty allowed the master actor in his approach to performance, particularly as it is demonstrated in movement patterns. "Learning Kabuki: The Training Program of the National Theatre of Japan" describes the disciplines studied by the young men accepted into the program initiated in 1970, and in which Pronko participated for fifteen months.

4. Bunraku

Almost concurrently with Kabuki, the puppet theatre now known as Bunraku was developing. During long years the influence of Bunraku was strongly felt in the Kabuki world, and at times Kabuki was imitated by the puppet operators as well. Doll movement, interesting in itself, is also therefore a major contribution to Kabuki movement patterns. (See Asian Puppet Theatre and Human Motion, by Mel Helstien.)

Dance

In the twentieth century, Kabuki and the world of Japanese dance have begun to go their separate ways. And yet Japanese dance, which is still called Kabuki dance, derives its performance style from Kabuki, along with almost its entire classic repertoire; and in the framework of a Kabuki performance one often sees the classic dances belonging to the repertoire of Nihonbuyō. Until the early twentieth century, the two were inseparable. Today dance is in large part, but by no means exclusively, a woman-dominated art, whereas Kabuki still is performed only by men. Studies on Japanese dance are rare, and none of them is thorough. Ashihara Eiryo's The Japanese Dance offers a good introduction, but it is short and some sections are sketchy or disorganized. It is packed with information, however, and is the best book on the subject in English. Gunji Masakatsu's Buyō: The Classical Dance is brief and desultory, although it touches on important aspects of history and aesthetics. The many color and black-and-white photographs, characteristic of the Weatherhill/Tankosha publications, are especially valuable.

Any student pursuing the subject of Kabuki movement or Kabuki dance should invest in the significant volume by Hanayagi Chiyo, Nihonbuyō No Kiso (Fundamentals of Kabuki Dance). There are plans for an English translation of this book which presents through photographs, drawings and text (in Japanese) the principles of movement, posture, and gesture used in Japanese dance and in Kabuki. The author, a distinguished dance teacher and performer in Tokyo, has devised exercises to be used in the study of fundamental movement, and these are available on records (see Audiovisual listings) with explanatory booklet (in Japanese).

Only a few articles deal with Kabuki dance movement, and then only incidentally. Frank Hoff's Song, Dance, Storytelling: Aspects of the Performing Arts in Japan has been mentioned above. About half the book deals with the dance that was performed by Okuni and her imitators in the earliest period of Kabuki's development. Hoff includes a translation of the collection of songs to which the performers danced. In his Introduction he studies a question that has fascinated him for many years, the relationship between words and movement. The same question is treated in Hoff's "Dance to Song in Japan," (Dance Research Journal) spanning the time from the earliest forms of dance in Japan up to Kabuki and the elegant dance of the Kyoto-Osaka region known as jiutamai.

A forthcoming volume of the Research Annual of the Congress on Research in Dance (CORD) under the general editorship of Betty True Jones, will include a number of papers on Asian dance forms. Three of them treat Kabuki dance at an early or late stage of its development. Yamaji Kozo's "Early Kabuki Dance" elaborates on the period when women were still allowed in Kabuki. Thomas R. H. Havens' "Freedom and the Woman in Contemporary Japanese Modern Dance" will give insights into what is happening with offshoots of Japanese dance or in reaction to it. Leonard Pronko's "Shinbuyō and Sosakubuyō: Tradition and Change in Japanese Dance," studies the revolution going on within the framework of classical dance.

Audiovisual Materials

The student interested in learning some fundamental Japanese movement cannot, of course, find models of such movement in books. Fortunately, there are audiovisual materials to help him in his studies, although they too can only take the novice a limited distance. There are endless records of Japanese theatre music, and actual recordings of plays, Nō, Kabuki and Bunraku. The only recording which is strictly pedagogic, however, is Hanayagi Chiyo's Nihonbuyō Kihon Renshū, issued by Japan Columbia Records along with a descriptive booklet in Japanese with instructions and line drawings. The exercises are an effective methodical system of studying the basic movement of Japanese dance, but they require a teacher, since they are intended for use under the guidance of a trained dancer.

Two of the Michigan State Asian Techniques videotapes feature A. C. Scott, author of a number of books on Chinese and Japanese traditional theatres. In "Asian Concepts of Stage Discipline and Western Actor Training," he relates Asian stage discipline to Western actor training, and draws on his own expertise in T'ai Chi Ch'uan. "Conversation with A. C. Scott," shows slides and film clips from his work with student actors and Asian performers, and reveals his own insights regarding the future of Asian performing arts in Western theatre.

More specifically Japanese are two tapes on Nō and three on Kabuki. "Acting Techniques of the Noh Theatre of Japan," features Akira Matsui, a Nō actor of the Kita School, in fundamental movement patterns from Nō, including gesture, fan usage, and variations for indicating role types. In "Noh, The Classical Theatre of Japan," he performs contrasting excerpts from Benkei on the Bridge and Lady Han. In the two tapes on "Kabuki Acting Techniques," Leonard Pronko demonstrates fundamental movement patterns for male and female roles in Kabuki (I), and vocal techniques used in Kabuki production (II) including a number of illustrations by Japanese actors. "Kabuki for Western Actors and Directors" presents Pronko's views on the application of Kabuki techniques to Western drama and a number of illustrations.

A more complete listing of films and tapes is given in the bibliography. Here it might be pointed out that the consulates general of Japan in a number of cities have available excellent introductory films on Nō, Kabuki, and the puppet theatre. Each is of a half-hour duration, in brilliant color, and contains effective explanations of a variety of scenes from major classics performed by artists of the highest rank. For those with a serious interest in the Nō drama, the two videotapes made under the direction of Bethe and Brazell (Cornell University), showing the second half of Yamamba and zeroing in on the kuse section of that play, are particularly enlightening.

Details of Kabuki productions are available in "Martial Arts of Kabuki from the National Theatre Institute of Japan," (Asia Society) and in the two (and hopefully, soon, more) films of James Brandon's productions of Kabuki in English at the University of Hawaii. Both Narukami and Sukeroku (Asian Theatre Film Library, University of Kansas) may be followed in Brandon's lively translations in Kabuki: Five Classic Plays.

Bibliographies

Brandon, James R. Asian Theatre: A Study Guide and Annotated
    Bibliography. American Theatre Association, 1980.
    Thirty-three densely packed pages are given to Japanese theatre in this very useful volume. Brandon gives a brief but carefully pointed outline of Japan's theatrical forms, then lists virtually every important book and article published on the subject. Each

is followed by a capsule description. After works on history, theory, and practice, he lists studies of each genre, collections of plays, reference works, and finally audiovisual materials. This volume is essential for anyone who wishes seriously to study Japanese theatre.

Pronko, Leonard C. Guide to Japanese Drama. Boston: G. K. Hall and Co., 1973.
A brief Introduction describes the development of Japan's rich theatrical forms. The bibliography lists some seventy-five works, divided by genre. Each is evaluated and described at some length. A new edition is under preparation, to include works published since 1973. A handy reference for the reader who wants to know what he will find where.

General Works on Japanese Theatre

Arnott, Peter D. The Theatres of Japan. London: Macmillan; New York: St. Martin's Press, 1969.

Inoura Yoshinobu and Toshio Kawatake. The Traditional Theatre of Japan. New York, Tokyo: Weatherhill/Tankosha, 1981.

1. Kagura, Folk Performances

Araki, James T. The Ballad-Drama of Medieval Japan. Berkeley and Los Angeles: University of California Press, 1964.

Hoff, Frank. Song, Dance, Storytelling: Aspects of the Perform-Arts in Japan. Cornell University East Asia Papers 15. Ithaca, NY: China-Japan Program, Cornell University, 1978.

Honda Yasuji. "Yamabushi kagura and bangaku: Performance in The Japanese Middle Ages and Contemporary Folk Performance," Frank Hoff, trans. Educational Theatre Journal, XXVI (May 1974), pp. 192-208.

King, Eleanor. Kagura. Sante Fe, NM: Gannon Press, 1980. Also published in Mime Mask and Marionette Journal, II, 2 (1980).

2. Bugaku

King, Eleanor. Bugaku. Sante Fe, NM: Gannon Press, 1980. Also published in Mime Mask and Marionette Journal, II, III, and IV (1980).
This volume is one chapter from King's lengthy treatment, The Way of Japanese Dance, which evokes in lively fashion the entire

range of dance in Japan, including the better-known forms like Nō, Kyōgen, Nihonbuyō, and Kabuki. It is to be hoped that the entire work will be published.

Wolz, Carl. Bugaku: Japanese Court Dance, with the Notation of Basic Movements and of 'Nasori.' Providence, RI: Asian Music Publications, 1971.

3. Nō

Bethe, Monica and Karen Brazell. Nō as Performance: An Analysis of the Kuse Scene of Yamamba. Cornell University East Asia Papers 16. Ithaca, NY: China-Japan Program, Cornell University, 1978.
  Two videotapes are available to use with this volume, one of the kuse, the other of the entire second part of Yamamba. (See Audiovisual listings.)

Keene, Donald. Nō: The Classical Theatre of Japan. Tokyo and Palo Alto, CA: Kodansha International, 1966.

Nakamura Yasuo. Noh: The Classical Theater. Don Kenny, trans. New York and Tokyo: Weatherhill/Tankosha, 1971.

Wolz, Carl. "The Spirit of Zen in Noh Dance," Dance Research Annual, VIII (CORD) (1977), pp. 55-64.

4. Nō Texts

Nippon Gakujutsu Shinkōkai. The Noh Drama: Ten Plays from the Japanese. Rutland, VT and Tokyo: Charles E. Tuttle Co., 1973 (Original edition, 1955).

Shimazaki Chifumi. The Noh, Vol. I "God Noh," Vol. III "Woman Noh" (Book One). Tokyo: Hinoki Shoten, 1972, 1976.

Tyler, Royall. Pining Wind: A Cycle of Nō Plays. Cornell University East Asia papers 17, and Granny Mountains: A Second Cycle of Nō Plays. Cornell University East Asia Papers 18. Ithaca, NY: China-Japan Program, Cornell University, 1978.

5. Kabuki

Brandon, James R. "Kabuki in English: Toward Authenticity." Japanese Tradition: Search and Research. 1981 Asian Performing Arts Summer Institute. Los Angeles: College of Fine Arts, University of California, 1981.

_____; William P. Malm; and Donald F. Shively. Studies in Kabuki: Its Acting, Music and Historical Context. Honolulu: University Press of Hawaii, 1978.

Bowers, Faubion. Japanese Theatre. Rutland, VT and Tokyo: Charles E. Tuttle Co., 1974. (Original edition, 1952)

Dunn, Charles J. and Bunzo Torigoe. The Actors' Analects. Tokyo: University of Tokyo Press, 1969.

Ernst, Earle. The Kabuki Theatre. Honolulu: The University Press of Hawaii, 1974. (Original edition, 1956)

Gunji Masakatsu. Kabuki. John Bester, trans. Tokyo and Palo Alto: Kodansha International, 1969. Photographs by Yoshida Chiaki.

Hamamura Yonezo; Sugawara Takashi; Kinoshita Junji; and Minami Hiroshi. Kabuki. Tokyo: Kenkyusha, 1956.

Leiter, Samuel L. "The Frozen Moment: A Kabuki Technique." Drama Survey, VI (Spring-Summer 1967), pp. 74-80.

_____. Kabuki Encyclopedia. Westport, CT: Greenwood Press, 1979.

_____. "Keren: Spectacle and Trickery in Kabuki Acting." Educational Theatre Journal, XXVIII (May 1976), pp. 175-188.

Pronko, Leonard C. "Freedom and Tradition in the Kabuki Actor's Art." Educational Theatre Journal, XXI (May 1969), pp. 139-146.

_____. "Learning Kabuki: The Training Program of the National Theatre of Japan." Educational Theatre Journal, XXIII (December 1, 1971), pp. 409-430.

Scott, A. C. The Kabuki Theatre of Japan. New York: Macmillan Co., 1966. (Original edition, 1955)

6. Kabuki Texts

Brandon, James R. Kabuki: Five Classic Plays. Cambridge: Harvard University Press, 1975.

_____ and Tamako Niwa. Kabuki Plays: Kanjinchō and The Zen Substitute. New York and Hollywood: Samuel French, 1966.

Leiter, Samuel L. The Art of Kabuki: Famous Plays in Performance. Berkeley and Los Angeles: University of California Press, 1979.

Scott, A. C. Genyadana, A Japanese Kabuki Play. Tokyo: Hokuseido Press, 1953. Kanjincho, A Kabuki Play. Tokyo: Hokuseido Press, 1953.

7. Bunraku

Adachi, Barbara. The Voices and Hands of Bunraku. Tokyo, New York and San Francisco: Kodansha International, 1978.

Keene, Donald. Bunraku: The Art of the Japanese Puppet Theatre. Tokyo and New York: Kodansha International, 1965.

8. Kabuki Dance--Nihonbuyō

Ashihara Eiryo, The Japanese Dance. Tokyo: Japan Travel Bureau, 1964.

Gunji Masakatsu. Buyō: The Classical Dance. Don Kenny, trans. Tokyo and New York: Weatherhill/Tankosha, 1967.

Hanayagi Chiyo. Nihonbuyō No Kiso (Fundamentals of Japanese Dance). Tokyo: Tokyo Shoseki, 1981. (Available from Kinokuniya Bookstore, Weller Street, Los Angeles, California.)

Hoff, Frank. "Dance to Song in Japan," Dance Research Journal, IC/1 (Fall/Winter 1976-77), pp. 1-15. (See also Frank Hoff's Song, Dance, Storytelling: Aspects of the Performing Arts in Japan, listed under Kagura.)

Jones, Betty True, ed. Research Annual, CORD (Conference on Research in Dance). Forthcoming.
This publication will include papers presented at the CORD/American Dance Guild meeting in Hawaii in 1978. Three of them contain material dealing specifically with Japanese dance movement: "Early Kabuki Dance" by Yamaji Kozō, "Freedom and the Woman in Contemporary Japanese Modern Dance," by Thomas R. H. Haven, and Leonard Pronko's "Shinbuyō and Sosakubuyō: Tradition and Change in Japanese Dance."

Audiovisual Materials

1. Kagura

"Edo Festival Music and Pantomime." 16mm. color film, 50 min. Asia Society.
Three dance pantomimes from Kagura repertoire.

2. Bugaku

"Bugaku: The Traditional Court, Temple and Shrine Dances from
    Japan." 3/4" videocassette, 30 min. Asia Society.

3. Nō

"Noh." 16mm. film, color, 30 min. Japanese Consulate.
    Excerpts from eight plays.

"The Style of the Classic Japanese Noh Theatre." 16mm. film,
    color, 17 min. IASTA.
    Demonstration of Nō movement by Kita Sadayo.

"Yamamba: The Kuse Scene." 3/4" video, color, 41 min. Cornell
    University.
    Kuse scene of Yamamba as discussed in text by Bethe and Bra-
zell.

"Yamamba: Act II." 3/4" video, color, 42 min. Cornell University.
    Performance in full costume of second part of Yamamba, with
Izumi Yoshi of Kanza school.

"Dance in Nō Theatre." 3/4" video, color. Announced, but not
    available as of end of 1981. Cornell University.

"Acting Techniques of the Noh Theatre of Japan." 3/4" U-matic
    video, 1/2" VHS 8310 or Betamax 1, color, 29 min. Michigan
    State University.
    Matsui Akira of Kita school of Nō demonstrates fundamentals of
movement.

"Noh, The Classical Theatre of Japan," 3/4" U-matic, 1/2" VHS
    8310 or Betamax 1 videocassettes, color, 29 min. Michigan
    State University.
    Matsui Akira of Kita school of Nō performs sections of Benkei on
the Bridge and Lady Han.

4. Kabuki

"Aspects of the Kabuki Theatre of Japan." 16 mm. film, color.
    15 min. IASTA.

"Kabuki." 16 mm. color film, 30 min. Japanese Consulate.
    An exciting selection of colorful scenes from major Kabuki plays
performed by top-ranking actors.

"Narukami: The Thundergod." 3/4" video, color, 2 hrs. Asian
    Theatre Film Library.

Performance in English of an important classic by students of the University of Hawaii.

"Sukeroku: Flower of Edo." 16 mm. film, color, 2 hrs. Asian
    Theatre Film Library.
Kabuki classic performed by students of the University of Hawaii.

"Martial Arts of Kabuki from the National Theatre Institute of
    Japan." 3/4" video, color, 30 min. Asia Society.
Demonstration of fighting techniques of Kabuki, including excerpts from two pieces.

"Kabuki Acting Techniques I: The Body," 3/4" U-matic, 1/2" VHS
    8310 or Betamax 1 video, color, 1 hr. Michigan State University.
Leonard Pronko demonstrates fundamental movement in Kabuki.

"Kabuki Acting Techniques II: The Voice." 3/4" U-matic, 1/2"
    VHS 8310 or Betamax 1, color, 29 min. Michigan State University.
Leonard Pronko explains filmed illustrations of vocal techniques, and demonstrates special effects.

"Kabuki for Western Actors and Directors." 3/4" U-matic, 1/2"
    VHS 8310 or Betamax 1, color, 40 min. Michigan State University.
Leonard Pronko outlines a multitude to ways Kabuki may be used in the West and illustrates with slides, films, and demonstrations from his own productions.

5. Kabuki Dance

"Chinese, Korean and Japanese Dance." 16 mm. color film, 30
    min. Asia Society.
Demonstration of dance patterns and excerpts, including some from Japanese classic dance performed by Hanayagi Suzushi.

"Saeko Ichinohe: Dance East and West." 3/4" video, color, 30
    min. Asia Society.
A comparison of Japanese and Western dance patterns by a well-known modern dancer; excerpts from her modern choreography influenced by Japanese dance.

Nihonbuyō Kihon Renshū (Fundamental Exercises in Japanese Dance).
    Japan Columbia Record CLS-5161-2. Available at Kinokuniya
    Bookstore, Weller Street, Los Angeles, California.
Hanayagi Chiyo's revolutionary systematic method of teaching fundamentals of Kabuki dance.

Chapter Fourteen

EAST ASIAN PERFORMANCE: CHINA

Alice Lo

The theater arts of China have never been popular in the
Western world and have drawn little attention from English-speaking
scholars. As a result, a relatively small amount of literature on
Chinese theater movement was produced until the beginning of the
last decade when China began to recover from the earth-shaking
Cultural Revolution and gradually opened her doors to the Western
world. It was only then that an increasing amount of literature on
Chinese theater movement was written in English by both westerners
and Chinese.

Selection for this bibliography is made to include English publications which deal with the Chinese theater history, stage conventions, dance movement, and performers. Publications which deal
solely with music and libretto are not included.

Classical Theater

The history of Chinese theater reaches back more than 2,000
years. Ancient records refer to performance of drama in religious
ceremonies and entertainment in the imperial courts as far back as
200 B.C. The most important imperial drama patron was Ming huang
(A.D. 712-56) of the T'ang dynasty (618-907), who established the
Pear Garden to train actors, actresses, and musicians. During the
Sung dynasty (960-1279) and Yuan dynasty (1280-1368), emerged
the northern style of drama called tsa-chu, and the southern style
called nan-hsi. The Ming dynasty (1368-1644) was a period of
flourishing diversification of regional drama. The kun-chu became
the most prominent and eventually developed into the Peking Opera
during the Ching dynasty (1644-1911). After the National Revolution liberated China from imperial rule in 1911, the classical theater
continued to flourish when the country was undergoing rapid modernization.

As standard works on the classical Chinese theater, A. C.
Scott's three descriptive studies and Cecilia Zung's Secrets of the

Chinese Drama have long been recognized. A. C. Scott, perhaps the most well-known Western writer on the Chinese classical theater, has contributed greatly in introducing Chinese theater to the Western world. His Introduction to the Chinese Theatre provides the novice with a general understanding of Chinese theater and its theatrical conventions as exemplified by twenty most popular plays. In The Classical Theatre of China he concentrates on the stage conventions, music, the actor and his roles, the technique of the actor, the plays, and the playhouse. Brief treatment is given to the history of the traditional theater and biographies of several famous actors. A glossary of technical terms is provided. An index is listed in English as well as in Chinese. His three-volume Traditional Chinese Plays published some ten years later is a descriptive analysis of acting techniques and costumes of two distinctive styles of the traditional Chinese theater: kun-chu and Peking Opera. Volume One includes translations of two plays of Peking Opera: The Butterfly Dream and Ssu Lang Visits His Mother, preceded by a short discussion of the stage conventions of this drama style. Volume Two introduces the drama style of kun-chu and its history and translates two of the most popular plays: Longing for Worldly Pleasures and Fifteen Strings of Cash. The third volume focuses on the comic actor in the Peking theater, the comic actor's technique, and includes translations of two plays: Picking Up the Jade Bracelet and A Girl Setting Out for Trial. An accomplished Peking Opera amateur actress, Cecilia Zung has written the best English explanatory guide to the performance of Chinese drama. This work explains the complex dance movements and symbolizations. The first part of her book provides the background information on Chinese theater conventions such as the architectural structure and function of the theater, costumes and stage properties, musical instruments, character types with face-painting illustrations, and a brief account of the history and development of the theater. The second part is the most detailed and thorough treatment of dance movement techniques in any English source. It describes the dance techniques of sleeve, hand, arm, foot, leg, waist, pheasant feather, and many symbolic actions. Part three provides classification and synopses of fifty plays. The 240 illustrations are most appropriate and reproduced in excellent quality. Terminology and play titles are given in English and Chinese. This book is well organized and very well written.

Four lesser known monographs are good introductions to classical Chinese theater history and stage conventions for a novice. Each monograph contains some unique features. Buss's Studies in the Chinese Drama discusses religious influences upon the Chinese drama. In Jack Chen's The Chinese Theatre, there is a discussion on Yanko--a folk dance style which greatly influenced the modern Chinese theater--a subject seldom dealt with in English sources. Halson's Peking Opera: A Short Guide introduces six different styles of Chinese opera besides Peking Opera. Eva Siao's photographic collection, Peking Opera: An Introduction Through Pictures, is an excellent visual introduction to Peking Opera, regardless of the sketchy and disorganized accompanying text. In addition to this introductory literature are two journal articles which appeared in the Ballet Today: "The Chinese Theatre" Part 1 (May 1953) and Part 2 (June 1953). The author's comparison of the Chinese theater and the European theater is most interesting. It is a pity that the intended series of articles stopped short at two issues.

The Chinese theater would be lifeless without its actors who are the core of the drama. The most celebrated of them all is the famous female impersonator Mei Lan-fang. A. C. Scott has written a detailed biography, Mei Lan-fang: Leader of the Pear Garden, studying the artist's family background, his theater training since childhood, his career against the confused social and political background of his time, his triumphant performing tours to Japan, the United States, and the Soviet Union, his contributions in revitalizing the Peking Opera tradition, and his effort in elevating actors to a higher social status. Mei Lan-fang's performing tour to the United States in 1930 was an historical event both for the American and Chinese theaters. His performances in San Francisco and Los Angeles were commemorated by a beautifully printed program titled The Pacific Coast Tour of Mei Lan-fang, in which his unique artistry was discussed and his dance skill described. The American dance world had high regard for this Chinese actor, singer, and dancer. In Dance Index (July 1942) is an article describing his dance technique and comparing the Chinese theater with the Western theater. Biographies of current opera actors and actresses can be found periodically in several Chinese journals published in English: China Pictorial, China Reconstructs, Chinese Literature, and People's China. One sample of them is "Sixty Years on the Stage" from China Reconstructs (November 1961). The seventy-five-year-old Peking Opera actor recounted his long career, started at the turn of this century. He described his performance and his physical and mental training to become an actor.

For readers who are interested in the historical aspects of the Chinese theater, Colin Mackerras' diligent research produces excellent materials. They provide insight into the social conditions and political environment of the Chinese societies from which the theater emerged and which the theatre reflects. The Rise of the Peking Opera, 1770-1870 and The Chinese Theatre in Modern Times: From 1840 to the Present Day are studies of the history of Peking Opera from its earliest time to the present Communist era. In the latter the author explores several opera styles in addition to the Peking Opera. More discussions on drama styles outside of Peking appeared in the Journal of Oriental Studies 9 (January 1971), "The Growth of the Chinese Regional Drama in the Ming and Ching." As always, his research is based largely on Chinese resources and his writings are scholarly and well documented. Bibliographic notes in his publications are valuable research guides for the serious student of Chinese theater. A History of Chinese Drama by William Dolby studies the history of Chinese drama from antiquity to the People's Republic. His extensive bibliography and list of Western language translations of Chinese dramas are invaluable research tools.

Yuan Drama--a theatrical form which flourished during the Mongol dynasty (1260-1368)--has scarcely been written about in English until the recent publication of two comprehensive works, The Golden Age of Chinese Drama: Yuan Tsa-chu and Chinese Theater in the Days of Kublai Khan. The former is a well-organized scholarly analysis drawing from Chinese, Japanese, and Western sources. It discusses the distinctive stage conventions of Yuan Drama: the four-act structure, musical system, character types, themes, and language. It is an important work. The latter is a thorough study resulting from James I. Crump's eighteen years of reading and writing on the subject, and his study in Japan, France, England, and Germany. The first half of his book deals with the historical background, the playwrights, the stages and theaters, the actors' art, and the background of the plays, and includes numerous excerpts translated from Chinese sources to il-lustrate his points. The second half includes the translation of three plays from the Chinese text Yuan-chu Hsuan (Taipei: Ching-wen, 1970): Li Kuei Carries Thorns, Rain on the Hsias-hsiang, and The Mo-ho-lo Doll. The touch of humor in the writing style of this exhaustive work helps to ease the "spasm" of reading it. All through the text, many commentaries which the author calls "di-gressions" are inserted. They break the main thrust of discussion but are important in explaining the author's arguments and his sources of research. To solve this problem, a pair of open and closed asterisks are inserted to indicate the beginning and ending of a "digression," so that the less-patient reader can skip over them and enjoy a smooth reading. A glossary lists more than 300 terms in Romanization and Chinese. The bibliographical entries in-clude sources in English and Chinese. This is a very important work and a masterpiece. For readers who do not wish to read through this large volume, the author's earlier articles can be con-sulted: "The Elements of Yuan Opera," Journal of Asian Studies 17/3 (1958) and "The Conventions and Craft of Yuan Drama," Journal of American Oriental Society 91/1 (1971).

Modern Theater

Since the collapse of the Ching dynasty in 1911, the new Re-public has undergone rapid modernization. During those years Peking Opera and regional dramas continued to flourish, along with experimental theatrical forms. At the same time a proletarian thea-ter movement was growing as the Communist revolution was gaining power. Many professional and countless amateur performing troupes made up of peasants, workers, and soldiers were organized. New dramas, songs, and dances were created, centering on proletarian revolutionary themes. Chairman Mao Tse-tung's Talks at the Yenan

Forum on Art and Literature set the direction for the theater development of the People's Republic.

The new theater movements are well surveyed by Howard Roger in Contemporary Chinese Theater, starting from the early years of this century to the 1970's. It explores various theatrical forms such as: Peking Operas, Spoken Plays (hua-chu), agitational sketches, variety shows, mobile theater, ballet, musicals, etc. Much attention is paid to the theater movements and the new theatrical productions of the Communist regime from 1949 through the Cultural Revolution to the present. Mackerras' The Chinese Theater in Modern Times: From 1840 to the Present Day studies the theaters inside and outside of Peking from the Republic to 1949 and the theater movement of the People's Republic. A chronological table, listing the parallel political events and events of the theater, is a tremendous help in organizing a clearer picture of the complicated theater movements. The uniquely Chinese Communist theater form--amateur theater, is discussed in his Amateur Theater in China 1949-1966. The Red Pear Garden contains three dramas: The White Snake and The Wild Boar Forest and Hai Jui Dismissed from Office. The first two dramas are modernized versions of the traditional Peking Opera, and the third is a new creation written by the then deputy mayor of Peking, Wu Han, based on Ming dynasty (A.D. 1368-1644) history. During the Cultural Revolution this once highly praised drama was banned with the accusation of using the Ming emperor to satirize Chairman Mao.

Peking Opera also underwent enormous reform to serve the People's Republic. Richard Yang, in his article, "The Reform of Peking Opera under the Communists," China Quarterly 11 (July-September 1962), discusses the many changes of Peking Opera which were based on the guiding principles of "pushing out the old, and producing the new."

Toward the mid-1960's the Maoist socialist leaders, seeing the revisionist middle-roaders were gaining political momentum, launched the Cultural Revolution to reeducate the nation. Classical dramas were reformed and new revolutionary dramas were created to serve this purpose. The translations of nine of those reformed dramas were collected in the Modern Drama from Communist China and most of them were revised since the end of the Cultural Revolution. Lois Snow's China on Stage: An American Actress in the People's Republic, plots the history of theater in China from the birth of Chinese Communism to the Cultural Revolution and explains the Maoist ideology in literature and art and the creation of model operas and ballet dramas. Included in full are libretti of three revolutionary operas: Taking Tiger Mountain by Strategy, Shachiapang, and The Red Lantern, and a ballet drama: The Red Detachment of Women with the author's comments on their political content, techniques, and style. A glossary of Peking Opera and ballet drama terminology are given with explanations. From the Chinese point

of view, an article from Chinese Literature, "How Our Revolution
Opera and Ballets Were Produced," briefly presents, in propaganda
overtones, the process of the production of the eight model theatri-
cal works. A more objective discussion of the model theatrical works
appears in H. Y. Li Mowry's Yan-pan Hsi, New Theater in China.
Peking Opera was reformed again to serve the Cultural Revolution.
Chiang Ching's (Mme. Mao Tse-tung) ideas "On the Revolution in
Peking Opera" were translated into English in Chinese Literature
(August 1967).

After almost ten years of political struggles, the Cultural
Revolution finally began dying down. Theater historian Colin
Mackerras examines the political ideology underlining the Chinese
theater movement after the Cultural Revolution in his article, "Chinese Opera after the Cultural Revolution (1970-72)" in China Quarterly (July-September 1973). He analyzes the main elements in the
theory of drama during the period of 1970-71. During the period
of 1972 continuing into 1973, he observes the Chinese theater showing increasing signs of similarity with the pre-Cultural Revolution
period.

From this period on, numerous new dramas not limited to
revolutionary themes are constantly being created. The most up-
to-date reports on new theatrical productions appear in China Pictorial, China Reconstructs, Chinese Literature, and People's China.

Dance

During the earlier time in Chinese history, dance was an independent artistic entity performed at tribal festivites, religious
rituals, court ceremonies, and as entertainment. During the Sung
dynasty (A.D. 960-1279) dance was incorporated with music into
operatic drama styles which were to become the dominant theatrical
form in China. Yuan drama and Peking Opera are two examples.
It was not until the 1940's that new dance forms, borrowing elements from traditional folk dance and previous theatrical styles,
emerged again as an independent art form.

What is dance? It is best defined by the most important
Chinese dancer and educator Tai Ai-lien in a short article, "The
Development of Chinese Dance," published in the Dancing Times
(March 1947). She also discussed the new directions of dance
movement in the 1940's which laid the foundation of the dance de-
velopments of today.

About the dance in the traditional theater, an American modern dancer, Sophia Delza, who had studied Peking Opera for several years in China, has analyzed in detail dance techniques in her
article, "The Art of Dance-action in the Classic Chinese Theatre,"
Dance Observer (November 1952). She also compared the philosophy

of Chinese dance with that of the American modern dance. Her article, "The Dance in the Chinese Theater," Journal of Aesthetics and Art Criticism (June 1958) is an expansion of the previous article. Here she gives a more comprehensive and detailed analysis of dance movement techniques in Peking Opera under the three categories which she has used in analyzing modern dance art: (1) Content-concept, (2) Body-behavior or Technique, (3) Arrangement-architecture. In her most current writing, "The Dance-arts in the People's Republic of China; the Contemporary Scene," Journal of Society for Asian Music (March 1974), she surveys the many different dance styles in the People's Republic after the Cultural Revolution: the traditional and new dances of the nationalities, new dances from city and country, dance-drama ballet, and the Peking Opera. This dancer-writer's own study of Chinese dance was written about in "Sophia Delza: American Modern Dancer Becomes Converted to Chinese Classical Dance," Dance Magazine (July 1954).

In classical theater, sleeve dance is an important and uniquely Chinese theatrical element. Gloria Strauss has pursued this subject in her monograph, The Art of the Sleeve in Chinese Dance, tracing its history back to antiquity. Much emphasis is given to the study of T'ang dynasty (A.D. 617-907) dance movement style and she traces its influence on the nineteenth-century operas. Her bibliography which includes works in English and other Western languages is a valuable research guide into the ancient history of dance movement through archeology, costumes, paintings, sculptures, rituals, and art history.

Ballet was brought into China in the early 1950's from the Soviet Union. "Ballet in Communist China," Dance Magazine (November 1967), gives a brief but thorough account of the first days of ballet in China and its development until the dawn of the Cultural Revolution. It introduces seven Chinese ballet works which incorporated Russian ballet technique and Chinese national and folk dances: Maid of the Sea, Magic Lotus Lantern, The Small Sword Society, Red Flag, The East Is Red, The White-haired Girl, and The Red Detachment of Women. A firsthand report on the Chinese ballet scene is found in Through the Bamboo Curtain by Beryl Grey, an English ballerina, who is the first Western ballerina to dance with the Chinese ballet company. Through this detailed travelogue of her three-week visit to China in 1964, one sees the birth and growth of the ballet theater in China, the ballet companies, schools, the dancers' training and life, their strength and weakness in ballet techniques. This book is a rare opportunity to see China at the period when her door was closed to the Western world. Dance scholar Gloria Strauss has written an excellent analysis on Chinese ballet, Dance and Ideology in China, Past and Present: A Study of Ballet in the People's Republic. She examines the relationship of dance and ideology through the history of China and finds "remarkable similarities ... between the Confucian rituals of the past and the ballet and spectacles of contemporary China," and

concludes that the basic link is the "notion that ideology should
command culture." With this conclusion she proceeds to analyze
why ballet, a genre evolved among the aristocrats of Europe, became the vehicle for the model revolutionary operas during the
Cultural Revolution. An excellent piece of analytical scholarship,
Strauss' book is logical, convincing, and well researched. The
dance manual of the ballet drama, Red Detachment of Women, published by the Foreign Languages Press in Peking, is a monumental
undertaking. It is a step-by-step instruction in a two-hour ballet
drama, accompanied by musical scores, drawings of dance gestures,
floor-movement plans, photographs of the performance, drawings of
dancer-characters, costumes, stage scenery and lighting instructions. It is a most interesting publication for dance notators and
choreographers. For the general dance reader, a much shorter
publication of less than ten pages, "Translated Excerpts of Chinese
Dance Notation," provides a glimpse of the dance notation of this
revolutionary ballet drama and that of the Ming dynasty (A.D. 1368-
1644) ritual dance. Frequent discussions of the current Chinese
dance scene and reports on new dance productions can be located
in the Chinese journals: China Pictorial, China Reconstructs, Chinese Literature, and People's China.

The Chinese population is 970,920,000, 94 percent of which is
made up by the Han people and the rest by fifty-five national minorities. From these national minorities stem a great variety of folk
dances and music which contribute to the richness of Chinese culture. Two articles from the January 1981 issue of China Pictorial
give a pictorial introduction of these national minorities and their
songs and dances. The two national minorities best represented in
songs and dances are introduced in articles from Chinese Literature,
"Tibetan Songs and Dances," (September 1978), and "Inner Mongolia
Dance and Music," (February 1979).

One particularly interesting Chinese folk-dance style is the
lion dance. Unfortunately not much has been written about it in
English. However, a few journal articles are available to provide
some general descriptions of lion dance techniques and its popularity among Chinese societies. "The Lion Dance," China Reconstructs
(December 1963) describes the different styles of lion dances and the
skills required to perform them. "Lion Dance," Chinese Literature
(July 1979) presents the history and the categories of the lion dance,
and reports on some new innovations. "On a Roof in Hong Kong,"
Dance Magazine (June 1967) reports on a lion dance practice session
on a roof of a refugees' housing settlement.

In Taiwan, dance and theater did not start to flourish until
the last decade. An open letter, "Al and I Spend a Year in Taiwan," in Dance Magazine (November 1967) reflects the barren field
of dance. Current dance and theater activities in Taiwan are frequently reported in the monthly bilingual (Chinese and English)
publication Sinorama. Most fascinating in the Taiwan dance scene

is that the oldest dance form and the newest modern dance coexist. The Confucian ceremonial dance, dating back more than 2,000 years has long been banned in mainland China, but is actively being practiced in Taiwan. "Honoring China's Greatest Sage," Sinorama (October 1978) describes vividly the process of a Confucian ceremonial dance ritual and its surroundings, and illustrates the ceremony and the Confucius temple with many colorful photographs. The origins and meaning of this ceremony are also discussed. A modern dance company, The Cloud Gate Dance Theater which was founded in 1973, is gaining international acclaim. Its repertoire of more than seventy dances integrates Chinese and Western dance techniques and philosophy. The October 1981 issue of Sinorama provides further discussion of the exciting dance group. In addition to ancient and modern dances are many tribal dances which are still being practiced in some villages. Madeline Kwok has surveyed and recorded sixty-two dances in twelve villages among the Paiwan Tribe, using Labanotation, film recording, interviewing, and participation. An abstract of her survey titled, "Dance and Cultural Identity Among the Paiwan Tribe of Pintung County, Taiwan," was published in the Dance Research Journal 3 (1978-79).

In Hong Kong, Cantonese Opera has long been the predominant theater art, but with the actors and actresses growing old and the young generation turning to Westernization, it has suffered severe decline in recent years. Replacing it is the increasing popularity of ballet, modern dance, and Chinese dance. Detailed information on Hong Kong theater activites is recorded in the publication commemorating The 6th Festival of Asian Arts held in Hong Kong in October 1981.

Martial Arts

The movement techniques from various styles of Chinese martial arts, especially T'ai Chi Ch'uan, have greatly influenced the dance movement in the classical theater and the new dance dramas. Some understanding of the Chinese martial arts enhances the understanding of the Chinese theater. For this reason selected publications on one of the martial arts, T'ai Chi Ch'uan, are included. Fundamentals of Tai Chi Chuan is the most comprehensive English text on the subject, written by a T'ai Chi Ch'uan authority and scholar in sociology and anthropology, Huang Wen-shan. It includes an in-depth discussion of T'ai Chi Ch'uan's history and philosophy, and its relation to science. The movement instructions teach the 108 forms of T'ai Chi Ch'uan, their application for self-defense, and the joint-hands operation. Extensive photo-illustrations help to clarify the instructions. Tai Chi Chuan; a Manual of Instruction, with step-by-step photo-illustrations, teaches the movement form of T'ai Chi Ch'uan without dealing with its philosophical contents. The American modern dancer Sophia Delza has written a manual of the Wu School of T'ai Chi Ch'uan, Body and Mind in

Harmony. Through her artistic and kinetic perception, she has absorbed, digested, and produced the most exacting movement instructions which are consciously analyzed by her personal aesthetic and psychological interpretations. Her discussion on the philosophical principles and movement characteristics of T'ai Chi Ch'uan provides valuable insight to the body movement of Chinese dance. For the less demanding dance readers, her earliest article, "Chinese Exercise-techniques: Kung Fu--Ancient Medical Gymnastics, Tai Chi Chuan--the Art of Gymnastic Movement," Dance Magazine (December 1953), presents a brief but comprehensive analysis of T'ai Chi Ch'uan, dealing with its shape and energy, and its physiological, emotional, intellectual, and psychological intent, and comparing it with modern dance.

Classical Theater

Bao Wenquing. "Guan Sushuang--Artist of Beijing." China Reconstructs, 29/7 (July 1980), pp. 72-77.

Buss, Kate. Studies in the Chinese Drama. Boston: The Four Seas Co., 1922.

Chen, Jack. The Chinese Theatre. New York: Roy Publishers, 1951, p. 63.

Crump, James Irving. Chinese Theater in the Days of Kublai Khan. Tucson, Arizona: University of Arizona Press, 1980.

_____. "The Conventions and Craft of Yuan Drama." Journal of American Oriental Society, 91/1 (1971), pp. 14-29.

_____. "The Elements of Yuan Opera." Journal of Asian Studies, 17/3 (1958), pp. 417-33.

Dolby, William. A History of Chinese Drama. New York: Harper & Row Publishers, Inc., 1976.

Fan Chih-lung. "Sixty Years on the Stage." China Reconstructs 10/11 (November 1961), pp. 40-42.

Halson, Elizabeth. Peking Opera: A Short Guide. Hong Kong: Oxford University Press, 1966.

Hawkes, David. "Reflections on Some Yuen Tsa-chu." Asia Major, 16 (1971), pp. 69-81.

_____. The Chinese in Modern Times: From 1840 to the Present Day. London: Thames and Hudson, 1975.

_____. "The Growth of the Chinese Regional Drama in the Ming and Ching." Journal of Oriental Studies, 9/1 (January 1971), pp. 58-91.

_____. The Rise of the Peking Opera 1770-1870: Social Aspects of the Theatre in Manchu China. London: Oxford University Press, 1972.

Mayor, Hyatt. "Mei Lan-fang." Dance Index, 1/7 (July 1942), pp. 107-9.

Moy, Ernest K., ed. The Pacific Coast Tour of Mei Lan-fang. San Francisco: The Pacific Chinese Dramatic Club, 1930.

Pratt, J. T. "The Chinese Theatre." (Part 1 and Part 2) Ballet Today 6/4 (May 1953), pp. 14-15; 6/5 (June 1953), pp. 10-11, 19.

Scott, Adolphe Clarence. The Classical Theatre of China. London: George Allen & Unwin, 1957.

_____. An Introduction to the Chinese Theatre. New York: Theatre Arts Books, 1958.

_____. Mei Lan-fang: Leader of the Pear Garden. Hong Kong: Hong Kong University Press, 1959.

_____. Traditional Chinese Plays. 3 vols. Madison: University of Wisconsin Press, 1967, 1969, 1975.

Shih Chung-wen. The Golden Age of Chinese Drama: Yuan tsa-chu. Princeton, N.J.: Princeton University Press, 1976.

Siao, Eva, and Rewi Alley. Peking Opera: An Introduction Through Pictures. Peking: New World Press, 1957.

Zung, Cecilia S. L. Secrets of the Chinese Drama, reprint ed. New York: Benjamin Blom, 1964; London: George G. Harrup Ltd., 1937.

Modern Theater

Chiang Ching. "On the Revolution in Peking Opera." Chinese Literature (August 1967), pp. 118-24.

Howard, Roger. Contemporary Chinese Theatre. Hong Kong: Heinemann, 1978.

Mackerras, Colin. Amateur Theatre in China 1949-1966. Canberra: Australian National University Press, 1973.

_____. "Chinese Opera After the Cultural Revolution (1970-72)" China Quarterly, 55 (July-September 1973), pp. 478-510.

Mao Tse-tung. Talks at the Yenan Forum on Art and Literature. Peking: Foreign Language Press, 1956.

Meserve, Walter J., and Ruth I. Meserve, eds. Modern Drama from Communist China. New York: New York University Press, 1970.

Mitchell, John D., ed. The Red Pear Garden: Three Great Dramas of Revolutionary China. Boston: David R. Godine, 1973.

Mowry, Hua-yuan Li. Yan-pan Hsi, New Theatre in China. Berkeley: University of California Press, 1973.

Snow, Lois Wheeler. China on Stage: An American Actress in the People's Republic. New York: Random House, 1972.

Wan Kung. "How Our Revolutionary Opera and Ballets were Produced." Chinese Literature (May-June 1977), pp. 66-72.

Yang, Richard F. S. "The Reform of Peking Opera Under the Communists." China Quarterly, 11 (July-September 1962), pp. 124-39.

Dance

"Anthropomorphic Dancing." China Pictorial (July 1981), pp. 32-33.

Chen Ta. "The Lion Dance." China Reconstructs, 12/12 (December 1963), pp. 35-36.

Chin Ming. "Popular National Dances Seen Again." China Reconstructs, 27/8 (August 1978), pp. 15-19.

"China's National Minorities." China Pictorial (January 1981), pp. 8-13.

Chung Shu-chih. "Tibetan Songs and Dances." Chinese Literature (September 1978), pp. 99-102.

"Dance of the People." China Reconstructs 4/10 (October 1955), pp. 15-7.

Delza, Sophia. "The Art of Dance-action in the Classic Chinese Theatre." Dance Observer, 19/9 (November 1952), pp. 148-50.

_____. "The Dance-arts in the People's Republic of China; the Contemporary Scene." Journal of Society for Asian Music (March 1974), pp. 28-39.

_____. "The Dance in the Chinese Theater." The Journal of Aesthetics and Art Criticism, 16/4 (June 1958), pp. 437-52.

"Festival in the Mountain." Sinorama (October 1980), pp. 58-67.

Festival of Asian Arts, the 6th. Hong Kong, October 15-31, 1981. Hong Kong: The Urban Council, 1981.

"For Cloud Gate, Tradition and Pioneers." Sinorama (October 1981), pp. 2-8.

Grey, Beryl. Through the Bamboo Curtain. New York: Reynal & Co., 1966.

"Honoring China's Greatest Sage." Sinorama (October 1978), pp. 20-7.

"A Hundred Flowers Bloom: Amateur Song and Dance Festival of China's National Minorities." China Reconstructs. Supp. (October 1965).

Kwok, Madline. "Dance and Cultural Identity Among the Paiwan Tribe of Pingtung County, Taiwan." Dance Research Journal, 2/1-2 (1978-79), pp. 35-40.

Lewis, Emery. "Sophia Delza: American Modern Dancer Becomes Converted to Chinese Classical Dance." Dance Magazine, (July 1954), pp. 36-7, 60.

Liu Enbo. "Sword-dance." Chinese Literature (November 1979), pp. 114-7.

Ouyang Yu-chien. "The Dance in China." People's China (July 1957), pp. 19-27.

Pierce, Suzanne. "Al and I Spend a Year in Taiwan." Dance Magazine (November 1967), pp. 47, 81-3.

Red Detachment of Women (Ballet). Peking: Foreign Languages Press, 1971-73.

Shu-chih, Chung. "Inner Mongolia Dance and Music." Chinese Literature (February 1979), pp. 114-117.

"The Sisters' Festival of the Miaos." China Pictorial (March 1981), pp. 81-3.

"Songs and Dances of National Minorities." China Pictorial (January 1981), pp. 1-5.

Strauss, Gloria B. The Art of the Sleeve in Chinese Dance. Dance

Perspective, no. 63. New York: Dance Perspectives Foundation, 1975.

_____. "Dance and Ideology in China. Past and Present: A Study of Ballet in the People's Republic." Dance Research Annual (Asian and Pacific Dance: Selected Papers from the 1979 CORD-SEM Conference) VIII (1977) pp. 19-53.

Sun Shengjun. "Village Songs and Dances." China Reconstructs, 29/11 (November 1980), pp. 46-8.

Sung Yang. "Proud Poplar, Yank Kai-hui's Story in Dance." China Reconstructs, 26/12 (December 1977), pp. 59-61.

Swift, Mary Grace. "Ballet in Communist China." Dance Magazine (November 1967), pp. 60-5.

Tai Ai-lien. "The Development of Chinese Dance." Dancing Times (March 1947), pp. 302-4.

"Tales of the Silk Roads--a Ballet." China Pictorial (February 1980), pp. 1-3.

Tan Aiqing. "The Oriental Song and Dance Ensemble." China Reconstructs, 28/5 (May 1979), pp. 60-5.

"Torch Festival of the Yi People." China Reconstructs, 28/9 (September 1976), pp. 62-5.

Tsui Chi. "Chinese Dancing." Dancing Times (February 1944), pp. 207-9.

"Ulan Muchir Troupes on the Grasslands." China Reconstructs, 27/12 (December 1978), pp. 48-9.

Wang Xi, and Liu Qingxia. "Along the Silk Road--Dance Drama." China Reconstructs, 29/3 (March 1980), pp. 24-9.

Wing, Camella, and Leung Yueh-wah, trans. "Translated Excerpts of Chinese Dance Notation, Instruction by Gloria B. Strauss." Dance Research Journal, 9/2 (Spring/Summer 1977), pp. 5-12.

Worth, Edith. "On a Roof in Hong Kong." Dance Magazine (June 1967), pp. 30-2.

Wu, Jimei. "Flying to the Moon." China Reconstructs, 29/12 (December 1980), pp. 21-5.

_____. "From Ballet to Folk Dance." China Reconstructs, 31/4 (April 1982), pp. 46-7.

Yang cheng-shih. "Tai Water Splash Festival." China Reconstructs, 27/11 (November 1978), pp. 18-21.

Yu, Hai-hai. "First Ballet Chinese Style." China Reconstructs, 7/5 (May 1958), pp. 10-2.

Zhang Shiling. "Lion Dance." Chinese Literature (July 1979), pp. 92-6.

Martial Arts

Delza, Sophia. Body and Mind in Harmony: Tai Chi Chuan, an Ancient Chinese Way of Exercise to Achieve Health and Tranquility. New York: Cornerstone Library, 1961.

_____. "Chinese Exercise--Techniques: Kung Fu--Ancient Medical Gymnastics, Tai Chi Chuan--the Art of Gymnastic Movement." Dance Observer, 20/10 (December 1953), pp. 6-8.

Huang Wen-shan. Fundamentals of Tai Chi Chuan. revised ed. Hong Kong: South Sky Book Co., 1973.

Lu Hui-ching. Tai Chi Chuan; a Manual of Instruction. New York: St. Martin's Press, 1973.

Audiovisual Material

Aspects of the Peking Opera. Color, 15 min. Produced and distributed by IASTA, New York.
Hu Hung-yen, star of the Peking Opera, demonstrates the style, movements and etiquette of China's classical theater. Miss Hu mimes the walking, sitting, flirting, weeping, and dancing of the hwa dan, or coquette role, her specialty. As a finale, she performs the ribbon dance, once the favorite of ancient emperors.

The Black Dragon Residence, Parts I and II. Part I, 60 min.; Part II, 90 min., color. Peking Opera in six scenes directed by Daniel S. P. Yang at the University of Hawaii, in 1972.
The production uses traditional costumes, makeup, properties, music, and movement patterns. Dialogues in English and arias in Chinese with English subtitles. Distributed by the Asian Theatre Film Lending Library, University of Kansas.

Chinese, Korean and Japanese Dance. Color, 28 min. Produced by the New York City Board of Education. Distributed by The Asia Society. 1965.
Demonstrates and interprets traditional Chinese, Korean, and Japanese dance steps and patterns.

Chinese Shadow Plays. Black and white, 30 min. Shadow plays as
performed by Master Chang Teh-ch'eng and his skin puppet
troupe from Taiwan. Available from the Asian Theatre Film
Lending Library, University of Kansas.

Martial Arts of Peking Opera. Black and white, 12 min. Produced
and distributed by IASTA, New York.
Shows the highly visual and acrobatic martial arts and sword
play of the traditional Peking Opera and is explained with detailed
English commentary.

A Night at the Peking Opera. Color, 18 min. Produced by Claude
Jaeger. Distributed by Film Images, Inc. France, 1957.
Selections from performances highlighting scenes of battle, dance,
and pantomime.

Tales of Silk Road. Color, 135 min. Produced by Pacific Audio &
Video Ltd. Distributed by Triocom Enterprises Ltd. Hong
Kong, 1980.
A dance-drama based on Duan-huang murals and Silk Road of
T'ang dynasty (A.D. 618-907), performed by the Gansu Song and
Dance Ensemble of the People's Republic of China. It combines
dance movements from Chinese classical dance, folk dance, and
ballet.

Chapter Fifteen

EAST ASIAN PERFORMANCE: KOREA

Oh-kon Cho

The exact origin of Korean theatre is lost in the history of the nation. Like the beginning of theatre in some countries, the source of Korean theatre may be found in some national ceremonies, folk, and shamanistic rituals.

Important civic observances, which might have included some elements of theatre, were held more than twenty centuries ago by some tribal states. Of these, the ch'ŏngun of Mahan (a tribal state which ruled the Korean peninsula roughly from the fourth century B.C. to the third century A.D.), the much'ŏn of Yae (another tribal state of the same period), and the yŏnggo of Puyŏ (a third state which was established much earlier and ended nearly in the same period) were the civic ceremonies of some importance which we think included participants who wore masks, sang, and danced in a style whose exact nature is still unknown.

It is possible that the forefathers of Korean theatre had their roots in the period of these early tribal states. But, unfortunately, it is quite impossible to recount with any certainty the early history of the theatrical activities from this period.

During the period of the Three Kingdoms (18 B.C.-935 A.D.), however, we find more historical documents although they are still extremely fragmentary. There were some important dance forms which employed masks in the performance in the Kingdom of Silla (57 B.C.-935 A.D.): the kŏmmu, the muaemu, and the ch'ŏyongmu, etc. The kŏmmu (or hwangchangmu) was a masked sword dance performed in honor of Hwangch'ang, a young warrior (hwarang) who was killed in battle. The Samguksagi (the history of the three kingdoms), written in 1185, contains some descriptions of this dance. According to another source, (the Samgukyusa, histories of the three kingdoms written in 1281 and 1283), the muaemu was a Buddhist ceremonial dance created by a famous monk, Wŏnhyo. The ch'ŏyongmu, a dance performed to chase away the spirits of disease, was also performed in the Silla period.

443

These masked dance-dramas of Silla were inherited by the
early Koryo dynasty (918-1392). In addition to these, some notable
national ceremonies of Koryo were the p'alkwanhoe, a ritual held in
midwinter to honor the spirits of heaven and earth, and the yŏndŭng-
hoe, a Buddhist service held on the first day of the lunar calendar.
The narae, a shamanistic rite, too, was performed in this period to
exorcise the animals by dance and conjuration, and with swords.
One more known drama of Koryŏ was the chohŭi, a spoken drama,
whose subject was mainly drawn from the lives of the heroic warriors who contributed to the founding of the dynasty.

During the Yi dynasty (1392-1910), theatre forms, four of
which we still have today, evolved and were performed for various
purposes. One category at least, was definitely influenced by shamanistic beliefs and rites, possibly having its origin in folk legends.
This theatre was a form of masked dance-drama performed as a part
of the program of a village festival called burakje. Of the many
examples of this type of play, the Hahoe pyŏlsin-kut is the most
well-known today. This play, which was customarily performed
every tenth year at the village of Hahoe, had several purposes:
the ensuring of prosperity, the relegation of evil spirits, and the
entertainment of the audience.

The masks, nine of which are still in existence, which are
employed for the performance of this drama are believed to be the
most refined among those of all other masked dance-dramas of Korea.
Some scholars have attempted to determine the origins of this folk
drama. Unfortunately, most of the documents which deal with this
subject are in Korean. For example, Song Sok-ha, in his Hanguk
minsokko (the study of Korean folk arts), written in 1957, briefly
discusses the pedigree of this drama. Yi Tu-hyŏn, another scholar
in the field, also talks about the mystery surrounding the origins
of this drama in his Hanguk kamyŏngŭk (Korean mask dance theatre) in 1973. However, there remains a great deal of mystery about
the beginning of this folk theatre.

The second category is made up of the various types of masked
dance-plays which are offshoots of sandaegŭk. This includes such
forms as: the pyŏlsandae, mainly in Yangju and Songp'a; the
t'alch'um, predominantly in Pongsan, Kangnyŏng, and Haeju; the
ogwangdae, chiefly in T'ongyŏng and Kosŏng; the yaryu, mostly in
Suyong and Tongrae. Today it is postulated that all of these forms
might have been developed by the itinerant performers who once
belonged to the sandae-togam (the Master of Revels), the office at
the Yi court which controlled the performers as well as the performances. Each regional theatre of this category has maintained
some of its uniqueness although the differences are never conspicuous. The same characters appear in different plays. All of them
employ dances of a similar pattern. The same themes are apparent
in almost all of them suggesting that their subject matter may have
been drawn from the same sources.

Until the end of World War II only a handful of research on these theatrical forms had been carried out. Since then, however, they have caught the attention as well as the interest of many scholars of folklore, literature, and theatre and, as a result, many more significant works have been printed. Regrettably, they are almost exclusively written in Korean. It is expected that Cho Oh-kon's new book, The Korean Traditional Theatre, will be published in English by UNESCO in 1984.

The third category is traditional puppet theatre which was performed by wayfaring professional players until just recently. Some historical documents suggest that the puppet theatre was already in existence as far back as in the Koryŏ period. The Namsatang players, who performed various types of entertainment, have been credited with the preservation of this theatre form as late as the end of World War II. Like the masked dance-drama, the puppet plays have common themes, that is, satirization of the privileged class such as the arrogant aristocrats, the corrupt Buddhist monks, and the nefarious officials. Choe Sang-su, in his The Study of Korean Puppet Plays, discusses and analyzes various aspects of this theatre. Cho Oh-kon's Korean Puppet Theatre: Kkoktu Kaksi (1979) is another notable publication on this subject.

The last important category is p'ansori, a form of single-man operatic theatre accompanied by a double barrel drum. In this theatre the singer performs all three theatrical elements: dialogue-narration, acting, and singing. The origins of p'ansori can be traced back to the early eighteenth century. Like the other theatrical forms, the p'ansori librettos, derived from well-known folk legends, had been preserved only orally until Sin Chae-hyo (1823-1884) began to document this theatre. Sin not only compiled the librettos in the now famous The Kwangdae-ka (the songs of kwangdae) but it is also believed that his work raised the status of this theatre and its performers. Unfortunately, not a single book on this subject in English is available except Kim U-ok's unpublished dissertation, P'ansori: An Indigenous Theatre of Korea (1980).

As we have noticed, the study of Korean theatre by English-speaking scholars has been limited resulting in the publication of only a few books. English translations of the folk and modern plays, too, have been few and far between. Recently, however, English translations of almost all folk plays have appeared in Korea Journal.

Kim, Tong-uk. "On P'ansori," Korea Journal, 13:3 (1973), pp. 10-17.
This short article begins with a brief history of kwangdae, the husbands of female shamans, whose sons often became the p'ansori performers. Kim also discusses the sources of p'ansori, the synopsis of nine librettos, and the plays. Then he adds that the songs

are more important than the plot itself which can be varied in the same p'ansori. According to the writer, Sin Chae-hyo, the first compiler of p'ansori, are the four important qualifications for kwangdae: beautiful voice, a talent for organizing the story, a talent for narration, and good-looking features. The article concluded with a few comments on some famous kwangdae. This is a good short article on the subject for the beginning student.

Song, Kyong-nin and Alan C. Heyman. "An Introduction to Korean Folk Dance," Korea Journal, 15:3 (1975), pp. 51-54.
The writers discuss the steps, expressiveness, and foot and arm movement of Korean dance.

Suh, Doo-soo. "Sandae-nori," Korea Journal, 10:11 (1970), pp. 13-16.
The article contains some basic information on the three forms of mask dance: ogwangdae, t'alch'um, and Yangju pyŏlsandae. If one were to point to the most notable aspect of this article, it lies in the comparative study of the three dance forms.

King, Eleanor. "Reflections on Korean Dance," Korea Journal, 17:8 1977, pp. 36-55.
In this refreshing article, King describes almost all forms of dance in Korea--from the court dance to the shaman's dance. It is written in a somewhat journalistic style, but no one would question that it is full of interesting information. The section on mask dance-drama is too brief to offer detailed information. Nevertheless, this is a good article on Korean dance.

Kim, Ch'on-hung and Alan C. Heyman. "Korean Traditional Dance," Korea Journal, 15:2 1975, pp. 51-55.
The two writers, who have often collaborated, briefly discuss the general aspects of the Chinju sword dance and the T'ongyŏng sungjŏn-mu. Regrettably, the writers do not make any connection between these dances and the dances which are employed in the performance of the folk plays.

Cho, Oh-kon. "Resistance Theatre and Motion Picture," Korea's Response to Japan: The Colonial Period 1910-1945. Kalamazoo, Michigan: The Center for Korean Studies, 1977, pp. 231-242.
This chapter deals mainly with the resistance theatre of Korea under and as a result of the Japanese occupation. The article begins with a brief discussion of the traditional theatre which was also used as a vehicle to express feelings of social injustice and oppression of the people in the old society. Then the writer proceeds to support his contention that the theatre between 1910 and 1945 was utilized as a tool of resistance against the occupying forces.

_____. "A Mask-dance Theatre of Northeastern Korea: Puckch'ŏng Lion Mask-dance Drama," Korea Journal, 21:12 (1981), pp. 45-48.

This article deals with one of the rarely performed folk theatre forms whose main purpose was to expel evil spirits and to insure the prosperity of the village. This pioneer article in English on the subject offers a good deal of information on this unique theatre which employs lion masks for the main characters in the performance.

_____. "Suyŏng Yaryu: A Mask-dance Theatre of Southwestern Korea," Korea Journal, 21:10 (1981), pp. 33-38.
This short article contains basic information on the folk theatre from the southeastern region of South Kyŏngsang Province. Included in the article are discussions of the theatre's origin, its masks, and the procession which preceded the performance of the masked play, the main feature of the program.

_____. "Ogwangdae: A Traditional Mask-dance Theatre of South Kyongsang Province," Korea Journal, 21:7 (1981), pp. 26-31.
An interesting and enlightening article on the southeastern folk theatre which was once popular in the region. The treatment of the origins of the theatre provides good background information. The rest of the discussion is also adequately prepared.

_____. "Yangju Pyŏlsandae: A Theatre of Traditional Korean Mask-dance Drama," Korea Journal, 21:4 (1981), pp. 27-34.
Like Cho's other article, "The Mask-dance Theatre from Hwanghae Province," this essay also contains a good deal of information. This well-organized article offers plenty of basic knowledge needed to understand this drama. The writer discusses almost all aspects of this theatre: the origins, players, stage, masks, dance, music, and play. Although the text is short, it goes a long way toward helping the reader in the comprehension of this folk theatre rarely introduced in the West.

_____. "The Mask-dance Theatre from Hwanghae Province," Korea Journal, 22:5 (1982), pp. 36-45.
The writer presents comprehensive information on almost every aspect of the folk theatre from this province, now in North Korea: the origins, history, performing company, players, stage, music, and play. As to the history of this theatre, the writer lists the possible origins and subsequent evolution which allegedly took place throughout its history. The portion on the discussion of the play is particularly convincing since he carefully supports his argument with historical events. This article may be one of the most succinct and comprehensive writings on the subject in a short form in the West.

_____. "The Traditional Korean Puppet Drama: A Mirror of Satire in the Feudal Society," Korea Journal, 20:10 (1980), pp. 4-13.
Cho takes the reader to the world of satire in two Korean puppet

plays. Especially, the use of the western definition of satire appears to fit neatly in the analyses of the plays. The writer attempts to show the reader that the inorganic structure and the disorderly, irrational view of the world contribute to the satiric nature of the play. He suggests that another important satiric element can be found in the use of extremely colloquial, antiliterary language which often startles the audience. In discussing the satiric elements, Cho enriches his subject by documenting with sociohistorical events.

Lee, Du-hyŏn. "Korean Masks and Mask-dance Drama," Korea Journal, 8:3 (1968), pp. 4-10.
As the title indicates, this article is mainly comprised of two parts: masks and mask dance-drama. The reader finds the first part far more interesting than the second. The definition of masks, the historical development of masks, the use of masks, and the information on various types of masks are well perceived. One also should not discount the writer's effort for the discussion on the historical influence on the development of the Korean masks. It is also interesting to note the writer's argument that the formation of the Korean mask drama can be attributed to the various forms of folk arts, the plays of ancient China, and miscellaneous plays of Korea.

Yoh, Suk-kee. "Traditional Korean Plays and Humor with Special Reference to Sandae," Korea Journal, 10:5 (1970), pp. 19-22.
This short article attracts the reader's attention mainly due to its approach to comic humor in the plays. A fairly large number of people have written about the Korean folk plays as being social dramas of satire, but not many have focused on their comic humor. The writer asserts that the truly important element of this theatre lies in comic humor created by "the extravagant fantasies and imagination of the common people" rather than in satire. The reader wishes that the article was longer so that it could include a further discussion on the subject.

Song, Bang-song. "Korean Kwangdae Musicians and Their Musical Tradition," Korea Journal, 14:9 (1974), pp. 12-29.
This article basically belongs to the field of Korean music. But the careful reader also finds some important study on the performers of the traditional theatre. The etymological discussion of the words for various entertainers such as kwangdae, chaein, shaman, and hwarang is enlightening. Also enlightening is the discussion that the various entertainers contributed to the development of the different types of entertainments. The study on the geneological development of entertainers throughout the history of Korea is valuable. Another noteworthy point is Song's attempt at the classification of kwandgae. According to him, kwangdae had a well-organized guild system. Thus the first-class performers, especially those of p'ansori, were often employed at the court, although most of the lesser ones could not enjoy such privileges. Song has succeeded

in drawing the drama student's attention to the study of musicians
who contributed to the field of theatre.

Chan, Amemiya. "Origins of Korean Mask Dance Drama," Korea
Journal, 17:1 (1977), pp. 57-64.
No one who is interested in the folk theatre of Korea should
overlook this short article. The essay begins with a concise discussion on the five types of primitive masks. In particular, the
discussion of the forefathers of mask dance-drama of the Three
Kingdoms period offers good introductory information. However,
the most enlightening aspect of this article may lie in the succinct
deliberation on the rise and fall of the sandae-togam, a govern-
mental agency which controlled theatrical performers of the Yi
dynasty. The two reasons for the abolishment of the agency which
the writer suggests are first, due to the depletion of the national
treasury; second, the change in court taste. This is an interesting article for the theatre student.

Ch'oe, Sang-su. "Mask Dance Charms Spirits, Ridicules Yangban
Class," Korea Journal, 3:2 (1963), pp. 11-13.
This three-page article consists of two parts: the classification
of mask plays and the principal themes of the Hahoe mask play.
The first part provides some information, but the second does not
go beyond a repetitive description of the synopses of these plays.

Ch'oe, Sun-u. "The Masks of Korea: The Case of Hahoe Masks,"
Korea Journal, 19:4 (1979), pp. 45-50.
This journalistic article offers basic information on the Korean
mask plays. The writer leads the reader to the contention that
the aesthetic quality of the Hahoe masks can be compared with
those of the Japanese Nō. The reader also finds a few more interesting as well as intriguing remarks. According to Ch'oe, the
mask frees the actor from any particular inhibition he is ordinarily
bound to by various cultural, social, and communal restrictions.
He goes further to say that once an actor puts on a mask and assumes the role, he quickly masters it. Although there are some
confusing points due to the inclusion of subjects which may be outside the topic, on the whole the article is informative.

_____. A Study of the Korean Puppet Play. Seoul: Korean
Folklore Studies Series, 1961.
Anyone who wishes to study the traditional Korean puppet theatre should not miss this book. Ch'oe, an eminent scholar, explores
almost every aspect of this theatre. The chapter on the origins of
the Korean puppet play is especially well documented. Another
chapter is devoted to an explanation of the beginning of the Korean
puppeteers who might have the same origins as those of China and
Japan. A brief section is also alloted to the explanation of the
etynological origin and meaning of the Korean puppet play. The
book is profusely documented with photographs of puppets, properties, and performance. Also included in the volume are the translations of two plays.

Lee, Du-hyŏn. "Korean Folk Play," Folk Culture in Korea (Korean Culture Series 4), Seoul: International Cultural Foundation, 1974, pp. 113-129, 139-148.

This article contains good introductory information on the Korean folk theatre in general. Not unlike many articles of this type, however, this essay, too, does not offer more than fundamental information. However, one interesting aspect of this article is that the writer attempts to draw the conclusion that there was some affinity between the Puckch'ong lion mask drama and the Japanese lion dance of the old days, presuming that the Japanese might have imported their art from Korea. Another interesting point is that the puppet theatre of Korea was imported from the Chinese continent.

Korean Center of ITI. The Korean Theatre Past and Present, 1981 (?).

This booklet was prepared for distribution to the delegates who attended the Fifth Third World Theatre Festival which was held in Seoul in March 1981. The publication, printed both in English and French, deals with almost every field of performing arts in Korea. Perhaps due to this fact, the chapter on masked dance plays and puppet drama does not go beyond the introductory stage which can be found in almost every book on Korean theatre. However, anyone who wants to have a quick overview of Korean theatre, both folk and modern, should choose this book at the present time.

Yoo, Chi-jin. "Report by Mr. Yoo Chi-jin," Proceedings of the International Symposium on the Theatre in the East and the West, Tokyo: Japanese National Commission for UNESCO, 1965, pp. 95-99.

This is a short report on the Korean theatre in general which was presented by Mr. Yoo at the International Symposium on Theatre in Tokyo. This article is too brief and lacks the in-depth study necessary to be seriously considered by a theatre student.

Korean Overseas Information Service, Ministry of Culture and Information. Masks of Korea. Seoul, 1981.

This is a booklet which apparently intended to give an overview of Korean masked dance-drama to the nonnative speaker whose speciality may lie in the theatre. The publication deals with eleven different types of folk theatre which employ masks for performance. The text on each theatre does not go beyond a brief description of titles of each act preceded by an almost equally condensed introduction. However, this compendium has some good points. That is, the rich and colorful photographic illustrations and the descriptions of the detailed dimensions of each mask. This is a good visual source book for introductory study.

Yoh, Suk-kee. "Korean Mask Plays," The Drama Review, 15:2 (1971), pp. 143-152.

Contrary to the title which suggests a broad content, the article mainly deals with the comic elements of two well-known mask dance-dramas--the Yangju pyŏlsandae and Pongsan T'alch'um. The major thrust of the essay is placed in the discussion of comic elements which, according to the writer, are derived mainly from the non-literary dialogue, awkward repetition, and comic gestures. This is a good article on the subject.

Korean National Commission for UNESCO. Traditional Performing Arts in Korea. Seoul, 1978.
The Korean National Commission for UNESCO has been credited with the publication of excellent books on Korean arts and culture. This is one of them. Included in the volume are not only the masked dance-dramas, but also other performing arts such as folk songs, farmers' music, and folk plays. This book provides good basic information on various masked dance-dramas in readable English. The abundant visually pleasing photographic illustrations furnish excellent visual materials.

Sim, Woo-Sung and Se-chung Kim. Introduction to Korean Folk Drama. Seoul: Korean Folk Theatre Troupe "Namsadang," 1970.
As the title suggests this is an introductory book on traditional Korean folk drama. The writers briefly introduce many aspects of ten different plays. Maybe due to limited space, the information appears to be sketchy. Although the organization of the book is less than desirable, a careful reader may find some useful information on the Korean folk dramas.

Cho, Oh-kon. Korean Puppet Theatre: Kkoktu Kaksi. East Lansing: Michigan State University/Asian Studies Center, 1979.
This is an introductory book on the traditional Korean puppet theatre. In the book, the author, who is a puppeteer himself, discusses many facets of this theatre: the origins, puppets, puppeteers, plays, etc. The translations of two plays by the author, which are included in the publication, are quite readable.

Hye-gu Lee. An Introduction to Korean Music and Dance. Seoul: Royal Asiatic Society Korea Branch, 1977.
This is a reissued version of an earlier publication, A History of Korean Music, obviously an erroneous title, by the Ministry of Culture and Information. This publication contains a good deal of information on Korean musical instruments and music, but less on dance, for the nonspecialist Western reader. Although the chapter on dance is brief, Lee describes six different forms of dance: court, folk, farmers', sword, priest, and drum dances. It is important to note that some of these dance forms, especially folk dance, are frequently employed in the production of various masked dance-dramas. The short annotations on the different types of dance are preceded by a concise introduction. This book provides good resource materials on Korean dance movements for the beginning student, but not for the serious scholar.

Audiovisual materials on Korean dance, music, and folk theatre are available from the Consulate General of Korea in major American cities.

In addition, The Asia Society Performing Arts Department, 726 Park Avenue, New York, N.Y. 10021, provides some films on these subjects upon request.

Chapter Sixteen

ASIAN MARTIAL ARTS AND PERFORMANCE

Phillip Zarrilli

No discussion of Asian movement or contemporary western performance training would be complete without at least an introduction to Asian martial arts and their relationship to both traditional forms of Asian performance as well as contemporary western concepts and techniques of training. This brief essay and the accompanying select bibliographical entries are limited to a few introductory sources in each of four main topical areas which essentially "introduce the field" of Asian martial arts and performance. It is beyond the scope of this work to attempt a comprehensive overview of the field. The four major topical areas covered in the following essay and entries include (1) an overview of the traditional historical relationship between Asian martial arts and performance; (2) sources for the study of the history and techniques of specific Asian martial techniques; (3) works covering philosophy, religion, spiritual and mental development, or cultural context of the martial arts; (4) and finally recent materials discussing the relationship between Asian martial arts and western performance.

Asian Martial Arts and Performance: An Overview

Combat systems and specific combat techniques have had a profound and lasting impact on the development of performance forms throughout human history. From simple decentralized tribal cultures to highly complex and politically centralized states, specific techniques of the hunt, or of battle have found their way into cultural performances enacted either by the warrior/soldiers themselves, or by performers who have transformed such techniques to fit an evolving aesthetic and performance style. In classical Greece the symbiotic relationship between martial training, dance, and performance is illustrated by both the pyrrhic and anapale. Plato described the pyrrhic as imitating

> the modes of avoiding blows and missiles by dropping or giving way, or springing aside, or rising up or falling down; also the opposite postures which are those of action

453

as, for example, the imitation of archery and the hurling of javelins, and of all sorts of blows. And, when the imitation is of brave bodies and souls, the action is direct and muscular, giving for the most part a straight movement of the limbs of the body.[1]

The pyrrhic was a part of the training of boys in Sparta from the age of five. Similar to the dramatic context where the chorus was trained at the expense of the choregus and performed as a part of the festival of Dionysus, at the Panathenaea competitions were held in the pyrrhic. While the pyrrhic was in essence a performance also serving as preparation for armed combat, the anapale, practiced at the gymnopaedia in Sparta, was a nude dance for boys "moving gracefully to the music of flute and lyre, displayed, postures and movements used in wrestling and boxing."[2]

The Greek example is but one of many of the close historical connection between festivals, performances, and combat techniques and systems of warfare. In extant western forms of performance, such as the English Morris dance, it is often difficult to discover the precise history and origin of the combat techniques. The legacy of the integral relationship between combat arts and cultural performance are clearer in Asian cultures. Through the centuries specific martial traditions in every Asian cultural area have spawned and/or been integrated within emerging forms of performance. Principles and practices of ancient martial systems are often closely linked with the development of performance methods and techniques. Observing the prepossessed presence of the martial arts master is identical to witnessing a virtuoso display of the highly skilled Asian classical performing artist. Asian cultural assumptions, principles, and techniques of physical and mental preparedness for combat and performance are often shared by both martial and performance systems.

The examples of specific historical linkage between martial systems, techniques, and performance genres are numerous. One of the most obvious historical connections is that in the traditional Chinese theatre which evolved its wu kung techniques employing both hand-to-hand fighting and manipulation of halberds, lances, and swords. Seen today in the spectacular acrobatic feats and mass stylized combat displays of the Peking stage, the process of accretion by which wu kung stage-combat techniques and choreography developed is presently lost in the maze of individual schools of Chinese martial traditions which found their way into the training and creation of choreography for the Chinese theatre. Without doubt, however, martial techniques and principles found their way into both the training as well as onstage combat choreography of traditional Chinese forms.

Likewise, the Kabuki theatre of Japan developed its tachima-wari or stylized fight-scene techniques. In kabuki the tateshi became the acting company's stage fight specialist responsible for combining various acrobatic moves, mie poses, and specific fighting techniques derived from the martial arts into Kabuki's exciting, fast-paced battle scenes. As with the traditional Chinese theatre, it is difficult to trace the exact development of specific stage fight techniques although most certainly the samurai sword techniques such as kenjutsu lie behind the development of Kabuki's stage combat.

A third of the many Asian examples of the close relationship between martial arts and performance is the Indian example. As early as the writing of the Natyasastra (between 200 B.C. and 200 A.D.), the link between martial techniques, performer training, and stage combat had been made. In the eleventh chapter of the encyclopaedic Natyasastra the performer is enjoined to prepare himself by taking

> exercise on the floor as well as high up in the air, and should have beforehand one's body massaged with the (seasamum) oil or with barley gruel. The floor is the proper place (lit. mother) for exercise. Hence one should resort to the floor, and stretching oneself over it one should take exercise.[3]

The neophyte receives further instructions to follow dietary restrictions as part of his training. This physical culture training was a traditional part of the Ayurvedic preventative health-care system, closely linked historically with the development and training of princes and members of the martial castes. In the same chapter the Natyasastra specifically describes the types of movements to be used onstage for "release of weapons," use of sword and shield in a variety of situations, and other weapons in the combat arsenal.

The legacy of this integral relationship between performer training, martial techniques, and stage combat in India is most vividly seen in Seraikella Chhau of Orissa, and Kathakali of Kerala. The basic techniques of Seraikella Chhau have been traced to the parikhanda system of exercise, a decidedly and obviously martial system traditionally used for the training of the warriors of Seraikella. While no separate extant practice of the martial system behind the parikhanda systems has yet been described in the literature, the kalarippayatt martial system of Kerala which influenced Kathakali is still practiced today, much as in the twelfth century when it evolved. In Kathakali the well-known preliminary rigorous physical culture system of exercise and massage was taken over directly from the martial practices of kalarippayatt. Both kalarippayatt and Kathakali exercises, when observed in person, are strikingly similar to the Natyasastra's description of exercise "on the floor as well as high up in the air," noted above.

These several brief descriptions of the close historical link

between Asian martial systems and performance genres could be
multiplied many times over. However, little has been written on
either the historical connections between combat and performance
systems or the comparative approach to and embodiment of techniques found in the martial and performing artist. Scattered references and brief descriptions are found in many of the major works
on individual forms of Asian performing arts. A. C. Scott, for example, in The Theatre in Asia (New York: Macmillan Publishing
Co., 1972, p. 16) notes in his introduction "on the Asian stage it
is often hard to draw the line where duel becomes pure dance and
performance in duel becomes combat." A few of the more specific
historical and descriptive studies of stage combat and/or dance
techniques and their martial legacy include two articles by Samuel
L. Leiter on Kabuki including, "Tachimawari: Stage Fighting in
the Kabuki Theatre," Monographs on Music, Dance, and Theater in
Asia (New York: The Asia Society, Vol. III, 1976); and "The Depiction of Violence on the Kabuki Stage," (Educational Theatre
Journal, 21, 2, 1969, pp. 147-155). In the Southeast Asia area
the most important studies include I Made Bandem's "The Baris
Dance," (Ethnomusicology, 19, 1975, 259ff; also in Dance in Af-
rica, Asia, and the Pacific: Selected Readings, edited by Judy
Van Zile. New York: MSS Info. Co., 1976), Mary Kathleen Foley,
"The Sundanese Wayang Golek: The Rod Puppet Theatre of West
Java," (Ph.D. diss., University of Hawaii, 1979, pp. 159-172 on
"Movement"); Max Harrell, "Penca, the Art of Self Defense, and
Topeng Babakan, Masked Dance, from Sunda, West Java," (Mono-
graphs on Music, Dance and Theatre in Asia, Vol. 4. New York:
Asia Society, 1977); Claire Holt, "Dance of Minangkabau: Notes by
Claire Holt," (Indonesia 14, 1972, pp. 73-88). For India a begin-
ning place is Rajeshwari Ghose's general article, "The Martial Element in the Dances of India," Festival of Asian Arts Souvenir Program (Hong Kong: 5th, 1980, pp. 125-127), but much more comprehensive in scope and coverage is Phillip Zarrilli's "From Martial
Art to Performance: Kalarippayatt and Performance in Kerala,
South India," in American Studies in Traditional Indian Theatre,
edited by Suresh Awasthi (Delhi: Vikas, in press). In this extensive chapter Zarrilli presents a detailed descriptive analysis of
the relationship between kalarippayatt and a wide variety of performing arts in Kerala including Kathakali dance-drama, the Christian folk-drama performances Cavittu Natakam, and numerous other
Kerala performing arts. Nearly all of the materials describing the
various forms of Chhau, and especially those covering Seraikella
Chhau, discuss the martial origins, exercises, and choreography of
the form. Kapila Vatsyayan in Traditions of Indian Folk Dance
(New Delhi: Indian Book Co., 1976) covers a wide range of folk-
dance forms from all regions of India and includes in her discussions descriptions of martial and hunting forms. These few sources
should provide a beginning place for the study of the historical relationship between combat arts and performance in Asia.

The Study of Specific Martial Arts

Since the American and western "discovery" of Asian martial arts in the 1940's, the first trickle of martial arts teachers in America and publications in English eventually turned to a flood in the 1960's when film stars like Bruce Lee popularized Asian martial arts. The number of forms currently taught in the United States, and the accompanying publications introducing and documenting specific forms is literally overwhelming. There are three main types of publications on specific martial arts and their history: (1) well-researched historical studies which include an introduction to specific techniques as a part of the history of forms; (2) manual books which document a specific form of martial art, or a specific set of techniques or style within one form; (3) and popular monthly martial arts magazines. What follows is a very limited selection and introduction to a few examples of each type of publication.

The best place to begin any study of the history and techniques of Asian martial arts is with the most comprehensive, sober, and authoritative overview of Asian martial arts, Comprehensive Asian Fighting Arts (Tokyo: Kodansha International, 1980. First published as Asian Fighting Arts, 1969), by two recognized experts in the field, Donn F. Draeger and Robert W. Smith. Draeger and Smith provide a straightforward historical overview of many of the major martial traditions from each cultural area of Asia. Specific techniques, schools, and great masters are described in this well-illustrated volume. A second general work of major importance is Pierre Huard and Ming Wong's Oriental Methods of Mental and Physical Fitness: The Complete Book of Meditation, Kineseitherapy and Martial Arts in China, India, and Japan (New York: Funk and Wagnalls, 1977). Huard and Wong place the martial arts in a wider context of Asian approaches to the body. Part I is a brief recapitulation of western concepts of the body and body care from classical Greek and Roman ideas and practices to the present. Parts II, III, and IV are devoted in turn to body care and body techniques in China, Japan, and India. While the Chinese and Japanese sections are carefully researched and balanced presentations of historical chronology, specific techniques, and undergirding religious principles governing attitudes toward the body, the final section on India is extremely brief and misleading in its almost total emphasis upon detachment and yoga. Other general "catalogues" or overviews of Asian martial arts do not offer the substantive scholarship and wide-ranging field work offered by either Draeger and Smith or Huard and Wong. Their differing approaches are complementary and will provide the neophyte with a solid basis for further reading.

While these are the most important and substantive general works, it is always important to be familiar with the full range of literature available. Typical of books for popular consumption, John Corcoran and Emil Farkas compiled The Complete Martial Arts Catalogue (New York: Simon and Schuster, 1977). Based on common questions about the martial arts, the catalogue addresses nearly everything in the contemporary world of the martial arts from "When did the first boom in the martial arts take place in America?" to questions about martial arts in television, movies, and the stars of the combat martial arts world.

When turning to studies of multiple forms within a culture area, again it is Donn Draeger's publications which set the standard for quality, accuracy, and sheer visual beauty in describing the martial forms of Japan. His three-volume series on the "Martial Arts and Ways of Japan," published by Weatherhill (New York and Tokyo) provide the most important and comprehensive total overview of the numerous Japanese martial arts placed in their historical and social contexts. The three volumes include Classical Bujutsu, Vol. I (1973), which surveys the classical combat forms of the Japanese warrior, his weapons, and their use; Classical Budo, Vol. II (1973) which tells the story of the Japanese "do" forms or "martial ways," concentrating on spiritual development; Modern Bujutsu and Budo, Vol. III (1974) traces the development of modern forms since the end of the feudal rule in 1868.

Little guidance can be given in this brief space through the maze of how-to manuals which have been written about specific martial techniques. No one can learn a martial art from a manual. They exist as documents which may be of some help to students of a particular teacher or a particular style of martial practice. In searching out information on particular forms, the best course of action is to begin with Draeger and Smith and Huard and Wong, and then to turn to specific manuals. Three major publishers in the martial arts business have produced a majority of the books in English: Kodansha International, Weatherhill, and Ohara. Contacting these companies for catalogues of current publications is one course of action. Kodansha and Weatherhill publications (which include those of Draeger and Smith) are well informed, well written, and well produced even when strictly focused on a specific martial form. Donn Draeger and Quinton Chamber's Javanese Silat (Tokyo: Kodansha, 1978) is an excellent example of such well-produced manuals which include a brief history of the form. Ohara Publications cover the widest spectrum of martial arts including everything from the soft T'ai Chi Ch'uan to the popular series of manuals, Bruce Lee's Fighting Method in four volumes, as well as specific books: Breaking, Kicking Techniques, Ninja (Vols. I and II), and Power Training.

Of the many martial forms of interest to the student of western performance, it may be of some help to provide a guide through suggested readings in three forms, one from each major Asian cultural area: the recently developed "gentle art" of Japanese aikido, the well-known and widely practiced "soft" form, Chinese T'ai Chi Ch'uan, and the little-known, highly physical and energetic Indian form, kalarippayatt. (Both aikido and T'ai Chi Ch'uan are covered in Comprehensive Asian Fighting Arts and Oriental Methods of Mental and Physical Fitness).

For aikido (the "way" of breathing and mental states), the basic principles and techniques of the form are best covered in Koichi Tohei's two books, Aikido in Daily Life (Tokyo: Rikugei Publishing House, 1973) and What is Aikido? (Tokyo: Rikugei Publishing House, 1962). These two introductory works can be supplemented by Robert Frager's "Aikido--A Japanese Approach to Self-Discovery and Mind-Body Harmony," (in Rediscovery of the Body, edited by Charles A. Garfield, New York: Dell Publishing Co., 1977) and Koichi Tohei's third volume, Book of Ki: Coordinating Mind and Body in Daily Life (Tokyo: Japan Publications, Inc., 1976). The final volume expands on the practical application of aikido principles and techniques to a variety of daily activities, emphasizing the implications for an individual's life style.

Of the many publications available on the Chinese T'ai Chi Ch'uan, the most comprehensive source is Wen-shan Huang's Fundamentals of T'ai Chi Ch'uan (Hong Kong: South Sky Book Company, 1973). Part I covers the history and philosophy of the form including its relationship to the I Ching, Confucianism, Taoism and Zen Buddhism. Part II includes methods and theories, covering fundamental postures, a summary of principles and methods, and an explanation of the extremely important breathing system. Part III includes a complete diagrammatic explanation of the basic forms of T'ai Chi Ch'uan, application to self-defense, and joint hands operation. Finally the volume concludes with some translations of T'ai Chi Ch'uan classics. In addition to Huang's text, students of western movement might look at the publications of Sophia Delza, a modern dancer who has studied the Wu style of T'ai Chi Ch'uan. Her publications have included her book-length T'ai Chi Ch'uan: Body and Mind in Harmony (North Canton, Ohio: Good News Publishing Co., 1961) and her later article, "T'ai Chi Ch'uan: The Integrated Exercise," (The Drama Review, 16, 1 1972, pp. 28-33).

The third form selected for this short review of available literature is the little-known kalarippayatt of Kerala, South India. While works like those of Draeger and Smith and Huard and Wong attempt to be "comprehensive" of "complete," forms like kalarippayatt are not included since they have only recently come to the attention of a wider public outside the indigenous culture of origin. Although sharing many of the same principles as many of the better known East Asian martial arts, this South Indian form is unique in its grounded fluidity of motion, gymnastic flexibility, and quickness of execution. Phillip Zarrilli has authored three introductory articles on the form including "Kalarippayatt, Martial Art of Kerala," (The Drama Review, 23, 2, 1979, pp. 113-124); "Kalarippayatt: The Combat Training of Ancient India," (Black Belt, 20, 1, 1982, pp. 56-59, 76-78); and "Kalarippayatt: The Sword and Shield of Ancient India," (Black Belt, 20, 8, 1982, pp. 40-44, 90, 92, 94, 96).

The most comprehensive history and documentation of the form is contained in Phillip Zarrilli's "Kalarippayatt and the Performing Artist East and West," (Ph.D. diss., University of Minnesota, 1978). E. H. Devi's "The Military System of Malabar," (Journal of Kerala Studies, 3, 1974, pp. 413-20) is an excellent overview of the medieval period when the kalarippayatt system was at the height of its prestige.

Popular martial arts trade magazines are just as numerous as books. The first martial arts magazine published was Black Belt magazine in 1961. Perhaps the most comprehensive and wide-ranging popular magazine in the field, Black Belt still has the largest national circulation, outdistancing some twenty rivals in the field. Magazines like Black Belt serve a broad-based public, and articles range from serious, well-written and knowledgeable articles on specific forms and their techniques to specious, over-exaggerated plaudits for individual stars or masters. Any reader needs to use his best judgement while wading through the martial arts magazine rack.

One six-times-yearly publication which deserves special mention is Hoplos, edited and published in Japan as a "Newsletter of the International Hoplological Research Center." The International Hoplological Research Center is under the direction of Donn F. Draeger. It is attempting to approach the study of weapons and combative systems in a systematic manner. Hoplos includes specific studies of weapons, specific forms of combat, and methods for the systematic study of martial and combat systems.

Religion, Philosophy, Spiritual/Mental Development, Cultural Context

A complete understanding of any Asian martial art is only gained through a study of the martial art in relation to its culture of origin. However, scholars from many disciplines have given little attention to the martial arts in the past. With the exception of a few earlier mediocre studies, the social sciences have given little, if any, attention to Asian martial arts until Jeffrey L. Dann's recent Ph.D. thesis, "Kendo in Japanese Martial Culture: Swordsmanship as Self-Cultivation," (University of Washington, 1978). This superb survey of the history and cultural significance of Kendo as an embodiment of Japanese modes of self-cultivation should serve as a model for future anthropological studies of Asian martial arts. Although the work presents no comprehensive or illustrated review of techniques of movement, the explanation of the significance of the body, including the central torso, eyes, feet, shoulders, hands, and face, is an outstanding explanation of Japanese cultural assumptions about the body. For the individual interested in martial arts in their cultural context and the place of kinesthetic analysis as one part of such studies, Dann's work is an excellent beginning place.

If the social sciences have given little attention to the martial arts, studies of religion and philosophy have consistently shown more interest in Asian physical and mental disciplines. In Japan, given the inseparable link between Zen Buddhism and Japanese culture and its arts, it is not surprising that the martial arts have been one of the major examples used to explain Zen. Daisetz Suzuki, Japan's foremost authority on Zen Buddhism, devotes two major chapters to the relationship between Zen and martial traditions in Zen and Japanese Culture (Princeton: Princeton University Press, 1959). Perhaps the most famous, popular, and influential publication on Zen and the martial arts is Eugen Herrigel's Zen in the Art of Archery (New York: Vintage Books, 1971. Originally published in 1953). Herrigel was a German philosopher who learned the Japanese art of archery (kyudo) in order to reach a better understanding of Zen. Herrigel's book is written from a personal point of view and is based on his own experience in learning archery.

In addition to serving as an insightful "insider's" view of the Japanese art of archery, Herrigel's personal account has popularly become something of an apologia on behalf of the spiritual benefits accruing to the practitioner of the martial arts. In essence, it has served as a model for a few more-recent general works which present the spiritual benefits of martial practice. Such works most often use a combination of art photographs; pithy, short quotations of sayings from martial art masters; and personal experience in the arts to convey their spiritual message. Two recent works of this type include Herman Kauz, The Martial Spirit (Woodstock, NY: Overlook Press, 1977) and Joe Hyams, Zen in the Martial Arts (Los Angeles: J. P. Tarcher, Inc., 1979).

Other important scholarly contributions in recent years have been translations of classic martial texts, mostly from Japan, which record the early thoughts of martial masters about their arts. The most important publications include Miyamoto Musashi's A Book of Five Rings (Translated by Victor Harris, Woodstock, NY: The Overlook Press, 1974), Zen and Confucius in the Art of Swordmanship: The Tengu-geijutsu-ron of Chozan Shissai (translated by Betty Fitzgerald, edited and with annotations by Reinhard Kammer. London: Routledge and Kegan Paul, 1978), and finally the Hagakure, The Book of the Samurai by Yamamoto Tsunetomo (translated by William S. Wilson, New York: Harper & Row, 1979). (Beyond the martial arts training place, these works have been extremely influential in guiding contemporary Japanese business practices, and in turn have become "must" readings for American business attempting to cut the Japanese competitive edge.)

Any attempt at a comprehensive understanding of the Asian martial arts must also include, as Huard and Wong have suggested in Oriental Methods of Physical and Spiritual Fitness, close attention to the process and phenomenon of centering and breathing.

All of the Asian martial arts in practice manifest the same centrality; physical movement emanating from a center in the "guts" below the navel. Likewise all systems of Asian martial arts employ important systems of breathing and breath control. In addition to the works on specific martial arts which discuss such techniques as they relate to the practice of a form, a number of publications have appeared on the center (hara in Japanese), breathing, and related body systems (most importantly, Indian yoga). A few introductory works in each of these important related areas include the following: on hara or the "vital center" see Haruo Yamaoka, Meditation Gut Enlightenment: The Way of Hara (San Francisco: Heian International Publ., Co., 1976), and Karlfried Graf von Durckheim, Hara: The Vital Centre of Man (London: Unwin, 1962). An introductory work on the Indian yoga system of breathing is Andre van Lysebeth, Pranayama, The Yoga of Breathing (London: Unwin, 1979). A solid general introduction to yoga is Ernest Wood, Yoga (Harmondsworth, Middlesex: Penguin, 1959) which should be followed by Mircea Eliade's classic work, Yoga: Immortality and Freedom (Princeton: Princeton University Press, 1958). For the individual interested in a manual of yoga techniques a good introduction is Swami Vishnudevananda's The Complete Illustrated Book of Yoga (New York: Bell Publishing Co., Inc., 1960).

Martial Arts and Western Performance

For the performing artist today, far more important than the historical connections between martial and performing arts is the practical use of martial principles, practices, and body/mind integration in training and/or performance. One of the most important developments in western performer training in the past twenty years has been an increased recognition of the importance of physical capabilities and discipline in training. Robert Benedetti noted,

> Freedom of conception for the actor must include free disposition of his weight. Karate, tumbling, T'ai Chi and the rest can liberate the actor by extending his range of choice. Imagine yourself onstage, knowing that you could, if you chose, leap into the air and flip over. This possibility so alters your range of choice that hosts of new possibilities, physical and spiritual, come into view. [Seeming, Being, and Becoming. New York: Drama Book Specialists Publishers, 1976, p. 93].

Benedetti is but one of many contemporary teachers, practitioners, and theorists who have rethought and redesigned training systems based on insights and techniques derived from or inspired by Asian martial, meditative, and medical arts. The consummate Asian martial and/or performing artist often stands before the westerner as a model virtuoso performer: self-possessed, egoless, in absolute control and command of his art, and able to infuse that art with absolute one-point concentration and focus.

The use of martial arts in western actor training began with the quiet work of such early innovators as A. C. Scott. In the course of his seventeen years at Wisconsin, Scott began to integrate T'ai Chi Ch'uan (which he had learned under a Chinese master in Hong Kong for a number of years) into his training of young western actors and as part of his work in establishing Wisconsin's Asian/Experimental Theatre Program. Others have followed the example of Scott and early innovators to the point where martial arts have been integrated into a number of actor training programs throughout the country.

In spite of the growing acceptance of martial arts in performer training today, little has been written about the specific function, use, and integration of martial techniques and principles into the western training process. One of the most significant early publications was Sophia Delza's "T'ai Chi Ch'uan: The Integrated Exercise," (The Drama Review, 16, 1, 1972, pp. 28-33). Delza's article was as important for the context in which it was published as for the substance of the article. Appearing in The Drama Review's 1972 special issue, "Acting: Some New Approaches," Delza's article appeared side by side with other innovative approaches to performer training in the early 1970's, including Lecoq techniques, Feldenkrais, circus, and several reflective articles on the processes of and approach to acting. Delza concentrated in her brief article on the calming influence of the practice of T'ai Chi Ch'uan which gives the actor an ability to "handle himself" and to become a "master of tranquility" (defined as "vigilant attention").

The most important and comprehensive work to appear is the recent publication, Martial Arts in Actor Training, edited by Phillip Zarrilli (New York: Drama Book Specialists Publishers, 1983). Zarrilli's Preface outlining the four basic methods of approaching martial arts in actor training is followed by Robert Benedetti's brief Foreword--a reflection on the continued place and importance of martial arts in the training of the contemporary performer. The volume opens with an Introduction by Richard Nichols which details nine ways in which the martial arts and performing interface, including, for example, "development of focused, intense concentration; staying in the moment, the 'here and now'; playing one action at a time; and unification of the mind and body." The substance of the book is given to four chapters focusing on five martial arts and their use in actor training. It is here that A. C. Scott unfolds in his chapter on T'ai Chi Ch'uan his early experience in the use of such martial techniques with western actors. Scott's chapter is followed by those on kalarippayatt (Phillip Zarrilli), kendo and iai-do (Richard Nichols), and aikido (Craig Turner). Each chapter briefly presents the history of the form, and then discusses techniques and exercises used in the context of actor training programs.

A few other significant articles have appeared on the convergence of Asian martial and related arts to performance. Linda

Conaway's "Image Idea, and Expression: T'ai Chi and Actor Training," (in Movement for the Actor, edited by Lucille Rubin, New
York: Drama Book Specialists Publishers, 1980) makes complimen-
tary reading to Scott's chapter in Martial Arts in Actor Training.
A brief glance at William H. Wegner's suggestive note, "The Creative Circle: Stanislavski and Yoga," (Educational Theatre Journal,
28, 1976, pp. 85-89) is worthwhile. Phillip Zarrilli's recent "Body
Work: Part I, The Physical Shape and Experience of Culture; Part
II, The Transmission and Transformation of Performance Knowledge,"
(New York: Wenner-Gren Foundation for Anthropological Research,
International Symposium on Theater and Ritual, 1982) explores the
process and implications for research of centering gained in his own
experience of studying the Indian kalarippayatt. (A series of articles chronicling the innovative work of A. C. Scott is due to appear
in the new Asian Theatre Journal).

A logical extension of the use of martial arts in actor training
is the use of Asian martial techniques in stage combat. Again, little has been written about the practical use of such techniques in
stage combat. One reason is obvious. Seldom are actual martial
techniques used in stage combat since learning live weapons techniques in which actual blows are delivered usually takes long-term
training. Some individuals teaching western stage combat have integrated into their teaching Asian martial exercises, principles, and
occasional techniques; but once again little has been written to explore this important area of cultural and technical interface. One
type of publication in which at least a glimpse is offered of the use
of Asian martial techniques in stage combat are production reviews.
Asian Theatre Bulletin contains a number of performance descriptions, especially of Kabuki productions, in which Kabuki's stylized
tachimawari have been used. Concerning the specific use of actual
martial techniques, Xerxes Mehta's "Notes From the Avant-Garde,"
(Theatre Journal, 31, 1, 1979, pp. 5-24) contains a review of Yoshi
and Company's production of Ame-Tsuchi (Japanese Mythological Exercises) in which the physical score and raw energy of the work was
directly derived from the company's study of kendo. More recently
Richard Schechner's Richard's Lear made use of the combat techniques of kalarippayatt for the battle scenes in his Shakespeare
adaptation (see "Richard Schechner's Richard's Lear," Phillip Zarrilli, The Drama Review, 25, 4, 1981, pp. 92-97).

Audiovisual Resources

A few important audiovisual resources exist in the field of
martial arts and performance. Three important resources document
specific techniques of martial forms incorporated into various performances. These include "Penca and Topeng Babakan from Sunda,
Indonesia," (Asia Society. 3/4" color videotape, 30 min.); "Martial
Arts of Kabuki from the National Theatre Institute of Japan," (Asia
Society, 3/4" color videotape, 30 min.); and "Martial Arts of Peking

Opera," (IASTA, 16 mm black-and-white film, 12 min.). Particularly important is the rare footage of Peking Opera training in the IASTA film taken on location in Taipei and including acrobatics, use of spears, set patterns of combat, and a variety of combination of weapons combat. "Martial Dances of Malabar" (a rare film available for viewing at the South Asia Center, University of Chicago, 16 mm black-and-white film, 21 min.) presents a romantic view of the Malabar coast of South India where kalarippayatt developed, but then shows some excellent footage of Velakali (sword and shield dance derived from the martial art) and of kalarippayatt itself including staff, spear, sword and shield, and empty hand combat.

In the area of interface between Asian martial arts and western performer training, Farley Richmond produced in his Michigan State series of videotapes, "Asian Acting Techniques for Western Actors and Directors," two sets of tapes featuring the use of martial arts in actor training. These include two tapes on the work of A. C. Scott ("Asian Concepts of Stage Discipline and Western Actor Training," and "Conversation with A. C. Scott"), and Phillip Zarrilli ("Kalarippayatt, Martial Art of India," and "Actor Training and Kalarippayatt, Martial Art of India").

Notes

1. Laws 7. 815 A.

2. Lillian B. Lawler. The Dance in Ancient Greece. Seattle: University of Washington, 1964, p. 108.

3. Manomohan Ghosh, ed. and tr. The Natyasastra Ascribed to Bharata-Muni. Calcutta: The Royal Asiatic Society of Bengal, 1950, Vol. I.

Chapter Seventeen

ASIAN PUPPET THEATRE AND HUMAN MOTION

Melvyn Helstien

> Abhinaya ... of the puppet master.... His shadowy form
> was perceptible in the darkness.... But it was only his
> hands which were really visible, his astonishing fingers
> manipulating the puppets and identified with their expres-
> sive life, of which indeed he was the source.... His art
> is abhinaya, like the mudras of the Hindu dancers.
>   Beryl de Zoete   The Other Mind

Though Heinrich Kleist had written of the movement of the
puppet as early as 1810 as reflecting the best in the art of the
dancer, and though Edward Gordon Craig proposed the ubermario-
nette as superior to the living actor in the early part of this century, western awareness of the puppet as an expressive force and
transformational device is only now beginning to make itself felt in
western theater. In Asia, the power of the puppet theater has
been acknowledged as an important though ephemeral art form for
centuries.

Unfortunately, there have been few discussions of the movement skills necessary to the puppeteer. Studies of the aesthetics
of the puppet theater have been principally confined to the design
of the figures. This is no doubt due to the fact that they are
more tangible than the manner in which the puppet artist speaks
for, or moves the puppet. In Asia the puppet performance only
exists when combined with dance movement, music, and voiced performance. But the ability to define the artistry of the puppeteer/
animator has rarely been considered. Part of my motivation for
what follows is to call attention to the dearth of such material.
Perhaps this will serve to inspire theater scholars to document performance techniques, using as a model the work of Roger Long,
Javanese Shadow Theatre: Movement and Characterization in
Ngayogyakarta Wayang Kulit.

Clearly the attention of scholars in the past has been focused
primarily on the way in which the Asian puppet reflected the "world

view" of the performers and their audiences. Scholars tended to be anthropologists, sociologists, folklorists or linguists. They did report on vocal, graphic, and plastic arts skills of the artists, but gave little attention to the techniques of performance. Improvisation and movement are mentioned as being complex, but the nitty-gritty of how the artist goes about acquiring these skills, how and why a movement is accomplished, are rarely examined.

Little has been written about the history of Asian forms of puppetry. This omission has to do with the transitory art of the puppet, with the fact that in most Asian locales the puppet is essentially a village entertainment, that comparatively few puppet plays have been written down or found their way into dramatic literature, and because history as we know it in the West does not conform to Asian ways of thinking. What we do know of the history of the puppet is derived from literary and epigraphical sources. Scholars have offered a variety of theories of puppet theater origins. In India, for example, Sanskrit scholars for two decades or more have debated Pischel's theory that India is the home of the puppet play. Other scholars of the theater arts have found mythology or folktales to support the existence of the puppet in India and China more than 2,000 years ago. But in Thailand, references to the puppet are much later, and Burmese scholars place the birth of puppetry as late as the eighteenth century.

While western historical research on Asian puppetry remains at times meager, in the mid-twentieth century there has been a marked revival of the practice of puppet theater, exemplified by the strength of excellent, sophisticated companies in many European countries both east and west, and the United States. There has been a growth of the teaching of the art in colleges and universities commensurate with that interest. Puppeteers and other western theater scholars have increasingly displayed an interest in Asian puppetry. Embracing as it does all of the arts of the theater --music, dance, acting, literature, production--puppetry has elements unique to its several different forms which bring insights to other modes of live production and means of production, in addition to its special attraction as a theatrical form all its own. However, traditional Asian puppet theater has rarely been seen by westerners. In the indigenous setting, performances tend to be in isolated villages rather than in population centers where other theater forms are often found.

The literature on Asian puppetry is diverse and vast. In China, Japan, and Indonesia, there has been scholarship as voluminous as that to be found on other theatrical forms, though less familiar to theater scholars. Much of this early published work in the first decades of the twentieth century was done by French, German, or Dutch scholars. But outside the continental European languages, a vast and comprehensive literature also exists in Indonesian on the wayang kulit (leather shadow puppet theater). An equally voluminous body of material delineates the graphic materials, the musical accompaniment, the relationship of this form of puppetry to the dance and other theatrical forms. A similar, though less comprehensive literature exists on the puppet theater of Bali. The data on other Indonesian islands is more sparse and tends to be less performance-oriented in nature.

Turning to the literature in English, it was only after the First World War with the renaissance of puppetry in Europe and America, that English and American investigators began to publish the results of their observations. They were goaded on by the American puppeteer and scholar Paul McPharlin.

In more recent years, four Asian areas have continued to elicit most interest: Java-Bali, China, Japan and Turkey. Lately India has also been the target of several scholars. Scholarship in English on the Chinese puppet theater has concentrated primarily on the operatic forms. But Chinese and European studies have focused on the leather shadow plays. These studies have concentrated on the literature, techniques of rendering the leather puppets, and the iconography of the figures. Little was known about other forms of Chinese puppetry until Russian puppeteer Sergei Obraztsov revealed such forms.

The major focus in Japanese puppet studies has been on the literary works of Chikamatsu and the relationship of that playwright to the joruriningyo plays known as "Bunraku." Much attention has been given to three areas: (1) the artistic value of the dolls; (2) their influence on the Kabuki theater when related to the dramas, and the movements and poses of Kabuki performance; and (3) the long period of training for the puppeteers. (However, in training studies in English, the manner in which the operators move the puppets is largely neglected.)

We know little about the Korean puppet theater except for two recent publications which generalize about the dramatic material, but have little data on the training or technical skills of the puppeteers.

References to the puppet theater in India have been generally confined to two particular genres: the Rajasthani string puppets, and the leather shadow figures of Andhra Pradesh. There has been little systematic study of either form, nor of the numerous other forms now known to exist. Some recent studies have been done by Friedrich Seltmann, Niels Roed Sorensen and Mel Helstien on the iconography, literary sources, and the making of the puppets. Seltmann's work is dense (see Stabpuppenspiel auf Java-Wayang Golek); Sorensen's is listed in the bibliography (see "Shadow Theatre in Andhra Pradesh"); my own has been only in the form of unpublished papers.

In other Southeast Asian countries, puppet theater is not as

well documented. Discursive references are to be found on the puppets of Burma, but no technical information. The puppet theater
of Thailand has been referred to in publications by the late Prince
Dhaninivat in the Journal of the Siam Society, with some efforts to
link the large Nang Yai figures to classical Thai dance (see Rutnin,
Mattani. The Siamese Theatre: A Collection of Reprints from the
Journal of the Siam Society). Cambodian puppetry, from the meager data available, appears to have been very exciting and in the
traditions of the Javanese-Thai-Malay orbit. But it is almost unknown in western literature. In Malaysia there has been an excellent study of the dramatic material drawn from the Ramayana, and
a discussion of the manner in which puppeteers acquire their expertise, by Amin Sweeney (see Malay Shadow Puppets: The Wayang
Siam of Kelantan), but he includes little on the manipulation skills
themselves. Most obscure is the information on the Vietnamese puppet theater. In recent years photographs have appeared in Vietnamese magazines, in World Theatre, and in a publication by Bharatiya
Natya Sangh, Puppet Theatre Around the World. The puppets of
the Middle East, save for Turkey, remain as obscure as ever insofar as accurate, current data on the types, the means of manipulation, the dramas, the acting skills required of the puppeteer.

There are also difficulties in the research process itself. If
one consults a library card catalogue under the heading "puppet,"
one soon discovers that there is precious little in English. There
are dozens of books on the construction of puppets and stages, in
what I categorize as "how-to" volumes, but little on the art. A
more sophisticated research approach recognizes that there are
many ways in which puppets are referenced. In English-speaking
countries the generic term "puppet" covers a minimum of four different types including rod, string, hand, and shadow. Generic
terms appear in other languages: "marionette" in France, "puppen"
in Germany, etc., with similar special terms for the four types
listed. In Indonesia, "ngruwat," "kekayon," "gunungan," "dalang,"
and the various specific forms of puppet theater known as "wayang"
("beber," "klitik," "kulit," "golek") all yield references. Folktales such as Amir Hamzah, Amor Singh Rathore, and the literary
epics Ramayana and Mahabharata will sometimes reveal data on the
puppet theater. In India, terms such as "tholu bommalatta," "to-
galu gombeyatta," and "thol pavai kuthu," refer to puppet types
in South India.

Indices of books dealing with various theater forms or histories of the theater also reveal a paucity of citations. And yet
Asian theater forms are so interrelated that materials on the puppet theaters reveal ties to the literature performed, the music and
instrumentation used in performances, and the movement patterns
of dance theater, derived from or adopted by puppeteers. It is
obvious that the Asian theater scholar needs to understand the
puppet theater.

Although the effect of puppet theater upon live theater and the interaction between the two has been discussed by scholars of both puppet and live theater, these revelations have had little influence on western interest or thought. This may be in part due to the difficulty in mastering the manipulation and language of any of the varied puppet forms. Westerners, until recently, have been deterred by the difficulties of the extensive training required to produce Asian theater. The dramatic works of the puppet theater are in most cases orally passed on from generation to generation. The western respect for the printed word has tended to ignore these dramas. The relative inaccessibility of the languages to westerners has contributed to the impression that these performing traditions are so exotic as to be incomprehensible.

But modern American Asian theater scholars have shown by their live productions that this need not be so. Through their influence artists are now beginning to find ways in which Asian theater techniques may be applied. From scholarly sources, and from field observation of puppet performances and the arts of the puppeteer, have come several general books which have surveyed Asian puppet theaters both in text and in photographs.

A number of important conferences on Asian puppet theater have been convened in the past fifteen years. Papers from some of these conferences have been published, but not all (see Osman, Traditional Drama and Music of Southeast Asia, and Sweeney, "An International Seminar on the Shadow Plays of Asia"). In most cases, these conferences reflect a growing interest in the puppet theater.

Still, the need for materials for theatrical producers and teachers in the classroom with respect to the puppet theater is great. Consciousness of the importance of bibliographic materials has given rise to some excellent bibliographies in the early part of this century. Unfortunately most of them tend to be rather old. A few new ones have appeared in the past ten years, but none concentrate specifically on Asian puppets.

The bibliography which follows has in common what can be gleaned of puppet movement. It is only very recently that theater scholars interested in the performing artist and the means by which such artists obtain results have begun to look at this most venerable art form as it affects audiences. This tendency should continue as new artists are being encouraged and trained to work in this medium.

Bibliographies

There are no bibliographies of the puppet theater which concentrate exclusively on Asia except for those found within the texts listed in the history, theory, practice section below. I know of no bibliography focused on the performance techniques of the puppeteer. I have included some of the most important more recent bibliographies in English in which I have attempted to delineate the number of references to Asian puppetry.

Baker, Blanche. Dramatic Bibliography. New York: Benjamin
    Blom, 1968, fifty-two puppet entries, reprinted, annotated.
    Thirty years of recent scholarship is missing, Some of the entries are still useful, however.

_____. Theatre and Allied Arts. New York: Benjamin Blom,
    1967, seventy-eight puppet entries, reprinted, annotated.
    Additions to puppet entries for an additional twenty years. As above.

Brandon, James R. "Asian Theatre: A Study Guide and Annotated Bibliography," Theatre Perspectives, No. 1. Washington,
    D.C.: American Theatre Association, 1980. 130+ puppet entries, annotated.
    The puppet entries are often useful, but the annotations sometimes miss important facts or appear to be unaware of more recent data.

Crothers, Frances J. The Puppeteer's Library Guide. Metuchen,
    N.J.: Scarecrow Press, 1971. Vol 1 (of a projected 6). 300 puppet entries.
    A very unreliable, though sometimes useful 237 pages of bibliography which is littered with gross errors and misspellings. It has a maddening organization and poor printing. The author's information on a given genre is frequently contradictory or buried in the mass of material.

Lewis, Elizabeth. The Rosalynde Stearn Puppet Collection.
    Montreal: McGill University Library, 1961. unpaged. Many unidentified Asian entries.
    A collection of more than 650 items from the private collection of a noted Canadian puppeteer and scholar.

Miller, George B., Jr., Janet S. Harris and William E. Hannaford,
    Jr. Puppetry Library. Westport, CT: Greenwood Press,
    1981. Fourteen puppet entries.
    A guide to the library of another former puppeteer and scholar, Marjorie Batchelder McPharlin. The annotations are minimal and of little use to one searching for specific information. Contains a section of books in the Cyrillic alphabet.

Pronko, Leonard C. Guide to Japanese Drama. Boston: G. K.
    Hall, 1973. Ten puppet entries, annotated.
    Pronko's enthusiastic and informative entries detail the usefulness of the materials he has chosen.

Richmond, Farley J. "Theatre in India," Journal of South Asian
    Literature. Triple issue, 10:2, 3, 4. East Lansing,
    Michigan: Asian Studies Center, 1975. Thirteen puppet en-
    tries.
    Briefly annotated. The issue also contains an article on the pup-
pets of Andhra Pradesh with passing data on the movement of these
figures, by Niels Roed Sorensen. (See below.)

History, Theory, and Practice

Asian Puppets: Wall of the World. Los Angeles: UCLA Museum of
    Cultural History, 1976. Reprinted 1979. Illustrated with
    black-and-white and color photographs, maps.
    An important general survey of Asian puppets, including essays
which contain historical data, discussions of puppet types, the variety of techniques for manipulation and vocal presentation, locales
in which the puppets are found, an appreciation of the social, ethical, and psychical aspects of the puppets. Covers India, Burma,
Java, Bali, Malaysia, Thailand, Cambodia, Sri Lanka, China, Korea,
Japan, and Vietnam.

Benegal, Som, ed. Puppet Theatre Around the World. New Delhi:
    Bharatya Natya Sangh, 1960. Illustrated with black-and-white
    and color photographs, drawings.
    Contains twelve summary articles on puppetry in India, China,
Turkey, Indonesia, Vietnam, Burma, Thailand, and Japan. Passing
references to movement and articulation techniques.

Buurman, Peter. Wayang Golek. Amsterdam: A. W. Sijthoff Alphen
    aan den Rijn, 1980. Illustrated with black-and-white and color
    photographs, drawings.
    Though in Dutch, this book, with its magnificent photographs,
drawings and charts, gives some sense of the movement and the
techniques of the dalang as manipulator, which supplements the
Foley dissertation below. As with the Seltmann volume below, a
major work, though inaccessible to those who read only English.
Remarkably, three important works on the wayang golek appeared
in 1979 and 1980, where there had been relatively little written
about them before.

Erda, Bettie. Shadow Images of Asia. New York: Katonah Gallery,
    1979. Illustrated with black-and-white photographs.
    Passing references to techniques of manipulation are to be found
in this catalog of puppets drawn from the collection of the American
Museum of Natural History.

Humphrey, Jo. Monkey King: A Celestial Heritage. Jamaica, NY:
    Chung-Cheng Art Gallery, St. John's University, 1980. Illus-
    trated with black-and-white photographs, map.
    One may glean some idea of the movement of the various and

wondrous forms of puppets illustrated in this catalog, drawn from a variety of collections in the United States.

Latshaw, George. Puppetry the Ultimate Disguise. New York:
    Richards Rosen Press, 1978. Illustrated with black-and-white
    photographs and drawings.
    In a straightforward manner, the author discusses the role of the puppeteer as actor-manipulator. There are excellent exercises which reveal the choreographic and interpretive complexities of the art in all its forms, and chapters explaining the construction and controls which further reveal how the movement of the puppet is accomplished. An excellent source of techniques.

Malkin, Michael R. Traditional and Folk Puppets of the World.
    Cranbury, NJ: A. S. Barnes, 1978. Illustrated with black-
    and-white and color photographs.
    Covers India, Sri Lanka, China, Indonesia, Japan, Korea, and Mainland Southeast Asia. Some discussion of the movement techniques in each of the areas discussed, though with little that would aid any save a practicing puppeteer.

Osman, Mohd. Taib, ed. Traditional Drama and Music of Southeast
    Asia. Kuala Lumpur: Dewan Bahasa dan Pustaka, 1974. Il-
    lustrated with drawings, music, and charts.
    Includes papers on Indonesia, Malaysia, Cambodia, Burma, Thailand, Philippines, and India, from the International Conference on Traditional Drama and Music of Southeast Asia, Kuala Lumpur, 1969. Movement techniques are referred to in passing in a number of the essays. References to various dance forms gives further clues to the manner of manipulation and movement.

Seltmann, Friedrich and Werner Gamper. Stabpuppenspiel auf Java-
    Wayang Golek. Zurich: W. Gamper, 1980. Illustrated with
    black-and-white and color photographs, drawings.
    This volume is in German, but the remarkably beautiful photographs and the diagrams offer insights into the Sundanese puppet theater form not accessible before now.

Spectacles d'Asie: Collection Kwok On. Paris: Bibliothéque Na-
    tionale, 1979. Illustrated with black-and-white photographs
    and drawings.
    Brief essays introduce the various forms in each country: India, Indonesia, China, Japan, Burma, Thailand, Malaysia, Cambodia, Turkey, and Greece. Passing references to manipulation. In French.

Sweeney, P. L. Amin, and Akira Goto. "An International Seminar
    on the Shadow Plays of Asia," East Asian Cultural Studies, 15,
    1-4 (March 1976).
    Includes papers presented at the seminar, which cover Malaysia, Indonesia, Thailand, Turkey, India, and Taiwan. Contains passing

references to manipulation techniques and the relationships of the puppet performances to dance and theatrical movement in the culture areas.

Tilakasiri, Jayadeva. <u>The Puppet Theatre of Asia</u>. Colombo: Department of Cultural Affairs, 1970. Illustrated with black-and-white and color photographs.
 Brief descriptions in a survey of puppetry in India, Sri Lanka (Ceylon), Indo-China, Indonesia, and Japan. China is not included. Later data make some references in this slim volume out of date. More information is now available on the Indian forms of puppetry.

Puppet Movement

With the single exception of Roger Long's work, there are no materials in English devoted to the explication of the art of the puppet manipulator. Found among the other documents which I have endeavored to explicate are the few written sources in English on the manipulation of the various forms of puppets.

1. Burma

Sein, Kenneth and Joseph A. Withey. <u>The Great Po Sein</u>. Bloomington: Indiana University Press, 1965. Illustrated with drawings by Ba Lone Lay.
 Chapter Two describes the puppet theater, remarks upon the movement of the puppets (marionettes) as the source of Burmese dance, and gives some conventions of the theater.

2. Cambodia

Brunet, Jacques. "Nang Sbek." Berlin: <u>Institut Internationale d'Etudes Comparatives de la Musique</u>, 1969. Illustrated with black-and-white and color photographs.
 This small pamphlet gives an excellent description (obtainable in French or German) of the manner in which these large figures are danced, comparing the movements to the Cambodian Royal Ballet. (<u>See also</u> Rutnin's work on the Thai <u>Nang Yai</u>.)

3. China

March, Benjamin. <u>Chinese Shadow-Figure Plays and Their Making</u>. Puppetry Imprints, Handbook 2. Detroit: Institute of the Arts, 1938. Illustrated with photographs and drawings.
 Provides technical information on the production and movement of the figures.

_____. "The Peiping Shadow Drama," Puppetry (1931), pp. 64-
71. Illustrated with black-and-white photographs.
A brief note on the way in which the figures are manipulated to
give movement characterization to the figures. Other types of movement and the uses for these specifics are given as well.

Obraztsov, Sergei Vladimirovich. The Chinese Puppet Theatre,
J. T. MacDermott, trans. London: Faber and Faber, 1961.
Illustrated with black-and-white photographs.
Discusses hand, rod, stick, marionette and shadow puppets. In-
formative insights, based on a trip to China, by a professional
Russian puppeteer. In passing, Obraztsov remarks on various
movement patterns as effected by the puppeteers and the relation-
ship of these movements to performers in the live theater.

Pimpaneau, Jacques. Das Poupées à l'Ombres. Paris: Université
Paris, 1977. Illustrated with black-and-white photographs,
drawings, prints.
Though in French, the illustrations give data on the many forms
of Chinese puppets. The text, for those conversant in the language, fills in many gaps in our knowledge of the techniques of
the puppeteers in the variety of forms of both shadow and three-
dimensional puppet forms.

4. India

Sorensen, Niels Roed. "Shadow Theatre in Andhra Pradesh,"
Sangeet Natak, 33 (July-September 1974), pp. 14-39. Illustrated with black-and-white photographs. Reprinted without
illustrations in Richmond, "Theatre in India."
Thoroughly describes the puppets, musical instruments and the
organization of a troupe. Contains brief hints of the movement of
the puppets.

5. Indonesia

Brandon, James R. Theatre in Southeast Asia. Cambridge: Harvard University Press, 1967. Illustrated with black-and-white
photographs.
It is intriguing to note that one of the longest lists of references
in the index of this noteworthy work is to the puppeteers and the
puppet theater. In a brief section, "Dance and the Puppet Theatre,"
there is a discussion of the interdependence of the movements of
the various forms of puppets and the dancers of Java, Thailand,
and Burma.

_____. On Thrones of Gold: Three Javanese Shadow Plays.
Cambridge: Harvard University Press, 1970. Illustrated with
black-and-white photographs.

In the excellent Introduction and Appendix C as well as the fine photographs accompanying the play texts, one derives a sense of the complexity and choreographic sophistication of the puppet movements of the Javanese wayang kulit.

Foley, Mary Kathleen. "The Sundanese 'Wayang Golek,'" Ph.D. diss., University of Hawaii, 1979. Illustrated with black-and-white photographs.

The West Javanese wooden rod-puppet theater is analyzed in terms of its social climate, performance techniques, repertory, and music. Chapter 6 contains a discussion of movement techniques and relates them to character types and scenes of action. In passing, mention is made of types of dances and their influence on the movement of puppets.

Long, Roger. Javanese Shadow Theatre: Movement and Characterization in Ngayogyakarta Wayang Kulit. Ann Arbor, MI: U.M.I. Research Press, 1982. Illustrated with black-and-white photographs, diagrams.

The movement patterns of Javanese wayang kulit vary from lyrical to gross in a complex, codified system which relates to the iconography of the individual puppet characters, the section of the play in which they are performed, the music accompanying the movements, the situation of the characters within the drama, and to some extent with the taste, skill and artistic development of the performer.

The author, using the system of Ngayogyakarta (Jogjakarta) and particularly of the Habirandha school, details the generalized types of movements of the range of characters from the most alus (refined) to the most kasar (crude) as well as those reserved for unique characters such as Ghatokacha and the comic punakawan. In splendidly explicit appendices he lists the battle movements by type and frequency of use for the range of characters which have previously been explained with great precision in the central work. He then delineates all of the movements used in thirty-two different prescribed battles.

The contribution to the understanding of the complexity of the art of wayang kulit, as found in Java, allows the reader, whether an aficionado or not, to follow the workings of this most sophisticated art form. For the expert it adds another dimension to the already layered complexity of wayang kulit and a further appreciation of the immense skill and knowledge of the dalang as artist.

6. Japan

Adachi, Barbara. The Voices and Hands of Bunraku. Introduction by Donald Keene. Tokyo, New York, San Francisco: Kodansha, 1978. Illustrated with black-and-white and color photographs.

An appreciation of the Bunraku which discusses the art of the puppeteer in relation to the movements and the training he receives. The book is beautifully illustrated with photographs both backstage and from the audience point of view which evoke the quality of the art and the artists involved.

Ando, Tsuruo. Bunraku, the Puppet Theatre. Don Kenny, trans. with an Introduction by Charles J. Dunn. New York: Walker/ Weatherhill, 1970. Illustrated with black-and-white and color photographs, drawings, paintings.

A general, largely historical viewpoint. Dunn's Introduction discusses the movement patterns of the puppeteer in a revealing if brief fashion, and the photographs offer many insights into the choreography and movement of the puppets.

Keene, Donald. Bunraku: The Art of the Japanese Puppet Theatre. Photographs by Kaneko Hiroshi, Introduction by Tanisaki Junichiro. Tokyo: Kodansha, 1965. Illustrated with superb black-and-white and color photographs, drawings and music.

Chapters 5 and 6 are devoted to a discussion of the arts of the puppeteer and techniques of moving the puppets. The carefully chosen illustrations further explicate the choreography involved when three puppeteers move the magnificently costumed puppets and show the kata (poses) which display the grace and beauty of line and posture of the dolls.

Scott, A. C. The Puppet Theatre of Japan. Rutland, VT: Tuttle, 1963. Illustrated with black-and-white photographs. Reprinted (paperback) 1973, with Index.

A useful introduction to the Bunraku with a brief appreciation of the movement techniques outlined from ancient texts. Unfortunately, there is neither a bibliography nor footnotes. The data only begin to suggest the complexity of the movement patterns, but lacks references to more complete information.

7. Korea

Cho, Oh-kon. "Korean Puppet Theatre: Kkoktu Kaksi," East Asia Series Occasional Paper, No. 6, Asian Studies Center, Michigan State University, 1979.

The author provides detailed description of production elements and also discusses extant plays.

8. Malaysia

Sweeney, Amin. Malay Shadow Puppets: The Wayang Siam of Kelantan. London: Trustees of the British Museum, 1972. Illustrated with black-and-white and color photographs.

Discussion of the repertory and performance methods, as well as description of the construction and types of puppets. There are interspersed references to techniques of movement, a diagram which explains the manner of choreography, and a discussion of the reasons for the way in which the puppets are held to the screen.

_____. The Ramayana and the Malay Shadow Play. Kuala Lumpur: National University of Malaya Press, 1972. Maps.
Essentially the same ground is covered with respect to movement in this larger, more detailed discussion of the repertory.

9.   Sri Lanka (Ceylon)

Tilakasiri, Jayadsva. Puppetry in Ceylon. Colombo: Department of Cultural Affairs, 1961. Illustrated with black-and-white photographs.
By inference only one can guess at the manner of manipulation of the puppets. Little specifics on movement.

10.   Thailand

Rutnin, Mattani. The Siamese Theatre: A Collection of Reprints from the Journal of the Siam Society. Bangkok: The Siam Society, 1975. Illustrated with black-and-white photographs.
Major articles on shadow and other forms of puppetry. That by René Nicolas, in French, offers the most hints as to what the movement patterns of the Nang Yai, the great leather shadow figures, are like as they relate to the khon and classical dance. Prince Dhaninivat's discussion of the relationship of the shadow play to the khon further explicates the borrowing from one to the other. (See Brunet's "Nang Sbek.") Other articles describe the small nang talung figures and some of the performance characteristics which are similar to those in Malaysia. (See Sweeney's work on Malay shadow puppets.)

Audiovisual

The films and videotapes listed below are readily available in the United States and offer the viewer an immediate perception of the complex technique of the puppeteers. Unfortunately, many Asian puppet forms have never been filmed or taped. Much of the material on film does not concentrate on performance techniques. However, the few titles listed, when supplemented with some of the materials listed in this bibliography, will reveal the interrelationship of music, dance, language and manipulation, which are integral to the Asian puppet theater forms.

The Awaji Puppet Theatre of Japan. 20 min. 16mm color. The Asia Society, New York.
Scenes from classic Japanese tales, Keisei Awa Naruto, The Miracle of Tsubosaka Temple and Egisu-Mai, as well as a demonstration of how the puppets are manipulated.

Bunraku. 30 min. 16 mm color. The Japanese Consulates, Tokyo.

An excellent film with good coverage of performances and puppet manipulation.

Chaya Nataka, Indian Shadow Puppets. 26 min. 16 mm color.
    Sangeet Natak Akademi, New Delhi.
A print of this film is held by the Department of Theater Arts, UCLA. Four types of leather shadow play are shown in performance. The manipulation of the puppets is frequently sacrificed to scenes of Indian landscape and other insigificant materials. An introduction to four of the six known forms.

Chinese Shadow Play. 30 min. Black-and-white videotape. The
    Asia Society, New York, also Bureau of Mass Comm., New York
    State Education Dept., Albany.
A lecture-demonstration presenting Chang Ten-cheng, fifth generation Chinese shadow-puppet master, making a typical puppet and then performing a scene from The Monkey, one of the most famous shadow plays. Taiwanese puppeteer.

Chinese Shadow Plays. 10 min. 16 mm. color. Contemporary
    Films, New York, and Pictura Film Distrubtion Corp., 43 W.
    16th St., New York.
An abbreviated performance of shadow puppet play, The White Snake. Some commentary on puppets, musical instruments and the manipulators.

Nang Yai. Asian Theatre Film Library, University of Kansas. 30
    min. 16 mm. black and white.
A documentary with English subtitles of a performance of the leather shadow puppets of Thailand, analogous to the Cambodian Nang Sbek, (large figures). Supplement to the dissertation of Stephanie Krebs, the filmmaker, from Harvard University's anthropology department.

Wayang Kulit. American Society for Eastern Arts, San Francisco.
    30 min. 16 mm. color. Also available, Glasscock Films, Los
    Angeles.
Scenes from a performance by a professional Javanese shadow puppeteer. The film was shot in California with the puppeteer Oemartopo as dalang.

Wayang Kulit. Eight-hour color videotape. University of California,
    Los Angeles.
A performance of Calonarang by dalang I Nyoman Sumandhi, which also includes interviews on techniques. There are also tapes on the teaching of the making and manipulation of the puppets during the Asian Performing Arts Summer Program at UCLA in 1979. Balinese wayang.

Wayang Kulit (Puppet Show). 15 min. 16 mm. color. Malaysian
    Embassy, Kuala Lumpur.

Chapter Eighteen

WESTERN ASIAN AND NORTH AFRICAN PERFORMANCE:
GENERAL INTRODUCTION

Peter J. Chelkowski
Section Editor

This bibliographical survey* covers the enormous area of
North Africa, Western Asia, the Caucasus, and Central Asia. Populated mainly by Arabs, Iranians, and Turkic peoples, the region
also includes numerous ethnic and religious minorities. Despite the
diversity of these peoples, Islam is the common unifying element of
culture and society. In addition, the region includes the three distinctive ethnic islands of Georgia, Armenia, and Israel.

Indigenous theatrical modalities such as storytelling, puppetry,
shadow plays, improvised comedy, and passion plays have existed
in these areas for hundreds of years, from the isolated mountain
villages of Anatolia to the courts of the caliphs. However, formal
theatre and dramatic literature in the area (with the exception of
Georgia and Armenia) were recent innovations, beginning only in
the early nineteenth century. Goethe in his "Noten und Abhandlungen" to Westösticher Divan noted with astonishment that no dramatic Persian literature existed. Had he been better acquainted
with the literature of the Arabs, Turks, and Jews, he may have
realized that the Iranians were not alone in this dramatic lack.
Much of this can be explained by the religions of the region. Judaism and Islam, with their restrictions on pictorial representation,
became the major obstacles to the development of the theatre in the
Middle East. Even today, the orthodox Jews of Israel and their
Muslim counterparts would never consider attending a theatrical
performance.

---

*Some of the chapters have been abridged to meet the special re-
strictions of this volume. Permission was requested and granted
for publication of some of the chapters prior to release of this volume and readers are directed to Middle East Studies Association
Bulletin (MESA).

Thus, it is not surprising that the religious minorities played a crucial role in the introduction of theatre to the Middle East. The Armenians, for example, were among the first to produce plays in Istanbul, and Christian and Jewish women were the first females to step on the stage, breaking the tradition of men playing women's roles.

Not only religious and social mores should be taken into consideration in the study of the development of drama and theatre, but the political climate as well. Because plays were vehicles for social commentary, the authorities either facilitated or repressed them according to circumstance. This has greatly influenced the development of the theatre from country to country. Turkey, for instance, experienced relatively little political censorship in its theatres, whereas the theatre in the countries of the Caucasus and Central Asia experienced the most, as they have been under foreign domination for more than a century, first under czarist Russia, and now under the Soviet Union. Ironically, however, this has encouraged the development of the theatre in the Soviet Muslim republics, for better or worse, since theatrical life in Russia is greatly developed and active.

Another obstacle to the development of theatre was not social but structural. Dramatic writing was a complex and novel import with little literary precedence in Middle Eastern belle lettres. Only the romantic epic (which may almost be referred to as closet drama) came close to the forms necessary for theatrical writing. Thus, indigenous writers, eager to adapt western forms, had tremendous structural and technical difficulties to overcome. Though gifted at stringing precious words together like pearls, and among the world's masters in their unsurpassed passion for poetry, writers at first lacked the dramatic structures and the artistic unity so essential in playwriting.

One way they circumvented this problem was by taking the skeleton of a western dramatic masterpiece and superimposing local situations and characters, reflecting extant social situations.

Language was another problem. The use of the formal literary language versus the vernacular was overcome more easily among the Iranians and the Turks than among the Arabs. The Jews also faced a similar problem, though they had the reverse task of translating from the vernacular languages into Hebrew.

Indigenous theatrical movements such as singing and dancing played an important role in the transition from entertainment and ritual to the spoken and acted drama, but ironically this success contributed to their decline. Western theatre has pushed aside the traditional forms of entertainment in the Middle East and North Africa. Before the modern era, entertainment, such as storytelling, improvised comedies, and puppetry were related to holidays, and seasonal and religious festivals, such as circumcisions, weddings, and births. Today, theatrical modalities have become mainly secular pastimes for people in all walks of life. There is, however, a growing nostalgia for the traditional indigenous forms. One can only hope that the growing interest in pastime entertainment and the growth of institutions devoted to the study and training of theatre crafts will encourage the preservation of the passing forms, if not in their entirety, then at least as an influence and inspiration to modern productions. It is noteworthy that the theatre in the West, which pushed aside the traditional Middle Eastern forms, is now looking towards them in hopes of borrowing means to revivify the actor-spectator relationship.

Chapter Nineteen

THEATRE IN TURKEY

Metin And

Theatrical art in Turkey today is a unique and complex blend of ancient indigenous traditions and western influences. The four major theatrical traditions--folk theatre, popular theatre, court theatre, and western theatre--have had such influence on one another that one must study them all in order to appreciate the significance of each.

Folk Theatre

Though dramatic art has existed among the Turks for thousands of years, its origins are obscure. Whatever its origins, the Turkish folk theatre has survived for centuries among the more than 40,000 villages scattered throughout the rugged countryside. The isolation of these villages and the homogeneity of the Turkish peasantry have encouraged the preservation of its unique dramatic forms.

Folk theatre consists largely of popular dramas performed by the villagers during family ceremonies or during the agricultural cycle, particularly at the time of the winter solstice. Because of gradual corruptions of the plays throughout the centuries, no standard versions exist. However, all folk dramas are based on two major plots. The first involves a battle between opponents who represent life and death, in which one is killed and subsequently restored to life by medicine or magic. The second plot concerns the abduction of a girl and her eventual return to a grieving mother, relatives, and friends.

Three main sequences usually seen within these elaborate rituals are the battle sequence, the procession or quest sequence, and finally the drama itself. Throughout these sequences, strong symbols constantly reinforce the life-versus-death themes.

These folk dramas, which are performed by the villagers themselves in the winter and are accompanied by pantomime, dances, and puppet performances, are a vast source of artistic energy which must be tapped if Turkey is to build up a strong national tradition.

Popular Theatre

Popular theatre was presented to the public by three classes of performers: (1) storytellers, (2) puppeteers (both shadow and puppet theatre), and (3) live actors, jesters, and pantomime dancers. These performers belonged to different guilds and companies called kol or cemaat, and included men (who also played women's roles) and dancing boys and girls.

Performances were given wherever they could be accommodated --in public squares, in the yards of inns, in coffee houses and taverns, and in private homes.

1. Storytelling is the most widely spread form of popular entertainment in the Islamic countries. In Turkey there are several terms for storytellers; the most common is meddah (literally praise-giver or panegyrist). Usually these storytellers represented many different persons. They could at times be so realistic that when telling stories, the audience would divide into two rival factions, sometimes fighting among themselves.

The storyteller knows many methods of creating and holding suspense and introducing surprise, and employs various techniques: inserting pauses, switching from conversational speech to chanting, moving the arms and head in sweeping gestures, whispering, screaming, and pounding the feet. He thus imparts to the audience the wide range of passions and feelings experienced by the characters.

2. Shadow and Puppet Theatre. The most widespread theatrical form in Turkey was the shadow theatre, which consisted of cut-out figures silhouetted against a lighted screen. It is believed to have developed during the Ayyubid dynasty (eleventh to thirteenth centuries) under the name of Khayal al-zil (shadow play), and later became known as Karagöz (The Black Eye) after the name of the main protagonist.

By the seventeenth century, Karagöz had fully developed into a purely Turkish phenomenon, but under the Ottoman rule became popular throughout the Near East, spreading to North Africa and the Balkan countries. Syria, Egypt, Algeria, Tunisia, and Greece all copied the Turkish Karagöz, and modeled plays and characters on the Turkish patterns.

Turkish shadow theatre was preceded by puppetry, a tradition about which little is known. There were five distinct kinds of puppets in Turkey; jiggling puppets (iskele kuklasi), presented by gypsy street showmen; hand or glove puppets (el kuklasi); marionettes (ipli kukla), held by hand; a rod puppet, presented from a carriage; and a variety of gigantic puppets used in some public festivals and guild processions, representing mythological figures or animals.

3. Ortaoyunu. The Turkish comedia dell'arte originated in the urban areas as a pastime for the middle classes. One of the earliest descriptions of such a performance may be found in a twelfth century epic prose poem.

Farces were frequently performed in an impromptu fashion whenever there was an audience or onlookers ready to participate: in the streets, at weddings or fairs, or at national or religious festivals. These were often prearranged comic situations, worked out in front of shops or houses largely through improvisations with practical jokes inserted on the spur of the moment.

These ortaoyunu performances have no plots in the Aristotelian sense. They have, to use the current terminology, an "open form." Because of this open form, and the special nature of the rapport with the audience, ortaoyunu can also be called presentational or nonillusionistic.

The Court Theatre

Unlike most Asiatic countries, Turkey has no individualized and distinctive court theatrical tradition. Until the westernized period, court theatre simply imitated the popular theatre, but in a more refined and literary way. The courts were the patrons of companies, dancers, actors, storytellers, clowns, puppet masters, and conjurers who would perform only for the aristocracy at the palaces.

The court sustained theatrical entertainment outside the palace as well. The birth of a new prince or his circumcision, a court marriage, the accession of a new ruler, triumph in a war, departure for a new conquest, or the arrival of a welcome foreign ambassador or guest all provided occasions for public festivities lasting as long as forty days and nights. These court-sponsored activities served the double purpose of amusing the courtiers and the people, and of impressing the world at large by a display of magnificence. The spectacles included not only processions, illuminations, fireworks, equestrian games, and hunting, but dancing, music, poetic recitations, and performances by jugglers, montebanks, and buffoons. Pageants were also presented on moving gaudy wagons or on ordinary carts fitted with large canopied platforms, each carrying a guild group performing scenes appropriate to its trade.

The Western Theatre Tradition

The development of the western theatre tradition in Turkey has always been closely related to political and constitutional changes. Indeed, the very names of the three periods of development reflect political, rather than theatrical themes: the reorganization and despotism period from 1839 to 1908; the constitutional period from 1908 to 1923; and the republican period from 1923 to the present.

In the early nineteenth century, western dramatic art in Turkey was found only in the private residences of foreign embassy personnel, performed exclusively by visiting European theatre and opera companies in their own languages. However, in 1839 a vast plan of reforms marked the fundamental constitutional change in Turkish political history, and the westerning climate which ensued proved favorable to the development of the western theatrical tradition.

Because western and Turkish dramatic forms were so different, it is not surprising that the fusion of the two was accomplished largely through the efforts of Armenian middlemen. The Armenians of Istanbul were the first to translate and adapt European plays for bilingual performances in Turkish and Armenian.

Modern writers and artists no longer approach western culture as an ideal model, but as a contrasting tradition. Some, including this writer, believe that it is vital to blend Turkish and western elements harmoniously in order to establish a national theatrical identity.

Books

(Ill. = illustrated, Bibl. = contains a bibliography)

Aki, Niyazi. XIX Yüzyil Türk Tiyatrosu Tarihi [History of the 19th century Turkish Theater]. Erzurum, 1963. Bibl.

_____. Çağdaş Türk Tiyatrosuna Toplu Bakis (1923-1962) [An Overview of Modern Turkish Theater]. Erzurum, 1968. Bibl.

This is an abridged version of the article scheduled for publication in Middle East Studies Association Bulletin (MESA).

An excellent companion study introducing Turkish dance forms is Dr. And's A Pictorial History of Turkish Dancing, Ankara, 1976. B.F., ed.

And, Metin. Dances of Anatolian Turkey. Dance Perspectives no. 3, New York, 1959. Ill., Bibl.

_____. Kirk Gün Kirk Gece [Forty Days and Forty Nights: A Survey of Ottoman]. Istanbul, 1959. Ill., Bibl.

_____. Dionisos ve Anadolu Köylüsü [Dionysus and the Anatolian Peasant]. Istanbul, 1962. Bibl.

_____. Ataç Tiyatroda [Literary Critic Atac on Drama]. Istanbul, 1963.

_____. A History of Theatre and Popular Entertainment in Turkey. Ankara, 1963-64. Ill., Bibl.

_____. 100 Soruda Türk Tiyatrosu [Turkish Theater in 100 Questions]. Istanbul, 1970.

_____. Geleneksel Türk Tiyatrosu [Traditional Turkish Theatre]. Ankara, 1969. Ill., Bibl.

_____. Tanzimat ve Istibdat Döneminde Türk Tiyatrosu 1839-1908. [Turkish Theater in the Age of Reforms and Despotism 1839-1908]. Ankara, 1972. Ill., Bibl.

_____. Meşrutiyet Döneminde Türk Tiyatrosu 1908-1923 [Turkish Theater in the Constitutional Period, 1908-1923]. Ankara, 1971. Ill., Bibl.

_____. 50 Yilin Türk Tiyatrosu [Turkish Theater of the Past 50 Years]. Istanbul, 1973. Ill., Bibl.

_____. Oyun ve Bügü. Türk Kültüründe Oyun Kavrami [Play and Magic. The Concept of Play in Turkish Culture]. Istanbul, 1974. Ill., Bibl.

_____. A Pictorial History of Turkish Dancing from Folk Dancing to Whirling Dervishes-Belly Dancing to Ballet. Ankara, 1976. Ill.

_____. Osmanli Tiyatrosu. Kuruluşu-Gelişimi-Katkisi [The Ottoman Theater Company. Its Foundation--Its Evolution--Its Contribution]. Akara, 1976. Bibl.

_____. Dünyada ve Bizde Gölge Oyunu [Shadow Theatre in the World and in Turkey]. Ankara, 1977. Ill., Bibl.

_____. Magic in Istanbul [A History of Stage Magic in Turkey]. Calgary/Alberta, 1978. Ill.

_____. Karagöz. Turkish Shadow Theatre. Rev. ed. [Appendix

on the History of Turkish Puppet Theatre]. Istanbul, 1979. Ill., Bibl.

Antoine, André. Chez les turcs. Metin And, ed. Ankara, 1965. Ill.

Cerulli, Paolo. Quattro Comedie del Teatro Turco di Oggi. Roma: Istituto Per l'Oriente, 1864.

Elcin, Şükrü. Anadolu Köy Orta Oyunlari [Anatolian Village Drama]. Ankara, 1964. Bibl.

Gerçek, Selim Nüzhet. Türk Temaşasi [Turkish Theatrical Arts]. Istanbul, 1942. Ill.

Halman, Talat Sait, ed. Modern Turkish Drama. An Anthology of Plays in Translation. Minneapolis and Chicago: Biblioetheca Islamica 1976. Bibl.

Jacob, Georg. Karagöz-Komödien. Berlin, 1899.

_____. Türkische Litteraturgeschichte in Einzeldarstellungen. Vol. 1. Das Türkische Schattentheater. Berlin, 1900.

_____. Türkische Volksliteratur. Berlin, 1901.

_____. Vorträge türkischer Meddah's. Leipzig, 1923.

_____. Geschichte des Schattentheaters in Morgen und Abendlands. Hannover, 1925. Ill., Bibl.

Karadağ, Nurhan. Köy Seyirlik Oyunlari [Peasants' Theatre]. Ankara, 1978.

Kudret, Cevdet. Karagöz [Shadow Plays] 3 vols. Ankara, 1968-1970. Ill.

_____. Ortaoyunu [Turkish Theater-in-the-round Plays] 2 vols. Ankara, 1975. Ill., Bibl.

Kunos, Ignaz. Das türkische Volksschauspiel-Orta ojnu. Leipzig, 1908. Ill.

Martinovitch, N. Turetsky theatr Karagöz. St. Petersburg, 1910.

_____. The Turkish Theatre. New York, 1933. Ill., Bibl.

Menzel, Theodor. Meddah, Schattentheater und Orta Ojnnu. Prag, 1941.

Nutku, Ozdemir. Tiyatro ve Yazar [The Theater and the Playwright]. Ankara, 1960. Ill.

_____. Darülbedayi'in Elli Yili [Fifty Years of the Istanbul City Theater]. Ankara, 1969. Ill., Bibl.

_____. Meddahlik ve Meddah Hikayeleri [Storytelling and Story-tellers' Stories]. Ankara, 1977. Ill., Bibl.

Özön, M. Nihat and Baha Dürder. Türk Tiyatro Ansiklopedisi [Encyclopedia of Turkish Theater]. Istanbul, 1967.

Poyraz, Türkan and Nurnisa Tuğrul. Tiyatro Bibliyografyasi 1859-1928 [Theater Bibliography 1859-1928]. Ankara, 1967.

Radloff, W. Proben der Volkslitteratur der türkischen Stamme. Vol 8. St. Petersburg, Berlin, 1903.

Reich, H. Der Mimus ein litterar-entwiklungsgeschicht-licher Versuch. Vol. 1. Berlin, 1903.

Ritter, Hellmut. Karagöz, türkische Schattenspiele. Vol. 1, Hannover, 1924; Vol. 2, Istanbul, 1941; Vol. 3, Wiesbaden, 1953. Ill.

Robson, Bruce. The Drum Beats Nightly: The Development of the Turkish Drama as a Vehicle for Social and Political Comment in the Post-revolutionary Period 1924 to the Present. The Centre for East Asian Cultural Studies. Tokyo, 1976. Bibl.

Şener, Sevda. Musahipzade Celal ve Tiyatrosu [Musahipzade Celal and His Drama]. Ankara, 1963. Bibl.

_____. Çağdaş Türk Tiyatrosunda Ahlâk, Ekonomi, Kültür Sorunlari (1923-1970) [Questions of Ethics, Economics and Culture in Contemporary Turkish Theater 1923-1970]. Ankara 1971. Bibl.

_____. Çağdaş Türk Tiyatrosunda Insan [Man in Contemporary Turkish Theater]. Ankara, 1972. Bibl.

Sevengil, Refik Ahmet. Yakin Çağlarda Türk Tiyatrosu [Turkish Theater in Recent Times]. 2 vols. Istanbul, 1934.

_____. Sur l'ancienneté de l'art dramatique turc. Istanbul, 1949.

_____. Eski Türklerde Drama Sanati [Dramatic Arts among the Ancient Turks]. Istanbul, 1959. Ill., Bibl.

_____. Opera Sanati ile Ilk Temaslarimiz [Our Early Contacts with Operatic Arts]. Istanbul, 1959. Ill., Bibl.

_____. Tanzimat Tiyatrosu [Theater in the Age of Reforms]. Istanbul, 1961. Ill., Bibl.

_____. Saray Tiyatrosu [The Court Theater]. Istanbul, 1962.
Ill., Bibl.

_____. Meşrutiyet Tiyatrosu [Theater in the Constitutional
Period]. Istanbul, 1968. Ill., Bibl.

Siyavuşgil, Sabri Esat. Karagöz. Psiko-sosyalojik bir deneme
[Shadow Theatre: A Psycho-sociological Treatise]. Istanbul,
1941.

_____. Karagöz. Son Histoire, ses personnages, son esprit
mystique et satirique. Istanbul, 1951. Ill.

_____. Karagöz, Its History, Its Characters, Its Mystic and
Satiric Spirit. Ankara, 1955. Ill.

Sokollu, Sevinç. Türk Tiyatrosunda Komedyanin Evrimi [The Evolution of Comedy in Turkish Theater]. Ankara, 1979. Bibl.

Spies, Otto. Türkisches Puppentheater. Emsdetten/Westf., 1959.
Ill.

Tecer, Ahmet Kutsi. Köylü Temsilleri [Peasants' Performances].
Ankara, 1940.

Tietze, Abdreas. The Turkish Shadow Theater and the Puppet
Collection of the L. A. Mayer Memorial Foundation. Berlin:
Gebr. Mann Verlag, 1977. Ill.

Turan, Semahat and Behire Abacioğlu. Tiyatro Bibliyografyasi
1928-1950 [Theater Bibliography 1928-1950]. Ankara, 1961.

Türkmen, Nihal. Orta Oyunu [Theatre-in-the-round]. Istanbul,
1971. Bibl.

Articles

Adjemian, J. H. "Le Théâtre Turc." La Revue Orientale, 2 (1886),
pp. 65-71.

And, Metin. "Turkish Dances." Dance Magazine, 8 (1958), pp. 54-
57, 62.

_____. "Turkey's Musical Theatre." The Music Magazine,
(February 1962), pp. 30-32.

_____. "Turchia" [Türkiye Cumhuriyeti Sommario: 1. Premessa;
2. Feste e spettacoli Popolari; 3. Teatro dramatico; 4. Teatro
musicale; 5. Danza e baletto]. Encyclopedia Dello Spettacolo,
Vol. 9 (1963), pp. 1167-1179.

_____. "Shakespeare in Turkey." Theatre Research: Recherches Théâtrales, 6, 2 (1964), pp. 75-84 and two pages of illustrations.

_____. "Türkiye'de Shakespeare." Bati Dili ve Edebiyatlari Araştirmalari Dergisi, 1 (1964), pp. 55-66.

_____. "Various Species of Shadow Theatre and Puppet Theatre in Turkey" in Atti del Secondo Congresso Internationale di Arte Turca. Naples, 1965.

_____. "Ballet in Turkey." The Dancing Times, Vol. 56. 665 (February 1965).

_____. "Twenty Years of Turkish Ballet." Dancing Times, 57, 680 (May 1967).

_____. "Turkish Ballet Delights in Classic and Native Works." Dance News 5 (May 1967).

_____. "Turkey" in The Oxford Companion to the Theatre, 3rd ed., Phyllis Hartnoll, ed. London, 1967.

_____. "Wie entstand das Türkische Orta Oyunu." Maske und Kothurn, 16 (1970), pp. 201-216 and eight pages of illustrations.

_____. "Türkiye'de Italyan Sahnesi." Italyan Filolojisi/Filologia Italiana, 2 (1970), pp. 127-142.

_____. "Eski Istanbul'da Fransiz Sahnesi." Tiyatro Araştirmalari Dergisi 2 (1971), pp. 77-102.

_____. "Eski Istanbul'da Yunan Sahnesi." Tiyatro Araştirmalari Dergisi "Dramatik Köylü Gösterilerinin Ritüel Niteligi." Türk Folkloru Araştirmalari Yilliği, 1 (1975), pp. 1-17.

_____. "Folklorda Gömü ve Karagöz'ün Mal Cikarma Ara Muhaveresi." Bogaziçi Universitesi Halkbilimi Yilliği, 1 (1975), pp. 113-123.

_____. "Türkiye'de Molière." Tiyatro Araştirmalari Dergisi, 5 (1975), pp. 47-64.

_____. "Origins and Early Development of the Turkish Theater." Review of National Literatures (Spring 1973), pp. 53-64.

_____. "DKT-Das Vogel-Strauss-Kabarett" in K. and Lissi Barisch, Istanbul, Köln: Verlag M. DuMont Schauberg, 1976, pp. 155-158.

_____. "Komşu Kültürlerde Dramatik Köylü Oyunlari ve Türk Rtkisi." Türk Folkloru Araştirmalari Yilliği, 2 (1976), pp. 1-25.

_____. "Islam Folklorunda Muharrem ve Taziye." Türk Folkloru Araştirmalari Yilliği, 3 (1976), pp. 1-38.

_____. "Dramatik Köylü Oyunlari Açisindan Muharrem, Asure ve Taziye." Tiyatro Araştirmalari Dergisi, 5 (1977), pp. 49-83.

_____. "Turkish Shadow Theatre: Karagöz." East Asian Cultural Studies, 15 (March 1976), pp. 77-86.

_____. "The Mevlana Ceremony." The Drama Review, 3 (1977), pp. 83-94.

_____. "On the Dramatic Fertility Rituals of Anatolian Turkey" in Studies in Turkish Folklore, Ilhab Basgöz and Mark Glazer, eds. Indiana University, Bloomington, 1 (1978), pp. 1-24.

_____. "Islam'da Tragedya Kahramani ve Tragedya Ornekleri." Ulusal Kültür 2 (1978), pp. 147-171.

_____. "Islam Ülkelerinde Geleneksel Tiyatrodan Bati Tiyatrosuna Geçiş." Ulusal Kültür, 6 (1979), pp. 69-118.

_____. "Un Essai de Classification des Jeux Dramatiques du Paysan d'Anatolie" in Quand le crible était dans la paille, Rémy Dor and Michèle Nicolas, eds. Paris (1978), pp. 25-36.

_____. "Türkei" in Schatten Theater, Fred Mayer, ed. Wurzburg: Edition Georg Popp, 1981, pp. 225-246.

_____. "Ta'zie-la tragédie en Islam, ses éléments conventionnels et rituels, ses valeurs dramatiques rapportés à la tragédie grecque et sa signification pour le théâtre moderne." Annuaire International du théâtre '79, Warszawa (1980), pp. 28-38.

_____. "The Turkish Folk Theatre." Asian Folklore Studies, 38 (1979), pp. 155-176.

_____. "On the Dramatic Fertility Rituals of Anatolian Turkey." Asian Folklore Studies, 39 (1980), pp. 86-104.

_____. "Two Approaches to Adaptation and Infusion of Folk Dances for the Stage: The Turkish State Ballet Company and the Turkish State Folk Dance Group" in The Sixth Festival of Asian Arts, Hong Kong (1981), pp. 158-165.

_____. "Ta'zie La Tragedia en el Islam. Sus elementos convencionales y rituales, sus valores dramáticos en relacion a la

tragedia griega y su significacion para el teatro moderno,"
Anuario Internacional de Teatro. Instituto Nacional de Bellas
Artes, Mexico, 1981, pp. 107-118.

_____. "La tradition des masques zoomorphiques et anthropo-
morphiques en Anatolie avec une référence spéciale aux pratiques
arméniennes et turques" in Le Long Voyage des Masques, Maison
de la Culture de Rennes, ed. Rennes, 1982, pp. 24-37.

Andreucci, Costanza. "Teatro in Turchiaierie oggi," Il Dramma, 41
(April-May 1965), pp. 46-61. [A paper based on Metin And's
A History of Theatre and Popular Entertainment in Turkey,
Ankara, 1963-64.]

d'Agostino, Charles. "Karageuz," Mercure de France, 49 (1938),
pp. 121-132.

Arrhe, M. "Macbeth unter Palmen," Unesco-Dients (Köln) 1 (1961),
pp. 24-36.

Ay, Lütfi. "Le Théâtre turc," Revue théâtrale (April-June 1951),
pp. 24-36.

Ballieu, Jacques. "Le Théâtre turc," Revue théâtrale (January-
March 1889), pp. 344-50.

Battersby, H. R. "The Karagöz Show or the Miniatures Theatres
of Turkey," Islamic Review, 43 (1955), pp. 28-29.

Bekri, Mustafa. "Ein türkisches Xajalspiel aus Brussa." Ztschr. der
Deutschen Morgenlandischen Gesellschaft, 53 (1899), pp. 621 ff.

Bergstrasser, G. "Türkische Schattenspieler," Orientalisches
Literatur-zeitung 28 (1925), pp. 424-31.

Bey, J. "Das türkische Theater," Die Volksbühne, 1, 15 (1926).

Bombaci, Alessio. "Ortaoyunu," Wiener Zeitschrift für die Kunde
des Morgenlandes, 56 (1960), pp. 285-97.

_____. "On Ancient Turkish Dramatic Performances" in Aspects
of Altaic Civilizations, Denis Sinor, ed. Ural Altaic Series,
Indiana University, 23 (1963), pp. 87-117.

_____. "Rappresentazioni Drammatiche di Anatolia," Oriens, 16
(1963), pp. 171-193.

Boratav, Pertev Naili. "Le type de Karagöz et ses correspondents
dans la tradition narratives" in Quand les marionnettes du
Monde se donnent la Main ..., Liège (1958), pp. 227-32.

Brands, Wilfrid. "Zum Stand des Theaterdichtung in der Türkei," Die Welt des Islams, 13, 21-22 (1970).

Bratter, C. A. "Die moderne türkische Bühne," Das Literarische Echo 11 (1908-09), pp. 396-400.

_____. "Die Wiedergeburt des türkischen Nationaltheaters," Bühne und Welt, 11 (1908-09), pp. 285-87.

Burian, Orhan. "Turquie," Revue Internationale de Théâtre (October-December 1947), pp. 146-48.

_____ and Perihan Çambel. "Theatre in Turkey," Players Magazine (May 1952).

Davey, R. "Karagheuz and the Stage in Turkey." The Theatre, 1 (1896), pp. 257-262.

Duda, Herbet W. "Das türkische Volkstheater," Bustan, 2 (1961), pp. 11-19.

_____. "Das Türkische Theater" in Das Atlantisbuch des Theaters, Martin Hürlimann, ed. Zürich/Freiburg (1966), pp. 842-850.

Evin, Ahmet Ö. "Turkey" in Modern World Drama, Byron Matlaw, ed. New York, 1972.

Gabain, A. "Ein türkisches Iphigenien-Drama" in Westöstliche Abhandlungen R. Tschudi. Fritz Meier, ed. Wiesbaden, 1912, pp. 278-285.

Germanus, J. "The Awakening of Turkish Literature." Islamic Culture, 7 (1933), pp. 177-194.

Gökyay, O. Şaik. "Ankara Devlet Konservatuvari Tarihçesi." Güzel Sanatlar, 3 (1941), pp. 49-64.

Graham, Caroline. "Albee to Bard in Ankara," New York Times, September 24, 1961.

Halman, Talat Sait. "Comic Spirit in the Turkish Theatre," The Theatre Annual, 31 (1975), pp. 16-42.

_____. "Turkey," in The Reader's Encyclopedia of Shakespeare Oscar James Campbell and Edward G. Quinn, eds. New York, 1966.

[Anonymous] "Das Hoftheater eines Sultan," Tagliche Rundschau, 237 (May 23, 1909).

Horn, P. "Das Theater," Geschichte des Türkischen Moderne. Leipzig, 1902, pp. 52-58.

Humphreys, A. R. "Shakespeare's Plays in Turkey," The Asiatic Review, 146 (1945), pp. 200-01.

Iz, Fahir. "On dokuzuncu yüzyil başinda yazilmis bir türkçe piyes," Türk Dili ve Edebiyati, 8 (1958), pp. 44-72.

Jackson, A. "Le Théâtre Ottoman," Osmanli 123 (1881).

"Jeu du Viel Homme" and "Jeu de Karagheuz Turc: La Balançoire," Bedrettin Tuncel and Ahmet Kutsi Tecer, trans., in Le Théâtre Populaire Européen, Léopold Schmidt, ed. Paris, 1965, pp. 33-37, 457-494.

Köhler, Fritz. "Das türkische Nationaltheater," Die Deutsche Rühne, 6 (1914), pp. 455-57.

[Koşay], H. Zübeyir. "Orta Oyununa Dair," Türk Yurdu, 10 (1928).

Köprülü [zade], F. "Meddahlar," Türkiyat Mecmuasi, 1 (1925), pp. 1-45.

Kunos, I. "Über türkische Schattenspiele," Ungarische Revue (1887), pp. 425-35.

_____. "Türkisches Puppentheater," Ethnologische Mitteilungen aus Ungarn, 2 (1889), pp. 148-158.

Labacka-Koecherowa, Malgorzata. "Une comédie turque inconnue dans les collections Polonaises" [An Unknown Turkish Comedy in Polish Collections], The Theater in Poland, 8 (1970).

Laqueur, K. "Theater und Music in der modernen Türkei," Ubersee-Rundachau, 11 (1959), pp. 22-23.

von Luschan, Felix. "Das türkische Schattenspiel," Internationales Archiv für Ethnographie, 2 (1889), pp. 125-144.

McAfee, Helen. "The Turkish Drama," The Forum, 50 (1913), pp. 230-38.

Macgowan, Kenneth. "Theatre à la Turkey," Theatre Arts (December 1958).

_____. "Notes on the Turkish Theatre," Drama Survey (Winter 1962), pp. 321-29.

Martinovitch, N. "Turkish Theatre. The Missing Link," The Moslem World (January 1944), pp. 54-55.

Meinecke, Max. "Hundert Jahre Türkisches Theater," Deutsch-Türkischen Gesellschaft, 31 (1959), pp. 1-4.

Melih, I. "Le Théâtre en Turquie," L'Oeuvre (December 1909).

_____. "Le Théâtre en Turquie," L'Oeuvre (December 1911).

Meller, Eugen. "Türkischen Theater," Das Theater 10 (1929).

Menzel, Theodor. "Türkische Schattenspiele," Die Scene (September 1925), pp. 178-182.

Mille, Pierre. "Le Théâtre en Turquie" in I. Melih, Leila (1912), pp. 16-89.

[Anonymous] "Modern Theatricals in Turkey," Journal of the Peking Society I-4 (1886), pp. 153-60.

Mühsam, Kurt. "Theater in der Türkei," Die Wage, 11 (1908), pp. 959-962.

Niessen, Carl. "Byzanz und Türkei" in Handbuch der Theater-Wissenschaft, 1, 3 (1958), pp. 1240-1258.

Nutku, Özdemir. "Darülbedayi'in Oyun Seçimindeki Tutum Uzerine Notlar," Tiyatro Araştirmalalari Dergisi, 1 (1970), pp. 69-139.

_____. "Die Verfremdung im Orta Oyunu," Masks und Kothurn, 16 (1970), pp. 217-228.

_____. "Original Turkish Meddah Stories of the Eighteenth Century" in Studies in Turkish Folklore. Indiana University, 1978, pp. 166-183.

Oestercheld, Erich. "Das Neue Drama der Turken," Die Deutsche Buhne 7 (1915), pp. 245-48.

_____. "Vom Drama der Türken," Vossiche Zeitung Morgenausgabe, 1-3 (1915), pp. 245-48.

Özdogru, Nüvit. "Turkey" in The Reader's Encyclopedia of World Drama, John Gassner and Edward G. Quinn, eds. New York, 1969.

Özgü, Melahat. "Türkei" in Heinz Kindermann's Theatergeschichte Europas Vol. X Salzburg, 1974, pp. 521-73.

Ronart, Stephan. "Das Theater in der Türkei," Das Theater des Welt 1-3 (1937), pp. 178-181.

Rossi, Ettore. "Karagöz" in Encyclopedia Dello Spettacolo (1954-1966), Vol. 6, pp. 861-63.

_____. "Orta Oyunu," ibid. Vol 7, pp. 1406-07.

Sakisian, Armenag. "Karagöz," Bulletin de l'Association française des amis de l'Orient, 14-15 (1933).

_____. "Le Théâtre de Karagheuz," l'Amour de L'art (March 1935), pp. 102-103.

Segebarth, I. "Vom türkischen Volkstheater," Der Neue Weg, 39/13 (1910).

Seif, T. "Drei Türkische Schattenspiele," Le Monde Oriental, 7 (1923), pp. 113-181.

Şener, Sevda. "Kurban üzerine bir inceleme," Tiyatro Araştirmalari Dergisi, 1 (1970), pp. 49-68.

_____. "Pir Sultan Abdal Oyunu Üzerine Bir Inceleme," Tiyatro Araştirmalari Dergisi, 2 (1971), pp. 11-27.

_____. "Cumhuriyet Dönemi Kadin Oyun Yazarlari," Tiyatro Araştirmalari Dergisi, 4 (1975), pp. 31-44.

_____. "Molière ve Türk Komedyasinin Gelişmesi." Tiyatro Araştirmalari Dergisi, 5 (1974), pp. 25-30.

[Anonymous] "The Stage in Turkey," Living Age, 328 (1926), pp. 332-3.

Spuler, Christa-Ursula. "Das türkische Drama der Gegenwart," Die Welt des Islams (1968), pp. 1-219.

Stewart, David C. "Recent Developments in the Theatre of Turkey," Educational Theatre Journal 6 (October 1954), pp. 213-216.

Stout, R. Elliot. "An Ottoman Festival," The Ohio State University Theatre Collection Bulletin, 14 (1967), pp. 30-42.

Süssheim, Karl. "Die Moderne Gestalt des türkischen Schattenspiels (Karagöz)," Ztschr. der Deutschen Morgenlandischen Gesellschaft, 63 (1909), pp. 739-773.

Thalasso, Adolphe. "Le Théâtre Turc," L'Avenir Dramatixue et littéraire (June-July 1894), pp. 193-206, 241-256.

_____. "Le Théâtre turc contemporain...," Revue encyclopédique Larousse (December 9, 1899), pp. 1038-44.

_____. "Le Théâtre turc," [special issue] and "Karageuz," Revue thétrale, 2 (1904), pp. 351 ff, 361-384.

_____. "Molière en Turquie," Le Molièriste (December 1887-January 1888).

[Anonymous] "Die Theuter zu Konstantinopel," Panaroma 17 (1850), pp. 278-282.

Turgay-Ahmad, Bedia. "Modern Turkish Theater," Review of National Literatures, 4-1 (Spring 1973), pp. 65-81.

[Anonymous] "Türkischer Theater," Hamburg Nachrichten, 7 (1904).

Uplegger, Helga. "Das Volksschauspiel," Philologiae Turcicae Fundamenta, Vol. 2 (1964), pp. 147-70.

[Anonymous] "Über Theaterwesen und Malerei in Stambul," Das Ausland, 40 (1886).

Yalman, Tunç. "Das türkische Theater," Europa Aeterna, 1 (1956), pp. 376-78.

_____. "Turkey" in A History of the Theatre, George Freedley and John A. Reeves, eds. (1968).

Chapter Twenty

THEATRICAL MOVEMENT OF THE ARABS

Laila Abou-Saif

The literature of ancient Egypt was religious and documentary. The belief that life continued after death was the source of inspiration of much Egyptian literature and drama. There were many myths concerning this. The most important of these was that of Osiris.[1,2] Osiris, son of Geb, the earth god, and Nut, the sky mother, is the god who reclaimed Egypt from savagery. Osiris also taught Egyptians how to worship. Together with Isis, his wife-sister, he also taught them the art of agricultural cultivation. He even committed the whole government of Egypt to Isis, while he, according to the myth, traveled all over the world diffusing the blessings of agriculture and civilization wherever he went. But, one day, Seth, Osiris's jealous brother, murdered him by putting him in a casket which was thrown into the Nile. The mourning Isis combed the river for the coffin. Finally, she found it off the Syrian shore. She carried it back to Egypt, mourning the dead king in private. Horus found the concealed corpse of his hated brother, while on a boar hunt one day. In a fury he dismembered it into fourteen pieces and scattered them throughout the land. But Isis found them all and buried them wherever she found them, erecting a monument over each of the pieces. Meanwhile, Osiris's son, Horus, had grown to maturity in the Delta swamps and was ready to avenge his father's murder. He confronted Seth in a terrible battle, in which Horus lost an eye, but emerged victorious, becoming the rightful heir and ruler of the kingdoms of lower and upper Egypt. Subsequently all pharoahs ruled as successors to Horus.

Meanwhile, Isis, with the help of the god Anubis, pieced together the broken pieces of the body of Osiris and performed rites due the dead. Thus revived, Osiris, reigned as king of the dead, judging at the trials of departed souls. The death, which according to the legend was suffered by Osiris, at the hands of his wicked brother Seth, became the portion of every human being; just as Osiris had risen again, so could each man also begin life anew, if only the same formulas were spoken and the same ceremonies performed by a faithful son, such as Osiris's son, Horus, had spoken for his father. To that end it was necessary for every Egyptian

499

to appear after death at a judgement in the presence of Osiris and before a court of forty-two, to declare himself innocent of wrongdoings.

Thus the idea of the conflict between good and evil, the incarnation of ethical and moral principles into human form, so essential to drama, are all present in this myth. In his study of ritual myths and drama in the ancient Near East, entitled Thespis, Theodore Gaster sees a connecting link between ritual and drama.[3] Myth, according to Gaster, is the connecting link between ritual and drama, and the interpretation of ritual and myth provide the key to the essential nature of drama. Working from this premise, Gaster examines the evidence of early drama in ancient Egypt in such sources as the Pyramid Texts, the Ramasseum Dramatic Papyrus, the Memphite Shabaka Stone, and the inscriptions on the Temple of Edfu.

Although he insists on referring to them as rituals, Gaster includes scenes from some of those Egyptian dramas which give a clear indication that they were dramatic texts.

It is to Kurt Sethe, the German egyptologist, that the credit must go for the discovery of the dramatic nature of these hieroglyphic texts. In his book, Die Altaegyptischen Dramtischen Texte (1928), Sethe explains that in normal hieroglyphic writing, all figures face the same direction, and may be written in four ways: facing left or right, either vertically or horizontally. They are read from the direction in which they face, and always from the top down. In drama the speaker's name faces one way, followed by the verb, to speak, and this is in turn followed by the listener's name, facing the opposite direction.[4] Here is an example of a scene, quoted in Gaster, from the Ramasseum Dramatic Papyrus from Thebes, from the so-called Coronation Play. The play, engraved in a papyrus, discovered in 1895, in a grave west of Thebes, is according to Yale scholar Dr. Ellsworth Laflin, "a prompt book of a theatrical producer."[5] The play is believed to have been presented for the accession of King Senwoseret I in 1970 B.C. The action includes a fencing match between Horus and Seth. A pillar, symbol of the Nilometer, is made to fall and rise again. The speaking roles are those of Horus, Thoth, Isis, Nephtys, and Geb. The text is careful to specify to whom each speech is addressed. The two principal actors are known: the king plays Horus, and the reader-priest, Thoth (the god of speech).

Scene 31

Ritual act: The chief officiant produces various pigments and cosmetics which are in turn conveyed to the king. Mythological interpretation (according to Gaster): This represents Thoth restoring the stolen eye of Horus and addressing him concerning it.

Says Thoth to Horus:	"I hearby convey the bright eye to thy face."
Stage properties:	A Horus Eye. Green pigment for the eyes.
Says Thoth to Horus:	"May thine eye never more be troubled or lose its winelike luster."
Stage properties:	Horus Eye. Wine red pigment for the eyes.
Says Thoth to Horus:	"I hearby convey unto thee the perfume of divinity and the pure eye which was wrested from thee."
Stage properties:	A Horus eye. Frankincense.
(Dialogue missing):	
Stage properties:	Double-plumed crown, to be placed on the king's head by the wardens of the great plumes.
Says Thoth to Horus:	Perfume thy face herewith, so that it be thoroughly perfumed." [6]

If we turn to another example of these early dramatic texts, the Pyramid Texts, we discover that there are more than fifty such texts, which date back to 4000 B.C. Some of these were to be found in the tombs of pharoahs, others in the tombs of the royals.[7] According to Ellsworth Laflin, who has written two dissertations on the subject of ancient Egyptian drama, Aristotle and the Egyptian Origins of Greek Drama (1938) and The Ancient Egyptian Drama (1941), which are probably the most extensive studies of that subject, the evidence that these texts were dramatic is in the hieroglyphics themselves. "If the hieroglyphic texts themselves are examined, the directions for action and the indications of various characters speaking become apparent as stage directions. On rare occasions, the characters' names precede the speeches, as 'I am Nut.' In most cases the character of Osiris was identified with the dead king (whose part, of course, had to be played by a priest), that of Horus, with the living king (who may have been played by himself)."[8]

The plot of many of the Pyramid Texts dealt with the ascent of the soul to become one of the imperishable stars or the resurection of the body, or both. "Ho, King Unis, thou didst not depart dead, thou didst depart living," runs a line of dialogue in one of those texts. Whereupon the king, or priest, playing the role of King Unis, would have to come to life. Acting would be involved as the priest, directing the actor-king, would say "throw off thy wrappings" and the actor-king, who had been a corpse up until then, would have to appear to come to life.[9]

According to Dr. Laflin, Egyptian drama seems to fall into four types of plays.

1. Coronation Festival Play. Often a Nativity play. Given at the king's coronation, such as the one quoted above.

2. Jubilee Play or Heb sed (Feast of the Lion's Tail). Given after thirty years rule; later given every five years after the coronation. Twin obelisks were set up to commemorate this. They represented shafts of sunlight on body and soul.

3. Resurrection Play (passion play), such as in the Pyramid Texts. The above plays were all about the king as a God, Horus, and were usually performed at twilight.

4. Medicine Play. The purpose of this drama was faith healing or psychological cures. The principal character here is Horus, as a child, bitten by a scorpion; his mother, Isis, administers artificial respiration and other magical cures to heal him. This play, entitled Horus of the Crocodiles (to be found inscribed on the Metternich stele located in the chateau Metternich, Bohemia, at Kynsvart), began a tradition of medicine shows which persists in Egypt to this very day.

The medicine shows were performed on brick boats or solar barks stages, which were boats floating in "sacred" lakes. The first three kinds of plays mentioned above were given at the "King's House of Millions of Years," a theatrical courtyard attached to every pyramid on the east side. Later, huge courtyards detached from tombs, as at Deir al Bahri, Madinet Habu and other tombs, were used as theatres.[10]

Every Egyptian king in the XXX dynasties, beginning 3000 B.C. probably had a special Coronation Festival Play, and a special version of the Jubilee Play (Heb sed) as well as the Resurrection of the Body Drama (Pyramid Texts). There were over 200 kings before 332 B.C., which means that there were 600 written dramatic texts. Many queens and princes probably had shorter texts. At least they had smaller pyramids with smaller theatrical courtyards attached.[11]

The pyramids have been used as a quarry for many years, and many buildings in modern Cairo are built out of their stones. Several minor pyramids have disappeared. The theatre courtyards were among the first to go, but their outlines are often traceable on the east side of the pyramid. When Horus, the mortal king (4000 B.C.), became deified as God-Born-On-Earth, and his house became the setting for plays depicting his Divine Birth, his Jubilee, and his Attainment of Immortality, in dramatic form, the building became more of a theatre than a temple, and the adjective "mortuary" was always misplaced. A god who is present in the flesh does not need a temple. When Osiris supplanted Horus as Supreme God in the new kingdom (about 3000 B.C.) the term "temple" again became appropriate as the earthly habitation of a remote deity. However, the fact that the plays were given in them tended to make the word "theatre" more appropriate to the purposes of the building. The ancient Egyptian's own term, the "House of the Millions of

Years," is a happy compromise which does not confine the building exclusively to ritual or to drama, but fits all circumstances. [12]

An important, early example of the play, given at the coronation of a king, is the Memphite Drama (3000 B.C.) inscribed on the "Shabaka stone," famous as the Rosetta stone of Egyptian drama (next to which it lies in the British Museum). The Memphite Drama commemorates the victory of the first King Horus over Seth and pays tribute to Ptah, the god of Memphis, and to Thoth, the god of speech.

Here is an example of the kind of action that took place within this dramatic context. What is noticeable here is that a narrator exists to present the action and then the scene is played out to the accompaniment of a libretto.

Presenter:	Howbeit Geb is saddened at the thought
	That though the son of his own favorite son,
	Horus should receive no more than Set.
	So he bestows on him his heritage.
	The story is enacted.
Geb:	(addressing Horus)
	Thee alone, do I appoint my heir.
Geb:	(addressing the nine Gods present)
	He and he alone shall be mine heir.
	In Upper Egypt and in Lower Egypt too
	Mine own son's son, my sole inheritor.
Presenter:	So Horus shines as sovereign of both realms
	United in this single Tenen-land. [13]

One of the most completely known plots of an ancient Egyptian play is, according to Professor Ellsworth Laflin, the Coronation Festival Play of Queen Hatchepsut as "king" of Egypt. It was one of the attempts of the famous queen to be considered as a "king," for in ancient Egypt, as well as in contemporary Egypt, the ruler must be a man, and the highest role in those days for an Egyptian woman was to become the Mother of the Supreme God.

In the Coronation Festival Play inscribed at the temple of Deir-al-Bahari in Luxor which took the form of a Nativity play, the Holy Spirit assumes the form of and shape of the previous Queen's husband to become the father of the present "King." The division into acts shows an excellent construction. [14]

Ancient Egyptian drama was presented for the benefit of the public. Mummies were taken to the passion plays and some of these plays were even peripatetic, and included a funeral procession with a coffin in which Isis stopped at various points to recover a severed limb or hand, which were then placed in the coffin. The audience evidently joined the procession. At the last stop, an actor concealed in the coffin rose up, his body seemingly reassembled. An early scene in this play could show Seth severing and distributing the limbs of Osiris, after having killed him. Another scene showed the blinding of Horus by Seth, the healing of the Horus eye by Thoth, the resurrection of Osiris by means of the healed Horus-eye, a magic amulet.

According to Dr. Laflin, the actors were both male and female and the audience sometimes included thousands at the larger pyramids. The texts apparently were memorized and even rehearsed. One theatre is known to have been endowed with the taxes of twelve towns. [15]

Professor Laflin asserts that at Abydos there is evidence of a roofed theatre (perhaps the earliest) formed by the body of Mother Sky herself. In the Louvre Museum in Paris there is a jackal head-mask with jaws that open and close by pulling strings. There is also evidence of the use of hairpieces and theatrical makeup. When a king or an actor impersonated a god, he wore a false beard which had a slight kick-up at the bottom. Wigs and false hairpieces survive. [16]

Drama in ancient Egypt lived and died in and around the temples. The gap between the human and the divine was too wide to bridge. Unlike the gods of Greek myths, the ancient Egyptian gods were never humanized. And thus, as ancient Egyptian civilization and religion came to an end, so did the drama.

The myth of Osiris, however, has persisted through the ages and has become imbedded in Egyptian folklore where it resonates to this very day. The ballad of "Hassan wa Naima" is an instance in case. The story of this popular ballad concerns a singer, Hassan, who falls in love with Naima, a rich peasant's daughter, but is not allowed to marry her because of his station in life. Naima runs away with him to his village where she is followed by her clan, who deceive Hassan into believing that they would consent to her marriage to him, provided he return to Naima's village for the wedding ceremony. Hassan complies. Upon arrival at the village, he is invited to sing for the entire village and then drawn into his future in-laws' home for refreshments. There, they murder him, dismembering his head from his body. Naima, who has witnessed the crime, keeps the head. The body is thrown into the Nile, from where it is eventually retrieved and identified by Naima, who denounces her own parents to the police.

The ballad has been the source of inspiration for many contemporary Egyptian plays. Shawki Abdel Hakim has written two versions of this ballad in dramatized form, Hassan wa Naima and Hassan wa Naima, 1976. [17] The Marxist poet and playwright Majik Serour has also treated this story in his colloquial verse play, From Where Shall Get People? (Menein Ajib Nass), written in the 1970's, as was Abdel Hakim's play. In these plays, Naima, echoing the ancient Egyptian heroine, Isis, is an archetypal character, symbolic of Egypt itself, vindictive and regenerative. Hassan is also a contemporary Horus, a fighter for his rights, mouthpiece for consciousness and social justice, and in the case of Serour, political rights.

Both Shawki and Serour remain faithful to the narrative nature of authentic Egyptian drama and folklore. In all the plays mentioned, a narrator is used, and then, as in the ancient Egyptian plays examined above, the scene is re-acted. The storyteller, or rawi, thus assumes a central role. This mingling of the narrative and dramatic is the closest thing to the approximation of a purely native construction in Egyptian drama, where the predominantly lyrical tradition, inherited from the love of recitation in Islamic and pre-Islamic poetry is juxtaposed and entwined with the mimetic, or dramatic, inherited from ancient times.

In Islamic times, the lyrical and narrative modes prevailed. The Arab poet, when he sang of the heroic deeds of his tribe, preferred the personal and the lyrical mode to the narrative or dramatic one. This was further encouraged by Islam's distrust of mimesis, since the representation of human and animal figures in art was generally considered as idolatrous. Consequently the predominant manifestation of Islamic art, aside from the lyrical, were the abstract, geometric, arabesque designs used for calligraphy and architectural designs. Nonetheless, the dramatic sense is as inherent to the Arab temperament as it is to other races, and in spite of these prohibitions and taboos, dramatic forms manifested themselves in the Islamic period. Most important of these was the shadow theatre.

There are three general categories of puppets: the hand puppets, the marionettes and the shadow puppets; the first two use three-dimensional figures, whereas the shadow puppet employs a two-dimensional effect created by the throwing of light and shadow on a translucent screen. The audience, in such theatre, sits on one side of the screen, while the puppets next to the surface are manipulated by control rods. A light source behind the screen shines past the puppet figures, thus enabling the audience on the opposite side of the screen to see shadow images cast there. In order to stress the nonhuman quality of the puppets of the shadow theatre, the puppeteer often punches holes in the puppet's body. In his book, Studies in the Arab Theatre and Cinema, Jacob Landau points out that shadow theatre originated in China and was introduced to Egypt in the twelfth and thirteenth centuries. [18] A manuscript of shadow plays, dating to that period, has been discovered under the authorship of Shams-al Din Mohammed Ibn Danyal. His shadow plays, published collectively as Tayf al-Khayal (The Spirit of Imagination), were written in poetry and versified prose. [19]

The first play in the collection, also called Tayf al-Khayal,

concerns an old soldier, Wisal, hustled by a matchmaker into marry-
ing a woman of extraordinary ugliness. "Prince" Wisal, who is ap-
pointed as a nominal ruler by the Caliph of Egypt, wishes to gain
moral support from the people. Wisal first appears dressed as a
soldier and describes himself in the most heroic language: as cun-
ning as a serpent, as ferocious as a lion, and as thirsty as the
sand. His clerk enters to read a decree appointing Wisel as king
of the lunatics, and confining his kingdom to include the relics of
Egypt, its hills and its tombs. The matchmaker, learning thus,
that the "king" has been impoverished, provides an ugly wife for
him, causing poor Wisal to go on pilgrimage to atone for his sins. [20]

Another play, Ajib wa Gharib (The Strange and the Amazing),
has very little plot and is described by Landau as a procession of
indigenous characters, who displace one another in a lengthy parade,
officiated by "two rogues." Thus we see various professionals who
display their skill and their wares: a snake charmer, a quack doctor, a hawker of medicinal herbs, an ophthalmic surgeon, two acrobats, an astrologer, a sorcerer trading in amulets, an epileptic, and
a phlebotomist with all her instruments. These are followed by animal tamers who present their animals and show off their tricks:
elephants, lions and bears appear on the shadow screen. Then
comes "Abou al-kitat" (the father of cats) who tries to reconcile
cats and dogs, a dancing teacher for dogs, a Sudanese buffoon, a
bayonet swallower, a monkey-performer and a rope-dancer. This
gallery of persona gesticulates and speaks, each in accordance to
its role, naturally. The play ends with the appearance on the
screen of an "enamored" man with self-inflicted wounds, a camel
driver, and a bearer of coal. [21]

The third play in the collection, Al-Mutayam (The Love-
Stricken), begins with a boxing match and ends with a feast attended by a carnival of dubious characters, such as: a debauchee
wild with carnal appetite, a man inclined to masturbation, a man who
snatches children from their beds in order to satisfy his fiendish
lust, an uninvited parasite, and finally the Angel of Death who
drives the guests away and takes al-Mutayam's soul, after the latter has duly repented. Music, bawdiness, caricatured or stereotypical characters thus provided the mainstay of Ibn Danyal's shadow theatre.

There existed alongside this form of shadow theatre, another,
which probably originated in Turkey and which became known by
the name of its chief protagonist: Karagoz. This was a kind of
proletarian Everyman who complained about everything and never
missed a chance to rail and rant against fortune. The Karagoz
plays probably date as far back as the eighth or ninth centuries
in Turkey and were probably a merger of the mime performance
and early shadow theatre entertainments. [22] The mime performances
were probably the mimetic performances of the Turkish meddah
(praise-singer) and the orta-oyunu (improvisational farce traveling

troupes) which were known to exist there between the ninth and fourteenth centuries.

The texts of shadow plays were transferred from one generation to another through the oral tradition. Consequently, extant shadow play scripts are primarily outlines of the dialogue and action, revolving around stereotypical characters, such as Karagoz and his companion, Hagivid. According to Landau, hundreds of Karagoz scripts have been recorded in modern times, such as the play The Muddle-Headed Watchman. Here, Hajivat arranges for the rental of the drunkard's house to a dame of doubtful morals. The drunkard hires Karagoz as night watchman, but instead of doing his duty, Karagoz tries repeatedly to enter the house against the lady's wishes. Meanwhile a dandy, and then an opium-smoker, and finally an Arab merchant gain entry by means of a password which Karagoz misunderstands and mispronounces. Finally, he manages to get into the house, where he becomes quite drunk and rowdy, upsetting the entire neighborhood. [23] Many of the Karagoz plays revolved around a couple of basic plots such as the one described, in which Karagoz gets a job at which he proves inadequate, or, Karagoz trying to do forbidden things, out of lust or curiosity, and getting caught by the police.

The comic effect in the Karagoz plays resulted not only from linguistic misunderstanding, but from the situations and the slapstick, which was extensive--Karagoz drinking, Karagoz getting involved in a brawl, etc. In addition to the characters of Karagoz and his companion, these plays provided a very colorful collection of dramatis personae, which included: dwarfs, rowdies, bathhouse-stokers, Negro slaves, Europeans, Jews and Armenians, madmen, sailors, hunchbacks, witches, wizards, demons, and devils.

The shadow theatre performances took place in cafés frequented by men in the popular parts of the city, such as the Hussein and were performed in the holy month of Ramadan, the month of fasting. These performances have all but disappeared, as a gradual conservatism has crept into Egyptian and Arab societies, especially after the sobering effect of the institutionalization of state-subsidized and supervised culture. Nonetheless performances of hand puppets of the Karagoz theatre could be seen in Cairo as late as the 1950's, in popular quarters of the city and during mulids or religious festivals. The manipulator of the puppets hid behind a curtain and mimicked the "human" voices of the hand puppets.

The shadow figures were usually made of leather, which was soaked and cut on a wooden frame to the shape of the various characters. The leather was then scraped with a piece of glass in order to make it transparent. Then the leather figure was put over a paper pattern and the details, such as the tarbouche (fez) of waistcoat, the sword, other accoutrements of Karagoz's apparel were filled out. The figures were about a foot in height and the limbs were connected to the body of the figure by means of gut thread, thus enabling the puppeteer to stimulate movement. The shadow puppets were controlled by rods, detachable from small sockets built into the figure. The screen was made of a semiopaque material. Props and scenery pieces were also used.[24]

The shadow theatre flourished in the Ottoman Empire during the seventeenth, eighteenth, and nineteenth centuries. There was, in all probability, an enduring tradition of shadow theatre in most Arabic countries, especially Egypt, where there have recently been discovered several new shadow plays dating to the eighteenth century. In the 1950's, the singer and "monologist" or speaker of comic monologues, Shukuku, revived the Karagoz puppet theatre successfully. The Egyptian ministry of culture fosters a puppet theatre, masrah al-arayes in al-Ezbekieh, to this very day.

More important, the techniques and characters of Karagoz theatre exercised a considerable influence on popular Egyptian comedy in the ensuing years. The following is an instance in case, taken from a play, entitled Karakosh's Reign by the comic actor-manager, Najib al-Rihani, written and produced in 1946. Karakosh was the name of a military leader who was made governor of Egypt by Salah-al-Din during the crusades. Jacob Landau suggests the name "Karagoz" may very well have been inspired by that historical figure.[25] The ensuing scene is strongly evident, however, of Karagoz techniques. "Bondok," the Karagoz-like protagonist, has just been insulted by his employer for his inefficiency in the job of rent collector. The employer, a Turkish Agha, declares that Bondok must be punished.

Kishk Agha:	Must punish. Must beat with sticks.
Bondok:	That would be a shame, sir, a shame.
Kiskh Agha:	Mr. Bondok.
Bondok:	O'Prophet of God, stand by me.
Kishk Agha:	Bondok, if dog incapable of watching over farm, over garden, must he not be punished?
Bondok:	Please, just let me hang around, sir.
Kishk Agha:	Bondok, nothing but dirt.
Bondok:	(to himself) It's coming now.[26]

In addition to the shadow theatre, there existed in the Arab world a tradition of improvisational comedy, such as the Orta Oyanu referred to above, in which indigenous comedy found its expression. Like the shadow theatre, it was physical and nonverbal, relying on situation and character for its effect and performed by and for a popular audience, especially in the countryside. In Egypt, such entertainments were called the fasl mudhik. Carsten Niebhur, the Danish traveler, reports having seen such a play in Cairo in 1780, about a woman who attracts travelers to a tent and then robs and strips them systematically.

The British orientalist, E. W. Lane, recording his observations on Egypt during the 1830's describes a similar farce, claiming that the "Egyptians are often amused by players of low and ridiculous farces, who are called 'Mohabbazeen.'"[27] The Mohabbazeen performed at weddings and at circumcision festivals, attracting an audience at the homes of the wealthy and in certain public places during religious festivals. Sometimes these "low and ridiculous" farces, were not so frivolous. The fasl mudhik which Lane had witnessed was not devoid of social and political comment: an innocent and naive peasant is thrown into jail for allegedly not paying his taxes. His wife, in order to obtain his release, must bribe the court clerk with food, the omda or village mayor with money, and the district governor with her body. The farce that Lane witnessed was performed before a high dignitary or pasha in order to open his eyes to the corruption of tax collectors.[28]

The troupe of performers of this fasl mudhik witnessed by Lane was accompanied by five musicians and dancers. Lane also described a variety of other entertainers he observed during his travels in Egypt including conjurors, jugglers, storytellers or rawis, who, to the accompaniment of their ruhbabbas (a horse-tail strung balalika kind of instrument), told legends of heroic figures such as Abou-Zayd al-Hilali.

These Egyptian troubadours, or commedia dell'arte troupes, continued to roam the rural countryside in Egypt well into the twentieth century. In an article, "Drama," in the Encyclopaedia of Religion and Ethics, Curt Prufer mentions the names of several popular performers who haunted Cairo cafés at the turn of the century, appearing in travelling circuses which performed during religious festivals and at Ramadan.[29] Ahmed Fahim al-Far was a noted imitator or muqalid of animal sounds. Ali Kaka, whose trademark was a cotton-worsted tail which he wore attached to his posterior, was famous for his monkey imitations. Mohammed Ali al-Iskandarani was known for his taqlid of Egyptian dialects, especially the southern or saidi dialect. Prufer also describes a fasl mudhik which he saw in Cairo, at the turn of the century, in which a servant, Hussein, cuckolded his own master. Western influence had begun to creep into the fasl mudhik by that time, and the Harlequinesque servant to become a recurrent figure.[30]

The troupe that Prufer witnessed could very well have been the company of George Dachoul, a Syrian comedian who presented his farces at Kamil's Café in the Hussein quarter of Cairo. Dachoul obtained his training in the shadow theatre, where he had worked with visiting Armenian and Turkish troupes. The stock characters of his skits were: the intriguing servant, Kamil, whom he played; a pair of lovers, usually singing lovers, referred to as the "amoroso"; a king or vizir, a villain character; a mother-in-law. The amoroso were played by young boys, women being forbidden to act.[31]

Kamil wore a patched suit and long Turkish fez. He clogged along with wooden slippers known in Arabic as <u>kobabe</u>, with which he administered beatings. His face was painted white, with clown-like red lips and nose. The Café Kamil was frequented by men, and is said to have had a small, cabaretlike stage. As Kamil became increasingly popular, his troupe was invited to perform in the theatres, as comic interlude. He also toured the countryside. [32]

Today, the fasl mudhik has all but disappeared from Cairo, where it has been replaced by comedies, television and the movies. However, it survives, in the repertory of traveling circuses, and in the retinue of belly dancers who animate rural weddings and festivals.

The following description summarizes one seen by this writer at the Helw circus in 1965 during a religious festival:

A lecherous looking old man appears informing the audience that it is time for him to look for a new bride. Yet such a bride is not easily found. His daughter, who would also like to get married, must wait because fathers come first and as long as he has not found a bride for himself, she may not dream of marriage. In order to speed things up the family servant decides to help the lovers. He will become the old man's bride! The daughter and her sweetheart dress him up in a long skirt, with a cushion for a behind, put rouge on his lips and cheeks and call him Anisa. The father is brought in and runs his hands approvingly over Anisa's padded beauty. Wedding guests (who are all in on the joke) file in to congratualte the couple. Finally the "bride" and groom are left alone and the inevitable happens. Anisa's shyness and coyness do not protect her. The old man corners her with a more than conspicuous broom stick and it is only when "she" flings off her disguise that "she" is saved. [33]

By the end of the nineteenth century and up to the period of World War I, there were three identifiable trends in Egyptian theatre: a trend towards melodrama, written in western style with Egyptian themes; a trend towards a musical theatre, also influenced by western revues, operettas and musicals; a trend towards a native, popular comedy, influenced by the West, but also, unlike the other genres mentioned above, influenced by the Karagoz and shadow theatre, as well as by the fasl mudhik.

According to Mohammed Manzalawi, Jacob Sanua (1839-1912), a Egyptian Jew, must be credited with creating the satiric stage and press in Egypt. Sanua, who established a small theatre from 1870 to 1872 where he produced comic skits in colloquial Arabic, was also heavily influenced by the techniques of the fasl mudhik. These plays, however, were also satiric of the Khedive's policies, as well as certain social institutions. [34] In his playlet, <u>The Two Con-cubines</u>, Sanua even made fun of polygamy. The following brief description of the play reveals the influence of the fasl mudhik and improvised comedy on Sanua:

> An old merchant marries a younger wife and brings her home to live with his first wife. The two women immediate-ly start to quarrel. Unable to handle the battling women, the merchant declares that he will go to the café and con-sole himself with some hashish. In the meantime, the two women continue to fight, this time over household duties. The merchant returns, and tries to reason with them. The women start to beat one another, and the merchant also gets a thoroughly good beating in the melee. He rushes out to get the help of his brother-in-law (the younger wife's brother), who has also been enjoying hashish at a nearby café. In an uproarious scene the two men try to take on the two women: beatings, verbal abuse, and slap-stick make the scene. The men retreat. Utterly frustrated, the merchant divorces both his wives by uttering "inti talqa" thrice. The women depart. The merchant takes a deep breath, faces his audience, and informs them that he now plans to revel in the peace of bachelor life. "But who will cook and clean for you?" asks someone in the audience. "Who has born your son?" asks someone else. Meanwhile, the first wife has crept on stage. "Take her back" volun-teers someone else in the audience. Alright, says the mer-chant, if only to please the audience. He will return his first wife to the marriage fold. [35]

Not unlike the fasl mudhik, with which it shares many simi-larities, such as slapstick, verbal invective, and the emphasis on physical action rather than dialogue, this play also abounds in musical entertainment. The brother-in-law enters onstage with a band of five musicians bearing a <u>darabukkeh</u> (earthen drum), a <u>nay</u> (vertical flute), <u>sagat</u> (brass castanets), a <u>mizmar</u> (a single-pipe woodwind instrument resembling an oboe), and a <u>tabla</u> (a small drum) to accompany the new wife in a belly dance. The social and moral satire intended by the author needs no comment.

The folk tradition described above never produced a full-fledged Egyptian drama. Even the attempts of Shawki Abdel Hakim and Najib Serour were sporadic. Between 1972 and 1979, this writer established a folk theatre at a caravanserai, in the Hussein district of Cairo, the Wekalat al-Ghouri--an attempt to perpetuate the folk tradition of Arab theatre. The courtyard of Islamic archi-tecture was used, along with the spanning tiers of balconies and <u>mashrabiyas</u> for the staging of folk plays, or plays dramatized from ballads such as <u>Shafika wa Metwalli</u>, <u>Hassan wa Naima</u>, and others. The theater was closed down in 1979. [36] Aside from that solitary attempt, the folk tradition sometimes emerges in the sophisticated, social comedies of later playwrights such as Twafik al-Hakim, Yussef Idris, and Yussri al-Ebiari. Modern Egyptian theatre has developed in direct result of contact with the West, a contact which began with Marun al-Naqqash's historic production in Arabic of Moliere's The Miser in 1847.

But today, there are some theatre practitioners and scholars (such as this writer) in the Egyptian theatre who look back into the heart of the ritual celebrations such as those which once characterized the evolution of theatre in ancient Egypt. There exist today, as an intrinsic part of the cultural ethos of the Arab world, certain rituals of quasi-religious nature, which contain theatrical elements which could revitalize the spontaneity and communality of the modern drama in the Middle East.

In his dissertation entitled "The Role of Ritual towards a Modern Egyptian Theatre," Professor Issam Abdel-Aziz of the Egyptian Institute of the Theatre identifies a potential "poor Egyptian theatre" in two such rituals: the zar and the zikr.[37]

The Arabic word zar signifies a "visitor of ill omen," or simply a visit of the spirits. The zar as performance refers to a collection of rituals whose purpose is to cast out spirits to the accompaniment of dancing, drum-beating, incantations and incense burning. As a popular entertainment, the function of the zar is to provide release for suppressed energy. Yet, according to Professor Abdel-Aziz, "the zar in form and content, reflects dramatic ideas and theatrical forms ... which associate this ritual with the popular theatre of the Egyptian environment."[38]

Although not intended as theatre, the zar is the closest movement-oriented performance in Arab culture which is even akin to Artaud's "theatre of cruelty."[39] The zar was imported to Egypt in the nineteenth century from northern Abyssinia, where it also survives. The driving out of spirits is relegated to a sheikha, a religious female, referred to in Egypt as the kodia. The handling of the spirits requires, according to popular belief, "specialists" for different kinds of spirits. Thus, there is a sheikha who deals with Sudanese spirits, and one who is specialized in southern Egyptian spirits, while a third could be the specialist in Cairene spirits.

The zar ritual proceeds roughly as follows: on the eve of the zar, a lamb is slaughtered and the patient is bathed in its blood. Thus, blood-soaked, the patient is brought the following morning before the kodia and her accompanying troupe of zarists. The kodia begins by asking questions to find out which spirit is inhabiting the patient. A young girl, reportedly, once claimed to be inhabited by the Virgin Mary, and upon probing from the kodia, demanded to have white robes, a cross and a halo, brought her. Costumed thus, the patient is then queried by the kodia, to the accompaniment of tambourines, castanets, and drums, in a dance which can reach trancelike climaxes. The zar is usually terminated with the exhaustion of the patient, who thus drained is conceived of having been rid of the inhabiting spirit--hers, the Virgin Mary.

As mentioned, the function of the zar is the release of energy. In achieving this purpose, the ritual assumes the many aspects of a theatrical performance. The patient is not only healed by the outlet of suppressed emotions, provided by the zar, but he is allowed a freedom of expression and an expansiveness in movement, which allows creativity. Thus the patient is allowed to express himself, not only in the ritual, but in the dances and other related movements of the zar. Movement plays an intrinsic role in this ritual. It starts at a slow rhythm, accelerating gradually, until it reaches an ecstatic, frenzied pace, which is accompanied by drums, music, incantations, and incense burning. The frenzied movement relaxes gradually, as the patient is seen to be getting rid of the spirit and the "purification" takes place.

Professor Abdel-Aziz goes so far as to claim in his study that the aim of the zar and the aim of drama are one and the same: catharsis. In the zar the patient is purified of all psychological conflicts latent in his subconscious and which hitherto were unable to find any form of outlet. Furthermore, the participants, as well as the audience, which may include members of the patient's family, also engage in the movement accompanying the ritual and are also, therefore, subject to its cathartic influence. [40]

Dramatic dialogue is also present in the zar. This is only too clear in the "impersonation" which occurs when the patient is gripped by the spirit which inhabits his body. Thus the patient begins to speak as the spirit does (in the case of the "Virgin Mary" quoting biblical verses, or even speaking in a classical, literary language which is normally inaccessible to an average young girl), adopts its movements, and overall, assumes a character entirely different from his own. The element of impersonation can only manifest itself through movement, that is, once the patient has been allowed to express the spirit physically.

A single patient may be inhabited by several spirits. They may engage in dialogue with one another. Or, with the kodia. At any rate, the person inhabited by a spirit becomes, in effect, two different characters: his own and that of the spirit. The spirit character may cause the patient to perform certain movements which are not his own, speak in a language which is not his, or indulge in physical feats which are beyond his normal capacity.

Conflict, as a dramatic element, is also present in the zar. There is usually some conflict between the patient and the inhabiting spirit, or there may be conflict between various spirits competing simultaneously to dominate the patient. When this occurs then the patient may speak in several languages at the same time, each language expressing one of those spirits. In one recorded case, the patient, a woman, assumed simultaneously four distinct characters: a prostitute, her baby, a judge, and a saint. Finally, and most dramatic, is the conflict between the kodia and the spirit, especially in the final paroxysm of the ritual when the kodia tries to master the spirit in order to dispel it.

In addition to all of these inherently dramatic elements, there is a participator-viewer relationship in the zar which is akin to the actor-audience relationship in the theatre. The viewers join in the singing and dancing and the incantations which often involve the evocation of saints and religious figures, common to Islam, Christianity and Judaism. The healing of the patient is also a triumph for the viewers, who have played an essential part in dispelling the spirits during this performance.

The dialogue in the zar is sacred and mythological. The spirits, who are for the most part of religious origin, are acted out by the patient through mimetic dancing and movement. The movement which expresses the spirit of Mary will undoubtedly be different from that movement which physicalizes the spirit of Judas.[41]

The other ritual, the zikr, concerns the performances of the dervishes, whose swirling dances have as their aim to "transport the body and soul to sublime horizons."[42] For the participant (the dervish), as well as the viewer (the audience), the zikr has as its aim the generation of religious enthusiasm.

The intrinsic purpose of the dervish performances is unification with God, the becoming one with the being of God. This, according to Professor Abdel-Aziz, cannot be achieved unless the dancer abandons the world, both physically and spiritually.[43] This is what the ritual achieves. In order to reach this noncorporality, the dervishes indulge in dancing and mimetic action. To the Sufis (a mystical philosophy of Islam arising in the late tenth century which emphasized personal union of the soul with God), words are inadequate to express God. One of the famous Sufis, Galal-al-Din al-Rumi, even went so far as to declare that he who knows God cannot express Him. Therefore, movement and mimetic action were chosen to express what the word was incapable of conveying.[44]

In the zikr, the performer first remains seated in intense concentration upon God, whom he invokes by the repetition of the word "Allah," over and over again and with different intonations. Finally, when he has reached a state of religious exaltation, he stands up and begins to revolve around himself. These revolutions which begin slowly at first, gain in speed and intensity. To the dervishes, these arduous movements are considered a spiritual exercise, yet, if we examine them objectively we shall see that they are also theatrical.

To begin with, the dancer has to be of exceptional agility and flexibility. He must have the capacity to dance or revolve around himself for hours. The ritual is accompanied by incantations, which are rehearsed and memorized. The music, which consists of tambourines, drums, and flutes, is also rehearsed and arranged in advance. The dervishes dance with a certain planned choreography: within a circle, called "the circle of light," in which they must remain, and in which all their movements must remain. The movement within this circle is mimetic, relating or expressing certain religious concepts and symbols. Thus, he dances to tell a story and movement becomes the vehicle through which this storyteller recounts his religious beliefs. Nothing is left to improvisation for these professional dancers, whose movements, insofar as they excel in their execution, are amply clear to their followers, in spite of their symbolic nature.

The followers, who may be seated around or dance with the dervishes, are also (ideally) transported to that ecstatic state which has already gripped the dervishes. Thus a "spiritual power" is conveyed from performer to viewer.

Thus, in these frenzied spiritual swirlings, we also find the oneness of the communal religious celebrations of ancient Egyptian drama. The exaltation of the spirit over the body, the triumph of good over evil, and of the transcendant over the corporal, takes us back in a full circle to those prehistoric days when drama served to regenerate the soul through the studied performances of theatrical celebrations.

Notes

1. Sir James Frazer, "Adonis, Attis, Osiris," Vol. 2. The Golden Bough (New York: Macmillan and Company, 1936), pp. 6-9.

2. George Steindorff and Keith Seele, When Egypt Ruled the East (Chicago: The University of Chicago Press, 1957), p. 147.

3. Theodore H. Gaster, Thespis (New York: Doubleday and Company, Inc., 1961), p. 3.

4. Kurt Sethe, Die Altaegyptischen Dramatischen Texte (Leipzig, 1928).

5. Ellsworth Laflin, Jr. unpublished ms. "Drama: From Egypt into Greece."

6. Gaster, p. 83.

7. Laflin, Ibid.

8. Freedley and Reeves, A History of the Theatre (New York: Crown Publishers, Inc., 1955), p. 2.

9. Ibid.

10. Laflin, unpublished ms. "Egypt: The Amount of Royal Drama."

11. Ibid.

12. Laflin, unpublished ms. "Egyptian Sources of Greek Tragedy."

13. Ibid.

14. Ibid.

15. Ibid.

16. Ibid.

17. Laila Abou-Saif, "Creating a Theatre of the Poor at Wekalat al-Ghouri in Cairo," The Literary Review: Arab Supplement (June 1982), p. 102.

18. Jacob Landau, Studies in the Arab Theatre and Cinema (Philadelphia: University of Pennsylvania Press, 1958), p. 12.

19. Ibrahim Hamada, Khayal al-Dhal was Tamthiliyat Ibn-Danyal (Cairo: Wizaret al-thaqafa was al-irshad al-quami, 1979), pp. 87-100.

20. Landau, p. 20.

21. Gassner and Quinn, The Reader's Encyclopaedia to World Drama (New York: Thomas Y. Crowell Company, 1969), p. 21.

22. Linda Suny Myrsiades, The Karaghiozis Tradition and Greek Shadow Theatre: History and Analysis (Ph.D. diss., Indiana University, 1973).

23. Olive Blackman, Shadow Puppets, (New York: Harper and Brothers, 1960), pp. 50-54.

24. Sotiris Spatharis, Behind the White Screen (New York: Red Dust, 1976), p. 135.

25. Landau, p. 20.

26. Laila Abou-Saif, Najib al-Rihani and the Development of Comedy in Egypt: 1914-1949 (Ph.D. diss., University of Illinois, Urbana, 1968).

27. E. W. Lane, An Account of the Manners and Customs of the Modern Egyptians (London: J. M. Dent and Co., 1908), pp. 395-97.

28. Ibid.

29. Curt Prufer, "Drama" in Encyclopaedia of Religion and Ethics, James Hastings, ed. (London, 1921), pp. 872-879.

30. Ibid.

31. Abou-Saif, Ph.D. diss.

32. Ibid.

33. Ibid.

34. Mohammed Manzalawi, Arabic Writing To-day: Drama (Cairo: American Research Center in Egypt, 1977), p. 22.

35. Mohammed Yussef Najm, Yacou'b Sanoua (Beirut: Dar el-thaqafa, 1963).

36. Laila Abou-Saif, "Creating a Theatre of the Poor at Wekalat al-Ghouri in Cairo," The Literary Review: Arab Supplement (June 1982), p. 102.

37. Issam Abdel-Aziz, "Al-zar wa al-masrah," Magalet al-masrah (July 1981), pp. 53-57.

38. Ibid.

39. Ibid.

40. Ibid.

41. Ibid.

42. Issam Abdel-Aziz, "Al-masrah al-Masri al-Faquir," Magalet al-masrah (June 1981), pp. 44-45.

43. Ibid.

44. Ibid.

General Works and Ancient Egyptian Drama

Breasted, James Henry. Ancient Records. Chicago: University of Chicago Press, 1906-1907.

_____. The Development of Religion and Thought in Ancient Egypt. New York: Scribner's, 1912.

Budge, Sir. E. A. W. Egyptian Hieroglyphic Dictionary (with index of English words, etc.). 2 vols. Philadelphia, 1920.

Driotone, Etienne. "Le Drame sacre dans l'antique Egypte" in Flambeau, I (January 1, 1928).

_____. "Une scene des Mysteres d'Horus" in Revue de L'Egypte Ancienne, Vol. II. Paris: Librarie Ancienne Honore Champion, 1929.

Frankfort, Henri. The Cenotaph of Seti I at Abydos, 2 vols. Adrienne de Buck, trans. 1933.

Gaster, Theodore, H. Thespis. New York: Henry Schuman, 1950.

Gropow, Hermann. "Die Publikation von Kurt Sethe der 'Pramidintexten' " in Zeitschrift der Deutschen Morgenlandischen Gesellschaft, 91 (1937).

Jequier, Gustave. Fouilles à Saqqarah; La Pyramide d'Aba. Cairo: L'Institut français d'archeologie orientale, 1935.

Laflin, Louis E. Aristotle and the Egyptian Origins of Greek Drama. M.A. thesis: Yale University, 1938.

_____. The Ancient Egyptian Drama. Ph.D. diss., Yale University, 1941.

Maspero, Gaston. Les inscriptions des pyramids de Saqqarah. Paris, 1894.

Petrie, Flinders. Seventy Years in Archeology. New York: Henry Holt and Co., 1932.

Schaefer, Kurt (Heinrich). "Die Mysterien des Osiris in Abydos unter konig Sesostris III" in Untersuchungen zur Geschichte und Altertumskune Aegptens, IV, 2, Leipzig: J. C. Hinrichs, 1904.

Spelers, Louis. Traduction, Index et Vocabulaire des Textes des Pyramides Egyptiennes. Bruxelles: Depot Avenue Marie-Jose, 159, 1936.

Steindorff, George, and Selle, Keith C. When Egypt Ruled the East. Chicago: The University of Chicago Press, 1968.

Arab Theatre

Abdel-Aziz, Issam. The Role of Ritual Towards a Modern Egyptian Theatre, Ph.D. diss. Hungarian Theatrical Institute, Budapest, 1980.

Abdel-Wahab, Farouk, ed. Modern Egyptian Drama. Minneapolis: Bibliotheca Islamica, 1974.

Abou-Saif, Laila. "Creating a Theatre of the Poor at Wekalat al-Ghouri in Cairo," The Literary Review, (June 1982).

_____. "Najib al-Rihani: From Buffoonery to Social Comedy" in Journal of Arabic Literature Vol. IV.

_____. Najib al-Rihani and the Development of Egyptian Comedy in Egypt. Ph.D. diss., The University of Illinois, Urbana, 1968.

Aboul Naga, Atia. Les Sources Françaises du Théâtre égyptian, 1870-1939. Algers: Bd. Zighoud Youcef, 1972.

Barbour, Neville. "The Arabic Theatre in Egypt" in Bulletin of the School of Oriental Studies, Vol. VIII, 1935-1937.

Blackman, Olive. Shadow Puppets. New York: Harper and Brothers, 1960.

Gassner, John and Edward Quinn, eds. The Reader's Encyclopedia to World Drama. New York: Thomas Y. Crowell Company, 1969.

Genzier, Irene L. The Practical Visions of Yaqub Sanu. Cambridge: Harvard University Press, 1966.

Hamalian, Leo, and John D. Yohanan, eds. New Writing from the Middle East. New York: Mentor, 1978.

Landau, Jacob. Studies in the Arab Theatre and Cinema. Philadelphia: University of Pennsylvania Press, 1958.

Lane, E. W. An Account of the Manners and Customs of the Modern Egyptians. London: J. M. Dent and Co., 1908.

Manzalawi, Mohammed, ed. Arabic Writing To-day: Drama. Cairo: American Research Center in Egypt, 1977.

Meserve, Walter J. "Some Observations on Modern Egyptian Drama," Al-Arabiyya: Journal of the American Association of Teachers of Arabic, 9, 1976-7?.

Myrsiades, Linda Suny. The Karaghiozis Tradition and Greek Shadow Puppet Theatre: History and Analysis. Ph.D. diss., Indiana University, 1973.

Niehbur, Carsten. Travels Through Arabic and Other Countries in the East. 2 vols. Edinburgh, 1792.

Peters, F. E. Aristotle and the Arabs. New York: New York University Press, 1968.

Prufer, Curt. "Drama" in Encyclopaedia of Religion and Ethics. James Hastings, ed. London: 1921.

Spatharis, Sotiris. Behind The White Screen. New York: Red Dust, 1976.

Tagher, Jeanette, "Les Debuts du théâtre moderne en Egypte" in Cahiers d'histoire égyptienne, I, 2, I (1949).

Tietze, Andreas. The Turkish Shadow Theatre and the Puppet Collection of the L. A. Meyer Memorial Foundation. Berlin: Mann Verlag, 1977.

Tomiche, Nada. Le Théâtre Arabe. Paris: UNESCO, 1969.

Woodman, David, ed. Egyptian One-Act Plays. Cairo: American University, 1974.

*   *   *

For a companion study dealing with Westernized drama of the Arabs, which was originally scheduled for publication in this volume, see The Theatrical Movement of the Arabs, by Pierre Cachia, published in Middle East Studies Association Bulletin. (MESA), Vol. XVI, No. 1, July 1982. B.F., ed.

Chapter Twenty-One

DEVELOPMENT OF THEATRE IN IRAN

Farrokh Gaffary

Rituals, Pageants, and Festivals

Although theatre forms as we know them in ancient Greece
(from 490 B.C.) or India (from first to fifth centuries A.D.) or
China (circa twelfth to fourteenth century A.D.) or Japan (circa
fourteenth to fifteenth century A.D.) did not exist in Iran, nevertheless for milleniums some very interesting forms of rituals and
entertainments were practiced by Iranians.[1]

Whereas the archeologists presume that certain figurines like
seals and stamps from western Iran of the fourth millenium B.C.,
depicting men with horned ibex heads, hairy bodies, wearing shoes
with upturned toes and carrying wide collars receding down the
back into bird tails, could be ibex gods or "masters and protectors
of game" or "mythical sorcerers playing the part of animals or humanized animals"[2]; it may also be proposed that they could be
masked men--half sacred, half profane--who served, as we shall
see later on, as entertainers.

In October of 522 B.C. a Magi who had usurped the Iranian
throne was killed by Darius of the Achaemenian dynasty and this
was followed by a general massacre of the Magis. About a hundred
years later Herodotus says: "this day was celebrated each year as
the feast of Magophonia or the day of the slaughter of the Magi....
The Persians observe this day with one accord, and keep it more
strictly than any other in the whole year ... this day is the greatest holy day that all Persians alike keep." This anticleric popular
festival was celebrated for over a hundred and twenty years.[3]
Certain scholars believe this feast could continue in the form of
other celebrations like Mir-e Noruzi or Day be Mehr and Omar Kos-
han which shall be mentioned later.

Since the invasion of Alexander (334-323 B.C.) and mainly
under the Parthians (third century B.C. to third century A.D.)
Greek theatre was performed in the original language in Iran. Objects remaining from the same Parthian period prove that the use

of animal masks depicting monkeys for example were common at the time. [4]

In the Mithra god cult, (from fourteenth century B.C. to fifth century A.D.) which expanded from India and Iran into Europe (as far as England) and Asia (China) and adapted itself with the varied surroundings, the access to different grades gave occasion to rituals or mysteries where the believers wore the guise and masks (perhaps due to Greek or Roman influence) of different animals (lions, crows, etc.) and imitated their cries and movements. [5]

At least as early as the Sassanian period (third to seventh centuries A.D.) buffoons, jugglers and tumblers, [6] musicians, and dancers [7] played an important part in the merry and grotesque procession of the Barneshastan-e Kuseh (the bride of the beardless man) mentioned at length by Iranian historians of the tenth and eleventh centuries. On a cold day at the brink of spring an ugly, half-naked beardless man, his body smeared with a warming ointment, a crow in one hand and fanning himself with the other pretending to be hot, rode through the village on an ass. The crowd threw snow and ice on him and at the same time bestowed him with gifts. The unfortunates who did not give donations were sprayed with ink and mud by the beardless. [8] This symbolic ceremony for seeing the winter out has survived for more than 1,700 years and is practiced even to this day in some Iranian villages. The Kuseh character is also well known in Turkey as Köse or Kosa. [9]

From pre-Islamic Iran (before seventh century) must also date the ritual of Dey be Mehr otherwise known in the tenth and eleventh centuries as Botikân (days of idols) during which dummies fabricated from mud or dough were left to harden against doorways in the streets. Passing crowds bowed to these as if to kings and finished by burning the effigies. Naturally with the arrival of Islam in Iran this custom was deemed "idolatrous" and banned.

The Mir-e Noruzi (the prince of the new year) ritual also originates from ancient Iran. In this carnival-like ceremony a farcical temporary king was elected for a few days. This rite which continued until sixty years ago was very similar to the Fete de Fous of western European Middle Ages, with its Abbot of Unreason (le Pape des Fous). [10]

In popular rejoicings Iranians continued to wear zoomorphic masks and disguises. The horned head of the ibex of the fourth millenium B.C. supposedly changed into the masks and skins of goats and bulls. Miniatures and drawings of these from the sixteenth and seventeenth centuries are frequent. [11] The grotesque parade described in Pantagruel by the French writer Rabelais (sixteenth century) is not very far from the Iranian zoomorphic dances.

In the same tradition, there existed (until the 1940's) in the forest of Gilan (northern Iran) a dance-pantomime which portrayed the story of a bride abandoning her groom to elope with her lover. The performers wore masks and apparel made of goat skin. Due to its amoral character this dance should be pre-Islamic.

In Bokhara in the mid-tenth century, according to an historian, took place, since milleniums (!), a mourning ritual with songs called "Kin-e Siyâvosh" (revenge of Siyâvosh). Siyâvosh was an Iranian legendary prince, innocently killed by his father-in-law. This ritual is also referred to as "the weeping of the Magi," hence its pre-Islamic origin.[12] Up to 1974 the ritual of Siyâvashun existed in the southern Iranian province of Fars.[13] Some consider the legend of Siyâvosh, a sinless hero killed unjustly, and his mourning, to be an influence on Tazieh, appearing some thousand years later (mentioned further on).[14]

The art of storytelling, Naqqâli, dates back to ancient Iran. In royal courts, public squares or tea houses, the Naqqâl recounted, as he does even today, tales of epic legends or popular picaresque romances by means of mime, hand movements, and varied vocal pitches. In the seventeenth century, a book entitled Tarâz-ol-akhbâr was devoted to the art and technique in this field. An attempt to reboost this genre was made in Mashhad, within the four Festivals of Tus (1975-78).

In the early twentieth century arrived from the West the Shahr-e Farang (city of Europe), a replica of what was known as the peep show or La Vue d'Optique in eighteenth century Europe. This was also adopted in the Arab world by the name of "Sundûq al Dunya."[15] It consisted of a large brass-bound box, standing on legs with three viewers of thick lenses through which Occidental pictures were shown, accompanied by amusing and colorful commentary. The advent of cinema and TV brought this medium to an end.

Shadow and Puppet Theatre

Spreading out from East Asia (Java, China, and India) shadow theatre, Khiyâl Bâzi (shadow plays) and Fanus-e Khiyâl (lantern of imagination) existed in Iran since long ago. The poet Omar Khayyam (died 1123), in a symbolic quatrain, compares the world to a lantern and its inhabitants to whirling figures. These images were supposedly painted on a form of lampshade rotating around a central light. Shadows and Fanus-e Khiyâl completely disappeared in Iran about eighty years ago.

Kheymeh Shabbâzi (the tent of the nocturne play), a puppet theatre with glove dolls (for daylight) and string puppets (for evening performances), has existed over many centuries, to the extent that Khayyam philosophically mentions: "We are the puppets (lo'bat) and the destiny is the puppeteer (lo'bat bâz). We

play on the spread of life and go again in the trunk of death."
The poet Attâr (died 1221) in his Oshtor Nâmeh (the book of camel)
mentions at length the puppet theatre, personifying the puppet
master as God. In the first half of the seventeenth century there
existed in Iran a sort of mobile puppeteer carrying "a large curtain
held up by a stretcher, hanging down to the puppeteer's knees con-
cealing him and serving as a back cloth for the puppets ... the
lower part of the curtain has a wide and deep pocket serving as
the stage. The puppeteer carries this pocket as a kangaroo her
pouch."[16] The main figure of the Iranian puppet theatre is Pahlavân Kachal (the bald hero) or Pahlavân Panbeh (the cottonwool
hero) a braggart, fake, and cowardly personage with an unfaith-
ful wife. Some authors find his characteristics and pseudoreligious
beliefs typically Iranian. Pahlavân Kachal seems more versatile and
cultivated than the Turkish Karagöz. According to the travelers of
the first half of the nineteenth century, in some of the Pahlavân
Kachal plays the molla (Shiite cleric) is represented as a false devotee more attached to earthly pleasures such as wine and dance
than to vigils. At the end of the same century, officialdom seems
more tolerant towards liberalities and obscenities of the puppet theatre.[17] Today this entertainment continues in a decayed form. The
manipulator hides behind the curtain whereas his companion sits on
the stage side playing an instrument and talking to and for the puppets using sometimes a small wind instrument placed between his
lips called Sutak, which produces a strident squeaky sound.

Religious Processions and Dramas

The Shiite sect of Islam became the official religion of Iran in
the early sixteenth century. The Shiites believe that Ali, the cousin and son-in-law of the Prophet Mohammad (died 632) should have
succeeded him as Khalif after his death. As this did not take place
the Shiites sectioned out claiming the legitimate succession for Ali
(died 661) and his sons Hasan (died 670) and Hoseyn; the latter
strongly opposed the Umayyad Khalif of Damascus and left Arabia
for Mesopotamia (and later perhaps Iran) where he had a following.
In the desert region of Karbela (actual Iraq) he was besieged by
Umayyad troops, left to thirst and eventually slain with many of his
companions (October 680).

The commander of the Umayyads was Omar ibn Sa'd (died
686). From the early sixteenth century the Iranians celebrated the
feast of Omar Koshân (the killing of Omar) a popular rejoicing in
which a giant effigy of Omar, stuffed with wood, straw, cloth, ma-
nure and fire crackers was burnt. As an act of provocation these
feasts took place particularly in Sunnite-inhabited areas. Gradually Omar ibn Sa'd was transformed by popular beliefs into Omar ibn
Khatâb, the second Khalif of Islam (died 644) who symbolized for
Iranians both the Arab invader and Sunnite enemy. Nowadays the
"Omar Koshân" is occasionally and secretly performed in Azarbaijan
in a satirical and erotic form by women.

Probably from the same period of the sixteenth century the Shamayel Gardân evolved: a man who went around exhibiting holy pictures painted on canvas, or on glass, narrating the fate of the martyrs of Shiism. Shamâyel Gardân or Pardedâri is still current in Iran.[18]

Since the murder of Imam Hoseyn (680) Shiites mourn him on the anniversary of his martyrdom. An Iranian king of the Shiite Buyid dynasty in the tenth century temporarily forced the Sunnite Khalif to officially commemorate the mourning of the Imam in Baghdad. In the following century preachings on the tragic end of the Prophet's grandson were instituted. In 1501 Hoseyn Vâ'ez Kâshefi wrote his Rozat ol Shohadâ (garden of the martyrs) on the sufferings and death of the Imam. Thereafter convincing orators recited extracts of this book, bringing from the believers cries and lamentations on the calamities of the Prophet's family. These sessions are called Rozeh Khâni (recitation of threnody).

The Safavid dynasty (sixteenth-eighteenth centuries) encouraged all the above-mentioned rites and moreover patronized the elaborate religious procession, Dasteh. Even from 1475 European travelers remark upon and later describe these processions which often took place on the first ten days of the Moslem month of Moharram, culminating on the tenth day (Ashura) with the martyrdom in Karbela. These Dasteh were most important coming from different neighborhoods (which caused frequent and bloody quarrels) composed of men beating their breasts, flagellating themselves with chains, attaching locks to their flesh and larding their heads with daggers (like the acts of the fanatic pilgrims of the holy city of Moulay-Idris in Morocco). All these represent pietistic exercises and mortifications to signify their remorse on not having helped Hoseyn.[19] Some individuals carried large heavy standards (Alam), decorated with tall flexible steel blades, lanterns and long ostrich feathers. Some of the people in the corteges personify events from the life of the Imam and his companions such as the journey and their tragic end. Camels bore the bridal chamber of the unfortunate Qâsem, nephew of Hoseyn, horses were decorated and sometimes artificially wounded by arrows, also huge wooden structures called "Nakhl" symbolizing the Imam's coffin were carried. The biggest Nakhl is in the city of Yazd usually carried by several hundred men. The entire train is accompanied by dirge singers beating themselves. Gradually these representations were transformed into mobile tableaux vivants. After the Safavids (approximately between 1722 and 1735) two travelers, Salamons and Van Goch, saw these tableaux carried on wheeled chariots, showing silent characters resembling (Shabih) the protagonists of the Karbela tragedy. Seemingly this must be the last stage of the lengthy evolution of ritual before becoming verbal and taking a dramatic form. In early 1770 Gmelin, a Russian traveler, used for the first time the word "theatre" in connection with these religious celebrations. But in fact it was in October 1787 that an Englishman, William Franklin, saw in Shiraz and described what may be considered up to now as one of the earliest performances of Tazieh.[20] The word "tazieh" originally meant condolences and mourning but eventually represented a dramatic play, Tazieh Khâni. But in fact the more correct term would be "Shabih Khani" (the play of resemblances).[21]

From this time on, due to piety, the Tazieh progressed and flourished under the patronage of the Qajar kings, particularly Naser-ed-Din Shah (1848-96) and was equally well received and actively supported by the general public.[22] This king constructed a huge round arenalike theatre--Takieh Dolat--in which the official and elaborate Taziehs were performed.[23] This ritual theatre genre became so renowned that an English Iranologist, Sir Lewis Pelly, wrote: "If the success of a drama is to be measured by the effects which it produces upon the people for whom it is composed or upon the audiences before it is represented, no play has ever surpassed the tragedy known in the Mussulman world as that of Hasan and Husain."[24] Other Englishmen, like Edward Gibbons, T. B. Macaulay and Matthew Arnold[25] and Frenchmen like Arthur Gobineau and Joseph Ernest Renan paid great tributes to the Persian religious drama.

The contents of these plays are essentially the narrative of the journey of the Imam and his people from Medina to Mesopotamia, his battles and his martyrdom. There are also plays concerning the Prophet Mohammad and his family, the Shiite saints and holy men, and koranic and biblical stories.

The most prominent character is Hoseyn, who personifies innocence and is the intercessor of the believers. His purity and unjust death (compared with the character of Siyâvosh and his funeral ritual mentioned earlier) and submission towards fate, cause him to be loved and worshipped. He is also (like Jesus) the intercessor of men on the day of judgement and for the redemption of Moslems he makes an offering of himself. To create an effect and make the people cry, authors of Tazieh not only took liberties in changing historical facts but also transformed the characters. Hoseyn, who in the books of the tenth century is presented as an audacious and self-assured person becomes, from the sixteenth century and particularly in the Tazieh, a man, while accepting his destiny, is also woeful and looks for sympathy to the extent that his moans become unbearably irritating today. So Hoseyn, by recounting his innocence and weakness, and by weeping, provokes cries and howls amongst the audience, who in this ritual performance in their turn also lament their own miseries (material needs and oppressions imposed by the authorities). The oppressed Mazlum is a personality most popular for arousing pity amongst the Iranians and this psychosociological phenomenon is visible throughout the Persian history and plays an important part in the Islamic Revolution since February 1979.[26]

Shabih Khâni takes place in public squares or courts of

caravansarais, mosques, or houses of rich people, but there is also a special construction for Tazieh called Tekiyeh or Hoseynieh where the audience sits around a square or round platform stage (Sakku). The surrounding loggias (alcoves) of the Tekiyeh were richly decorated with carpets, shawls adorned with inscriptions and crystal chandeliers, etc., lent by the Shah, the dignitaries, and also the people. The performers, more correctly termed the executants, playing the holy men and their followers dress in green or white, their adversaries or the villains in red. The plays are always in Persian verse, sung by the good and recited by the bad ones. The executants are not generally professional actors, they are from all walks of life and play on occasions. Some masks, specially of the demon, are also used.

Thanks to Rozeh Khâni and especially Tazieh, Persian classical music survived under religious cover and pretext. The current instruments are various large kettle drums, different trumpets, an elongated horn (Karnâ) heralding the sorrow, and cymbals.

Since 1808 foreign travelers compared Tazieh with the mystery and passion plays of the European Middle Ages. There are two kinds of Tazieh performances: the stationary, as mentioned above and the mobile, in which the executants roam around the streets playing consecutive episodes as they move on through the standing crowds. There is a resemblance between the Iranian processions and Shabin Khâni and for example the Passion Week Celebrations in Guatemala or the Corpus Domini in Sicily or the Easter Procession at Sezze Romano, near Rome.

The stage or the Sakku has no curtains but at times it bears elaborate arrangements.[27] For example, the hell scenes give the opportunity to present an impressive show of people painted entirely in black, chained to each other and carrying on their heads bowls in which long flames burn. Since 1812 travelers mention simulated battle scenes in open places where more than "four thousand" (!) horsemen fought without accidents.

Tazieh mise en scene has special rules: circling around the Sakku on foot or horseback means going from one place to another, a race around the Sakku by armed horsemen symbolizes a battle, a person turning around signifies a change of place, a large basin of water represents the river Euphrates and straw plays the role of the Mesopotamian Desert sand. The parts of women are played by veiled men who are not supposed to act in an effeminate manner.[28] The person directing the performance is called Moin ol Bokâ (the one who helps to bring tears) or Tazieh Gardân; he is constantly on the platform distributing written texts amongst the executants who do not necessarily know them by heart, he orders the protagonists around, sometimes even by prodding them with his club, he brings and removes the stage properties: for example by dipping a piece of cotton wool in sheep blood and throwing it across the stage it represents a piece of flesh. The audacity in Tazieh is remarkable in the sense that the allusion to the tragedy of Karbela is some times shown in flashback (as in the Tamerlane play) and other times as an event to come or a flash-forward (as in Moses play where the Jewish prophet foresees the martyrdom of Hoseyn). The unconscious modernity of such a drama is also apparent on other occasions: like the absence of a back stage which leaves the players to wait their turn on the sides; also the permanent contact between the stage and the audience who participate constantly by weeping and breast beating in sign of sorrow or laughing loudly and even molesting the villains (on very rare occasions the executant playing the part of Yazid, the killer of Hoseyn, has been lynched). All these peculiarities attracted the attention of today's stage directors, such as Jerzy Grotowski and Peter Brook.[29] An important feature of the Tazieh is the fact that for all people involved (executants and audience) the performance in the foremost is a religious ritual, therefore the men acting the villains feel guilty of their parts and before killing their innocent victims, weep in sorrowful apology. This consciousness of the actors who are essentially deeply religious is compared by certain authors with Bertolt Brecht's Verfremdungs effekt.[30] Even if such a comparison should be made with reserve it is an interesting phenomenon to note that in Europe at the end of the nineteenth century and the beginning of the twentieth century the trend reacting against realism and naturalism in the theatre (mainly in the works of V. E. Meyerhold, E. B. Vakhtangov, L. Pirandello, O. Krejca, G. Strehler, and T. Kantor, etc.) utilized the same techniques without actually knowing Persian religious drama. Nevertheless there is a case directly influenced by Tazieh, that of Claude Confortès, a French playwright and director, in his Le Marathon (1972).

From the beginning the Shiite clergy held a contradictory attitude towards the Shabih Khâni. It has been authorized and patronized by some and rejected and condemned by others for different reasons (portraying of holy men and thus ridiculing their personalities, the use of music, and the show of some nudity, etc.). Right from the start there were also comical plays included in the repertoires called Gusheh or Shabih-e Mozhek like The Tying of the Demon's Thumb or The Impositions of Moin ol Bokâ or The Adventures of Shirafkan.[31] These plays could have gradually separated off from the religious drama to become an authentic secular national theatre but with the arrival of western novelties and their strong impact unfortunately this never happened and moreover, Tazieh entered an age of decay and was finally banned in the early 1930's during the reign of Rezâ Shah Pahlavi (1925-41) under the pretext of avoiding "barbaric acts of mass exaltation" and for consideration towards the Turkish Sunnite State. Tazieh barely survived in a decayed and clandestine form in out-of-the-way villages and only resurfaced with the revival of religious sentiments after the abdication of the Shah in 1941, but it remained in a poor state until the beginning of the 1960's when an intellectual movement based on traditions began scholarly research and gave encouragements culminating in the Shiraz Arts Festival where in 1976 an International Seminar animated by P. J. Chelkowski[32] and seven Passion plays in fourteen performances (gathered by Mohammad Baqer Ghaffari) in Shiraz and a nearby village were attended by a hundred thousand spectators including Queen Farah Pahlavi.

Jesters and Traditional Comedy

Since pre-Islamic times Iranian kings had jesters and buffoons (Dalqak or Maskhareh). Shah Abbas (1587-1628) had a celebrated entertainer, Kal Enâyat (Enâyat the Bald), and it seems that this talented clown was the first to start mimicked sketches (Bâzi or play) namely: The Canvas Shop, The Eye Healing, The Saving of the Life of the Shah's Falconer.

In the seventeenth century, troops of musicians and dancers performed amorous and comic singing sketches which ended in brawl and escape. Dialogue buffoonary called Taqlid (imitations) came next. A traveler of the same period admiring the ability of Persian acrobats and conjurers whom he considered superior to the French ones, also mentions actors wearing masks and performing three-hour comedies full of "insolence" and "lewdity." In the beginning of the eighteenth century as the Shiite clergy forbade the appearance of women as dancers and players, young boys with unbroken voices replaced them en travesti creating much ambiguity.

There were also other forms of comedy: Kachalak Bâzi (the play of the bald), Baqqâl Bâzi (the play of the grocer), and Ruband Bâzi (the play of the mask). In the latter, actors walked on stilts wearing long robes. These comedies were performed in tea houses as well as in private houses on occasions of marriages, births, and circumcisions.

To obtain a central stage in public places or to gain space in the courtyards of houses, the pool in the center was covered by wooden platform beds and carpets. So the term Ruhozi (over the pool) or Takht-e Hozi (wooden beds over the pool) became the generic names for the improvisatory Persian traditional comedy both in the cities and rural areas. The principal character of this genre is the Siyâh (black man) whose date of appearance is unknown. He blackens his face and hands with soot and grease, speaks with the accent of former Iranian black slaves, using an indecent and obscene vocabulary (like his counterparts in traditional Arabian comedies or in Turkish Karagöz and Oratayunu). He freely criticizes the dignitaries, the rich men, and the social defects and behind the guise of an "irresponsible simpleton Negro" he is able to be very daring. Other characters of the Ruhozi are the rich and aged haji, his wife, son, daughter and her suitor. In the beginning of the nineteenth century Chodzko mentions that these plays mock the mollas and their

act of ablution and leeching.[33]   In the twentieth century, in order
to avoid a clash with the authorities, the plays performed in the
tea houses were mainly of pseudohistorical subjects but included a
flavor of contemporary criticism by the Siyâh, who double-deals his
master, favors the lovers, acts generally silly and at the end gives
the moral conclusion of the play. Alongside the Ruhozi existed the
pantomime genre Lâl Bâzi (play of the mute) which emerged from
dance. About 1917, theatres of popular comedies opened in Tehran
and survived a precarious period of closures and openings due to
prudish elements. The stages were at first square, surrounded by
the audience, then three-sided with a large painted canvas of a
garden scene hanging as backdrop. Famous animators of the 1920's
were Akbar Sarshâr, Ahmad Moayed, Babrâz Soltâni, and two formidable Siyâhs: Zabiollâh Mâheri and Mehdi Mesri. The players
joked with the audience and musicians accompanied them from time
to time. A new character emerged mocking the westernized Iranians: Fokoli (from the French Faux col). Women had their own
traditional theatre with entirely female casts (acting even the male
parts). Performed in harems were such daring comedies as Khaleh
Roro (Auntie Roro). About 1930 Reza Shah Pahlavi's censorship
demanded texts for the Ruhozi plays, which was against the spirit
of improvisation and moreover restricted its critical aspect. At the
end of the 1930's entertainers (comedians, musicians, and puppeteers) performing for private parties were based in shops on Cyrus
Avenue in Tehran. In the religious uprising of June 1963 some of
these agencies (mainly managed by Jews) were targets of looting
and fire, but they survived. When the last stronghold of popular
comedies Tamâshâkhân-e Iran (Iran theatre) closed down in 1963
due to lack of subsidies, it was succeeded by the Hâfez nô theatre
in the red-light district of Tehran, with Sadi Afshâr as Siyâh. In
August 1977 at the Shiraz Art Festival, a tribute was rendered to
the improvisatory popular comedies by an International Symposium
and the performances of Ruhozi by groups from all over Iran.[34]
During the Islamic Revolution of 1979 the Hâfez nô Theatre was
burnt down along with the destruction of the district. Since this
time the group has occasionally performed on the Islamic TV.

Naser ed Din Shah (1848-96) was interested in both Iranian
traditional performances, and as it was seen later, western-style
theatre. He had famous court jesters and like all monarchs encouraged these to ridicule some of the courtiers and statemen.
The most well-known of his buffoons was Karim Shirei (Karim the
Treacle) who specialized in Baqqâl Bâzi and to whom was attributed
a certain text called Baqqâl Bâzi in Presence of the Shah. He never performed this but it contained interesting direction on this type
of acting. The other well-known entertainer of the same king was
Esmâil Bazzâz, who in his plays changed the classical grocer (Baqqâl)
into other characters such as a court physician, a colonel and even
the chief of the Tehran Police who in 1883 reacted and had him
beaten, but the comedian complained to the Shah and received
justice.

The Comedy in Western Manner

Almost every diary-keeping Iranian traveler to Europe between 1799 and 1870 mentioned with much admiration all kinds of western theatrical performances. As these narratives were unpublished in Iran, the public had no knowledge of them.

Mirza Fath Ali Akhundzadeh (1812-78) was not only the first Iranian, but the first Asian (even before the Turks, Indians, and Japanese) to write plays in western-style theatre. He became a Russian citizen under the name of Akhundov and was a critical-minded progressive writer whose pamphlets exercised great influence in Oriental liberal circles. He was fluent in Persian, Arabic, Turkish, and Russian and became interpreter of the Russian Vice-Roy of the Caucasus. He wrote his six comedies in Turkish Azari (between 1850-57), later translated them into Russian to be performed in Tiflis, St. Petersburg, and Moscow. Akhundzadeh's comedies are: Mollâ Khalil the Alchemist, denouncing a charlatan swindling ignorant people; Monsieur Jordan, the Botanist, opposing science to superstition; The Vizer of the Khân of Sarâb (or Lankarân), criticizing the corrupt governors; The Thief-Catching Bear, an amorous intrigue among peasants; The Miser, portraying a greedy merchant; and a skit on Russian occupation of southern Caucasus, The Barristers, takes place in Tabriz about unscrupulous lawyers who try to swindle a woman.[35] In these amusing comedies he gives a preeminent place to women and denounces the abuse of power, the evils of banditry and the hypocrisy of the clergy against whom he wrote a pamphlet, Letters of Kamâl od Doleh. He complains that the Moslem law has forbidden the theatre this beautiful gift. Akhundzadeh, the first Asian to have shown the importance of a new theatre in European style, has been called the Molière and the Gogol of the East. The text of his plays, Tamsilât, was published in Turkish Azari (Tiflis, 1859) and read in Iran and translated into Persian by Mirza Mohammad Qarâjedâghi (published in Tehran, 1874). The translator claimed it as the first example of theatre in Persian. Both the Turkish and the Persian texts were written in colloquial everyday language rather than the literary affected style.

In fact the first plays written directly in Persian were by Mirzâ Aqâ Tabrizi, who was on a brief government mission in Constantinople; he also knew a little Russian and was fluent in Turkish Azari and French to the extent that for more than seven years he was the local chief secretary at the French Legation in Tehran.

He had read Akhundzadeh's plays in Turkish Azari and the author had requested him to translate them into Persian, but Mirzâ Aqâ had replied (letter of June 1871) that he preferred to write dramatic pieces himself in Persian and to give his people a chance to see "examples in this new manner."[36] Nevertheless his plays were much influenced by Akhundzadeh who gave him advice of restraint which he fortunately did not heed. His highly amusing comedies are: Ashraf Khân, about forced gifts and bribes; The Government of Zamân Khân, on extortion of money from simple people; The Pilgrimage of Shâh Qoli Mirzâ, a tale of tricks and pranks; and Aqâ Hâsem's Love Affair, the weakest plot. Mirzâ Aqâ shocked the conformists and the believers of classical conventions (starting with Akhundzadeh through to 1960), who criticized his free language and disregard of the rule of the three unities. Precisely these "mistakes" gave his work involuntary boldness and modernity and A. Bricteux believes that the comical situations and funny everyday dialogues, make these masterpieces of humor comparable with Gogol's Revizor and Jules Romains' Knock. These plays denounce, in an uninhibited way, moral simperings, corruption of absolute rulers, and the sheepishness of the people. Probably Akhundzadeh with the intention of protecting Mirzâ Aqâ from the dangers of the Shah's authorities, proposed that his works be attributed to Mirzâ Malkam Khan (1833-1908), a liberal Iranian politician exiled in Europe and out of reach of the Shah's vengeance. So Malkam Khan, who was very close to Akhundzadeh and had the habit of using dialogues in some of his political pamphlets, could feasibly have written these and was erroneously known as the author of Mirzâ Aqâ's plays, right up to 1956 when two Soviet Azarbayjanian scholars disclosed the truth.

Another liberal, Mirzâ Aqâ Khan Kermâni (1853-96), also used dialogues in his book, Three Letters, which included "Susmar od doleh" (The Lizard of the State), a tale of a nineteenth-century governor's tyranny. This was adapted for the stage in 1977 (directed by M. Hashemi) at the Festival of Popular Traditions in Isfahan.

Introduction of European Theatre

Naser ed Din Shah on his journey of 1873 to Europe was impressed by performances of circuses, operas, and theatres and published his diary the following year. But it was only in March 1886 that the first European-style auditorium (a l'Italienne) was constructed in the higher school of Dar ol Fonun. It was managed by Mirza Ali Akbar Khan, Mozayen od Doleh (1843-1932), who had studied painting in France, and Monsieur LeMaire, the French music professor. The first production was cast by nonprofessional Europeans who recited the Persian lines badly in parrot fashion. Due to the pressure of the mollas, the auditorium was restricted to the royal family and entourage. The first translation of The Misanthrope (Sargozasht-e Mardomgoriz) by Mirza Habib Esfahâni (printed in Istanbul, 1869) and some of Molière's other plays were performed in this hall. Imitating a mode current in Turkish theatre, French characters were Persianized and given Iranian names and manners. Although it seemed favored by the Shah, the Dar ol Fonun Hall lasted only six years and was probably closed because of the dangers of its relative liberty.

Iranian Theatre in the Twentieth Century

Since 1911 some theatrical companies were formed with on-and-off activities and relative success. Their repertoires consisted of works by Iranian authors in the western style or translations and adaptations from foreign pieces. In a brief space it is not possible to cover this period in detail so only the more important names and titles shall be noted. [37] The subject matter of most of these plays was either based on criticizing the old-fashioned customs of the past and the praising of modern western manners, or patriotic pieces like that of Mirzadeh Eshqi's (1893-1925) opera poem, "The Resurrection of Iranian Kings" (1916). In 1923 Hasan Moqaddam made fun of the overwesternized Iranians in "Jafar Khan has returned from Europe." To avoid Reza Shah Pahlavi's (1925-41) censorship, authors escaped into historical subjects, fairytales and vaudeville, and women who appeared on the stage were usually of Armenian or Jewish origin.

After the departure of Reza Shah and the entry of Anglo-Soviet and later American troops, political rights were established. Abdolhoseyn Nushin (1905-70), a member of the Tudeh Communist party, translated and staged Iranianized versions of Molière, M. Maeterlinck, M. Pagnol, and Ben Jonson plays. By taking seriously his work as a director and using the possibilities of stage craft to advantage, Nushin was the first to attract both a bourgeois and an intellectual audience. Antidemocratic repression (first in 1949 and then in 1953) restrained liberties. In the reign of Mohammad Reza Shah Pahlavi (1941-79) a contradictory phenomenon took place: on the one hand there was greed for riches culminating in corruption, oppression and superficial westernization, and on the other hand, the official trend emphasizing a national cultural identity and the revival of the traditional heritage. Many interesting plays were produced during this period.

Ali Nasirian and Abbas Javânmard (both actors, playwrights, and directors) produced good adaptations of the works of an important writer, Sādeq Hedāyat (1903-51): The Provisory Husband and The Necrophagous (1957). Nasirian alone wrote and played The Golden Serpent (1957), inspired by the patterns and gestures of the traditional public place animators (M'arekegir). His Wondering Nightingale (1959) is taken from a folktale and in Siyâh (1960) his deep interest in the principal character of the popular comedy is evident.

A high school for actor training, Honarestân-e Honarpishegi, was founded in 1938 and in the beginning of 1958 a General Office of Dramatic Arts was instituted and then integrated with the Ministry of Culture and Arts. A school of dramatic arts (issuing B.A. degrees) was founded and later the faculty of fine arts of Tehran University opened a department for theatre. Both these schools have been closed since 1980, due to the revolution. An official theatre, the 25th Shahrivar Hall, opened in the 1960's, where many plays were performed. Also the Festival of Provincial Theatre Groupes took place between 1976 and 1978 and five issues of the Theatre Quarterly were published over the period of 1977-78. Since March 1981, another magazine, Sahne-ye Ma'âser, about theatre has appeared.

Among well-known playwrights there is: Gholamhoseyn Sâedi (born 1935), physician, amateur anthropologist, writer, and opponent to the Shah's regime. His Stickweilders of Varazil (1965) is a premonitory tale of villagers, first befriended then threatened by hunters (foreigners?) who take refuge in a Moslem shrine. (Some other plays by Sâedi are A without accent and A with accent, 1968; Dikeh va Zavieh, 1968; and Woe to the Vanquished, 1971.

Bahrâm Beyzâi (born 1938), playwright, film director and theatre historian, employs symbolism in search of personal beliefs. In Sunset in a Strange Land and Tale of the Hidden Moon (1963) he uses the puppet theatre form with live actors ending with the puppet master (Demon or God as in Attâr, seven centuries before) tearing up the dolls who will to choose their own destinies. (Other plays by Beyzâi are Pahlavan Akbar Dies, 1965; and Death of Yazdegerd, 1979.)

More dramatists to be mentioned are: Akbar Râdi, Bahman Forsi, Parviz Kârdân and Arhâm Sadr, the latter animated his own theatre in Isfahan.

The National Iranian Television (NIRT), founded in 1966, emphasized cultural life and promoted traditional and contemporary theatre. The NIRT founded the Festival of Arts in Shiraz (1967-77), concentrating mainly on theatre and music in an atmosphere of bold creations unique of its kind because of the bringing together of authentic traditional performances from Asia, Africa, and Latin America and the latest of contemporary creations (Peter Brook, Robert Wilson, Jerzy Grotowski, Shuji Terayama, Victor Garcia, Joe Chakin, Andrei Serben, Tadeus Kantor, Peter Schumann, André Gregory, etc.).[38]

Moreover, the NIRT and the festival promoted a theatre workshop of the Kargâhe Namâyesh (1969), in which worked Arby Ovanessian (born 1942), a talented stage and film director who created many varied foreign and Iranian works including those of the playwright Abbas Nalbandiân (born 1947), A Profound Research ... (Shiraz, 1968), about a group of people gathered in a sparse space waiting for an answer; and Suddenly (Shiraz, 1972), the story of an outsider killed by fanatics.

Other directors of this group are: Bijan Mofid with the City of Tales (Shiraz, 1968), under the guise of children's tales and animal masks, mocks the society of his time; Esmâil Khalaj with How are you Mash Rahim? and Golduneh Khanum (Shiraz, 1977), a knowledgeable description of the simple people of Tehran; and

Ashurbanipal Bâbella, with To-Night is Moonlight (Shiraz, 1974), a contemporary satire inspired by Ruhozi.

Apart from the above group there are: Iraj Saghiri with Qalandar Khuneh, (Shiraz, 1975) containing a mixture of folklore and Tazieh; Khojasteh Kia, who wrote and directed Testimony on the Martyrdom of Hallaj (Tehran, 1969); and Parviz Sayyâd, popular actor and film director who staged Eavesdroppers (Shiraz, 1973), written by poet and painter Manuchehr Yektâi.

The festival of Shiraz also organized two other festivals, one of Tus (1975-78), in the city of Mashhad, devoted to oral and written literature, mainly epic, and the other, that of popular traditions, in Isfahan (1977).

Immediately after the revolution of February 1979, there was a short-lived period of theatrical fervor including the staging of Abbâs Aqâ, the Worker by S. Soltanpur, a leftist writer, executed by the Islamic authorities on June 21, 1981.

Notes

1. Unfortunately no general history of Iranian rituals, performance and theatre exists in English. The only book in a European language is in French by Medjia Rezvani, Le théâtre et la danse en Iran. Paris: Maisonneuve, 1962, containing useful information but inaccurate. There are two general and compact articles in English by Peter J. Chelkowski, "The Religious Drama in Iran," and Farrokh Gaffary, "The Secular Theatre in Iran," in the McGraw-Hill Encyclopedia of World Drama, III, (1984), pp. 55-65. Also, two informative bibliographies by P. J. Chelkowski, "Popular Shia Islam," and F. Gaffary, "Secular Theatre, Dance, Film, Radio, T.V. and Zurkhaneh in Iran" in L. P. Elwell-Sutton, ed. Bibliographical Guide to Iran. New York: Cambridge University Press, 1981. Another source is P. J. Chelkowski, "Popular Entertainment, Media and Social Change in Twentieth Century Iran," in Cambridge History of Iran, Vol. VII, (to be published). The best book on the history of Iranian theatre is in Persian: Bahrâm Beyzāi, Namāyesh dar Irān (Tehran, 1965); (revised and corrected edition to be published).

2. R. D. Barnett, "Homme masqué ou Dieu-Ibex?" in Syria, XLIII, (1966), Fasc. 3-4, and P. Amiet, "L'iconographie archaique de l'Iran" in Syria, LVI, (1979), Fasc. 3-4.

3. S. H. Taqizadeh, Articles and essays in English, Vol. VI, Tehran, 1978, pp. 99, 105, 336.

4. Richard Ettinghausen, "The dance with zoomorphic masks" in

George Makdisi, ed., Arabic and Islamic Studies in honour of H. A. R. Gibb. Leiden: E. J. Brill, 1965. This article gives information mainly about masks in Islamic Iranian art.

5. Franz Cumont, The Mysteries of Mithra (1903) New York: Dover publications; Martin Vermaserren, Mithra. London, 1963; R. A. Turcan, Mithra et le mithriacisme. Paris, 1981.

6. Roman Ghirshman, Iran. New York: Penguin Books, 1954.

7. R. Ghirshman, Iran: Parthians and Sassanians. London: Thames & Hudson, 1962, Illustration numbers 256, 257, 258.

8. Ahmad Biruni, The Chronology of Ancient Nations (translated into English by E. Sachau). London, 1879 (reprint, 1969), pp. 199-226.

9. M. And, "The Turkish Folk Theatre" in Asian Folklore Studies Vol XXXVIII, 2 (1979), pp. 155-176.

10. Paul Ginisty, Le Théâtre de la rue. Paris: A. Moroncé, 1925, p. 5.

11. R. Ettinghausen, op. cit., and S. C. Welch, Royal Persian Manuscripts. London: Thames & Hudson, 1978, p. 69. The latter has mistaken musicians and buffoons for mystics.

12. E. Yarshater's article in P. J. Chelkowski, ed. Ta'ziyeh: Ritual and Drama in Iran. New York: New York University Press, 1979.

13. S. Daneshvar, Suvashun (a novel in Persian). 9th ed. Tehran, 1978.

14. Sh. Meskub, Sug-e Siyavush. 5th ed. Tehran, 1978. An intelligent study of martyrs, in Persian.

15. N. Tomiche and Ch. Khaznadar, Le Théâtre Arabe. Paris: Unesco, 1969.

16. M. And, Karagöz. Istanbul: Dost, 1979, p. 104. An excellent resume on west Asian shadows and puppets.

17. The oldest references to "Pahlavân Kachal" are in French, A. Chodzko (c1833), Le Théâtre Persan, Paris, 1878, and in Russian, I. K. Berezin (1842-43), Puteshestwi po sieviernoy Persi, Kazan, 1852. Also in French, R. Dozy, Essai sur l'histoire de l'Islamisme, Leyden, 1879, and A. Cellière, Deux Comedies Turques, Paris, 1888.

18. E. Yarshater, Development of Persian Drama, in P. J.

Chelkowski, ed. Iran: Continuity and Variety. New York: New York University Press, 1971. This article is a concise narrative of Iranian theatre.

19. M. J. Fischer, Iran: From Religious Dispute to Revolution. Harvard University Press, 1980. Contains valuable information on Tazieh.

20. W. Franklin, Observations Made on a Tour from Bengal to Persia in the Year 1786-1787. London, 1790.

21. P. J. Chelkowski, ed., Ta'ziyeh: Ritual and Drama in Iran. New York: New York University Press, 1979. The best and most recent general book on the subject. A. Krymsky, Persian Theatre (published in Ukranian, in Kiev, 1925, and translated into English by V. Pechenuk, unpublished) contains very important extracts of western travelers witnessing these rituals. M. Forough, Abraham's Sacrifice in Persian Passion Plays, in A. U. Pope, ed., A Survey of Persian Art; Vol XIV, 3rd ed., Tehran, Tokyo, 1977. E. Rossie and A. Bombaci, Elenco di drammi religiosi Persiani, Vatican, 1961. An important list in Italian, in the Vatican Library Collection consisting of more than a thousand Tazieh texts. A. de Gobineau, Religions et philosophies dans l'Asie Centrale. Paris, 1865, reprinted many times since. A. Chodzko, Le Théâtre Persan. Paris, 1878. Also, in Persian, the general book of B. Beyzâi, op. cit. The Persian text of Tazieh plays was published by Z. Eqbal and M. J. Mahjub, Jong-e Shahâdat, Vol. 1. Tehran, 1976.

22. J. Calmard, "Le Mécénat des Représentations de Tazieh" in Le Monde Iranien et l'Islam, Vol II, 1974, and Vol. IV, 1976-77, Paris. These remarkable articles give an account of the performances in the nineteenth century.

23. S. G. W. Benjamin, Persia and the Persians. London and Boston, 1886. As the first American diplomatic envoy to Iran, he gives a good description of this theatre.

24. L. Pelly, The Miracle Play of Hasan and Husain. London, 1879, recently reprinted, containing the English translation of thirty-seven plays.

25. M. Arnold, "A Persian Passion Play" in Essays in Criticism, Vol. II, London, 1871.

26. P. J. Chelkowski, "Iran: Mourning becomes Revolution" in Asia, May-June 1980. M. J. Fischer, op. cit.

27. A. Gobineau, op. cit., gives vivid description of the sceneries.

28. Mayel Baktash's article, in P. J. Chelkowski, ed., Ta'ziyeh: Ritual and Drama in Iran, op. cit.

29. See the article (sometimes partial) of Peter Book, "Leaning on the Moment" in Parabola, May 1979.

30. P. Mamnoun's article in Ta'ziyeh: Ritual and Drama in Iran, op. cit.

31. Published in Persian, F. Gaffary, Teâtr-e Irâni. Tehran, 1971.

32. The proceedings of this symposium can be found in Ta'ziyeh: Ritual and Drama in Iran, op. cit.

33. For a resume of such a play see James Mew, "The Modern Persian Stage" in the Fortnightly Review, LIX, January-June, 1896.

34. W. O. Beeman, "A Full Arena: The development and meaning of popular performance traditions in Iran" in M. Bonine & N. Keddie, eds., Modern Iran, State University of New York Press, 1981. Also an excellent description of Ruhozi and rural comedies by W. O. Beeman, "Why do they laugh?" in Journal of American Folklore, a special issue on folk theatre, to be published.

35. Translated into French by L. Bazin, M. F. A. Akhundzadeh's Comedies, Paris, 1962. The best biography and study is in Persian by F. Admiyat, Andisnehây-e M. F. Akhundzâdeh, Tehran, 1970. The Persian text of his plays, Tamsilât, was republished in Tehran, 1970. In my chapter on theatre in L. P. Elwell-Sutton, ed., Bibliographical Guide to Iran, there is a list of his comedies translated into foreign languages.

36. In Persian, H. Sadiq, Panj namâyeshnâmeh as Mirzâ Aqâ Tabrizi, Tehran, 1977. A. Bricteux translated the plays into French, Les Comédies de Malkom Knan, Biege & Paris, 1933.

37. For a more detailed resume refer to my article on "Iranian Secular Theatre" in McGraw-Hill Encyclopedia, op. cit.

38. See the English Album, "Festival of Arts of Shiraz-Persepolis. The First Ten Years (1969-76)," Tehran.

Chapter Twenty-Two

DRAMA AND THEATRE IN THE RUSSIAN EAST

Edward Allworth

On the dramaturgical map of western Asia, the huge section
long held by Czarist and Soviet Russia deserves attentive scrutiny.
Theatrical life has been especially rich in the multiethnic Transcaucasus, and, to a lesser degree, in the Tatar homelands and
central Asia, at least since medieval times. The area leads the
entire Middle East in this field in certain respects. Theatre in the
region is abundant, as well as versatile in form. It has given to
both players and audiences literary religious performances, a secular neoclassical drama, folk comedy, modern European-style stage
works, an ideologically committed theatre, plus numerous plays
translated or adapted from the West and East. But how far this
modern variety may be identified either as local Asian or international western remains a serious question for every specialist.

In part, this bibliographical survey means to designate
sources to forward that discussion. While sketching out the main
lines taken by stage art development in the area, concise information about key dramatists and plays will be provided, with reference to English- and European-language translations and commentaries whenever they are available. However, because very few
separate monographs on dramaturgy in this area have yet been published in English, French, or German, most citations refer to articles or chapters within larger studies. Readers should be aware
that there is a rich lode of original material in the languages of the
Russian East, upon which future research may focus. In addition,
a fair amount of published drama, theatrical history, and related
writing in those languages may be found in research libraries in the
United States and western Europe. Strong collections are located
in the New York Public Library, Columbia University Libraries, the
Library of Congress, and the Library of the University of California
at Los Angeles. Similarly important are those in the British Museum
in London; l'Ecole des Langues Orientales Vivantes, Paris; Bayerische
Staatsbibliothek, Munich; and Istanbul Universities.

Religious Genres

By the eighteenth century, in the area between the Black and Caspian seas, north of Iran, three well-established versions of religious drama or mystery play and theater fascinated believers and foreign travelers alike. Antiquity is often claimed for its Christian ritual dramas. Earliest may have been the Armenian tradition, in this area, with the Georgian close behind, but only one Georgian play, entitled The Annunciation, still exists which dates from the tenth century or before.

In Azerbaijan, the performance of Muslim religious drama, called shabi among local Shiites, reaches back at least to the late eighteenth century according to Ivor Lassy, who conducted field research on the Apsheron peninsula jutting into the Caspian Sea from 1913 to 1915. His dissertation, published in 1916 at Helsingfors by Lilius and Hertzbert, Ltd., is the most original source for this genre in Azerbaijan, and is called The Muharram Mysteries among the Azerbeijan Turks of Caucasia. Lassy, throughout his 284-page book, never speaks of a single episode of the dozens of known ritual dramas by title but he describes the content and action of many in detail. These Muslim religious dramas center upon the martyrdom of Hassan and especially of Hussein, the Prophet Muhammad's grandsons.

Several eminent visitors to the Transcaucasus have left valuable impressions of these performances in print. The Russian artist Basile Vereschagine provides many sketches of performances observed at Shusha around 1864 in his "Voyage dans les Provinces du Caucase ... Seconde partie--la Transcaucasie de Tiflis a Schoucha ...," in Le Tour du Monde 1 er trim (1869), pp. 241-288, translated from Russian. French author Alexandre Dumas likewise visited the Shiite region of Azerbaijan, witnessing the religious drama of the Muslims at Derbend, Baku and Shamakha. His report appears in Chapter XXV of his Impressions de Voyage: Le Caucase (Paris: Calmann Levy, 1880), pp. 63-72f. There is also an 1879 edition. The Russian writer Maxim Gorky, exiled to Tbilisi (Tiflis), saw parts of extensive Muharram celebrations there in May 1898, though he recorded no drama at the time in his article "Prazdnik shiitov," (Sobranie sochinenii v tridtsati tomakh, Tom 23, Moscow: Gosizdat Khudozhestvennoi Literatury, 1953), pp. 273-284. British journalist Edmond O'Donovan describes in detail performances of this drama seen during 1879-1881 among the Tekke Turkmens of central Asia in a village quite near the Iranian frontier. His book, The Merv Oasis. Travels and Adventures East of the Caspian during the years 1879-80-81, including Five Months' Residence among the Tekkes of Merv (London: Smith, Elder & Co., 1882), Vol. II, Chapter XXXII, echoes the reports of many Russians and Europeans, all of which reflect the stunning experience of witnessing these extraordinary indigenous theatrical performances. For the best source of bibliography concerning texts of the episodes of

Muslim religious drama as well as analyses and criticism of the genre, see Peter Chelkowski, "Bibliographical Spectrum" in Ta'ziyeh: Ritual and Drama in Iran (New York: New York University Press and Soroush Press, 1979), pp. 255-268, though not devoted specifically to Azerbaijan, the tradition there was very close to that of Iran.

Texts for thirty-seven of these episodes from the Muslim Passion play, taken from the Iranian tradition by Lewis Pelly, have appeared in English translation in his book, The Miracle Play of Hasan and Husain (London: Wm. H. Allen and Co., 1879, reprinted by Gregg International Publishers, Ltd., 1970), 2 vols., 650 pp. Also, almost thirty manuscripts of shabis in the Azerbaijanian (Azeri) language are located in the Vatican Library treating the episodes about Amir Timur, Shahrbanu, Hussein and many others. In the same collection there are more than 1,000 manuscripts in Persian, a language formerly widely used and understood in Russian Azerbaijan. See the annotated listing in Elenco di Drammi Religiosi Persiani (Fondo Mss. Vaticani Cerulli), by Ettore Rossi and Alessio Bombaci (Vatican City: Biblioteca Apostolica Vaticana, 1961), lx and 416 pp. Also, see Chapter Twenty-One in this book, entitled "Development of Theatre in Iran."

Although antireligious policies of the USSR's regime make presentations of shabi unusual today, compared with the period before 1920, performances in Soviet Azerbaijan have been seen occasionally as recently as the early 1970's. A negative but revealing account of such a presentation in 1970 was reported in Räfail Haghiyev's article "The Event in the Village of Alar," translated from Azeri from Kommunist (Baku), September 4, 1970, by David Nissman, A Radio Liberty Translation (New York: Radio Liberty Committee, 1970), 6 pp.

Classical Theatre and Drama

Aside from sacred theater, Armenia and Georgia also enjoyed some serious historical drama of a classical style from the late seventeenth century until about the mid-nineteenth century. Armenian classical drama was known in Tbilisi as well as among concentrations of Armenians in Istanbul and elsewhere outside the Transcaucasus.

Azerbaijanian sources reveal no comparable classical development for that period in the Azeri or Persian languages used in the Transcaucasus, either in Tbilisi or Baku. Nor is this neoclassical phase to be found in any other parts of Czarist Russian Asia.

Folk Plays and Theatre

Constants in the theatrical life of the Transcaucasus and Central Asia were species of verbal and stage art in wide variety.

While religious, late classical, modern, and even ideological drama evolved in the area, folk theatre continued to be acted. Aside from the gynastics, juggling, stilt-walking, dancing, and similar forms, there were several kinds of puppet theatre and live skits. Some of these were fairly extended and were put on in most of the Eastern regions of what has become the USSR. In the Middle Ages, Georgia had its folk revels (keenoba) and Armenia a comic gusan-mimos and vartzak, male and female folk actors. In Azerbaijan until recently, for example, survived a playlet called "Khan-Khan" which often has entertained people at wedding celebrations. In "Khan-Khan," a no-body is enthroned and obliged to exact clever punishment and for-feits from petitioners or defendants in response to fanciful complaints, riddles, and the like. In central Asia by the mid-nineteenth century sizeable folk troupes, working without scripts or other chapbooks, were very well established at the court of the Qoqan Khanate in the Farghana Valley. The standard repertoire of those groups closely resembled that of Tajik and Uzbek itinerant players who offered presentations (tamashas), usually in open-air, unstaged perform-ances. Invariably comic and usually ribald, some well-known skits involved considerable dialogue and action. Prominent were "The Moralskeeper" (Rais), "Seminary Instructor" (Mudarris), "The Tomb" (Mazar), and "The Wedding" (Uylänish). Travelers, who have often observed this kind of theatrical life, include Eugene Schuyler, a United States' diplomat in the Czarist Empire, who records his ex-perience in Turkistan. Notes of a Journey in Russian Turkistan ... (New York: Scribner, Armstrong & Co., 1877), Vol. I, pp. 133-137; see also Henry Lansdell, Through Central Asia (London: Sampson, Low, Marston, Searle and Rivington, 1887), pp. 304-305. Lansdell, a missionary who visited the town of Kitab, in the Buk-haran Amirate, in 1882, almost a decade after Schuyler's trip to Tashkent and Farqhana, was repelled by the "nastiness" of the playlets. For details, consult Uzbekskii sovetskii teatr (Tashkent: Izdatel'stvo "Nauka" Uzbekskoi SSR, 1966), pp. 50-54; A. L. Troitskaia, "Ferganskaia teatral'naia ekspeditsiia," Sovetskaia etnografiia, 1 (1937), pp. 163-164; M. Arif, "Äzarbayjanda khalg teatrī (bä'zi geydlär). Khalg oyun vä märasimlarindä teatr vä tamasha unsurläri," Ädabiyyat mäjmuäsi, I (Baku 1946), pp. 4-5; Georg Goyan, Two Thousand Years of the Armenian Theater (c1954), pp. 17, 26. When the new, European-style stage arose in central Asia, it openly and explicitly reacted against the rowdi-ness of the folk theatricals.

The Modern Stage

The rich tradition possessed by the three major, but ethnical-ly unrelated cultural groups of the Transcaucasus--Armenians, Azerbaijanians and Georgians--must have played a role in later theatre life. But that heritage by itself insufficiently explains the first, striking emergence in the mid-nineteenth century of a modern Middle Eastern drama and stagecraft among those groups. Persia had simultaneously shared almost the same medieval religious drama and folk comedy with Azerbaijan, but no original Persian drama of a modern variety was seen onstage in Iran until well into the twentieth century.

The special ingredient that appears to explain the difference between the Transcaucasus and the greater Middle East seemed to come along with European encroachment into certain old centers of civilization.

Between 1840 and 1850 an extraordinary phenomenon occurred there. One playwright from each major Transcaucasus nationality wrote an original play in his language before any rivals entered the scene. Chronologically, Prince Georgii D. Eristavi (1811-1864) came out first with his Georgian play, The Lawsuit (Dava) in 1840. In the following year appeared the adaptation in Armenian from a Russian work, the Armenian version by Khachatur Abovian (1805-1848), Theodora, or a Daughter's Devotion (Theodora Kam Vodiakan Seruh). Mirza Fath Ali Akhunzada (1812-1878), though far from his Azerbaijan homeland, offered Tbilisi's theatre directors an initial work, Mullah Ibrahim Khälil, Alchemist (Hekayät-i mollah Ibrahimkhälil kimyagär), in 1850 in his native Azeri language, followed promptly by his own translation of it to Russian.

Ideological Theatre

An insistent didacticism permeated new playwrights' works in Tartarstan and central Asia starting around the turn of the twentieth century. Onstage, the Jadids (reformists) gained surprising popularity among mostly illiterate audiences with short plays about such virtues as hard work and education or the evils of forced marriage and drug addiction. More important, a number of historical tableaus effectively championed patriotism, like Tamerlane's Mausoleum (Timurning saghanasi) (1919), by Abdalrauf Fitrat, introducing politics to the scene.

The onset of the Soviet era continued the preeminently didactic uses of drama and stage throughout Russian Asia now under the Communists. The ideological bases for all writing and performing drastically changed from the Buddhist (Buryat and Kalmyk), Christian or Muslim ethical-religious systems to Marxism as interpreted by Vladimir I. Lenin and Joseph V. Stalin. The former freedom, only relative under Czarist censorship, to compose and to stage works using subjects chosen by playwrights, disappeared almost entirely. Likewise, written theatre history and criticism has become thoroughly controlled. All these limitations carve a lamentable hollow in the literature available to students of the region and field of knowledge. Worse yet, western handbooks or encyclopedic reference books often suffer from indifference or dependence upon tainted Soviet sources.

In addition, themes and subjects of the repertory inside the USSR predictably conform to Communist party slogans of the day, whether stressing "anti-imperialism," advancing the contemporary Five-Year Plan, or displaying approved Russian ethnocentrism. By specifying acceptable themes, the political authorities, who manage all publishing and stage affairs, restrict and censor at the source, systematically shaping theatrical life. The inventiveness of dedicated creative artists is therefore all the more striking.

Quantitatively, the output of plays and organizing of paid troupes has been large in the Soviet East. But, until after the death of Stalin in 1953 and the widespread expression of dissent clandestinely in samizdat (self-publication) and publicly among Georgians, Armenians, Turkmens and many other nationalities there, prescription stifled most initiative. In the 1960's and 1970's, however, new dramatists started to experiment a little in a slowly altering climate of opinion. Some interesting efforts, apolitical but nevertheless intellectually and aesthetically rewarding, have been made.

The most telling illustration of this trend came from two central Asian writers, Chingiz Aitmatov and Kaltai Muhammedjanov, in the early 1970's. Their play, The Ascent of Mount Fuji (Köktepaga shïghu) (New York: Farrar, Straus and Giroux, 1975), was written in Kazakh by its Kirgiz and Kazakh authors, translated by them into Russian, and performed first at Moscow's Sovremennik Theater in that language. Its scathing treatment of post-Stalin-era dishonesty and "morality" among educated central Asians caused a sensation. The English version gained attention abroad immediately in performances at the Arena Theater, Washington, D.C., and repeatedly on US Public Television. To the ethical problems it poses, more than to the rather static, overly verbal drama, has the two-act play owed its fame. Thus, it remained true to the ideological genre of theatre and drama, begun by the Jadid reformists and sustained throughout the ensuing Soviet decades, that initiated modern stage art in that portion of the Middle East.

Note: This is an abridged version of the article scheduled for publication in Middle East Studies Association Bulletin (MESA). B.F., ed.

Chapter Twenty-Three

THEATRICAL MOVEMENT IN THE HEBREW THEATRE

Freddie Rokem

Today's Hebrew theatre is almost as multifaceted and varied
as the number of individuals and institutions which comprise it. It
is quite a complicated matter to trace its origin since the cultural
roots of the modern Israeli society are a multiplicity of ethnic cultures from all over the world. And it is only natural that this
ethnic and cultural diversity should be expressed in the theatre in
general and in all its linguistic, pictorial, and gestural components
in particular.

Before discussing theatrical movement in the Hebrew theatre
however, a number of basic distinctions have to be made. For example, theatrical activity in the State of Israel since 1948, the year
of national independence which marks the beginning of what is
called Israeli theatre, has used a number of languages onstage.

It is not sufficient however to attempt to define Israeli and
pre-Israeli theatre on the basis of the language used onstage within
a certain geographical area (Palestine-Israel) because the same languages have also been used by Jews onstage in other places too.
Thus the most important Hebrew theatre company in present-day
Israel, Habima, was established in Moscow in 1917 and arrived in
Palestine for the first time only in 1928, performing in Hebrew.

The most international language of what we can call the Jewish theatre was probably Yiddish, Yiddish having been the lingua
franca of the Jews in eastern Europe until the Second World War.
Today, for historical and cultural reasons, Yiddish is no longer
central to the Jewish theatre. [1]

In addition to the linguistic and geographical influences on
the development of Israeli theatre, religion has also played a part.
The Jewish religion and law have traditionally considered the theatre as alien, and this has certainly been an important inhibiting
component in the early development of the Jewish theatre, which
started to take form only around 1870. Jews who assimilated into
the gentile cultures and became important for their contributions

545

to the national theatrical tradition they joined were always very strongly criticized by the orthodox Jewish establishment. In present-day Israel strictly orthodox Jews would never go to the theatre. Traditionally of course, the Purim-play performed at the Jewish festival commemorating the rescue of the Persian Jews through the intervention of Queen Esther, has a very strong standing among the orthodox Jews, but it is of course only the exception which confirms the rule.[2]

The Enlightenment period (nineteenth century) saw the growth of literary works written in Hebrew, and in fact there were also many plays written during this period, but they were composed in such an elevated style that they were completely unfit for theatrical performance.[3]

The most important Hebrew theatre, Habima, was founded in Moscow in 1917, where it eventually developed into one of the studios of Stanislavski. It was preceded by various minor attempts to perform in Hebrew but it meant the first real breakthrough for an artistic Hebrew stage. Habima's most important and most famous production was An-Ski's The Dybbuk which was staged by the well-known Armenian director Vakhtangov, premiered in January 1922. This play depicts the religious life in a small Jewish village in eastern Europe and focuses on the dilemma of a young bride who is possessed by the spirit of a dead lover on the eve of her marriage to another suitor. The Dybbuk was performed by Habima more than 1,300 times, in more or less the same manner, virtually all over the world until the middle of the 1950's.

The great challenge for the young Hebrew stage was to find a way of depicting artistically, through a reinvigorated language, how Jews lived in past times and in the present. But with the language both so ancient and so new and foreign, the theatre companies also sought to convey meaning and emotion through dance and movement, and this was something for which there was also no existing Jewish artistic tradition model. So the first practitioners and visionaries of Hebrew theatre had to create a completely new means of artistic communication, a process which is still continuing in modern Israel. Thus it is no exaggeration to claim that with regard to the Hebrew theatre, no tradition existed before the twentieth century. Therefore, it is useful to see what kind of theatrical development took place in the early part of this century when the tradition was actually formed, with interest in tracing briefly the forms which physical movement and gesture were assuming in the Hebrew theatre of this time, especially in the 1920's.[4]

We find that gesture and movement patterns which can clearly be identified as expressionistic in the early twentieth century central and eastern European theatre were interpreted as patterns which were distinctly "Jewish" and "Hebrew" and thus found their way into the emerging tradition of the Hebrew stage.[5] We also find some traditionally Jewish religious gestural patterns, and together they all make up the basis for the creation of a new tradition--the Hebrew theatre. Thus, the manner in which theatrical components are transferred from one cultural system to another is of utmost importance for the understanding of the theatrical movement of the Hebrew theatre.

The Habima Theatre of Moscow made its real breakthrough with the famous production of The Dybbuk.[6] In general, critical opinion praised the production and pointed to it as the quintessential example not only of the Hebrew theatre, but of Jewish theatre. With regard to physical movement, one of the most applauded elements was the beggars' dance in the second act. Vakhtangov added five beggars to the original seven. "Their gestures and make-up were exaggerated and mask-like. The actors modeled their characterizations by using specific images of animals (frog, monkey, fox, hyena, ape). The beggars--one-armed, lame, deaf, imbecillic, consumptive, hunch-backed, round and froglike and blind--had individual musical rhythms that allowed for greater exaggeration and contrast. The dance was divided into three parts, and after the first and second section each beggar returned to a specific place at the tables and sat in a characteristic sculptural pose, creating a bas-relief for the downstage action."[7] The beggars were conceived as a symbol of the suffering of the Jewish people investing the otherwise apolitical and mystical play with a revolutionary element. Among Jewish critics opinions were more ambivalent with regard to the Jewish nature of this dance.[8]

While Habima was making an enthusiastically received tour of Europe in the middle of the 1920's, two of its former members, Menahem Gnessin and Moshe Ha-Levy, arrived in Palestine in order to establish their own theatres. The Palestine Theatre (Teatron Eretz-Israel) which was founded by Menahem Gnessin, went to Berlin for an intensive period of study (with M. Reinhardt and others) and to hold rehearsals for a production of the biblical play Belshazar by Heine Rochet. This performance had its premiere in Berlin (1924) and was later shown for the first time in Tel Aviv (1925).

The "originality of the Hebrew movements on stage" in Belshazar were enthusiastically hailed.[9] Shimon Finkel, who had joined the Palestine Theatre in Berlin and was later to become one of the major actors of Habima, claims that what was special about the movements in this performance was the manner in which the hands and the head were turned against the natural inclinations of the body in relieflike positions and angles. The hands were turned back and forth to stress their presence and according to Finkel this was something that the director and the actors had picked up from their studies of expressionism in Berlin during their visit there.[10]

Both in Belshazar and The Dybbuk the expressionistic movements were assisted by the use of make-up, costumes, and stage setting which stressed the irregular, the unnatural and the non-conventional.

The Palestine Theatre also mounted a production of The Dybbuk (1926) which was more or less a copy of the renowned Habima production, and in Palestine this production was received with quite a large measure of animosity on the part of the critics. The dances were considered to be Christian or Armenian and quite foreign to the Jewish or Hebrew spirit. The director Menahem Gnessin, in response to this criticism, gradually revised the performance and some of its more grotesque elements were removed, a decision which made the performance in general, and the movements of the dances in particular, come closer to the Jewish folk dance and more distant from the expressionistic theatre.[11]

In the expressionistic theatre, the dance primarily serves as a metaphoric element externalizing a general situation, a state of mind, or a mood. It can of course be realistically motivated through the plot or the situation of the play, e.g., a wedding dance, but its concrete design is generally not based on realistic observation--hence the grotesqueness and exaggeration. But it was the expressionism of The Dybbuk by Habima which was recorded in the annals of theatre history as one of the truly great innovations of the early Hebrew theatre. Gradually, from the 1930's on and until the beginning of the 1950's, the Habima production of The Dybbuk grows into what could be called the "myth" of the Hebrew theatre. It seems however that also in this production some of the grotesqueness and intensity of the production, including the dances and movement patterns, were gradually moderated over the years.

Moshe Ha-Levy founded the Ohel Studio which, after a period of studies and rehearsals in Palestine, opened its first production in Tel Aviv in 1926. Ha-Levy developed a lyrical realistic style in his theatre, and this influenced his search for a form for movement patterns; lyric realism and ethnographic authenticity was the stylistic basis for the production of Krasninnikov's biblical play Jacob and Rachel (1928),[12] for which Ha-Levy went to the local beduin, as the closest counterpart to the biblical characters in order to copy their movement patterns.

An interesting example of a mixture of the realistic/ethnic and the expressionistic movement patterns can be found in the work of the dancer Baruh Agadati who appeared in a large number of solo performances in the 1920's. Agadati presented dances which he called Yemenite, Arab, Chassidic, etc. in which two of the decisive factors of differentiation among them were the dress and the accompanying music: he probably also made an attempt to find distinctive ethnic choreographic patterns for the different communities.[13] His contribution moreover lies in his search for a specific ethnic artistic expression which was Jewish and Hebrew at the same time.

In theatrical performances the movement patterns must be seen as a dynamic relationship between the individual and the group present onstage. This was especially true when the spirit of Habima, The Palestine Theatre, the Ohel as well as other Hebrew theatres in Palestine was a collective one, where the influence of the individual actors on questions of repertoire and directing was quite great. It seems that what came to be known generally as "the ensemble," as an aesthetic condition, can here be broadened to include a cultural meaning since "ensemble" was probably also a reflection of the larger collective spirit of the emerging society of new settlers in Palestine at the time.

The major trend of the Hebrew theatre from its very beginnings until today can be summarized as an attempt to form and create a theatrical tradition where there is a multitude and richness of cultural roots. Sometimes these cultural roots, whether they were ethnical or generally Jewish, could be transferred to the shape and thus be incorporated into the theatrical tradition and sometimes the theatrical tradition had to be formed by elements belonging to the general theatre, like expressionism and naturalism which in their new cultural contexts sometimes were embedded with a new significance. This then is part of the dynamics of the development of Hebrew theatrical tradition as it started to take definite form in the 1920's and as it is still developing today.

Notes

1. Nahma Sandrow, Vagabond Stars, New York, 1977. An absurd comment on this condition is seen in present-day Poland where there are virtually no Jews (there were 3.3 million in 1939) but where there is a Yiddish state theatre, the actors of which are almost all non-Jews who learn to perform in Yiddish in the theatre's school.

2. Khone Shmeruk, Yiddish Literature: Aspects of its History, Tel Aviv, 1978 (in Hebrew).

3. Gershon Shaked, The Hebrew Historical Play at the Time of the Revival, Jerusalem, 1970 (in Hebrew).

4. "Hebrew" is in this context not restricted to the language alone, and at the time of the first important steps towards the development of the theatre it was often used to point at the general cultural revival taking place in Palestine.

Note: This is an abridged version of the article scheduled for publication in Middle East Studies Association Bulletin (MESA). B.F., ed.

5. Denis Calandra, "Jessner's 'Hiutertreppe': A Semiotic Approach to Expressionist Performance," Theatre Quarterly, IX, 35 (1979), pp. 31-42; and Mel Gordon, "German Expressionist Acting," The Drama Review, 19, 3 (T 67) (1975), pp. 34-50.

6. E. Levy, The Habima--Israel's National Theatre 1917-1977, New York, 1979; and M. Kohansky, The Hebrew Theatre-- The First Fifty Years, Jerusalem 1969.

7. Pearl Fishman, "Vakhtangov's The Dybbuk," Modern Drama, XXIV, 3 (T 87) (1980), pp. 51-52.

8. Uri Haklai, The Life of Nahum Zemach Against the Background of Jewish Culture in Russia, Ph.D. diss. Hebrew University, Jerusalem 1974, p. 164 (in Hebrew).

9. In various articles in the Hebrew journal Teatron ve-Omanut (Theatre and Art), 1, 17/6 (1925), p. 13; and 4-5, 15/10 (1925), p. 7.

10. In an interview in his home in Tel Aviv, June 1, 1981.

11. The Hassidic dance, which was of course also influenced by eastern European local traditions, won acceptance in Palestine; it was more formal and regular and much less agressive than the theatrical expressionism of the beggars' dance in Vakhtangov's production of The Dybbuk. See "Dance," Encyclopedia Judaica, V, (1970). There had also been a famous Yiddish production of The Dybbuk produced by the Vilna Troup in Poland (premiere December 1920) which stressed the folkloristic aspects of the play. A copy of this production had also been staged in Hebrew in Palestine directed by Michael Gov (premiere June 1922). See also Freddie Rokem, "The reception of The Dybbuk in Palestine 1922-1928," Katedra (in press, in Hebrew).

12. M. Kohansky, op. cit., 104 according to Ha-Levy's memoirs Darki ale bamot (My road on stages), Tel Aviv, 1955-56 (in Hebrew).

13. Photographs from the 1920's as evidence for movement patterns in dance and in the theatre are often not completely reliable because the dancers and actors often posed for the photographer while in the performance itself they were never frozen in this manner.

Chapter Twenty-Four

DANCES OF THE MIDDLE EAST

Maxine Leeds Snow

A dance performance is an experience, for the audience and the dancer, which exists in a moment and then is gone. Despite the possibility of recording movement through notation, on film or on videotape, the vast majority of dance performances go unrecorded. This is one reason why it is difficult to find information about dance.

A history of religious and social prohibitions against expressions of the body have made dance a suspect form. It is not serious, or worse, it is an evil practice. It has not been given the amount of serious critical analysis that one finds in literature or the fine arts.

The researcher looking for information on the dance forms of western Asia, the Middle East, and North Africa has an especially difficult task. Many of the articles available in English are popular accounts of strange and exotic hootchy-kootchy dancers.

The publication, in 1974, of the Dictionary Catalog of the Dance Collection, Performing Arts Research Center (Boston: G. K. Hall & Co., 1974), provided a tremendous resource. The catalog gave bibliographic access to the books, periodical articles and nonprint media in their excellent collection. It has been updated to include the library's latest acquisitions through regular supplements.

The following articles and books were found in the Dictionary Catalog of the Dance Collection. This bibliography is intended to be a starting point for anyone investigating dance in the Arab and Jewish cultures of the Middle East and western Asia.

Islamic Culture

1. General

Davison, Ian. "Arabian Dances," The Dancing Times (February 1922), pp. 443-445. Illus.

Faruqi, al-Lois Ibsen. "Dance as an Expression of Islamic Culture," Journal of Dance Research, 10 (Spring-Summer), pp. 6-13.

_____. "Dances of the Muslim Peoples," Dance Scope, 11 (Fall/ Winter 1976-77), pp. 43-51. Illus.

Juana (Stage name). "From the High Atlas to the Desert's Shore," Dance Magazine (December 1951), pp. 17-19, 43-46. Illus.

Shawn, Ted. "Dancing in North Africa," The Dance Magazine (December 1925), pp. 30-32, 62. Illus.

Story, Sommerville. "Arab Dancing Girls," The Dancing Times (March 1936), pp. 759-762. Illus.

Young, R. Clemson. "Arab Music and Dancing in North Africa," The Dancing Times (June 1931), pp. 220-221.

2. Afghanistan

Heitzig, Rupert. "Culture in Kabul," Dance Magazine (April 1963), pp. 28, 63-64. Illus.

Jan, Mirza Abdullah. "Oriental Dancing, Syria, Afghanistan and Ceylon," The Dancing Times (December 1931), pp. 263-264. Illus.

3. Algeria

Hofmann, Wilfried. "Folk and Theatre Dancing in Present Day Algeria," Ballet Today (April 1962), pp. 16-18. Illus.

4. Egypt

Grieg, Leon. "Dance With the Pharohs," Ballet Today (December 1955), pp. 12-13, 27. Illus.

Knapp, Bettina L. "Mystery and Wonderment in Egyptian Music and Dance," Arabesque, 3 (November-December 1977), pp. 14-16. Illus.

Terry, Walter. "Egyptians Turn to Dance for Folk and Theater Expression," Dance Scrapbook. New York Herald Tribune, July 14, 1946.

_____. "Religious Ceremony in Egypt Conducted by Dervish Dancers," Dance Scrapbook. New York Herald Tribune, July 7, 1946.

5. Iran

Caron, Nelly. "The Ta'zieh, the Sacred Theatre of Iran" in The World of Music, 17, 4 Mainz: B. Schott's Sohne, 1975.

DeWarren, Robert. "Discovery in Persia: An Interview on the Search for Persian Folklore in Forming the Mahalli Dancers of Iran"; and Williams, Peter. "The Mahalli Dancers in London," Dance and Dancers (January 1973), pp. 28-34. Illus.

Nettl, Bruno. "The Classical Music of Iran," Essays on the Asian Theater, Music and Dance, 3 New York: Performing Arts Program of the Asia Society, 1973?

"Persian Dancing Girls and Their Dances," The Dancing Times (September 1918), pp. 355-357.

6. Morocco

Anderson, Jack. "National Dance Company of Morocco, Brooklyn Academy of Music, November 2, 1971." Dance Magazine (January 1972), p. 25.

Grame, Theodore C. "Music in the Jma al-Fna of Marrakesh," The Musical Quarterly (January 1970), pp. 74-87. Illus.

7. Pakistan

Ishaq, Shahid. Evolution of Classical Dancing in Pakistan: A Study. Karachi: Printer's Combine (Mercantile), 1969, 29 p. Illus.

Massey, Reginald. "The Dance and Music of Pakistan," The Dancing Times (January 1967), pp. 188-189, 195. Illus.

8. Saudi Arabia

Deaver, Sherri. "Concealment versus Display: The Modern Saudi Woman," Dance Research Journal of CORD, 10 (Spring-Summer 1978), pp. 14-18.

9. Tunisia

Alport, Erich. "The Dancers of Kerkennah," Ballet, 4 (September 1947), pp. 41-43. Illus.

Kinney, Try. "A Romantic Look at Oriental Dance," Arabesque, 6 (May-June 1980), pp. 6-10, 22. Illus.

10. Turkey

Akdik, Ergi. "A Compilation of Turkish Folk Dances," M.A. thesis, Women's College, University of North Carolina, 1961.

Ali, Pasa. "A Dance from Western Turkey," Let's Dance (April 1973), pp. 20-21.

And, Metin. "Dances of Anatolian Turkey," Dance Perspectives, 3 (1959), 76 p. Illus. Map.

_____. A History of Theatre and Popular Entertainment in Turkey. Ankara, 1963-64. 144 p. Illus.

_____. A Practical History of Turkish Dancing. Ankara, 1976.

Conville, D. "Turkish Dream," Drama, 140 (1981), pp. 7-9.

James, David W. "Turkish Folk Dances," The Dancing Times (October 1946), pp. 14-15, 19.

"Llangollen," The Dancing Times (September 1960), p. 629.

Martinovich, Nicholas M. The Turkish Theatre. New York: Arno, 1968.

11. Dervish Dances

Baker, Robb. "The Whirling Dervishes of Turkey; Brooklyn Academy of Music, Nov. 14-19, 1972," Dance Magazine (February 1973), p. 20.

Barnett, Albert. "The Holy Dances of the Dervishes," The Dancing Times (June 1929), pp. 238-239. Illus.

Bhattacharya, Deben. "The Forbidden and Ecstatic Circle: Banned Whirling Dervish Dancers Can Still Be Seen Once a Year in Turkey," Dance Magazine (February 1965), pp. 44-45. Illus.

Dickerman, Watson B. "Whirling Dervishes," Theatre Arts (January 1934); pp. 67-72. Illus.

Faulkner, Trader. "Dervishes of Konya," The Dancing Times (December 1973), pp. 154-155, 157. Illus.

Farrah, Ibrahim. "The Whirling Dervishes: Living the Dance," Arabesque, 4 (January-February 1979), pp. 10-11, 16. Illus.

Friedlander, Ira. The Whirling Dervishes, London: Macmillan, 1975. 159 p. Illus.

Gordon, Mel. "Gurdjieff's Movement Demonstrations: The Theatre of the Miraculous," The Drama Review: Occult and the Bizarre Issue, 22 (June 1978), pp. 33-44. Illus.

Knapp, Bettina L. "Dervish Dances in Iran," Arabesque, 4 (January-February 1979), pp. 3-4, 17. Illus.

Jan, Mirza Abdullah. "Oriental Dancing," The Dancing Times (November 1931), pp. 129-132.

McGowan, Kate. "Turkish Dance." (In 4 parts) Arabesque Part 1, 1 (March-April 1976), pp. 10-12; Part 2, 2 (May-June 1976), pp. 10-11, 16; Part 3, 2 (July-August 1976), pp. 14-15, 21; Part 4, 2 (September-October 1976), pp. 7-8. Illus.

Massey, Reginald. "Dervish Dancers; Friend House, Euston, England, November 18-25, 1971," The Dancing Times (January 1972), p. 207.

Percival, John. "Unusual Visitors," Dance and Dancers (December 1974), pp. 31-32.

Sadler, A. W. "Mysticism and Devotion in the Music of the Qawwali," Monographs on Music, Dance and Theater in Asia. New York: Performing Arts Program of the Asia Society, 1974.

Stoody, Ralph. "The Chorus of the Dervishes; Like Human Gyroscopes the Dancing Priests of Islam Whirl and Turn in Strange Religious Ecstasies," Dance Magazine (March 1927), pp. 32, 60. Illus.

Terry, Walter. "Religious Ceremony in Egypt Conducted by Dervish Dancers," Dance Scrapbook. New York Herald Tribune, July 7, 1946.

12. Belly Dancing

Ali, Aisha. "Meetings in the Middle East," Arabesque, 5 (January-February 1980), pp. 18-20, 25. Illus.

Aradoon, Zarifa. The Belly Dance Costume Book, Stanford, CA: Dream Place Publications, c1978. 202 p. Illus.

Balladine, Roman and Sula Balladine. The Secrets of Belly Dancing. Millbrae, CA: Celestial Arts Publishing, c1972. 96 p. Illus.

Berger, Morrore. "The Arab Danse du Ventre," Dance Perspectives 10 (1961), 48 p. Illus.

Deaver, Sherri. "Concealment Versus Display: The Modern Saudi

Woman," Dance Research Journal (of) CORD, 10 (Spring-Summer 1978), pp. 14-18.

Farrah, Ibrahim. "Impressions of Cairo," Arabesque, 2 (July-August 1976), pp. 6-7, 19. Illus.

Lahm, Adam. "Oriental Dance: The Techniques of Ibrahim Farrah," Dance Teacher Now, 2 (Summer 1980), pp. 18-22. Illus.

La Meri. "Learning the Danse du Ventre," Dance Perspectives (Spring 1961), pp. 43-47. Illus.

Mishkin, Julie Russo. The Compleat Belly Dancer. Garden City, NY: Doubleday, 1973. 160 p. Illus.

Muir, Leily Lori. "Costumes of the Ouled Nail," Arabesque, 3 (July-August 1977), pp. 6-17. Illus.

_____ and Jean Wood. "Costumes of the Ghawazee," Arabesque, 2 (March-April 1977), pp. 18-20. Illus.

Mustacchi, Marianna M. "Flaubert and the Oriental Dance," Arabesque, 2 (January-February 1977), pp. 9-21. Illus.

"On the Gypsy Circuit," Dance Magazine (May 1965), p. 20. Illus.

Ross, Betty. "One Arabian Night: A Personally Conducted Tour of a Modern Egyptian Cabaret," Dance Magazine (November 1926), pp. 14, 61.

Saretta, Phyllis. "Arab Dancing Girls: Dances of the Ouled Nail," Arabesque, 3 (July-August 1980), pp. 18-23. Illus.

_____. "The Clubs, Charisma and Technique," Arabesque, 6 (July-August 1980), pp. 4-7. Illus.

Sklar, Vivian. "Interview with Nakhla," Wind and Spirit, 1 (October-November 1979), pp. 8-12. Ports.

_____ and Linda Soloman. "Vocabulary of Movement," Wind and Spirit, 1 (August-September 1979), p. 22. Illus.

Sobel, Bernard. "This Historic Hootchy-kootchy," Dance Magazine (October 1946), pp. 13-15, 46. Illus.

Soloman, Linda. "An interview with Anahid Sofian," Wind and Spirit, 1 (August-September 1979), pp. 8-10.

_____. "Women in Middle Eastern Dance--Beginnings," Wind and Spirit 1 (August-September 1979), pp. 23, 25.

Stewart, Joan. "Womandance," Arabesque, 6 (July-August 1980),
   pp. 3, 14, 19-20.

Wood, Leona. "Danse du Ventre: A Fresh Appraisal. Part I,"
   Arabesque, 5 (January-February 1980), pp. 8-13. Illus.

_____ and Anthony Shay. "Danse du Ventre: A Fresh Appraisal." Dance Research Journal of the Committee on Research in
   Dance, 8 (Spring/Summer 1976), pp. 18-30. Illus.

Worell, Sabiha and Hayatt (Harriet Trevas). "An interview with
   Tahia Carioca," Arabesque, 2 (November-December 1976), pp.
   5, 8-9. Illus.

Jewish Culture

1. Hasidism

Baral, Lillian. "Folk Dancing in Israel a Lure to Tourists," Rosin
   the Bow, 5 (Winter-Spring 1956), pp. 39-40. Illus.

Berk, Fred, ed. The Chassidic Dance. New York: American
   Zionist Youth Foundation, 1975. 64 p.

Gellerman, Jill Marsha. "With Body and Soul; an Introduction to
   the Ecstatic Dance of the Hasidim," M.A. thesis, Ohio State
   University, 1972, 195 p. Illus.

"Hadassah. Dance Themes of Hassidism and Hinduism; a lecture
   delivered at a consultation on religion and dance at the River-
   side Church, New York City." Dance Observer (March 1963),
   pp. 37-39. Illus.

"Hassidic Sher," Let's Dance (July 1956), p. 13.

Lapson, Dvora. "The Chassidic Dance," Dance Observer (1937),
   pp. 109-110.

2. Israel

"Al Gemali," Let's Dance (August-September 1972), pp. 20-21.

"At va'ani," Let's Dance (May 1969), p. 18.

Baral, Lillian. "Folk Dancing in Israel a Lure to Tourists," Rosin
   the Bow, 5 (Winter-Spring 1956), pp. 39-40. Illus.

Berk, Fred. Ha-rikud: The Jewish Dance. New York: American
   Zionist Youth Foundation, 1972. 101 p. Illus.

_____. Machol ha'am (Dance of the Jewish People). New York: American Zionist Youth Foundation, 1978.

_____ and Katya Delakova. The Jewish Folk Dance Book. New York: National Jewish Welfare Board, 1948.

"Bona Habanoth; Come Here Maidens," Let's Dance (July 1956), p. 14.

"Erev Ba: I and II," Let's Dance (May 1966), pp. 19-22.

Fifield, Audrey. "Costumes of Israel," Let's Dance (May 1966), pp. 8-10. Illus.

Folk Dance Federation of California. "Lech Lamidbar, (Let's Go to the Desert)," Folk Dances From Near and Far, 8 (1957), p. 12.

Folk Dance Federation of California. "Mayim (Water)," Folk Dances From Near and Far, 7 (1952), p. 15.

Frehof, Florence. "The Dancing People of Israel," Let's Dance (July 1956), pp. 12, 15. Illus.

_____. A Guide for Israeli-Jewish Folk Dancers. New York: Bloch Pub. Co., c1963. 31 p. Illus.

"Haro's Haktana Min Hagai," Let's Dance (August-September 1972), pp. 18, 23.

Hoppe, Hilda. "Israeli Folk Dancing," Let's Dance (April 1958), pp. 7-9. Illus.

"Im Hoopalnu," Rosin the Bow, 5 (2nd Quarter 1954), p. 24.

Ingber, J. B. "Shorashim: The Roots of Israeli Folk Dance," Dance Perspectives, 59 (Autumn 1974), pp. 1-60. Illus.

"Israeli Team Tour Here With Authentic Folk Dances," Dance News (January 1957), p. 9. Illus.

Kadman, Gurit. "The Folk Dance of Israel," The Folk Dancer (March-April 1956), p. 165.

Kaufman, Ayalah. "Summary of a Paper on Indigenous and Imported Elements in the New Folk Dance in Israel," International Folk Music Council Journal (May 3, 1951), pp. 55-57.

"Le'or chi yu chech, (Brilliance of Your Smile; Israel)," Let's Dance (April 1958), pp. 17, 20.

"Machar," Let's Dance (May 1969), p. 14.

Mason, Nancy. "Inbal Dance Theater of Israel: New York City, Feb. 9, 1971," Dance Magazine (April 1971), p. 100.

Meyers, Therese. "Dancing in a Biblical Land," Dance Magazine (January 1959), pp. 50-53, 64-65, 75-76, 92.

Puretz, Susan Luskin. "Israeli Folk Dance: Where It's Been and Where It's Going," Let's Dance (May-June 1974), pp. 6-8.

Rosen, Lillie F. "Israeli Folk Festival 1974, Felt Forum, N.Y.C., Oct. 17-20, 1974," Dance News (December 1974), p. 12.

"Sham Hareh Golan," Let's Dance (October 1973), pp. 20-21.

"Shiboley Paz," Let's Dance (June-July 1973), pp. 18, 23.

Shoshani, Michael. Folk Dances of Israel. Tel Aviv: Israel Music Institute, c1970. 111 p. Illus.

Sorrell, Walter. "Dancing in Israel," Dance Magazine (February 1949), pp. 12-17, 37. Illus.

"Ta'am Haman," Let's Dance (July-August 1961), pp. 14+.

"Tzadik Katamar," Let's Dance (October 1973), pp. 18, 23.

3. Palestine

Blumenfeld, Leon. "Dance Pioneering in Palestine," Dance Magazine (March 1929), pp. 17, 56-57. Illus.

Chochem, Corinne. Palestine Dances! New York: Behrman's Jewish Book House, 1951. 63 p. Illus. (Reprint. Westport, CT: Greenwood Press, 1978.)

Delakova, Katya. Dances of Palestine. New York: Hillel Resources, 1947. 32 p. Illus.

Folk Dance Federation of California. "Scherr," Folk Dances From Near and Far, 2 (1946), p. 21.

Folk Dance Federation of California. "Tel Avivia," Folk Dances From Near and Far, 5 (1950), p. 31.

Levy, Hassia. "Dance in Palestine." Dance Observer (February 1948), pp. 16-17. Port.

Terry, Walter. "Arab-Jewish Cultural Bonds are Found in New Palestine Dances," Dance Scrapbook. New York Herald Tribune Feb. 1, 1948.

4. Yemen

Hoppe, Hilda. "Israeli Folk Dancing," Let's Dance (April 1958), pp. 7-9. Illus.

"Inbalim," Let's Dance (August-September 1963), pp. 23+.

Joel, Lydia. "Sara Levi-Tanai: Dreamer and Doer," Dance Magazine (January 1960), pp. 16-17. Illus. Port.

Kadman, Gurit. "Yemenite Dances and Their Influence on the New Israeli Folk Dances," International Folk Music Council Journal 4 (1952), pp. 27-30.

Staub, Shalom. "A Man Has Brains Until He Gets Up to Dance, (a Yemenite Proverb)," Israel: Dance 1975 (1976), pp. 15-18. 1st section.

_____. "Just an Echo? The Dances of Yemenite Women," Israeli Dance, 2 (1976), pp. 15-17.

Chapter Twenty-Five

MOVEMENT IN AFRICAN PERFORMANCE*

Judith Lynne Hanna

There is progressive movement toward understanding nonverbal performance in Africa as cultural, social, and physical human expression. This state of the art essay will explain the context for the growth of African movement studies--essentially dance and dance-drama, describe theoretical approaches (some of which perpetuate old stereotypes and ethnocentric views), indicate the kinds of dance events that have been studied, propose new directions, and suggest further references for the study of movement in African performance.

Pervasive in Africa, dancing is often mentioned in conjunction with religious ritual, music, storytelling, masking, dress, festivals, play, recreation, and war. Such movement in African performance is described with varying detail and sophistication. From an extensive literature, I will select work that illustrates different points of view, facts, and fantasy. The discussion is neither comprehensive nor exhaustive and concentrates on material in English.

Due to the growing understanding of both Africa and dance, the literature on these subjects is less fixated on dance as pornography, war, or savagery than it was in the past. Recent research tends to reflect a concern for the perspectives of the movement performers and audiences and to present a fuller picture of what actually happens. In addition, there is a growing recognition of the intertwining of the aesthetic or artistic with the utilitarian as well as the blurring of the sacred and secular. The change in

*This chapter is an expanded and updated version of an earlier assessment of movement in African performance entitled "African Dance Research: Past, Present, and Future," Africana Journal, 11 (1-2), 1980. Permission from Africana Publishing Company to use this material is gratefully acknowledged. I wish to thank Daniel Biebuyck, Robert Garfias, Joseph Hickerson, Boniface Obichere, Simon Ottenberg, Beverly Robinson, Bennetta Jules-Rosette, and Keyan Tomaselli for their reference suggestions.

dance reporting parallels the change in western morality, values, and technology.

Prior to the 1960's the limited state of dance study was due to a Puritan ethic, Victorian morality, concepts of masculinity, ethnocentrism, Christian missionary recognition of the relationship of African dance and religion, European occupation of Africa, capitalist social stratification, primitive recording technology, and the social science need to emphasize seemingly scientific subjects in their disciplines, which meant the neglect of the arts. (See Hanna 1966, 1979b, 1979c, 1983a, 1983b.) The Puritan distrust of gaiety and body beauty gave an inferior status to dancers who used the repudiated body in ways equated with the Devil's handiwork, with animal instincts, and with lower forms of life.

African dance was too licentious within the Victorian frame of reference. Furthermore, men's dancing in Anglo-Saxon culture had effeminate, homosexual overtones. Because scholars of an art form usually need some experience in it, many avoided dance because this was disparaged. Thus observers of dance in Africa, unacquainted with how the human body could use the space, rhythm, and dynamic dance elements and choreographic processes, had difficulty describing movement. European ethnocentrism led scholars to exclude from the category of dance any nonballet or jig movement. The missionaries in Africa, aware of the deeply rooted intertwining of African dancing with pagan religion, tried to eliminate dancing, and thereby more readily propagate Christianity. Sometimes dances disturbed the colonialists' sleep, distracted Africans from working for Europeans, or showed independence and virility and thus anti-imperialism as in warrior dances (Hanna 1977; 1979c, Ch. 7); therefore administrators banned dances. Consequently the study of dance, which might legitimize it, was not encouraged. And detailed movement analyses could not be expected until the advent of portable, tropicalized film and videotape equipment. A visual recording permits multiple viewing. Notation upon perceiving a once-a-year ritual performance or festival can only be incomplete.

Factors that now retard the growth of studies of movement in African performance include the current economics of scarcity and inflation with its resulting decrease in funding for area studies research, increase in cost of audiovisual recording, and slowly developing research training in the relatively new departments of dance and more established departments of theatre. However, interest in the combination of the theoretical perspectives and methods of the social sciences, humanities, and arts with the skills of movement analysis is realistically foreseeable. Let us now turn to the scope and limitations of approaches that explore dance in culture and society, dance as movement description, dance as an entity apart from its context, and dance as part of the African culture area.

Dance in Culture and Society

Although it is difficult to generalize about a continental area as huge as Africa, one common observation is that dance is not a segmented and minor aspect of life as it tends to be in western industrialized societies. In Africa, dances are enmeshed to a greater extent in nondance aspects of individual and group life. With their holistic perspective, anthropologists lead in the study of African dance as part of these processes. They have tended to emphasize the context of dance. Evans-Pritchard's 1928 article on the Azande beer dance is a landmark. He describes the social functions, song structure, muscular movements, spatial dance patterns, dance participants, leaders, training, and occasions for dance. In his widely recognized classic study, Mitchell (1956) used the Kalela dance event as an incisive wedge to elucidate the dynamics of the society of which the dance is part and to help explain the dance itself. He portrays dance as an emblem of the social class aspirations of an African group in a Zambian urban setting.

Social scientists have explored a variety of dance topics related to basic aspects of individual and group life. I will mention some of these topics which are not, however, mutually exclusive. Everyday life, morality, myths, and legends provide feelings, attitudes, concepts, and stories that are enacted in dance.

Fernandez (1966, 1982) describes aesthetics in Fang dance, and Horton (1960, 1963, 1966, 1967) portrays Kalabari notions of dance appropriateness and competency. The latter's work is also related to the communications of belief systems. Griaule (1965) records a Dogon elder's notions of dance as part of a coherent system of thought. Dogon dance is a cosmological representation and vehicle for moving the world to order after the disorder of death. Dance teams and masked societies perform choreography that depicts the Dogon conception of the world's progress. Hanna (1976, 1979c, 1982a, 1982e) describes how the Ubakala's dance reflects the key tenets of their value system, mediates conflict and social relations, and also introduces change. She explores why dance is a widespread medium humans use to relate to the supernatural and summarizes the range of dance religious practices in Africa: worship or honor, conducting supernatural beneficence, effecting change, and embodying the supernatural (1979c, 1984). Ten Raa (1969) describes the moon as a symbol of life and fertility in Sandawe thought and the communication of this belief through dance.

Discussions of economic behavior and dance are in Nadel (1942), Little (1951), and Imperato (1970), who is a specialist in tropical diseases. Dance may be intimately connected with work, yet interrupt or follow it as an incentive to the successful completion of a day's activities or future endeavors. Among the Fang, dance is a form of economic exchange combining elements of the defunct competitive gift exchange (ensuring the distribution of trade goods and uniting alien social units in so doing) and competitive relations involving notions of opposition and alliance that are dramatized in marriage ceremonies (Fernandez 1975-1976). The role of dance in education appears in Raum (1940), Hanna (1965b, 1976, 1979a, 1979c), and Drewal (1973). Fortes (1938) describes the developmental nature of dance performance. Nketia (1957) for possession and Ottenberg (1982a) for masquerades suggest how children acquire a cultural heritage and learn adult forms (see Hanna 1982d). Initiation dances are special forms of education and symbolic action; see Biebuyck (1973), Blacking (1969), Mair (1951), Ravenhill (1978), Stayt (1931), Turner (1967, 1969), Weil (1971), and White (1953). Dances in initiation ceremonies usually mark its phases, communicate the value of fertility, and pass on lore about the individual's newly developed sexual powers and the social responsibilities arising therefrom. Initiates may be "danced" and thus magically protected against malevolence and given the promise of fertility (Richards 1956). Jacobs' (1961) study of puberty rites provides insights on courtship.

Studies on healing dances include Marshall (1969, 1976) on the !Kung Bushmen, who also use the curing dance to drive away evil which might be present but unseen; Katz (1982) on the Kalahari !Kung; Lewis-Williams (1982) who links the Bushmen curing dance to economic production and visual art; and Hanna (1978) who suggests the relevance of Ubakala's "preventative medicine" to Americans. Ottenberg (1982b) offers a western psychological interpretation of Afikpo masquerade dances. By stressing noneveryday kinesic activity that permits the performer to deal with repressed early life experience, the masquerades hold special fascination for performers and audience. Possession dance is often related to physical or mental health. See Lindblom (1920), Messing (1958), Nketia (1957), Werbner (1964) and Hanna (1979c; Ch. 5). A number of researchers have focused on the relationship between dance and politics: Blacking (1962, 1965), Hanna (1979c, Ch. 6; 1982a), Cornet (1980), and Siroto (1969, 1972). In Africa as in Europe, the production of dance provides the opportunity to gain prestige by showing wealth. Some African groups use the dance medium as a political lobby to convey grievances and propose solutions. From Siroto we learn that mask dancing helps an individual in attaining leadership and social control (see also Sieber 1971, Wembah-Rashid 1971). Kuper reports (1968) that the Swazi believe their warriors keep the king alive and healthy by their own dance movements. The Kikuyu way to promulgate a new constitution is to call for dances to be held in every district (Kenyatta 1962). Ranger (1975) pursues his past work on resistance, compulsion, and protest, seeing the dance as a "very impressionistic scale of balance of emasculation and creativity, of accommodation and independence" (p. 4). Communicating power relationships and strategically playing a role in politics, dance creates and validates leaders and is a vehicle of competition for power, social control, coping with subordination, constraining the exercise of power, and redress and transformation. Dance is a coping mechanism for many situations: marriage and birth (Hanna 1978), death (Wilson 1954), and the foibles of humanity. Among the Kalabari, the ikaki (tortoise) masquerade is a representation of human psychology in animal guise; the playing of ikaki is a taming of human behavior (Horton 1967). Tomaselli (1980, 1981) raises issues about the meaning of theatrical movement in the political context of contemporary apartheid in South Africa. The black dramatist, he argues, provides a group therapy which proceeds outwards from the performer to the wider society to lay reality bare. Theatre is not a commodity traded off in terms of integrity for profit; rather the traditional function of performance carries over. To wit: the war dance spontaneously enacted by discontented striking workers in front of the Department of Labour officials at an iron foundary later coalesced into the play Ilanga. Theatre is a medium of working class expression. Steadman (1981) provides a select bibliography of information relevant to the development of performance in South Africa.

After European contact with Africa, traditional theatrical events continued in the festival, ritual, and social genres. Western theatre forms soon made their appearance through university education. Herein Africans both moved like westerners and also like themselves when they incorporated indigenous movement. In addition to traditional and western performance patterns, there were syncretistic blends such as the Ghanaian Concert Party (similar to the western commedia dell'arte or vaudeville) and Nigerian Folk Opera (renowned representatives include Duro Ladipo, Kola Ogunmola, Chief Hubert Ogunde, and the Alarinjo Theatre).

In these eclectic forms, dance and mimetic movement constitute active components. Dance may either be an aside, as in the Ghana Drama Studio presentation of Mother's Tears, or dance may be an integral part of a production. Illustrative is the work of Wole Soyinka which is more westernized than the folk opera although it has similar elements. The Lion and the Jewel uses several arts, including dance; Dance of the Forest presents its climax through dance; and Death and the King's Horseman also draws upon Yoruba dance tradition.

In such dance companies as Guinea National Ballet or National Dance Theatre of Zaire, the common pattern is to develop a simple story line into which a series of traditional dances are performed. The traditional materials, of course, appear in shortened and otherwise modified format (see section on continuity and change).

Another transformation of traditional type dances are those dances performed in the contemporary school or government-sponsored competition or festival. National independence celebrations are common occasions for official government-organized festivals.

Dance in traditional Africa communicates the people's concerns. This function carries over into modern times. Consequently, the westernized theatre often has the manifest function of entertainment at the same time that it had the convert function of encouraging nationalism (Traore 1972, Ranger 1975). Overviews of contemporary African Theatre appear in Carpenter (1962), Kennedy (1972), Traore (1972), Jones (1976), and Banham (1976).

Dance Movement Description

Because most scholars do not have dance movement analysis training, their descriptions of the physical actions of dance are limited. The work of an historian like Ranger (1975), for example, only focuses on the context of dance. Drewal (1973), an art historian whose dance-trained colleague Margaret Drewal described Yoruba movement, and Hanna (1976, 1973, 1982a), an anthropologist also trained in dance, attempt to describe and relate the context of the dance to the text or movement. Collaboration between an anthropologist and movement analyst using Benesh notation appears in Blacking (1977).

Notational ideographs, representations in graphic symbols, are a shorthand for data, as is academic jargon meaningful and rapidly used by a small coterie of "experts." Even if one does not choose to use notation, the mastery of the concepts for notation sharpens one's abilities to observe variations in movement patterns and qualities. The four major dance notation systems (Labanotation, Laban's effort-shape analysis, Benesh, and Eshkol-Wachman) do not specify the distinctive structural units but provide symbols for the description of dances so that they can be performed, the purpose for which the systems developed. Moving to contrastive patterns and to digital coding for computer analysis to show quantitative patterning, clusters, and correlation, a direction for the future, is as easy from verbal as graphic transcriptions.

Kubik (1977), an ethnomusicologist, evolved his own system of dance transcription through transcribing the actions of African music-making from silent film. Some African dances have been described using Labanotation. References to notated scores, primarily written by Odette Blum and Nadia Chilkovsky Nahumck, appear in Warner (1983); see also Vadassy (1973). Irmgard Bartenieff and Forrestine Pauley developed a choreometric movement coding scheme (Lomax 1968, pp. 222-247, 262-273). They based their selection of movement characteristics upon what they perceived to be salient after viewing films. Other researchers might choose different characteristics. Harper (1968a, 1968b), a dancer, and Frank Speed, a filmmaker, collaborated in recording dances and providing an accompanying verbal description of aspects of the text and context. (See Keil 1979, p. 251, on Harper 1968a.) Although movement can be notated graphically or verbally or recorded on film or videotape, in each of these transformations dance loses some of the dimensions that it has in performance.

Dance Structure Apart from Its Context

Contrary to those who view dance as intermeshed with non-dance aspects of social life or describe movement in detail, Armstrong (1971) sees dance as a phenomenon in itself and primarily a work of the feelings. This is actually a notion long held in the nonanthropological dance world (see Hanna 1983a, 1983b). Assuming that people respond to form, Armstrong does not explain how what he calls "the affecting presence" works as does, for example, Berlyne in his empirical studies of aesthetic psychology. Psychologists have found that emotion and thought are intertwined. Berlyne (1971), Turner (1969), and Hanna (1979c) argue that this interpenetration allows aesthetic forms to move people to social action. Armstrong does not consider that other cultures may respond to an affecting presence in ways uncommon to him.

Rejecting the concept of such artistic media as languages (p. 29), Armstrong denies an affecting reference to something external to dance (pp. 31, 122). Most of the work on dance in culture and society and the arts generally refutes this position (Sebeok 1982). For example, among the Afikpo, heightened aesthetic interest occurs when there is a high level of skill and also when there is much symbolism, "usually a congruence of cultural, social, and psychological symbols" (Ottenberg 1973, p. 33).

While rejecting ethnocentric theory for analysis, Armstrong puts forth his own scheme apart from any African interpretations. The scheme, comprised of dichotomous intension/extension and continuity/discontinuity, is illustrated with Yoruba Dance. While most Yoruba dance does exhibit intension, limbs remaining close to the body, and continuity, the body maintaining a columnar quality, Armstrong does not consider cases that do not fit this pattern. Eshu Elegba, a "deity universally recognized and appealed to by all Yoruba regardless of their affiliation to other cults" (Wescott 1962, p. 337), engages in much "wide side-stepping, high kicks, and sudden and violent contractions" (ibid. p. 344).

Keil (1979, p. 197) suggests that Armstrong's "exclusion of masculine and feminine modes of expression and dimensions of feeling from the entire theory" to be a major flaw. He found Tiv, as Hanna found Ubakala, dance to have gender distinctions.

Dance and the African Culture Area Concept

Perhaps because of the colonialist heritage, some scholars seek a distinctively African expression common to the approximately

1,000 societies with peoples as diverse as the agricultural Igbo of Nigeria, pastoral Massai of Kenya, and hunter/gatherer Bushmen of Namibia. Unfortunately, the generalizations put forth lack empirical support according to ethnographers and film records (Feld 1972; Stone 1982a; M. Drewal 1980). Lomax, a folk music specialist, generalizes to all of Africa on the basis of a few selected films from a sample of four groups (!Kung, Bahima, Fulani, Dogon). Let us examine Lomax's propositions apart from what Keil (1979, p. 187) refers to as "the inevitable associations of static, ill-defined, and semi-isolated variables, the loss of each culture's complex internal relationships, which makes the study of the arts interesting in the first place; and so on." Keil found most of Lomax's hypotheses about dance and music to be inapplicable to Tiv culture. Lomax asserts that technologically simple societies have simple dance styles and structures; dance evolves, he assumes, unlinearly. This position is countered by evidence, e.g., Hanna's study of Ubakala dance (1976, 1979b, 1979c, 1979d) which shows the complexity in pragmatics (purpose and function), syntax or grammar, semantics (meaning of the physical movement), and the manipulation of space, time, and effort in multimedia presentations. Furthermore, there is a variety of styles and structures within the Ubakala's repertoire. For example, when the age of both sexes is relatively close, but their biological and social role differentiation is greatest, when women are seen as life-givers and men as life-takers, the dance movement patterns diverge most markedly. Reanalyzing some of Lomax's data, Erickson (1976) shows that Lomax has failed to support his hypotheses of universal associations between song-style features and the process of cultural evolution. Erickson's use of multivariate techniques to analyze the dance-style data would probably yield similar results.

African folk dance, according to Lomax, has a static, closed tradition. This assumption is fallacious in light of the Ubakala emphasis on change which may occur in movement, song, music, and costume. The Ubakala ethos and behavior are antithetical to maintaining a rigid status quo.

Lomax states that there is a simple causal explanation for dance: everyday movement patterns generate and animate dance movement. The relation between dance movement and economic activity has long been recognized by dance scholars. Lomax's implicit theoretical formulation is a stimulus-response model in which the human dancer has no cognitive choice. Lomax does not recognize that dance may incarnate reality as well as escape or counter it. There is no evidence that everyday movement patterns generate many Ubakala dance movements; birth, coitus, and killing are not daily occurrences for everyone. And the fighting portrayed in the Ese dance is prohibited under the present system of law and order. Dance movement style and structure may be generated by a variety of body processes and structures, by music, and by current events. Choice, innovation, and borrowing epitomize Ubakala dance-plays. Feeling is usually involved in the Ubakala dances, but one cannot deny the importance of the cognitive, instrumental aspects of performances, whether "to sit on a man" or motivate proper attitudes and actions--the dance-play form has many dynamics. The Dogon view the rapid Gôna dance movement as a relief, like vomiting, which is not a dancer's everyday movement (Griaule 1965). By setting up constraints on activity, costume may be another causal explanation for dance movement.

Lomax assumes a sexual romanticism and lumps all African dance into the category of "wildly, energetic, hip-swinging dances," and "speed" supposedly flows through all African movement (1968, p. 234). The wild, panting expenditures of energy are countermanded by the intracultural dance diversity within Ubakala. If all the dancing women (many pregnant or nursing) engaged in wild dance, the demographers would tell a different story than they do. Rather than an orgiastic effect, Ubakala women display tender concern for life continuity and succor for young and old. Ogotommêlie (Griaule 1965) suggested that sex is one of many dimensions of dance and that recreation of the cosmology involves far more than orgy. From his film sample, Lomax describes the Bushmen as having a "flowing sensuous style" empty of "group controlling content" (1972). Yet Marshall (1969, p. 363), on the basis of field observation over time, describes contrary behavior: "Many of the men move their bodies so little that they are like statues being carried by the dancing legs."

Lomax assumes that dance promotes solidarity, the individual submitting to the communal rhythmic unison to produce a harmony of the whole (1968, p. 170). Yet the occasion of dance or dance itself may also lead to conflict. Second burials among the Ubakala, where reminders of unsettled scores surfaced, often led to fighting. The dances Evans-Pritchard observed in central Africa were the most frequent occasion of disharmony (1965, p. 74). Turner noticed quarrels and fights during public dances in the intervals between phases of the rituals of the Ndembu (1967, pp. 40, 256). In the Sudan, the Anuak have a partner couple dance in which men would cut in on each other during the dance, latecomers trying to wrest their partners from those who were already dancing. This gave rise to much fighting and many people were said to have been killed (Lienhardt 1957, p. 352).

Thompson (1974), an art historian, spotlights some meaning of masks in motional context, focuses on the interrelationship of the arts, and presents verbal transcripts of some African's evaluations of art. Always "inviting reasons for the beauty of a given dance" (p. 3), Thompson concluded that there are ten "criteria of fine form which seem to be shared among makers of sculpture, music, and the dance" (p. xii). His canons are "ephebism: the stronger power that comes from youth; 'Afrikanische Aufheben': simultaneous suspending and preserving of the beat; the 'get-down quality':

descending direction in melody, sculpture, dance; multiple meter: dancing many drums; looking smart: playing the patterns with nature and with line; correct entrance and exit: 'Killing the song,' 'cutting the dance,' 'lining the face'; vividness cast into equilibrium: personal and representational balance; call-and-response: the politics of perfection; ancestorism: ability to incarnate destiny; coolness: truth and generosity regained" (pp. 5-48). Unfortunately Thompson's African informants do not support his ten canons (Hanna 1975). The highest support for any of the canons is about 20 percent of his respondents. Furthermore, there are methodological problems with the selection of informants: the sample is sexist and gerontocratic. Ninety-six informants selected haphazardly within a nine-year period from thirty-two locales which include five countries were asked different questions. Here, as in the Armstrong and Lomax work, there is no consideration of variation within a group of people. Projects that work toward a synthesis of a large body of data are important. However, they cannot ignore the data that do not fit the key argument.

Surveys of African Movement

There are several surveys of movement in African performance. They tend, however, to be superficial. Brelsford (1959) surveys dances of Northern Rhodesia. Darbois's (1962) photographs are from French-speaking West Africa. Goer (1935) has perceptive commentary from his travels. Harper (1969) provides an overview of Yoruba dance. An insightful journalistic photographer, Huet (1978) brings together 256 images of dances and ceremonies of forty indigenous peoples of Africa's Guinea Coast, western Sudan, and Equatorial Africa. Jean-Louis Paudrat provides ethnographic interpretations. Martin (1967) summarizes dance types in Ethiopia. Chokwe dance is described in Museo do Dundo (1961). Tracey presents dances of the Chopi (1948) and of the gold mines (1952). H. Drewal (1975) provides an introduction to masked movement, and Brink (1981), to forms of theatre among the Beledugu Bamana of Mali.

Interrelation of the Arts

Dance and its intermesh with the verbal arts is described in Clark (1965), Scheub (1971), and Vidal (1969) who also comments on music. Calame-Griaule examines, with photographs and by means of a text, the expressive gestures of a narrator called Ahmaden Ag-Assala who is from the Tuareg of Azawaq (1977). Distinctions exist between these functions: "phatic" to establish or maintain communication, "explicative" to give redundant information, "dramatization" to animate, and "information" to go beyond what is said. Olofson (1974) elicited terms for facial expressions of gaze and hand gestures. These pertain to sternness, annoyance, social withdrawal,

anger, and contempt: nonverbal means of communicating inaccepta-
ble feelings. These gestures might be used in theatrical performance.

Perspectives on dance and music appear in Blacking (1973),
Jones and Kombe (1952), Chernoff (1979), Echezona (1966), Keil
(1979), Laoye (1966), Nketia (1965, 1975), Nzewi (1971), and
Tracey (1948). Thompson (1971a, 1971b, 1974) considers sculpture and masks as elements of dance. See also Ottenberg (1975).

Continuity and Change

Relevant articles in this category include Anonymous (1965),
Beier (1954), Binet (1972), Camara (1967), Decock (1968), Dorsinville (1970), Fabian (1978), Ferguson (1962), Fodeba (1958), Hanna
(1965a, 1974) Hanna and Hanna (1968), Harper (1967), Hopkins
(1965, 1972), Imperato (1971), Meillassoux (1965, 1968), Merriam
(1964), Nzekwu (1962), Opoku (1966), and Skelton (1964). See
the last section of Dance in Culture and Society, above.

Directions for the Future

At this point in the study of movement in African performance, present writings on the subject should be critically examined
so that quality scholarship may increase. The research cited in
this essay provides perspectives and presents propositions that
should be further pursued, but with care to avoid pitfalls discovered upon reflection. Williams (1976-77) examines her own work on
African dance (1968, 1970) and proposes another approach which
Gell (1979) sharply faults. Keil (1979), although primarily concerned with Tiv song, learned that dance, which makes songs
"juicier," may be the primary expressive form among the Tiv.
Viewing his own work as an introduction to future research, he
raises many stimulating questions. Hanna, too, reflects over a
fifteen-year period and gropes toward a theory of dance (see 1979b
for a model and several scholars' comments, and 1979c, 1979d, 1981
and 1983b; Montagu 1980).

We need to know how the movement cultural heritage is taught
and learned (Hanna 1982d). What is the meaning of movement? Although there are several methods for notating the physical progression of a dance, as mentioned above, only recently has attention
focused on the various devices and spheres of conveying meaning
in movement performance.

I have discovered that there are at least six symbolic devices
for conveying meaning that may be utilized in dance. Each device
may be conventional (customary, shared legacy) or autographic
(idiosyncratic or creative expression of a thing, event, or condition).

A concretization is a device that produces the outward aspect
of something. A war dance, for example, imitates or replicates advance and retreat tactics in a battle. An icon represents most
properties or formal characteristics of something and is responded
to as if it were what it represents. An example is a possessed human being manifesting the supernatural through dancing and being
treated with genuine awe by his or her social group. A stylization
encompasses somewhat arbitrary gestures or movements which are
the result of convention. Illustrations are pointing to the heart as
a sign of love or using dance to create abstract images within a
conceptual structure of form as in many of George Balanchine's
"pure" ballets. A metonym is a motional conceptualization of one
thing representing another of which it is a part or with which it
is associated in the same frame of experience. A war dance as
part of a battle is illustrative. A metaphor expresses one thought,
experience, or phenomenon in place of another that it resembles to
suggest an analogy between the two: one can dance the role of a
leopard to denote the power of death. An actualization is a portrayal of one or several of the dancer's usual roles. When Louis
XIV danced the role of king he was treated as king.

The devices for encapsulating meaning in dance seem to operate within one or more of seven spheres: the sociocultural event
and/or situation, e.g., people may go to the ballet to be seen socially, dance-viewing being incidental; the total human body in action; the whole pattern of the performance; the sequence of unfolding movement; specific movements; the intermesh of movements with
other communication modes such as speech or costume; and dance
movement as a vehicle for another medium, like dance serving as a
backdrop for a performer's poetry recitation. Elsewhere (1979b) I
elaborate on searching for meaning in movement and provide illustrations from Ubakala dance-play performance.

The cognitive and the emotional are intertwined in dance. We
have little knowledge of these dimensions in dance. In addition to
probing meaning of movement, as above, an area to explore is
whether performers get across the messages they intend to convey.
In a non-African setting I asked performers what feelings they
wanted to impart in a particular dance and how they thought they
conveyed the emotions. Then at the performance, I asked audience
members what emotions they perceived and what were the clues to
them. This kind of investigation is appropriate for Africa (Hanna
1983b).

Because it is reality and is about past, present, or future
reality, dance should be examined as an entity in itself as well as
in relationship to the individual and the group within a model that
draws upon current thinking and empirical findings in the arts,
humanities, and social sciences. A model should have the under-
pinning of psychobiological bases and combine textual (analysis of
system of movement), contextual (analysis of social, cultural, his-

torical, and environmental catalysts for dance, its process, and its impact), and symbolic interaction (analysis of perspectives of participants--both dancers and observers) approaches. Dance involves concept (notions about dance), process (behavior in relation to dance), result or product (performance with its style, structure, and meaning), and function (consequence for the dancer, audience, and broader society). These aspects of dance may be considered as prisms through which to view whole societies or subgroups; conversely these may be seen as prisms through which to view dance. Usually considered as dependent on other sociocultural factors, dance encapsulates culture, and situations, and structures in discrete performance. Dance should, however, also be considered as an independent factor generating culture and situations. Through their parody of the Western waltz, young Ubakala girls, for example, introduce new patterns of heterosexual behavior.

It is important to identify relationships between dance and other aspects of life and to specify the conditions under which they occur. Research should take into account observations of what is done, what doers think about it, and the relationship of research recordings and dance participant (performers, assisting personnel, and audience) perspectives, and the relationship to other aspects of culture, society, history, and environment.

Empirical case studies are the essential building blocks of knowledge about movement in African performance. Comparative, empirical studies are also necessary to assist in determining the generality of a proposition. The comparative approach is a useful strategy to force the analyst to try to account for the effect of different variables in similar societies, and thus deepen description, analysis, and explanation. Obviously a single study of African dance cannot encompass everything relevant to dance. But in circumscribing a study for strategic purposes, it is valuable for building a body of knowledge to place the research project's specific concepts and findings within a broad theoretical framework of human movement and recognize the limits of evidence and conclusions. A theory, interrelated sets of propositions which guide observation and other research and explain findings, must of course be generative.

Bibliographies and Other Research Resources

Further sources on African dance can be found in the bibliographies of Aning (1967), Briginshaw (1979), Drewal and Jackson (1974), Gaskin (1965), and Human Relations Area Files. Panofsky (1975) is a general African bibliography.

See Feld (1972), M. Drewal (1980), and Stone (1982) for filmographies of movement in African performance. Feld provides a conceptual discussion of visual recording (1976) and recommends Lipton (1976) and Weinstein and Booth (1977) for technical guides.

Krebs (1973) describes a technique for using film or video to elicit meaning. Rouch (1978), who has made several films with Gilbert Rouget and Germaine Dieterlen, discusses the issue of filming when the dancer considers the sound and visual images to be reflections of themselves and of their gods.

Guides to physical movement analyses include Arend and Higgins (1976), Benesh and Benesh (1956), Dell (1970), Eshkol (1958), Hutchinson (1970), Nahumck (1978), and Martin and Pesovár (1963). Hanna illustrates verbal transcriptions using Laban's concepts and includes a movement glossary (1976), and as mentioned earlier, provides a research tool for probing meaning in movement (1979d).

. Commentary on dance research methods and problems is interlaced through Hanna (1979c). A useful introduction to social science research methods is Pelto and Pelto (1977).

Aning, B. A. An Annotated Bibliography of Music and Dance in English-speaking Africa. Legon: Institute of African Studies, University of Ghana, 1967.

Anonymous. "Palaver: Dance and Music in Senegal," Présence Africaine, 26 (54) (1965), pp. 243-271.

Arend, Susan and Joseph R. Higgins. "A Strategy for the Classification, Subjective Analysis, and Observation of Human Movement," Journal of Human Movement Studies, 2 (1) (1976), pp. 36-52.

Armstrong, Robert P. The Affecting Presence: An Essay in Humanistic Anthropology. Urbana: University of Illinois Press, 1971.

Banham, Martin, with Clive Wake. African Theatre Today. London: Pitman, 1976.

Beier, Ulli. "Yoruba Folk Operas," African Music Society Journal, 1 (1) (1954), pp. 32-34.

Benesh, Rudolf and Joan Benesh. An Introduction to Benesh Dance Notation. London: A. & C. Black, 1956.

Berlyne, D. E. Aesthetics and Psychobiology. New York: Appleton-Century-Crofts, 1971.

Biebuyck, Daniel. Lega Culture: Art, Initiation, and Moral Philosophy Among a Central African People. Berkeley: University of California Press, 1973.

Binet, J. Sociétés de Danse Chez Les Fang du Gabon. Paris: l'ORSTOM, 1972.

Blacking, John. "Musical Expeditions of the Venda," African Music, 3 (1) (1962), pp. 54-78.

_____. "The Role of Music in the Culture of the Venda of the Northern Transvaal" in Studies in Ethnomusicology 2. M. Kolinski, ed. New York: Oak Publications, 1965, pp. 20-53.

_____. "Songs, Dances, Mimes and Symbolism of Venda Girls' Initiation Schools," Parts I, II, III, IV. African Studies, 28 (1, 2, 3, 4) (1969), pp. 3-35, 69-118, 149-199, 215-266.

_____. How Musical is Man? Seattle: University of Washington, 1973.

_____. "An Introduction to Venda Traditional Dances (Notation and Descriptions of Some Venda Dance Movements, Dora Frankel)," Dance Studies, 2 (1977), pp. 36-56.

Brelsford, W. V. "African Dances of Northern Rhodesia," The Occasional Papers, No. 2 Lusaka: Government Printer for the Rhodes-Livingstone Museum, 1959.

Briginshaw, Valeria A. "African Dance Bibliography," Africana Journal, 10 (1) (1979), pp. 14-33.

Brink, James T. "The Conceptual Meaning of Theater among the Beledugu Bamana: An Ethnographic Overview" in Discourse in Ethnomusicology II. Caroline Card, ed. Bloomington, Indiana: Ethnomusicology Publications Group, Archives of Traditional Music, 1981, pp. 67-82.

Calame-Griaule, Geneviève. "Pour ane étude des geste narratifs" in Langage et Cultures Africaines: Essais d'ethnolinguistique. Geneviève Calame-Griaule, ed. Paris: F. Maspero, 1977, pp. 303-359.

Camara, Condetto Nenekhaly. "Revolution and Culture in Guinea," Horoya, Sept. 2, 1967, pp. 1-2; Sept. 3-4, pp. 1-2; Sept. 6, pp. 1-2; Sept. 8, pp. 1-2 (Translated in Transactions on Africa, 646 (1967), pp. 20-33).

Carpenter, Peter. "Theater in Ghana," Universitas, 5 (1962), pp. 35-37.

Chernoff, John Miller. African Rhythm and African Sensibility. Chicago: University of Chicago, 1979.

Clark, J. P. "Poetry of the Urhobo Dance Udje," Nigeria Magazine, 87 (1965), pp. 282-287.

Cornet, Joseph. "The Itul Celebration of the Kuba," African Arts, 13 (3) (1980), pp. 29-32, 92.

Darbois, Dominique. African Dance: A Book of Photographs (Text by V. Vašut). Prague: Artia, 1962.

Decock, Jean. "Pre-theatre et rituel (National Folk Troupe of Mali)," African Arts, 1 (3) (1968), pp. 31-37.

Dell, Cecily. A Primer for Movement Description Using Effort-Shape and Supplementary Concepts. New York: Dance Notation Bureau, 1970.

Dorsinville, Roger. "The Making of Liberian Ballet," African Arts, 4 (1) (1970), pp. 36-39.

Drewal, Henry John. "Ẹfẹ/Gẹlẹde: The Educative Role of the Arts in Traditional Yoruba Culture," Ph.D. diss., Columbia University, 1973.

_____. "African Masked Theatre," Mime Journal, 2 (1975), pp. 36-53.

Drewal, Margaret T. "Films on Music and Dance in Southern-Africa: Bibliography Review," Dance Research Journal, 12 (1) (1980), pp. 30-33.

_____ and Glorianne Jackson. Sources on African and African-Related Dance. New York: American Dance Guild, 1974.

Echezona, W. W. C. "Compositional Technique of Nigerian Traditional Music," Composer, 19 (1966), pp. 41, 43, 45-47, 49.

Erickson, Edwin E. "Tradition and Evolution in Song Style: A Reanalysis of Cantometric Data," Behavior Science Research, 11 (4) (1976), pp. 227-308.

Eshkol, Noa. Movement Notation. London: Weidenfeld & J. Harries, 1958.

Evans-Pritchard, E. E. "The Dance," Africa, 1 (1928), pp. 436-462.

_____. Theories of Primitive Religion. Oxford: Clarendon Press, 1965.

Fabian, Johannes. "Popular Culture in Africa: Findings and Conjectures," Africa, 48 (4) (1978), pp. 315-334.

Feld, Steve. Filmography of the African Humanities. Bloomington, IN: African Studies Program, Indiana University, 1972.

_____. "Ethnomusicology and Visual Communication," Ethnomusicology, 20 (2) (1976), pp. 293-325.

Ferguson, Isabel. "Dancers of the Ivory Coast," African Music Society Journal, 3 (1) (1962), pp. 18-19.

Fernandez, James W. "Principles of Opposition and Vitality in Fang Aesthetics," Journal of Aesthetics and Art Criticism, 25 (1966), pp. 53-64.

_____. "Dance Exchange in Western Equatorial Africa," Dance Research Journal, 8 (1) (1975-76), pp. 1-6.

_____. Bwiti: An Ethnography of the Religious Imagination in Africa. Princeton: Princeton University Press, 1982.

Fodeba, Keita. "African Dance and the Stage," World Theatre, 7 (3) (1958), pp. 164-178.

Fortes, M. "Social and Psychological Aspects of Education in Taleland." Supplement to Africa, 11 (4) (1938), pp. 61-64.

Gaskin, L. J. P. A Select Bibliography of Music in Africa. London: International African Institute, 1965.

Gell, Alfred. "On Dance Structures: A Reply to Williams," Journal of Human Movement Studies, 5 (1979), pp. 18-31.

Gorer, Geoffrey. Africa Dances. New York: W. W. Norton, 1972 (1935 orig.).

Griaule, Marcel. Conversations with Ogotemmêli. London: Oxford University Press, 1965.

Hanna, Judith Lynne. "Africa's New Traditional Dance," Ethnomusicology, 9 (1965a), pp. 13-21.

_____. "African Dance as Education," Impulse: Dance and Education Now (1965b), pp. 48-52.

_____. "The Status of African Dance Studies," Africa, 36 (1966), pp. 303-307.

_____. "The Highlife: A West African Urban Dance" in Dance Research Monograph One. Patricia A. Rowe and Ernestine Stodelle, eds. New York: Committee on Research in Dance, 1973, pp. 138-152.

_____. "African Dance: The Continuity of Change," Yearbook of the International Folk Music Council, 5 (1974), pp. 164-174.

_____. "Review of Robert Farris Thompson's African Art in Motion." African Studies Association Review of Books, 1 (1975), pp. 5-9.

_____. "The Anthology of Dance-Ritual: Nigeria's Ubakala Nkwa di Iche Iche," Ph.D. diss., Columbia University, 1976.

_____. "African Dance and the Warrior Tradition" in The Warrior Tradition in Modern Africa. Special Issue of Journal of Asian and African Studies. Ali A. Mazrui, ed., 12 (1-2) (1977), pp. 111-133; Leiden: E. J. Brill.

_____. "African Dance: Some Implications for Dance Therapy," American Journal of Dance Therapy, 2 (1) (1978), pp. 3-15.

_____. "Dance and Its Social Structure: The Ubakala of Nigeria," Journal of Communication, 29 (4) (1979a), pp. 184-191.

_____. "Movements Toward Understanding Humans Through the Anthropological Study of Dance," Current Anthropology, 20 (2) (1979b), pp. 313-339.

_____. To Dance is Human: A Theory of Nonverbal Communication. Austin: University of Texas Press, 1979c.

_____. "Toward Semantic Analysis of Movement Behavior: Concepts and Problems," Semiotica, 25 (1-2) (1979d), pp. 77-110.

_____. "The Anthropology of Dance: Or, Who Collects Butterflies?," American Ethnologist, 8 (4) (1981), pp. 808-810.

_____. "Dance and the Women's War," Dance Research Journal, 14 (1-2) (1982a), pp. 25-28.

_____. "Is Dance Music? Resemblances and Relationships," The World of Music, 24 (1) (1982b), pp. 57-71.

_____. "Dance" in Encyclopedic Dictionary of Semiotics. Thomas A. Sebeok, ed. London and Bloomington: Macmillan and Indiana University Press, 1982c.

_____. "Dance and the Cultural Heritage" in Dance and the Child. Conference Proceedings, 1982d.

_____. "Nigeria's Ubakala Dance-Plays: Performance, Culture, and Society," rev. of 1976, under publication review, 1982e.

_____. "The Mentality and Matter of Dance," Art Education: Art and the Mind. Martin Engel, ed. of special issue (1983a).

_____. The Performer-Audience Connection: Emotion to Metaphor in Dance and Society. Austin: University of Texas Press, 1983b.

_____. "Dance and Religion" in The Encyclopedia of Religion. Mircea Eliade, ed. New York: The Free Press, 1984.

_____ and William John Hanna. "Heart Beat of Uganda," African Arts, 1 (3) (1968), pp. 42-45, 85.

Harper, Peggy. "Dance in a Changing Society," African Arts, 1 (1) (1967), pp. 10-13, 76-77, 79-80.

_____. "Tiv Women: The Icough Dance," Studies in Nigerian Dance, 1 (1968a) (Frank Speed, filmmaker).

_____. "The Miagno Dancers," Studies in Nigerian Dance, 2 (1968b) (Frank Speed, filmmaker).

_____. "Dance in Nigeria," Ethnomusicology, 13 (1969), pp. 280-295.

Hopkins, Nicholas S. "The Modern Theater in Mali," Présence Africaine, 25 (53) (1965), pp. 159-193.

_____. "The Persuasion and Satire in the Malian Theater," Africa, 42 (1972), pp. 217-226.

Horton, Robin. The Gods as Guests: An Aspect of Kalabari Religious Life. Lagos: Nigeria Magazine Special Publication, 1960.

_____. "The Kalabari Ekine Society: A Borderland of Religion and Art," Africa, 33 (2) (1963), pp. 94-114.

_____. "Igbo: An Ordeal for Aristocrats," Nigeria Magazine, 90 (1966), pp. 168-183.

_____. "Ikaki--The Tortoise Masquerade," Nigeria Magazine, 94 (1967), pp. 226-239.

Huet, Michel. The Dance, Art and Ritual of Africa. Introduction by Jean Laude, Text by Jean-Louis Paudrat (trans. from the French). New York: Pantheon Books, 1978.

Hutchinson, Ann. Labanotation. Rev. and Exp. 1954 ed. New York: Theatre Arts Books, 1970.

Imperato, Pascal James. "The Dance of the Tyi Wara," African Arts, 4 (1) (1970), pp. 8-13.

_____. "Contemporary Adapted Dances of the Dogon," African Arts, 5 (1) (1971), pp. 28-33, 68-71.

Jacobs, Rev. Donald Reiman. "The Culture Themes and Puberty Rites of the Akamba, a Bantu Tribe of East Africa," Unpublished doctoral dissertation, New York University, 1961.

Jones, A. M. and L. Kombe. The Icila Dance Old Style: A Study in African Music and Dance of the Lala Tribe of Northern Rhodesia. London: Longmans Green-African Music Society, 1952.

Jones, Eldred Durosimi, ed. "Drama in Africa," African Literature Today, No. 8. New York: Africana Publishing Co., 1976.

Katz, Richard. Boiling Energy: Community Healing Among the Kalahari Kung. Cambridge: Harvard University Press, 1982.

Keil, Charles. Tiv Song. Chicago: University of Chicago, 1979.

Kennedy, Scott. In Search of African Theatre. New York: Scribner's Sons, 1972.

Kenyatta, Jomo. Facing Mt. Kenya. New York: Vintage Books, 1962.

Krebs, Stephanie. "The Film Elicitation Technique: Using Film to Elicit Conceptual Categories of Culture" in Principles of Visual Anthropology. Paul Hockings, ed. The Hague: Mouton, 1975, pp. 283-302.

Kubik, Gerhard. "Patterns of Body Movement in the Music of Boys' Initiation in South-East Angola" in The Anthropology of the Body. John Blacking, ed. New York: Academic Press, 1977, pp. 253-274.

Kuper, Hilda. "Celebration of Growth and Kingship: Incwala in Swaziland," African Arts, 1 (3) (1968), pp. 57-59, 90.

Laoye I, Oba Adetoyese. "Music of Western Nigeria: Origin and Use." Composer, 19 (1966), pp. 34-41.

Lewis-Williams, J. D. "The Economic and Social Context of Southern San Rock Art," Current Anthropology, 23 (4) (1982), pp. 429-449.

Lienhardt, Godfrey. "Anuak Village Headmen," Africa 27 (4) (1957), pp. 341-355.

Lindblom, Gerhard. The Akamba. 2nd ed., Vol 17. Uppsala: Archives d'Etudes Orientales, 1920.

Lipton, Lenny. Independent Filmmaking. San Francisco: Straight Arrow (rev. ed.), 1976.

Little, Kenneth L. The Mende of Sierra Leone. London: Routledge and Kegan Paul, 1951.

Lomax, Alan. Folk Song Style and Structure. Washington, D.C.: American Association for the Advancement of Science, 1968.

_____ (with Norman Berkowitz). "The Evolutionary Taxonomy of Culture," Science, 177 (1972), pp. 228-239.

Africa / 581

Mair, Lucy. "A Yao Girl's Initiation," Man, 50 (1951), pp. 60-63.

Marshall, Lorna. "The Medicine Dance of the !Kung Bushmen,"
Africa, 39 (1969), pp. 347-381.

_____. The !Kung of Nyae Nyae. Cambridge: Harvard Univer-
sity Press, 1976.

Martin, György. "Dance Types in Ethiopia," Journal of the International Folk Music Council, 19 (1967), pp. 23-27.

_____ and Erno Pesovár. "Determination of Motive Types in
Dance Folklore," Acta Ethnographica, 12 (1963), pp. 295-331.

Meillassoux, Claude. "The 'Koteba' of Bamako," Présence Africaine,
24 (52) (1965), pp. 159-193.

_____. Urbanization of an African Community: Voluntary Asso-
ciations in Bamako. Seattle: University of Washington, 1968.

Merriam, Aplan P. "Music [dances at the University of Ibadan],"
Africa Report, 9 (8) (1964), p. 31.

Messing, Simon D. "Group Therapy and Social Status in the Zar
Cult of Ethiopia," American Anthropologist, 60 (1958), pp.
1120-1126.

Mitchell, J. Clyde. "The Kalela Dance," Paper No. 27. Manchester:
Manchester University for the Rhodes-Livingstone Institute,
1956.

Montagu, Ashley. "Dance, Dance, Dance," The Sciences, 20 (4)
(1980), pp. 20-21.

Museo do Dundo. Angolan Folk Music: Chokwe People. Lisboa:
Companhia de Diamantes de Angola, 1961.

Nadel, S. F. A Black Byzantium: The Kingdom of Nupe in Nigeria.
London: Oxford University Press, 1942.

Nahumck, Nadia Chilkovsky. Introduction to Dance Literacy: Perception and Notation of Dance Patterns. Transvaal, South
Africa: International Library of African Music, 1978.

Nketia, J. H. Kwabena. "Possession Dances in African Societies,"
Journal of the International Folk Music Council, 9 (1957),
pp. 4-9.

_____. "The Interrelations of African Music and Dance," Studia
Musicologica 7, Journal of the International Folk Music Council,
17 (1965), pp. 91-101.

_____. The Music of Africa. London: Victor Gollancz, 1975.

Nzewi, Mezi. "The Rhythm of Dance," Ibadan, 25 (1968), pp. 36-38 (also in The Conch, 3 (2) (1971), pp. 104-108).

Nzekwu, Onuoara. "Ibo Dancing," Nigeria Magazine, 73 (1962), pp. 35-43.

Olofson, Harold. "Hausa Language About Gesture," Anthropological Linguistics, 16 (1974), pp. 25-39.

Opoku, Albert A. "Choreography and the African Dance," University of Ghana Institute of African Studies Research Review, 3 (1) (1966), pp. 53-59.

Ottenberg, Simon. "Afikpo Masquerades: Audience and Performers," African Arts, 6 (4) (1973), pp. 32-36.

_____. Masked Rituals of Afikpo: The Context of an African Art. Seattle: University of Washington, 1975.

_____. "Boys' Secret Societies at Afikpo" in African Religious Groups and Beliefs: Papers in Honor of William R. Bascom. Simon Ottenberg, ed. Meerut, India: Archana Publications for Folklore Institute, 1982a, pp. 170-184.

_____. "Illusion, Communication, and Psychology in West African Masquerades," Ethos, 10 (2) (1982b), pp. 149-185.

Panofsky, Hans E. A Bibliography of Africana. Westport, CT: Greenwood Press, 1975.

Pelto, Pertti J. and Gretel H. Pelto. Anthropological Research: The Structure of Inquiry. 2nd ed. New York: Cambridge University Press, 1977.

Ranger, T. O. Dance and Society in Eastern Africa 1890-1970: The Beni Ngoma. Berkeley: University of California Press, 1975.

Raum, Otto. Chaga Childhood. London: Oxford University Press, 1940.

Ravenhill, Phillip L. "The Interpretation of Symbolism in Wan Female Initiation," Africa, 48 (1) (1978), pp. 66-78.

Richards, Audrey I. Chisungu: A Girls' Initiation Ceremony Among the Bemba of Northern Rhodesia. New York: Grove Press, 1956.

Rouch, Jean. "On the Vicissitudes of the Self: The Possessed

Dancer, the Magician, The Sorcerer, the Filmmaker, and the Ethnographer." Steve Feld and Shari Robertson, trans. Studies in the Anthropology of Visual Communication, 5 (1) (1978), pp. 2-8.

Sangree, Walter H. "Dancers as Emissaries in Irigwe, Nigeria," Dance Research Journal, 8 (2) (1976), pp. 31-35.

Scheub, Harold. "The Technique of the Expansible Image in Xhosa Ntsomi-Performances," Research in African Literature, 1 (1970), pp. 119-146.

Sebeok, Thomas A., ed. Encyclopedic Dictionary of Semiotics. London and Bloomington: Macmillan and Indiana University Press, 1982.

Sieber, Roy. "Masks as Agents of Social Control" in Man in Adaptation: The Institutional Framework. Yehudi A. Cohen, ed. Chicago: Aldine-Atherton, 1971. pp. 434-438.

Siroto, Leon. "Masks and Social Organization Among the Bakwele People of Western Equatorial Africa," Ph.D. diss., Columbia University, 1969.

_____. "Gon: A Mask Used in Competition for Leadership Among the Bakwele" in African Art and Leadership. Douglas Fraser and Herbert M. Cole, eds. Madison: University of Wisconsin Press, 1972, pp. 57-77.

Skelton, Thomas R. "Staging Ethnic Dance--the Dance and the Dancers," Impulse: International Exchange in Dance (1963-64), pp. 64-70.

Stayt, Hugh. The Bavenda. London: Oxford University Press, 1931.

Steadman, Ian. "Performance Research: A Select Bibliography," Critical Arts, 2 (1) (1981), pp. 60-65.

Stone, Ruth M. "Twenty-five Years of Selected Films in Ethnomusicology: Africa (1955-1980)," Ethnomusicology, 26 (1) (1982a), pp. 147-159.

_____. Let the Inside be Sweet: The Interpretation of Music Event among the Kpelle of Liberia. Bloomington: Indiana University Press, 1982b.

Ten Raa, Eric. "The Moon as a Symbol of Life and Fertility in Sandawe Thought," Africa, 39 (1969), pp. 24-53.

Thompson, Robert Farris. Black Gods and Kings. Los Angeles:

UCLA Museum and Laboratories of Ethnic Arts and Technology, 1971a.

_____. "Sons of Thunder: Twin Images Among the Oyo and Other Yoruba Groups," African Arts, 4 (3) (1971b), pp. 8-13, 77-80.

Tomaselli, Keyan G. "Black South African Theatre: Text and Context," English in Africa, 8 (1) (1980), pp. 51-57.

_____. "From Laser to the Candle," South African Labour Bulletin (Sustaining the Working Class), 6 (8) (1981), pp. 64-70.

_____. African Art in Motion. Berkeley: University of California Press, 1974.

Tracey, Hugh. Chopi Musicians. London: Oxford University Press, 1948.

_____. African Dances of the Witwatersrand Gold Mines. Johannesburg: African Music Society, 1952.

Traore, Bakary. The Black African Theatre and its Social Functions. Trans. and with a preface by Dapo ADeluga. Ibadan: Ibadan University Press, 1972.

Turner, Victor W. The Forest of Symbols: Aspects of Ndembu Ritual. Ithaca: Cornell University Press, 1967.

_____. The Ritual Process: Structure and Anti-Structure. Chicago: Aldine, 1969.

Vadasy, Tibor. "Ethiopian Folk Dance III: Wallo and Galla," Journal of Ethiopian Studies, 11 (1) (1973), pp. 213-231.

Vidal, Tunji. "Oriki in Traditional Yoruba Music," African Arts, 3 (1) (1969), pp. 56-59.

Warner, Mary Jane. Laban Notation Scores: An International Bibliography. London: International Council of Kinetography Laban, 1983. (Available through the Dance Notation Bureau, Ohio State University.)

Weil, Peter M. "The Masked Figure and Social Control: The Mandinka Case," Africa, 41 (1971), pp. 279-293.

Weinstein, Robert and Larry Booth. Collection, Use and Care of Historical Photographs. Nashville: American Association for State and Local History, 1977.

Wembah-Rashid, J. A. R. "Isinyago and Midimu: Masked Dancers of Tanzania and Mozambique," African Arts, 4 (2) (1971), pp. 38-44.

Werbner, Richard P. "Atonement Ritual and Guardian-Spirit Possession Among Kalanga," Africa, 34 (1964), pp. 206-223.

Wescott, Joan. "The Sculpture and Myths of Eshu-Elegba, the Yoruba Trickster: Definition and Interpretation in Yoruba Iconography," Africa, 32 (1962), pp. 336-354.

White, C. M. N. "Conservatism and Modern Adaptation in Luvale Female Puberty Ritual," Africa, 23 (1953), pp. 15-24.

Williams, Drid. "The Dance of the Bedu Moon," African Arts, 2 (1) (1968), pp. 18-21.

_____. "An Exercise in Applied Personal Anthropology," Dance Research Journal, 9 (1) (1976-77), pp. 16-29.

Williams, Rev. J. S.; and J. E. K. Kumah. "Sokodae: Come and Dance," African Arts, 3 (3) (1970), pp. 36-39.

Wilson, Monica. "Nyakyusa Ritual and Symbolism," American Anthropologist, 56 (1954), pp. 228-241.

Chapter Twenty-Six

MOVEMENT IN THE PERFORMING ARTS
OF THE PACIFIC ISLANDS

Adrienne L. Kaeppler

The performing arts of the Pacific and the societies that created them were brought to the attention of the Western world in the
published reports of the seventeenth- and eighteenth-century voyages of exploration organized primarily by Spain, France, and England. The best of these early descriptions were from individuals
who traveled with Captain James Cook on his three Pacific voyages
and focus primarily on selected areas of Polynesia. During the
nineteenth century, German, Russian, and American explorers described performances in other areas of the Pacific, followed by
Japanese reports beginning near the turn of this century (much of
this early material is quoted in Anderson, 1933). Although certainly sketchy, these early eyewitness accounts are invaluable sources
when used in conjunction with published and manuscript reports
from missionaries, whalers, traders, beachcombers, and anthropologists.

Until this century, the performing arts of the Pacific could
not easily be "captured" for nonimmediate analysis except for the
written word, drawings, and still photography. Some of the earliest performances by Pacific Islanders that could have been studied
away from their homelands include a New Zealand Maori troupe that
performed in England in 1862 as well as Hawaiian and Western Polynesian entertainers who performed at the World's Columbian Exposition in Chicago in 1893.* Unfortunately these opportunites for
study of movement seem to have been missed.** The earliest re-

---

*Wax cylinder recordings of the Western Polynesian group, includ-
ing Samoan Uvean, and Fijian dance songs, are now in the Library
of Congress.

**Aoutouru, the Tahitian taken to France by Bougainville; Omai
from Huahine taken to England by Captain Furneaux at the completion of Cook's second voyage; Lee Boo, the Palauan   (cont.)

cordings (on wax cylinders) and moving pictures in situ appear to be those made during the Cambridge Torres Straits' expedition of 1898. Only recently have field studies in the Pacific focused specifically on dance, music, or theater except as part of broader anthropologically oriented research.

This chapter will deal with the three large geographical/ cultural areas of the Pacific--Polynesia, Melanesia, and Micronesia. The movement forms will be delineated in conjunction with the sociocultural backgrounds of which they are an inextricable part. While satire and ridicule were occasionally part of Pacific performances, dramatic encounter or the presentation of abstract morals were not usually part of traditional performance practice. On the other hand theatrical "showmanship" was a traditional part of ritual display such as during the mixing of kava for important Tongan political events or burning dancers with torches during ceremonies among the Kaluli of New Guinea.

A distinction can be made between performances aimed primarily at presentation and those which focus primarily on participation. Even this is not clear cut, however, for even performances of presentation require active mental participation by the audience. They are not simply a sequence of beautiful movements but often are a composer's challenge to his audience to understand the deeper meanings embodied in allusive poetry or dance movements.

Melanesia

Comprised of New Guinea (Papua New Guinea and Irian Jaya), New Britain, New Ireland, Manus (formerly Admiralty Islands), Vanuatu (formerly New Hebrides), New Caledonia, and the Solomon Islands, Melanesia has had few studies which focus on movement. The performing arts in which movement plays a prominent role are often associated with rites of passage and secret society rituals and although this information has been well presented, the movement itself has not. Sociopolitical systems in Melanesia can be characterized primarily as "bigmen" societies. The leader or bigman in most New Guinea societies and in many other Melanesian areas is often a self-made man. He often becomes a bigman by aligning followers who help him amass goods for great public giveaways to other bigmen and their followers, which they in turn will try to outdo. Successful bigmen succeed because they command respect in their societies--oratory, bravery, gardening ability, and magical power.

---

taken to England by Captain Wilson, and other eighteenth-century Pacific visitors to Europe probably gave casual dance performances for their hosts, but apparently they were not described (although Madame d'Arblay describes the singing of Omai).

Large-scale ceremonies, which might take ten years to prepare, were traditionally held in conjunction with the erection of large men's houses (New Guinea), the purchase of higher rank in secret societies (Vanuatu), the making and consecration of slit gongs (Solomons), the sponsorship of ceremonies for the dead (New Ireland), or simply reactivating social relationships. Today ceremonies in which movement plays a predominant role include "sing-sings," other local and intertribal dance or "arts" festivals, presentations by national theater groups, and performances for tourists.

Movement in Melanesia was, and often still is, a vehicle for the presentation of masks and other costume constructions or the display of body decoration and ceremonial finery. These spectacles are events of visual and aural display--a kind of total theater in which there are many participants and few observers. Central performers may wear unwieldy masks and costumes impersonating spirits of the bush or the sea, close or remote ancestors, mythical beings, or birds and other animals.

Characteristic movements in many parts of Melanesia are up/down "bouncing" movements of legs and body created by alternately bending the knees and lifting the heels in place, or by step-bend-step-bend progressing forward or back. The torso is often used as one unit and a dance leader may simply begin by starting his knee bending and straightening and then the others join in down the line or around a circle until the whole group moves up and down together in place or in a prearranged choreographed pattern. Often the function of the movement is to transport a group of people ceremonially from one place to another, for example, from the men's house to the beach. The movements are usually accompanied by one or more rhythmic instruments, such as a slit drum, hourglass-shaped drums, or rattles. In some areas melodic instruments such as panpipes, flutes, and today imported stringed instruments furnish the aural dimension. The movement itself, however, is often a visual and aesthetic elaboration of rhythmic pulse.

Dramatic ceremonies in which movement played an important part were characteristic of the Papuan Gulf area of New Guinea, studied and analyzed by F. E. Williams. Long cyclical hevehe ceremonies which he describes for Orokolo centered on sea spirits which manifested themselves periodically at certain stages during the building of a men's house. Huge hevehe masks, constructed of rattan cane and covered with bark cloth, appeared when the house was completed. At sunrise mask after mask emerged from a huge never-opened door. To a rhythmic drum accompaniment, these masked spirits were joined by their clansmen who imitated their steps as they danced their way back to the sea. Their movements were influenced by the facts that these were supernatural beings and that they wore difficult-to-move-in attire. Stylized walking and rhythmic changes in elevation were important. Arms of the sea spirits might be covered and used to steady the masks or

joined by their clansmen, they carried drums. This massed rhythmic environment of sound and moving bodies is a classic example of
the Melanesian emphasis on visual rhythm.

Such visual extensions of rhythm can be found in many parts
of New Guinea, for example, in the Highlands where the costumes
are composed primarily of attachments. Bird of paradise plumes
and other feathers extend from headdresses, back, bustle, or arms;
rattles of seeds or shells are attached to legs, costumes, or arms;
cuscus skin ripples like vertical waves and shredded leaves and
fibers cascade and bounce; penis coverings of gourd, shell, or
bark are curved forward and upward to emphasize the up/down
movement of this part of the body. Recent studies by Strathern,
Gell, Jablonko, and Schieffelin among the Melpa, Umeda, Maring
and Kaluli present some of this important material on ritual, movement, and world view. A film, The Red Bowman, done in association with Gell illustrates the relationship of movement to sexual
antagonism and the life cycles of humans and birds.

New theater groups, especially the New Guinea National
Theatre based in Port Moresby and the Raun Raun Theatre based
in Goroka, have developed traditional world views and movement
concepts in ways appropriate to the diverse stages of the modern
world from New Guinea village spaces to the sterile concert halls
of Sydney, New York, and San Francisco. Although movements
are based on traditional ones, women participate almost equally
with men. Here there is a hero or star of the production which
unfolds a dramatic story line conceptually different from the more
abstract timeless encounters between sea spirits and their descen-
dants. This new form of dance drama is an appropriate medium
for the perpetuation of traditional movements in a new setting. The
addition of a story line and the emphasis on dramatic encounter has
at the same time encapsulated the traditional emphasis on movement
as a visual extension of rhythm.

For other parts of Melanesia information on movement, if it
exists at all, is so far available primarily in anthropological studies,
such as Layard for Malekula, Vanuatu (e.g., 1942, pp. 316-343;
1944, pp. 121-122) and Oliver for the Solomon Islands (e.g., 1955,
p. 369). Other areas are great gaps in our knowledge of theatrical movement of Pacific Islanders. Some of the most exciting movement forms that still await recording and analysis are those of New
Britain and New Ireland. Wearing huge bark cloth masks with insect and other animal features or carrying 5 by 8 foot bark cloth
constructions, men of the Baining tribe of New Britain saunter or
run through a gigantic bonfire, appearing and disappearing, scattering sparks into the darkness. In contrast, as part of the ma-
langgan rituals of New Ireland, participants wearing tatanua masks
perform elegant measured movements using head and shoulders in
such a way as to give the appearance of other-worldly beings peer-
ing into these unknown surroundings.

The Solomon Islanders, too, retain many of their traditional movement forms varying from women bending their torsos forward at the hips at about a 45° angle while stamping and striking the ground with decorated staffs, to men dancing in lines and columns with woven shields, to groups that dance in intricate patterns around and amongst themselves while carrying carved hornbill birds, to modern "bamboo bands" which include dancing with huge panpipes in a kind of Melanesian calypso.

Polynesia

Culturally Polynesia can be separated into two major groupings, West Polynesia comprised of Tonga, Samoa, Uvea (Wallis), Futuna, Niue, Tuvalu (formerly Ellice Islands) Tokelau, and Fiji (a transitional area between Polynesia and Melanesia in which the performing arts are more closely related to Polynesia) and East Polynesia comprised of the Society Islands (Tahiti), Marquesas Islands, Austral Islands, Mangareva, Tuamotu Islands, Cook Islands, Easter Island, New Zealand, and Hawai'i. The performing arts in which movement plays a predominant role are traditionally, as well as today, associated with oral literature as a vehicle for the praise and honor of high-ranking chiefs, the recognition of national or local events, the praise of places and people, and for entertainment. Other occasions were the welcoming of visitors which sometimes included traditional challenges.

In Polynesia power and prestige are derived from genealogical descent which is often traceable to the gods. Rank is an important feature of Polynesian societies and the performing arts pay allegiance to the rank-based sociopolitical system honoring and validating social distinctions. Power resides in chiefly office into which one is born. Performances are included as gifts to those with prestige and power. Specialists compose poetry, add music and movement, and rehearse the performers for an audience who will bring to the performance a critical aesthetic evaluation of poetic composition, musical sound and appropriateness, and movement allusion, as well as overall performance and appropriateness for the occasion. Although the occasions were sometimes religious, more important were the sociological features and the social relationships between people. In addition to the texts and their visual interpretations through movement, these sociological distinctions could be seen in the order of the performances, the placement of individuals within the group, and the costumes which imparted information about the performers and their genealogical lines. Today occasions in which movement plays a predominant role are festivals of competition such as the Bastille Day Fête in French Polynesia, the Merrie Monarch and other dance festivals in Hawai'i, "concert parties" as well as more traditional ceremonial meetings on the marae in New Zealand, and the ubiquitous performances for tourists where allusive danced poetry has been superseded by engaging pantomime with universal appeal.

Traditionally, much theatrical movement in Polynesia was a visual enhancement of oral literature. The performer was essentially a storyteller who rendered poetry into visual form by alluding to selected words of the text. The lack of the essential involvement of legs and body in helping to convey a story differentiates a storyteller from an actor. Actors, except for buffoons, are almost entirely absent in the traditional movement repertoire of Polynesia. Probably the closest to actors were members of the Arioi in the Society Islands. In Arioi performances social comment in the form of satire and ridicule were said to be part of danced dramas. Unfortunately the Arioi were entirely suppressed by missionaries before these performances were understood or described by outsiders. Indigenous knowledge about the performances that was still remembered at the end of the nineteenth century was recorded by Teuira Henry.

The most important movement dimensions in Polynesia are those of the hands and arms. The performer does not become a character in a dramatic interchange and stylized gestures do not correspond to words or ideas put together in a narrative sequence. Performances are usually by large or small groups in which all do the same sequence of choreographed movements, or occasionally the men and women do separate sets of movements simultaneously. Many of the performances take place in a seated position. When standing, the body and legs add a rhythmic and aesthetic dimension but do not usually advance the "story," except, perhaps, for the haka (posture dances) of New Zealand.

The main movement difference between West and East Polynesia is the use of the lower body. Hip movements are not a significant dimension in West Polynesia--hip motions being subdued and indeed often hidden by voluminous costumes. In much of East Polynesia, however, the lower body may include side-to-side hip movements with upper legs parallel for women which contrast with an opening and closing of the legs with knees bent for men. In the Society and Cook Islands these movements are very rapid and in some genres, such as 'ōte'a, have become the main movements of the dance. In Hawai'i, although the hip movements are slower, they enhance the side-to-side stepping as an aesthetic element in their own right.

More important throughout Polynesia are the movements of the hands, wrists, and arms. The rotation of the lower arm, flexion and extension of the wrist, curling of the fingers, flexion at the knuckles, and placement of the upper arm are the significant dimensions. Characteristic of Tonga, for example, is the complex interplay between rotation of the lower arm, flexion and extension of the wrist, and the curling of the fingers. Samoan arm movements are based on a combination of bending the elbow, extension of the wrist, and flexion at the knuckle. While rather stiff wrists in conjunction with lower arm rotations placed in bilaterally symmetrical arm positions are characteristic of Tahiti; soft wrist movements without lower arm rotation with both arms placed either to the right or to the left are more characteristic of Hawai'i. In contrast, the more forceful movement styling of New Zealand is tied to a stronger rhythmic pulse, the wrists are stiff and the hands quiver, while the placement of the arms is more often straight or the elbow emphasizes a more definite angle.

The combination of these two bodily complexes--the amount and velocity of side-to-side hip movement, and the interplay of hand/wrist/arm movement and placement--gives each Polynesian movement tradition its distinctive style.

The study of movement in Polynesia is very uneven, ranging from Tonga where the movement structure has been studied in minute detail along with its sociological significance by Kaeppler to Samoa where only general descriptions of movement or function can be gleaned from the writings of Margaret Mead and other anthropologists and ethnomusicologists. Or in East Polynesia the detailed study of Tahitian dance by Moulin contrasts with no published study for the Marquesas or Cook Islands. In New Zealand, although there are several historical and terminological works and books which give detailed instructions on how to perform Maori dances and games, there is virtually no analysis available in published form (but see Shennan, 1977). In Hawai'i there are many studies of the historical sources but few studies of movement analysis (there are, however, at least two in process by Kaeppler and Stillman).

In many parts of Polynesia analysis has been hampered by the literary nature of the performances and the complexity of the arm movements. In order to fully understand a Polynesian performance tradition, performers, spectators, and analysts must understand the language, have an ethnoaesthetic appreciation of the rhythm and meter of poetry and song, be familiar with the literary and movement allusions, and understand the sociopolitical context as well as the cultural philosophy of that society over time. Although this is true for other parts of the Pacific--or indeed anywhere--it is particularly exacerbated in Polynesia. Most movement analysts trained to cope with the complex arm movements cannot speak the languages to which these movements are tied in a literary/aesthetic form. Or most speakers or learners of Polynesian languages such as Polynesians or anthropologists are not trained to cope with the analysis of complex arm movement systems. Such individuals are being trained, however, and within a few years other Polynesian movement traditions should be better known.

Although based on literature, Polynesian movement does not adapt well to staged theatrical forms appreciated by outsiders. Two relatively successful theatrical performances with which I am familiar were based on the life of Hawaiian Princess Ka'iulani and a Tongan myth. Both of these, however, combined Western modern dance with Polynesian "atmosphere" movement rather than adhering to strictly Polynesian movement--which, because of its basis in a foreign language text, easily becomes boring to outsiders unless changed to pantomime. Accordingly, Polynesian theater groups have not yet emerged and touring national dance groups have changed their style and repertoire to an evolved form which is not based so strongly on language and knowledge of cultural traditions.

Micronesia

Comprised of the Federated States of Micronesia (Yap, Truk, Ponage, and Kosrae--formerly the Caroline Islands), Marshall Islands, Marianas Islands (including Guam), Belau (Palau), Kiribati (formerly the Gilbert Islands), and Nauru, Micronesia is little known as far as its movement systems are concerned. There has been little research devoted strictly to the study of movement and our knowledge is based primarily on information from anthropologists, ethnomusicologists, and linguists, as well as on the accounts of casual observers and travelers.

Many Micronesian islands are extremely small and isolated. The sea could be bountiful with food or destructive with hurricanes and tropical storms and was a great influence on their cultural traditions. Thus, small islands were often allied with larger ones in complex systems of tribute and exchange. For example, the large island Yap was in an overlord position to Ulithi, Woleai, Ifalik, and other islands. Performances including poetry, music, and dance were given as tribute to Yap. These productions could then be performed by the Yapese, but the texts were in languages that were unintelligible to them. The movements apparently did not illustrate the text or render it into visual form but were primarily decorative. Dance groups were often large and performers (and sometimes observers) were only of one sex. Dances for the fertility of land, sea, and people were important as were activities associated with the sea and canoes. There was a concern with social rank in the placement of performers and spectators and an emphasis on perfectly rehearsed execution of the decorative movements.

The sung and danced poems of Ifalik have been studied by Burrows. They are performed either sitting or standing by large groups. Knees, waist, and elbows are all slightly bent, and small steps turn the body from side to side. The synchronized, sweeping movements of arms and hands are emphasized. Occasionally an individual will stand and become a frigate bird in movement while the others are seated. The quite different performance tradition in Palau includes high pitched singing by women who advance in long lines with side-to-side hip movements with knees bent.

In Kiribati the stage alternates among men, women, and children in a sequence of standing and sitting dances. Although hip movements for women--culminating in a series of strong side pulses which sends their long grass skirts ascending to their head and shoulders--and a bent knee stance for men are important, the movement dimensions of more significance are those of hands and arms. The arms, extended to forward side diagonals at various levels with hands extended, make slow, elegant movements consisting primarily of arm rotations which alternate palm facings and knuckle flexions between poses which focus on head facings. Although expressive of a theme, the movements do not interpret the texts which were traditionally received from ancestor spirits during special rituals or in trance.

In many parts of Micronesia ritual movement was associated with tattooing, seafaring, and fertility. In recent years, however, the virtual demise of tattoo, the introduction of Western shipping and supplies, as well as new concepts of medicine and overpopulation have made these traditional functions less important. Other introduced movement forms based on the marching of German soldiers and stick dances which are borrowed from island to island are the more usual parts of the repertoire today. These "Micronesian dances," rather than performances more characteristic of specific islands, are performed for United Nations Day programs and tourists. It is likely, however, that the traditional forms still exist and, indeed, surface on such occasions as Pacific Arts Festivals. Perhaps there is still time to put on record and to perpetuate the style so admired by Robert Louis Stevenson in 1889 (1971, pp. 253-254):

> Of all so-called dancing in the South Seas that which I saw in Butaritari [Kiribati] stands easily the first. The hula, as it may be viewed by the speedy globe-trotter in Honolulu, is surely the most dull of man's inventions, and the spectator yawns under its length as at a college lecture or a parliamentary debate. But the Gilbert Island dance leads on the mind; it thrills, rouses, subjugates; it has the essence of all art, an unexplored imminent significance.

In an engaging ethnocentric manner Stevenson has described what was important in theatrical movement in the Western world. Movement was to be theatrical and an art form. Micronesian decorative movement, at least in some areas, has similarities to this view. Melanesia and Polynesia, however, with their emphases on rhythmic pulse or the visual dimension of allusive poetry have entirely different aims and manifestations. In all such areas outside our immediate purview a thorough cultural grounding is the first necessary step for understanding the movements of ritual, dance, and theater. The Pacific Islands still offer promise for such research.

The bibliography which follows includes primarily the works that were used in the preparation of this chapter along with other publications in which movement is described in some detail. These publications should be consulted when carrying out further research. Many other works mention dance and ritual movement in passing, but have little research potential for the specialist in theatrical movement. For those who do want to pursue further written works, however, two available bibliographies (McLean and Gourlay) should be consulted. These well-annotated reference works will lead the interested researcher to even the shortest references to dance and movement.

Much of the information included in this chapter comes from my own field research including extended intensive work in Tonga and Hawaii, shorter field investigations in Tahiti, Fiji, New Zealand, the Solomon Islands, and New Guinea, attendance at Pacific Festivals of Art, Bastille Day Fête competitions, Hawaiian dance festivals, and attending Pacific Island dance performances of troupes visiting Hawaii, the mainland United States, and England.

Pacific

Baessler, Arthur. 1895. Südsee-Bilder. Berlin: Reimer.

Beaglehole, J. C. (ed.). 1955-1967. The Journals of Captain James Cook on his Voyages of Discovery. Cambridge University Press for the Hakluyt Society.

Christensen, Dieter, and Adrienne L. Kaeppler. 1974. "Oceania, Arts of (Music and Dance)." Encyclopaedia Britannica, 15th ed. 13:456-61.

McLean, Mervyn. 1977. An Annotated Bibliography of Oceanic Music and Dance. Wellington: The Polynesian Society.

Sadie, Stanley, ed. 1980. The New Grove Dictionary of Music and Musicians. London: Macmillan. Entries on "Pacific Islands," "Melanesia," "Micronesia," and "Polynesia."

Thompson, Laura. 1957. Dance around the World: The South Pacific Islands. Dance Magazine 31:28-35.

Wilkes, Charles. 1845. Narrative of the United States Exploring Expedition During the Years 1838, 1839, 1840, 1841, 1842. Philadelphia: Lea and Blanchard.

Melanesia

Bateson, Gregory. 1932. Further Notes on a Snake Dance of the Baining. Oceania 2:334-41.

_____. 1958. Naven. Stanford University Press.

Clarke, William C. 1973. Temporary Madness as Theatre: Wild-
Man Behaviour in New Guinea. Oceania 43(3):198-214.

Gell, Alfred. 1975. Metamorphoses of the Cassowaries: Umeda
Society, Language and Ritual. London: Athlone Press.

_____. In press. Style and Meaning in Umeda Dance. In Paul
Spencer, editor, Society and the Dance. New York: Cambridge University Press.

Gourlay, Ken. 1974. A Bibliography of Traditional Music in Papua
New Guinea. Port Moresby: Institute of Papua New Guinea
Studies.

Haddon, Alfred C. 1912. Reports of the Cambridge Anthropological Expedition to Torres Strait. Vol. 4. Cambridge University
Press.

Jablonko, A. P. 1968. Dance and Daily Activities Among the Maring People of New Guinea: A Cinematographic Analysis of
Body Movement Style. Columbia University Unpublished dissertation.

Layard, John. 1936. Maze-Dances and the Ritual of the Labyrinth.
Folklore 47:123-170.

_____. 1942. Stone Men of Malekula. London: Chatto and
Windus.

_____. 1944. Song and Dance in Malekula. Man 44(97):121-122.

Oliver, D. 1955. A Solomon Island Society. Cambridge, Mass.:
Cambridge University Press.

Parkinson, Richard. 1887. Im Bismarck-Archipel: Erlebnisse und
Beobachtungen auf der Insel Neu-Pommern (Neu-Britannien).
Leipzig: Brockhaus.

Peekel, Gerhard. 1931. Religiöse Tänze auf Neu-Irland (Neu-
Mecklenburg). Anthropos 26:513-32.

Pool, Jean. 1943. Still Further Notes on a Snake Dance of the
Baining. Oceania 13:224-7.

Read, W. J. 1931. A Snake Dance of the Baining. Oceania
2:232-6.

Schieffelin, Edward L. 1976. The Sorrow of the Lonely and the
Burning of the Dancers. New York: St. Martin's Press.

Strathern, Andrew and Marilyn. 1971. Self-Decoration in Mount
Hagen. London: Duckworth.

Strathern, Andrew. In press. "A Line of Boys": Melpa Dance as a Symbol of Maturation. In Paul Spencer, editor, Society and the Dance. New York: Cambridge University Press.

Williams, F. E. 1940. Drama of Orokolo: The Social and Ceremonial Life of the Elema. Oxford: Clarendon Press.

Polynesia

Anderson, Johannes C. 1933. Maori Music with Its Polynesian Background. Polynesian Society Memoir 10.

Armstrong, Alan. 1964. Maori Games and Hakas. Wellington: A. H. and A. W. Reed.

Armstrong, Alan, and Reupena Ngata. 1960. Maori Action Songs. Wellington: A. H. and A. W. Reed.

Beechey, R. W. 1831. Narrative of a Voyage ... Performed in the Years 1825, 26, 27, 28. London: Colburn & Bentley.

Buck, Peter (Te Rangi Hiroa). 1938. Ethnology of Mangareva. Honolulu: Bishop Museum Bulletin 157.

Burrows, Edwin G. 1940. Polynesian Music and Dancing. Journal of the Polynesian Society 49 (September):331-46.

Costa, M. K. 1951. Dance in the Society and Hawaiian Islands as Presented by the Early Writers, 1767-1842. Unpublished Masters Thesis, University of Hawaii.

Ellis, William. 1969. Polynesian Researches: Polynesia. Rutland, Vermont and Tokyo: Charles E. Tuttle.

Emerson, Nathaniel B. 1909. Unwritten Literature of Hawaii. The Sacred Songs of the Hula. Washington: Bureau of American Ethnology Bulletin 38.

Forster, J. R. 1778. Observations made during a voyage round the world.... London.

Handy, E. S. Craighill. 1927. Polynesian Religion. Honolulu: Bishop Museum Bulletin 34.

_____. 1930. History and Culture in the Society Islands. Honolulu: Bishop Museum Bulletin 79.

Henry, Teuira. 1928. Ancient Tahiti. Honolulu: Bishop Museum Bulletin 48.

Kaeppler, Adrienne L. 1967. Folklore as Expressed in the

Dance in Tonga. Journal of American Folklore 80(316):160-168.

_____. 1967. Preservation and Evolution of Form and Function in Two Types of Tongan Dance. In Genevieve A. Highland, et al., editors, Polynesian Culture History: Essays in Honor of Kenneth P. Emory, pp. 503-536. Bernice P. Bishop Museum Special Publication 56.

_____. 1970. Tongan Dance: A Study in Cultural Change. Ethnomusicology 14(2):266-277.

_____. 1971. Aesthetics of Tongan Dance. Ethnomusicology 15(2):175-185.

_____. 1972. Method and Theory in Analyzing Dance Structure with an Analysis of Tongan Dance. Ethnomusicology 16(2): 173-217.

_____. 1973. Acculturation in Hawaiian Dance. Yearbook of the International Folk Music Council for 1972 4:38-46.

_____. 1976. Dance and Interpretation of Pacific Traditional Literature. In Adrienne L. Kaeppler and H. Arlo Nimmo, editors, Directions in Pacific Traditional Literature: Essays in Honor of Katharine Luomala, pp. 195-216. Bishop Museum Special Publication 62.

_____. 1976. Dance in Tonga: The Communication of Social Values Through an Artistic Medium. In Daniel Lerner and Jim Richstad, editors, Communication in the Pacific, pp. 15-22. Honolulu: East-West Communication Institute.

_____. 1977. Polynesian Dance as "Airport Art," in Asian and Pacific Dance: Selected Papers from the 1974 CORD Conference, pp. 71-84. CORD Annual VIII. New York: Committee on Research in Dance.

_____. 1978. Melody, Drone, and Decoration: Underlying Structures and Surface Manifestations in Tongan Art and Society. In Michael Greenhalgh, and Vincent Megaw, editors, Art in Society: Studies in Styles, Culture and Aesthetics, pp. 261-274. London: Duckworth.

_____. 1982. Polynesian Dances: A Selection for Contemporary Performance. Honolulu: Alpha Delta Kappa.

_____. In press. Structured Movement Systems in Tonga. In Paul Spencer, editor, Society and the Dance. New York: Cambridge University Press.

_____. In preparation. Hula and Ha'a: The Movements of Dance and Ritual.

Kanahele, George S., ed. 1979. Hawaiian Music and Musicians. Honolulu: The University Press of Hawaii.

Karetu, Sam. 1975. Language and Protocol of the Marae. In Michael King, editor, Te Ao Hurihuri: The World Moves On. Wellington: Hicks Smith, pp. 35-54.

Kealiinohomoku, Joann. 1965. Dance and Self Accompaniment. Ethnomusicology 9(3):292-5.

Kramer, Augustin. 1903. Die Samoa Inseln. Stuttgart: Schweizerbartsche Verlag.

Loeb, Edwin. 1926. History and Traditions of Niue. Honolulu: Bishop Museum Bulletin 32.

Metraux, Alfred. 1957. Easter Island. New York: Oxford University Press.

Moulin, Jane Freeman. 1979. The Dance of Tahiti. Papeete, Tahiti: Christian Gleizel/Les Editions du Pacifique.

Oliver, Douglas L. 1974. Ancient Tahitian Society. Honolulu: University Press of Hawaii.

O'Reilly, Patrick. 1980. Dancing Tahiti. Paris: Scop-Sadag. Dossier 22.

Roberts, Helen H. 1967. Ancient Hawaiian Music. Honolulu: Bishop Museum Bulletin 29, 1926. New York: Dover (reprint, 1967).

Rossen, Jane Mink and Margot Mink Colbert. 1981. Dance on Bellona, Solomon Islands: A Preliminary Study of Style and Concept. Ethnomusicology 15(3):447-466.

Rougier, Emmanuel. 1916. Fijian Dances and Games. Fijian Society Transactions, pp. 16-36.

Salmond, Anne. 1975. Hui: A Study of Maori Ceremonial Gatherings. Wellington: Reed.

Shennan, Jennifer. 1977. Waiata-a-ringa: A Movement Study of Action-Songs. Unpublished M.A. Thesis, University of Auckland, Anthropology Department.

Stillman, Amy K. 1982. The Hula Ku'i: A Tradition in

Hawaiian Music and Dance. Unpublished M.A. Thesis, University of Hawaii Music Department.

Thompson, Chris. 1971. Fijian Music and Dance. Fiji Society Transactions and Proceedings 11:14-21.

Youngerman, Suzanne. 1974. Maori Dancing Since the Eighteenth Century. Ethnomusicology 18(1):75-100.

Micronesia

Born, Regierungsarzt L. 1903. Einige Bemerkungen über Musik, Dichkunst und Tanz der Yapleute. Zeitschrift für Ethnologie 35:134-42.

Browning, Mary. 1970. Micronesian Heritage. Dance Perspectives 43. New York.

Burrows, Edwin G. 1963. Flower in my Ear: Arts and Ethos of Ifaluk Atoll. Seattle: University of Washington Press.

Furness, William Henry. 1910. The Island of Stone Money: Uap of the Carolines. Philadelphia and London: Lippincott.

Hambruch, P. and A. Eilers. 1936. Musik und Tanz, Ponape ii. Ergebnisse der Südsee-Expedition 1908-1910. Hamburg. Pp. 184-225.

Koch, Gerd and S. 1969. Kultur der Gilbert-Inseln. Encyclopaedia cinematographica. Göttingen. "Tanze," pp. 277-319.

Laxton, P. B. and Te Kantu Kamoriki. 1953. 'Ruoia', a Gilbertese Dance. Journal of the Polynesian Society 62:57-71.

Müller, Wilhelm. 1917. Yap. Ergebnisse der Südsee-Expedition 1908-1910. Hamburg. Vol. 2.

Stevenson, Robert Louis. 1971. In the South Seas. Honolulu: University of Hawaii Press.

Chapter Twenty-Seven

AUSTRALIAN ABORIGINAL THEATRICAL MOVEMENT

Stephen A. Wild

Relevance of the Term "Theatrical Movement" to Australian
Aboriginal Performances

The term "theatrical movement" requires some consideration
of its meaning before applying it to traditions of performance belonging to cultures so different from our own as that of Australian
Aboriginal society. It may well be argued that Aboriginal performance traditions are not theatrical, in which case we would have
nothing to contribute to this anthology. Such a position would be
an injustice to the many brilliant traditional Aboriginal performances
described in the literature and which may still today be observed in
more traditionally oriented Aboriginal communities, however these
performances may be characterized. It behooves us, then, to view
"theatrical movement" in terms broad enough to encompass Aboriginal performances, and to show in what ways they differ from theatrical performances with which we are more familiar.[1]

Let us restate the term "theatrical movement" as "movement
performed in the context of theatre," since it is the term "theatre"
which particularly requires definition. What we might regard as the
"common view" of theatre implies, usually, performers and an audience. Immediately we are in difficulty when applying the concept
to Aboriginal society, since in Aboriginal performances all the participants are usually also performers in one way or another. Also,
paradoxically, some participants may not be permitted to actually
see or even hear the main part of the performance, but they are
nonetheless participating in some other way somewhere else. Commonly in Aboriginal performances there is a category of participants
often referred to in the literature as "managers," but such participants are not behind a stage anxiously watching the performers,
they are part of the performance and often provide musical accompaniment. In short, although in Aboriginal performances roles are
clearly differentiated, they often differ from theatrical roles with
which we are familiar.

What may be referred to as "staging" of Aboriginal performances also often differs from the common view of theatre. While
some Aboriginal performances have a recognizable "stage" or bounded
area in which all of the action takes place, many do not. In the
latter cases the performances may occur in several places, sometimes simultaneously, sometimes by the performers moving from one
place to another as the performance proceeds. Important parts of
the entire performance may occur during the movement from one
place to another. This characteristic of many Aboriginal performances poses obvious difficulties in adapting them to a Western stage.
A definition of theatre which encompasses all Aboriginal performances
which we would want to include in any consideration of Aboriginal
theatrical movement should not be restricted by the concept of a
"stage."

The use of time in Aboriginal performances often varies considerably from its use in Western theatrical performance. A performance may last for days, weeks or even months, consisting of a
series of shorter performances with rest periods between. A non-
Aboriginal observer may have difficulty in perceiving the beginning
of a performance, although endings are usually well marked. A
performance generally consists of a long period of preparation which
passes often almost imperceptibly into what may be considered the
main part of the performance; the dividing line between them is often so blurred that it is impossible to establish unambiguously. This
is not to imply that, once under way, an Aboriginal performance
cannot be precisely coordinated. Indeed, some writers have commented on the brilliant coordination of Aboriginal performances, often involving a number of performers and a complex set of performance roles (see Eyre 1964 [1845]; Clunies Ross and Wild 1981).
Perhaps performances are often so spectacularly executed partly
because of elaborate and careful preparation, during which performance roles and actions are discussed, participants remind themselves of themes to be enacted by singing relevant songs and discussing myths, objects to be used in the performance are prepared
and bodies of participants are decorated.

Elements common to both Aboriginal performances and the common conception of theatre do, however, exist. They include music,
dance, body decoration, and objects manufactured and decorated
specifically for the performance occasion. They are integrated by
specific themes. They are special occasions set apart from everyday life for which special invitations are sent out. Despite the
blurring of the distinction between Aboriginal performers and audience, performers (in the broadest sense, producers of visual art
as well) are held accountable for "a display of communicative competence" over and above their responsibility for conveying the referential content of the communication, and thus, it can be held,
performances are aesthetically evaluated. There are formal stylistic
devices for which special descriptive terms (a technical vocabulary)
exist.[2] These common elements justify the characterization of

Aboriginal performances whose descriptions are reviewed in this
essay and listed in the accompanying bibliography as theatrical.

State of Available Resources and Selection of Items

The resources available on Australian Aboriginal theatrical
movement are both a feast and a famine. Under the heading of
"Ritual, Ceremonial, and Dramatic Performances," Catherine Berndt
commented in 1961 "... apart from numerous scattered observations
of this sort, there has been no thorough research into this topic
as a separate area of study" (Berndt, C. H. 1963:269). The situation is almost no better today, more than twenty years later. And
yet, in preparing for our task we received on request almost 200
foolscap photocopied pages of card catalogue entries under the subject "Dance" from the Library of the Australian Institute of Aboriginal Studies (hereafter referred to as AIAS). Some of the items
included therein contained only brief mentions of the subject, but
many contained substantial descriptions and many more could be included if the subject is to encompass more than strictly dance.
From the earliest accounts of European observations of Australian
Aborigines to the present mixture of casual, popular and professional accounts, spanning a period of about 200 years, probably a
majority have included descriptions of what could be characterized
as "theatrical movement."

This situation poses a problem for the bibliographer: a list
of sources which focus primarily on theatrical movement as such
would be extremely meagre, yet where to draw the line beyond that
point requires rather arbitrary decisions. One obvious criterion is
the extent of material on theatrical movement in each source, but
the sheer volume of sources on Aborigines and the obscurity of
many of them effectively precludes its fully systematic application
short of carrying out a substantial research project. A thorough
literature search and summary of sources in Aboriginal theatrical
movement would be a valuable exercise, but since none has been
done what has been included and excluded in the bibliography is
the result of a less than fully systematic procedure. Nevertheless,
some general statements about selection criteria and the procedure
adopted may be made.

The major criterion for selection of items for the bibliography
was the inclusion of substantial analyses and/or descriptions of theatrical performance. Generally items which refer to performances
but do not actually describe or analyze them, of which there are
many, were excluded. Also generally excluded were accounts of
phenomena associated with theatrical movement (music and/or texts
of songs, myths and beliefs, and various forms of visual art) but
which do not deal with movement itself.

We began our task by reviewing the AIAS card catalogue

entries under "dance." Since the AIAS Library is the major repository of Australian Aboriginal sources and the entries in its uniquely
classified catalogue are quite elaborate and detailed, this procedure
seemed the most promising, as well as the most convenient. Decisions on what to include and exclude on the basis of the amount of
material on dance were facilitated by the detailed summaries of the
content for each entry. Also, of course, many items were known
to the compilers, and in many cases of uncertainty the sources were
consulted. Nevertheless, not all sources excluded were known or
consulted, and some significant items may have been missed. On
the other hand, we also added some items missed by the cataloguers.

A bibliography of Aboriginal theatrical movement, as we have
defined it, would be substantially incomplete were it to focus nar-
rowly on dance. Furthermore, the compilers of the AIAS Library
catalogue are dependent to a large extent on the conception of dance
held by the authors of papers and books deposited in the Library.
Thus the initial bibliography on dance was expanded to include
items known to have substantial accounts of ceremonial action which
may or may not be identified as dance or drama. The major categories of sources so included are the main ethnographic studies and
anthropological testbooks on Australian Aborigines. The selection
of these items was dependent mainly on our collective knowledge of
the literature and on checking sources listed in other bibliographies
and mentioned in texts known to us. Completeness cannot, of course,
be guaranteed; even as the bibliography was being finalized, ready
for typing, other sources occurred to us.

Finally, although categories of sources are discussed in this
chapter, it was decided not to impose a categorization on the bibliography. This was for several reasons. Firstly, almost any categorization would necessitate multiple listings of many items under
several categories, i.e. no exclusive categorization would be possible. Such a procedure would unnecessarily expand an already
rather long bibliography. Secondly, any categorization adopted
would impose an organization which would exclude other organizations, any of which may be equally or more appropriate to a particular user depending on his or her interests. For example, categories may be established on the basis of publication dates, culture
areas, exclusiveness of treatment of the subject, types of theatrical
performance, or qualitative evaluations of the sources. Instead, we
have ordered the bibliography alphabetically by author and the date
of publication, and in the essay readers are directed to items judged
as significant for particular reasons.

Recent and Current Research

Most of the serious studies of theatrical movement among Australian Aborigines have appeared since 1969, and in the main these
have taken a dance and/or ethnomusicological perspective rather

than a more general theatrical perspective. Of particular note is the excellent study of Andagarinja women's ceremonies in central Australia by Catherine Ellis (1970), who provided a detailed description of body painting, dance movements and songs and their performance relationships. Also noteworthy is T. G. H. Strehlow's monumental study of Aranda songs of central Australia (1971), which includes many descriptions of associated theatrical movement; however, the focus is on song texts. The first serious attempt to study Aboriginal dance movements per se was made by Alice Moyle and Elphine Allen (Moyle, A. M. 1972), when Aboriginal dances were filmed for the expressed purpose of combined music and dance notations (see also Moyle, A. M. 1977a, 1977b; Allen 1973; and Groote Eylandt Field Project: Aboriginal Dances, (8.3), Groote Eylandt Field Project: Five Brogla Dances, (8.4) under Films). A number of dance notations were made from these films and were deposited in the AIAS Library. The technical care taken to optimize the notation potential of the films precluded a more general theatrical component to the study.

Several theses based on extended field research and including dance as a primary or secondary focus were completed during the 1970's. Two were primarily ethnomusicological theses but took a broad approach to performance which included dance and theatrical movement in general (Shannon 1971; Wild 1975; see also Wild 1977, 1977-78). The research by Shannon and Wild was conducted in one Aboriginal community in central Australia in the same period of time, one focussing on women's performances and the other on men's. Two other theses were based on research in Arnhem Land, the central north coastal region of Australia, although in different communities (Boorsboom 1978; Quisenberry 1973). Aside from the popular account by dancer Beth Dean and her husband Victor Carell (1955), Quisenberry's thesis remains the only completed substantial study of Aboriginal dance to date, and it is a useful introduction to Aboriginal dance and ceremony in one area of Australia. Boorsboom's thesis is a study of an exchange ritual with a considerably more substantial description and analysis of theatrical movement than most studies of Aboriginal ritual.

The immediate future offers a more promising outlook. Two dance researchers, Andrée Grau and Megan Dail-Jones, are currently conducting extended field research on grants from AIAS.[3] Both are graduates from the Institute of Choreology in London and trained in anthropology. Also, Margaret Clunies Ross and the present writer are engaged in a collaborative study of the relationship among music, song texts and dance of a song series from north central Arnhem Land, taking into account the ritual context of its performance (see Clunies Ross and Wild 1981). Important to this research is the analysis of material on sound-synchronized 16mm camera rolls shot for Waiting for Harry (1980), a film of a mortuary ceremony whose central song series is the subject of the analysis. A monograph is projected as the final result of this research.

Importance of Studying Aboriginal Theatrical Movement

Traditionally, most Aboriginal theatrical movement is intimately associated with religious ritual. Secular performance is limited in occurrence and often related in some way to religion. Many early reports of Aboriginal performances did not mention their religious intent, either because of the authors' ignorance or ethnocentric prejudice (see Berndt, R. M. 1974: 1). Underlying and unifying ritual performances are religious myths of ancestral spirits whose activities continue to shape the patterns of Aboriginal life and of the world in which they live. Myths also relate people to people, and people to land, through circumstances surrounding conception and through descent. Although the ethnographic literature abounds with translated accounts of myths as narratives, there is a dearth of information about how they were originally presented and collected. It may be that many well-formed narratives appearing in the literature are approximations of nonnarrative genres of Aboriginal expression in a narrative genre characteristic of Western society.[4] Commonly, though not in all cases, myths are presented through dramatic performances and through piecemeal exegeses associated with performances. (See Stanner 1966 and Berndt, R. M. 1974 for discussions of the relationship between myths and ritual performances.)

The importance of theatrical performance in Aboriginal society has had two seemingly contradictory effects--feast and famine--on the sources of information available. Despite the plethora of descriptive accounts of religious rituals, there has been a dearth of analyses from a performance perspective. One explanation arises out of widespread Aboriginal restrictions on access to culturally important religious rituals: sexual segregation in ritual life is common, and noninitiates are commonly excluded from all but the least valued rituals. The great developments which have occurred in Aboriginal studies in the two decades since the founding of the AIAS have coincided with increased access of Aborigines to the printed word and to audio-visual media, and to increasing reluctance of Aborigines to permit the content of restricted rituals to become public knowledge.[5] As specializations in Aboriginal studies have become increasingly differentiated and analytically honed, the opportunities to study theatrical performance have diminished. Referring to the time prior to the founding of the AIAS, Catherine Berndt suggested other reasons for this lack: "Research into the ritual-myth-song-drama complex is perhaps less unobtrusive, or more conspicuous, than an interest in, say, social structure and organization: it is certainly more suspect to those who hold the view that this aspect of Aboriginal culture must go, and the sooner the better" (1963: 272).

The difficulties of studying Aboriginal theatrical performance must be weighed against its importance, and one mitigating factor. The increasing availability of convenient audiovisual technology to assist in field studies, both to record theatrical performances and to elicit information in the field, facilitates more detailed analyses than were possible hitherto. Sound-synchronized Super-8 filming equipment and portable video recorders are compact, lightweight, easy to operate and produce good results. Most Aboriginal communities now possess film projection and video playback equipment so that information can be readily obtained from film and videotape in the field. Aside from the general academic value of studying this important aspect of Aboriginal culture, improvements in Aboriginal education may depend on its greater consonance with Aboriginal culture, including traditional modes and styles of transmission of knowledge. An improved understanding of Aboriginal theatrical performance may lead to more effective transmission of knowledge than results achieved from the present heavy reliance on written modes of transmission and be more in keeping with the maintenance of an Aboriginal identity.

The Contemporary Situation

It would be wrong to assume that all Australian Aborigines are uniformly oriented towards traditional modes of existence. The current norm of more traditionally oriented Aborigines in the more remote areas of Australia is sedentary life on a government-supported settlement, or small town, with satellite hamlets or "homeland centers" in the surrounding countryside. Current Aboriginal lifestyles range from fairly traditional life at homeland centers through a working life on pastoral properties, life in small, predominantly White Australian towns, to ghetto or more integrated life in large urban centers. This is reflected in styles of Aboriginal performing arts, from traditional rituals performed in their home territories to Black theatre in Sydney, and there is much in between. Sansom (1980) has analyzed the patterns of life in Aboriginal camps on the fringes of Darwin, administrative capital of the sparsely populated Northern Territory; although he does not describe theatrical performance, the author gives a detailed account of the organization of and motivation for a ceremony performed by the inhabitants of "the camp at Wallaby Cross." One pattern which has developed, especially since the establishment of the Aboriginal Artists Agency, is of semi-professional or ad hoc performance troupes whose members normally reside at or near remote government settlements touring Australian country towns, schools and cities and occasionally overseas; tours are generally organized by the Agency.[6] No research has been directed at this phenomenon, although some popular accounts have been published (see below).

Categories of Sources

This is not intended to be an exhaustive categorization of sources listed in the bibliography, but rather an indication of some important sources in major categories. The major items since 1969 have been mentioned above. Other items specifically on theatrical movement are as follows. There is a scattering of serious items prior to 1969 (Bates n.d.; Berndt, C. H. 1952; Berndt, R. M. & C. H. 1962; Campbell 1940; Haddon 1893; Hiatt, B. 1966; Kemp 1968-69; Laade 1968; McCarthy 1964; Morse 1968) and a few on the arts which specifically include theatrical movement (Berndt, C. H. 1962, 1963). Popular accounts include items on Aboriginal performance troupes and festivals (Anon. 1971, 1972, 1975; Durack 1971; Edwards 1971) and others (Church 1945; Dean 1955; Ewers 1964 [1947]; Jones 1979, 1980; Long 1937; MacFarlane 1950; Simpson 1971; Thorne 1939). I am aware of only one substantial recent bibliography which includes theatrical movement (Moyle 1978; see also the bibliography in Berndt, C. H. 1963).

Next in importance are the major ethnographic sources which include substantial descriptions of theatrical movement or ceremonies. In earlier times ethnographic summaries of regions were in vogue, and they usually included ceremonial descriptions (Howitt 1904; Roth 1897, 1902; Smyth 1878; Spencer 1914; Spencer and Gillen 1899, 1904; see also Massola 1971). Recollections, reminiscences, journals and memoirs of travelers, missionaries and settlers are a useful source (Angas 1967 [1847]a; Curr 1883; Daley 1925; Eyre 1964 [1845]; Hassell [1975]; Major 1900; Salvado 1977 [1851]). Worthy of particular note is Eyre's journals whose detailed descriptions of dances could easily be realized in performance (see pp. 228-43). Hardly mentioned in the bibliography, but potentially an important historical source, are early illustrations of Aboriginal performances, of which Angas (1967 [1847]b), with its four plates of ten paintings of dance figures or performances and accompanying descriptive text, is an excellent example (see also Berndt, R. M. 1974 for early as well as more recent photographs of dances). Most of the important general ethnographies and theses contain descriptions of major ceremonies (Berndt, R. M. and C. H. 1942-45, 1951, 1970; Goodale 1971; Haddon 1901; Hiatt, L. 1965; Kaberry 1939; McConnell 1930-34; Meggitt 1965 [1962]; Róheim 1943; Spencer and Gillen 1927; Tonkinson 1978; Turner 1974; Warner 1958 [1937]). Also, there are studies of particular ceremonies, summaries of types of ceremonies and studies of ritual life (Bell 1980; Berndt, C. H. 1950, 1965; Berndt, R. M. 1951, 1952; Elkin 1972; Howitt 1884, 1885; Meggitt 1955, 1966; Munn 1973; Róheim 1933; Stanner 1966; Thomson 1934). Finally, textbooks and general summaries on Australian Aborigines have always included sections or chapters on ritual performance and sometimes dance in particular (Basedow 1925; Berndt, R. M. and C. H. 1977 [1964]; Curr 1886-87; Elkin 1974 [1938]; Maddock 1972; Mathew 1889, 1899; McCarthy 1957; Thomas 1906).

By far the most direct way of acquiring knowledge of theatrical movement, aside from seeing the actual events, is through audiovisual media. Added to the bibliography is a list of films which

contain significant sequences of Aboriginal theatrical movement.
Not included is the large amount of unedited archival film footage
in existence (particularly in the AIAS Film Archive) which is available to researchers. Also not included are the large collections of
still photographs and sound recordings in the AIAS and other re-
positories in Australia (for a list of commercially available AIAS
records see Wild 1981). Most of the readily available and useful
films were produced by the AIAS Film Unit, some of which may be
restricted in their use because of their sacred-secret contents. A
few lists of audiovisual material exist which identify items on Aboriginal dance (Barlow 1980; Coppell 1978; Kennedy 1970; see also
Moyle 1978).

Location and Availability of Sources

Most major published works will be readily found in large libraries in North America, Britain and Australia. The most important source of material on Australian Aborigines is the AIAS, through
its Publication Unit, its Film Unit and its Library. Some items in
the bibliography are published by the AIAS, and virtually all items
are deposited in the AIAS Library. Small items and short sections
of books in the AIAS Library may be photocopied for private use,
and some titles are available through interlibrary loan within Australia. Unpublished manuscripts in the AIAS Library are deposited
under a system of options which specify the conditions of access
and use; options selected by depositors vary from open access and
free availability to users, to various degrees of restriction. Readers should direct inquiries to the Senior Bibliographer, AIAS Library (see note 3 for address). In Australia, AIAS films may be
purchased or rented directly from the AIAS Film Unit, and the
Australian National Library and State Film Centres lend AIAS films
and other films on Aborigines free of charge to schools, universities
and community groups. AIAS films are distributed in North America by Extension Media Center, University of California, Berkeley;
and in Britain by the Royal Anthropological Institute, London.

Notes

1. I wish especially to acknowledge the help of Andrée Grau, who
   is jointly responsible for the bibliography, in discussing ideas
   for this essay. I also thank Margaret Clunies Ross and Megan
   Dail-Jones for reading a draft of the paper and for their
   suggestions. Michael Leigh, AIAS Film Archivist, compiled
   the list of films.

2. See Bauman, Richard 1975, "Verbal art as performance,"
   American Anthropologist 77(2): 290-311; also Wild 1977.

3. AIAS grants for field research in Aboriginal Studies are awarded

to qualified applicants from anywhere in the world. Travel
funds to and from Australia are not generally made available.
Inquiries should be sent to The Principal, AIAS, P.O. Box
553, Canberra City, A.C.T. 2601, Australia.

4. The suggestion applies only to narrative discourse. For an
analysis of a formal Aboriginal speech see Margaret Clunies
Ross, "Two Aboriginal oral texts from Arnhem Land, north
Australia, and their cultural context," to be published in
S. T. Knight and S. Mukherjee, eds. The Social Relations
of Literary Texts (forthcoming). There are also some suggestions in Capell, A., "Myths and tales of the Nunggubuyu,
southeast Arnhem Land," Oceania 31: 31-62.

5. Aboriginal reticence on the subject of initiation ceremonies is
mentioned in nineteenth-century literature, e.g. Hodgkinson
1845: 231-2; Howitt 1884: 432, 455 footnote 1; 1885: 311-2.

6. Further information on the Agency can be obtained from Aboriginal Artists Agency, 8 Church Street, North Sydney 2060,
Australia. One overseas tour was to the United States in
the summer of 1980. The troupe performed in Los Angeles,
New York, Washington and San Francisco. Some film footage
was shot and the occasion received considerable media coverage. Readers may wish to write to the U.S. organizer of
the tour, Mr. Spider Kedelsky, Orinoco Dance Foundation,
943½ Lucille Ave., Los Angeles, CA 90026.

Allen, Elphine
1973 "Australian Aboriginal Dance." In Ronald M. Berndt
and E. S. Phillips, eds. The Australian Aboriginal Heritage, an Introduction Through the Arts. Sydney: Australian Society for Education Through the Arts, in association with Ure Smith. Pp. 275-90.

Angas, George F.
1967 [1847]a "Savage Life and Scenes in Australia and New
Zealand." Landmarks in Anthropology, Weston LaBarre,
general editor. New York, London: Johnson Reprint
Corp. Originally published by Smith, Elder, and Co.,
London.
1967 [1847]b South Australia: Illustrated. Facsimile edition,
Sydney: A. H. and A. W. Reed. Originally published by
Thomas McLean, London.

Anonymous
1971 "Mowanjum Dance Group." Department of Native Welfare
Newsletter 1(10): 28-39.
1972 "The Yelangi and Waiben Dancers." Identity 1(5): 18-23.
1975 "Cairns Festival." Identity 2(6): 19-22.

Barlow, Alex
1980 Aboriginal Studies Resource List. Canberra: AIAS.

Basedow, Herbert
1925 The Australian Aboriginal. Adelaide: Preece.

Bates, Daisy M.
1905-6 "The Marriage Laws and Some Customs of the West
Australian Aborigines." Victorian Geographical Journal
13-14: 36-60.
n.d. "Songs, Dances, etc.--Corroborees and Songs, Murchison." Unpublished ms. deposited in Australian National
Library, Canberra; copy deposited in AIAS, Canberra.

Bell, Diane
1980 Daughters of the Dreaming. Australian National University, Canberra: Ph.D. Thesis.

Berndt, Catherine H.
1950 Women's Changing Ceremonies in Northern Australia.
L'Homme 1. Paris: Hermann et Cie.
1952 "A Drama of North-Eastern Arnhem Land." Oceania
22: 216-39, 275-89.
1962 "The Arts of Life: An Australian Aboriginal Perspective." Westerly 1(2-3): 82-8.
1963 "Art and Aesthetic Expression." In Helen Sheils, ed.
Australian Aboriginal Studies. A symposium of papers
presented at the 1961 research conference. Melbourne:
OUP. Pp. 256-77.
1965 "Women and the 'Secret Life.'" In R. M. and C. H.
Berndt, eds. Aboriginal Man in Australia, Essays in
Honour of Emeritus Professor A. P. Elkin. Sydney, Melbourne, London: Angus and Robertson. Pp. 238-82.

Berndt, Ronald M.
1951 Kunapipi. Melbourne: Cheshire.
1952 Djanggawul. London: Routledge and Kegan Paul.
1974 "Australian Aboriginal Religion." In Th. P. van Baaren,
L. Leertouwer and H. Buning, eds. Iconography of Religions, Section V. Leiden: E. J. Brill.

Berndt, Ronald M. and Catherine H. Berndt
1942-45 "A Preliminary Report of Field Work in the Ooldea
Region, Western South Australia." Oceania 12-15.
1951 Sexual Behaviour in Western Arnhem Land. New York:
Viking Fund Publications in Anthropology no. 16.
1962 "Aborigines: Dancing." In Australian Encyclopaedia,
second edition. Sydney: Grolier Society. Vol 1: 62-4.
1970 Man, Land and Myth in North Australia: The Gunwinggu
People. Sydney: Ure Smith.
1977 [1964] The World of the First Australians. Second edition. Sydney: Ure Smith.

Black, L.
1944 The Bora Ground. Sydney: Booth.

Boorsboom, Adrianus P.
1978 Maradjiri: A Modern Ritual Complex in Arnhem Land,
North Australia. Nijmegen, Katholieke Universiteit, Central Reprographie, Directoraat A-Facultieten.

Campbell, Tomas D.
1940 "The Drama and Theatre Arts of the Aborigines."
Mankind 2(9): 329-30.

Chase, Athol
1980 Which Way Now?: Tradition, Continuity and Change in
a North Queensland Aboriginal Community [Lockhart River].
University of Queensland: Ph.D. Thesis.

Church, A. E.
1945 "Ballet at Badu." Walkabout 11(9): 33-4.

Clunies Ross, Margaret and Stephen A. Wild
1981 "The Relations of Music, Text and Dance in Arnhem
Land Clan Songs." Unpublished paper presented at the
Conference on Transmission in Oral and Written Traditions,
Humanities Research Centre, Australian National University,
Canberra, August 1981.

Coppell, W. G.
1978 Audio-Visual Resource Material Relating to the Aboriginal
Australians. Canberra: Curriculum Development Centre.

Curr, Edward M.
1883 Recollections of Squatting in Victoria: Then Called the
Port Phillip District (From 1841-1851). Melbourne: Robertson.
1886-87 The Australian Race. Melbourne: Ferres. (4 vols).

Daley, Charles
1925 "Reminiscences from 1841 of William Kyle, a Pioneer."
Victorian Historical Magazine 10(3): 158-72.

Dawson, James
1981 [1881] Australian Aborigines: The Languages and Customs of Several Tribes of Aborigines in the Western District of Victoria, Australia. Canberra: AIAS. Originally
published by George Robertson, Melbourne, Sydney, Adelaide.

Dean, Beth
1955 "In Search of Stone-Age Dance." Walkabout 21(5): 15-20.

Dean, Beth and Victor Carell
1955 Dust for the Dancers. Sydney: Ure Smith.

Durack, Mary
1971 "No Longer Just a Dream: The Aboriginal Theatre
Foundation Gets to Work." Identity 1(2): 17-22.

Edwards, Gregson
1971 "Dancing for the Future." Northern Territory Affairs
2: 14-16.

Elkin, A. P.
1972 "Two Rituals in South and Central Arnhem Land"
[Yabuduruwa and Maraian]. Sydney: University of
Sydney. Oceania Monographs no. 19. Originally published in Oceania 31-2, 42.
1974 [1938] The Australian Aborigines. Fifth edition. Sydney: Angus and Robertson.

Ellis, Catherine
1970 "The Role of the Ethnomusicologist in the Study of
Andagarinja Women's Ceremonies." Miscellanea Musicologica
5: 76-208.

Ewers, John K.
1954 [1953] With the Sun on My Back. Second revised edition. Sydney: Angus and Robertson.
1964 [1947] "Aboriginal Ballet." In A. T. Bolton, ed. Walkabout's Australia: An Anthology of Articles and Photographs from Walkabout Magazine. Sydney: Ure Smith in
association with the Australian National Travel Association.
Pp. 62-75. Reprinted from Walkabout 14(2): 29-34.

Eyre, Edward J.
1964 [1845] "Manners and Customs of the Aborigines of Australia." In His Journals of Expeditions of Discovery into
Central Australia. Australiana Facsimile Editions no. 7.
Adelaide: Libraries Board of South Australia. Vol. II:
145-507. Originally published by T. & W. Boone, London.

Fink, Ruth A.
1960 The Changing Status and Cultural Identity of Western
Australian Aborigines: A Field Study of Aborigines in the
Murchison District, Western Australia, 1955-1957. Columbia
University, New York: Ph.D. Thesis.

Goodale, Jane C.
1971 Tiwi Wives: A Study of Women of Melville Island, Northern Australia. Seattle: University of Washington Press.

Goodale, Jane and J. D. Koss
1966 "The Cultural Context of Creativity Among Tiwi." American Ethnological Society Proceedings, 1966: 175-91.

Haddon, Alfred C.
1893 "The Secular and Ceremonial Dances of Torres Straits." Internationales Archiv für Ethnographic 6: 131-62.
1901 Head-Hunters, Black, White and Brown. London: Methuen.

Hassell, Ethel
[1975] My Dusky Friends: Aboriginal Life, Customs and Legends and Glimpses of Life at Jarramungup in the 1880s; With an Introduction by Sara Meagher. Fremantle, Western Australia: C. W. Hassell.

Hiatt, Betty
1966 "Report on the Female Aboriginal Dancing Associated with the Bora Ceremony at Lockhart River Mission in the Cape York Peninsula." Unpublished ms. deposited in AIAS, Canberra.

Hiatt, L. R.
1965 Kingship and Conflict: A Study of an Aboriginal Community in Northeast Arnhem Land. Canberra: Australian National University Press.

Hodgkinson, Clement
1845 Australia from Port MacQuarie to Moreton Bay. London: T. & W. Boone.

Howitt, Alfred W.
1844 "On Some Australian Ceremonies of Initiation." Royal Anthropological Institute Journal 13: 432-59.
1855 "The Jeraeil or Initiation Ceremonies of the Kurnai Tribes." Royal Anthropological Institute Journal 14: 301-25.
1904 The Native Tribes of South-East Australia. London: Macmillan & Co.

Jones, Mary
1979 "Dancing Feet?: The History of Sacred Dance." Zadoc Central News, October 1979: 13-25.
1980 "The History of Sacred and Biblically-Inspired Dance in Australia." Nelen Yubu 6: 3-18.

Kaberry, Phyllis M.
1939 Aboriginal Woman, Sacred and Profane. London: Routledge.

Kartomi, Margaret
1970 "Tjitji Inma at Yalata." Hemisphere 14(6): 33-7.

Keen, Ian
1978 One Ceremony, One Song: An Economy of Religious Knowledge Among the Yolngu of North-East Arnhem Land. Australian National University, Canberra: Ph.D. Thesis.

Kemp, Thérèse B.
1968-69 "A Propos de Certaines Danses des Aborigènes de la Tasmanie." Ethnographie, Paris 63(3): 156-9.

Kennedy, Peter (ed.)
1970 Films on Traditional Music and Dance, a First International Catalogue. Paris: UNESCO for International Folk Music Council.

Laade, Walfgang
1968 "Etwas über Musik und Tanz bei den Insulanern der Torres-Strasse." Kontakte 4: 121-5.

Lockwood, Douglas W.
1963 Crocodiles and Other People. Adelaide: Rigby.

Long, G. MacDonald
1937 "Corroboree." Walkabout, September 1937: 49, 51, 53, 55.

MacFarlane, Philip H.
1950 "The Wild-Fowl and the Devil: A Legend of the Torres Strait." Walkabout 16(1): 46-8.

Maddock, Kenneth
1972 The Australian Aborigines: A Portrait of Their Society. Penguin Books.
n.d. "Report on Field Work in the Northern Territory 1964-65." Unpublished ms. deposited in AIAS, Canberra.

Major, Thomas
1900 Leaves from a Squatter's Notebook. London: Sands.

Massola, Aldo
1971 The Aborigines of South-Eastern Australia as They Were. Melbourne: Heinemann.

Mathew, John
1887 "Mary River and Bunya Bunya Country." In E. M. Curr. The Australian Race. Melbourne: Ferres. Vol. 3: 152-209.
1889 "The Australian Aborigines." In Royal Society of New South Wales Journal and Proceedings 23: 335-449.
1899 Eaglehawk and Crow: A Study of the Australian Aborigines Including an Inquiry into their Origin and a Survey of Australian Languages. Melbourne: Melville, Mullen and Slade.

Mathews, Robert H.
1898 "Initiation Ceremonies of Australian Tribes." American Philosophical Society Proceedings 37: 54-73.

McCarthy, Frederick D.
1957 Australia's Aborigines: Their Life and Culture. Melbourne: Colorgravure Publishers.
1964 "The Dancers of Arukun." Australian Natural History 14(9): 296-300.
1978 "Aurukun Dances." Northbridge, NSW. Unpublished ms. deposited in AIAS, Canberra.

McConnel, Ursula H.
1930-34 "The Wik-munkan Tribe of Cape York Peninsula." Oceania 1(1): 97-194; 1(2): 181-205; 4(3): 310-67.

Meggitt. M. J.
1955 "Djanba Among the Walbiri, Central Australia." Anthropos 50: 375-403.
1965 [1962] Desert People: A Study of the Walbiri Aborigines of Central Australia. Chicago and London: The University of Chicago Press. Originally published by Angus and Robertson, Sydney.
1966 "Gadjari Among the Walbiri of Central Australia." Sydney: The University of Sydney. The Oceania Monographs no. 14. Originally published in Oceania 36-7.

Morphy, Howard
1977 "Too Many Meanings": An Analysis of the Artistic System of the Yolngu of North-East Arnhem Land. Australian National University, Canberra: Ph.D. Thesis. (2 vols)

Morse, Babette
1968 "Dance Notation and Aboriginal Culture." Hemisphere 12(11): 2-6.

Mountford, Charles P.
1956 "Expedition to the Land of the Tiwi." National Geographic Magazine 109: 417-40.
1958 The Tiwi, Their Art, Myth and Ceremony. London: Phoenix House; Melbourne: Georgian House.
1962 Brown Men and Red Sand: Journeyings in Wild Australia. Sydney: Angus and Robertson.
1976 Nomads of the Australian Desert. Adelaide: Rigby.

Moyle, Alice M.
1972 "Sound Films for Combined Notation: The Groote Eylandt Field Project, 1969." International Folk Music Council Yearbook 4: 104-18.
1977a "Aborigines: Music, Song and Dance." In The Australian Encyclopaedia, third edition. Sydney: Grolier Society of Australia. Vol. 1: 37-40.

1977b "Music and Dance: Mastersingers of the Bush." In
P. Stanbury, ed. The Moving Frontier: Aspects of
Aboriginal-European Interaction in Australia. Sydney:
Reed.
1978 "Song and Dance." In M. C. Hill and A. P. C. Barlow,
comps. Black Australia: An Annotated Bibliography and
Teachers' Guide to Resources on Aborigines and Torres
Strait Islanders. Canberra: AIAS; New Jersey: Humani-
ties Press. Pp. 63-6.

Moyle, Richard M.
1979 Songs of the Pintupi: Musical Life in a Central Australian Society. Canberra: AIAS.

Munn, Nancy D.
1973 Walbiri Iconography: Graphic Representations and Cultural Symbolism in a Central Australian Society. Ithaca
and London: Cornell University Press.

Peterson, Nicolas
1970 "Buluwandi: A Central Australian Ceremony for the
Resolution of Conflict." In R. M. Berndt, ed. Australian
Aboriginal Anthropology. Nedlands, Western Australia:
University of Western Australia Press for AIAS. Pp. 200-
15.

Plomley, N. J. B., (ed.)
[1966] Friendly Mission: The Tasmanian Journals and Papers
of George Augustus Robinson, 1829-1834. Hobart: Tasmanian Historical Research Association.

Quisenberry, Kay
1973 Dance in Arnhem Land: A Field Study Project 1970-72.
Southern Methodist University, Dallas: M.F.A. Thesis.

Raven-Hart, R.
1948 "Islands of Torres Strait." Walkabout 14(12): 14-16.
1949 The Happy Isles. Melbourne: Georgian House.

Richard, Francis
1925 "Customs and Language of the Western Hodgkinson Abo-
riginals." Queensland Museum Memoirs 8(3): 249-65.

Róheim, Géza
1933 "Women and Their Life in Central Australia." Royal
Anthropological Institute Journal 63: 207-65.
1943 The Eternal Ones of the Dream. New York: International
Universities Press.

Roth, Walter
1897 Ethnological Studies Among the North-West Central
Queensland Aborigines. Brisbane: Government Printer.

1902 "Games, Sports and Amusements." North Queensland Ethnography: Bulletin no. 4. Brisbane: Government Printer.

Salvado, Rosendo
1977 [1851] The Salvado Memoirs: Historical Memoirs of Australia and Particularly of the Benedictine Mission of New Norcia and of the Habits and Customs of the Australian Natives. Translated and edited by E. J. Storman. Nedlands, Western Australia: University of Western Australia Press. Originally published by Society for the Propagation of the Faith, Rome.

Sansom, Basil
1980 The Camp at Wallaby Cross. Canberra: AIAS.

Shannon, Cynthia
1971 Walpiri Women's Music. Monash University, Clayton, Victoria: B.A. Honours Thesis.

Simpson, Colin
1971 "The Balnooknook Corroboree." In Reader's Digest Association Australia. This Land--These People. Sydney.

Smyth, Robert B.
1878 The Aborigines of Victoria. Melbourne: Government Printer.

Spencer, Sir Walter Baldwin
1896 "Through Larapinta Land: A Narrative of the Expedition." In Report on the Work of the Horn Scientific Expedition ..., Vol. 1: 1-136.
1914 Native Tribes of the Northern Territory of Australia. London: Macmillan.
1928 Wanderings in Wild Australia. London: Macmillan. (2 vols).

Spencer, Sir Walter Baldwin and F. J. Gillen
1899 The Native Tribes of Central Australia. London: Macmillan.
1904 The Northern Tribes of Central Australia. London: Macmillan.
1927 The Arunta: A Study of a Stone Age People. London: Macmillan. (2 vols).

Stanner, W. E. H.
1966 On Aboriginal Religion. Sydney: The University of Sydney. The Oceania Monographs no. 11. Originally published in Oceania 30-4.

Stirling, Edward C.
    1896 "Anthropology." In Report on the Work of the Horn
        Scientific Expedition ..., Vol. 4: 1-157.

Strehlow, T. G. H.
    1971 Songs of Central Australia. Sydney: Angus and
        Robertson.

Stubington, Jill
    1977 "Songs to Live By." Hemisphere 21(8): 25-30.
    1979 "North Australian Aboriginal Music." In Jennifer Isaacs,
        ed. Australian Aboriginal Music. Sydney: Aboriginal
        Artists Agency.

Taplin, G.
    1879 The Folklore, Manners, Customs, and Languages of the
        South Australian Aborigines. Adelaide: Government
        Printer.

Thomas, N. W.
    1906 Natives of Australia. London: Archibald Constable &
        Company.

Thomson, Donald
    1934 "Notes on a Hero Cult from the Gulf of Carpentaria,
        North Queensland." Royal Anthropological Institute Jour-
        nal 64: 217-35.

Thorne, Jessie C.
    1939 "'Playabout' Corroboree." Wildlife 1(14): 12-13.

Tonkinson, Robert
    1970 "Aboriginal Dream-Spirit Beliefs in a Contact Situation:
        Jigalong, Western Australia." In R. M. Berndt, ed.
        Australian Aboriginal Anthropology. Nedlands, Western
        Australia: University of Western Australia Press for AIAS.
        Pp. 277-91.
    1978 The Mardudjara Aborigines. New York: Holt, Rinehart
        and Winston.

Travers, Robert
    1968 The Tasmanians: The Story of a Doomed Race. Mel-
        bourne: Cassell.

Turner, David H.
    1974 Tradition and Transformation: A Study of the Groote
        Eylandt Area Aborigines of Northern Australia. Canberra:
        AIAS.

Von Sturmer, John R.
    1980 "Notes on Dancing at Cannon Hill, Thursday 18 December

1980: A Demonstration of the Character of <u>Mulil</u> Before the Aboriginal Land Commissioner, Mr. Justice Toohey, at the Alligator Rivers Stage 2 Land Claim Hearing." Unpublished ms. deposited in AIAS, Canberra.

Warner, W. Lloyd
1958 [1937] <u>A Black Civilization</u>. New York: Harper & Row.

West, Lamont
1964 "Notes on Tapes in AIAS Archives." Unpublished ms. deposited in AIAS, Canberra.

Wild, Stephen A.
1975 <u>Walbiri Music and Dance in Their Social and Cultural Nexus</u>. Indiana University, Bloomington, Indiana: Ph.D. Thesis.
1977 "Australian Ritual as Performance: Structure of Communication in Men's Mimetic Dance Among Walbiri Aborigines of Central Australia." Paper presented at Conference on Culture and Communication, Temple University, March 1977. Unpublished ms. deposited at AIAS, Canberra.
1977-78 "Men as Women: Female Dance Symbolism in Walbiri Men's Rituals." <u>Dance Research Journal</u> 10(1): 14-22.
1980 "Australian Aboriginal Performances, Past and Present." <u>In</u> Souvenir Programme Book, The Festival of Asian Arts, Hong Kong.
1981 "Aboriginal Music and the Australian Institute of Aboriginal Studies." <u>The Australian Journal of Music Eduation</u> 28: 33-8.

Wolff, H.
1938 "Nachrichten von der 2 Frobenius--Expedition in Nordwest-Australien." [Communications from the Second Frobenius Expedition in North-West Australia, Collated from the Journals of H. Wolff.] <u>Paideuma bd.</u> 1: 89-99.

<u>Films</u>* (compiled by Michael Leigh)

Arnhem Land. Sydney: Australian Commonwealth Film Unit, 1950. 25 min., sd., col., 16mm. Credits: Director, Charles P. Mountford; Photographer, Peter Bassett-Smith; Music, Alfred F. Hill.

---

*The format adopted for FILMS follows that of Anglo-American Cataloguing Rules II. The editor's name is given only if different from that of the director. AIAS means Australian Institute of Aboriginal Studies (as in the Bibliography).

<u>R</u> at the end of a citation refers to the classification (cont.)

Arnhem Land Dances. Sydney: A. P. Elkin, 1950. 20 min., sil.,
    col., 16mm. Credits: Director, A. P. Elkin; Photographer,
    J. H. Buffum; Sound, T. Dale; Advisors, A. Capell, N. W. M.
    Macintosh, W. E. Harney.

Australian Aborigines: Songs and Dances. Sydney: Australian
    Instructional Films, 1952. 6½ min, sd., b.&w., col., 16mm.
    (Modern Social Studies Series, 14.) Credits: Director, A. P.
    Elkin.

Buffalo, Geese and Men. Great Britain: British Broadcasting Cor-
    poration, 1963. 30 min., sd, b.&w., 16mm. (Quest Under
    Capricorn, no. 3.) Credits: Director, David Attenborough;
    Photographers, Eugene Carr and Charles Lagus; Sound, Bob
    Saunders; Editor, Larry Toft.

Dance of the Buffalo Hunt. Sydney: Australian Commonwealth
    Film Unit for Department of Territories, 1963. 4½ min., sd.,
    b.&w., 16mm. Credits: Producer, Jack S. Allen; Director,
    Jack Rogers; Photographer, Richard Mace; Sound, Barry
    Bowden.

Dances at Aurukun. Sydney: Australian Commonwealth Film Unit
    for AIAS, 1964. 28 min., sd., col., 16mm. Credits: Direc-
    tor, Ian Dunlop; Photographers, E. Cranstone, R. Bailie-Mace,
    B. Hillyard; Sound, Frank White.

Djalambu. Canberra: AIAS, 1964. 55 min., sd., col., 16mm.
    Credits: Director, Cecil Holmes; Photographer, Bryce Hig-
    gins; Sound, Sandra Holmes. R.

The Djungguan at Yirrkala. Canberra: AIAS, 1966. 55 min., sd.,
    col., 16mm. Credits: Director, Roger Sandall; Photographers,
    Roger Sandall, Bill Grey; Sound, Ken Pounsett. R.

Emu Ritual at Ruguri. Canberra: AIAS, 1967. 35 min., sd.,
    col., 16mm. Credits: Director, Roger Sandall; Photographers,
    Roger Sandall, Lester Bartholomew; Sound, Jim Branford,
    Laurie Fitzgerald; Anthropological Advisor, T. D. Campbell,
    M. Barrett, N. Peterson. R.

---

restricted (because of its sacred-secret contents) given by the
AIAS on expert advice and following Aboriginal classification. Out
of respect for Aboriginal wishes, caution should be exercised in
selection of audiences for films so classified and they should not
be given open public screenings. Film lending libraries in Australia impose strict borrowing conditions on restricted films on advice from AIAS.

Five Aboriginal Dances from Cape York. Sydney: Australian Commonwealth Film Unit, 1966. 8 min., sd., col., 16mm. Credits: Director, Ian Dunlop; Photographers, E. Cranstone, B. Hillyard; Sound, Frank White; Editor, Richard Mitchell.

Goodbye Old Man. Canberra: AIAS, 1977. 70 min., sd., col., 16mm. Credits: Director, Photographer, David MacDougall; Sound, Bryan Butler; Anthropological Advisor, Maria Brandl.

Groote Eylandt Field Project: Aboriginal Dances, (8.3). Canberra: AIAS, 1969. 30 min., sd., col., 16mm. Credits: Directors, Alice Moyle, E. C. Snell; Photographers, Don Hauser, Rod Power; Sound, Graham Ivey; Editor, Nicholas Alexander; Advisor, Elphine Allen.

Groote Eylandt Field Project: Five Brolga Dances, (8.4). Canberra: AIAS, 1969. 15 min., sd., b.&w., 16mm. Credits: Directors, Alice Moyle, E. C. Snell; Photographers, Don Hauser, Rod Power; Sound, Graham Ivey; Editor, Nicholas Alexander; Advisor, Elphine Allen.

Gunabibi--An Aboriginal Fertility Cult. Canberra: AIAS, 1968. 55 min., sd., col., 16mm. Credits: Director, Photographer, Roger Sandall; Sound, Doug Grant; Anthropological Advisor, Nicolas Peterson. R.

The House-Opening. Canberra: AIAS, 1980. 45 min., sd., col., 16mm. (Aurukun Project Series.) Credits: Director, Sound, Judith MacDougall; Photographer, David MacDougall.

In Song and Dance. Sydney: Waratah Films for Australian Commonwealth Film Unit, 1964. 28 min., sd., b.&w., 16/35mm. Credits: Director, Lee Robinson; Photographers, Mike Molloy, Kerry Bown, Ross Nichols; Sound, John Heath; Editor, Don Saunders.

The Islanders. Sydney: Australian Commonwealth Film Unit, 1968. 22 min., sd., col., 16/35mm. Credits: Director, Cecil Holmes; Photographer, Raeburn Trindall; Sound, Julian Ellingsworth; Editor, Alan Harkness; Anthropological Advisor, Jeremy Beckett.

Larwari and Walkara. Canberra: AIAS, 1975. 45 min., sd., col., 16mm. Credits: Director, Photographer, Roger Sandall; Sound, Lauri Fitzgerald; Anthropological Advisor, Stephen Wild. R.

Lockhart Dance Festival. Canberra: AIAS, 1974. 30 min., sd., col., 16mm. Credits: Director, Curtis Levy; Photographer, Richard Tucker; Sound, Kevin Kerney, Editor, Ronda MacGregor; Anthropological Advisors, John Von Sturmer, Athol Chase.

The Lorrkun Ceremony. Canberra: AIAS, 1968. 40 min., sd., col., 16mm. Credits: Director, Cecil Holmes; Photographer, Andrew Fraser; Sound, Sandra Le Brun Holmes; Anthropological Advisor, Kenneth Maddock. R.

Lurugu (long version). Canberra: AIAS, 1974. 75 min., sd., col., 16mm. Credits: Director, Curtis Levy; Photographer, Geoffrey Burton; Sound, Fred Pickering; Editor, Stewart Young; Anthropological Advisor, John Von Sturmer. R.

Lurugu (short version). As above. 59 min. (not restricted).

Madarrpa Funeral at Gurka'wuy. Sydney: Film Australia, 1979. 88 min., sd., col., 16mm. Credits: Director, Ian Dunlop; Photographer, Dean Semmler; Sound, Rodney Simmons; Editors, Ian Dunlop, Gunnar Iassaacson; Anthropological Advisors, Dundiwuy Wanambi, Narritjin Maymurru, Warrpandiya Marawili, Dyambalipu Munungurr, Howard Morphy, Frances Morphy, Ngalawurr Munungurr, Nancy Williams.

The Maraian Ceremony. Sydney: University of Sydney, 1950. 35 min., sd., col., 16mm. Credits: Director, A. P. Elkin; Photographer, J. H. Buffum; Sound, T. Dale; Advisors, A. Capell, N. W. M. Macintosh, W. E. Harney. R.

The Maraian Ceremony of Croker. Canberra: AIAS, 1968. 49 min., sd., col., 16mm. Credits: Director, Roger Sandall; Photographer, Richard H. Tucker; Sound, Ken Pounsett; Editor, Rod Adamson; Anthropological Advisor, Nicolas Peterson. R.

Mourning for Mangatopi. Canberra: AIAS, 1975. 56 min., sd., col., 16mm. Credits: Director, Curtis Levy; Photographer, Oscar Scherl; Sound, Ric James; Editor, Ronda MacGregor; Anthropological Advisor, Maria Brandl.

The Mulga Seed Ceremony. Canberra: AIAS, 1968. 25 min., sd., col., 16mm. Credits: Director, Roger Sandall; Photographers, Roger Sandall, Lester Bartholomew; Anthropological Advisors, Nicholas Peterson, Jeremy Long. R.

Native Australia. Sydney: Brooke Nicholls for Kodak Australia, 1922. 12 min., sil., b.&w., 16mm. Credits: Director, Photographer, Brooke Nicholls.

Pintubi Revisit Yaru Yaru. Canberra: AIAS, 1971. 30 min., sd., col., 16mm. Credits: Director, Photographer, Roger Sandall; Sound, Laurie Fitzgerald; Anthropological Advisors, Ken Hanson, Jeremy Long. R.

Pintubi Revisit Yumari. Canberra: AIAS, 1969. 30 min., sd., col., 16mm. Credits: Director, Photographer, Roger Sandall;

Sound, Laurie Fitzgerald; Anthropological Advisors, Ken Hanson, Jeremy Long. R.

Pitjantjara Ritual at Areyonga. Canberra: AIAS, 1969. 25 min., sd., col., 16mm. Credits: Director, Photographer, Roger Sandall; Sound, Laurie Fitzgerald; Editor, Rod Adamson; Anthropological Advisor, Nicolas Peterson. R.

Primitive People--Australian Aborigines, Part III: The Corroboree. Great Britain: Gaumont British Instructional Films, Ltd., 1949. 7 min., sd., b.&w., 16mm. Credits: Director, Ralph Smart; Photographer, George Heath; Editor, Brian Salt. R.

Ubar Ceremony of Goulburn Island. Canberra: AIAS, 1964. 48 min., sd., col., 16mm. Credits: Director, Cecil Holmes; Photographer, Allan Keen; Sound, Sandra Le Brun Holmes; Editor, Rod Adamson; Anthropological Advisor, Jeremy Long. R.

Waiting for Harry. Canberra: AIAS, 1980. 57 min., sd., col., 16mm. Credits: Director, Photographer, Kim McKenzie; Sound, Peter Barker; Anthropological Advisor, Les Hiatt.

A Walbiri Fire Ceremony: Ngatjakula. Canberra: AIAS, 1977. 21 min., sd., col., 16mm. Credits: Director, Photographer, Roger Sandall; Sound, Laurie Fitzgerald; Editor, Kim McKenzie; Anthropological Advisor, Nicolas Peterson.

Walbiri Ritual at Gunadjari. Canberra: AIAS, 1968. 28 min., sd., col., 16mm. Credits: Director, Photographer, Roger Sandall; Sound, Ken Pounsett; Anthropological Advisor, Nicolas Peterson. R.

Walbiri Ritual at Ngama. Canberra: AIAS, 1966. 24 min., sd., col., 16mm. Credits: Director, Roger Sandall; Photographers, M. J. Barrett, R. Sandall; Sound, Jim Banford; Advisors, Nicolas Peterson, M. J. Barrett, T. K. Campbell. R.

Walya Ngamardiki: The Land My Mother. Sydney: Film Australia, 1978. 20 min., sd., col., 16/35mm. Credits: Director, David Roberts; Photographer, Andrew Fraser; Sound, Max Hensser, George Hart, Colin Waddy.

The Yabuduruwa Ceremony of the Roper River. Canberra: AIAS, 1965. 48 min., sd., col., 16mm. Credits: Director, Cecil Holmes; Photographer, Mike Molloy; Sound, Sandra Le Brun Holmes; Editor, Ron Adamson; Anthropological Advisor, A. P. Elkin. R.

Chapter Twenty-Eight

NATIVE AMERICAN DANCE AND DRAMA

Marcia Herndon

There are many possible approaches to compiling a bibliographic essay on American Indian dance and drama. Depending
on one's point of view, and how both "dance" and "drama" are
defined, one approach would be to simply state that there is no
Native American drama and very little dance, if these are defined
as activities set apart from usual and necessary human activities.
If the area of interest is kept to a narrow definition of dance, the
half-dozen Indians who have had careers in ballet could be cited--
particularly Maria Tallchief.

A focus on the available literature in the infant field of
dance ethnography would produce references to only three scholars
--Gertrude Prokosch Kurath, Joan Kealiinohomoku, and Jill Sweet.
The contributions of Kurath, both to dance ethnography and to the
study of American Indian music and dance, have been enormous.
Since her 1949 articles on Iroquois matriarchal dances, particularly
from the Seneca tribe (Kurath, 1949b, 1949c), she has contributed
a number of dictionary and encyclopedia entries (Kurath, 1949a,
1950a, for example), contributed a number of articles to anthropological sources, particularly Pueblo Indian ethnography, and to
folklore studies of expressive culture (see bibliography). In contrast, the contributions of Joann Kealiinohomoku focus on Hopi dance
and cross-cultural comparisons, as in her thoughtful article on
Hopi and Polynesian dance forms (1967). In addition, Kealiinohomoku
has been concerned with theoretical approaches more than ethnographic descriptions (see, e.g., 1978a, 1978b), and development of
methodology. Her article on field guides (1974a) remains one of the
most valuable sources for the study of ethnic dance in general.
Jill Sweet represents the latest generation of dance ethnographers,
specializes in American Indian dance, and promises to make valuable
contributions to the development of the field.

If anthropology or folklore is the area of focus for a bibliographical essay on American Indian dance and drama, there is a
much wider body of literature. However, anthropologists and

625

folklorists, as well as ethnomusicologists, lack the specific expertise which allows for precise ethnographic description, resulting in much less specificity of description of the dance movements themselves. These contributions will be discussed in some detail later.

Concentration on amateur interest in Indian dance would produce several publications containing informative, if often naive, descriptions of dances. Notable among these are such publications as The American Indian Hobbyist, The Folk Dancer, Folk Musician and Singer, American Indian Tradition, and The Folklorist. These and other, similar, publications often provide surprisingly good descriptions of dances, often sufficient to induce the reader to attempt their performance. Such articles, however, rarely even consider the place of dance or drama in the particular Indian society from which they come.

If attention is centered on American Indian authors who have written about their music, dance, or drama, the field is narrow indeed. In the nineteenth century, Washington Matthews wrote extensively on Navajo ceremonial activities (1887, 1889, 1894a, 1894b, 1896, 1897). He considered not only ceremonial contexts but also such areas as musical instruments, mythological background, and dance genres in his attempt to refute Letterman's assertion, in 1856, that Navajo singing was merely a "succession of grunts" (Matthews, 1896). His classic description and analysis of the "Navajo Night Chant" was published in 1902. In the 1940's, a Hopi, Nequatewa (1946) was published on a Hotevilla Flute Ceremony. More recently, Cherokees such as Charlotte Heth (see, e.g. Heth, 1973) and Marcia Herndon (see, e.g. Herndon 1971, 1979, 1980) and Choctaw David Draper have completed doctoral work in ethnomusicology and have begun to contribute to the published literature.

An historical approach predictably yields no dearth of printed commentaries, descriptions, and analyses of Indian dance and drama. For the most part, these represent the thoughts of European or Euro-American travelers, priests, settlers, missionaries, or adventurers. They reveal the boredom of the uninitiated outsider or, worse, the opinionated smugness of an author who is convinced that his or her dance and drama forms are superior to anything existing elsewhere.

Finally, a focus on topical approaches or surveys of the subject area yields several different kinds of contributions. Herndon's general text, Native American Music (1980), does not treat dance specifically, but incorporates the movement and dramatic aspects of Indian dance into her general presentations of ceremonial activities. In contrast, the CORD Research Annual, No. VI (1972), an issue that was devoted specifically to the anthropology of American Indian dance, both honors the contributions of Kurath to the field, and considers conceptual approaches, change, and dance as expressive behavior. Kurath (1953) and Nettl (1954, 1969) have provided useful schemes for dividing the vast range of styles of Indian music, dance, and expressive culture into geographic regions. In terms of specific area coverage, Charlotte Frisbie's Southwestern Indian Ritual Drama (1980) sets new standards for in-depth studies. Unfortunately, as yet it remains as both the prototype and sole example of such regional scholarship.

Given the diversity of possible approaches to preparing a bibliographic essay on Native American dance and drama, which approach should be taken? In addition, what kind of scholar should write it? For the present volume, the editor, due to various factors, eventually chose an American Indian author who is not a specialist in dance ethnography but an ethnomusicologist. Consequently, some effort will be made, in this chapter, to focus on the complexity and diversity of Native American dance and drama as they are perceived by Indians themselves.

What, then, is Native American dance and drama? To begin with, cultural multiplicity must be taken into consideration. There are almost 200 distinct tribal groups within the territory of the United States. In addition, distinction must be made between tribal and urban groups, between traditional and modern, and between Christian and non-Christian factions, as well as mixed-blood communities, and the various pan-Indian manifestations. Despite all of the differences there are some basic overall features of Native American dance and drama.

It is very important to know that the dance, medicine, philosophy, literature, drama, and graphic arts of American Indian peoples are inextricably bound together. In Native American thought, nature is viewed as sovereign, and human beings rank below nature, as objectifications of that which creates and governs the behavior of all existence. The imperatives of nature are articulated to people through dreams, visions, intuition, or transcendent experiences, and the transcendent is sought through music, dance, art, and drama. As McAllester has pointed out, "Music is a force in life, not a matter of taste" (1977:161). Native American dance and drama, then, are not separable entities, but are parts of life, expressed in an intuitive-experiential mode. Any art form is seen as an extension of nature:

> The cultural imperative toward the unity of art and Nature is evident ... in the use of multifunctional musical instruments, such as gourds; in the mimicry of animal cries typical of some styles; and in the imitation of everyday kinaesthetic mannerism, such as walking, in dance. (Herndon, 1980:86).

It is not surprising, then, that Indian dance and drama are utilitarian and are created simply as another functional and pragmatic activity. Although they are normal, rather than special,

activities, the arts are viewed as a medium of change or transformation. The efforts of specialists bring about several different kinds
of transformations, including the healing of illness, the lessening of
stress, communication with the Spirit World, or an increase in competence or well-being. Thus, American Indian dance, theatrical forms,
music, and art transcend "art for art's sake," and are not necessarily concerned with pleasing, diverting or entertaining a group of
people.

As McAllester points out, there is little descriptive vocabulary,
in the technical sense, and performances are not assessed in terms
of a good, versus a bad, performance (1977:162). Instead, a performance is a matter of efficacy and of participation through action:

> In Native American culture, no artwork is complete without
> the active and committed participation of the audience. Ac-
> tive involvement demands that the audience participate--
> whether actively or passively--rather than judge ... the
> proper emotional vantage point for the audience is in the
> "heat of the flame," rather than apart from it. No distance
> of perspective is desirable. (Herndon, 1980:89).

American Indian art forms are subjective, pragmatic, and directly reflective of cultural values and the way in which Indians
view themselves and their place in the universe of time, space, and
motion. This has a direct effect upon the nature of Indian dance:

> With certain dramatic exceptions, Native American dance is
> traditionally earth-bound and earth-oriented. Dance is flat-
> footed. Accented movements tend to be earth-directed in
> body momentum and foot motion. Postures are walking or
> stooped with muscle tension either body centered or earth
> focused. These things are neither arbitrary nor accidental.
> They are inherent reflections of Native American cultural
> values. The dance incorporates and expresses the mother-
> earth and certain egalitarian social relationships.
>   It is significant that the older male or man-dominated
> forms of the Plains, and of the Navajo and Hopi, too, for
> example, are the most earth-bound, and make up a conserva-
> tive element in both the dance and general cultures. Exam-
> ples are the Navajo ye'iibicheii, Hopikachina and bean dances,
> and Plains warrior and chiefs dances. On the other hand,
> those partner and social dances in which women have a role
> equal to that of the men (or even dominating as in selecting
> their partners) tend to have less flat-footed and more bouncy
> steps. Examples might include the Navajo squaw dances,
> Hopi butterfly dance, and Plains rabbit and two-step dances.
>   All of this contrasts directly with that epitome of classi-
> cal dance of dominant Euro-American culture, the ballet.
> The ballet is heaven-oriented, aspiring constantly to get
> away from the earth through toe-tip steps, stretched body

postures, and high flying leaps. Again, such forms are
not accidental. They reflect a vertically conceptualizing
culture and a society where people strive to rise "above"
their circumstances or each other. (Huenemann, 1978:202).

As Kealiinohomoku points out, American Indian dance is the
affective expression of strongly held cultural values:

> ... dance crystallizes strongly held ideational aspects of a
> culture into tangible expressions, and galvanizes peoples'
> thoughts into emotion. The total dance event, and the spe-
> cific phenomenon likewise, is a transforming mechanism that
> makes religious thought become religious behavior. (Keali-
> inohomoku, 1977:148).

Since the dance event is a transforming mechanism, it is not
unreasonable to assume that dance forms reflect cultural change,
through time. That is, as the pervasive influence of Euro-American
thought and culture is exerted on Native American cultures, newer
dance forms will reflect the degree and extent of culture change
present in Native American cultures. The logical area in which to
explore this proposition is the pan-Indian pow-wow.

Although the inception of the pow-wow is obscure, Oklahoma
is recognized as the origin-point of Pan-Indianism in general (Petrullo, 1934; Newcomb, 1955; Howard, 1955, 1965b, 1983). Where
formerly there were many distinct cultures and world views, one
effect of domination by "White" culture has been the development
of a generalized pantribal "Indian" culture, which is a mixture of
a number of diverse elements:

> The principal manifestations of Pan-Indianism that involve
> music and dance are the intertribal pow-wow in the secular
> sphere and peyotism in the religious sphere. In the pow-
> wow the principal dance forms are a modified version of the
> Hethuskha or War dance (also known as Omaha dance, Grass
> dance, Hot dance and Wolf dance in various tribal settings),
> which has been stripped of most of its warrior society and
> religious features and has been opened to participation by
> both sexes; the Round dance; and, since 1970, the Gourd
> dance. It may be followed, depending upon the locale, by
> the Leading or Stomp dance, the Forty-nine dance, or the
> Owl dance as an after-pow-wow feature. All of these dance
> forms have an accompanying repertoire of music as does the
> Peyote religion. (Howard, 1983:71).

There have been several descriptions of pow-wow dances,
notably those by James H. Howard (1955, 1965a, 1965b, 1976a, 1976b,
1983), and William W. Newcomb, Jr. (1955). Costumes have received
attention from Norman Feder (1957, 1958), and particular pow-wow
dancers have received media coverage (e.g., Debnam, 1980).

Theoretical considerations have been relatively slow in coming for the pow-wow, but Samuel Corrigan's discussion of Canadian Plains pow-wows in the framework of cultural integration (1970) and J. Anthony Paredes' discussion of synthesis and change in Eastern Creek Indian expressive culture are welcome exceptions. It is Lynn Huenemann, however, who captures the essence, for Indians, of the pow-wow dance forms. As mentioned above, traditional Native American dance forms tend to be earth-bound and earth-oriented. In contrast,

> Plains pow-wow dancing has seen the rise ... of a form that tends toward vertical (upward) orientation. Its steps are on the toes; its posture is often tall and extended. This is the modern "fancy" dance which certainly is less earth-bound than the "traditional" and "straight" dances. Similar comments could be made about the ladies fancy "shawl" dance. Argument could [also] be made that there has been an increase in the number of dances where women have roles of equal prominence with men. (Huenemann, 1978: 202).

It might well be maintained that, given the strong connection between religion and dance, dance is generally resistant to change through time and is retained as an area in which cultural identity can be maintained and expressed. Since the pow-wow is a relatively recent phenomenon, however, it reflects not only cultural maintenance but also cultural adaptations. Since the advent of a more vertical orientation in pow-wow dance types, there has also been a corresponding resurgence of more traditional dance types, styles, costumes, and associated behavior. As Huenemann points out,

> More and more younger dancers are dancing "traditional" or "straight" styles, while certain tribes have maintained a conscious preference for traditional styles over fancy styles all along. Likewise, certain conservative traits have continued to survive even in new pow-wow developments. One significant social behavior is the performance ... custom in which lady singers enter a song after the men start the song. This practice does not seem to be weakened even by the few female drum (singing) groups that have existed from time to time ... both the form and the function of Plains music and dance are continually evolving in subtle ways to reflect and fulfill the social ... needs, the cultural values, and the contemporary aesthetic of the people. (Huenemann, 1978:203).

The evolution of Pan-Indian music, dance, and drama in the realm of the sacred is not a simple matter to discuss. Within the pow-wow tradition, for example, some performances would have to be characterized as basically religious in nature. More clearly religious is the Native American Church, often called the "Peyote

Cult," or "Peyote religion" in the literature. The use of the non-addictive but hallucinogenic peyote cactus in Native American Church ceremonies accounts for the degree of interest exhibited by more sensational anthropological popularizers. More restrained considerations can be found in La Barre (1969), Slotkin (1975), Hertzberg (1971), Deloria (1973), and Herndon (1980). Although the ceremonies of the Native American Church cannot really be said to contain dance elements, they do include dramatic elements. In addition, the Native American Church, like the Indian Shakerism in the Northwestern United States, combine traditional and particular beliefs with elements borrowed from Christianity. Indeed, it is the long and uneasy relationship between Christian missionaries and Indians that accounts for most changes in traditional dance and drama. Most often, the main pressure by missionaries was for Indians to abandon their customary dance forms.

The Native American Church, which spread widely among Indian tribes just before the turn of the century, replaced most earlier forms. There have been, since White contact, a number of movements, variously labeled by scholars as "Nativistic movements," "charismatic movements," "revitalization movements," "reform movements," or "religious revivals." Some of these movements, on which data are available are: the Handsome Lake Case (Seneca, 1799-1815); the Delaware Prophet (1762-1765); the Shawnee Prophet (1805-1814); the Ghost Dance (1888-1896), and the Native American Church.

The Ghost Dance is perhaps the best known of these movements. James Mooney, an ethnographer, produced the most comprehensive report (1896). Unfortunately, his account, while sympathetic and understanding, is not explicit in its descriptions of the dance itself:

> ... the dance ... with its scenes of intense excitement, spasmodic actions, and physical exhaustion even to unconsciousness ... always accompanied religious upheavals (Mooney, 1896:783).

The message of the Ghost Dance was quite simple. By following the rules of the ceremony a time would come when all Indians, both living and dead, would be reunited on a regenerated earth, free from stress, enemies, disease, and misery. Believing, people danced. Their dancing was not understood by nervous federal troops, and as a result, several groups of Indian Ghost Dancers were shot down during their ceremonies, most notably in the encounter at Wounded Knee, South Dakota on December 22, 1890. For a dominated people, then, dancing is not only integrated into life, but also may bring about death.

While it might seem logical, given the development of film and recording technologies as well as the introduction of dance notation systems, to assume that Pan-Indian dance and drama would receive intense scholarly attention, this has not thus far been the case. The influence of the assumption, by folklorists and early ethnographers, that only "aboriginal" forms were truly worthy of study seems to have prevailed in this area as well. Since many ceremonial activities appear to be falling into disuse, for a number of reasons, scholarly concentration on traditional dance and drama is well justified.

By far, the bulk of accounts of traditional Indian music, dance, art, and ceremonial activities focus on the tribal groups of the Southwestern United States. Of these, coverage of the Navajo is most extensive. Beginning with the publications of Washington Matthews (1887, 1889, 1894a, 1894b, 1896, 1897), and continuing through the work of Father Berard Haile (1938, 1940, 1946, 1950, 1957), work has focused on the complex of Navajo ceremonial practices, or "ways," which include, but are not limited to, the following:

> Blessingway
> Holyway chant ceremonial complexes
>   Shooting chant subgroup
>   Shootingways
>   Red Antway
>   Big Starway
>   Hailway
>   Waterway
>   Mountain chant subgroup
>   Mountaintopways
>   Beautyways (male and female)
>   Excessways
>   Mothways
>   God-impersonators subgroup
>   Nightway
>   Big Godway
>   Plumeway
>   Coyoteway
>   Dogway
>   Ravenway
>   Wind chant subgroup
>   Navajo Windway
>   Chiricahua Apache Windway
>   Handtremblingway
>   Eagle Trapping subgroup
>   Eagleway
>   Beadway
> Ghostway ceremonial complexes
>   Ghostways subgroup
>   Upward-reachingway
>   Red Antway (Ghostway form)
>   Big Starway (Ghostway form)

Shootingways (Ghostway form)
Handtremblingway (Ghostway form)
Reared-in-Earthway (Ghostway form)
Enemyway
Lifeway
Flintways
Shootingway (Lifeway form)
Handtremblingway (Lifeway form).

Leland Wyman (1957, 1965, 1972), Haile (see references above), and Wyman and Clyde Kluckhohn (1938) have all made valuable contributions to the understanding of Navajo classification of their song ceremonials. In particular, Father Haile and Maude Oakes' account of Beautyway (1957) includes a helpful bibliography of Navajo music, dance, and ceremonial practice.

Myths underlying and explaining various Navajo chantways have been examined by Katherine Spencer (1957). Sensitive, probing accounts of various aspects of specific Navajo chantways have been done by David McAllester (1949, 1952, 1954, 1955, 1956a, 1956b, 1956c, 1961, 1962, 1968, 1969, 1970, 1971a, 1971b, 1971c, 1972), and Charlotte Frisbie (1967, 1968, 1970). Working in collaboration, Frisbie and McAllester have produced a valuable "autobiography" of Frank Mitchell, a Navajo Blessingway singer (1978).

For the nearby Pueblo tribes, Gertrude Kurath and Antonio Garcia have produced Music and Dance of the Tewa Pueblos (1969), a complex consideration of ceremonial ecology, choreographic and musical patterns, and symbolic pageantry which is intended to "lead to a deeper esthetic and cultural understanding of the Tewa people" (1969:1). There have also been numerous articles in El Palacio, some of which are anonymous, concerning Pueblo dances. Donald N. Brown has concerned himself with Pueblo dance costumes (1962) and Taos dance (1961). George Herzog compared Pueblo and Pima musical styles (1936), while Kurath has provided numerous articles on various aspects of Pueblo dance styles. For the Hopi, Kealiinohomoku has done cross-cultural comparisons (1967), functional pieces on social dance events (1978a), and work on the religious character of Hopi dance (1978b).

Charlotte Frisbie's Southwestern Indian Ritual Drama (1980), represents the "state of the art" in Southwestern Indian scholarship. It contains tightly focused pieces by Frisbie on the Navajo house blessing ceremony, by McAllester on Shootingway, by Haefer on the Papago Skipping Dance, by Hinton on Havasupai vocables, by Farrer on the Mescalero Apache girls' puberty rites, by Brown on the Picuris Deer Dance, by Kealiinohomoku on Hopi public representational drama, and by Tedlock on Zuni kachina songs. Other contributions, by Kurath and Roberts, are more general in nature. The important contribution of the book, however, in addition to the articles themselves and a useful bibliography, is the distillation, by

Frisbie, of discussions on Southwestern ritual drama which delineates the nature of ritual drama and makes regional characterizations.
This book is an invaluable source of detail, theoretical stimulation,
and sensitive presentation.

For the most part, perceptive accounts of the dance, drama,
and ceremonial activities of American Indian tribes in the remainder
of North America are lacking. Although a selection of available publications has been compiled in this bibliography, the reader will note
that many articles and books have been hampered by their authors'
training, cultural background, and theoretical bent. For example,
training in music, but not dance, tends to produce publications
which focus on the singing or the musical instruments and ignores
the dance itself. Training in anthropology, history, sociology, or
folklore, but not in music, produces contextual publications which
usually ignore or minimize the presence of both music and movement.
Cultural bias is perhaps most evident in Huenemann's fine resource
text, Songs and Dances of Native America (1978). A faculty member at Navajo Community College, Huenemann's emphasis on Navajo
music and dance is quite evident in the amount and prominence of
Navajo, versus other tribal, coverage.

Perhaps the most important single factor hampering the study
of Native American dance and drama is their interconnection with religion. Most study has been undertaken by outsiders with various
kinds and degrees of training and interest. Significantly, most of
these outsiders have been members of the dominant White culture;
they have come in droves to examine aspects of Indian life, behavior,
and thought as if Indians were objects. Consequently, as is true of
all dominated populations, Indian groups have tended to react to
scholars with suspicion and to withhold information or to alter it in
some way. Thus, descriptions of Indian dances must be taken as
partial, at best. It is often the case that especially religious ceremonies are totally restricted to Indian participation; sometimes, both
a public and a private version of a ceremony will be held, with the
public celebration hiding the existence of the private one.

In conclusion, it can be said that much has been written
about Native American dance, music, drama, and ceremony, but
little is really known. False impressions abound, and much remains
to be accomplished before it can be said that scholarship has grasped
the essence of Indian dance or drama. The interdisciplinary, intercultural nature of this area of study makes the task all the more
formidable. Even so, a determined individual can benefit greatly
from a careful, somewhat skeptical, excursion into the available literature. The following bibliography has been prepared with that
possibility in mind.

Aberle, David F.
1966 The Peyote Religion Among the Navajo. Chicago: Aldine.
1967 "The Navajo Singer's 'Fee': Payment or Prestation?" in
Studies in Southwestern Ethnolinguistics. Dell Hymes and
W. Bittle, eds. The Hague: Mouton.

Abrahams, Roger and George Foss
1968 Anglo-American Folksong Style. Englewood Cliffs, New
Jersey: Prentice-Hall.

Adair, James
1775 The History of the American Indians, particularly those
Nations Adjoining to the Mississippi, East and West Florida,
Georgia, South and North Carolina, and Virginia. London:
Edward and Charles Dilly.

Alexander, H. B.
1929 "Field Notes at Jemez." El Palacio, 27:98-101.

Altman, G. J.
1946-7 "Yaqui Easter Play of Guadalupe, Arizona." Masterkey,
20:181-9; 21:19-23; 67-72.

American Anthropological Association
1954 American Anthropologist, Southwest Issue. E. W. Haury,
ed. Vol. 56(4):I.

Anderson, Frank G.
1955 "The Pueblos Kachina Cult: A Historical Reconstruction."
Southwest Journal of Anthropology, 11:404-19.

Anonymous
1823 "The Busk." Niles' Weekly Register, November 15(25):
169.
1827a "Dancing School Among the Indians." New York Mirror,
March 21(4):285-6.
1827b "Indian War Dance." North American Review, October
27(1):190.
1837 "The Pole Cat, or Shell Dance." Southern Literary Messenger, June (3):390-1.
1844 "Eagle Dance." Army and Navy Chronicle, May 2(3):553.
1847 "An Indian Dance." Dwight's American Magazine,
August 13(3):520.
1849 "The Ancient Cherokee Traditions and Religious Rites."
American Quarterly Register and Magazine, December
3:444-50.
1879 Report: United States Geographical Survey, Vol. 7:334-6.
1898 "Music of the Zuni Indians of New Mexico." Musical
Courier, 37:1.
1928a "The Animal Dance at San Ildefonso." El Palacio, 24:
119-22.

1928b "Santo Domingo and San Felipe." El Palacio, 24:427-8;
       435.
1929   "The Green Corn Ceremony." El Palacio, 27:48-50.
1934   "Navajo Goat Song." Masterkey, 8:188.
1952   "Masked Kachinas in Spanish Times." Masterkey, 26:
       17-20.
1956   "Program of the 11th Annual Pawnee Indian Homecoming."
       July 12-15, Pawnee, Oklahoma.
1958   "Cochiti Parrot Dance." American Indian Hobbyist,
       4(7-8):78-9.
1962   Program of the 11th Annual Tulsa Pow-wow. July 27-9,
       Tulsa, Oklahoma.
1965   "Internal Revenue Service Rules Navajo Sings' Medical
       Expense." Indian Voices, April:5-6.
1967   "Our Lady of Guadalupe Day in Taos." El Palacio, 74:4,
       34.
1972   "Facts About the Papago Indian Reservation and the
       Papago People." Sells: Papago Tribal Office.

Apel, Willi
1969   Harvard Dictionary of Music, 2nd Edition. Cambridge,
       Massachusetts: The Belknap Press of Harvard University
       Press.

Arnold, Charlotte
1928   "The Dance at Nambe." El Palacio, 24:26-8.

Astrov, Margot
1950   "The Concept of Motion as the Psychological Leitmotif of
       Navajo Life and Literature." Journal of American Folklore,
       63(247):45-56.

Auden, W. H.
1950   Collected Shorter Poems, 1930-1944. London: Faber
       and Faber.
1956   The Age of Anxiety, A Baroque Ecologue. London:
       Faber and Faber.
1966   Marginalia. Cambridge, Massachusetts: Ibex.

Austin, Mary
1930   "American Indian Dance Drama." Yale Review (Battle-
       boro) 29:732-45.

Bahr, Donald, Juan Gregorio, David Lopez, and Albert Alvarez
1974   Piman Shamanism and Staying Sickness (Ka:cim Mumkidag).
       Tucson: University of Arizona Press.

Bahti, Tom
1970   Southwestern Indian Ceremonials. Las Vegas, Nevada:
       K. C. Publications.

Bailey, Florence M.
1924 "Some Plays and Dances of the Taos Indians." Journal,
American Museum of Natural History, 24:86-95.

Bailey, Virginia
1938 "Indian Music of the Southwest." El Palacio, 44:1-3.

Baker, Theodor
1882 Uber die Musik der nordamerikanischen Wilden. Leipzig
Braithopf & Hartel. English translation: On the Music of
the North American Indians. Ann Buckley, trans. Buren,
The Netherlands: Knuf. 1976.

Bakkegard, B. M.
1960 "Music in Arizona Before 1912." Journal of Research in
Music Education, 8(2):67-74.

Bakkegard, B. M. and E. A. Morris
1961 "Seventh Century Flutes from Arizona." Ethnomusicology,
5(3):134-86.

Balikei, Ansen
1970 The Netsilik Eskimo. Garden City, New York: Natural
History Press.

Ballard, K.
1970 The American Indian Sings. Book 1. Santa Fe: Ballard Music Company.

Bancroft, Hubert Howe
1875 "Manner of Singing and Dancing." in The Native Races
of the Pacific States of North America, Vol. III. New
York: D. Appleton and Company.

Bandelier, Aldred F.
1890 "Final Report: Investigations Among the Indians of the
Southwestern United States." Papers of the Archaeological
Institute of America, Vol. 3:67-9; 151-2; 307-8.

Barbeau, Marius
1951 "The Dragon Myths and Ritual Songs of the Iroquoians."
Journal of the International Folk Music Council, 3:81-5.
1958 Medicine Men of the North Pacific Coast. Bulletin 152.
Ottawa: National Museum of Man of the National Museum
of Canada.

Barker, G. C.
1957a "The Yaqui Easter Ceremony at Hernosillo." Western
Folklore, 16:256-62.
1957b "Some Aspects of Penitential Processions in Spain and

the American Southwest." Journal of American Folklore, 70:137-42.
1958 "Some Functions of Catholic Processions in Pueblo and Yaqui Culture Change." American Anthropologist, 60:445-9.

Barrett, S. A.
1911 "The Dream Dance of the Chippewa and Menominee Indians of Northern Wisconsin." Bulletin of the Milwaukee Public Museum, 1(2):250-415.

Bartlett, Charles R.
1955 "Some Seneca Songs from Tonawanda Reservation." Bulletin of the New York State Archaeological Association, 5:8-16.

Bartoli, J. F.
1955 "The Apache 'Devil Dance.'" Musical Courier, 152(8): 8-10.

Bartram, William
1791 Travels Through North and South Carolina, Georgia, East and West Florida, the Cherokee Country, The Extensive Territories of the Muscogulges, or Creek Confederacy, and the Country of the Choctaws. James and Johnson, Philadelphia. Reprinted by the Dover Press, 1928.

Basso, K.
1973 "Southwestern Ethnology: A Critical Review." in Annual Review of Anthropology, No. 2. B. Siegel, ed. Palo Alto, California: Annual Reviews, Inc.

Baxter, R. H.
1895 "The Moqui Snake Dance." American Antiquarian (and Oriental Journal), 17:205-7.

Beauchamp, William M.
1891 "Iroquois Notes." Journal of American Folklore, 4:39-46; 5(1892):223-9.
1893 "Notes on Onondaga Dances." Journal of American Folklore, 6:181-4.
1895a "Onondaga Notes." Journal of American Folklore, 8: 209-16.
1895b "Notes on the Onondaga Dances." Journal of American Folklore, 6:181-4.
1907 "Civil Religious and Scouting Councils and Ceremonies of Adoption of the New York Indians." New York State Museum Bulletin 113.

Becker, D. M.
1954 "Music of the Papago." Smoke Signals, 6(5):2-4.

Beckwith, M. W.
1906 "Dance Forms of the Moqui and Kwakiutl Indians." Proceedings of International Congress of Americanists, 15(2): 79-114.

Bell, Clive
1914 Art. London: Chatto and Windus.

Benedict, Ruth
1931 Tales of the Cochiti Indians. Bureau of American Ethnology, Bulletin 98. Washington, D.C.: U.S. Government Printing Office.
1938 "Comments." in General Anthropology. Franz Boas, ed. Boston: D. C. Heath and Company.
1959 "They Dance for Rain in Zuni." in An Anthropologist at Work, M. Mead, ed. Boston: Houghton-Mifflin Company.

Bennett, John W.
1944 "The Development of Ethnological Theory as Illustrated by Studies of the Plains Sun Dance." American Anthropologist, 46:162-82.

Black, R. A.
1964 "A Content-Analysis of Eighty-one Hopi Indian Chants." Unpublished Ph.D. Dissertation: Indiana University.
1965 "Ethnomusicology Research in the American Southwest." Paper presented at Annual Meeting of Society for Ethnomusicology, Albuquerque, New Mexico.
1966 "Hopi Rabbit-hunt Chants: A Ritualized Language." in Essays on the Verbal and Visual Arts. J. Helm, ed. American Ethnological Society Proceedings. The Hague: Mouton.

Bloomfield, Leonard
1962 The Menomini Language. New Haven, Connecticut: Yale University Press.

Boas, Franz
1895 "Social Organization and Secret Societies of the Kwakiutl." Annual Report, Bureau of American Ethnology, for 1895. Washington, D.C.: The Smithsonian Institution.
1921 "Ethnology of the Kwakiutl." Bureau of American Ethnology, 35th Annual Report, 1913, Vol. 35(2). Washington, D.C.: The Smithsonian Institution.
1927 Primitive Art. Cambridge, Massachusetts: Harvard University Press.
1930 Religion of the Kwakiutl Indians. New York: Columbia University Press.
1938 "Literature, Music, and Dance." in General Anthropology. Franz Boas, ed. Boston: D. C. Heath and Company.

1966 Kwakiutl Ethnography. Helen Codere, ed. Chicago: University of Chicago Press.

Boekelman, H. J.
1936 "Shell Trumpet from Arizona." American Antiquity, 2:27-31.

Bogert, C. M.
1942 "The Hopi Snake Dance." Natural History, 47:276-83.

Bolton, Herbert
1930 Anza's California Expedition. Berkeley: University of California Press.

Boulton, L.
1941 "Recent Recordings in Southwestern Music." Teacher's National Association Proceedings (1940), Series 35:128-31.
1968 "La musique rituelle des Indiens de l'Amerique du Sud-Ouest." in Encyclopedie de musiques sacress, Vol. 1. J. Porte, ed. Paris: Labergeria.

Bourke, J. G.
1884 The Snake-Dance of the Moquis of Arizona. New York: Charles Scribner's Sons.
1885 "The Urine Dance of the Zunis." Proceedings of American Association for Advancement of Science, 34:400-04.
1888 "Compilation of Notes and Memoranda Bearing upon the Use of Human Ordure and Human Urine in Rites of a Religious or Semi-religious Character Among Various Nations." Washington, D.C.
1895 "The Snake Ceremonials at Walpi." American Anthropologist, 8:192-6.

Boyle, David
1898a "Mid-Winter Festival." Ontario Education Department Archaeological Report (Toronto):82-91.
1898b "Iroquois Music." Ontario Archaeological Museum Report, 143-56.
1899 "The Pagan Iroquois." in Annual Archaeological Report, 1898, being part of the Appendix to the Report of the Minister of Education, Ontario, Toronto, 1899. 54-143; 166-8.
1900 "Music of the Pagan Iroquois." in Annual Archaeological Report, 1899, being part of the Appendix to the Report of the Minister of Education, Ontario, Toronto, 1900. 166-8.

Briegleb, A. (Compiler)
1971 Director of Ethnomusicological Sound Recordings Collections in the United States and Canada. Special Series in Ethnomusicology, No. 2. Middletown: Wesleyan University Press.

Brown, D. N.
1959 "The Dance of Taos Pueblo." Unpublished Senior Honors
Thesis: Harvard University.
1960 "Taos Dance Classification." El Palacio, 67(6):203-9.
1961 "The Development of Taos Dance." Ethnomusicology,
5(1):33-41.
1962 Masks, Mantas, and Moccasins: Dance Costumes of the
Pueblo Indians. Colorado Springs: Taylor Museum.
1963 "Museums and Dance Ethnology." in "Dance Ethnology,
Dance Education and the Public--A Symposium Organized
by G. P. Kurath." Ethnomusicology, 7(3):239-43.
1967 "Distribution of Sound Instruments in the Prehistoric
Southwestern United States." Ethnomusicology, 11(1):
71-90.
1968 "Review of Two Indian House Records: Round Dance
Songs of Taos Pueblo." Ethnomusicology, 12(2):304-5;
211.
1971 "Ethnomusicology and the Prehistoric Southwest." Ethnomusicology, 15(3):363-78.
1974 "Evidence for Dance from the Prehistoric Southwest."
CORD Research Annual, 6:263-84.
1976 "The Dance of Taos Pueblos." CORD Research Annual,
7:182-272.

Brown, H.
1906 "A Pima-Maricopa Ceremony." American Anthropologist,
8:689-90.

Brown, John Mason
1950 "A Trip to the Northwest in 1861." Filson Club Historical Quarterly, XXIV:103-36.

Brown, Mary E.
1892 "Chief-making Among the Passamauoddy Indians."
Journal of American Folklore, 5:57-89.

Buckland, A. W.
1891 "The Indian Ghost Dance." Theological Monthly,
5:122-6.

Bullough, E.
1957 Aesthetics. London: Bowes and Bowes.

Bunzel, R.
1932 Introduction to Zuni Ceremonialism. 47th Annual Report,
Bureau of American Ethnology, No. 47. Washington, D.C.:
U.S. Government Printing Office.

Burford, C. C.
1948 "Sauk and Fox Ceremonials Attract Large Attendance and
Widespread Interest." Journal of the Illinois State Archaeological Society, 5(3):39-41.

Burton, Frederick R.
1902 "Hiawatha, the Indian Musical Play." Concert-Goer, 208:8-9.

Bushnell, David I.
1909 "Dances and Music." in The Choctaws of Bayou Lacomb St. Tammany Parish, Louisiana, Bulletin 48. Washington, D.C.: U.S. Government Printing Office.

Buttree, Julia M.
1930 The Rhythm of the Redman. New York: A. S. Barnes and Company.

Cadman, Charles Wakefield
1909 "The Decadence of the Indian Pow-Wow. Tribal Music and Something About It." Musical Courier, 59(23):59-60.

Capron, L.
1953 The Medicine Bundles of the Florida Seminole and the Green Corn Dance. Anthropological Papers, 35, Bureau of American Ethnology Bulletin, No. 151. Washington, D.C.: U.S. Government Printing Office.

Carter, John G.
1938 The Northern Arapaho Flat Pipe and the Ceremony of Covering the Pipe. Anthropological Papers 2, Bureau of American Ethnology, Bulletin 119. Washington, D.C.: U.S. Government Printing Office.

Castetter, Edward F. and Willis H. Bell
1942 Pima and Papago Indian Agriculture. Albuquerque: University of New Mexico Press.

Casual (Anonymous?)
1898 "Ceremonial Dances of the American Indians." Nature, 58:490-1.

Catlin, George
1841 Illustrations of the Manners, Customs and Conditions of the North American Indian. New York: n.p.

Caudwell, Christopher
1965 Poetry's Dream Work, A Modern Book of Esthetics. Melvin Rader, ed. New York: Holt, Rinehart and Winston.

Cazeneuve, J.
1955 "Some Observations on Zuni Shalako." El Palacio, 62:347-56.

Chafe, Wallace L.
1961 Seneca Thanksgiving Rituals. BAE Bulletin 183. Washington, D.C.: The Smithsonian Institution.

Chapman, Date M. and O. S. Galseth
1925 "Sun Basket Dance at Santa Clara." El Palacio,
18:45-6.

Chapman, J. M.
1927 "The Shalako Ceremony at Zuni." El Palacio, 23:622-7.

Charlevoix, Pierra F. X.
1744 "Histoire et description generals de la Nouvell-France"
avec le Journal d'un voyage fait par ordre du roi dans
l'Amerique Septentrionnale. Paris. 6 Vols. Vol. 3.

Chauvenet, B.
1929 "A Zuni Shalako." El Palacio, 27:299-306.

Chesky, Jane
1941 "Indian Music of the Southeast." Kiva, 7:9-12.
1943 "The Nature and Function of Papago Music." Unpublished M.A. Thesis: The University of Arizona.

Ch'iao, C.
1971 Continuation of Tradition in Navajo Society. Academia
Sinica, Monograph Series B., No. 3. Taipei: Institute
of Ethnology.

Clark, L. H.
1966 They Sang for Horses: Impact of the Horse on Navajo
and Apache Folklore. Tucson: University of Arizona.

Clements, F.
1931 "Plains Indian Tribal Correlations with Sun Dance Data."
American Anthropologist, 33:216-27.
1943 "The Sun Dance of the Plains Indians." American
Indigena, 3(4):359-64.

Collaer, P. (Editor)
1973 Music of the Americas. New York: Praeger Publishers.

Collier, Donald
1943 "The Sun Dance of the Plains Indians." American Indigena, 3(4):359-64.

Collier, F. B. M.
1936 "Ojibwa Dances." Dancing Times, London, April:12-15.

Collier, John
1972 American Indian Ceremonial Dances: Navajo, Pueblo,
Apache. New York: Crown Publishers.

Collins, J. J.
1968 "A Descriptive Introduction to the Taos Peyote Ceremony." Ethnology, 7:427-49.

Colton, H. S. and E. Nequatewa
   1933 "The Ladder Dance." Museum Notes, Museum of Northern Arizona, 5:4-12.

Committee on Research in Dance
   1974 "New Dimensions in Dance Research: Anthropology and
   Dance--The American Indian." CORD Research Annual, 6.

Cone, Edward
   1968 Musical Form and Musical Performance. New York:
   W. W. Norton.

Conklin, Harold C., and William C. Sturtevant
   1953 "Seneca Indian Singing Tools at the Coldspring Long-
   House: Musical Instruments of the Modern Iroquois."
   Proceedings of American Philosophical Society, 97:262-90.

Converse, Harriet M.
   1891 "Iroquois Green Corn Festival of 1890." Journal of
   American Folklore, 4:72-8.
   1895 "The Seneca New Year Ceremony and Other Customs."
   in Indian Notes, Museum of the American Indian: Heye
   Foundation.

Coomaraswami, A. K.
   1934 The Transformation of Nature in Art. New York: Dover.

Cornplanter, Jesse
   1903 Iroquois Indian Games and Dances. Chicago: F. Starr.

Corrigan, Samuel W.
   1970. "The Plains Indian Pow-Wow: Cultural Integration in
   Manitoba and Saskatchewan." Anthropologica, (n.s.),
   12(2):253-77.

Coze, Paul
   1952 "Of Clowns and Mudheads." Arizona Highways, 28(8):
   18-29.

Crawford, D. E.
   1967 "The Jesuit Relations and Allied Documents: Early
   Sources for an Ethnography of Music Among American
   Indians." Ethnomusicology, 11(2):199-206.

Cringan, Alexander T.
   1899a "Pagan Dance Songs of the Iroquois." in Archaeological
   Report, Appendix to the Report of the Minister of Education, Ontario, Toronto. 166-89.
   1899b "Iroquois Music." in Annual Archaeological Report, 1898:
   being part of the Appendix to the Report of the Minister
   of Education, Ontario, Toronto, 1899. 143-56.

1900a "Pagan Dance Songs of the Iroquois." in Annual Ar-
       chaeological Report, 1899, being part of the Appendix to
       the Report of the Minister of Education, Ontario, Toronto,
       1900. 168-89.
1900b "Traditional Songs of the Iroquois Indians." Musical
       Times, 41:114.
1903   "Iroquois Folk Songs." in Annual Archaeological Report,
       1902, being part of the Appendix to the Report of the
       Minister of Education, Ontario, Toronto, 1903. 137-52.
1906   "Indian Music." in Annual Archaeological Report, 1905,
       being part of the Appendix to the Report of the Minister
       of Education, Ontario, Toronto, 1906. 158-61.

Crowell, S.
    1877   "The Dog Sacrifice of the Seneca." in Indian Miscellany,
           W. W. Beach, ed. Albany, New York.

Curtis, Edward S.
    1930   The North American Indian, Vol. 19. Norwood, Massa-
           chusetts: Plimpton Press.

Curtis, N.
    1904   "A Bit of American Folk Music: Two Pueblo Indian
           Grinding Songs." Craftsman, 7:35-41.
    1906a "Isleta: Hunting Song." Southern Workman, 35:144.
    1906b "Indian Song: Seneca." Southern Workman, 35:45.
    1907   The Indians Book. New York: Harper and Brothers.
    1911   "Feather Dance Song." Southern Workman, 40:599.
    1921   "American Indian Griddle Songs." Musical Quarterly,
           7:549-58.

Davis, A. L.
    1933   "American Apostle: Ghost Dance of Religion." American
           Mercury, 30:210-77.

Davis, E. H.
    1920   The Papago Ceremony of Vikita. Indian Notes and Mono-
           graphs, Heye Foundation. New York: Museum of the
           American Indian.

Dellenbaugh, F. S.
    1915   "The Somaikoli Dance Sichumovi." American Museum
           Journal, 15:256-8.

Deloria, Vine
    1973   God Is Red. New York: Grosset and Dunlop.

Densmore, Frances
    n.d.   "Songs of the Condoling and Installation Council of the
           League of the Iroquois." Recorded and described by
           J. N. B. Hewitt, 1932. Unpublished ms in the Bureau
           of American Ethnology.

1906   "Geronimo's Song." Indian School Journal, 6(6):30-1.
1907a "An Onondaga Thanksgiving Song." Indian School
       Journal, 7:23-4.
1907b "An Ojibwa Prayer Ceremony." American Anthropologist,
       9:433-4.
1918   "Teton Sioux Music." Bureau of American Ethnology,
       Bulletin 61. Washington, D.C.: U.S. Government Printing
       Office.
1921   "Music of the Papago and Pawnee." in Explorations and
       Fieldwork of the Smithsonian Institution in 1920. Washing-
       ton, D.C.: Smithsonian Institution.
1926   "Poems from Desert Indians." Nation, 122-407.
1927a "Desert Indian Rain Chant." World Review, 5:151.
1927b "Study of Indian Music in the Nineteenth Century."
       American Anthropologist, 29:77-86.
1927c "Music of the Winnebago Indians." in Explorations and
       Fieldwork of the Smithsonian Institution. Washington,
       D.C.: Smithsonian Institution.
1927d "The Use of Music in the Treatment of the Sick by the
       American Indians." Musical Quarterly, 13:555-65.
1929a Papago Music. Bureau of American Ethnology, Bulletin
       90. Washington, D.C.: U.S. Government Printing Office.
1929b "Tribal Customs of the Menominee Indians of Wisconsin."
       in Explorations and Fieldwork of the Smithsonian Institution.
       Washington, D.C.: The Smithsonian Institution.
1931a "Music of the Winnebago, Chippewa and Pueblo Indians."
       in Explorations and Fieldwork of the Smithsonian Institution.
       Washington, D.C.: The Smithsonian Institution.
1931b "Music of American Indians at Public Gatherings."
       Musical Quarterly, 17:464-79.
1932a "Resemblance Between Yuman and Pueblo Songs."
       American Anthropologist, 34:694-700.
1932b "Yuman and Yaqui Music." Bureau of American Ethnol-
       ogy, Bulletin 110. Washington, D.C.: U.S. Government
       Printing Office.
1932c "Menominee Music." Bureau of American Ethnology, Bul-
       letin 102. Washington, D.C.: U.S. Government Printing
       Office.
1936   The American Indians and Their Music. New York:
       Woman's Press.
1937   "The Alabama Indians and Their Music." in Straight
       Texas. J. Frank Dobie and Mody Boatright, eds. Austin,
       Texas: Steck Company.
1938a "Influence of Hymns on Forms of Indian Songs."
       American Anthropologist, 40:175-7.
1938b "Music of Santo Domingo Pueblo." Southwest Museum
       Papers, 12:1-186.
1941   "Native Songs of Two Hybrid Ceremonies Among the
       American Indians." American Anthropologist, 43:77-82.
1943a "Use of Meaningless Syllables in Indian Songs."
       American Anthropologist, 45:160-2.

1943b "Choctaw Music." Bureau of American Ethnology, Bulletin 136. Washington, D.C.: U.S. Government Printing Office.

1943c "A Search for Songs Among the Chitimacha Indians in Lousiana." Bureau of American Ethnology, Bulletin 133. Washington, D.C.: U.S. Government Printing Office.

1944 "Traces of Foreign Influences in the Music of the American Indians." American Anthropologist, 46:106-12; 213.

1945 "Importance of Recordings of Indian Songs." American Anthropologist, 47:637-9.

1947 "Imitative Dances Among the American Indians." Journal of American Folklore, 60:73-8.

1950 "Words of Indian Songs as Unwritten Literature." Journal of American Folklore, 63:450-8.

1953 "Use of Indian Music." Musical America, 73(5):15.

1954a "Importance of Rhythm in Songs for the Treatment of the Sick by American Indians." Scientific Monthly, 79: 109-12.

1954b "Music of the American Indian." Southern Folklore Quarterly, 18:133-56.

1956 "Seminole Music." Bureau of American Ethnology, Bulletin 161. Washington, D.C.: U.S. Government Printing Office.

1957 "Music of Acoma, Isleta, Cochiti and Zuni Pueblos." Bureau of American Ethnology, Bulletin 165. Washington, D.C.: U.S. Government Printing Office.

Dewey, John
1925 Experience and Nature. Chicago: Open Court.
1934 Art As Experience. New York: Balsh and Company.

Di Peso, C.
1956 The Upper Pima of San Cayetano del Tumacacori, An Archaeological Reconstruction of the Ootam of Pimeria Alta. Dragoon, Arizona: Amerind Foundation Pub.

Dobyns, Henry, and Robert Euler
1967 The Ghost Dance of 1889 Among the Pai Indians of Northwestern Arizona. Prescott, Arizona: Prescott College Press.

Dockstader, F. J.
1953 "Origin of the Shalako." Desert Magazine, 16(1):29-30.
1957 "The American Indian in Graduate Studies. A Bibliography of Theses and Dissertations." Contributions from the Museum of the American Indian, Heye Foundation, No. 15.

Doeser, Anthony G.
1963-4 "The Iroquois Water Drum." American Indian Tradition, 9:24-6.

Dorsey, A. and H. R. Voth
1901 "The Oraibi Soyal Ceremony." Field Museum, Anthropological Series, 3:5-59.
1902 "The Mishongnovi Ceremonies of the Snake and Antelope Fraternities." Field Museum, Anthropological Series, 3:16-261.

Dorsey, Ella Lorraine
1908 "The Forbidden Dance (Da-H-pi-ke)." Messenger, 50: 466-85.

Dorsey, George A.
1910 "Sun Dance." Handbook of American Indians, Vol. II. Bureau of American Ethnology, Bulletin 30. Washington, D.C.: U.S. Government Printing Office.

Douglas, F. H.
1939 "The Shaking-Tent Rite Among the Montagnais of James Bay." Primitive Man, 12:11-16.

Downey, J. C.
1970 "Review Essay of A. Lomax, Folk Song Style and Culture." Ethnomusicology, 14(1):63-7.

Dozier, Edward P.
1958 "Spanish-Catholic Influences on Rio Grande Pueblo Religion." American Anthropologist, 60:442-5.

Draper, W. H.
1901 "Indian Dances of the Southwest." Outing, 37:659-66.

Driberg, J. H.
1936 "The Secular Aspect of Ancestor-Worship in Africa." in Journal of the Royal African Society, Vol. 35, No. 138.

Driver, H.
1970 "Review Essay of A. Lomax, Folk Song Style and Culture." Ethnomusicology, 14(1):57-62.

Drucker, Philip
1955 Indians of the Northwest Coast. Garden City, New York: Natural History Press.
1965 Cultures of the North Pacific Coast. Scranton, Pennsylvania: Chandler.
1940 "Kwakiutl Dancing Societies." Anthropological Records, Vol. II, #6. Berkeley: University of California Press.

Dubois, Cora
1932 "Tolowa Notes." American Anthropologist, 34:248-62.

Ducasse, C. J.
1953 "The Aesthetic Attitude." in The Problems of Aesthetics.

Eliseo Vivas and Murray Krieger, eds. New York: Rinehart.

Dumarest, Noel
1919 "Notes on the Cochiti, New Mexico." Memoirs of the American Anthropological Association, 6:147-86; 188; 190-3; 203-8.

Dutton, B. P.
1936 "Hopi Dance to the Jemez Indians." Research, 1:70-84.
1955 "Pueblo Fiestas, Navaho Ceremonies, Apache Ceremonies." in New Mexico Indians and Their Arizona Neighbors. Santa Fe: New Mexico Association on Indian Affairs.

Eickemeyer, Carl, and Lillian W. Eickemeyer
1895 Among the Pueblo Indians. New York: Merriam Company.

Eliade, M.
1957 The Sacred and the Profane. New York: Harcourt, Brace and World.
1964 Shamanism: Archaic Techniques of Ecstasy. New York: Bolligen Series, No. 76.

Ellis, Florence Hawley
1951 "Patterns of Aggression and the War Cult in Southwest Pueblos." Southwestern Journal of Anthropology, 7:183-95.
1952 "Jemez Kiva Magic and Its Relation to Features of Prehistoric Kivas." Southwestern Journal of Anthropology, 8:148; 151; 155; 157; 163.
1953 "Authoritative Control and the Society System in Jemez Pueblo." Southwestern Journal of Anthropology, 9:390.

Espinosa, A. M.
1918 "All Souls' Day at Zuni, Acoma and Laguna." Journal of American Folklore, 31:550-2.

Estergreen, Marion
1950 "When Taos Dances." New Mexico Magazine, 28:16; 40-1.

Evans, B. and M. Evans
1931 American Indian Dance Steps. New York: A. S. Barnes and Company.

Farrer, Claire R.
1978 "Mescalero Ritual Dance: A Four-Part Fugue." Discovery, 1-13.

Fay, C. E.
1912 "Some Notes on the Cow Dance, Santa Clara Pueblo." El Palacio, 59:186-8.

Fecokes, J. Walter
1890 "Passamoquoddy--Snake Dance and Song--Music and Description." Journal of American Folklore, 3:261-3.

Feder, Norman
1957 "Costume of the Oklahoma Straight Dancer." American Indian Hobbyist, 4(1-2):3-17.
1958 "Oklahoma Fancy Dance Costume." American Indian Hobbyist, 4(5-6):52-7.
1962 "Matachines, A Photo Essay." American Indian Hobbyist, 8(2):79-82.
1964 "Origin of the Oklahoma Forty-Nine Dance." Ethnomusicology, Vol. III:3.

Federal Writers' Project of the Works Progress Administration
1939a Montana, A State Guide Book. New York: Viking Press.
1939b The Papago. Vol. 20, No. 3. Flagstaff: Arizona State Teachers' College.

Fenton, William N.
1936 An Outline of Seneca Ceremonies at Coldspring Longhouse. Yale University Publications in Anthropology, No. 9. New Haven: Yale University Press.
1937 "The Seneca Eagle Dance: A Study of Personality Expression in Ritual." Discussion, Yale University.
1940 "Masked Medicine Societies of the Iroquois." Annual Report of the Smithsonian Institution, Publication 3606. Washington, D.C.: The Smithsonian Institution.
1941 "Tonawanda Longhouse Ceremonies: Ninety Years After Lewis Henry Morgan." Bureau of American Ethnology, Bulletin 128. Washington, D.C.: U.S. Government Printing Office.
1942 Songs from the Iroquois Longhouse. Smithsonian Publication 3691, Album 6. Archive of American Folk Song. Washington, D.C.: Library of Congress.
1948 "Seneca Songs from Coldspring Longhouse." Album 17, Folk Music of the U.S., Washington, D.C.: Library of Congress.
1953 "Iroquois Eagle Dance: An Offshoot of the Calument Dance." Bureau of American Ethnology, Bulletin 156. Washington, D.C.: U.S. Government Printing Office.
1961 "Iroquois Studies at the Mid-Century." Proceedings of the American Philosophical Society, 95:296-310.
1963 "The Seneca Green Corn Ceremony." The Conservationist, 18:20-2.

_____ and Gertrude P. Kurath
1951 "The Feast of the Dead, or Ghost Dance, at Six Nations Reserve, Canada." in Symposium on Local Diversity in Iroquois Culture. William Fenton, ed. Bureau of American

Ethnology, Bulletin 149. Washington, D.C.: U.S. Government Printing Office.

Fergusson, Erna
1931 Dancing Gods: Indian Ceremonials of New Mexico and Arizona. Albuquerque: University of New Mexico Press.

Fewkes, J. W.
1890a "On the Use of the Phonograph Among Zuni Indians." American Naturalist, 24:687-91.
1890b "Additional Studies of Zuni Songs and Rituals with the Phonograph." American Naturalist, 24:1094-8.
1890c "A Study of Summer Ceremonials at Zuni and Moqui Pueblos." Bulletin of the Essex Institute, 22(7):89-113.
1890d "A Contribution to Passamaquoddy Folklore." Journal of American Folklore, 3:257-80.
1891a "A Suggestion as to the Meaning of the Moki Snake Dance." Journal of American Folklore, 4:129-38.
1891b "A Few Summer Ceremonies at Zuni Pueblo." Journal of American Ethnology and Archaeology, 1:1-61.
1893 "A Central American Ceremony Which Suggests the Snake Dance of the Tusayan Villagers." American Anthropologist, 6:285-306.
1894a "The Walpi Flute Observance." Journal of American Folklore, 7:265-87.
1894b "Snake Ceremonies at Walpi." Journal of American Ethnology and Archaeology, 4(1):1-126.
1895a "The Oraibi Flute Altar." Journal of American Folklore, 8:265-82.
1895b "Provisional List of Annual Ceremonies at Walpi." Internationale Archiv fur Ethnographie, 8:215-38.
1895c "A Comparison of Sia and Tusayan Snake Ceremonies." American Anthropologist, 8:118-41.
1899 "Hopi Basket Dances." Journal of American Folklore, 12:81-96.
1900 "The New Fire Ceremony at Walpi." American Anthropologist, 2:80-138.
1901 "The Lesser New Fire Ceremony at Walpi." American Anthropologist, 3:438-53.
1902 "Minor Hopi Festivals." American Anthropologist, 4:482-511.
1910 "Butterfly Dances of the Hopi." in The Butterfly in Hopi Myth and Ritual. American Anthropologist, 12:576-94.

_____ and J. G. Owens
1892 "The La-la-kon-ta: A Tusayan Dance." American Anthropologist, 5:105-29.

_____ and A. M. Stephen
1892 "The Man-Zrau-Ti: A Tusayan Ceremony." American Anthropologist, 5:217-45.

Fillmore, J. G.
1896a "Two Tiqua Folk-Songs." Land of Sunshine, 4:273-80.
1896b "Songs of the Navajos." Land of Sunshine, 5:238-41.
1897 "Forms Spontaneously Assumed by Folk-Songs." Music,
12:289-94.

Fletcher, Alice Cunningham
1915 Indian Games and Dances with Native Indian Songs.
Boston: C. C. Birchard and Company.
1934 "Study of Indian Music." American Anthropologist,
36:487-8.

Fogelson, Raymond
1971 "The Cherokee Ballgame Cycle: An Ethnographer's
View." Ethnomusicology, 15(3):327-38.
1977 "Cherokee Notions of Power." in The Anthropology of
Power. Richard N. Adams, ed. New York: Academic
Press.

Forde, C. D.
1931 "Ethnography of the Yuma Indians." University of
California Publications in American Archaeology and Ethnology, 28(4):83-278.

Forrest, E. R.
1961 Snake Dance of the Hopi Indians. Los Angeles:
Westernlore Press.

Frederich, Douglas
1931 The Menomini Indian--A Woodland Tribe. Denver:
Denver Art Museum.

Frisbie, C. J., and D. P. McAllester (Editors)
1978 Oltai Tsch: Autobiography of Frank Mitchell, Navajo
Blessingway Singer from Chinle, Arizona.

Frisbie, Charlotte J.
1967a "An Analysis of the Worked Bone and Antler Artifacts
from Sapawe." Musical Instruments.
1967b Kinaalda. A Study of the Navajo Girl's Puberty Ceremony. Middletown: Wesleyan University Press.
1968 "The Navajo House Blessing Ceremony." El Palacio,
75(3):26-35.
1970 The Navajo House Blessing Ceremony: A Study of Cultural Change. University of New Mexico Ph.D. Dissertation. Ann Arbor: University Microfilms.
1977 Music and Dance Research of Southwestern United States
Indians. Detroit Studies in Music Bibliography, No. 36.
Detroit, Michigan: Information Coordinates.
1980 "An Approach to the Ethnography of Navajo Ceremonial
Performance." in The Ethnography of Musical Performance.

Marcia Herndon and Norma McLeod, eds. Darby, Pennsylvania: Norwood Editions.

———— (Editor)
1980 Southwestern Indian Ritual Drama. School of American Research Advanced Seminar Series. Albuquerque: University of New Mexico Press.

Frisch, Jack Aaron
1970 "Revitalization, Nativism and Tribalism Among the St. Regis Mohawks." Discussion, Indiana University.

Fry, Roger
1924 Vision and Design. New York: Brentano.

Fuentes, Eduardo Sanchez
1939 La Musica Aborigen de America. La Habana: Molina Y Cia.

Furst, Peter
1973 "An Indian Journey to Life's Source." Natural History, 82:34-43.

Gallenkamp, C.
1954 "Raphael's Last Deer Dance." Desert Magazine, 17(5): 11-14.
1955 "The Pueblo Indians of New Mexico." Canadian Geographical Journal, 50:206-15.

Gamble, John S.
1960 "Forty-Nine, a Modern Social Dance." American Indian Hobbyist, 6(7-8):86-8.

Garcia, A., and C. Garcia
1968 "Ritual Preludes to Tewa Dances." Ethnomusicology, 12(2):239-44.
1970 "Ritual Preludes and Postludes." in Music and Dance of the Tewa Pueblos, by G. Kurath. Museum of New Mexico Research Records, No. 8. Santa Fe: Museum of New Mexico Press.

Garcia, A., and J. and G. Trujillo
1966 "Tanoan Gestures of Invocation." Ethnomusicology, 10(2):206-7.

Gaus, Dorothy Shipley
1976 "Change in Social Dance Song Style at Allegany Reservation, 1962-1973: The Rabbit Dance." Discussion, Catholic University of America.

Gianini, C.
1928 "The Hopi Snake Dance." El Palacio, 25:439-49.

Gifford, E.
1931 "The Southeastern Yavapai." University of California
Publications in American Archaeology and Ethnology, 29:
177-252.

Gill, Sam D.
1983 Sacred Words: A Study of Navajo Religion and Prayer.
Westport, Connecticut: Greenwood Press.

Gillis, F., and A. Merriam
1966 Ethnomusicology and Folk Music: An International Bibliography of Dissertations and Theses. Special Series in
Ethnomusicology, No. 1. Middletown: Wesleyan University
Press.

Gilman, B. I.
1891 "Zuni Melodies." Journal of American Ethnology and
Archaeology, 1:63-91.
1908 "Hopi Songs." Journal of American Ethnology and Archaeology, 5:1-226.

Gluckman, Max
1962 Essays on the Ritual of Social Relations. Manchester:
University of Manchester Press.

Goddard, Pliny E.
1913 Indians of the Southwest. Handbook Series, Vol. 2.
New York: American Museum of Natural History.
1919 "Notes on the Sun Dance of the Cree of Alberta." in
Anthropological Papers, Vol. 16, Publications in Anthropology. New York: The American Museum of Natural
History.

Goggin, J. M.
1939 "Additional Pueblo Ceremonies." New Mexico Anthropologist, 3:62-3.

Goldfrank, Ester S.
1923 "Notes on Two Pueblo Feasts." American Anthropologist,
25:188-96.
1927 "The Social and Ceremonial Organization of Cochiti."
Memoirs of the American Anthropologist Association, 33:47;
54-6; 57; 61; 72-5; 77; 103-13.

Gonzales, C.
1966 "The Shalakos Are Coming." El Palacio, 73(3):5-17.

Goodlander, M. R.
1908 "Primitive Songs and Dances: A Second Grade Assem-
bly." Elementary School Teacher, 9:65-9.

Goodwin, G.
1942 The Social Organization of the Western Apache. Chicago:
University of Chicago Press.

Gordon, D.
1972 "An Early Fiesta at Laguna." Masterkey, 46(1):34-7.

Gotshalk, D. W.
1947 Art and the Social Order. Chicago: University of
Chicago Press.

Graham, S.
1923 "The Shalako Dance." El Palacio, 15:139-40.

Guernsey, S. J.
1920 "Notes on a Navajo War Dance." American Anthropologist,
22:304-7.

Gunther, Erna
1966 Art in the Life of the Northwest Coast Indian. Portland,
Oregon: Portland Art Museum.

Haas, Mary R.
1950 "Tunica Texts." University of California Publications in
Linguistics. Vol. 6, No. 1. Berkeley: University of
California Press.

Hackett, Charles W.
1942 Revolt of the Pueblo Indians of New Mexico. Vol. 8 and
9. Coronado Cuarto Centennial Publications.

Hagberlin, H. K.
1916 "The Idea of Fertilization in the Culture of the Pueblo
Indians." Memoirs of American Anthropological Association,
3:26-8; 29-30; 34-5.

Haile, B. (O.F.M.)
1938 "Navaho Chantways and Ceremonials." American
Anthropologist, 40:639-52.
1946a The Navaho Fire Dance or Corral Dance. Saint
Michaels, Arizona: Saint Michaels Mission Press.
1946b The Navaho War Dance. Saint Michaels, Arizona:
Saint Michaels Mission Press.

Hall, T. B.
1953 "Dancing the Snakes." Arizona Highways, 29(7):4-11.

Hallowell, A. Irving
1926 "Bear Ceremonialism in the Northern Hemisphere."
American Anthropologist, 28:1-175.

1934a "Some Empirical Aspects of Northern Saulteaux Religion." American Anthropologist, 36:389-404.
1934b "Culture and Mental Disorder." Journal of Abnormal and Social Psychology, 29:1-9.
1936 "Psychic Stresses and Culture Patterns." American Journal of Psychiatry, 92:1291-1310.
1951a "Cultural Factors in the Structuralization of Perception." in Social Psychology at the Crossroads, John Rohver and Muzafer Sherif, eds. New York: Harper.
1951b "Frank Gouldsmith Speck, 1881-1950." American Anthropologist, 53:67-87.
1955 Culture and Experience. Philadelphia: University of Pennsylvania Press.

Harrington, J. P.
1908 "Yuma Account of Origins." Journal of American Folklore, 21:324-48.
1912a "The Tewa Indian Game of Canute." American Anthropologist, 14:243-86.
1912b "The Devil Dance of the Apache." Museum Journal, University of Pennsylvania, 3:6-10.

_____ and H. H. Roberts
1928 Picuris Children's Stories with Texts and Songs. 43rd Annual Report, Bureau of American Ethnology. Washington, D.C.: U.S. Government Printing Office.

Harrington, Mark R.
1891 "Iroquois Dance in Green Corn Festival." Journal of American Folklore, 4:73-5.
1921 "Religion and Ceremonies of the Lenape." Indian Notes and Monographs, Publication 9. Museum of the American Indians, Heye Foundation.
1933 "The Dark Dance of the Ji-ge-onh." Masterkey, 7:76-9.

Hartley, Marsden
1918 "Tribal Esthetics." The Dial, 45:399-401.
1920 "Red Man Ceremonials." Art and Archaeology, 9:7-15.

Harvey, B.
1966 "Song of the Dog Kachina." Masterkey, 40(3):106-8.

Haury, Emil W., et al.
1950 The Stratigraphy and Archaeology of Ventana Cave. Tucson, Arizona: University of Arizona.

Hawley, Florence E.
1937 "Kokopelli of the Prehistoric Southwestern Pueblo Pantheon." American Anthropologist, 39:644-6.
1948 "Dance of the Devil Chasers." New Mexico Magazine, 26(9):16.

1950 "Big Kivas, Little Kivas, and Moiety Houses in Historical
Reconstruction." Southwestern Journal of Anthropology,
6:287-8; 290-5.

Hayden, J. and C. R. Steen
1937 "The Vikita Ceremony of the Papago." Southwestern
Monuments Monthly Reports, (April), 263-83.

Haywood, C.
1951 A Bibliography of North American Folklore and Folksong.
New York: Greenberg Publishers.

Heckewelder, John (Rev.)
1876 "History, Manners and Customs of the Indian Nations
who once inhabited Pennsylvania and the Neighboring
States." Pennsylvania Historical Society Memoirs, Vol. 12.
Philadelphia: Historical Society of Pennsylvania.

Hegel, G. W. F.
1920 The Philosophy of Fine Art. F. P. B. Osmaston, London: G. Bell & Sons.

Heizer, R. F.
1944 "The Hopi Snake Dance." Ciba Symposium, 5:1681-4.

Herndon, Marcia
1980 Field Notes.
1971 "The Cherokee Ballgame Cycle: An Ethnomusicologist's
Viewpoint." Ethnomusicology, September, 1971.
1979 "Play Elements in the Myth of North American Indians."
in Forms of Play in Native North America. Edward Norbeck
and Claire R. Farrer, eds. 1977 Proceedings of the American Ethnological Society, St. Paul, Minnesota: West Publishing Co.

_____ and Norma McLeod
1979 Music As Culture. Darby, Pennsylvania: Norwood
Editions.

Hertzberg, Hazel W.
1971 The Search for an American Indian Identity. Syracuse,
New York: Syracuse University Press.

Herzog, George
1928a "The Yuman Musical Style." Journal of American Folklore, 2:183-231.
1928b "Music Styles in North America." in Proceedings of the
23rd International Congress of Americanists.
1931 "Transcriptions of Four Pueblo Melodies." in American
Indian Dance Steps, by B. and M. Evans." New York:
A. S. Barnes and Company.

1933 "Maricopa Music." in Yuman Tribe of the Gila River, by
L. Spier. Chicago: University of Chicago Press.
1934 "Speech Melody and Primitive Music." Musical Quarterly,
20:452-66.
1935a "Special Song Types in North American Indian Music."
Zeitschrift fur Vergleichende Musikwissenschaft, 3:32-3.
1935b "Plains Ghost Dance and Great Basin Music." American
Anthropologist, 37:403-19.
1936a "Research in Primitive and Folk Music in the United
States." American Council of Learned Societies, Bulletin
24.
1936b "A Comparison of Pueblo and Pima Musical Styles."
Journal of American Folklore, 49:283-417.
1938 "Music in the Thinking of the American Indian." Peabody
Bulletin, May:1-5.
1942 "Study of Native Music in America." Washington: Proceedings of the 8th American Scientific Congress, Vol. II:
203-9.
1946 "Some Linguistic Aspects of American Indian Poetry."
Word, 2:82-3.
1950 "Song." in Funk and Wagnalls Dictionary of Folklore.

Heth, C.
1973 "Bibliography on Native American Indian Music." Paper
presented at the Meeting of the Modern Language Association, June.

Hewett, Edgar L.
1918 "The Corn Ceremony at Santo Domingo." El Palacio,
5:69-76.
1925 "The Fiesta Book." Papers of the Archaeological Institute of America, Vol. 13.

Hewitt, J. N. B.
1906 "Otkon." in Handbook of American Indians North of
Mexico, II. F. W. Hodge, ed. Bureau of American
Ethnology, Bulletin 30. Washington, D.C.: Smithsonian
Institution.
1907 "Indian Dance." in Handbook of American Indians North
of Mexico, F. W. Hodge, ed. Washington, D.C.: U.S.
Government Printing Office.

Hickerson, J. C.
1961 "Annotated Bibliography of North American Indian Music
North of Mexico." Unpublished M.A. Thesis: Indiana
University.

Hieb, L.
1974 "Rhythms of Significance: Towards a Symbolic Analysis
of Dance in Ritual." CORD Research Annual, 6:225-33.

Hight, B.
    1953 "Koyemshi: The Mudheads." New Mexico Sun Trails,
        6(0):2-3.

Hill, G.
    1954 Bibliography of Pueblo Indian Dances and Ceremonies.
        Santa Fe: Museum of New Mexico.

Hinchman, Fred K.
    1931 "Among the Pueblos." Masterkey, (5):112.

Hinton, L.
    1974 Personal Communication.

_____ and D. Hanna
    1971 "Havasupai Medicine Song." Alcheringa, 3:68-75.

Hodge, F. W.
    1896 "Pueblo Snake Ceremonials." American Anthropologist,
        old series, Vol. 9:133-6.
    1920 "Hawikuh Bonework." Indian Notes and Monographs,
        Heye Foundation 3(3).

Hoebel, E. Adamson
    1961 The Law of Primitive Man. Cambridge: Harvard Uni-
        versity Press.
    1967 "Song Duels Among the Eskimo." in Law and Warfare,
        Paul Bohannon, ed. Garden City, NY: The Natural His-
        tory Press.

Hofmann, C.
    1946 "Frances Densmore and the Music of the American Indian."
        Journal of American Folklore, 59:45-50.
    1970 Musical Instruments of the Indians of the Americas.
        Rochester, New York: Rochester Museum and Science
        Center.

Hoffman, Walter James
    1888 "Pictography and Shamanistic Rites of the Ojibwa."
        American Anthropologist, 1:209-31.
    1891 "The Midewiwin or 'Grand Medicine Society' of the Ojib-
        wa." 7th Annual Report, 1885-1886. Bureau of American
        Ethnology. Washington, D.C.: U.S. Government Printing
        Office.
    1892 "The Menominee Indians." Annual Report of the Bureau
        of American Ethnology, Part 1. Washington, D.C.: U.S.
        Government Printing Office.

Hogue, Alexander
    1929 "Picturesque Games and Ceremonials of Indians." El
        Palacio, 26:177-9; 181-2.

Holm, Bill
1972 Crooked Beak of Heaven. Seattle: University of Washington Press.

Hood, Mantle
1963 "Music, the Unknown." in Musicology. Frank Harrison, Mantle Hood, and Claude Palisca, eds. Englewood Cliffs, New Jersey: Prentice-Hall.
1971 The Ethnomusicologist. New York: McGraw-Hill.

Hough, W.
1897 "Music of the Hopi Flute Ceremony." American Anthropologist, 10:162-3.
1899 The Moki Snake Dance. Chicago: University of Chicago Press.
1915 "The Hopi Indians." Little Histories of the North American Indians, 4.
1919 "The Hopi Indian Collection in the U.S. National Museum." Proceedings of the U.S. National Museum, 54:235-96.

Howard, James H.
1951 "Notes on the Dakota Grass Dance." Southwest Journal of Anthropology, Vol. 7, No. 1.
1955 "The Pan-Indian Culture of Oklahoma." The Scientific Monthly, Vol. XVIII, No. 5.
1965a "The Compleat Stomp Dancer." Museum News, South Dakota Museum, Vermillion, Vol. 26, No. 5-6.
1965b "The Ponca Tribe." Bureau of American Ethnology, Bulletin 195. Washington, D.C.: U.S. Government Printing Office.
1976a "The Plains Gourd Dance as a Revitalization Movement." American Ethnologist, 3(2):243-59.
1976b "Oklahoma Choctaw Revive Native Dances." Actes du XLif Congrès International des Americanistes, Paris 2-9 Septembre.
1983 "Pan-Indianism in Native American Music and Dance." Ethnomusicology, 27(1):71-82.

Hridlicka, A.
1905 "Notes on the San Carlos Apache." American Anthropologist, 7:480-95.
1906 "Notes on Pima of Arizona." American Anthropologist, 8:39-46.

Hubert, W. and M. Mauss
1902-3 "Theorie generale de la Magic." L'Annee Sociologique.

Huebner, G.
1938 "The Green Corn Dance at Santo Domingo." El Palacio, 45:1-17.

Huenemann, Lynn
1978 Songs and Dances of Native America. Sibley, Iowa: Education House.

Hume, David
1963 Of Standards of Taste. The Philosophy of David Hume,
V. C. Chapell, ed. New York: Modern Library.

Hunt, Wesley R.
1941 "Notes on the Santa Ana Indians." El Palacio, (48):
135-40.

Hurt, W. R.
1952 "Christmas Eve Ceremonies of the Pueblo Indians of New
Mexico." Hobbies, 57:139.
1966 "The Spanish-American Comanche Dance." Journal of
Folklore Institute, 3(2):116-32.

Innis, Harold
1951 The Bias of Communication. Toronto: University of
Toronto Press.

Jaancon, J. A.
1927 "Indian Music of the Southwest." El Palacio, 23:438-47.

James, G. M.
1954 Stolen Legacy. New York: Philosophical Books.

Jameson, Mrs.
1839 "A Red Indian Dance." Niles' Weekley Register, 56:135
(April).

Johnson, C. I.
1964 "Navaho Corn Grinding Songs." Ethnomusicology, 8(2):
101-20.

Johnson, J. B.
1940 "The Piman Foot Drum and Fertility Rites." El Mexico
Antiqua, 5:140-1.

Jones, A. W.
1937 "Additional Information about the Vikita." Southwestern
Monument Monthly Reports, May:338-41.

Jones, H.
1931a "Zuni Shalako Ceremony." El Palacio, 30:1-10.
1931b "The Fiesta of San Geronimo at Taos." El Palacio,
31:300-2.
1932 "Niman Katcina Dance at Walpi." El Palacio, 33:68-71.

Jones, Owen R.
1972 "Music of the Algonkians: Cree, Montagnais, Naskapi."
Folkways, PE, 4253.

Jones, W.
1951 "Prayer for Rain." New Mexico, 29(6):23; 53-5.

Jorgensen, Joseph Gilbert
1972 The Sun Dance Religion: Power for the Powerless.
Chicago: University of Chicago Press.

Joseph, Alice, Rosamond B. Spicer, and Jane Chesky
1949 The Desert People: A Study of the Papago Indians.
Chicago: University of Chicago Press.

Kanellos, V.
1953 "Prayer to Mother Earth." New Mexico, 31(4):18-19; 45.
1956 "Rituals in the Old Tradition." New Mexico, 34(12):24;
59.

Kant, Immanuel
1960 Observations on the Feeling of the Beautiful and Sublime.
John T. Toldthwait, trans. Berkeley: University of
California Press.

Karpeles, Maud
1968 "The Distinction Between Folk and Popular Music."
Journal of the International Folk Music Council, Vol. XX,
9-12.

Kealiinohomoku, J.
1967 "Hopi and Polynesian Dance: A Study in Cross-Cultural
Comparisons." Ethnomusicology, 11(3):343-58.
1974a "Field Guides." CORD Research Annual, 6:245-60.
1974b "Dance Culture as a Microcosm of Holistic Culture."
CORD Research Annual, 6:99-106.
1974c Personal Communication.
1978a "Hopi Social Dance Events and How They Function."
Discovery, 27-40.
1978b "Ethnodance." in The Religious Character of Native
American Humanities, Sam D. Gill, ed. Tempe: Arizona
State University, Dept. of Humanities and Religious
Studies.

_____ and F. Gillis
1970 "Special Bibliography. G. P. Kurath." Ethnomusicology,
14(1):114-28.

Keech, Roy A.
1933 "Two Days and Nights in a Pueblo." El Palacio, 35:
189-92.
1934a "The Pecos Ceremony at Jemez, August 1, 1932." El
Palacio, 36:129-134.
1934b "Green Corn Ceremony at the Pueblo of Zia, 1932." El
Palacio, 36:145-9.
1937 "The Blue Corn Dance." National Archaeological News,
1(9):26-8.

Keesing, Felix M.
    1939 "The Menomini Indians of Wisconsin." American Philo-
        sophical Society Memoirs, Vol. X, Philadelphia.
    1953 Social Anthropology in Polynesia. London & NY: Ox-
        ford University Press.

Keil, Charles
    1966 Urban Blues. Chicago: University of Chicago Press.
    1979 Tiv Song. Chicago: University of Chicago Press.

Kennedy, Keith
    1928 "Some Musical Instruments of the Southwest Indians."
        Masterkey, 1(8):17-18.

Kidder, A. V.
    1951 "Whistles From Arizona." American Antiquity, 16:256.

King, B. M.
    1935 "A Study of Form and Expression in American Indian
        Music as Exemplified in the Songs of Jemez Pueblo." Un-
        published M.A. Thesis: University of Minnesota.

Klah, H.
    1942 Navajo Creation Myth. Navajo Religious Series, Vol. 1.
        Santa Fe: Museum of Navajo Ceremonial Art.

Klett, F.
    1879 "The Cachina: A Dance of the Pueblo at Zuni," Report
        upon U.S. Geographic Surveys West of the 100th Meridian.
        7:332-6.

Kluckhohn, C.
    1923 "The Dance of Hasjelti." El Palacio, 15:187-92.
    1933 "Great Chants of the Navajo." Theatre Arts Monthly,
        17:639-45.
    1938a "Participants in Ceremonials in a Navaho Community."
        American Anthropologist, 40:359-69.
    1938b "Navaho Women's Knowledge of Their Song Ceremonials."
        El Palacio, 45:87-92.

    _____ and L. Wyman
    1940 "An Introduction to Navaho Chant Practices." Memoirs
        of the American Anthropological Association, No. 53.

Kluckhohn, Florence
    1955 "Dominant and Variant Value Orientations." in Personal-
        ity in Nature, Society, and Culture. Clyde Kluckhohn,
        et al, eds. New York: Knopf.

Kolinski, Mieczyalaw
    1970 "Two Iroquois Rabbit Dance Song Cycles." Newsletter

of the Canadian Folk Music Society, 5:11-38.
1972a "An Apache Rabbit Dance Song Cycle as Sung by the Iroquois." Ethnomusicology, 16:415-64.
1927b "An Iroquois War Dance Song Cycle." CAUSM, 2:51-64.

Kool, Jaap
1921 Tanze der Naturvolker; ein Deutungsversuch Primitiver Tanzkatte und Kultgebrauche. Berlin: A. Furstner.

Korson, R. and J. Hickerson
1969 "The Willard Rhodes Collection of American Indian Music in the Archives of Folk Song." Ethnomusicology, 13(2): 196-304. A Special Bibliography: Willard Rhodes-Fellows.

Krader, B.
1956 "Bibliography of George Herzog." Society for Ethnomusicology Newsletter, No. 6:11-20 and No. 8:10.

Kroeber, A. L.
1926 "Handbook of the Indians of California." Washington, D.C.: Smithsonian Institution, BAE Bulletin 78.
1931 "Walapai Ethnography." Memoirs of the American Anthropological Association, No. 42.
1935 Walapai Ethnography. Menasha, Wisconsin: American Anthropological Association.

Kroeber, Alfred L.
1904 "The Arapaho, III. Ceremonial Organization." Bulletins: Vol. 18, Part II: 151-229. Publications in Anthropology, New York: American Museum of Natural History.
1906 "Ceremonial Organization of the Plains Indians of North America." Proceedings of the 15th Session of the International Congress of Americanists, 2:53-65.
1923 Anthropology. New York: Harcourt, Brace.
1953 "Native Culture of the Southwest." American Archaeology and Ethnology, 23(9):375-98.

Kroeber, H. R.
1909 "Papago Coyote Tales." Journal of American Folklore, 22:339-42.

Krutch, Joseph W.
1963 "The Tragic Fallacy." in Aesthetics and the Philosophy of Criticism. Martin Levic, ed. New York: Random House.

Kurath, Gertrude P.
1949a "Dance--Folk and Primitive." in Dictionary of Folklore, Mythology, and Legend. Maria Leach, ed. 1:276-96. New York: Funk and Wagnalls.
1949b "Matriarchal Dances of the Iroquois." in Indian Tribes

of Aboriginal America. Vol. 3 of Selected Papers, 29th
International Congress of Americanists, New York. Sol
Tax, ed. Chicago: University of Chicago Press.
1949c "Structural Types of Seneca Dance." in Conference of
Iroquois Research, Proceedings, 14:25-7.
1950a "Ritual Drama." in Dictionary of Folklore, Mythology
and Legend, 2:946-9. New York: Funk and Wagnalls.
1950b "New Method of Choreographic Notation." American
Anthropologist, 52:120-3.
1951a "The Feast of the Dead, or Ghost Dance, at Six Nations
Reserve, Canada." in Symposium on Local Diversity in
Iroquois Culture. William Fenton, ed. BAE Bulletin 149:
139-65.
1951b "Iroquois Midwinter Medicine Rites." Journal of the International Folk Music Council, 3:96-100.
1951c "Local Diversity in Iroquois Music and Dance." in
Symposium on Local Diversity in Iroquois Culture. William
Fenton, ed. BAE Bulletin 149:109-37.
1953a "Native Choreographic Areas of North America."
American Anthropologist, 55:60-73.
1953b "Analysis of the Iroquois Eagle Dance and Songs."
BAE Bulletin, 156:223-306.
1953c "The Tutelo Harvest Rites: A Musical and Choreographic Analysis." Scientific Monthly, 76:153-62.
1954 "The Tutelo Fourth Night Spirit Release Singing."
Midwest Folklore, 4:87-105.
1955 "Aboriginal American Folk Dance." Folk Dance, 2(5):
117-18.
1956a "Choreography and Anthropology." American Anthropologist, 58:177-9.
1956b "Masked Clowns." Tomorrow, 4(3):108-12.
1956c "Songs and Dances of Great Lakes Indians." Folkways,
F-4003.
1956d "Antiphocal Songs of Eastern Woodland Indians."
Musical Quarterly, 42:520-6.
1957a "Basic Techniques of Amerindian Dance." Dance Notation Record, 8(4):2-8.
1957b "Notation of a Pueblo Indian Corn Dance." Dance Notation Record 8(4):9-10.
1957c "The Origin of the Pueblo Indian Matachines." El
Palacio, 64(9-10):259-64.
1957d "Dance Styles of the Rio Grande Pueblo Indians."
The Folklorist, 4(3):89.
1957e "Pan-Indianism in Great Lakes Tribal Festivals." Journal of American Folklore, 9(1):31-8.
1958a "Plaza Circuits of Tewa Indian Dancers." El Palacio,
65(1-2):16-28.
1958b "Game Animal Dances of the Rio Grande Pueblos."
Southwestern Journal of Anthropology, 14(4):438-48.
1958c "Buffalo Dances at Cochiti Pueblo, New Mexico." The
Folklorist, 4(5):149-50.

1958d "Two Line Dances of San Juan Pueblo, New Mexico."
       Midwest Folklore, 8(3):155-8.
1959a "Menominee Indian Dance Songs in a Changing Cul-
       ture." Midwest Folklore, 9(1):31-8.
1959b "Cochiti Choreographies and Songs." in Cochiti, C. H.
       Lange, ed. Austin: University of Texas Press.
1960a "Panorama of Dance Ethnology." Current Anthropology,
       1(3):233-54.
1960b "Calling the Rain Gods." Journal of American Folklore,
       73:312-16.
1960c "The Sena'asom Rattle of the Yaqui Indian Pascolas."
       Ethnomusicology, 4(2):60-3.
1960d "Dance, Music, and Daily Bread." Ethnomusicology,
       4(1):1-9.
1961   "The Effects of Environment on Cherokee-Iroquois Cere-
       monialism Music, and Dance." in Symposium on Cherokee
       and Iroquois Culture. William N. Fenton and John Gulick,
       eds. BAE Bulletin 190:173-195.
1962   "American Indian Dance in Ritual and Life." Folklorist,
       6(4,5,6):428-35, 446-9, 479-82, and 7(1,2,3):8-11, 41-7,
       70-7.
1962a "American Indian Ritual Dances for Sustenance: Har-
       vest Rites of Woodland Agriculturalists." Folklorist, 7:70-
       78.
1962b "The Iroquois Bear Society Ritual Drama." American
       Indian Tradition, 8:84-5.
1963   "Tewa Plaza Dances." American Indian Tradition,
       9:16-21.
1964   "Iroquois Music and Dance: Ceremonial Arts of Two
       Seneca Longhouses." BAE Bulletin 187. Washington.
1965   "Tewa Choreographic Music." in Studies in Ethnomusi-
       cology, M. Kolinski, ed. New York: Oak Publications.
1966a "The Kinetic Ecology of Yaqui Dance Instrumentation."
       Ethnomusicology, 10(1):23-42.
1966b "Review of One Folkways Record: Healing Songs of
       the American Indian." Ethnomusicology, 10(3):372.
1968   "Dance and Song Rituals of Six Nations Reserve, On-
       tario." National Museum of Canada Bulletin 220.
1969   "A Comparison of Plains and Pueblo Songs." Ethno-
       musicology, 13(3):512-17.
1970   "Review of Iroquois Social Dance Songs of William Guy
       Spittal." Ethnomusicology, 14:188-90.
1972   "Research Methods and Background of Gertrude Kurath."
       in New Dimensions in Dance Research: Anthropology and
       Dance--The American Indian. CORD Research Annual, VI
       pp. 35-6.
1981   Tutelo Rituals on Six Nations Reserve, Ontario. Special
       Series No. 5, Society for Ethnomusicology. Stephen A.
       Wild, ed. Ann Arbor, Michigan.

_____ and Antonio Garcia
1970   Music and Dance of the Tewa Pueblos. Museum of New

Mexico Research Records, No. 8. Santa Fe: Museum of New Mexico Press.

La Barre, Weston
1969 The Peyote Cult. New York: Schocken.

Lahmer, D. M.
1929 "Music and Poetry of American Indians." Poetry Review, 20:333-40.

Lamphere, L.
1969 "Symbolic Elements in Navajo Ritual." Southwestern Journal of Anthropology, 25:279-305.

Lane, C.
1887 "The Sun Dance of the Cree Indian." Canadian Record of Science, 2:22-6.

Lange, C. H.
1951 "King's Day Ceremonies at a Rio Grande Pueblo, Jan. 6, 1940." El Palacio, 58(12):398-406.
1952a "San Juan's Day at Cochiti Pueblo, New Mexico, 1894 and 1947." El Palacio, 6:175-82.
1952b "The Feast Day Dance at Zia Pueblo." Texas Journal of Science, 4:19-26.
1953a "Notes on a Winter Ceremony at Isleta Pueblo, Jan. 7, 1940." El Palacio, 60(3):116-23.
1953b "Economics in Cochiti Cultural Change." American Anthropologist, 55(5):674-94.
1953c "Reappraisal of Evidence of Plains Influences Among the Rio Grande Pueblos." Southwestern Journal of Anthropology, 9:212-30.
1954 "An Animal Dance at Santo Domingo Pueblo, Jan. 26, 1940." El Palacio, 61(5):151-55.
1957 "Tablita, or Corn, Dances of the Rio Grande Pueblo Indians." Texas Journal of Science, 9(1):59-74.
1959 Cochiti: A New Mexico Pueblo, Past and Present. Austin: University of Texas Press.
1974 "A Time Capsule from the 1880s: Bandelier's 'Memoranda of Investigations Required.'" in Collected Papers in Honor of Florence Hawley Ellis. T. R. Frisbie, ed. Papers of the Archaeological Society of New Mexico, No. 4. Norman: Hooper Publishing Company.

Laski, Vera
1957 "The Raingod Ceremony at Tewa, A Religious Drama." Masterkey, 31:76-84.

Laubin, Reginald and Gladys
1948 "The Indian Dance." Musical Digest, 30(3):34-7.

Lawrence, D. H.
 1934 "Indinishe Mysterien: der tanz des spaessenden Korns; der schlangentanz der Hopi-Indianer." Neus Rundschan 45(1):79-94.

Lawson, John
 1718 History of Carolina. London: T. Warner and Co., Reprinted, Raleigh, N.C.: O. H. Percy and Company, 1860.

Lea, H.
 1953 "The Basket Dance." New Mexico, 31(5):18, 55.
 1954 "Prayer to the Sun." New Mexico, 32(3):22, 37.
 1963-4 "More About the Matachines." New Mexico Folklore Record 11:7-10.

Lesser, Alexander
 1933 "Cultural Significance of the Ghost Dance." American Anthropologist, 35:108-15.

Levich, Marvin (Editor)
 1963 Aesthetics and the Philosophy of Criticism. New York: Random House.

Lewis, Orian Louise
 1953 "Fiesta at Nambo Pueblo." El Palacio, 60(12):409-13.

Lewis, William S.
 1931 "Red Man's Farewell Song As He Went Forth to Battle; Tribal Sin-ka-has of Northwestern Tribes Translated Into English." Frontier, XI:368-75.

Liberty, Margot
 1980 "The Sun Dance." in Anthropology on the Great Plains. W. Raymond and Margot Liberty, eds. Lincoln: University of Nebraska Press.

Link, M. S.
 1960 "From the Desk of Washington Matthews." Journal of American Folklore, 73:317-25.

Linton, Ralph
 1943 "Nativistic Movement." American Anthropologist, 45(43): 230-40.

List, G.
 1962 "Songs in Hopi Culture, Past and Present." Journal of International Folk Music Council, 14:30-5.
 1963 "The Boundaries of Speech and Song." Ethnomusicology, 7:1-16.
 1964 "The Hopi and the White Man's Music." Sing Out, 14(2):47-9.

1965 "Review of One Folkways Record: Hopi Katchina Songs and Six Other Songs by Hopi Chanters." Ethnomusicology, 10(3):373.
1968 "Hopi as Composer and Poet." in Proceedings of Centennial Workshop in Ethnomusicology, University of British Columbia, Vancouver. Third Edition, P. Crossley-Holland, ed. (1970).

Litvinoff, V.
1973 "Yaqui Easter." Drama Review, 17:52-63.

Lloyd, E.
1940 "The Papago Feast of Saint Francis." Southwestern Monuments Monthly Reports, 389-92.

Lomax, A.
1959 "Folk Song Style." American Anthropologist, 61:927-54.
1962 "Song Structure and Social Structure." Ethnology, 1(4):425-51.
1968 "Folk Song Style and Culture." American Association for Advancement of Science Publication, No. 88.

_____ and I. Bartenieff, and F. Paulay
1974 "Choreometrics: A Method for the Study of Cross-Cultural Pattern in Film." CORD Research Annual, 6:193-212.

Longacre, W.
1973 "Current Directions in Southwestern Archaeology." in Annual Review of Anthropology, No. 2. B. Siegel, ed. Palo Alto, California: Annual Reviews, Inc.

Lowie, Robert H.
1914 "Ceremonialism in North America." American Anthropologist, 16:602-31.
1938 "The Emergence Hole and the Foot Drum." American Anthropologist, 40:174.

Lujan, R. and J. Lujan
1962 "The Hoop Dance." New Mexico Magazine, 40(11-12):37, 39.

Lumholtz, Carl
1912 New Trails in Mexico. New York: Scribner's.

Lummis, Charles Fletcher
1905 "Catching our Archaeology Alive." Out-West, 22:35-45.

Lurie, Nancy Oestreich
1964 "Iroquois Music and Dance." Bureau of American Ethnology Bulletin 187.

1965 "An American Indian Renascence?" Midcontinent American Studies Journal, Vol. 6, No. 2.

MacCauley, Clay
1887 "The Seminole Indians of Florida." Bureau of American Ethnology, 5th Annual Report. Washington, D.C.: U.S. Government Printing Office.

MacLeish, K.
1941 "A Few Hopi Songs from Moenkopi." Masterkey, 15:178-84.

Maillard, A. S.
1758 An Account of the Customs and Manners of the Micnakis and Maricheets. London: S. Hooper & A. Morley.

Malinowski, B.
1926 "Magic, Science, and Religion." in Science, Religion and Reality, J. A. Needham, ed.

Maritain, Jacques
1962 "The Purity of Art" in Art and Scholasticism and the Frontiers of Poetry. Joseph Evans, trans. New York: Charles Scribner & Sons.

Marriott, Alice L.
1944 "Dancing Makes Rain." TFSP, 19:88-93.
1945 "When You Go to the Indian Fair." The Southwest Review, 30(4):335-8.

_____ and Carol Rachlin
1971 Peyote. New York: Crowell.

Marpurg, F. W.
1760 Aaneliding tot het clavier-speelen. Amsterdam: J. U. Hummel.
1795 Anleitung zum Claverspielen. New York: G. Olms.

Marshall, L. R.
1941 "A Drum for the Navajo Chorus." Etude, 59:126.

Martindale, Don A. (Editor)
1967 National Character in the Perspective of the Social Sciences. Philadelphia: American Academy of Political and Social Sciences.

Mason, J. A.
1920 "Papago Harvest Festival." American Anthropologist, 22:13-25.

Mason, O. T.
1897 "Geographical Distributions of the Musical Bow." American Anthropologist, 10:377-80.

Matthews, Washington
1887 "The Mountain Chant: A Navajo Ceremony." Fifth Annual Report, Bureau of American Ethnology.
1889 "Navaho Gambling Songs." American Anthropologist, 2:1-19.
1892 "A Study of Butts and Tips." American Anthropologist, 5:345-50.
1894a "Songs of Sequence of the Navajos." Journal of American Folklore, 7:185-94.
1894b "The Basket Drum." American Anthropologist, 7:202-8.
1896 "Songs of the Navajos." Land of Sunshine, 5:197-201.
1897 "Navaho Legends." Memoirs of American Folklore Society, No. 5.
1902 "The Night Chant." Memoirs of American Museum of Natural History, No. 6.

McAllester, D. P.
1949 Peyote Music. Viking Fund Publications in Anthropology, No. 13. New York: Viking Fund, Inc.
1952 "Navajo Creation Chants." Pamphlet to accompany Album of 5 Records produced by Peabody Museum, Harvard University.
1954 Enemy Way Music. Papers of the Peabody Museum of American Archaeology and Ethnology, Harvard University, Vol. 41(3).
1955 "American Indian Songs and Pan Tribalism." Midwest Folklore, 5:132-6.
1956a "The Role of Music in Western Apache Culture." in Selected Papers of the Fifth International Congress of Anthropological and Ethnological Sciences, Philadelphia.
1956b Myth and Prayers of the Great Star Chant and the Myth of the Coyote Chant. Editor and author of commentaries on material recorded by Mary C. Wheelwright. Museum of Navajo Ceremonial Art, Navajo Religion Series. Santa Fe.
1956c "An Apache Fiddle." Society for Ethnomusicology Newsletter, No. 8:1-5.
1961 Indian Music in the Southwest. Colorado Springs: Taylor Museum.
1962 Music of the Pueblos, Apache and Navajo. LP Record (with D. N. Brown) and booklet. Colorado Springs: Taylor Museum.
1968 "Review of Two Canyon Records: Navajo--Songs of the Dine, and Apache--Songs by Philip and Patsy Cassadore of the San Carlos Tribe." Ethnomusicology, 12(3):401-3.
1970 "Blessingway Songs." in Blessingway, by L. Wyman. Tucson: University of Arizona.
1971a "Review of Two Canyon Records and One Indian House

Recording: Memories of Navajoland, sung by Ed Lee Natay; Philip Cassadore Sings Apache Songs; and Night and Day Yeibichai, sung by Navajo singers from Klagetoh" Ethnomusicology, 15(1):164-70.

1971b "Review of Indian House Record: Navajo Skip Dance and Two-Step Songs." Ethnomusicology, 15(2):296-7.

1971c Readings in Ethnomusicology. New York: Johnson Reprint Corporation.

1972 "Review of Music and Dance of the Tewa Pueblos by G. P. Kurath." Ethnomusicology, 16(3):546-7.

1978 "A Different Drum: A Consideration of Music in the Native American Humanities." in The Religious Character of Native American Humanities, Sam D. Gill, ed. Tempe: Arizona State University, Dept. of Humanities and Religious Studies.

_____ and D. Mitchell
n.d. "Navajo Music." in Handbook of North American Indians, Vol. 9, pt. 2. A. Ortiz, Vol. ed.

McElvary, May F.
1951 "The Deer Dance at Christmas." New Mexico, 29(12): 13, 34-5.

1953 "Shepherd's Fires." New Mexico, 31(12):21, 33.

McGillycuddy, V. T.
1942 "The Significance of the Indian Ghost Dance Religion." in When People Meet: A Study in Race and Culture Contacts. Alain Locke and Bernhard J. Stern, eds. New York: Progressive Education Association.

McLeod, Norma
1974 "Ethnomusicological Research and Anthropology." in Annual Review of Anthropology, No. 2. B. Siegel, ed. Palo Alto, California: Annual Reviews, Inc.

1979 "Play Elements in the Music of North American Indians." in Forms of Play in Native North America, Edward Norbeck and Claire R. Farrer, eds. Proceedings of the American Ethnological Society. St. Paul, Minnesota: West Publishing Co.

McLuhan, Marshall
1962 The Gutenberg Galaxy. London: Routledge and Kegan Paul.

Mead, M.
1959 An Anthropologist at Work: Writings of Ruth Benedict. Boston: Houghton Mifflin Co.

Mead, S. M. and J. E. Mead
1968-9 "The Southwest, U.S.A.: The Indians and Some of

Their Dances." Te Ao How, 65:10-12. (Wellington, New Zealand).

Mechling, W. H.
1958-9 "The Malecite Indians, with Notes on the Micmacs." Anthropologica, 7:1-160 and 8:151-274.

Merriam, Alan P.
1951 "Flathead Indian Instruments and Their Music." Musical Quarterly, XXXVII:368-75.
1964a The Anthropology of Music. Evanston: Northwestern University Press.
1964b "The Arts and Anthropology." in Horizons of Anthropology, S. Tax, ed. Chicago: Aldine Press.
1966 "The Anthropology of Music. Current Anthropology Book Review with Comments." Current Anthropology, 7(2):217-30.
1967 Ethnomusicology of the Flathead Indians. Chicago: Aldine Press.
1974 "Anthropology and the Dance." CORD Research Annual, 6:9-27.

Michelson, Truman
1918 The Mythical Origin of the White Buffalo Dance of the Fox Indians. Bureau of American Ethnology, 40th Annual Report. Washington, D.C.: U.S. Government Printing Office.
1924 "Further Remarks on the Origin of the So-Called Dream Dance of the Central Algonkians." American Anthropologist, 26:293-4.
1928a "Notes on the Buffalo-head Dance of the Thunder Gens of the Fox Indians." Bureau of American Ethnology, Bulletin 87. Washington, D.C.: U.S. Government Printing Office.
1928b "Notes on the Fox Gens Festivals." Proceedings of the 23rd Session of the International Congress of Americanists.
1929a "The Changing Character of Fox Adoption Feasts." American Journal of Sociology, 34:890-2.
1929b "Observations on Thunder Dance of Bear Gens of Fox Indians." Bureau of American Ethnology, Bulletin 89. Washington, D.C.: U.S. Government Printing Office.

Michener, B.
1966a "Yei-be-chai." Viltia, 25(1):20-1.
1966b "The Fire Dance." Viltia, 25(2):7-9.

Miles, A.
1953 "Aboriginal Musical Instruments in North America." Hobbies, 57:134-7.

Miller, J.
1976 "Kokopelli." in Collected Papers in Honor of Florence

Hawley Ellis. T. R. Frisbie, ed. Papers of the Archaeological Society of New Mexico, No. 2. Norman: Hooper Publishing Company.

Mindeleff, C.
1886 "An Indian Dance." Science, 7:507-14.
1898 "Navaho Houses." Seventeenth Annual Report, Bureau of American Ethnology, 2:469-517.

Montell, G.
1938 "Yaqui Dances." Ethnos, 3(6):145-66.

Mooney, James
1886 "The Sacred Formulas of the Cherokees." Seventh Annual Report of the Bureau of American Ethnology. Washington, D.C.
1890a "The Cherokee Ball Play." American Anthropologist, 3(1890):105-32.
1890b "Cherokee Theory and Practice of Medicine." Journal of American Folklore, 3(1890):44-50.
1893 "The Ghost-Dance Religion and the Sioux Outbreak of 1890." Fourteenth Annual Report, Bureau of American Ethnology. Washington, D.C.: U.S. Government Printing Office.
1894 "The Siouan Tribes of the East." Bureau of American Ethnology Bulletin No. 22, Washington, D.C.
1896 "The Ghost-Dance Religion." in The 14th Annual Report of the Bureau of American Ethnology, Part 2. Washington, D.C.: U.S. Government Printing Office.
1900 "Myths of the Cherokee." Nineteenth Annual Report of the Bureau of American Ethnology, Washington, D.C.

_____ and Frans M. Olbrechts
1932 "The Swimmer Manuscript: Cherokee Sacred Formulas and Medicinal Prescriptions." Bureau of American Ethnology, Bulletin No. 99, Washington, D.C.

Morgan, Lewis Henry
1851 "Musical Performances." in League of the Ho-De-No-Sau-Nee, or Iroquois. Reprinted, 1954. Rochester: Sage and Brother.

Morris, E. A.
1959 "Basketmaker Flutes from Prayer Rock District, Arizona." American Antiquity, 24:406-11.

Moskowitz, I. and J. Collier
1972 American Indian Ceremonial Dances. New York: Bounty.

Mullins, Cora Phebe
1929 Songs of the Indian Dances. Omaha: Citizen Printing Co.

Munro, Theodore
1949 The Arts and Their Interrelations. New York: Liberal
Arts.

Murdock, George Peter
1941 Ethnographic Bibliography of North America. Anthropological Studies, Vol. I. New Haven: Yale University
Press.

Murie, James R.
1981 Ceremonies of the Pawnee. Smithsonian Contributions to
Anthropology, No. 27. Washington, D.C.: Smithsonian
Institution Press.

Music Educators Journal
1972 "Music in World Cultures." (October).

Nabokov, Peter
1969 "The Peyote Road." New York Times Magazine, March,
9:30-1.

Nequatewa, E.
1946 "The Flute Ceremony at Hotevilla." Plateau, 19:35-6.

Nettl, B.
1953a "Review of Three LP's by Densmore and the Library of
Congress." Midwest Folklore, 3:124-5.
1953b "Observations on Meaningless Peyote Song Texts."
Journal of American Folklore, 66:161-4.
1953c "Stylistic Variety in North American Indian Music."
Journal of American Musicological Society, 6:160-8.
1954 "North American Indian Musical Styles." Memoirs of the
American Folklore Society, No. 45.
1955 "Musicological Studies in American Ethnological Journals."
Music Library Association Notes, 12:205-9.
1956 Music in Primitive Culture. Cambridge: Harvard University Press.
1959 "Review of Densmore's Music of Acoma, Isleta, Cochiti
and Zuni Pueblos." Ethnomusicology, 3(1):34-5.
1960a An Introduction to Folk Music in the United States.
Wayne State University, Studies No. 7. Detroit: Wayne
University Press.
1960b Cheremis Musical Styles. Bloomington, Indiana Press.
1961 "Polyphony in North American Indian Music." Musical
Quarterly, 47:354-62.
1964 Theory and Method in Ethnomusicology. New York:
Free Press of Glencoe.
1965 Folk and Traditional Music of the Western Continents.
Englewood Cliffs, New Jersey: Prentice-Hall, 2nd ed.,
1973.
1966 "Some Influences of Western Civilization on North

American Music." in New Voices in American Studies. R. Browne, et al., eds.

1969 "Musical Areas Reconsidered: A Critique of North American Indian Research." in Essays in Musicology in Honor of Dragan Plamenac on His 70th Birthday. Gustave Reece and Robin Snow, eds. Pittsburgh: University of Pittsburgh Press.

1970 "Review of A. Lomax's Folk Song Style and Culture." American Anthropologist, 72:438-41.

1975 "The State of Research in Ethnomusicology and Recent Developments." Current Musicology, 20:76-78.

Newcomb, W. W.
1974 North American Indians: An Anthropological Perspective. Pacific Palisades, California: Goodyear Publishing Company.

Nicholas, D.
1939 "Mescalero Apache Girl's Puberty Ceremony." El Palacio, 46:193-204.

Nicholson, H. S.
1945 "Four Songs from a Yuma Version of Los Pastores." University of Arizona General Bulletin, 9:25-8.

Norbeck, E. and Claire R. Farrer
1979 "Forms of Play in Native North America." 1977 Proceedings of the American Ethnological Society. St. Paul, Minnesota: West Publishing Co.

Northrop, F. S. C.
1947 The Logic of the Sciences and the Humanities. New York: Meridian Press.

Oakden, E. C. and M. Sturt
1927 "The Snake Dance of the Hopi Indians." Scottish Geographical Magazine, 43:41-4.

Oliver, M. L.
1911 "The Snake Dance." National Geographic Magazine, 22(2):107-37.

Olson, Ronald L.
n.d. The Social Organization of the Haisla of British Columbia. University of California Anthropological Records, V. 2, No. 5.

Opler, M. E.
1941 An Apache Life-Way. Chicago: University of Chicago Press.

1942 "Adolescence Rite of the Jicarilla." El Palacio, 49:25-38.

1946 Childhood and Youth in Jicarilla Apache Society.

Publications of the Frederick Webb Hodge Anniversary Publications Fund, Vol. 5. Los Angeles: Southwest Museum.
1969a "Remuneration to Supernaturals and Man in Apachean Ceremonialism." Ethnology, 7:356-93.
1969b "Western Apache and Kiowa Apache Materials Relating to Ceremonial Payment." Ethnology, 8:122-4.

Ortega y Gasset, José
1956 The Dehumanization of Art, and Other Writings on Art and Culture. trans., Willard R. Trask. Garden City, New York: Doubleday.

Ortiz, Alfonso
1969a The Tewa World. Chicago: University of Chicago Press.
1969b "Review of One Taos Recordings and Publications Record: So These Won't Be Forgotten: Music of Picuris Pueblo, New Mexico." Ethnomusicology, 13(3):586-8.
1972 "Ritual Drama and Pueblo World View." in New Perspectives on the Pueblos. Alfonso Ortiz, ed. Albuquerque: University of New Mexico Press.

Owen, Mary A.
1919 "The Mythical Origin of the White Buffalo Dance of the Fox Indians." Annual Report, Bureau of American Ethnology, 40.

Painter, M. T.
1974 "A Yaqui Easter." CORD Research Annual, 6:347-50.

Palmer, Rose A.
1929 "North American Indians." Smithsonian Scientific Services, Vol. 4:134-5.

Pancoast, C. L.
1918 "Last Dance of the Picuris." American Museum Journal, 18:308-11.

Parker, Arthur C.
1909 "Secret Medicine Societies of the Seneca." American Anthropologist, 11:165-85.

Parkes, Henry B.
1947 The American Experience. New York: Knopf.

Parsons, Elsie C.
1917 "All-Souls' Day at Zuni, Acoma and Laguna." Journal of American Folklore, 30:495-6.
1919 "Note on a Navajo War Dance." American Anthropologist, 21:465-7.
1920 "Notes on Isleta, Santa Ana, and Acoma." American Anthropologist, 22:57-8, 63.

1921a "Note on the Night Chant at Tuwelchedu." American Anthropologist, 23:240-3.
1921b "Further Notes on Isleta." American Anthropologist, 23:156-65.
1922a "Winter and Summer Dance Series in Zuni." University of California Publications in American Archaeology and Ethnology, 17:169-216.
1922b "Ceremonial Dances at Zuni." El Palacio, 13:119-22.
1923a "Notes on San Felipe and Santo Domingo." American Anthropologist, 25:489-93.
1923b "The Hopi Buffalo Dance." Man, 23:21-7.
1923c "Fiesta at Santa Ana." Scientific Monthly, 16:178-83.
1924 "The Scalp Ceremonial of Zuni." Memoirs of the American Anthropological Association, No. 31:1-42.
1925 "A Pueblo Indian Journal 1920-1921." Memoirs of the American Anthropological Association, No. 32. Menasha, Wisconsin: American Anthropological Association.
1926 "The Ceremonial Calender of the Tewa of Arizona." American Anthropologist, 28:209-29.
1927 "Notes on Jemez Ethnography." American Anthropologist, 29:719.
1928 "The Laguna Migration to Isleta." American Anthropologist, 30:608-10.
1930a "The Social Organization of the Tewa of New Mexico." Memoirs of the American Anthropological Association, No. 37. Menasha, Wisconsin: American Anthropological Association.
1930b "Some Aztec and Pueblo Parallels." American Anthropologist, 35:611-36.
1932 "Isleta, New Mexico." Bureau of American Ethnology Annual Report, No. 47. Washington, D.C.: U.S. Government Printing Office.
1933 "Hopi and Zuni Ceremonialism." Memoirs of the American Anthropological Association, No. 39. Menasha, Wisconsin: American Anthropological Association.
1938 "Humpbacked Flute Player of the Southwest." American Anthropologist, 40:337-8.
1939 Pueblo Indian Religion. 2 Vols. Chicago: University of Chicago Press.

Parsons, McIlvania
1926 "The San Juan Turtle Dance." Horae Scholasticae, 59:177-9.

Peabody, C.
1917 "A Prehistoric Wind-Instrument From Pecos, New Mexico." American Anthropologist, 19:30-3.

Peek, A. M. and E. Johnson
1932 "Red Drums of Christmas: Indian Dance that Celebrates the Birth of Jesus." Pictorial Review, 34:18-19.

Petrullo, Vincenzo
1934 The Diabolic Root. Philadelphia: University of Pennsylvania Press.

Pilling, Arnold E.
1962 "Some Questions on Taos Dancing." Ethnomusicology,
6(2):88-92.

Pillsbury, Dorothy L.
1952 "Christmas Eve in San Felipe." Desert Magazine, 14(12):
22-4.

Poe, Edgar Allan
1950 Edgar Allan Poe: Selected Prose and Poetry. W. H.
Auden, ed. New York: Holt, Rinehart and Winston.

Poley, Horace S.
1920 "An American Wedding." El Palacio, 8:75.

Pollenz, Philippa
1947 "Some Problems in the Notation of Seneca Dances." M.A.
Thesis: Columbia University.
1949 "Methods for the Comparative Study of the Dance."
American Anthropologist, 51:431.

Powers, William K.
1961a "American Indian Music, Part Three: The Social
Dances." American Indian Tradition, 7(3):97-104.
1961b "American-Indian Music, Part Five: Contemporary
Music and Dance of the Western Sioux." American Indian
Tradition, 7(5):158-65.
1961c "The Sioux Omaha Dance." American Indian Tradition,
8(1).
1962a "The Rabbit Dance." American Indian Tradition, 8(3).
1962b "Sneak-Up Dance, Drum Dance, and Flag Dance."
American Indian Tradition, 8(4).
1966 "Feathers' Costume." Pow-wow Trails, Vol. III, No. 7-8.
1981 "Toward a Sound Ethnography of Native American Music."
Ethnomusicology, 25(1):159-62.

Prall, David
1967 Aesthetic Judgment. New York: Crowell.

Prince, J. D. and Frank G. Speck
1903 "The Modern Pequots and Their Language." American
Anthropologist, 5:193-212.

Rader, Melvin (Editor)
1965 A Modern Book of Esthetics. New York: Holt, Rinehart
and Winston.

Radin, Paul
    1911 "Ritual and Significance of the Winnebago Medicine
          Dance." Journal of American Folklore, 24:149-208.
    1945 The Road of Life and Death: A Ritual Drama of the
          American Indian. The Bollingen Series, No. 5. New
          York: Pantheon Books, Inc.

Raymond, J.
    1960-1 "Kumanche of the Zuni Indians of New Mexico."
            Folklorist, 6(3):400-02.

Reade, John
    1877 "Some Wabanski Songs." Transactions of the Royal So-
          ciety of Canada, 5:1-8.

Reagan, Albert B.
    1904 "The Matachina Dance." Proceedings of the Indiana
          Academy of Science, Vol. 1903-07:293.
    1906 "Dances of the Jemez Pueblo Indians." Transactions of
          the Kansas Academy of Science, 23:241-72.
    1910 "Notes on the Shaker Church of the Indians." Proceed-
          ings of the Indiana Academy of Science, Vol. 1908-10:115.
    1911 "Sketches of Indian Life and Character." Transactions
          of the Kansas Academy of Science, 23:141.
    1914 Don Diego or the Pueblo Uprising of 1680. New York:
          Harriman.
    1915 "The Corn Dance at Jemez." Southern Workman, 44:481-4.
    1929 "Fourth of July Summer Solstice Ceremony of the Nava-
          jos." Southern Workman, 58:310-13.
    1934 "A Navaho Fire Dance." American Anthropologist, 36:
          434-7.

Redfield, Robert
    1962 "Primitive World View." in Human Nature and the Study
          of Society. Vol. 1, Margaret Park Redfield, ed. Chicago:
          University of Chicago Press.

Reed, Erik
    1954 "Transition to History in the Pueblo Southeast." Ameri-
          can Anthropologist, 56:595.

Reichard, G.
    1934 Spider Woman. New York: Macmillan.
    1939 Dezba. New York: J. U. Augustin.
    1950 Navaho Religion. 2 Vols. New York: Bollingen Founda-
          tion.

Reilly, P. T.
    1970 "The Disappearing Havasupai Corn-planting Ceremony."
          Masterkey, 44(1):30-4.

Rexroth, K.
 1956 "American Indian Songs: U.S. Bureau of Ethnology Collection." Perspectives U.S.A., 16:197-201.

Reyman, J.
 1974 "Evidence for the Influence of Natural Rhythms in Southwestern Pueblo Dance Patterns." Paper presented at 19th Annual Meeting of Society for Ethnomusicology, held jointly with Committee on Research in Dance, October, San Francisco.

Rhodes, Willard
 1949 "Sioux and Navajo." New York: Folkways Records and Service. Album Notes for Ethnic Folkways Library Album No. 1401:6.
 1952 "North American Indian Music: A Bibliographic Survey of Anthropological Theory." Music Library Association Notes, 10:33-45.
 1956a "American Indian Music." Tomorrow, 4:97-102.
 1956b "Bibliography of Frances Densmore, with Introduction." Society for Ethnomusicology Newsletter No. 7, (April):13-29.
 1963a "North American Indian Music in Transition." Journal of International Folk Music Council, 15:9-14.
 1963b "Selected Hopi Secular Music." Arizona State University: Unpublished Ph.D. Dissertation.
 1967a "Acculturation in North American Indian Music." in Acculturation in the Americas. Proceedings and Selected Papers of the 19th International Congress of Americanists. S. Tax, ed. New York: Cooper Square Publishers.
 1967b "Special Bibliography: Helen Heffron Roberts." Ethnomusicology, 14(1):114-28.

Riemer, Mary Frances
 1980 "Seneca Social Dance Music." Folkways, FE 4072.

Risner, V.
 1973 Dance Ethnography Data Inventory. Los Angeles: University of California at Los Angeles, Dept. of Dance.

Robb, John D.
 1952-3 "The J. D. Robb Collection of Folk Music Recordings." New Mexico Folklore, 7:6-20.
 1961 "The Matachines Dance--A Ritual Folk Dance." Western Folklore, 20(2):87-101.
 1964 "Rhythmic Patterns of the Santo Domingo Corn Dance." Ethnomusicology, 8(2):154-60.

Roberts, D. L.
 1964 "A Brief Guide to Rio Grande Pueblo Dances." Quarterly of the Southwestern Association on Indian Affairs, 1(2): 12-15.

1965 "Review of Six Taos Recordings and Publications Records: Taos Indian Songs, Taos Spanish Songs, New Mexican Alabados, Taos Matachines Music, Picuris Indian Songs, and Bailes de Taos." Ethnomusicology, 9(2):205-6.

1970 "Tewa Pueblo Round Dances." in Music and Dance of the Tewa Pueblos, by G. Kurath. Museum of New Mexico Research Records, No. 8. Santa Fe: Museum of New Mexico Press.

1972 "The Ethnomusicology of the Eastern Pueblos." in New Perspectives on the Pueblos. A. Ortiz, ed. Albuquerque: University of New Mexico Press.

Roberts, Helen H.
1923 "Chakwena Songs of Zuni and Laguna." Journal of American Folklore, 36:177-84.

1927 "Indian Music from the Southwest." Natural History, 27:257-65.

1928 "Analysis of Picuris Songs." 43rd Annual Report, Bureau of American Ethnology: 399-447.

1933 "The Pattern Phenomenon in Primitive Music." Zeitschrift fur vergleichende Musikwissenschaft, p. 49-52. Notenbeispiele, p. 25-30.

1936 Musical Areas in Aboriginal North America. Yale University Publications in Anthropology, No. 12.

Rothenberg, J.
1972 Shaking the Pumpkin. New York: Doubleday.

Russell, F.
1898 "An Apache Medicine Dance." American Anthropologist, 11:367-72.

1908 "The Pima." 26th Annual Report, Bureau of American Ethnology, 3-389.

Russell, Frank
1975 The Pima Indians. Re-edition with Introduction, etc., by Bernard L. Fontana. Tucson: University of Arizona Press.

Rust, H. W.
1896 "The Moqui Snake Dance." Land of Sunshine, 4:70-6.

Sachs, C.
1937 World History of the Dance. New York: W. Norton & Company.

1940 The History of Musical Instruments. New York: W. Norton & Company.

Sargent, Margaret
1950 "Seven Songs from Loretta." Journal of American Folklore, 63:175-80.

Saxton, Dean and Lucille
1969 Dictionary: Papago and Pima to English and English to Papago and Pima. Tucson: University of Arizona Press.

Schevill, M.
1947 Beautiful on the Earth. Tucson: University of Arizona Press.

Schoolcraft, Henry R.
1821 Narrative Journal of Travels from Detroit Northwest through the Great Chain of American Lakes to the Sources of the Mississippi River in the year 1820. Albany: E. & E. Hosford.

Schweitzer, J. and R. K. Thomas
1952 "Fiesta of St. Francis at San Francisquito, Sonora." Kiva, 18(1-2):1-7.

Seder, T.
1952 "Old World Overtones in the New World: Some Parallels with North American Musical Instruments." University Museum Bulletin, University of Pennsylvania, No. 16-4.

Seton, Ernest T.
1910 The War Dance and the Fire-fly Dance. New York: Doubleday Page Co.

Shafter, Mary Severance
1927 American Indian and Other Folk: Dances for Schools, Pageants and Playgrounds. New York: A. S. Barnes & Company.

Shimony, Annemarie
1961 "Conservations among the Iroquois at the Six Nations Reserve." Yale University Publications in Anthropology 65. New Haven: Yale University Press.

Skinner, Alanson
1909 "The Iroquois Indians of Western New York." Southern Workman, 38:206-11.
1911 "Dances and Music of the Northern Saulteau." in Notes on the Eastern Cree and Northern Saulteaux. Anthropological Papers of the American Museum of Natural History, Vol. IX, New York: American Museum.
1915 "Associations and Ceremonies of the Menomoni Indians." Anthropological Papers, Vol. 13. New York: The American Museum of Natural History.
1919 "The Sun Dance of the Plains Ojibwa." Anthropological Papers, Vol. 16. Publications in Anthropology. New York: The American Museum of Natural History.
1920 "Medicine Ceremonies of the Menominee, Iowa, and

Wahpeton Dakota." Indian Notes and Monographs #4.
Museum of the American Indian. Heye Foundation.
1925 "Songs of the Menominee Medicine Ceremony." American
Anthropology, Vol. 27:290-314.

Sloane, E.
1962 "Hoop Dance." New Mexico Magazine, 40(11-12):39.

Slotkin, James Sidney
1957 "The Menomini Pow-wow." Milwaukee Public Bulletin No.
4. Milwaukee.
1975 "The Peyote Way." in Teachings from the American Earth,
Dennis and Barbara Tedlock, eds. New York: Liveright.

Smith, H. E.
1971 "Southeastern Studies--A View to the Future." Human
Organization, 30:427-36.

Smith, H. I.
1896 "Certain Shamanistic Ceremonies Among the Ojibwas."
American Antiquity, 18:282-4.

Smith, Nicholas, N.
1955 "Wabanaki Dances." Bulletin of the Massachusetts
Archaeological Society, 16:29-37.
1962 "Saint Francis Indian Dances--1960." Ethnomusicology,
6:15-19.

Smith, Seba
1846a "The Religion and Superstition of the North American
Indians, No. II." The Literary Emporium, 3:97-100 (April).
1846b "The Religion and Superstition of the North American
Indians, No. III, IV, V." The Literary Emporium, 3:129-
33; 170-4; 230-3 (May, June, August).

Smithson, C. L.
1959 "The Havasupai Woman." University of Utah Anthropological Papers, No. 38.

Snyder, A. F.
1966 "Navajo Night Dances and Ballet's Golden Age." Film
News, 23(5):12.
1974 "The Dance Symbol." CORD Research Annual, 6:213-24.

Sonneck, O. G. T., and William Treat Upton
1945 A Bibliography of Early Secular American Music (18th
Century). Washington: Library of Congress, Music Division.

Sorokin, Pitirim
1941 The Crisis of Our Age: The Social and Cultural Outlook.
New York: Dutton.

1957 Social and Cultural Dynamics. Boston: Porter Sargent.

Speck, Frank G.
1909 "Ethnology of the Yuchi Indians." University of Pennsylvania Museum Anthropological Publications. 1:1-154. Philadelphia: University of Pennsylvania Museum.
1911 Ceremonial Songs of the Creek and Yuchi Indians, with Music transcribed by Jacob D. Sapir. University of Pennsylvania Museum Anthropological Publication 1 (No. 1). Philadelphia: University Museum.
1922 Beothuk and Micmac: Notes and Monographs. Museum of the American Indian. Heye Foundation Misc. Series 22.
1931 A Study of the Delaware Big House Indian Ceremony. Pennsylvania Historical Commission (Harrisburg), Vol. II.
1935 Naskapi: The Savage Hunters of the Labrador Peninsula. Norman: University of Oklahoma Press.
1937 "Oklahoma-Delaware Ceremonies, Feasts and Dances." Memoirs of the American Philosophical Society, Vol. 7. Philadelphia: University of Pennsylvania Press.
1939 "Catawba Religious Beliefs, Mortuary Customs and Dances." Primitive Man, 12(2):21-57.
1940 Penobscot Man. Philadelphia: University of Pennsylvania Press.
1945 "The Iroquois: A Study in Cultural Evolution." Cranbrook Institute of Science Bulletin 23. Detroit: Cranbrook Institute of Science.
1949 Midwinter Rites of the Cayga Long House. Philadelphia: University of Pennsylvania Press.

_____ and Leonard Broom
1951 Cherokee Dance and Drama. Berkeley and Los Angeles: University of California Press.

_____ and George Herzog
1942 The Tutelo Spirit Adoption Ceremony. Harrisburg, Pennsylvania: Pennsylvania Historical Commission.

Spence, Lewis
1947 Myth and Ritual in Dance, Game and Rhyme. London: Watts & Co.

Spengler, Oswald
1926 The Decline of the West. New York: Knopf.

Spicer, Edward H.
1974 "Context of the Yaqui Easter Ceremony." CORD Research Annual, 6:309-46.

Spicer, L.
1928 "Havasupai Ethnography." American Museum of Natural History, Anthropological Papers, 29(3):81-392.

Spier, Leslie
    1921 "The Sun Dance of the Plains Indians: Its Development
        and Diffusion." Anthropological Papers, 16. Publications
        in Anthropology, The American Museum of Natural History.

Spinden, Herbert Joseph
    1908 "The Nez Percé Indians." Memoirs, American Anthropo-
        logical Association, Vol. II, Part 3. Lancaster, Pennsyl-
        vania.
    1915a "Home Songs of the Tewa Indians." American Museum
        Journal, 15:73-8.
    1915b "Indian Dances of the Southwest." American Museum
        Journal, 15:103-15.

Stacey, R.
    1907 "Some Zuni Ceremonies and Melodies." Music Lover's
        Calendar, 2:54-61.

Steiger, Brad
    1974 Medicine Power. Garden City, New York: Doubleday.

Stephen, A. M.
    1936 Hopi Journal. E. C. Parsons, ed. New York: Colum-
        bia University Press.
    1937 "Clowns in Hopi Ceremonial Dances." Nature, 139:888.
    1939-40 "The Hopi Indians of Arizona." Masterkey, 13 and
        14.

Sterling, M. W.
    1941 "Snake Bites and the Hopi Snake Dance." Annual Re-
        ports, Bureau of Regents, Smithsonian Institution.

Stevenson, M. C.
    1894 "The Sia." 11th Annual Report, Bureau of American
        Ethnology.
    1904 "The Zuni Indians." 23rd Annual Report, Bureau of
        American Ethnology.

Stevenson, R.
    1973a "Written Sources for Indian Music until 1882."
        Ethnomusicology, 17(1):1-40.
    1973b "English Sources for Indian Music until 1881."
        Ethnomusicology, 17(3):399-42.

Stricklen, E. G.
    1923 "Notes on Eight Papago Songs." University of California
        Publications in American Archaeology and Ethnology, 20.

Sturtevant, William
    1961 "Comment on Gertrude P. Kurath's 'Effects of Environ-
        ment on Cherokee-Iroquois Ceremonialism, Music and

Dance.'" in Symposium on Cherokee and Iroquois Culture. William Fenton and John Gulick, eds. BAE Bulletin 180. Washington, D.C.

Swanton, John R.
1925 "Social Organization and Social Usages of the Indians of the Creek Confederacy." Bureau of American Ethnology, Annual Report 42. Washington, D.C.: U.S. Government Printing Office.
1928a "Social and Religious Beliefs and Usages of the Chickasaw Indians." Bureau of American Ethnology, Annual Report 44. Washington, D.C.: U.S. Government Printing Office.
1928b "Religious Beliefs and Medical Practices of the Creek Indians." 42nd Annual Report, Bureau of American Ethnology. Washington, D.C.: U.S. Government Printing Office.
1931 "Source Material for the Social and Ceremonial Life of the Choctaw Indians." Bulletin 103, Bureau of American Ethnology. Washington, D.C.: U.S. Government Printing Office.

Tait, W. M.
1915 "Indian Dances." Overland Monthly, 65:88-92.

Taylor, B.
1974 "The Physical Values and Physiological Function of American Indian Dance." CORD Research Annual, 6:149-65.

Tedlock, B. J.
1973 "Kachina Dance Songs in Zuni Society: The Role of Aesthetics in Social Integration." Wesleyan University: Unpublished M.A. thesis.

Tedlock, D.
1972 Finding the Green: Narrative Poetry of Zuni Indians. New York: Dial Press.

Tedlock, Dennis and Barbara Tedlock
1975 Teachings from the American Earth. New York: Liveright.

Teit, James
1927-8 "The Flathead Group." in The Salishan Tribes of the Western Plateaus. 45th Annual Report of the Bureau of American Ethnology. Washington, D.C.: U.S. Government Printing Office.

Thomas, Robert K.
1961 "The Redbird Smith Movement." in Symposium on Cherokee and Iroquois Culture. William N. Fenton and John Gulick, eds. Bureau of American Ethnology, Bulletin 180. Washington, D.C.: U.S. Printing Office.

1965 "Pan-Indianism." Midcontinent American Studies Journal, Vol. 6, No. 2.

Thompson, G.
1889 "An Indian Dance at Jemez." American Anthropologist, 2:351-55.

Thwaites, Reuben Gold (Editor)
1959 The Jesuit Relations and Allied Documents. Travels and Explorations of the Jesuit Missionaries in New France 1610-1791. New York: Pageant Books.

Tooker, Elizabeth
1964 "An Ethnography of the Huron Indians, 1615-1649." BAE Bulletin 190. Washington, D.C.
1970 The Iroquois Ceremonial of Midwinter. Syracuse: Syracuse University Press.
1978 The Indians of the Northeast: A Critical Bibliography. Bloomington: Indiana University Press.

Tress, A.
1968 "Deer Dances I Have Seen." Dance Magazine, 42(9): 58-61; 84-5.

Trigger, Bruce G. (Editor)
1978 Handbook of North American Indians. Vol. 15: Northeast. Washington, D.C.: Smithsonian Institution.

Troyer, C.
1913 The Zuni Indians and Their Music. Philadelphia: Theodore Presser Co.

Turner, Victor
1969 The Ritual Process. Chicago: Aldine Press.

Turney-High, Harry
1933 "The Bluejay Dance." American Anthropologist, XXXV, Jan.-Mar. 103-7.

Underhill, Ruth M.
1938 Singing for Power: The Song Magic of the Papago Indians. Berkeley: University of California Press.
1946 Papago Indian Religion. New York: Columbia University Contributions to Anthropology, #33.
1948 "Ceremonial Patterns in the Greater Southwest." Monographs of the American Ethnological Society, Vol. 13.

Valenzuela, J.
1974 "Roots, Branches and Blossoms." CORD Research Annual, 6:299-306.

Van Gennep, Arnold
1972 The Rites of Passage. Chicago: University of Chicago
Press.

Van Stone, M. R.
1941 "Songs of the Indians." El Palacio, 48:149-54.

Vivas, Eliseo and Murray Krieger (Editors)
1953 The Problems of Aesthetics. New York: Rinehart.

Voegelin, C. F. and R. C. Euler
1957 "Introduction to Hopi Chants." Journal of American
Folklore, 70:115-36.

Voegelin, Erminie W.
1942 "Shawnee Musical Instruments." American Anthropologist, 44:463-75.

Vogt, E. Z.
1955 "Study of the Southwestern Fiesta Systems as Exemplified by the Laguna Fiesta." American Anthropologist,
57:820-39.

von Hornbostel, E. M.
1923 "Musik und Musikinstrumente." in Vom Rorima zum
Orinoko, Kock-Gruenberg, Stuttgart. III.

Voth, H. R.
1901 "Oraibi Powamu Ceremony." Field Museum, Anthropological Series, 3:67-158.
1903a "Oraibi Oaqol Ceremony." Field Museum, Anthropological Series, 6:1-46.
1903b "Oraibi Summer Snake Ceremonies." Field Museum,
Anthropological Series, 3:267-358.
1912a "Oraibi Marau." Field Museum, Anthropological Series,
11-88.
1912b "Oraibi New Year Ceremony." Field Museum, Anthropological Series, 11:111-19.
1912c "Tawa Baholawu of the Oraibi Flute Societies." Field
Museum, Anthropological Series, 11:121-36.

Wallace, Anthony
1951 "The Frank G. Speck Collection." American Philosophical Society Proceedings, 95:286-9.
1955 "The Disruption of the Individual's Identification with
His Culture in Disasters and Other Extreme Situations."
Paper read at National Research Council, Committee on
Disaster Studies, Conference on Theories of Human Behavior in Extreme Situations. Vassar.
1956 "Revitalization Movements." American Anthropologist,
58:264-81.

1970 The Death and Rebirth of the Seneca. New York: Knopf.

Walsh, Dorothy
    1953 "The Cognitive Content of Art." in The Problems of Aesthetics. Eliseo Vivas and Murray Krieger, eds. New York: Rinehart.

Walter, Paul, Jr.
    1930 "Notes on a Trip to Jemez." El Palacio, 29:207.

Walton, L. L.
    1926 Dawn Boy: Blackfoot and Navaho Songs. New York: Dutton.
    1930 "Navajo Song Patterning." Journal of American Folklore, 43:105-18.

Ware, N.
    1970 "Survival and Change in Pima Indian Music." Ethnomusicology, 14(1):100-113.

Weber, Max
    1958 The Rational and Social Foundations of Music. Don Martindale, et al., trans. and eds. New York: American Book-Stratford Press.

Weinman, J.
    1970 "The Influence of Pueblo Worldview on the Construction of its Vocal Music." Ethnology, 14(2):313-15.

White, Leslie A.
    1927 "Ancient Indians and Modern Pueblos." Buffalo Society of Natural Science Hobbies, 8(6):7-10; 13-16.
    1932 "The Pueblo of San Felipe." Memoirs of the American Anthropological Association, 38:21-40; 50-5; 56-60.
    1935 "The Pueblo of Santo Domingo, New Mexico." Memoirs of the American Anthropological Association, 43:47-54; 60; 88-120; 136-44; 150-5; 159-60.
    1942 "The Pueblo of Santa Ana, New Mexico." American Anthropologist, 44(2):115-44; 204-79; 296-302; 305-16.
    1945 "Ethnography of Sandia." Papers of the Michigan Academy of Science, Arts and Letters, 31:220.
    1962 "The Pueblo of Sia, New Mexico." Bureau of American Ethnology, 184:125; 150; 156; 166; 170; 177; 183; 226-7; 233; 236-62; 265-70; 271-4; 276; 282-3.

Wilder, C. S.
    1968 "The Yaqui Deer Dance: A Study in Cultural Change." Bureau of American Ethnology, 186:145-210.

Williamson, G., et al.
    1940 "The Fiesta of Saint Francis Xavier." Kiva, 16(1-2).

Winship, George Parker
1901 "A Maine Indian Ceremony in 1605." American Anthropologist, 3:387-8.

Wissler, Clark
1912 "Societies and Ceremonial Associations in the Oglala Division of Teton-Dakota." American Museum of Natural History, Anthropological Papers, Vol. XI, Part I.
1916 "General Discussion of Shamanistic and Dancing Societies." Anthropological Papers of the American Museum of Natural History, Part 2, 11:853-6.
1933 "Year's Calendar of Indian Dances." Theatre Arts Monthly, 17:663.
1938 The American Indian. Third Edition, New York: Oxford University Press.

Witthoft, John
1946 "Cayuga Midwinter Festival." New York Folklore Quarterly, 2:24-39.
1949 Green Corn Ceremonialism in the Eastern Woodlands. Occasional Papers of the Museum of Anthropology, University of Michigan, No. 13. Ann Arbor: University of Michigan Press.

Woodward, A.
1937 "A Song of the Navaho War." Masterkey 11(1);26-8.

Wyman, L.
1962 The Windways of the Navaho. Colorado Spring: Taylor Museum.
1965 The Red Antway of the Navaho. Santa Fe: Museum of Navajo Ceremonial Art, Navajo Religion Series 5.
1970 Blessingway. Tucson: University of Arizona Press.

_____ and C. Kluckhohn
1938 Navaho Classification of Their Song Ceremonials. Memoirs of American Anthropological Association, No. 50.

Chapter Twenty-Nine

DANCE AND DRAMA-DANCE OF LATIN AMERICAN INDIANS

Pamela Howard

> "And thus they danced: they
> did not leap nor make great
> movements; they did not make
> dance gestures; they did not
> move throwing themselves about,
> nor dance making arm-movements,
> nor go bending their bodies,
> nor whirling, nor wander from
> side to side, nor fall back."

> From, "The Flowers are Of-
> fered, Ceremony of the Ninth
> Month," Tlazochimaco, Flo-
> rentine Codex as translated
> by A. J. O. Anderson and
> C. E. Dibble.

And just how did they dance? In this particular case, as a
serpent; quietly, calmly and evenly. However, that is not to say
that all Indian dances of today display such controlled, somber
movements or even that all dances of the past were similarly low
keyed. To the contrary, Indian dance and dance-dramas of Latin
America fluctuate between the cacophonous "Sicuri" dance of Bolivia, the daring flying pole dance of Mexico and Mesoamerica, and
the aforementioned Ninth Month Ceremony.

The distinction between "folk" and "Indian" dance is, at
times, difficult to discern which in turn leads to difficulties in
definition. It has also been difficult, or nearly impossible, to study
Indian dance as a pure form free of Western influence. The overwhelming dominance of the conquistadors, and the persistant, all
pervasive, Catholic infiltration into and synthesis with the religious
structure of Indian culture renders it impossible, and undesirable,
to study Indian dance and dance-dramas without considering Hispanic

culture and influence. However, generally speaking, one can consider "Indian" those dances performed by Indians to musical instruments made of natural elements such as wood, seed and animal skins, and masks and costumes using feathers or body paint.

Events that give rise to Indian performances are usually either religious, medicinal or ceremonial in nature. Dancing for the sake of dance or social pleasure is unknown in the purer Indian cultures of Latin America.

To study adequately the dance of a people one must employ skills from a broad range of social science disciplines including ethnology, linguistics, musicology, history, sociology, and anthropology or else work as a team with specialists from those disciplines. The dances of very few Latin American Indian cultures have been so thoroughly studied, if any at all, and the field is open for such comprehensive studies.

The earliest evidence of dance and dramatic performance in Latin America can be seen in the fascinating, colorful frescoes on the walls of Bonampak, Mayan archaeological ruins located in southern Mexico; on petroglyphs of other ruins; and in the few remaining animal skin or bark codices laboriously produced by the scribes of ancient American civilizations. Examples of dancing figures may be seen in, among others, the Aztec codices Florentino, Borbonicus and Magliabecchiano and the Mixtec Codex Vindobinensis. These same sources can also be used to study the costumes, ornaments, musical instruments, masks and choreography of the ancestors of today's Mexican Indian dancers.

Further documentation of the prevalence and importance of ceremonial dance or dramatic performance is offered by the prolific chroniclers, who were for the most part, priests who accompanied the Spanish and Portuguese conquistadors to the New World. Among the numerous chroniclers, those who described at greater length the dances and ceremonies they witnessed were Bernardo de Sahagún in his Historia General de las Cosas de Nueva España,[1] José de Anchieta in Cartas, informações, fragmentos históricos e sermões do Padre ..., José de Acosta in Historia natural y moral de las Indias, Juan de Torquemada in Los Veintiún libros rituales y Monarchia Indiana and Francisco López de Gómara in Historia de México.

Once the chroniclers had, to their satisfaction, described the so-called pagan rites, ceremonies, and dances of the New World and their reactions to them, the recording of such activities experienced a lull, with the exception of occasional church edicts prohibiting such acts. It was not until 1862, with the appearance of Gramática de la lengua Quiché that there was a resurgence of recorded dance observations. The adventurous French priest, Charles Etiènne Brasseur de Bourbourg, discovered the Rabinal Achí and later recorded several dance-dramas of the Indians of Guatemala, most of which he surely had witnessed, others of which he may not have.

Shortly thereafter, in 1881, the thoroughly Brazilian brazilianist João Barbosa Rodriguez published his article, "O Canto e dança selvícola" (The Song and Dance of the Jungle), in the Revista Brazileira in which he provides minute details of many dances and semi-dances of Amazonian head-hunters and other, more civilized, tribes.

The period from the turn of the century until the 1920's saw many adventurous expeditions into the lesser explored regions of Mexico, Central and South America that resulted in the unearthing and rediscovery of ancient ruins as well as an increased interest in the contemporary vestiges of ancient cultural practices. Ethnological studies experienced a great surge and Indian dance movement observations figured frequently in these studies. A lengthy report to the Institut Ethnographique International de Paris in 1913 by Auguste Genin entitled, "Notes on the Dances, Music and Songs of the Ancient and Modern Mexicans"[2] is an earlier work containing many good photographs thereby rendering it an excellent source for costume verification. Another notable, albeit brief, article of the period is Jean Charlot's "Esthetics of Indian Dances" (Mexican Folkways, 1925, 1(2):4-8). Charlot combines his observations and deep appreciation of foreign art forms with acute sensitivity and perception.

Many more reports, articles and slim tomes continued to appear steadily throughout the 1930's and 1940's emanating from European, North and South American anthropologists, and ethnographers. One notable work of the period is Enrique Llano's Danses indiennes du Mexique in which he focuses on pre-Columbian Maya and Aztec dance. From 1946 to 1959 a truly outstanding source for its time came to light through the efforts of a number of scholars in conjunction with the United States Bureau of Ethnology. The Handbook of South American Indians, edited by Julian Steward, is a key English language source to Indian dance movement, and tribal culture as a whole, for that region. Due to its classified arrangement, information on dance is scattered throughout the seven-volume set. However, it is a gold mine for many lesser studied tribes and dances. Also noteworthy is Felicitas Barreto's Danças indígenas no Brasil with concise descriptions of dozens of Indian dances accompanied by photographs.

It was with the numerous key publications of the 1960's and early 1970's that the study of Indian dance came of age. The first major work of the period was a Middle American Institute compilation of articles entitled Native Theatre in Middle America, which included, among others, "Dance of the Conquest of Guatemala" by Barbara Bode, and "The Calderonian Auto Sacramental = El Gran Teatro del Mundo" by William Hunter.

Later, Samuel Martí and Gertrude P. Kurath, both of whom
are leading scholars in this field and have written numerous articles dating from the 1940's, combined their efforts and talents to
publish another outstanding source, Dances of Anáhuac, which
appeared in 1964. The work is well illustrated with diagrams and
pictographs from codices, chronicler's engravings, and photographs
of ancient musical instruments and contemporary performances. Theoretical considerations of religion and art; ceremonial and secular
dances and choreography; symbolism; and regional comparisons are
treated with insight gained from years of study. Gertrude Kurath
also wrote the lengthy bibliographic essay, "Drama, Dance and Music," in Volume Six of the Handbook of Middle American Indians
(1967). Either of these two works could be used as a point of departure for the study of this topic.

The major work to appear in the 1970's deals only with Mexican Indian dance. Historia general del arte mexicano: danzas y
bailes populares (México: Editorial Hermes, 1976) by Electra Mompradé and Tonatiúh Gutiérrez contains descriptions of nearly 100
dances, supplemented by more than 250 photographs. The evolution of Indian dance is explored thoroughly from its pre-Columbian
roots to contemporary Mestizo dances.

The following bibliography is, by no means, to be considered
comprehensive. It is intended to serve only as a guide or stepping
stone to the major sources and selected, good minor sources on Latin American Indian dance. The inclusion of many foreign language
sources was necessitated by the simple fact that a great portion of
the scholarship in the field has been carried out by persons whose
native language is not English. All annotated items were reviewed
by the bibliographer (with one noted exception); other items were
not readily available. Especially useful sources are marked with an
asterisk (*).

All geographical regions of continental Latin America have
been covered, although unavoidably in varying depths. The pre-
ponderance of entries for Mexico in the bibliography reflects its
place as the leading subject for studies of indigenous dance and
drama. Logically, the trend appears to have been that the countries with the greater Indian populations have inspired a greater
percentage of the literature on Indian dance.

The methodology implemented for this bibliography included a
thorough search of the card catalog of Tulane University's Latin
American Library and consultation of numerous subject bibliographies and indices. Library of Congress subject headings that provided the best leads were:

    Dancing--Folk and national dance
    Festivals
    Folk dancing
    Folk drama

Indians of Central America--Dances
Indians of South America--Dances
Indians of (Specific country)--Dances
(Specific Indian group)--Rites and ceremonies

Particularly useful bibliographies and indices not previously mentioned were:

Handbook of Latin American Studies. Gainesville: University of
Florida Press, 1935- .

Hispanic American Periodicals Index. Tempe, Az: Arizona State
University Library, 1974- .

Bibliographic Guide to Latin American Studies. Boston: G. K.
Hall, 1978- .

Gropp, Arthur. Bibliography of Latin American Bibliographies
Published in Periodicals. Metuchen, N.J.: Scarecrow Press,
1968.

Bibliographic Guide to Dance. Boston: G. K. Hall, 1976- .

Guide to Dance Periodicals. Gainesville: University of Florida
Press, 1931-1935. Volume 4.

Dictionary Catalog of the Dance Collection. New York Public Library. Boston: G. K. Hall, 1974.

Notes

1. This work includes a Spanish translation of the Florentine Codex
   originally composed in Aztec. Arthur J. O. Anderson and
   Charles E. Dibble have translated the thirteen parts from
   the Aztec into English. See: Florentine Codex: General
   History of the Things of New Spain. (Santa Fe, N.M.:
   School of American Research, 1950-1955).

2. This was later published in the Annual Report (1920) of the
   Smithsonian Institution, in English.

Mexico

Acuña, René. Farsas y representaciones escénicas de los mayas
antiguos. México: Universidad Nacional Autónoma de
México, 1978. (Centro de Estudios Mayas, cuaderno 15).
75p.

A glossary of Maya "voces" relating to Mayan games, dance

and farces extracted from the Diccionario de Motul (Vol. 1).
Also contains a section on "unknown" dances based on historical sources such as Diego de Landa's and Sahagún's
works. Bibliography.

Adán, Elfego. "Las Danzas de Coatetelco." Anuario del Museo
Nacional de Arqueología, Historia y Etnología, 2(1910):133-134.

Alcaraz, Angela. "La Canacuas; the canacuas." Mexican Folkways,
1930, 6(3):117-118.

Brief description of dance as performed in Uruguay. Contends that dance is post-conquest in origin. Spanish and
English.

Alvarez y Alvarez de la Cadena, Luis. México: leyendas-costumbres,
trajes y danzas. [2nd. ed. (facsimile) Mexico]: Jesus Medina (Editor), 1970. 458p.

The chapter on costumes and dance (pages 304-418) is most
useful, however there is a good deal of information scattered
throughout the volume. Detailed descriptions of Indian dance
are provided for each of many groups and regions of Mexico.
Color sketches are very good although the models look decidedly European.

Amezquita Borja, Francisco. Música y danza de la Sierra Norte de
Puebla. Puebla, Mexico: n.p., 1943.

Barrera Vasquez, Alfredo. "El Teatro y la danza entre los antiguos
mayas de Yucatan." El Libro de los cantares de Dzitbalche.
Mexico: n.p., 1960.

Bennet, W. C. and R. M. Zingg. "Native fiestas," "Peyote" and
"Church fiestas." In, The Tarahumara: An Indian Tribe of
Northern Mexico. Chicago: University of Chicago Press,
1935. (Pp. 268-90; 296-318).

Very good descriptions of several Tarahumara fiestas including configurations, and ceremonial paraphernalia. Some dances
are "pure" Indian, others are church-inspired dances. Descriptions of curing, green-corn, rain, harvest, peyote,
Matachines, and Guadalupe fiestas are provided. In the
summary of the chapter "Church fiestas," primitive aspects
of performances are contrasted with church-inspired movements. Illustrations.

Bricker, Victoria R. "Historical Dramas in Chiapas, Mexico."
Journal of Latin American Lore, 3(2):227-248.

Attempts to document survival of the Dance of the Conquest

and the Dance of Moors and Christians in highland Chiapas. Includes some text excerpts of dramas and discusses performers, history, structure and content of the Dance of Moors and Christians.

Bricker, Victoria Reifler. Ritual humor in highland Chiapas. Austin: University of Texas Press [1973]. 257p.

Contains good descriptions of many Mexican Indian dances throughout the text. Reader must use index to locate scattered descriptions of specific dances. Also contains many photographs depicting costumes and masks. Illustrations. Bibliography.

Bruno Ruiz, Luis. Breve historia de la danza en México. México: Libro-Mex [cover 1956]. 140p.

Brief descriptions of Aztec dance and instruments based on Sahagún, Clavijero, and Códices Borbónico, Florentino, and Mexicas given on pages 19-34.

Campobello, Nellie. Ritmos indígenas de México. México: n.p. 1940. 246p.

Detailed descriptions of movements and rhythms particular to various Mexican regions, i.e. Oaxaca, Northern Mexico, Michoacan. Includes many indigenous movements (Mayan, Yaqui, Tarascan) as well as folkloric ones. Unfortunately, configurations are not given and stick-figure drawings are useless as examples of movements.

Campos, Rubén M. "Las Danzas aztecas." Gaceta Musical (Paris). Part 1, 1(2):8-14 (February 1928) and Part 2, 1(3):19-24 (March 1928).

The place of dance in the life of the ancient Aztecs and the place of Aztec dance in modern Mexico. Contains music and text of songs.

_____. "Las Danzas mexicanas." Nuestro México, 1932, (1):25-29.

Carrasco, P. "Tarascan folk religion: an analysis of economic, social and religious interactions." Tulane University. Middle American Research Institute. Publication No. 17. (Pp. 1-64).

Charlot, Jean. "Esthetics of Indian dances;" Mexican Folkways, 1925, 1(2):4-8.

Charlot praises and elevates Indian dance by espousing that the "Indian dance proceeds from a certain taste of beauty

residing in proportion, and giving to their best works the
feature of mathematic passion, which puts them on a much
higher plane than the works we are accustomed to call
beautiful." States his theories on gestures, dress and exhorts further study on Indian taste in dress and dance.

Christensen, Bodil. "The Acatlaxqui Dance of Mexico." Ethnos,
1937, 4:133-36.

Succinct, first-hand description of the dance which takes
place on November 25 to celebrate St. Catherine's Day.
Illustrations.

Danzas mexicanas auténticas. México, D.F.: Palacio de Bellas
Artes, Monografías de las danzas, 1937.

Dominguez, Francisco. "Canacuas, danza antigua de Guaris; ancient
dance of the Guaris." Mexican Folkways, 1930, 6(3):110-16.

Description of the pre-conquest origins of this Tarascan
wedding dance and songs in Paracho, Michoacan. Includes
themes of "guaris" (unmarried girls), tata niño (good father,
little friend), compadrito (good little friend) and Flor de
Changunga. Illustrations.

Erasmus, Charles John. "A raindance in northwest Mexico; the
causal analysis of an event." In: Manners, Robert A., ed.
Process and pattern in culture, pp. 84-98.

Fergusson, Erna. Fiesta in Mexico. New York: A. A. Knopf,
1934.

Fernández, J. and V. T. Mendoza. Danzas de los concheros de
San Miguel de Allende, México. México: n.p., 1941. (Pp.
12-17.)

Flores Barnes, Alura. "The Jarana yucateca." Real Mexico, 1934,
3(7):24-25.

Gallop, Rodney. "Aerial dances of the Otomis." The Geographical
Magazine 6(2):73-88.

Concise, well-written description of the "juego de los voladores" performed in Metepec, Pahuatlan, and Huehuetlilla,
Mexico. Uses several excerpts from Torquemada's De la
monarchia Indiana to describe religious significance of
dance. Includes speculation regarding the appearance of
Malinche in some dances. Map, illustrations.

_____. "Dances of Indian Mexico." [Parts 1-5]. The Dancing
Times. (London), 1937, p. 11-13; continued in subsequent
issues.

Part 1. Ancient Aztec dances. Part 2. Among the Yaqui Indians. Part 3. The flying dance. Part 4. Where West Meets East. Part 5. Moors and Christians.

Genin, Auguste. "Notes on the dances, music and songs of the ancient and modern Mexicans." Smithsonian Institution. Annual Report, 1920. Washington, D.C. 1922. Also Publication de l'Institute Ethnographique International de Paris (1913).

Divided into three sections, this work focuses on the music and dances of the ancient Mexicans, musical instruments and modern Indian dances. The many photographs make it a good source for costume verification.

Gillmore, Frances. "The Dance Dramas of Mexican Villages." University of Arizona. Bulletin, 1943, 14(2):1-28.

_____. "Spanish texts of three dance dramas from Mexican villages." University of Arizona, Bulletin, 1942, 13(4) and 1943, 14(2).

Gonzáles, Carlos. "La Danza de las sonajas o del Señor." Mexican Folkways, 1925, 1(2):13-15.

A dance that dates from colonial times, it is similar to other "Moors and Christian" dances but ends with highly exciting general movement. Describes personages, costumes and music.

Guerrero, José E. "Danzas chontalpeñas." Nuestra música (México), 1947, pages 192-198. Illustrations, music.

Gutierrez, Electra and Tonatiuh. "La Danza ritual de los voladores." Mexico Quarterly Review, 1973, 4(2):27-38.

Gyles, Anna Benson and Chloë Sayer. Of Gods and Men: Mexico and the Mexican Indian. London: British Broadcasting Corporation, 1980.

Describes many Huichol dances including the Pascola Dance. The text relating to contemporary Indian dance is scattered requiring use of the index. Contains many good photographs and a bibliography.

Haggard, J. V. "Matachines of Mexico and the Southwest." Theatre Arts Monthly, April 1937, 21:293-299.

Hanna, Judith Lynne. To Dance is Human. Houston and London: University of Texas Press, 1979.

See chapter entitled "Dance and Political Thoughts and Action. Case A--Dance of Anáhuac: For God or Man in Prehistory?" Discusses the relationship of politics to religion. "Assesses the use of dance representation as correlative data in understanding processual change in time and space." Hypothesizes that dance performance and later representation in artifacts served sociopolitical designs. Specifically that dance was used as a communicative symbolic system to create, reflect, and reinforce social stratification and a centralized, integrated political organization encompassing diverse, geographically dispersed ethnic groups. The author supports this hypothesis in sections dealing with factors contributing to a stratified behavior; stratification among the Aztecs; and dance, stratification and integration.

Horcasitas Pimental, Fernando. "Piezas teatrales en lengua Nahuatl: Bibliografía descriptiva." Boletín bibliográfico de antropología americana (México), 1949, 11:154-164.

Annotated bibliography of theatrical texts. About one-half relate to Indian culture, others are nationalist or Catholic pieces written in Nahuatl. Gives type of work, whether or not photocopies exist, translations, origin, topic, characters, and editions.

Huerta, Jorge. A Bibliography of Chicano and Mexican Dance, Drama and Music. Oxnard, CA: Colegio Quetzalcoatl, 1972. 59p.

For the most part, contains articles from non-scholarly journals such as Travel and National Geographic.

Icaza, Francisco A. de. "Orígenes del teatro en México." Boletín de la Real Academia Espanola. (Madrid), 2:57-76.

Jenkins, Ruth Elizabeth. An Historical study of the dances of the Mexican Indians in the latter pre-Hispanic, colonial and modern periods of Mexico. [New York] 1932.

Jiménez, Guillermo. La Danza en México [Mexico] 1932. 18p.

Delightful treatise on why Mexican Indians dance. Includes use of some natural drugs and spirits; peyote, jiculí, marijuana and pulque.

Kendrick, Edith. Regional Dances of Mexico. Dallas: B. Upshaw, 1935. 78p.

Kurath, G. P. "Los Arrieros of Acopilco, Mexico." Western Folklore, 1947, 6:232-36.

_____. "Los Concheros." Journal of American Folklore, 1946, 59:387-99.

* _____. "Dance Acculturation." In: Heritage of Conquest: The Ethnology of Middle America. Edited by Sol Tax. Glencoe, Ill.: Free Press, 1952 (Viking Fund Seminar on Middle America Ethnology). Pages 233-242.

Succinct description of various aspects of dance acculturation including: dance functions and forms, geographical distribution, provenience, social distribution, organization, historical perspective, acculturation, and study of the fiesta pattern. Focus is on Mexican pre-Hispanic cultures. Mentions dance names of many indigenous groups such as Yaquis, Otomí, Mixtecs, Zapotecs, Maya, Aztec, Tarahumara, and Chichimeca.

_____. "Mexican Moriscas" Journal of American Folklore, 1949, 62:87-106.

Larsen, H. "The Mexican Indian Flying Pole Dance." National Geographic 1937, 71:387-400.

Well-written travel account of Pahuatlán ceremony of the volador that is believed to represent the Indian "century" or cycle of 52 years. Describes accidents that may happen. Also gives a brief description of the Acatlaxqui (Reed Throwing Dance). Photographs are of excellent quality.

* Llano, Enrique. Danses indiennes du Mexique. Bruxelles: Academie Royale de Belgique, 1939. 138p.

This survey of indigenous dance in Mexico focuses on pre-Columbian dance of the Mayas and Aztecs, however also includes sections dealing with colonial Spanish influence. An excellent source for readers of French. Illustrations. Bibliography.

Mansfield, Portia. The Conchero Dancers of Mexico. Master's Thesis, New York University, 1953. 289p.

Includes directions and tunes for the dances. Bibliography.

Martí, Samuel. Canto, danza y música precortesianos. México: Fondo de Cultura Económica, 1961. 379p.

_____. "Danza precortesiana." Cuadernos Americanos (México), September 1959, 106(5):129-51. Bibliography.

_____. "Netotiliztli o danzas de placer y regocijo." Cuadernos Americanos (Mexico), 1967, 26(4):171-74.

_____. "Teatro, danza y música precolombinos." In: Novedades (Mexico en la cultura), No. 847, 3rd. epoca.

* _____ and Gertrude Prokosch Kurath. Dances of Anáhuac; The Choreography and Music of Pre-Cortesian Dances. Chicago, Aldine Publishing Company, 1964. 251p. (Viking Fund Publications in Anthropology, No. 38).

Consistent theme is the relationship of dance to beliefs, social structure and life of pre-Cortesian peoples of the Anáhuac, the Nahuatl name for the Basin of Mexico. This well-illustrated source uses many codices and historical documents to trace the sources, motions and branches of Mayan and Aztec dance. Appendixes include glossaries of Maya and Aztec dance terms, lists of Aztec songs and dances and films of modern Meso-American fiestas.

Matos Moctezuma, Eduardo. "La Danza de los Montezumas." Anales. Instituto Nacional de Antropología e Historia (México), 1965, 18(47):71-92.

A conquest dance of Mexico. Bibliography.

Mattlage, Louise. "Dance Drama: Mayan Sacrifice." Dance Magazine May 1971, pages 20-22.

Mendoza, Vicente T. "Supervivencias de la cultura azteca; la canción y baile del Xochipitzahua." Revista Mexicana de Sociología, 1942, 4(4):87-98.

Contains a brief description and music of the Dance of the Aztec Pilgrimage that was performed, until recently, in the Valley of Mexico. Bibliography.

Mérida, Carlos. "Pre-Hispanic Dance and Theatre." Theatre Arts Monthly, August 1938, 29(8):561-68.

Well-illustrated short article on the contemporary native dance scene. Describes "The Virgin and the Beasts."

"Mexican Whirlers." Life, October 1947, 23:119.

* Mompradé, Electra and Tonatiúh Gutiérrez. Historia general del arte mexicano: danzas y bailes populares. México: Editorial Hermes, 1976. 239p.

Excellent source with over 250 marvelous photos and etchings. Chapters include: formative roots of dance and bailes of Mexico, including pre-Hispanic dance, evolution of dance after the conquest and dances performed today. Over 95 dances are described individually; however, there is a total absence of step patterns. Other chapters are: agricultural and "petitoria" ceremonial dances, dances relating to the ancient Huehueteote cult, dances with totemic character or relating to Nahuatlism, cycle of Moors and Christians, and popular Mestizo dance. Bibliography.

Montell, G. "Yaqui Dances." Ethnos (Stockholm), 1938, 3:145-166.

Noting the retention of much of their primitiveness, the author comments on several Yaqui dances as performed in the 1930's. Dances described are: Pascolas, The Deer Dance, and Matachines. Excellent illustrations and photographs. Bibliography.

Montes de Oca, José G. Danzas indígenas mexicanas. Tlaxcala, Tlax.: Imprenta del gobierno del estado, 1926.

Peterson, Anya. Mexican Dance Forms: A Bibliography with Annotations. Stanford, CA: Stanford University, Institute for the Study of Contemporary Cultures of the Institute of International Relations, 1967. 12p.

116 briefly annotated entries. Contains several citations dealing with Indian dance and drama. However, most are folkloric.

Richards, Annette. "The Dancers of Monte Albán." Pacific Discovery (San Francisco), 1955, 38(4):12-17.

Robb, J. D. "The Matachines Dance: A Ritual Folk Dance." Western Folklore, 1961, 20:87-101.

Schwendener, Norma. Legends and Dances of Old Mexico. New York: A. S. Barnes & Co., Inc. 1934, 111p.

More folkloric than Indian. Describes configurations of ten Mexican dances based on Indian legends. Los Tecomates, Las Sembradores [sic], Los Matlanchines, Los moros, Los Viejetos [sic], Los Negritos, La Virgen y las Fieras, Los Apaches, Los Inditos, Danza de la Mujer Apaches [sic]. Illustrations.

Solórzano, Armando and Raul Guerrero. "Ensayo para un estudio sobre la Danza de los Concheros de la gran Tenochtitlán." Boletín Latinoamericano de Música, 5(1941):449-476.

Discusses pagan origin of the dance, costumes, music and choreography.

Spicer, E. H. "Potam: A Yaqui Village in Sonora." American Anthropological Association, Memoires 77. (1954).

Pages 72-77, 159-160 are the most interesting. Descriptions of Coyote Dance and Pascola dancers.

Spicer, Edward H. "La Danza Yaqui del venado en la cultura mexicana." América Indígena, 1965, 25(1):117-39.

The author studies and analyzes the mythical context (symbolism of words of the songs that accompany the dance); manner in which the dance is represented; training necessary for the appearance of new dances. He then proceeds to note the transcendency of the dance into the repertoire of the Ballet Folklórico de México. English summary. Bibliography.

Stresser-Péan, Guy. "Danse des aigles et danse des jaguars chez lez Indiens Huastèques de la région de Tantoyuca." Proceedings, International Congress of Americanists, 28th, Paris 1947. Pp. 335-38.

A good description of the Dance of the Eagles and the Dance of the Jaguars including costumes and musical instruments. Illustrations.

Toor, Frances. "Nota sobre las Canacuas." Mexican Folkways, 1930, 6(3):108-109.

Toro, Alfonso. "The 'Marismas': The Indian Dances of the Moors and Christians." Mexican Folkways, 1925, (2):8-9.

Brief description of the picturesque three-day festival of Zacatecas which records the battles between Moors and Christians.

Torres Quintero, Gregorio. Fiestas y costumbres aztecas. Mexico, n.p., 1927. 232p.

"Tula. Dance Tradition and Creation of the Modern Indian." Dance Observer. (New York), February 1955, p. 23; May 1948, p. 53-54; October 1952, p. 117-18.

"Tula. The Yaqui Fiesta de Gloria." Dance Observer, February 1947, p. 16-18.

Valdiosera Berman, Ramón and William C. Boone (Translator). "Danzantes/Dancers." Artes de México, 21(184):78-96.

Vera Cruz, México. Sección de Asuntos Indígenas. "Calendar of Indian Dances," Boletín indigenista (México), 1947, 7(1): 50-55.

Chronological list of dances performed in the State of Veracruz, Mexico. Place, Indian language and dance.

Wilder, Carleton Stafford. "The Yaqui Deer Dance: A Study in Cultural Change." U.S. Bureau of American Ethnology, Bulletin, No. 186, (1963), Washington, D.C.

Well-researched, in-depth study of the dance as observed in 1939-40 in Pascua, Arizona, a settlement founded by Yaquis from the tribal homeland in Sonora, México. Sections cover the ethnographic position of the Yaqui; fiesta pattern with reference to the Deer Dance; costumes and musical instruments used in the dance; twenty deer songs with modern native and English translations; discussion of the songs; dance variations and meaning. Bibliography. Illustrations. Diagrams.

Yanaguana Society. Presentation of the Matachine Dance by Chichimec and Other Indians. San Antonio, Texas: The Society, 1934.

Brief description of dance imposed upon Mexican Indians by either missionaries from the Philippines or Spanish conquerors. Etymology of Matachine is given.

Mesoamerica

Alexander, Hartley Burr. "The Singing Girl of Copán; A Ballet in the Maya Mode." Theatre Arts (New York), August 1933, pp. 595-98.

* Armas Lara, Marcial. El Renacimiento de la danza guatemalteca y el origen de la marimba. Guatemala: Centro Editorial "José de Pineda Ibarra," Ministerio de Educación Pública, 1964. 424p.

An excellent source of dance and dance-drama in Guatemala written by the president of the Sociedad Folklórica Guatemalteca. The work is well illustrated and contains photos of contemporary renditions of ancient dances showing costumes, steps and props. It is evenly divided between indigenous dance and folkloric (costumbrista) dance. Provides dialog for the Dance of the Conquest and Rabinal Achí.

Barrientos Castillo, José. El Baile de la Conquista como elemento de investigación histórica: Tecum Umam. Guatemala: Tipografía Sánchez and de Guise, 1941.

Pages 9-27 contain description of dance with verses. Subsequent pages deal with controversial history of the Quiché King Tecum Umam and a description of the Baile de los Toritos.

Bode, Barbara Ora. The Dance of the Conquest in Guatemala. New Orleans: Middle American Research Institute, Tulane University, 1961.

Dance-drama that depicts the Conquest of Guatemala by Spanish in 1524. Dramatizes warning of old king of Utatlán that the Spanish forces were heading toward Quiché Kingdom; preparations for battle in Xelajú; hand-to-hand encounter in which Conquistador Pedro de Alvarado kills young king Tecum. The Río Xequiquel runs red with blood of Spanish and Indians as Quiché warriors embrace religion of "hijos del sol." Bibliography.

Brasseur de Bourbourg, Charles Etiènne. "Essai sur la poésie et la musique, sur la danse et l'art dramatique des anciennes populations mexicaines et guatémaltèques." Gramática de la lengua quiché. Paris, 1862. V. 2, pp. 5-23.

Brasseur de Bourbourg's description of the "Rabinal Achí" has inspired great controversy revolving around whether or not he actually witnessed the dance. In this work he not only treats the Rabinal Achí, but some Aztec and Mayan dances as well.

Chinchilla Aguilar, Ernesto. La Danza de sacrificio y otros estudios. Guatemala: Centro Editorial "José de Pineda Ibarra," Ministerio de Educación Pública, 1963. 169p.

Describes seventeenth-century religious document that prohibits Indian dance of Tum-Teleche o Loj-Tum, (pages 9-19).

_____. "La Danza del 'Tum-Telecha' o 'Loj-Tum.'" Antropología e Historia de Guatemala, 1951, 3(2):17-20.

About the Act of Prohibition of the dance. Letters to and from inquisition officials.

The Güengüence; A Comedy Ballet in the Nahuatl-Spanish Dialect of Nicaragua. Edited by Daniel G. Brinton. Philadelphia: D. G. Brinton, 1883.

Jensen, P. Daniel. "Baile del Venado: Santa Eulalia Huehuetenango." Guatemala Indígena, January 1971, 12(1-2):203-221.

Text of the baile. States that the bailes have been presented three times in recent years: 1947, 1957, and 1970.

Kurath, G. P. "Dance Relatives of Mid-Europe and Middle America." Journal of American Folklore, 1956, 69:286-298.

La Farge, Oliver and Douglas Byers. "The Year Bearer's People."

Middle American Research Institute, Publication No. 3. New Orleans: Tulane University, 1931. Pages 99-111.

Well-illustrated, detailed description of the Deer Dance as performed at San Marcos. An outstanding feature of the work are two floor plans of the First Chief Prayer-Maker's house during a Cahampal ceremony and the Capitan del Bailes house during the ceremony before the Deer Dance. Illustrations.

Lemmon, Alfred E. "Maya music and dance." National Studies (St. John's College, Belize) 1(4):4-11.

This brief survey focuses on music, but includes a few pertinent paragraphs on the Monkey Dance, Deer Dance, Xol Moro, and Cortez Dance. Lacks citation of sources.

Lothrop, Samuel Kirkland. "Further Notes on Indian Ceremonies in Guatemala." Indian Notes, January 1929, 6(1):1-25.

Miscellaneous brief comments on the Dance of the Deer, a Guatemalan Snake Dance, Uajzaqip Vats (Festival of Eight Thread), and Maximen. Illustrations.

McArthur, Enrique. "Los Bailes de Aguacatán y el culto a los muertos." Anales de la Sociedad de Geografía e Historia (Guatemala), 1972, 65:68-85. Also in Estudios Centroamericanos, May 1972, 27(283):255-271.

Explores the motivation behind the performance of dances. Agrees with Bode on some points, but expands upon theories she presented. Describes the history of dance groups; outstanding features of local dance; various sections of the dance and expenses to dancers. Concludes that fear of sudden illness or dishonorable death summoned by the "Mam" (religious leader) is the reason for continuation of dance performances. Bibliography.

Mace, Carroll Edward. "Los Negritos: The Black Messengers." Xavier Review, 1/2 (September 1981).

Describes nine short one act pre-Columbian dance dramas that occur during ritual processions from December 20-25 and during Epiphany.

_____. "New Information About Dance Dramas of Rabinal and the 'Rabinal-Achí.'" Xavier University Studies (New Orleans), February 1967, 6(1):1-19.

An authority on dance-dramas in Guatemala, Dr. Mace presents information to support the authenticity of the Rabinal-Achí and Patzcá "bailes."

_____. "The Patzcá Dance of Rabinal." El Palacio (Santa Fe), 1961, 68(3):151-67.

Traces Mexican influence on the Patzcá Indian dance in the region of Rabinal, Guatemala. Also gives music and poems of the Patzcá in English, Spanish and Quiché. Heavily footnoted. Illustrations.

_____. Two Spanish-Quiché Dance-Dramas of Rabinal. [New Orleans, Tulane University] 1970. 221p. (Tulane Studies in Romance Languages and Literature, No. 3).

Monterde, Francisco. Teatro indígena pre-hispánico: Rabinal Achi. México: Universidad Nacional Autónoma de México, 1955.

Text of Rabinal Achi as translated by Raynaud. Monterde has added many readers' notes to both the text and Raynaud's appendix.

Montoya, Matilde. Estudio sobre cuatro manuscritos del Baile de la conquista. Guatemala: Editorial Universitaria, 1970. 422p.

Analytical and comparative study of four texts of the Conquest Dance: Cobán, Cantel, Sacapulas and San Andés Xecul. Also explores themes, roles and acts of the dance.

* The Native Theatre in Middle America. By Gustavo Correa. Middle American Research Institute. Publication No. 27. New Orleans: Tulane University, 1961. 296p.

A collection of four works dealing with various aspects of indigenous, pre-Cortesan and colonial dance and theatre. Includes the works: "La Loa en Guatemala" (with English summary) by Gustavo Correa and Calvin Cannon; "Texto de un baile de diablos" by G. Correa; "The Calderonian auto sacramental," "El Gran Teatro del Mundo" by William Hunter and "The Dance of the Conquest of Guatemala" by Barbara Bode. Bibliography. Illustrations.

Paret-Limardo de Vela, Lise. La Danza del venado en Guatemala. Guatemala: Centro Editorial "José de Pineda Ibarra," Ministerio de Educación Pública, 1963.

Reynolds, Dorothy. "Guatemalan Dances at Colorful Highland Festivals." Americas, January 1956, 8(1):31-35.

Rodríguez Ronaret, Francisco. "Notas sobre una representación actual del Rabinal Achi o Baile del Tum." Guatemala Indígena, 1962, 1a. época, 2(1):45-56.

Describes preparation, characters, costume, dance, instruments and objects of the dance as viewed in 1955.

Saquic Calel, Rosalio. "Baile de Gracejos." Guatemala indígena,
1970, 5(1):203-206.

Dance of Mirth in which participants poke fun at neighboring
villages.

Stookey, Margaret M. "Guatemala Dance the Quiché Quadrille."
The American Dancer (Los Angeles), March 1942, p. 16.

Termer, F. "Los Bailes de culebra entre los indios quichés en
Guatemala." Proceedings. 23rd. International Congress of
Americanists, 1930. Pages 661-67.

In depth descriptions of the "Baile de Culebra (snake)" as
performed in Santa Cruz Quiché, San Bartolo, and Pologuá.
Includes similarities and differences. Also describes the
"Fiesta of the Atamalqualiztli" (water tamales) celebrated
every eight years. Illustrations. Bibliography.

_____. "Der Palo de Volador in Guatemala." El Mexico Antiguo,
1931-36, 3:13-23.

Vela, David. "Danzas y primeras manifestaciones dramáticas del
indígena mayaquiché." América Indígena, Abril/Junio 1972,
32(2):515-521.

Proposes that vernacular dances remain unchanged and little understood because each form is the product of regional
tradition. Discusses problems encountered by missionaries
desiring to discourage indigenous dances. Bibliography.

* _____. Traditional and Folkloric Music in Central America.
Paris: United Nations Educational, Scientific and Cultural
Organization, 1971. 12p.

Very good overview of Indian dance and music. Includes
sections on secularized music and dance, organography and
ritual music, characteristics of native music, bird imitation,
survival and cross-fertilization.

Yurchenko, Henrietta. "Taping History in Guatemala; Being a Report on the Ancient Ritual Ballet of the Ixil Indians."
American Record Guide (New York), December 1958, 25(4):
228-229, 282-284. Illustrations.

Panama, Colombia, and Venezuela

Acosta Saignes, Miguel. "El Maremare: Baile del Jaguar y la Luna."
Archivos venezolanos de folklore (Caracas), 1952, 1:266-82.

Presents arguments, pro and con, the indigenous roots of
the dances of the Maremare of the Orinoco Basin. Bibliography.

Cartagena, Alberto de. "Apuntes sobre danzas indígenas de algunas
tribus de la Amazonia Colombiana." Antropología y etnología
(Madrid), 1953, 8:83-113.

Domínguez, Luis Arturo. Fiestas y danzas folklóricas de Venezuela.
Caracas: Monte Avila Editores, 1969. 327p.

González Cajias, Fernando. "Atabi: en muchos sentidos, un hom-
bre contemporáneo." Conjunto, 1977, 32:25-31.

_____. "Atabi: Primer montaje en Colombia sobre tradiciones
precolombinas." Latin American Theater Review, 1977, 1(1):
75-80.

Laval, Ramon. "Native Rhythms in Venezuela." Pan American
Union Bulletin, 72:646-49.

Tejeira Jáen, Bertilda. "El Festival de danzas cunas en Ustupo."
América Indígena, 1972, 32(1):139-146.

Ecuador, Peru, Bolivia, and Chile

Bandelier, Adolph F. A. "La Danse des 'Sicuri' des Indiens Aymará
de la Bolivie." Boas Anniversary Volume, New York: Stechert,
1906. (Pp. 272-282).

Deriving its name from the "sicu," small pan pipes, the
Sicuri is performed to dozens of such flutes emitting whatever melody the flute players favor. Added to this caco-
phony are beautiful, mushroom-shaped headdresses of ostrich
feathers resulting in one of the more unique visual and audi-
tory experiences of Indian dance performance.

Bandizzone, Luis M. (Editor). Poesía, música y danza inca.
Buenos Aires: n.p., 1943.

Bonilla del Valle, Ernesto. Tierra chola: el valle de Jauja-Huancayo.
Lima: Imprenta Editores Tipo-offset, 1973, 263p.

Brown, Michael F. "Notas sobre la chonguinada de Junin."
América Indígena, 1976, 36(2):375-384.

A mixture of pre-Columbian and colonial traditions, the
Peruvian "chonguinada" gained in popularity as a direct result of mining development theorizes the author. A brief

description of the dance performance is given and the author concludes that the dance serves as a mechanism to reinforce relations between emigrant workers. Bibliography.

Caballero F., Policarpo. "Auqa Tusuy o la danza guerrera inkaika." Cuzco. Universidad. Sección arqueológica. Revista, 1959, 48:84-93.

Coba, Carlos. "Nuevos planteamientos a la etnomúsica y al folklore." Sarance [Instituto Otavaleño de Antropología, Otavalo, Ecuador], 1976, 2:50-62.

Coimbra, Gil. "La Música y la danza del pueblo Aymara." Revista geográfica americana (Buenos Aries), 1941, 12:89-96 and 15: 331-338.

Fortún de Ponce, Julia Elena. La Danza de los diablos. [La Paz: Ministerio de Educación y Bellas Artes, Oficialía Mayor de Cultura Nacional, 1961.] 108p. Illustrated.

Gonzalez Bravo, Antonio. "Música, Instrumentos y Danzas Indígenas." In: La Paz en su cuarto centenario, 1548-1948. Vol. 3: 403-460. Illustrations.

Harcourt, Raoul d'. La Musique des Incas et ses survivances.... Paris: n.p., 1925. 2 v. Illustration. Music. Plates.

Helfritz, Hans. "Musik und tänze der Aimaras und Quechuas." Mexico antiguo, 1955, 8:283-292.

In spite of strong Christian influence, the author considers those dances in which skins, masks and feathers are utilized to be classified as pre-Columbian. He points out that when Indian festivals coincide with the Catholic, the Indians often substitute their festival appellation for Catholic terms. Music and instruments are also discussed. English and Spanish summaries. Illustrations.

Jiménez Borja, Arturo. "La Danza en el antiguo Perú(epoca inca)." Revista, Museo Nacional (Lima), 1946, 15:122-161. Illustrations.

_____. "La Danza en el antiguo Perú (epoca pre-inca)." Revista, Museo Nacional (Lima), 1955, 24:111-136. Illustrations.

Ladron de Guevara, Blanca A. "Transformación de las danzas incaicas." Cultura Peruana, 1942, 2(11):36-37.

La Meri. "The Children of Inti: Peru, Bolivia." Dance Magazine (New York), June 1949, pp. 30-35. Illustrations.

Merino de Zela, Mildred. "Artes coreográficos tradicionales." In, Busto D., Jose Antonio del (Editor). Historia de la cultura peruana. Lima: Editorial Arica, 1973, Pp. 258-260.

Navarro del Aguila, Victor. Folklore nactional: calendario de fiestas populares del Departamento del Cusco. Cusco: n.p., 1947 (i.e., 1977).

Chronological listing of dances performed in Cuzco. Also regional department, province, and district lists.

* Paredes Candia, Antonio. La Danza folklórica en Bolivia. La Paz: Ediciones ISLA, 1966. 253p.

A key source for the Indian dances of Bolivia. A full one-half of the text is dedicated to descriptions of Indian dances based on original source material. The origin, legend, number of participants, classification, props, choreography and musical instruments are described for many Aymara and Inca dances. Each dance description is followed by a short bibliography. Excellent costume illustrations.

Paredes, Manuel Rigoberto. El Arte folklórico de Bolivia. 2d. edition. La Paz: Gamarra, 1949.

The Kachua, a dance of love, Chunchus, Loco-pallapallas, Liphes are a few of the dances of Bolivian Indians described in this work. Also describes musical instruments, songs, parades and literature.

Ramiro Beltrán, Luis. "Bolivia's Dancing Devils." Dance Magazine (New York), August 1954, pp. 18-20. Illustrations.

Sassoon, Hamo. "Dancers at Pisac." Geographical Magazine (London), 1949, 22:177-181.

Thompkins, William David. The Marinera: A Historic and Analytical Study of the Dance of Peru. Los Angeles: Master's thesis, University of California, 1973.

Uribe-Echevarria, Juan. Fiesta de la Tirana de Tarapacá. Valparaiso: Universidad Católica de Valparaiso, 197? 93p.

Vásquez, Emilio. "Coreografia puneña; la pandilla." Revista, Museo Nacional (Lima), 1946, 15:81-121. Illustrations. Music.

_____. "Coreografia Titikaka: los Chokelas." Revista, Museo Nacional (Lima), 1945, 13:65-83.

Survival of traditional dance in the Puno area, with

accompanying pentaphonic examples in 2/4 (tempo de huayno), 2/4 (allegro), 3/8 (huayno, lento) and 2/4 (moderato) to show the character of the music. (HLAS annotation.)

* Verger, Pierre. Fiestas y danzas en el Cuzco y en los Andes. Buenos Aires: Editorial sudamericana, [1945]. 199p.

An excellent source for costumes and masks, this photographic essay of the festivals and dances of the Andean people captures several religious dance festivals from dawn to sunset. The text is tri-lingual; English, Spanish and French. Appendices include a calendar of festivals with type and place and indexes of dances, and places.

Argentina and Paraguay

Cadogán, León. "Como interpretan los Chiripá (Avá Guarani) la danza Ritual." Revista de Antropología (São Paulo), 1959, 7(112):65-99.

A study of the Chiripá group of Paraguayan Guaranís. This article seeks to explain the "raison d'être" of their dances. Economics, mythology and religion, cultism and vocabulary are treated.

Flury, Lázaro. "Danzas, costumbres y creencias de los indios del Gran Chaco." América Indígena, 1956, 16:111-121.

Provides brief descriptions of the dances and ceremonies of various tribes indigenous to northern Argentina. Includes the Danza del Gualañí, Danza de la Algarroba, Spring Dance and others. English summary.

_____. "Danzas de los indígenas chaqueños de la República Argentina." Estudios antropológicos publicados en homenaje al doctor Manuel Gamio. México, D.F., 1956, Pp. 331-32.

Indicates the universal characteristics of chaqueño dance and compares them with some African, Asian and Incan dances. This article is frustratingly brief.

_____. "El 'Selamatac,' una danza ritual de los indígenas chaqueños." América Indígena, 1949, 9:343-48.

Brief article describing the most significant dance of the Toba Indians of Argentina. Probable origins, motivation and choreography are discussed. Includes music.

Gonzalez, Joaquín Víctor. Música y danzas nativas. Buenos Aires: S. Glusberg, 1920.

Strelnikov, I. D. "La Música y danza de las tribus indias Kaáihwuá (Guaraní) y Botocudo." Proceedings, International Congress of Americanists, 23rd. New York, 1928. Pp. 796-802.

It is rare that one encounters a description of Paraguayan Indians, much less of their dance. This paper describes the music and dance of two tribes in great detail.

Viviani, Alberto. "Música e danza nel Gran Chaco." La Scala (Milano), July 1956, 80:47-53; 77-78.

Contains illustrations, music and portraits. Summaries in French, English and German.

Brazil

Baldus, Herbert. "As Danças dos Tapirapé," Proceedings. International Congress of Americanists, 31st. São Paulo, 1954, 1:89-98.

Twelve years of cultural changes following contact with outsiders did not lessen the Tupí Indians' love of dance. Various dance movements of several Tupí tribes are described. This is also a good bibliographical source for Portuguese language sources.

Barreto, Felícitas. Danças do Brasil, 2a. ed. Rio de Janeiro: Typy, 1959. 171p.

_____. Danzas indígenas del Brasil. Translated by Alberto Estrada Quevedo. México: Instituto Indigenista Interamericano, 1960. 138pp.

Concise descriptions of major dances of numerous Indian tribes throughout Brazil. Contains many beautiful black-and-white photographs, however text is very brief. No configurations, music or lyrics given. Bibliography. Illustrated.

Cândido, Antônio. "Possíveis raizes indígenas de uma dança popular." Revista de Antropologia, 1956, 4(1):1-24.

Explores and analyzes the indigenous roots of present-day Brazilian dance, in particular the "Cururu" of Mato Grosso, São Paulo and Goiás. Discusses Tupi-Guarani movements, culture and the later effect of Jesuit contact. Bibliography.

Dietschy, Hans. "Die Tanzmasken der Karaja Indianer Zentralbrasiliens und der Aruaña Fisch." Schweizerische Gesellschaft für Anthropologie und Ethnologie. Bulletin, 1970-71, 47:48-53.

Rodrigues, An'Augusta. "O Jaraguá." Revista Brasileira do Folclore, September 1971, 11(31):319-322.

Rodrigues, João Barbosa. "O Canto e dança selvícola." Revista
Brasileira, 9(1881):32-60.

Silva, Francisco Pereira da. "Tontinha." Revista Brasileira do
Folclore, January 1972, 12(32):63-65.

Cross- and Multi-Cultural Sources

Austin, Mary. "The Dramatic Arts of the American Indians."
Theatre Arts Monthly, August 1933.

Davis, Martha Ellen. Music and Dance in Latin American Urban
Contexts: A Selective Bibliography. [Brockport: New
York, 1973] 20p.

Contains a few citations dealing with history of dance.

Dirkson, A. "Introduction to Religious Dance." Dance Magazine,
1962, 36:14-17.

Handbook of South American Indians, edited by Julian Haynes
Steward. Washington, D.C.: United States Government
Printing Office, 1946-59. (Bureau of American Ethnology
Bulletin 143) 7 Vols.

A key English language source to South American Indian
dance movement, as well as tribal culture in whole. The
set is divided by cultural region, then by tribe. Each article is arranged according to a standard sequence with
minor exceptions as dictated by unique cultural facets.
For the topic of dance, one is heavily dependent upon the
Index (in volume 7) due to the work's classified arrangement. The subject headings--"Dance accessories," "Dancers," "Dances," and "Dancing"--reveal the greatest amount
of information in volumes 1-5. Although the source contains
a great deal of information, be forewarned that it is scattered and requires patience to ferret it out. A wide variety
of dances are described in varying detail including the
Chuncho, Kururu, Nomi, Itsa-kó and other lesser-known
dances.

Henríquez Ureña, P. "El teatro de la America Española en la Epoca
Colonial." Obra crítica, Mexico: Fondo de Cultura Economica,
1960. Pages 698-718.
Also Conferencias del ciclo de 1936 dictadas en el Teatro
Nacional de Comedia. Buenos Aires: Comisión Nacional de
Cultura, 1936.

Using excerpts from historical sources, Henríquez Ureña briefly summarizes Indian drama and dance in the pre-conquest period and the effects of Catholic infusion of the colonial period on Indian ceremonies.

Jaraba-Pardo, Enisberto. "El Teatro indígena y campesino." Latin American Theatre Review, 1977, 11(1):81-83.

Kurath, Gertrude P. "Aboriginal American Folk Dance." The Folk Dancer (Manchester, England), November-December 1955, pp. 117-118.

_____. "Basic Techniques of Amerindian Dance." Dance Notation Record, 1957, 8(4):2-8.

_____. "Drama, Dance and Music." Handbook of Middle American Indians (vol. 6, Social Anthropology), edited by Robert Wauchope. Austin: University of Texas Press, 1967. Pages 158-190.

An outstanding source for dance/drama research written by a leading authority. This should be used as a departure point for any study on indigenous dance in Mexico and Middle America. The generously illustrated article provides information on fiesta, ecological, ecclesiastical, secular calendars of dances, types of dances and dramas, characters, instruments and celebrations. The useful bibliography contains many English-language sources.

Pierre, Dorathi Bock. "Dance Evolution." Educational Dance (Hollywood), October 1938, 1(3):10-11.

Parts 3-5 (November 1938, December 1938, January 1939) deal with American Indians.

Potvin, Charles. "Le Théâtre barbare." Revue de Belgique (Bruxelles), September 1895, Series 2, 7(15):166-183. Bibliographic footnotes.

Stresser-Pean, Guy. "Les Origines du volador et du comelagatoazte." Proceedings, International Congress of Americanists, 28th. Paris, 1947. Pages 327-334.

Comparative analysis of pole flying in Mexico, Nicaragua and Guatemala based on historical documents and first-hand observations. Includes some uncommon illustrations.

Chapter Thirty

ESKIMO* PERFORMANCE

Maija M. Lutz

Although performance in Eskimo society is by no means restricted to forms which involve movement, one of the primary vehicles for the expression of both cultural and artistic values of the
Eskimos has always been the dance. Not only does traditional Eskimo dance interrelate with the other performing and visual arts,
but it is also inseparable from areas of Eskimo social culture such
as religion and folklore. In addition, Eskimo dance can be viewed
as simultaneously existing on several different levels, including the
personal, the communal, and the supernatural. Whereas the songs
which accompany dance can be individually owned and the execution
of these songs and dances reflects the capabilities of each individual
performer and composer, the primary importance of a performance
lies in its ability to solidify relations among members of a group and
to fuse the earthly world with the spiritual one.

In view of the importance that has always been attached to
dance by the Eskimos, it is almost ironic to observe the general
lack of a thorough treatment of dance in most writings dealing with
the subject. Just as the various Eskimo arts should not be viewed
in isolation but rather as interrelated components of a larger whole,

---

*The term "Inuit" (meaning "the people") has received wide accept-
ance both among scholars of Eskimo culture as well as among the
Eskimos themselves as a preferential designation for this group of
people. The term "Eskimo" means "eaters of raw flesh" and was
probably used by the Algonkian Indians who originated it as a
derogatory word. Since, however, the term "Inuit" can be correctly applied only to those Eskimos who speak the Inupik language,
it is not all inclusive and the use of it as a generic term to denote
all Eskimos is not linguistically appropriate. Thus, in the interests
of accuracy I have chosen to retain the word "Eskimo," using it by
itself when referring to Eskimos in general or together with a qual-
ifying word (e.g., Alaskan Eskimo) when referring to specific groups.

so also dance should be regarded as a total event with every phase of it from the dance movements themselves to the reaction of the audience toward the dancers being accorded equal importance. Unfortunately, such is not the case and the one area which falls especially short of adequate treatment and coverage has been that of dance per se, namely the movements themselves and their relationship to the music which accompanies them. Given the fact that dance by definition implies movement through time and space, this lacuna appears especially puzzling until one realizes that most discussions of Eskimo dance in printed sources can be attributed to scholars whose primary interest is not dance. Thus, it is not surprising that a source which includes very detailed musical analysis of the dance song repertoire of a particular community, for example, might include only a few cursory remarks on the dancing itself. Fortunately, most current scholars dealing with the Eskimo arts recognize the necessity for both an interdisciplinary and comprehensive approach to them and are beginning to fill in some of these gaps.

Before proceeding with an assessment of the available resources on Eskimo dance, ceremony, and related areas, I would like to present a brief overview of dance and music in Eskimo society for those who may be totally unfamiliar with this geographical area. Two crucial points must be kept in mind throughout any discussion of Eskimo culture in general, as well as music and dance in particular. The first concerns the tremendous amount of diversity present in all phases of Eskimo culture. Not only are there differences among the four major geographical (or political) groupings of Eskimos (Alaskan, Canadian, Greenlandic, and Siberian), but there are discernible differences within these major groupings as well. Thus, generalizations about any aspect of Eskimo culture, including music and dance, must be introduced with caution, since scholars are constantly presenting us with new findings and insights concerning characteristics which may be unique to specific Eskimo communities or subgroups.

The second point concerns changes which have occurred in Eskimo society as a result of contact with Euro-Americans. In the case of some Eskimo groups this contact can be traced as far back as the eighteenth or nineteenth centuries, whereas in the case of others it has taken place only within the last twenty or thirty years. What is important to remember is that, as a result of these contacts, music and dance of certain areas have been transformed into something quite different from what they were prior to contact times. In some areas, for example, the traditional drum dance has been supplemented with or entirely replaced by European-type dances such as the square dance done to accordion accompaniment. Or a festival which occurred in a specific village in the early part of the century may be obsolete and forgotten in that same village today. Thus, it is necessary for the reader of material concerning these arts to always be aware of the time period under discussion as well as of acculturative factors which may have been at work in a particular community or region.

Although Eskimo dance and music have always exhibited variations and differences from one group to the next, certain practices were common throughout the Arctic area. One of these was dancing, usually in the context of a festival or celebration, done to the accompaniment of monophonic singing, i.e., singing in unison or octaves, and the beating of a frame drum. This single-headed, shallow drum, which can range in shape from round to slightly oval and measure anywhere from one foot to more than three feet in diameter, is held by a lateral handle, which is attached to the outer rim of the frame, and is played with a stick or beater. In former times the materials used in the construction of the drum depended on what was accessible in each locale, and environmental factors such as availability of foodstuffs often determined the nature of performance. In parts of Alaska, where people were able to develop more elaborate ceremonial patterns due to a more dependable food supply, group performances involving several drummer-singers and a group of dancers were common. In the central Arctic, however, where the effort to subsist often involved great mobility of the individual family unit, the solo drummer-dancer was the norm.

Drum dancing in the western Arctic was part of an organized and structured ceremonial complex incorporating a variety of festivals and celebrations. In southern Alaska, for instance, no less than five major feasts took place--the Annual Feast to the Dead, the Great Feast to the Dead, the Bladder Feast, the Inviting-In Feast, and the Asking Festival. Although ceremonialism was somewhat less complex in northern Alaska, hunting festivals such as the Messenger Feast and others associated with whaling and caribou drives played an equally important role. Dancing was often of a mimetic nature and portrayed both human activities and animal behavior. The performances were enriched by the addition of paraphernalia such as finger masks, feather wands, dance mittens, headdresses, and wooden face masks. Sometimes special or new clothing was worn during ceremonies and in some parts of Alaska women stripped to the waist when dancing.

Even though celebrations took a less structured form in the eastern Arctic, many occasions such as the arrival of visitors, success in hunting, or the need to drive away evil spirits during stormy weather called for a festival. The solo drummer-dancer was usually accompanied by a chorus of women, who in some areas wore special clothing and had their hair fixed in pigtails. As was also the case with the Alaskan festivals, various symbolic acts could take place during these festivals, as for instance the killing of evil spirits which were represented by masked and costumed men.

Traditionally, the drum dance served many functions. Not only was it necessary for maintaining good relations with both fellow

human behings and a variety of spirits, but it also served as an
important tool for teaching and reaffirming cultural values. In
those communities where drum dances are still held today, the purpose seems to be primarily a social one. However, even though
many of the contexts of drum dancing have disappeared, many Eskimos still view this form of entertainment as an important link with
their past.

In Greenland, and to a lesser degree among some Eskimo
groups in Canada, the drum played an important role in song con-
tests. Among the Canadian groups the derision exhibited by the
song partners during the singing of these songs was of a friendly
nature, whereas among the Greenland Eskimos drum fights could
become somewhat violent and were used for settling serious dis-
putes that had arisen out of crimes such as theft or murder.

Drums were also used by the shaman or medicine man to
heighten the excitement of a shamanistic performance, which could
be part of a festival, and to enable the shaman to communicate with
the supernatural. It was partially because of the association that
the drum had with traditional Eskimo religious practices that many
Christian missionaries discouraged its use to the extent that it
eventually disappeared from many communities.

In addition to a large repertoire of drum-dance songs, Eskimos utilized many other types of songs which did not involve any
instrumental accompaniment. One genre of song which seems to be
especially prevalent throughout the Arctic is the juggling song.
Once used to accompany the actual game of juggling, this type of
song, which often consists of a nonsensical array of words, sounds,
or references, is often sung nowadays without its accompanying activity. Other activities, such as making string figures (cat's cra-
dle), playing hide and seek, and putting a child to sleep, were accompanied by singing. Songs were often incorporated into stories
or legends; sometimes entire tales were told in a rhythmical fashion
bordering between speech and song. Usually prior knowledge of
the story was needed in order to understand the allusions or archaic language of the story. Storytelling was often enhanced by
such factors as the dimly lit surroundings and the appearance and
mannerisms of the storyteller. Among the Eskimos of Baffin Island,
for instance, the storyteller would sit in the back of the snow house
facing the wall, with his hood pulled over his head and mittens on
his hands.

A rather unusual type of activity which has received wide attention among researchers during the past several years has been
the Eskimo throat game. This type of performance involves pairs
of women who face each other and exchange a series of fast, rhythmical vocal patterns using both voiced and voiceless pitch to produce various levels of intonation. This type of game, which ex-
hibits an infinite variety of these vocal and rhythmical patterns,
seems to have been restricted to the Canadian Arctic.

It is virtually impossible to present an overall description of traditional Eskimo musical style, since all features of this style such as range, scale structure, form, rhythm, and relationship of melody to drum beat vary so greatly from one region to the next. Thus, it is important for the reader who is not generally familiar with Eskimo music and dance to realize that the characteristics of the style of one area are not necessarily transferable to another area and that it is not possible to speak of Eskimo music or dance as one entity without making allowances for many exceptions. Even the traits which seem to apply to most Eskimo areas need qualification. For instance, most traditional Eskimo singing is done in unison or octaves and the use of part-singing is normally associated with music that has been borrowed from outsiders. This is true for most Eskimo groups but not the Caribou Eskimo, who use a form of polyphony in their traditional drum songs and do not attribute it to any outside influences.

As mentioned previously, acculturative factors have been responsible for many changes in Eskimo performance. In areas where missionary activity has succeeded in suppressing the native dances, various forms of European dance have arisen as substitutes. Christian church music, ranging from revival hymns to sophisticated four-part chorales, has become an important component of all Eskimo communities, even those which have retained much of their traditional music and dance. Eskimo familiarity with Western popular music has given rise to composers and performers of this type of music among the Eskimos themselves. And ethnic awareness, which has pervaded the North American continent as a whole during the last decade or so, has resulted in a kind of cultural awakening among many Eskimo groups. One sees a renewed interest in the preservation or revival of native dance and music and the teaching of these arts to the young. This interesting combination of the old and the new, which can be perceived in music and dance of all areas of the Arctic, attests to the fact that music and dance change and evolve in all societies to reflect other transformations and developments within those particular cultures. Just as Western dance and music have gone through periods of radical change and innovation as well as experienced revivals of earlier forms and ideas (e.g., neoclassicism), the same may be said of music and dance in Eskimo culture.

The following discussion of published literature and other sources on Eskimo performance will be divided into the four major geographical/political Eskimo areas--Canada, Alaska, Greenland, and Siberia, with an introductory section being devoted to general works dealing with Eskimo performance as a whole. In addition, I have included a list of selected recordings of Eskimo music following the bibliography. Complete bibliographical citations for all works referred to in the essay, where they are often listed only by the author's last name and date, are to be found in the bibliography.

Although an attempt will be made to emphasize those sources focusing heavily on dance and other theatrical movement, important sources dealing with all types of performance will be pointed out.

General Works

Until the 1970's, general sources dealing with Eskimo perform-ance were at a premium. The Swiss musicologist Zygmunt Estreicher was one of the few scholars involved in viewing Eskimo music in its entirety. In "Die Musik der Eskimos" (1950), the earliest of two general articles written by him in the 1950's, Estreicher attempts to reconstruct the evolution of Eskimo music as well as to compare it with American Indian and Paleo-Siberian music. Although his theo-ries are very interesting, they are based solely on musical evidence without consideration of sociocultural factors. In his short and suc-cinct encyclopedia article entitled "Eskimo-Musik" (1954) Estreicher discusses musical styles, musical contexts, previous research on Es-kimo music, as well as reasons for interest in Eskimo music.

The next two general sources, both published in the 1970's, are indispensable for anyone doing research on Eskimo dance and music. The first is an annotated bibliography of Eskimo music com-piled by Cavanagh in 1972. Although many important publications have appeared since that time, this bibliography is very thorough in its listing of works dealing extensively with music, dance, and ceremony. The second source, Eskimo Music by Region by Johnston (1976a), is intended to be a comparative study of all Eskimo musical areas. The work is somewhat unbalanced in quality, since Johnston's first-hand experience with and knowledge of Alaskan Eskimo music and dance make the chapters dealing with Alaska much more reliable than the others, which are based on secondary sources. Neverthe-less, it is a valuable work, especially since our knowledge of Alaskan Eskimo music and dance was quite incomplete until Johnston joined the music faculty at the University of Alaska in 1973 and began ex-tensive research on Alaskan Eskimo and Indian music and dance. Es-pecially noteworthy in this publication are the numerous illustrations of dance and dance-related paraphernalia.

The New Grove Dictionary of Music and Musicians, published in 1980, contains three entries having to do with Eskimo music and dance (see Binnington and Liang 1980a and b, and Olsen 1980 in bibliography). In addition to these separate entries, there are two brief references to Eskimo music and dance in the subsection deal-ing with Siberian folk music under the Union of Soviet Socialist Re-publics entry. In my opinion, several omissions, ambiguities, and inconsistencies in the sections by Binnington and Liang prevent this from being a totally reliable source. Unfortunately, as with any large-scale work such as the 20-volume New Grove, the time lapse between submission of material and publication makes portions of the work outdated even before they are published. I think a far more satisfactory and up-to-date encyclopedia article on Eskimo music is one by Cavanagh (1981) in the Encyclopedia of Music in Canada. Cavanagh's article is very clearly organized into sections dealing with style areas, dance songs and rituals, other traditional musical genres, and acculturation.

An unpublished paper which might be of interest to individuals concerned with movement forms is one entitled "An Examination of Musical and Cultural Contexts of the Frame Drum Among the Eskimos" by Lutz (1972). In addition to a discussion of physical characteristics and performance techniques of the drum, the paper also contains information on the role of the drum in dance as well as other contexts.

The only general source dealing with Eskimo dance of which I am aware is the article "Dance in Eskimo Society: An Historical Perspective" by R. and G. Luttmann (1977). However, the emphasis of this article, which is primarily a review of the literature in the field, is on Alaska.

In reference to the short discography which I have included following the bibliography should be mentioned a recent article by Nattiez (1980a), in which he assesses available recordings of Eskimo music by pointing out their assets and shortcomings.

Canada

It was not until the last decade that ethnomusicologists began to visit the Canadian north for the sole purpose of investigating Eskimo music and dance. Prior to this time much of our knowledge concerning these activities came from ethnographers and others whose primary interests often lay in directions other than performance. Three of these early contributors are especially important. Franz Boas, the German scientist whose original purpose for undertaking a journey to Baffin Island in 1883 was to do a geographical survey of the area, provided us with one of the first scientific monographs on the Eskimo. In his The Central Eskimo, which was originally published in 1888, Boas presents the reader not only with information concerning Eskimo music, dance, and ceremony, but includes transcriptions of songs as well. The work of Boas served as the basis for an ethnomusicological study done in the same vicinity by Lutz in 1973-1974 (see Lutz 1978 in bibliography). The latter work will be discussed later in the chapter.

Diamond Jenness, the renowned Canadian eskimologist who was on the staff of the Canadian Arctic Expedition, recorded over 100 songs between the years 1914 and 1916 as part of his anthropological research on the Copper Eskimos. This collection served as the basis for Eskimo Songs: Songs of the Copper Eskimos, published in 1925 in collaboration with Helen H. Roberts (see Roberts and Jenness in bibliography). Although the major portion of this work consists of song texts (and their translations), musical transcriptions, and musical analyses, included also is a discussion of the various types of Copper Eskimo songs and dances. Rather detailed information on Copper Eskimo games, songs, dances, musical instruments, and ceremonies can be found in a general ethnological report by Jenness entitled The Life of the Copper Eskimos (1922, republished in 1970).

Probably the best known of the early ethnographers who reported on Eskimo performance is Knud Rasmussen, who led the Fifth Thule Expedition, a Danish undertaking, to Arctic North America in the years 1921-24. Rasmussen, whose mother was part Eskimo, was born in Greenland and grew up speaking Eskimo as his native tongue. Because of his command of the language, he was not only able to communicate more easily with the Eskimos whom he visited, but he was also able to develop a far better understanding of such things as meaning and symbolism in song texts or native concepts concerning the process of musical composition than most other researchers. Rasmussen's works on the intellectual and spiritual culture of the Iglulik Eskimos (1929), the Caribou Eskimos (1930), the Netsilik Eskimos (1931), and the Copper Eskimos (1932) all contain valuable information on musical events and their function in each society. Kaj Birket-Smith, also a member of the Fifth Thule Expedition, provides us with additional information on music and dance in his publication on the material and social life of the Caribou Eskimos (1929).

The 1970's marked an unprecedented interest in Eskimo music and dance of all areas, including Canada. Because of the continuously rising costs of doing any kind of research in the Arctic as well as the difficulty in obtaining monetary grants to do such research, it is not surprising that much of the field work that is currently being carried out in the Canadian Arctic is being done by Canadians. Two universities with strong programs in Eskimo music studies are the University of Montreal and Laval University. Especially noteworthy at the University of Montreal has been the work on katajjait, or throat games of Eskimo women, conducted by the Research Group in Musical Semiotics under the direction of Jean-Jacques Nattiez. The National Museum of Man in Ottawa has sponsored several ethnomusicological field trips to the Arctic and the Museum's archives contain valuable audiovisual material from these trips.

Many recent books, articles, and papers have greatly expanded our knowledge of both music and dance of specific locales as well as particular types of performance. The aforementioned women's throat game has received attention in articles by Beaudry (1978) and Saldin d'Anglure (1978), as well as in an unpublished paper by Nattiez (1980b). Beaudry (1980) has also written a short article geared toward the general reader on throat games and other Eskimo games which involve music.

Several major ethnomusicological studies of specific Canadian Eskimo communities have been done within the last few years. Cavanagh's study of the music of the Netsilik Eskimo was done in the three communities of Gjoa Haven, Pelly Bay, and Spence Bay. Her Ph.D. dissertation, a two-volume work entitled Music of the Netsilik Eskimo: A Study of Stability and Change (1978), is soon to be published by the National Museum of Man in their Mercury Series. In this work Cavanagh focuses on the current drum dance repertoire of the three communities. Although she includes in her dissertation some discussion of dance itself, it is in a subsequent unpublished paper (1980) that she approaches the problem of what it actually means to dance to the music. In order to understand the relationship between the dance steps and the music and to prove that there indeed is a relationship between these two elements, Cavanagh uses a combination of traditional Western music notation and Labanotation. Although Cavanagh's work in this area is in its preliminary stages, it is a major step toward looking at dance as a total event.

Pelinski has conducted fieldwork among the Caribou Eskimos in the communities of Rankin Inlet and Eskimo Point. In his article "Inuit A Ja Jai Songs: On Music Tradition and Change in Rankin Inlet" (1977) he discusses the changes that have taken place in the performance, compositional process, and formal structure of the "a ja jai" songs, which were traditionally used for drum dancing, as a result of interaction with the European musical tradition. A revised French version of the above article is also included as one of five chapters in a recent publication by Pelinski in which he applies various methodological approaches, such as the use of linguistic models and computer technology, to a single genre of Caribou Eskimo song, namely the "a ja jai." This work, entitled La Musique des Inuit du Caribou: cinq perspectives methodologiques (1981), makes a significant contribution to our knowledge of Caribou Eskimo music as well as ethnomusicological theory. Pelinski's publication Inuit Songs from Eskimo Point (see Pelinski, Suluk, and Amarook in bibliography), which was done in collaboration with two Eskimos, is a songbook containing Eskimo texts, English translations, and musical notation of 41 traditional songs, including "a ja jai" songs, animal songs, and children's game songs. A recording is included with this publication.

The work of Lutz in the Cumberland Sound vicinity of Baffin Island has already been mentioned in connection with Boas' work in the same area. Since this region, including the settlement of Pangnirtung where Lutz did her fieldwork, is a very acculturated one, the dominant types of music and dance are Euro-American ones. Lutz devotes a major portion of her publication The Effect of Acculturation on Eskimo Music of Cumberland Peninsula (1978) to a discussion of these borrowed genres of music and dance and the factors which were responsible for their adoption and integration into the social culture of the Eskimos. Lutz's publication is also accompanied by a recording. In addition, Lutz has conducted fieldwork in Labrador, another very acculturated area, and her monograph surveying both traditional and borrowed genres of Labrador Eskimo music will be published by the National Museum of Man in the near future (see Lutz, in press).

In closing the section on Canada, two final articles should be mentioned. "Music of the Canadian Inuit" by Crowe (1976) is an excellent survey article on both traditional and modern music and dance of the Canadian Eskimos. "Music of the Inuit" by O'Connell (1979) looks into the relatively recent practice among Eskimo young people of composing and performing contemporary music which reflects the thoughts and ideas of present-day Eskimos. These guitar-accompanied songs, which are patterned after folk or country-western models, are gaining popularity among the Eskimos through radio broadcasting and are bringing recognition to the composers who write them and the performers who sing them.

Alaska

Although recent studies of Alaskan Eskimo performance have demonstrated the existence of an even greater diversity in Eskimo music and dance than was previously thought to be the case and have certainly expanded our knowledge of Alaskan Eskimo music and dance, several important scientific reports and ethnographic accounts from the late nineteenth century and first half of the twentieth century provide us with no longer obtainable descriptions of festivals and ceremonies which have either been abandoned entirely or have lost much of their original significance. Three reports from the late nineteenth century which focus on dancing and festivals are Murdoch's Ethnological Results of the Point Barrow Expedition (1892), Nelson's The Eskimo About Bering Strait (1899), and Edmonds' report from 1899 on the Eskimo of St. Michael and vicinity, which was published for the first time by Ray in 1966 under the title "The Eskimo of St. Michael and vicinity as related by H. M. W. Edmonds" (see Ray 1966 in bibliography). The reports of Nelson and Edmonds are especially interesting for comparative purposes, since both make observations on dancing and festivals of the same approximate geographical area during the same time period.

Two publications by Hawkes from the early twentieth century go into somewhat greater detail on Alaskan Eskimo dance festivals. The "Inviting-In" Feast of the Alaskan Eskimo (1913) is primarily a discussion of the types of dances performed and dance songs sung during one particular festival. The Dance Festivals of the Alaskan Eskimo (1914) is a more general discussion of dance festivals in the Bering Strait region of Alaska. The year 1947 saw the publication

of two important works dealing with ceremonialism. Alaskan Eskimo
Ceremonialism by Lantis is an excellent survey based both on secondary sources and Lantis' own fieldwork. It goes into specific
rituals and ceremonies as well as the elements which make up these
ceremonies such as dances, songs, masks, and musical instruments.
The Whale Hunters of Tigara by Rainey includes a detailed account
of ceremonies connected with hunting as they occurred in the vicinity of the present-day village of Point Hope prior to 1900. Among
the activities described is the famed "blanket-toss," which traditionally occurred in conjunction with the end of the whaling season.
Since the ceremonial life of the Alaskan Eskimo was traditionally
very rich and structured in comparison with other Eskimo areas,
the above publications are especially important for the reader whose
knowledge about Eskimo culture is limited in scope and is based on
stereotyped impressions.

Two other ethnographic accounts which include valuable information about Alaskan Eskimo music, dance, and ceremony are Nunamiut: Among Alaska's Inland Eskimos by Ingstad (1954) and The
North Alaskan Eskimo: A Study in Ecology and Society by Spencer
(1959, republished in 1976). Ingstad's work, which is a popular
account of his one winter's stay among the Nunamiut Eskimos of
Anaktuvuk Pass in Northern Alaska, includes interesting descriptions of feasts, dances, songs, and musical instruments. The work
by Spencer has valuable information on the karigi, or ceremonial
house, and the festivals and dances that were connected with it, as
well as the nature and function of songs.

The publication Eskimo Masks: Art and Ceremony by Ray
(1967) should be of interest to scholars of movement forms, since
it deals with an important component of Alaskan Eskimo dance.
Both face and finger masks were used in complex ceremonies involving song, dance, and story to interpret the great variety of
deities and spirits present in Eskimo cosmology. Contrary to contemporary Eskimo art such as printmaking and soapstone carving,
these wooden masks were much more than artistic creations; they
were an integral part of a ceremonial life which fused the supernatural world of the Eskimo with the earthly one.

As mentioned previously, Thomas Johnston of the University
of Alaska has been a prolific contributor to the literature on Alaskan Eskimo performance. His numerous articles on the subject have
appeared in journals and periodicals as diverse as the Indian Historian and the Tennessee Folklore Society Bulletin. I have chosen
to refer to four of Johnston's articles, although many of the others
would be of interest to dance and theater scholars.

"Songs and Dances of the Alaskan Eskimo, With a Foreword
on Both Eskimo and Indian Music in Alaska" (1975b) is a useful general article on the traditional and contemporary functions of Alaskan
Eskimo and Indian musical performance and the principles behind

the organization of Eskimo musical sound. Also given are musical transcriptions and analyses of seven North Alaskan Eskimo dance-songs--two for which the dance movements are known and fixed, three for which the dance movements are improvised freely, and one which is used for the whaling feast skin-toss. The next two articles deal specifically with dance. In "Alaskan Eskimo Dance in Cultural Context" (1975a), which is a study of traditional dance in contemporary Eskimo society, Johnston looks at various facets of dance such as dance classification, dance function, criteria for a good dancer, the learning process in dance, religious beliefs connected with dance, and dance as a vehicle for bringing about altered states of consciousness. "Humor, Drama, and Play in Alaskan Eskimo Mimetic Dance" (1978) is a study of the modern Alaskan Eskimo "Inviting-In" dance festival. This festival, which was suppressed for many years by Christian missionaries, has been revitalized and today serves to affirm native Alaskan Eskimo unity. It is interesting to note that the "Inviting-In" festival which was attended by Hawkes in 1912 (see Hawkes 1913 in bibliography) almost did not take place because of the objections of the local missionary.

Alaska, more than any other Eskimo area, has experienced a kind of cultural renaissance which has resulted in very concerted efforts among the Eskimos to introduce traditional music and dance to children and young people. Johnston's article "Eskimo Drum Clinics: The Winds of Change in Eskimo Music" (1980) discusses one way of bringing native music and dance to village schoolchildren, namely through the traveling drum-and-dance clinic. These clinics, which are funded by the National Endowment for the Humanities, visit various communities by invitation from the local village council and bring to the schools an Eskimo music and dance curriculum which is relevant to the children and helps to reinforce their ethnic identity.

In closing the section on Alaska I would like to mention two other articles pertaining to dance. A brief article by Honigmann entitled "Dance of the Ancient Ones" (1968) discusses drum dancing of the Mackenzie Delta Eskimo. Although the Mackenzie Delta Eskimos are a Canadian group, their music and dance are more closely allied with Alaskan Eskimo styles than with those of the eastern Arctic. This article is accompanied by some excellent illustrations of dancing and drumming. Ager's article "Eskimo Dance and Cultural Values in an Alaskan Village" (1975-1976), which is based on her fieldwork in the village of Tununak located on Nelson Island in southwestern Alaska, is an excellent example of the treatment of dance as an entire event made up of many interrelated parts. Although the main thrust of Ager's article is the incorporation of highly regarded Eskimo values, such as humor and hospitality, into the dance forms of this particular community, she also focuses on areas such as music, costume, dance setting, and the methodology she used in learning the dances herself and in obtaining information about them.

Greenland

At the same time that Franz Boas undertook his geographical survey in the Cumberland Sound area of Baffin Island, the Dane Gustav Holm began a similar exploration in the Angmagssalik area of East Greenland. The results of Holm's research were first published in Danish in 1888 (see Holm 1914 in bibliography for English translation) and this work together with Boas' The Central Eskimo represents the earliest scholarly presentation of information about Eskimo culture to the scientific community. Holm's publication, just like Boas', includes substantial material on musical practices. Holm discusses shamanistic rituals, drum matches for settling feuds, the telling of tales, and the singing of songs. It is interesting to note that, although Holm is obviously describing drum dancing in one section of the work, he never refers to this activity as dance. Rather, he simply states that if the singer is a man he does not stand still but bends his knees more or less in time with the music, takes an occasional step forward or back, makes a half turn, or twists the upper part of his body in a number of different ways. If the singer is a woman, she stands quite firmly but keeps moving her hips in a figure 8. The reader of early accounts such as this must be aware of differences in interpretation by various observers and be able to synthesize and sometimes even decode the material which is presented to him.

The names of William Carl Thalbitzer and Hjalmar Thuren stand out not only in reference to research on Eskimo music of Greenland but of Eskimo music as a whole. Thalbitzer, a Danish linguist who did extensive fieldwork among the Eskimos of both the east and west coasts of Greenland in the early years of this century, was among the first to make field recordings of Eskimo music. He collaborated with Thuren, a Danish musician, and the two were responsible for producing some of the most thorough and detailed writings on Eskimo music up to that time. Thuren provided the reader with very careful musical transcriptions and analyses, and Thalbitzer placed great emphasis on the contextual aspects of music as well as meanings of song texts. Thalbitzer and Thuren's publications include those which discuss the music of particular Eskimo groups in Greenland (Thalbitzer 1923 and 1941; Thalbitzer and Thuren 1923), those which discuss Eskimo music of Greenland as a whole (Thuren 1923), and more general sources on Eskimo music incorporating some information about other Eskimo areas as well (Thuren 1911).

Another individual whose writings on Eskimo music of Greenland should be mentioned in reference to research done in the early part of this century is Christian Leden, a Norwegian composer. Leden visited both the Polar Eskimos in the northwest part of Greenland and the Angmagssalik Eskimos of East Greenland. Although some of his publications are very technical in nature, consisting primarily of musical transcriptions and their analyses, his first publication from 1911, in which he discusses music and dance of both West and East Greenland, would be of interest to the dance and theater scholar.

Two individuals who have made consistent contributions to knowledge about the music of Greenland since 1960 are Olsen and Hauser, both of whom have been connected with the Danish Folklore Archives in Copenhagen. Unfortunately, some of their publications are in Danish and thus not easily accessible to most English speakers. Olsen's article "Intervals and Rhythm in the Music of the Eskimos of East Greenland" (1968), which is based on his own fieldwork in East Greenland, discusses the melodic and rhythmic flexibility or license which exists in Eskimo music of that area and contrasts this situation with that in Western art music. Without a doubt many a scholar has run into difficulties in researching or even discussing the music of another culture because of just such differences in the criteria used in assessing this music by the native people themselves. In his article "Acculturation in the Eskimo Songs of the Greenlanders" (1972) Olsen makes the observation that, although the general tendency in Greenland has been to separate traditional Eskimo music from occidental music, there is a certain amount of mixing of the two styles in West Greenland.

Some of Hauser's most recent work has included the investigation of Eskimo migration patterns from southern Baffin Island to the northern part of Greenland by analyzing melodic materials from both areas (Hauser 1978a and b). The Baffin Island influence on certain Polar Eskimo drumsongs is discussed in an earlier article by Hauser (1977), in which he formulates three types of structure (or form types) for songs of the Polar Eskimos.

Finally, an excellent ethnohistorical treatment of the Eskimo song contest in West Greenland is found in Kleivan's article "Song Duels in West Greenland: Joking Relationship and Avoidance" (1971). Kleivan discusses the function of these song duels as well as the attitudes of various early missionaries toward this type of activity. He also delves into some of the tensions and problems which evolved among the West Greenland Eskimos when this important form of social control was abandoned.

Siberia

We probably know less about music and dance of the Siberian Eskimos than of the other major Eskimo groups discussed above. Since Western fieldworkers have been denied access to this group of Eskimos by the Soviet administration, very little published material is available in the English language. We do know that there

are some similarities between the traditional musical practices of
Siberian Eskimos and those of the Alaskan Eskimos. This is not
surprising since until relatively recently there was contact between
these two groups of people.

One important source dealing with Siberian Eskimo rites and
ceremonies is Hughes' English translation of a Russian article by
Voblov, in which Voblov describes Eskimo ceremonies that were already losing much of their original significance when this research
was being done in the 1930's (Hughes 1959). Dancing and singing
were important components of several of these ceremonies. Another
article of interest is one by Johnston (1976b), in which he examines
Siberian Eskimo music and musical practices with respect to circumpolar musical diffusion. Johnston also incorporates in his article
Voblov's material having to do with music and dance.

As can be seen in the preceding pages, the literature on Eskimo performance is vast and diverse. The 63 entries which follow
represent only a selective bibliography. Both the scope and length
of this essay have necessitated the omission of many worthwhile contributions in the field. In addition, other sources such as journals
of explorers, missionaries, or traders often provide the researcher
with interesting observations concerning various performance activities. It is hoped that this essay will bring the reader to a closer
understanding of music, dance, and drama as indispensable elements
of Eskimo culture.

Ager, Lynn Price
    1975-
    1976 "Eskimo Dance and Cultural Values in an Alaskan Vil-
          lage," Dance Research Journal 8(1):7-12.

Beaudry, Nicole
    1978 "Le Katajjaq: un jeu inuit traditionnel," Etudes/Inuit/
          Studies 2(1):35-53.
    1980 "Arctic Throat-Games: A Contest of Song," Performing
          Arts in Canada 17(3):26-28.

Binnington, Doreen, and Ming-Yueh Liang
    1980a "Eskimo Music," in The New Grove Dictionary of Music
          and Musicians, Vol. 6, edited by Stanley Sadie. London:
          Macmillan Publishers Limited, pp. 247-248.
    1980b "North America, #II,4: Eskimo," in The New Grove
          Dictionary of Music and Musicians, Vol. 13, edited by
          Stanley Sadie. London: Macmillan Publishers Limited, pp.
          318-320.

Birket-Smith, Kaj
    1929 The Caribou Eskimos: Material and Social Life and Their

Cultural Position. Copenhagen: Gyldendal. Report of the Fifth Thule Expedition, 1921-1924, Vol. 5, Parts I and II.

Boas, Franz
1964 [1888] The Central Eskimo. Lincoln: University of Nebraska Press. Originally published in 1888 in Washington as part of the Sixth Annual Report of the U.S. Bureau of Ethnology.

Cavanagh, Beverley
1972 "Annotated Bibliography: Eskimo Music," Ethnomusicology 16(3):479-487.
1978 Music of the Netsilik Eskimo: A Study of Stability and Change. Unpublished Ph.D. dissertation, University of Toronto. To be published by the National Museum of Man, Ottawa, in their Mercury Series.
1980 "To Dance to the Music?" Unpublished paper presented at the Canadian Folklore Studies Association Meeting in Montreal, June 1980.
1981 "Inuit," in Encyclopedia of Music in Canada, edited by Helmut Kallmann, Gilles Potvin, and Kenneth Winters. Toronto: University of Toronto Press, pp. 458-460.

Crowe, Keith
1976 "Music of the Canadian Inuit," North/Nord 23(6):52-56.

Estreicher, Zygmunt
1950 "Die Musik der Eskimos," Anthropos 45:659-720.
1954 "Eskimo-Musik," in Die Musik in Geschichte und Gegenwart, edited by Friedrich Blume. Kassel u. Basel: Bärenreiter-Verlag, Vol. 3, pp. 1526-1533.

Hauser, Michael
1977 "Formal Structure in Polar Eskimo Drumsongs," Ethnomusicology 21(1):33-53.
1978a "Inuit Songs from Southwest Baffin Island in Cross-Cultural Context, I," Etudes/Inuit/Studies 2(1):55-83.
1978b "Inuit Songs from Southwest Baffin Island in Cross-Cultural Context, II," Etudes/Inuit/Studies 2(2):71-105.

Hawkes, Ernest William
1913 The "Inviting-In" Feast of the Alaskan Eskimo. Ottawa: Department of Mines, Geological Survey, Memoir 45.
1914 The Dance Festivals of the Alaskan Eskimo. Philadelphia: University Museum Anthropological Publications, Vol. 6, No. 2.

Holm, Gustav Frederik
1914 "Ethnological Sketch of the Angmagsalik Eskimo," Meddelelser om Grønland 39:1-147. The Ammassalik Eskimo, Pt. 1, No. 1, edited by William Thalbitzer.

Honigmann, John J.
1968 "Dance of the Ancient Ones," The Beaver 299:44-47.

Hughes, Charles Campbell
1959 "Translation of I. K. Voblov's 'Eskimo Ceremonies,'"
Anthropological Papers of the University of Alaska 7(2):
71-90.

Ingstad, Helge
1954 Nunamiut: Among Alaska's Inland Eskimos. Translated
from the Norwegian by F. H. Lyon. London: George
Allen and Unwin Ltd.

Jenness, Diamond
1970 [1922] The Life of the Copper Eskimos. New York:
Johnson Reprint Corporation. Originally published in 1922
in Ottawa as vol. 12, pt. A of the Report of the Canadian
Arctic Expedition, 1913-1918.

Johnston, Thomas F.
1975a "Alaskan Eskimo Dance in Cultural Context," Dance
Research Journal 7(2):1-11.
1975b "Songs and Dances of the Alaskan Eskimo, with a Foreword on Both Eskimo and Indian Music in Alaska," Viltis
33(5):6-18.
1976a Eskimo Music by Region: A Comparative Circumpolar
Study. Ottawa: National Museum of Man, Ethnology Division Mercury Series Paper No. 32.
1976b "Siberian Eskimo Music," Journal of Asian and African
Studies 11(3-4):208-214.
1978 "Humor, Drama, and Play in Alaskan Eskimo Mimetic
Dance," The Western Canadian Journal of Anthropology
8(1):47-64.
1980 "Eskimo Drum Clinics: The Winds of Change in Eskimo
Music," North/Nord 27(3):18-21.

Kleivan, Inge
1971 "Song Duels in West Greenland: Joking Relationship and
Avoidance," Folk 13:9-36.

Lantis, Margaret
1947 Alaskan Eskimo Ceremonialism. Seattle: American Ethnological Society Monograph No. 11.

Leden, Christian
1911 "Musik und Tänze der grönländischen Eskimos und die
Verwandtschaft der Musik der Polareskimos mit der Indianer," Zeitschrift für Ethnologie 43:261-270.

Luttmann, Rick and Gail
1977 "Dance in Eskimo Society: An Historical Perspective,"
Focus on Dance 8:15-22.

Lutz, Maija M.
    1972 "An Examination of Musical and Cultural Contexts of the
    Frame Drum Among the Eskimos." Unpublished paper pre-
    sented at the Society for Ethnomusicology Meeting in Toron-
    to, Nov. 30-Dec. 3, 1972.
    1978 The Effects of Acculturation on Eskimo Music of Cumber-
    land Peninsula. Ottawa: National Museum of Man, Ethnol-
    ogy Division Mercury Series Paper No. 41. (Accompany-
    ing recording.)
    In press Musical Traditions of the Labrador Coast Inuit.
    Ottawa: National Museum of Man, Ethnology Division
    Mercury Series Paper.

Murdoch, John
    1892 Ethnological Results of the Point Barrow Expedition.
    Washington, D.C.: Ninth Annual Report of the Bureau of
    Ethnology.

Nattiez, Jean-Jacques
    1980a "Le disque de musique amérindienne, II: Introduction
    à l'écoute des disques de musique inuit," Recherches
    Amerindiennes au Quebec 10(1-2):111-122.
    1980b "Inuit Vocal Games: The State of the Art." Unpub-
    lished paper presented at the Society for Ethnomusicology
    Meeting in Bloomington, Indiana, November 1980.

Nelson, Edward William
    1899 The Eskimo About Bering Strait. Washington, D.C.:
    Eighteenth Annual Report of the Bureau of American
    Ethnology, Part I.

O'Connell, Sheldon
    1979 "Music of the Inuit," The Beaver 310(2):12-17.

Olsen, Paul Rovsing
    1968 "Intervals and Rhythm in the Music of the Eskimos of
    East Greenland," in Proceedings of the Centennial Work-
    shop on Ethnomusicology held at University of British
    Columbia, Vancouver, June 19 to 23, 1967, edited by
    Peter Crossley-Holland. Vancouver: Government of the
    Province of British Columbia, pp. 54-59.
    1972 "Acculturation in the Eskimo Songs of the Greenlanders,"
    Yearbook of the International Folk Music Council 4:32-37.
    1980 "Greenland," in The New Grove Dictionary of Music and
    Musicians, Vol. 7, edited by Stanley Sadie. London:
    Macmillan Publishers Limited, pp. 688-689.

Pelinski, Ramon
    1977 "Inuit a ja jai Songs: On Music Tradition and Change
    in Rankin Inlet," The Western Canadian Journal of Anthro-
    pology 7(3):1-15.
    1981 La musique des Inuit du Caribou: cinq perspectives

méthodologiques. Montréal: Les Presses de l'Universite
de Montréal, Sémiologie et Analyse Musicales.

_____, Luke Suluk, and Lucy Amarook
1979 Inuit Songs from Eskimo Point. Ottawa: National Museum of Man, Ethnology Division Mercury Series Paper No.
60. (Accompanying recording.)

Rainey, Forelich G.
1947 "The Whale Hunters of Tigara," Anthropological Papers
of the American Museum of Natural History 41:229-283.

Rasmussen, Knud
1929 Intellectual Culture of the Iglulik Eskimos. Copenhagen:
Gyldendal. Report of the Fifth Thule Expedition, 1921-
1924, Vol. 7, No. 1.
1930 Observations on the Intellectual Culture of the Caribou
Eskimos. Copenhagen: Gyldendal. Report of the Fifth
Thule Expedition, 1921-1924, Vol. 7, No. 2.
1931 The Netsilik Eskimos: Social Life and Spiritual Culture.
Copenhagen: Gyldendal. Report of the Fifth Thule Expedition, 1921-1924, Vol. 8, Nos. 1 and 2.
1932 Intellectual Culture of the Copper Eskimos. Copenhagen:
Gyldendal. Report of the Fifth Thule Expedition, 1921-
1924, Vol. 9.

Ray, Dorothy Jean
1967 Eskimo Masks: Art and Ceremony. Seattle: University
of Washington Press.

_____, ed.
1966 "The Eskimo of St. Michael and Vicinity as Related by
H. M. W. Edmonds," Anthropological Papers of the University of Alaska 13(2):1-143.

Roberts, Helen Heffron, and Diamond Jenness
1925 Eskimo Songs: Songs of the Copper Eskimos. Ottawa:
Report of the Canadian Arctic Expedition, 1913-1918, Vol.
14.

Saladin d'Anglure, Bernard
1978 "Entre cri et chant: les Katajjait, un genre musical
féminin," Etudes/Inuit/Studies 2(1):85-94.

Spencer, Robert F.
1976 [1959] The North Alaskan Eskimo: A Study in Ecology
and Society. New York: Dover Publications, Inc. Originally published in 1959 in Washington as Bulletin 171 of
the Bureau of American Ethnology.

Thalbitzer, William Carl
1923 "Language and Folklore," Meddelelser om Grønland

40:113-564. The Ammassalik Eskimo, Pt. 2, No. 3, edited
by William Thalbitzer.
1941 "Social Customs and Mutual Aid," Meddelelser om Grønland
40:569-739. The Ammassalik Eskimo, Pt. 2, No. 4, edited
by William Thalbitzer.

_____ and Hjalmar Thuren
1923 "Melodies from East Greenland, with a Supplement Containing Melodies from North-West Greenland," Meddelelser
om Grønland 40:47-112. The Ammassalik Eskimo, Pt. 2,
No. 2, edited by William Thalbitzer.

Thuren, Hjalmar
1911 "La musique chez les Eskimos," S.I.M. Revue Musicale
Mensuelle 7:36-56.
1923 "On the Eskimo Music of Greenland," Meddelelser om
Grønland 40:1-45. The Ammassalik Eskimo, Pt. 2, No. 1,
edited by William Thalbitzer.

Recordings

Folkways FE 4069
Eskimo Songs from Alaska. Recorded by Miriam C. Stryker.
Notes by Miriam C. Stryker. Edited by Charles Hofmann.

Folkways FE 4444
The Eskimos of Hudson Bay and Alaska. Recorded by Laura
Boulton. Notes by Laura Boulton and Henry Cowell.

Hudson's Bay Company and Boot Records Limited
#'s NCB500-NCB505 (Records) or #'s 5NCB500-5NCB505 (Cas-
settes) Six albums of contemporary works by some of the
most popular native musicians of Northern Canada. Produced by the Northern Service of the Canadian Broadcasting Corporation. Available from: The Beaver, 77 Main
Street, Winnipeg, Canada R3C 2R1.

Philips 6586 036
Inuit Games and Songs. (In UNESCO collection "Musical
Sources.") Produced by the Research Group in Musical
Semiotics, Faculty of Music, University of Montreal under
the direction of Jean-Jacques Nattiez.

University of Washington Press UWP 902
Alaskan Eskimo Songs and Stories. Recorded by Lorraine
Donoghue Koranda. 32-page booklet by Lorraine Donoghue
Koranda.

CONTRIBUTORS

LAILA ABOU-SAIF, Ph.D. Egyptian Institute of Theatre, Academy of Arts, Cairo. Dr. Abou-Saif is author of Najeb al-Rihani and the Development of Comedy in Egypt and Egyptian Women, plus many articles on Egyptian theatre. She is also a filmmaker, theatre director and actress.

EDWARD ALLWORTH, Ph.D. Department of Middle East Languages and Culture, and Center for the Study of Central Asia (Head), Columbia University. Among Dr. Allworth's many publications on Central Asia are articles on drama and theatre, including "Introduction to the Modern Drama of the Transcaucasus" and "Murder as Metaphor in the First Central Asian Drama," plus the translation of several plays. Through the American Council of Learned Societies and the Soviet Academy of Science, Dr. Allworth began research in 1983 at the Institutes for Theatres in the Uzbekistan SSR of the Soviet Union.

METIN AND, Ph.D. University of Ankara, Turkey. In addition to his university teaching, Dr. And is well known as a drama and dance critic and public lecturer. He has published over 1,000 articles in various languages, and is author of such books as Dances of Anatolian Turkey, A History of Theatre and Popular Entertainment in Turkey, Karagöz: Turkish Shadow Theatre, and many others.

JILL BECK, M.A. Department of Theatre Arts, City College of New York; Director of Education, Dance Notation Bureau, New York City. Professor Beck has a varied background in the dance field and is involved at present in doctoral studies at New York University.

DAVID BEST, Ph.D. Department of Philosophy, University College of Swansea, U.K. Dr. Best has published widely, including Expression in Movement and the Arts and Philosophy and Human Movement. He has traveled to several continents for lecture tours and his professional credits include keynote addresses for various conferences on human movement, both athletic and aesthetic.

PETER CHELKOWSKI, Ph.D. Department of Near Eastern Languages and Literatures, New York University. Dr. Chelkowski has published many books, articles, and monographs, in various languages, on the performing arts in the Middle East and North Africa. Among his published books are Ta'ziyeh: Ritual and Drama in Iran and Mirror of the Invisible World.

OH-KON CHO, Ph.D. Department of Theatre, State University of New York at Brockport. He has published numerous scholarly articles on the traditional Korean theatre, and his major study, Korean Puppet Theatre, was published by the Asian Studies Center of Michigan State University. He is currently continuing research in Korea.

KATHY FOLEY, Ph.D. Department of Theatre Arts, University of California-Santa Cruz. She is Southeast Asia editor for the Asian Theatre Journal and specializes in Indonesian puppet theatre. Her research for this bibliography was facilitated by a grant from the Regents of the University of California.

FARROKH GAFFARY, Ph.D. For many years Dr. Gaffary served as the director of Shiraz Art Festival and the Institute for Traditional Performance and Ritual, in Tehran. His published works in French, English and Persian deal mainly with the development of drama and theatre in Iran. A recent work, to be published in England as Bibliography of Iranian Studies, is a bibliography of works on Iranian drama, theatre, film and television.

JUDITH LYNNE HANNA, Ph.D. Center for Family and Community Development, University of Maryland. As an anthropologist with a dance background, Dr. Hanna has published broadly in the various areas of human movement performance, with two recent books to her credit, To Dance is Human and The Performance-Audience Connection.

RANDALL HARRISON, Ph.D. Department of Psychiatry, University of California-San Francisco. Dr. Harrison is active in his area of psychology of communication and is the author of various works including the books Beyond Words and The Nonverbal Domain.

MELVYN HELSTIEN, Ph.D. Department of Theatre Arts, University of California-Los Angeles. He is a two-time Fellow of the American Institute of Indian Studies and a Senior Fellow of the Indo-U.S. Subcomission on Cultural Exchange. He served as curator of Asian Puppets: Wall of the World, UCLA Museum of Cultural History, Catalog and Exhibition, 1976.

MARCIA HERNDON, Ph.D. Native American Studies, University of California-Berkeley. As a Native American herself, and as a ethnomusicologist, Dr. Herndon has published extensively on the subject of Music of Native Americans.

PAMELA HOWARD, M.A. and M.L.S. Librarian (cataloger-Spanish Civil War), University of California-San Diego. (When this work was completed, Ms. Howard worked as Reference Librarian, Latin American Library, Tulane University.) She has published bibliographies on Latin American subjects. Because of a special interest, she participates in folk dances of other cultures.

ADRIENNE L. KAEPPLER, Ph.D. Curator of Oceanic Ethnology, Smithsonian Institution. For many years, Dr. Kaeppler was Research Anthropologist at the Bishop Museum and on the faculty of University of Hawaii. As an anthropologist who studied dance from childhood, Dr. Kaeppler has brought unique insight to her many publications on the arts and dances of the Pacific Islands.

RHEA LEHMAN. Ms. Lehman is currently completing her Ph.D. at the Department of Theatre and Drama at the University of Wisconsin-Madison. She has had extensive experience in dance and movement techniques, including studies and training in several Indian performance forms. She has worked professionally as an editor.

ALICE LO, M.A. Ms. Lo received her Chinese classical and folk dance training during her early years in Hong Kong; her instructors included dance masters of Taiwan and Mainland China. She received her M.L.S. from University of Southern California and M.A. in Dance Ethnology from University of California-Los Angeles. Currently she is active in teaching, performing and creating Chinese dances.

ANNETTE LUST, Ph.D. Modern Foreign Languages (Chair), Dominican College-San Rafael, California. Trained in mime as well as foreign languages, Dr. Lust has written extensively on mime in America and Europe, including a history of the mime, From the Greek Mimes to Marcel Marceau. She is considered one of the major mime critics in this country and is active in national and international organizations that promote the mime.

MAIJA M. LUTZ, Ph.D. Tozzer Library, Harvard University. As an ethnomusicologist, Dr. Lutz has been published in areas of her interest--music and dance of the Eskimo and North American Indian cultures, and acculturative processes and musical change.

MARTHA MYERS, M.S. Dance Department (former Chair), Connecticut College, and Dean of the American Dance Festival. Professor Myers organized the first National Body Therapy Conference in 1980 and authored a series of articles in Dance Magazine, upon which her chapter here is based. Through writings and workshops, Professor Myers has promoted scientific links to the arts of the dance through an understanding of the human body.

MARGARET PIERPONT. Associate Editor/Education, Dance Magazine. Ms. Pierpont was the editor for the series "Body Therapies and the

Modern Dancer," and has written or edited many articles on such subjects as dance education, injury prevention, nutrition, and non-verbal communication. She has been a student of the four systems described in her chapter in this volume.

LEONARD PRONKO, Ph.D. Department of Modern Languages and Literatures, Pomona College, Claremont, California. At Pomona he has directed more than a dozen Kabuki productions. He was the first non-Japanese in the Kabuki training program of the National Theatre of Japan. Professor Pronko has held fellowships from the Guggenheim Foundation, the Japan Foundation and the French Government. His books on Western theatre include The World of Jean Anouilh, Avant-garde, and other studies of contemporary and nineteenth-century French authors. He has been visiting professor at the University of California, and the University of Hawaii, and in 1981-82 he was a Phi Beta Kappa Visiting Scholar.

FREDDIE ROKEM, Ph.D. Department of Theatre Studies, Hebrew University of Jerusalem. Dr. Rokem's publications deal mainly with the development of the Hebrew Theatre and the role of the Bible in the development of the Hebrew Theatre.

BARI ROLFE. Conservatory of Mime, Chablot College, Hayward, California. Professor Rolfe has authored several books on the mime and commedia dell'arte, including Mimes on Miming and Mime Directory Bibliography. She is considered one of the major mime critics and she is active in all areas of promotion of the mime and movement theatre.

DIANA SCHNITT, M.F.A. Dance Department (Chair), Connecticut College. Professor Schnitt is also on the faculty of the American Dance Festival, and member of the Labon Institute of Movement Studies and the Institute for Nonverbal Communication.

MAXINE LEEDS SNOW, M.S. Library, Loyola University, New Orleans. Ms. Snow has published works in children's literature and dance criticism. With extensive training in classical and ethnic dance forms, Ms. Snow is a dancer and choreographer.

CRAIG TURNER, M.F.A. Professional Actor Training Program (Director-Movement Training), University of Washington, Seattle. Professor Turner has published numerous articles on movement in actor training. He is active in professional organizations and in the promotion of theatrical movement.

H. T. A. WHITING, Ph.D. Department of Psychology (Chair), Interfaculty of Physical Education (Dean), The Free University, Amsterdam. Dr. Whiting is a Fellow of the British Psychological Society. He is editor and founder of the Journal of Human Movement Studies. He has written many books and numerous articles on psychology and physical education, and is active in other areas of publishing, administration and promotion.

STEPHEN A. WILD, Ph.D. Ethnomusicology Research Office, Australian Institute of Aboriginal Studies, Canberra City. Besides his administrative duties as research officer, Dr. Wild supervises the training of new workers in the field. He has numerous publications to his credit.

DRID WILLIAMS, Ph.D. Anthropology of Human Movement Program (Director), New York University. Dr. Williams is Faculty Editor of the Journal for Anthropological Study of Human Movement (JASHM), and has published many articles on dance and anthropology of human movement. She came to the field of anthropology after a professional career in dance. (Since this writing, Dr. Williams has moved from N.Y.U. to pursue post-doctoral studies at Indiana University, in Bloomington.)

PHILLIP ZARRILLI, Ph.D. Department of Theatre and Drama; South Asian Studies (Adjunct Faculty), Asian-Experimental Theatre Program (Director), University of Wisconsin-Madison. Among his numerous publications are (editor) Martial Arts in Actor Training, and The Kathakali Complex: Actor, Performance, Structure. Dr. Zarrilli received training in Kathakali at the Kerala Kalamandalam, and specialized in advanced martial arts training (kalarippayattu) at the C.V.N. Karli, Trivandrum, Kerala. He has been the recipient of Fulbright and American Institute of Indian Studies research fellowships. Partial funding for his contribution to this volume was made possible by a grant from the University of Wisconsin's graduate school.

\